Going
Critical

Going Critical

The First North Korean Nuclear Crisis

Joel S. Wit

Daniel B. Poneman

Robert L. Gallucci

BROOKINGS INSTITUTION PRESS
Washington, D.C.

Copyright © 2004
THE BROOKINGS INSTITUTION
1775 Massachusetts Avenue, N.W., Washington, D.C. 20036
www.brookings.edu

Library of Congress Cataloging-in-Publication data
Wit, Joel S.
  Going critical : the first North Korean nuclear crisis / Joel S. Wit, Daniel B. Poneman, and Robert L. Gallucci.
    p. cm.
  Includes bibliographical references and index.
  ISBN 0-8157-9386-3 (cloth : alk. paper) — ISBN 0-8157-9386-3
    1. Korea (North)—Politics and government. 2. Nuclear weapons—Korea (North) 3. Korea (North)—Military policy. 4. Korea (North)—Foreign relations. 5. World politics—20th century. I. Poneman, Daniel. II. Gallucci, Robert L. III. Title.

  DS935.5.W57 2004
  327.7305193'09'049—dc22   2004002321

9 8 7 6 5 4 3 2 1

The paper used in this publication meets minimum requirements of the American National Standard for Information Sciences—Permanence of Paper for Printed Library Materials: ANSI Z39.48-1992.

Map images copyright © Mountain High Maps®

Typeset in Minion

Composition by Cynthia Stock
Silver Spring, Maryland

Printed by R. R. Donnelley
Harrisonburg, Virginia

Dedicated to the memory of

MEYER PONEMAN

ALBERT G. SIMS

MAURICE CARL WIT

ELISE WIT

Contents

Preface

THE concept for this book emerged from an interview granted by two of the authors to a Japanese publication on the occasion of the fifth anniversary of the 1994 agreement that, for a time, resolved the nuclear dispute dividing North Korea from the world. The authors were asked to reflect on their involvement in the negotiations leading to that agreement. The interview stirred dormant memories that might soon fade beyond recovery. A number of other treatments and interpretations of that crisis have been written, many of which contain unique insights and perspectives, but none of which draw from the full record of the crisis available to the individuals who served in the U.S. government during that period.

This realization was troubling for, as Napoleon said, "History is the version of past events that people have decided to agree upon," which may vary greatly from what occurred in fact. If the histories are inaccurate, or colored by predispositions or ideologies that distort understanding of the actual events, then subsequent decisionmakers could easily learn the wrong lessons and err in confronting future crises. The consequences of such error could be disastrous when the matter at issue relates to nuclear weapons, which have the power to kill hundreds of thousands of people in a flash.

The task of presenting an inside account of the first North Korean nuclear crisis, however, would be a massive undertaking, so another author—also deeply involved in the negotiations leading to the 1994 agreement—joined the team. We then requested and were granted access to our former government files related to Korea, to form the backbone of documentary evidence required to tell the story thoroughly and accurately. The research entailed an exhaustive review of decision memoranda, minutes, and summaries of conclusions from meetings of cabinet and subcabinet officials under the auspices of the National Security Council (NSC); memoranda of conversations involving U.S. officials from the president on down; contemporaneous notes scribbled during the actual negotiations with the North Koreans; and diplomatic correspondence, reporting cables, and more. It was supplemented by material that has been available to the public, as well as dozens of interviews with key players from several nations involved in the crisis. This research encompassed not just U.S. policy but also that of other key participants, including North Korea.

The book that eventually emerged from this process took longer than any of us had wished or hoped, a product of the complexity of the material, the difficulty of juggling drafts and redrafts among the three authors, and the time-consuming process of undergoing a government review. As a largely personal account, this book does not purport to be encyclopedic in its treatment of the Korean Peninsula, nor does it attempt to serve as an omnibus history of peninsular relations over the past ten years. Readers with broader interests in the peninsula are strongly encouraged to refer to the outstanding history, *The Two Koreas,* by Don Oberdorfer; we certainly did. We have focused instead on the period during which the peninsula faced its most serious threat: the possible acquisition of nuclear weapons by North Korea.

Apart from the research, analysis, and writing, our greatest challenges were stylistic: how could three authors offer a firsthand account without becoming hopelessly entangled in a welter of dueling pronouns or vainly seeking to integrate three unique perspectives into a coherent whole? Eventually we opted for the simplest, if somewhat awkward, solution: the three authors would describe the crisis—and each other—in the third person. At least that way the reader would not be saddled with figuring out whose point of view was being conveyed at any point in the book. This approach also imposed a discipline to find common ground in describing events for which we sometimes had three divergent interpretations.

A further word on sourcing. We could only take the third person approach so far; although some of the specific statements and quotations in the book represent our own memories, we refrained from footnoting ourselves as interviewees. Also, we fully recognize the uncertainties involved in analyzing North Korean behavior, especially what or how particular North Korean leaders or factions may think about any given issue or option. Nevertheless, many of these and other passages express judgments reflecting information contained in files that remain in official government archives unavailable to the public, which we were unable to footnote.

Another stylistic challenge not unique to this book was how to describe the same people and things over and over again without terminally boring the reader. Following many other authors, at times we resort to the convenience of referring to longtime North Korean dictator Kim Il Sung and his heir, Kim Jong Il, as the "Great Leader" and the "Dear Leader," but it should be understood as a reference to a nom de guerre and not acceptance of either their personal qualities or party propaganda.

Many people helped us bring all the threads of this story together. First and foremost, we thank Bob Gallucci's executive assistant, Clare Ogden, for her encouragement, not to mention her constant efforts to ensure that the three of us would meet periodically to work on this project. Alice Brennan helped meld together comments and editing changes during the hectic final stages of this project. A hearty band of energetic and dedicated research assistants managed to wade through the reams of unclassified materials available to the public: Hanseul Kang, Yuki Tatsumi, Marsha Lee Lewis, Brent Wolfort, Miyuki Onchi, Alex Chopan, Jennifer Butte-Dahl, Kerry McCormack, Sarah Debbink, Michael di-Paula-Coyle, Peter De Nesnera, Sarah Clanton, Matt Lewis, Shannon Cadagan, Megan Tapper, Melanie Hart, Corey Dyckman, Matthew LePage, Jillian Ryan, and Maria-Teresa Nogales. Finally, Doug and Keiko Morris provided Joel Wit with a quiet shelter as he raced to complete the manuscript.

We are deeply grateful to Michael Armacost, Strobe Talbott, Richard Haass, James Steinberg, and the Brookings Institution for their support, particularly in allowing Joel Wit to do much of the research under their roof and for publishing our manuscript. Bob Faherty, Janet Walker, Vicky Macintyre, Renuka Deonarain, Becky Clark, and Susan Woollen of the Brookings Institution Press have been patient yet energetic in their efforts to bring the manuscript to the light of day. John Hamre and Kurt Campbell at the Center for Strategic and International Studies (CSIS) were kind enough, aside from employing Joel Wit, to allow him to complete the manuscript while working at their institution. Finally, we also gratefully acknowledge the financial support of Carnegie Corporation of New York and the Korea Foundation, which enabled us to complete our work. In that connection, we are most grateful to David Speedie for his early and sustained support and encouragement.

The classification review process was arduous, and we never would have survived it without the professionalism and dedication of the State Department team that managed it, led first by the late Ambassador William Gleysteen and then by Robert Rich, as well as their National Security Council colleagues William Leary, Rod Soubers, and Michael Smith. We would also like to thank Bernard Crawford at the NSC as well as Alice Richey and her staff at the State Department for their tireless efforts in retrieving relevant files and documents.

Thanks also go to the other agencies that reviewed the manuscript. Of course, the opinions and characterizations in this book are those of the authors, and do not represent official positions of the U.S. government.

Tragically, in the midst of his efforts, Ambassador Gleysteen suddenly fell ill and passed away. It was typical of this dedicated and distinguished diplomat that he ensured a smooth hand-off of the project even as he faced his own final battle with courage and dignity.

In addition, many experts or participants in the events described generously offered to contribute their reflections and recollections or to review or comment on part or all of the manuscript, including John Akers, Samuel Berger, Robert Carlin, Victor Cha, Arnold Kanter, Charles Kartman, Anthony Lake, James Laney, Gary Luck, William Perry, Charles ("Jack") Pritchard, Gary Samore, Brent Scowcroft, John Shalikashvili, and James Steinberg. Sharon Squassoni deserves a special thanks for reviewing and commenting on the draft manuscript. Our thanks also go to the many who provided interviews or commented on the text but requested anonymity.

Bob Gallucci and Dan Poneman are deeply grateful to their wives, Jennifer Sims and Susan Poneman, and their children, Jessica and Nicholas Gallucci and Claire, Michael, and William Poneman, for their sustained patience, good humor, and support.

Finally, as in all undertakings of this nature, the authors reserve to themselves full responsibility for all errors of fact or interpretation in the pages that follow.

Introduction

A LARGE conference room occupies the top floor of the building housing the U.S. mission to the United Nations in New York City. Three of its four sides are walled in glass, giving spectacular vistas of Manhattan. On a warm June morning in 1993, the rays of the rising sun warmed the room, yielding no sign of the impending chill brought by the serious demeanor of the officials who quietly filed in for a momentous meeting. Sitting on one side of the negotiating table were eight members of a sixteen-person delegation from the Democratic People's Republic of Korea; on the other, the same number of Americans. The rest of each delegation sat in chairs behind them.

None of the U.S. delegates in the front row had ever met a North Korean before. Robert Gallucci, the chief negotiator for the United States, was struck by the grim faces of the North Koreans, girding to defend their right to develop the most awesome weapons known to humankind. The only spot of color on their gray suits was a small lapel pin each wore bearing a picture of Kim Il Sung, proclaimed the Great Leader of his people. This negotiation was the first critical test in the most serious nuclear crisis the world had experienced since the superpower confrontation over Soviet missiles in Cuba some three decades earlier.

The story of that crisis and its resolution is one of intense struggle by the newly minted Clinton administration to block a grave threat—the acquisition of nuclear weapons by a country locked in hostility with the United States and its allies. The narrative is shaped by Washington's alliances with the Republic of Korea and Japan; by its enduring efforts to uphold the Nuclear Non-Proliferation Treaty (NPT) and to prevent the spread of nuclear weapons; by its support for the organization responsible for policing the nuclear nonproliferation regime, the International Atomic Energy Agency (IAEA); by its still uneasy but improving relations with Pyongyang's powerful neighbor, China; and by U.S. domestic and bureaucratic politics. The story relates to the most vital interests of the United States, and how Washington makes policy when the vital—yet distinct—interests of others are also at stake.

Sixteen months would pass between the meeting in New York that day and a signing ceremony in Geneva, Switzerland, that would end the nuclear stalemate. For the United States, the stakes were high from the outset. The American government estimated that North Korea would be able to produce about 150 kilograms of plutonium a year once all three of its nuclear reactors were operating. That would be enough to build more than thirty Nagasaki-sized nuclear weapons annually, and more than enough to export. Indeed, there was good reason to believe that rogue states and terrorist groups would pay the needy regime in Pyongyang well for fissile material or finished weapons.

The crisis arose when the North Koreans refused to honor their safeguards agreement with the IAEA, and it threatened to spin out of control when Pyongyang declared its intention to withdraw from the NPT. Failure by the international community to rise successfully to the challenge would inevitably damage the treaty and its safeguards system, the cornerstone of a nearly universal regime establishing a global norm against the spread of nuclear weapons. The timing could not have been worse; the NPT was to undergo a twenty-five-year review in 1995, at which time its members could decide whether to extend, amend, or abandon the treaty. If North Korea could walk away from the treaty's obligations with impunity at the very moment its nuclear program appeared poised for weapons' production, it would have dealt a devastating blow from which the treaty might never recover. Moreover, a North Korea armed with nuclear weapons and ballistic missiles could in time lead the governments in Tokyo and Seoul to reconsider their relations with the United States as well as their own commitments to refrain from developing nuclear weapons.

The United States entered into negotiations on the theory that Pyongyang might be "talked down" from its defiant nuclear posture. This did not imply that American decisionmakers had any illusions about North Korea's stance—since the deaths of Josef Stalin and Mao Zedong, the regime was unrivaled in its totalitarianism. No one believed that Pyongyang could be "trusted" to carry out its agreements. But when viewed in the cold, calculating light of not only U.S. national interests but also those of America's close allies in the region, the quest for a negotiated settlement seemed to be the "least worst alternative" as the first line of defense against North Korean acquisition of nuclear weapons—compared to military action against North Korea, containing Pyongyang through isolation, or forcing its collapse. Importantly, resorting to the diplomatic option precluded no others. To the contrary, in order to be effective a strategy of coercive diplomacy would require an integrated use of carrots and sticks. And if diplomacy failed, American officials would be ready—and justified—to switch from carrots to sticks.

While U.S. officials all agreed that the North should not be rewarded for simply honoring its existing international commitments, some face-saving offerings could make it easier for the North to step back from the brink. When the North Koreans showed little interest in token concessions but a great deal of interest in a substantial deal that would bring them modern, more proliferation-resistant nuclear reactor technology, the game was on—in capitals, among the allies, and with Pyongyang.

For the Clinton administration, the politics in Washington and with Seoul were often as challenging as dealing with the North. South Korean president Kim Young Sam dealt with the nuclear crisis as a critical domestic issue for his government, which it surely was. But his political needs led him at times to take positions or make inflammatory statements that undermined his American ally in its negotiations with the North, if they played well in the South. And more often than not, they did.

In Washington, the dramatic confrontation with the Stalinist regime in Pyongyang drew the press like a magnet. Observers in Congress and think tanks called on the administration to take a tough line in dealing with the North while showing great deference to America's ally in the South. At times this line was hard to tread, as the tougher the United States acted toward North Korea, the more unnerved the South became in understandable anxiety at the prospect of war. For it was clear to all that, if the North's plutonium production program could not be stopped by negotiations, the only real alternative was military action. Perhaps the United States could strike and destroy Pyongyang's nuclear facilities from the air without suffering retaliation, but that was not the assessment of the U.S. intelligence community or its military leaders.

When negotiations aimed at settling the dispute stalled in the spring of 1994, the United States dusted off plans for an air strike on the North's nuclear facilities and for sending more troops to the Korean peninsula, while also preparing to seek sanctions from the UN Security Council. Either course of action could have precipitated a full-blown war on the Korean peninsula. With 37,000 Americans already deployed in the South and 10 million people living in Seoul within artillery range of the North, war would be costly for all. Thus, the president and his senior advisers had to reckon with the possibility that a surgical strike could well lead to armed conflict. U.S. military leaders estimated that a clash could have incurred one million casualties in South Korea alone, claiming mainly Korean lives but also tens of thousands of American soldiers and many more American expatriates. If war came, it would be another Korean War, not another Gulf War.

The crisis peaked on June 16, 1994. There has been much debate over just how close we came to war in the dark days of June; readers of this book will be able to form their own judgments based on the historical record. The potential *casus belli* occurred when North Korea defied U.S. warnings and unloaded fuel rods laden with bomb-making plutonium from its operating nuclear reactor. Washington responded by moving steadily toward imposing sanctions against the North at the United Nations and reviewing a decision to send significant military reinforcements to the peninsula. Such a deployment would have been the culmination of a steady, slow buildup that had started at the beginning of the year. These developments led to growing pressure to evacuate thousands of American citizens from South Korea. That would have been a sure sign to both Seoul and Pyongyang that the crisis could soon boil over.

No one will ever know how close the two sides were to a catastrophic second Korean War, because just as the president was weighing a decision to send more American troops to defend Korea, former president Jimmy Carter intervened in the crisis through a fateful meeting with North Korea's aging leader, Kim Il Sung. But for Carter's involvement, the North Koreans might have miscalculated by carrying through with their threats to expel international inspectors monitoring the unloaded fuel rods. They might have begun separating bomb-usable plutonium from those rods. That might have triggered a U.S. decision to launch a preemptive attack that would have destroyed Pyongyang's known nuclear facilities. Or the crisis could have reached a fever pitch when the United Nations imposed sanctions, probably within the next month. By then, the United States would have begun to deploy tens of thousands of additional troops to Korea to deter North Korea from following through on its threat that the imposition of sanctions was tantamount to a declaration of war. Whether Pyongyang would have waited for those reinforcements to arrive or would have attacked beforehand will remain a matter for historical debate.

In any event, war did not come, and over the next four months U.S. officials, working closely with their allies and others, forged a diplomatic solution to the North Korean nuclear crisis. This required the Americans to work hard to set priorities, calculate trade-offs, and resolve disputes within the national security community in order to develop and execute a coherent proposal. That laid the groundwork for intense, virtually continuous negotiations among Washington, Seoul, and Tokyo over what would be demanded of—and offered to—the North. Only then could the negotiations with North Korea in Geneva lead to the agreement on reciprocal, sequential steps laid out in the short, four-page document known as the Agreed Framework. Supporters of the deal argued that the accord met the principal allied objectives regarding the North's plutonium production program. Others complained that the costs outweighed the benefits, and that the deal did not address all issues of concern regarding North Korea.

The story told in the following pages seeks to illuminate the debates surrounding this period in American history. In so doing, the authors hope that much can still be learned that will bear on efforts to resolve the renewed nuclear crisis in North Korea. Some aspects of North Korea's strategy in 1993 and 1994 may provide clues to its calculations today, or to how much may be achieved in any negotiation with the North, through the optimal combination of carrots and sticks. The domestic context in the Republic of Korea and the United States must also be taken into account. Injecting emotionally charged labels such as "blackmail" and "appeasement" into the discussion powerfully affects how much room political leaders have to maneuver in seeking a diplomatic solution. Any administration wishing to engage the North in discussions will need to buttress its support from the political center, protect its right flank, and show toughness and commitment to principle, even as it searches for practical solutions that may stray from dogma in new and perhaps untried ways. Indeed, the history, politics, and details of the negotiation of the Agreed Framework may hold important lessons for any administration attempting to engage an unsavory government over a matter of critical national security importance.

The political situation in the major capitals today is substantially different from ten years ago. In Washington, the tragedy of September 11 has converted catastrophic terrorism from nightmare to reality, giving rise to a presidential doctrine preserving the right to take military action to preempt those—such as North Korea—who could bring nuclear destruction to our homeland. In Seoul, attitudes toward North Korea and the United States have changed dramatically: many South Koreans now see their American allies as a greater threat than their North Korean rivals. In Japan, attitudes toward North Korea have hardened over concerns about Pyongyang's missiles and its confessed abduction of Japanese citizens. Russia and China have witnessed the passing of the political baton to a new generation of leaders, who view security, nuclear weapons, and alliances differently than their predecessors.

The need to address the nuclear threat in all its dimensions with all relevant parties ineluctably has led this book to examine diplomatic and bureaucratic processes. It tells the inside story of how the United States makes decisions and manages relations with allies and adversaries. The authors participated in almost every aspect of the policy process leading up to the signing of the Geneva accord and to its implementation. They therefore cannot claim the objectivity or perspective that derives from detachment, only that which follows from the passage of time. They have tried to be balanced and fair in their assessments, and in what they have chosen to include in these pages. The reader will decide how well they have succeeded.

Going Critical

1

A Cornered Dog
Will Sometimes Bite

Fʟʏɪɴɢ over North Korea in 1980, an American spy satellite spotted something alarming: the foundations of what would become a 5-megawatt nuclear reactor. U.S. satellites had been watching the Yongbyon area, located about 100 kilometers north of Pyongyang, since the "Corona" program successfully orbited its first photo-reconnaissance mission in 1960. Initially the satellites spotted nothing at the site except a few small buildings. By 1965 construction activity was evident. A few years later, a small nuclear research reactor, provided to North Korea by the Soviet Union, was up and running.[1] Although the reactor was not viewed as a direct threat, under Soviet pressure North Korea ultimately placed it and other related facilities under International Atomic Energy Agency safeguards, to provide assurance of their exclusively peaceful use. Throughout the 1970s, Yongbyon showed little additional activity. Then came the 1980 photographs showing the components of what appeared to be an even larger reactor near a large hole, presumably dug to accommodate its foundation.[2] The discovery would eventually lead to a confrontation between Pyongyang and Washington over North Korea's nuclear weapons program.

The specter of nuclear weapons has contributed significantly to tensions and misperceptions on the peninsula ever since the Korean War. In November 1950 President Truman stated that the United States would take "whatever steps are necessary" to deter Chinese aggression, and warned that the use of nuclear weapons had been actively considered. There is evidence to suggest that Washington in subsequent months was prepared to drop these weapons on Korean and Chinese targets if Beijing had thrown more troops into the war.[3] In February 1953 President Eisenhower began dropping "discreet hints" that nuclear weapons might be used. Later that year Secretary of State John Foster Dulles told India's leader, Jawaharal Nehru, that the United States would use "stronger rather than lesser" military means to end the war if negotiations failed. The administration hoped that this would be interpreted as an implied nuclear threat. Eisenhower and Dulles later maintained that threat was a major factor in bringing an end to the conflict.[4]

More than twenty years later, in 1975, Secretary of Defense James Schlesinger publicly warned North Korea that the use of tactical nuclear weapons would be carefully considered in case of aggression.[5] That danger may have seemed real a year later; after North Koreans killed two American soldiers, nuclear-capable bombers from Guam flew up the peninsula toward the Demilitarized Zone ("DMZ") dividing North from South Korea. A U.S. intelligence analyst recalled that the incident "blew their . . . minds" in Pyongyang.[6] That same year, presidential candidate Jimmy Carter asserted that the United States already had 700 atomic weapons in Korea.[7] One observer later noted that Pyongyang might have viewed its acquisition of nuclear weapons as a necessity because the United States "had exposed North Korea, during its infancy as a nation, to the fearsome power and enormous political value of nuclear weapons."[8]

On the surface, the North's nuclear activities evolved in the usual way, starting with peaceful cooperation agreements. In 1956 Pyongyang and Moscow signed two agreements designed to increase cooperation; North Korean scientists began receiving extensive training on nuclear physics at the Soviet Dubna Nuclear Research Complex. In 1959 Moscow and Pyongyang agreed to set up a research center in North Korea. Established on the right bank of the Kuryong River, 8 kilometers from the town of Yongbyon, the new center was called the "furniture factory," perhaps to hide its real purpose from the prying eyes of the outside world. In 1965, three years after a visit by Premier Alexei Kosygin, the Soviet Union delivered North Korea's first research reactor. It entered operation around 1967.[9]

North Korea's interest in nuclear weapons emerged from the shadows in the early 1960s. Kim Il Sung announced a new self-reliant military policy, stimulated by what he saw as Moscow's capitulation to Washington during the Cuban missile crisis. Part of the strategy was to build deep and heavy fortifications in case of an American nuclear attack. But Pyongyang also wanted its own nuclear arsenal. In 1964 a North Korean delegation visiting China carried a letter to Mao Zedong from Kim observing that since the two communist countries had shared the burden of war, they should also share atomic secrets. China responded that such weapons were unnecessary for a small country. Another appeal to Beijing later on was also rejected.[10]

Around the world, nuclear ambitions intensified in the 1970s. The 1973 oil crisis spiked international interest in nuclear energy as an alternative to dependence on the vagaries of Middle East politics. The 1974 test by India of what it disingenuously described as a "peaceful nuclear explosive"—derived from plutonium produced in a research reactor imported from Canada, with heavy water imported from the United States—demonstrated that nuclear technology acquired under the flag of peaceful nuclear cooperation could be diverted to military use. The Indian nuclear test drove American policymakers to redouble their efforts to curb worrisome nuclear efforts in a host of other nations, including Argentina, Brazil, South Africa, Pakistan, Taiwan, North Korea, South Korea, and several Middle Eastern nations.

Government decisions to pursue nuclear weapons tend to be most heavily influenced by their security environment. In South Korea, the perception of a growing threat from the North combined with President Richard Nixon's decision to withdraw the Seventh Infantry Division led President Park Chung Hee to launch a covert program to develop a nuclear bomb. Central to this effort was an agreement to purchase a plutonium reprocessing plant from France. Under strong diplomatic pressure from the Ford administration, the South reluctantly curbed its weapons program and abandoned the reprocessing plant. U.S. pressure to block South Korean efforts to advance its nuclear weapons option continued into the Carter administration.[11]

North Korea's response to the altered nuclear equation in the 1970s was equally predictable. Pyongyang sought to upgrade its modest program when it negotiated with the Soviet Union for a much larger, 5-megawatt research reactor.[12] Eventually, Pyongyang decided to build the reactor itself, using its previous experience and whatever technology it could get overseas. The new gas-graphite moderated design, based on declassified British blueprints, enabled it to use natural uranium fuel which, when irradiated, served as an ideal source for weapons plutonium. Each core load would produce about 30 kilograms of plutonium—enough for about five nuclear warheads. This facility, spotted by the American spy satellite, began operation in the mid-1980s, but by then work had begun on another reactor, ten times as powerful. Belatedly, the United States pressed Moscow, as North Korea's key ally, to exert pressure on Pyongyang to join the Nuclear Non-Proliferation Treaty. In 1985, persuaded by a Soviet pledge to provide it with four full-size nuclear power plants, the Pyongyang government did just that.

Under the provisions of the treaty, within eighteen months of accession a new member must conclude a comprehensive safeguards agreement with the International Atomic Energy Agency. This did not happen. The IAEA mistakenly sent the wrong form of agreement to North Korea, an error that was not remedied until the end of the eighteen months.[13] It was only discovered when the North Koreans rejected the agreement as transgressing their national sovereignty. That neither North Korean, IAEA, nor U.S. officials had even bothered to look closely enough at the draft agreement to recognize such an obvious blunder demonstrates a mystifyingly lackadaisical attitude toward North Korea's nonproliferation obligations. When the correct form was finally sent to Pyongyang, a further eighteen months passed without obtaining North Korean acceptance of a safeguards agreement, much less implementation of its safeguards obligations. And when *those* eighteen months had passed, the United States prodded the IAEA but it took no serious action to press North Korea to comply with its nonproliferation commitments. The North Korean program metastasized during this period of indifference into a full-scale plutonium production effort that would require radical surgery to dismantle.

Pyongyang's drive toward nuclear weapons may also have been intensified because of its increasing sense of isolation, due in part to the widening gap between the North and South Korean economies. Per capita incomes in the South did not overtake those in the North until the mid-1970s. Year after year little changed in the North—a lonely bastion of Stalinism, insulated from the forces of change that ultimately destroyed the Soviet Union and its East European satellites. By the mid-1980s annual economic growth sputtered along at about 2 to 3 percent a year, then declined 3 to 5 percent a year beginning in 1989. With the collapse of outside economic support from Pyongyang's erstwhile communist allies—themselves shuffling into oblivion—the decline rate hit 10 to 15 percent in the early 1990s.[14]

The story in South Korea stood in stark contrast, as a series of politically repressive but economically dynamic leaders led Seoul to follow Japan's footsteps as the next "Asian miracle." Between 1962 and 1995 the South Korean economy expanded at an average annual rate of 8.5 percent. Its gross national product grew from $2.3 billion to $437.4 billion, corresponding to a per capita rise from $87 to $9,511 at current prices. The economic revolution coursed through many sectors; between 1980 and 1990 annual growth rates exceeded 11 percent for industry, 12 percent for manufacturing, and 8 percent for services.[15] By 1992 South Korea exceeded North Korean GNP by more than a factor of 10, a gap that continued to widen as Pyongyang's economy struggled and the South hummed along at 5 percent annual growth rates.[16] And while military governments continued to rule, they had gained enough respectability to win the right to host the Summer Olympic Games in 1988.

Of equal or greater importance, North Korea's traditional allies had forever changed in ways that undermined its few pillars of foreign support. Maoist China, source of the Cultural Revolution and inspiration to the anti-imperialist opponents of the "capitalist-roaders," had given way to a more pragmatic regime that sought better relations with Seoul. The changes in the Soviet Union were more profound, as Gorbachev struggled through calibrated political and economic reform—perestroika—to keep his country from collapsing under the weight of tyranny and communist economics. In the words of the widely respected Korea expert Don Oberdorfer, the Soviet Union evolved from godfather and benefactor of North Korea to partner and client of South Korea.[17] By 1991 the 38th parallel had become a lonely, isolated outpost of armed, cold war confrontation. Meeting in Pyongyang with William Taylor, a prominent American expert on Korea, the North Korean leader Kim Il Sung observed: "The world is changing all around us."[18]

The fall of the Berlin Wall, the collapse of communism in Eastern Europe, and the rapprochement between South Korea and China and the Soviet Union probably had a profound effect on North Korea's leaders. Kim Il Sung must have been alarmed by the whirlwind of events throughout the communist world, questioning whether his regime could survive the newly unleashed centripetal forces of democracy and free markets that were beginning to take root. North Korea had already begun in the mid-1980s to show signs of opening to the outside world and experimenting with its stagnating economy. By 1985 the two Koreas were engaged in a dialogue that reflected a serious and much debated policy in Pyongyang of seeking limited accommodation with Seoul and engaging the United States. At the same time, there also seemed to emerge in the leadership a group of economic "realists" who tinkered with the system to get it moving and favored some foreign entry into the economy.

Further complicating matters, Kim Il Sung was preparing for the succession of his son Kim Jong Il. The elder Kim, born in 1912 near Pyongyang, gained notoriety as a guerilla leader against Japanese occupation forces. He rose to power after World War II in the Russian-occupied half of the peninsula, becoming chairman of the Korean Workers Party in 1949. Kim would hold that position until his death in 1994, presiding over the Democratic People's Republic of Korea and called the "Great Leader" by his people. His son, Kim Jong Il, the "Dear Leader" while his father was alive, was born in 1942 in the Russian Far East. Until high school he was known by his Russian name,

Yuri. After he graduated from Kim Il Sung University, his first real job was chief of his father's bodyguards. The younger Kim seems to have begun his rise to power in 1971 in what promised to be the first communist dynasty.

That process had been under way for two decades as the younger Kim was brought up through the party ranks, giving him experience at successively higher levels of leadership and building his base of support from the bottom up. By the end of the 1980s, he had taken control of party affairs and the economy. Kim Jong Il was also increasingly influential in running North Korea's national security and foreign policy affairs—including its nuclear program—although his father still maintained some undetermined role. Conventional wisdom at the time portrayed the younger Kim as spoiled, erratic, and cruel. But other sources indicated that he appeared to take a consistent approach, supporting "economic realists," presiding over the North's policy of limited opening to Seoul and Washington and initiatives to improve ties with Japan, Western Europe, and even Israel. In short, Kim Jong Il remained an enigma.

The First Bush Administration

This was the Korean reality inherited by the new Bush administration in 1989, a reality that became more disturbing with the discovery of a reprocessing facility at Yongbyon. The rectangular building would have been hard to miss; located in a complex south of the 5-megawatt reactor, it was about the length of two football fields and six stories high. Incredibly in retrospect, some analysts posited that the building housed a production line for vinalon, a synthetic material similar to nylon, though why such a facility would be collocated with heavily protected nuclear plants was never adequately explained. On the other hand, building a reprocessing facility alongside the production reactors made great sense. The spent fuel from those units could be dissolved through reprocessing, leading to the separation of plutonium well suited for the production of nuclear weapons from the uranium and fission products contained in irradiated fuel elements.

Just as disturbing was information that North Korea might be working on a nuclear weapon design. To detonate a plutonium bomb, a hollow sphere of plutonium must be rapidly and symmetrically compressed in order to achieve a supercritical mass that would produce a significant nuclear yield. Evidence of powerful conventional explosives tests at the Yongbyon facility in the late 1980s persuaded the Bush administration that North Korea was working on an implosion-based weapon.

These developments suggested that the U.S. policy of isolating Pyongyang—which had been in place for three decades following the Korean War—could not alone prevent North Korea from going nuclear. In that spirit, the Reagan administration had already proposed a "modest initiative" in recognition of the end of the cold war and of South Korea's move to establish diplomatic relations with Pyongyang's communist allies. It called for reduced restrictions on travel and contact, improved economic cooperation, diplomatic discussion, and humanitarian assistance to North Korea. The theory was that by engaging Pyongyang, it might be possible both to persuade the North to join the community of nations and to refrain from building nuclear weapons.

The Bush administration took that initiative further and launched a policy of "comprehensive engagement," intended to inch toward better relations once North Korea abandoned its nuclear weapons development.[19] The administration's study of American policy toward Korea—National Security Review 28—proposed to achieve that goal by maintaining a strong deterrent against North Korean aggression, promoting North-South dialogue, and locking Pyongyang into its nuclear nonproliferation obligations while preventing its access to dangerous enrichment or reprocessing technologies. Another goal was to persuade North Korea to abjure terrorism and to constrain sales related to nuclear and chemical weapons as well as ballistic missiles. The prize for progress in these areas would be gradual movement toward normalized U.S.–North Korean relations.[20] In a bow to domestic interests and recognizing the North's need for food assistance, the administration put in place laws allowing the export to Pyongyang of $1.2 billion of American goods in 1991, primarily food, and medical or humanitarian equipment, even before the nuclear problem was resolved.[21]

National Security Review 28 also recognized that the reported presence of U.S. nuclear weapons in Korea would continue to dog American diplomacy. According to one nongovernmental expert, President Jimmy Carter's strong inclination to withdraw American troops from Korea implied that tactical nuclear weapons would also be removed. But the military was divided on the wisdom of such a move. Some officers felt nuclear weapons were militarily irrelevant and only created political headaches; others believed they were essential in view of Pyongyang's strong conventional forces. When the Carter administration backed away from withdrawing American troops, their tactical nuclear weapons stayed. Under the Bush administration respected officials such as General Robert RisCassi, the commander of U.S. forces in Korea, and Donald Gregg, ambassador to South Korea, supported their withdrawal.[22] But the proposal foundered at the White House. National Security Adviser Brent Scowcroft did not want to appear to reward Pyongyang's aggressive behavior.

Another divisive issue was how far to press the North in securing an end to its nuclear program. Should the United States ask North *and South* Korea to forswear plutonium reprocessing, and enlist Japan in that effort? One school of thought, dubbed the "arms controllers" and led by the State Department's ambassador-at-large Richard Kennedy, advocated bringing Pyongyang into compliance with the NPT and persuading it to accept safeguards inspections conducted by the IAEA. This group resisted any steps aimed at curtailing North Korean nuclear activities *if* those steps had the collateral effect of undermining the NPT and the IAEA. Hence it opposed either asking the Koreans to forswear reprocessing or even discussing the proposal with Japan since the NPT did not proscribe that activity, which in theory could be part of a purely peaceful nuclear energy program. The issue was especially sensitive in Japan, where it was a matter of long-standing national energy policy to reprocess spent fuel from its commercial nuclear reactors, in order to extract the plutonium and recycle that material in Japanese reactors. An earlier attempt by the Carter administration to muscle Tokyo out of the plutonium fuel cycle had ended in U.S. failure and diplomatic retreat.

On the other side of the debate were the "security pragmatists," who were less concerned with nonproliferation theology and more with blocking physical access to weapon-usable materials. They were skeptical that the NPT, enforced by the IAEA, could constrain North Korean proliferation activities. The Office of the Secretary of Defense was the most prominent member of this camp, led by Under Secretary of Defense Paul Wolfowitz. This position also found support in the State Department, where the Political-Military Bureau tempered its concerns for maintaining the nonproliferation regime with a security pragmatism based on the same considerations as the Pentagon. The Department of State's East Asia Bureau—its lead player on Korea—tended to favor protecting U.S. bilateral relationships over multilateral obligations that threatened to irritate those relations.

The pragmatists' approach informed a July 1991 meeting in the office of Under Secretary of State Reginald Bartholomew to discuss American policy toward North Korea. North and South Korea were weeks away from their admission to the UN. Bartholomew and Assistant Secretary of Defense Jim Lilley agreed that the United States should press Japan to condition normalization of its own relations with Pyongyang on a North Korean pledge not to reprocess—a pledge beyond the requirements of the NPT and based on the implicit premise that the existing IAEA system was inadequate. Wolfowitz added that Washington needed a club to get North Korea's attention. Bartholomew stressed that if the United States agreed to "pay" to persuade North Korea simply to observe its existing NPT obligations then the NPT might as well be discarded, because once one started to pay others to live up to freely accepted international obligations there would be no stop to it. A mutually verifiable ban on reprocessing, however, would go beyond the NPT and therefore could justify some reciprocal benefit.

Since there was no way to reconcile the pragmatists' goal—denying physical access by North Korea to weapon-usable materials—with allowing reprocessing in North Korea, Washington decided to float the idea in Tokyo of a reprocessing ban in Korea. If Japan balked that such a ban would force it to curtail its own reprocessing program, the administration would reconsider. When approached by the State Department, to the happy surprise of U.S. officials, the Japanese *supported* the proposal. Evidently they were more concerned with the nuclear threat from Korea than with preserving the principle that plutonium reprocessing was not only legal but also an appropriate way to close the nuclear fuel cycle.

There Do Not Exist Any Nuclear Weapons Whatsoever

As the Korean nuclear situation grew ever more worrisome, the international community continued its process of radical transformation. In 1989 the Berlin Wall had fallen, and Czechoslovakia had regained its liberty in the Velvet Revolution. In August 1991, Soviet leader Mikhail Gorbachev was seized at his dacha in Sochi, near the Black Sea, by conspirators bent on restoring traditional communist discipline in reaction to the libertinage and uncertainties of perestroika. The attempted coup ultimately failed, but the crumbling Soviet Union was destined to vanish before the New Year, a victim of the internal contradictions of a communist ideology that sought to build a society and a government upon a fundamental misunderstanding of human nature.

The cold war effectively over, leaders were left with the question: what role should nuclear weapons retain in a post–cold war era? Administration officials argued over how to respond to the unfolding events. As President Bush later wrote, the "overriding debate within the administration remained what we wanted to see emerge, and how best to make the most of the greatly increased influence of the reformers while we could."[23] A central concern that required urgent attention with the breakup of the Soviet Union was the fate of the collapsing superpower's nuclear arsenal.

On September 27, 1991, shortly after the attempted Soviet coup, President Bush announced the unilateral withdrawal of all U.S. ground-launched tactical nuclear weapons around the world, calling on the Soviets to reciprocate. This path-breaking confidence-building measure would constitute an important diplomatic gesture to the Soviet leaders, while substantially reducing the threat that conventional conflict could somehow escalate to nuclear holo-caust.[24] According to Don Oberdorfer, President Bush also secretly ordered the removal of all nuclear weapons in South Korea delivered by aircraft.[25]

The president's stunning initiative triggered a burst of diplomatic progress on the Korean Peninsula. As North-South relations gathered momentum, by December 1991 the prime ministers of the two Koreas negotiated a mutual nonaggression pact, each pledging to avoid interference in the internal affairs of the other. Prodded by the United States, President Roh Tae Woo followed the Bush announcement with his own proposal, pledging to refrain from plutonium reprocessing as well as from the manufacture, possession, or stor-age of nuclear weapons. But the dam broke when Roh stated, "As I speak, there do not exist any nuclear weapons whatsoever, anywhere in the Republic of Korea."[26] President Bush artfully skirted long-standing U.S. policy to neither confirm nor deny the presence or absence of nuclear weapons at any place and time: "I heard what [he] said and I'm not about to argue with him."[27]

By the last day of 1991, the surge of nuclear diplomacy had produced the North-South Denuclearization Declaration (NSDD). Though proliferation concerns had to date focused on the plutonium path to weapons, the White House urged that the evolving draft of the NSDD be modified also to include a ban on uranium enrichment, another path to building the bomb. In the end, the NSDD codified the Roh initiative and proscribed both plutonium repro-cessing and uranium enrichment on the Korean Peninsula, shutting down both principal avenues to nuclear weapons manufacture, at least on paper.[28]

The Denuclearization Declaration represented a double victory for the security pragmatists. First, it represented a symbolic victory over the arms controllers, by curtailing the freedom that both Koreas otherwise would have enjoyed as NPT parties: the right to enrich uranium and separate plutonium provided these activities were undertaken under IAEA safeguards. Second, it represented a victory for muscular American diplomacy over the preferences of both North and South Korea, who never would have concluded the NSDD—with its enrichment and reprocessing bans—without U.S. encouragement.

Aside from agreeing to the Denuclearization Declaration, in December 1991 Pyongyang also ended five years of heel dragging by announcing its intention to sign its long-overdue IAEA safeguards agreement once the United States confirmed there were no American nuclear weapons in Korea. For its part, the United States signaled quietly to the North through talks between its diplomats in the Chinese capital, the "Beijing channel," and elsewhere that if Pyongyang took that step it would be rewarded with a high-level meeting with a senior American diplomat. The North had sought such contact for years, not only to foster an improved bilateral relationship, but also as a mark of respect and an opportunity to drive a wedge between the United States and South Korea.

The United States kept the momentum going when President Bush visited Seoul in the first week of 1992, offering to cancel the annual Team Spirit military exercise for that year once Pyongyang redeemed its pledge to sign its safeguards agreement. Called "our Super Bowl" by one U.S. officer, Team Spirit began in 1976 after the Vietnam withdrawal to reassure South Korea and bolster deterrence against the North. The exercise often involved hundreds of thousands of troops and, some suspected, even nuclear weapons.[29] Not surprisingly, North Korea viewed Team Spirit as a dress rehearsal for an invasion.

Team Spirit's utility had been hotly debated in the United States. Many senior military officers had considered eliminating it since other exercises could accomplish the same objectives at far lower cost and less political clamor from the North. The skeptics seemed to be making headway when, on January 7, after consultations between South Korean and American officials, Seoul announced that Team Spirit would be canceled for that year. In order to maintain pressure on North Korea, however, Secretary of Defense Dick Cheney took other steps to ensure a strong military posture in the South, including delaying the planned withdrawal of 6,000 U.S. troops from the peninsula and enlarging other military exercises.[30]

In a further, unprecedented move, two days later National Security Adviser Brent Scowcroft announced that the United States and North Korea would hold direct talks later that month.[31] Under Secretary of State for Political Affairs Arnold Kanter, the third-ranking official in the Department of State, would lead the U.S. delegation. Kanter, whose government service began in 1977, first at State and then at the National Security Council (NSC), held a doctorate from Yale. Before entering government, he had worked at think tanks—the RAND Corporation and the Brookings Institution—and had been a university professor. His counterpart was Kim Yong Sun, the Worker's Party secretary for international affairs. The six-foot-tall Kim—humorous, charming, and quite polished—had at one point in his career been sent to a coal mine for teaching his colleagues Western dances. Now, after rising through the diplomatic ranks, he appeared to have more influence than the North Korean foreign minister, courtesy of his close relationship with Kim Jong Il.

Preparations for those talks had, in fact, been under way throughout late 1991. The head of the State Department's Korea Desk—Charles Kartman—and an officer stationed at the U.S. Mission to the United Nations—Danny Russel—had been meeting with a North Korean official stationed in New York—Ho Jong—sometimes in a basement conference room at the United

Nations. (All three would later play important roles in the nuclear crisis.) The back and forth, which continued for some time, was both novel and significant enough to lead the State Department to take great care in how Washington's positions were presented. Kartman would dictate verbatim over the telephone the phrases Russel was supposed to use with the North Koreans. One participant recalled that "it seemed that we were more orthodox than the North Koreans! I suspect the concern was not to upgrade from the Beijing channel until the North Koreans had earned it, so we were being careful to make sure only non-substantive administrative details were discussed."[32]

During preparations for the Kanter-Kim meeting, differences surfaced once again, this time between those who believed that diplomacy offered the best path to persuade North Korea to give up its nuclear weapons option and those who believed that Pyongyang would see direct talks as a sign of weakness and an opportunity to disrupt solidarity with South Korea. Agencies wrestled over every point and nuance in Kanter's draft presentation, producing a carefully negotiated document.

Kanter's presentation was based, according to one American participant, on the "good-doggie, bad-doggie" principle. If North Korea complied fully with its nonproliferation obligations, including full implementation of the recently signed Denuclearization Declaration, it could look forward to a future of greater communication and commerce with the United States and the rest of the international community.[33] But the inability of U.S. agencies to agree on exactly how many benefits to open to the North prevented Kanter from being too specific about the bright future. The U.S. position excluded even mentioning the possibility of "normalization" of bilateral relations. The choice between dialogue and confrontation, concluded Kanter, lay with Pyongyang.

Not surprisingly, Pyongyang declined to accept that burden; the U.S. promise of greater communication and commerce was so vague and intangible that it held little to attract North Korean cooperation. At the same time, the North Koreans—having witnessed the collapse of East Germany and Romania through greater exposure to the freedom and prosperity of Western Europe—viewed Kanter's vision with some ambivalence, if not downright fear. In his presentation, Kim Yong Sun, also appearing to hew closely to a script, laid the responsibility for the tensions dividing Korea at the doorstep of the Americans and their South Korean and Japanese allies. Aside from proposing that both Koreas and the United States work together to deal with the greatest danger in Asia—namely, Japan—the North Korean negotiator pressed unsuccessfully for further meetings between the two sides.

But Kim also dropped some tantalizing hints. He said point blank that North Korea would have no objections to U.S. troops remaining on the peninsula even after national unification, citing the Japanese again as an important consideration. The Americans—used to years of North Korean rhetoric aimed at ending their military alliance with Seoul and pushing them off the peninsula—were surprised.

Not an inspiring encounter, the New York meeting was significant for occurring at all, while the tone—if somewhat stiff and restrained—was not outwardly hostile. The United States, having delivered the promised high-level meeting, now saw North Korea do its part. After Pyongyang initialed IAEA safeguards and ratified the agreement in April, Director General Hans Blix (later head of the UN inspection effort in Iraq) paid a six-day visit to North Korea to tour the facilities that now would be subject to inspection. Subsequently he told the U.S. Congress that Pyongyang was cooperating, but any definitive judgments about its nuclear program were several months away. His caution would prove justified.[34]

Stalling Out: Three Blind Alleys

Though no one knew it at the time, the Blix visit represented a high-water mark of cooperation as the peninsula now began to tip toward crisis. By the end of 1992, every avenue that had opened to new promise following the Bush nuclear initiative of September 1991—North Korean channels with the South, IAEA, and the United States, respectively—had narrowed and closed. For some time, positive momentum continued; for instance, the North-South meeting of prime ministers in September 1992 made further progress in promoting reconciliation. But talks held under the auspices of the Joint Nuclear Control Commission slowly ground to a halt, failing to resolve any of the contentious inspection issues related to verification of the North-South Denuclearization Declaration.

The issue of inspections was also souring Pyongyang's budding relationship with the IAEA. In its May 1992 declaration to the IAEA—required from states entering a safeguards agreement—the North confirmed the existence of a reprocessing plant at Yongbyon and the separation of 90 grams of plutonium two years earlier from damaged reactor fuel, an action it characterized as a scientific experiment. But inspections in July and September began to reveal some discrepancies in the declaration. Scientific analysis of the data gathered during these visits showed that North Korea recovered more batches of plutonium than it had declared and that reprocessing occurred over a much longer period of time than Pyongyang had admitted. As IAEA director general Blix pressed for access to additional sites and information to help solve the mystery, tensions rose between Vienna and Pyongyang.[35]

For the IAEA, the growing challenge of North Korea was an important test of its own credibility. Only a few years earlier, the Gulf War had revealed that a covert nuclear weapons program existed in Iraq despite IAEA inspections of Baghdad's known nuclear facilities. The soul-searching that followed in Vienna produced a number of innovations. One was an emphasis on an already existing but never used right of "special inspections," which meant the IAEA could seek to visit declared and undeclared locations and facilities if evidence suggested they held nuclear material. Although such inspections were still a last resort, the agency was not going to make the same mistake with North Korea that it had made with Iraq. Moreover, the IAEA's determination was only reinforced by the contrasting experience with South Africa, which had recently revealed the existence of its nuclear weapons program and was cooperating in coming clean.[36]

The slowing of progress with the IAEA and South Korea blocked the last avenue for meaningful dialogue: talks with the United States. In September, as hope for progress dimmed, Kim Yong Sun sent a letter to Under Secretary Kanter through the Beijing channel trying to arrange another bilateral meeting. While Kim predictably patted his country on the back, noting that Pyongyang had opened its facilities to the IAEA, he blamed the South's intransigence for the lack of progress on the bilateral nuclear inspection regime. Kanter called the proposal "interesting" but, also predictably, rejected talks absent progress on North-South inspections and cooperation with the IAEA.

Chafing under the IAEA's scrutiny, thwarted in its desire for talks with Washington, and pressed to accept inspections by South Korea, the North was about to experience yet another blow: the resumption of the Team Spirit exercise. While the United States and South Korea had insisted that the suspension of Team Spirit 1992 was an isolated decision unlinked to future exercises, the North had vigorously urged that the suspension become permanent. The South Koreans, however, were so exasperated with the deepening stalemate that they favored going ahead with Team Spirit 1993. At the annual Security Consultative Meeting held in early October 1992, Secretary of Defense Dick Cheney agreed, since the Pentagon was reluctant to get into a dispute with South Korea. But some wiggle room remained. Although the communiqué issued after the annual meeting stated that preparations for the 1993 exercise would continue, a final decision would not be made until December or January.[37] Unassuaged, Pyongyang blasted the decision. Donald Gregg, the U.S. ambassador to Seoul, called the move "one of the biggest mistakes" of American policy toward Korea.[38]

Making matters worse, the day before the Team Spirit announcement, South Korea declared it had uncovered a massive North Korean spy ring. Employing a sure-fire tool to inflame Pyongyang, the South's intelligence agency claimed that the North was employing some 400 agents in the South to cause agitation and disrupt politics.[39] The announcement may have been a deliberate attempt by South Korean intelligence to slow the pace of nuclear diplomacy and by the campaign managers of presidential candidate Kim Young Sam's ruling party to prevent better relations with the North. Electoral politics also may have played a role; a staff member of his opponent, Kim Dae Jung, was arrested in the affair. In any case, once the scandal broke, President Roh canceled a trip to North Korea by senior economic officials in his government. The chilling effect on inter-Korean relations was unmistakable.[40]

The twin blows of the resumption of Team Spirit and the spy scandal produced predictable results. Within weeks North Korea suspended all contacts with Seoul, with the exception of the Joint Nuclear Control Commission, where the two countries continued to spar over an inspection regime for the Denuclearization Declaration. The North also threatened to suspend IAEA inspections, but its warnings were by and large ignored. Charles Kartman, the State Department Korean country director, recalled that the "advantages of using Team Spirit as a club appealed to many people, and the advantages of satisfying South Korean demands that we use a club were obvious." While he and others argued that this was counterproductive, Kartman wryly observed that "the voice of caution was rather low level."[41]

On the eve of the 1992 presidential elections in the United States and South Korea, the East Asian Policy Coordinating Committee (PCC) of the National Security Council, chaired by Assistant Secretary of State William Clark, took stock of the Bush administration's policy. The October 28 meeting reaffirmed the conclusions of National Security Review 28: cautious engagement and not isolation of North Korea would best advance American goals. The members of the committee agreed that the nuclear issue should be the first order of business, followed by resolution of the problem of North Korea's missile exports. Once the nuclear problem was solved, a U.S.–North Korean political-level dialogue could begin. Washington also could consider phasing out selected economic sanctions, starting with the Trading with the Enemy Act, which had become law after the Korean War and was designed to cut off all economic contact with Pyongyang. In short, the administration seemed to believe that once short-term problems were resolved, its policy of engagement would continue to move forward.

Steady as She Goes

On November 4, William Jefferson Clinton was elected the forty-second president of the United States. In South Korea, former opposition leader Kim Young Sam emerged victorious from elections on December 18. Looking ahead, the State Department predicted that the coming to power of the two new presidents, and the ongoing transition of power to Kim Jong Il in North Korea, would likely lead to a period of adjustment and a "feeling out" of one another in the first half of 1993.

As the two presidents prepared to take office, the outgoing Deputies Committee met just before Christmas to discuss Korea. Since the Policy Coordinating Committee had met two months earlier, the situation had continued to deteriorate. The intense North Korean reaction to the resumption of the Team Spirit exercise had paralyzed the already sluggish inter-Korean negotiations concerning a bilateral nuclear inspection regime. The North had refused to grant the IAEA access to a site called "Building 500," which stored nuclear waste that might help establish whether North Korea had separated more plutonium than it had declared. If its efforts continued to fall short of the mark, the agency planned to hold a special Board of Governors meeting and then to refer the nuclear issue to the UN Security Council.[42] In November, Washington rebuffed a proposal by North Korea's deputy ambassador to the United Nations, Ho Jong, for another Kanter-Kim session, again insisting that the North first meet its nonproliferation obligations.

Concerned but not alarmed, the Deputies Committee, consisting of senior officials just a step below cabinet level, discussed reducing or delaying Team Spirit to allow the new administration to decide whether or not to hold the exercise. But changes at this late date would be logistically difficult. It seemed more practical to use public diplomacy to deflect the North's attempts to blame the United States and South Korea for the stalemate. In the end, the deputies agreed on a "steady as she goes" approach; once the new administrations in Washington and Seoul took office and Team Spirit concluded, they believed the situation would calm. But in Seoul, a South Korean official warned a visiting American that "a cornered dog will sometimes bite in addition to barking."

"Steady as she goes" also seemed to describe the course plotted by Pyongyang. While Washington, Seoul, and Vienna tried to nudge the nonproliferation agenda forward, for the second year in a row Kim Il Sung's annual New Year's address did not betray any deep concerns over the nuclear issue. Refraining from direct criticism of the United States and South Korea, Kim Il Sung offered to meet with anyone who takes a "sincere" stand on reunification "without questioning his or her past." He also called on other countries, the United States, and Japan, to help solve problems on the peninsula. The speech came at a time when Pyongyang was sending officials to Asia, Europe, Latin America, and the Middle East to break out of its isolation and to improve trade ties given the food shortages and economic problems that bedeviled North Korea.

While Kim Il Sung's conciliatory foreign policy stance was coupled with an airing of conservative domestic political themes that may have been meant to appease hard line elements, there were no signs that the North was preparing for an impending crisis. To the contrary, officials believed to favor greater opening to the outside world had received promotions at a meeting of the Supreme People's Assembly held a few weeks earlier. Indeed, in January the North Koreans announced a greater emphasis on light industry, in an effort to raise the standard of living and to prepare for at least some economic restructuring.[43] U.S. government analysts speculated that Kim Jong Il, more like Gorbachev than Yeltsin, wanted to tinker with the status quo while preserving the system.

On January 21, 1993, incoming national security adviser Anthony ("Tony") Lake convened the NSC staff in Room 208 of the Old Executive Office Building. Lake had served as a young Foreign Service officer in Saigon in 1963 and first joined the NSC staff in 1969 as a special assistant to then national security adviser Henry Kissinger, before resigning in protest over the secret bombing of Cambodia. During the Carter administration he returned to government as the director of policy planning at the State Department, and spent most of the 1980s teaching and writing about foreign policy. Beneath his amiable demeanor and dry sense of humor lay a sharp intellect, deep knowledge of history, and a keen sense of the use of power.

After a few remarks about the new president's foreign policy, Lake introduced the senior staff. One official who was to play a key role in the unfolding crisis was Deputy National Security Adviser Samuel R. ("Sandy") Berger, a longtime associate of the new president and a successful trade lawyer in Washington, D.C. Berger had been Lake's deputy on the State Department's Policy Planning Staff under President Carter and would later succeed him as national security adviser. He had a keen intellect, an intuitive sense of the art of the possible, and a seemingly endless capacity for work. Next to Berger sat Leon Fuerth, a former Foreign Service officer who had helped Al Gore become one of the Senate's leading arms control experts. Fuerth's insights and creativity would contribute significantly to the administration's Korea policy throughout the crisis.

Lake invited the senior directors to highlight critical issues facing the new administration. North Korea was near but not at the top of the new administration's busy nonproliferation agenda. Daniel Poneman was one of the few holdovers from the Bush administration. Also a lawyer by training, Poneman had served in the Department of Energy for a year before joining the NSC staff to work on nonproliferation issues under Senior Director for Defense Policy and Arms Control Arnold Kanter, before Kanter moved over to the State Department as under secretary. The incoming Clinton administration decided to establish a separate office for Non-Proliferation and Export Controls and appointed Poneman as its first senior director.

When his turn came, Poneman first addressed the cluster of proliferation issues relating to Russia but then turned to North Korea, reporting that IAEA inspectors were at that moment on the ground at Yongbyon; a special Board of Governors meeting would likely be held in February to address the North Korean issue. On January 26, Poneman told Lake that the critical question of the day was whether the announcement reaffirming that Team Spirit would be held would in turn lead Pyongyang to throw out the IAEA inspectors who were still completing their work. If not, he predicted that the next critical point would be reached in two to three weeks, when the IAEA Board of Governors would take up the issue.

The initial steps of the new Clinton administration maintained continuity with the approach of its predecessor, though they were hardly calculated to win hearts and minds in North Korea. The administration did not revisit, much less reverse, Defense Secretary Cheney's agreement to conduct the Team Spirit exercise in 1993. Moreover, Under Secretary Kanter's interlocutor from the high-level talks of January 1992—Kim Yong Sun—and five other members of a delegation that was planning to participate in a February 3 meeting of parliamentarians in Washington were denied visas.[44] The decision came as a disappointment to some State Department officials who were hoping somehow to jump-start relations with Pyongyang by allowing Kim to come to Washington.[45]

In part, the continuity in U.S. policy resulted from inertia; the Clinton administration was still getting organized. As was customary since the Kennedy administration, the president had quickly issued a number of directives, launching a series of policy reviews that aimed to shape the new administration's policy and, implicitly, to foster the interagency consensus and teamwork that would be critical to their effective implementation. Among the earliest of these reviews were Presidential Review Directive 8, the nonproliferation policy review chaired by Poneman, and a separate review of East Asian policy, chaired by Assistant Secretary of State for East Asian Affairs William Clark. He was also a holdover from the Bush administration, as was Assistant Secretary of State for Political-Military Affairs Robert Gallucci, who would later emerge as the administration's point man on North Korea. Indeed, many of the key decisionmakers on North Korea had been working on the problem during the Bush administration.

Continuity was not only the result of a need to get organized. Strong backing for the IAEA would be critical to a president who had campaigned on the need to elevate nonproliferation to the top of the national security agenda.

Other elements of the Bush policy—a strong commitment to the security of South Korea, close coordination with Seoul and Tokyo, and careful diplomacy to enlist Pyongyang's traditional friends in Beijing and Moscow in rolling back the North Korean nuclear program—would have seemed equally natural to Republicans or Democrats. The first interagency meetings on the evolving standoff elicited a consistent response: North Korea must comply with its nonproliferation obligations, including not only IAEA special inspections but also the inspections required by its agreement with South Korea. Some thought was given to whether it was wise to allow the conflict with the IAEA to come to a head during the Team Spirit exercise; Japan believed the confluence of the two might provoke an especially negative North Korean reaction. But the standard (albeit erroneous) wisdom was the situation would cool down once Team Spirit was over.

Events already set in motion by the time President Clinton assumed office appeared to follow an inexorable course. In late January, following the announcement reaffirming that Team Spirit would be held as scheduled, Hans Blix issued his first request ever for special inspections. Then talks at the end of the month in Pyongyang between the IAEA and North Koreans made no progress, prompting Blix to call for a special Board of Governors meeting to endorse his request.[46]

The agency tried one last time to make progress when North Korea's minister of atomic energy, Choi Hak Gun, visited Vienna the weekend of February 20–21. During ten hours of meetings, Blix made every effort to give the North Koreans an opportunity to address the problem with their plutonium production declaration, even warning that at its upcoming meeting the board would be shown satellite pictures of North Korea trying to hide nuclear activities. But Choi would not budge. Although the IAEA inspectors had considered taking the North Koreans to lunch in town since most restaurants nearby were closed on weekends, a frustrated Blix told his team, "No agreement, no lunch."[47]

As its differences with the IAEA came into sharper focus, it was unclear whether Pyongyang was mobilizing for a crisis. Its initial posture of preparing the North Korean populace for progress in ties with the United States and South Korea shifted somewhat after the January 26 Team Spirit announcement. The next day, the North Korean Foreign Ministry issued a statement that moved its differences with the IAEA into the open and seemed to throw some cold water on hopes for a diplomatic solution. It claimed that the United States could not escape responsibility for preventing North Korea from fulfilling its obligations under the NPT and that Team Spirit was a "nuclear threat" contradictory to the treaty. Some inferred that Pyongyang might be able to fulfill its obligations once the exercise was over.[48] There were also signs Pyong-yang wanted to avoid derailing efforts to improve ties with the United States and South Korea. In an unusual, carefully calculated gesture, the statement contained an unattributed quotation from Clinton's inaugural address, sug-gesting that the North was paying close attention to the new administration's pronouncements.[49]

But a showdown had become inevitable. In mid-February, Seoul's ambas-sador to the United States, Hyun Hong Choo, met with Lake, Poneman, and NSC director for Asian affairs, Torkel Patterson, at the White House. Lake mused that the North Koreans may have thought that merely accepting inspec-tions would have been enough to satisfy the international community. But now that the IAEA had actually caught them in a deception, the North seemed unable to find a way out of the box. And Hans Blix, determined not to repeat the agency's embarrassment over its failure in Iraq, insisted on pressing for spe-cial inspections once North Korea's lack of cooperation had become clear.

On February 22, the thirty-five member states of the IAEA Board of Gov-ernors met in an extraordinary closed session to look at satellite photographs showing the apparent nuclear waste sites where the IAEA sought access. The scene was reminiscent of the UN Security Council session held during the Cuban Missile Crisis three decades earlier, when U.S. Ambassador Adlai Stevenson unveiled photos of Soviet missiles in Cuba. This was the first time that the agency had used intelligence information from a member state in such a graphic way. It was an extraordinary sight, as IAEA officials displayed grainy black-and-white photographs taken from space to the assembled rep-resentatives, including those of countries (such as Libya) known to be inter-ested in acquiring their own nuclear weapons.

The United States had quietly begun briefing the IAEA at the end of 1992 on developments at Yongbyon using satellite photography. Central Intelli-gence Agency analysts had battled the State Department to prevent disclosure of the photographs. Finally, CIA director Robert Gates had authorized the dis-closure to strengthen the international case against North Korea, a decision that the incoming administration sustained. Now, as IAEA officials and repre-sentatives peered at the photographs, they saw a storage facility under con-struction and what appeared to be an older facility at the Yongbyon nuclear complex being covered with a mound of dirt, which then appeared with trees and shrubs planted on top. The implication was obvious; North Korea seemed to have buried some nuclear waste under the camouflaged mound and built a newer facility to serve as a decoy.

The North Korean delegation soldiered on despite the damning evidence, but Blix argued that information obtained from a member state could not be ignored if relevant to IAEA implementation of its responsibilities under the safeguards agreement. Moreover, the North Korean explanations did not clear up the inconsistencies between their declaration and the IAEA inspectors' own observations. In fact, explanations for some discrepancies made sense but did not change the final assessment that the North's declaration was wrong. The agency chose, in the words of one IAEA official, to "express certainty" about its analysis since the North could claim that if Pyongyang was right about one minor inconsistency, the IAEA was wrong about others.[50]

Faced with a solidly documented case and a North Korean rebuttal that left the central evidence unchallenged, the board adopted a resolution on February 25 calling on North Korea to comply with its IAEA safeguards obligations within one month. The resolution contained two compromises that were required to secure China's support, since Beijing was loath to put too much pressure on its traditional ally. First, the North Koreans were given one month to comply, essentially allowing them to resume their cooperation with the IAEA after the Team Spirit exercise had concluded. Second, the resolution did not require North Korea to agree to "special inspections," but rather only to grant the IAEA access to the two sites.

Blix immediately telexed the text to Pyongyang along with a request for an inspection beginning on March 16. The North Koreans ominously warned that the new situation would require them to take countermeasures of self-defense to safeguard their sovereignty and supreme national interests.[51] That statement, in retrospect, seemed to refer to the prospect of North Korea exercising the "supreme national interest" clause in the NPT in order to withdraw from the treaty.

The Sunshine Policy

The IAEA resolution could not have come at a worse time for the new South Korean government. Only the day before, Kim Young Sam had taken office as president. Born in 1927 on Koje Island off southern Korea, Kim was a long-time politician, opposition leader, and dissident. In a political masterstroke, he had merged his opposition party with the ruling party of President Roh Tae Woo, which led to his nomination and eventual election over longtime rival Kim Dae Jung. As president, Kim would be a driving force for change, entering office with a vision of a "New Korea" built on the promise of sweeping political, economic, and social reform.

The new president had a flair for daring political moves and a sensitivity to public opinion. One of Kim's first speaking forays was in the cafeteria of the Agency for National Security Planning (NSP), South Korea's seemingly ubiquitous intelligence service, which had dogged him for many years. Kim would later boast that he had hired for his own staff a policeman who had spent a decade watching him. By his own admission, he was more a politician than an intellectual, claiming that he "borrowed other people's brains." This led some South Koreans to joke that Kim "borrowed too many people's brains," which explained why his policies were inconsistent.

More comfortable with domestic politics than foreign policy, Kim had conservative views on North Korea that may have been influenced by the fact that its agents, in committing an armed robbery, had killed his mother four decades earlier.[52] On the other hand, the new president surrounded himself with advisers drawn from outside the bureaucracy, who were not tainted by connections to past military regimes. Academics with views ranging from progressive to moderate, Kim's "Gang of Four" was at the center of his foreign policy team.

Of the four, Han Sung Joo, the new foreign minister, would play Kissinger to President Kim's Nixon. A well-known professor at Korea University with a doctorate from the University of California at Berkeley, Han had taught in New York City and then returned to Seoul. He had been a government adviser on North-South relations and written extensively on that subject, the United States, and foreign policy, both as an academic and as a columnist for *Newsweek*. He was soft spoken, thoughtful, and even bookish. Han would emerge as the most influential voice in shaping South Korean policy during the nuclear crisis.[53]

President Kim's most controversial appointment was Han Wan Sang, the new deputy prime minister and unification minister. A former campus radical and dissident, Han was also a rumpled academic who believed that real North-South dialogue would only take place if Pyongyang had confidence that Seoul was neither trying to change nor absorb it. According to Han, because of South Korea's strength, it was in a position to make bold gestures that would convince the North Koreans of its sincerity.[54] Years later, he would recall his efforts as the first attempt at a "sunshine policy" toward North Korea, a phrase that would subsequently become famous in describing President Kim Dae Jung's policies toward Pyongyang.[55]

The new foreign policy team was rounded off by two additional academics turned policymakers. The first, Chung Chong Wook, was a professor at Seoul National University before being tapped for the job of Blue House national security adviser. A "moderate centrist," he was viewed by some critics as being too pro-American. The second, Kim Deok, was the first academic appointed head of South Korea's intelligence organization. Previous directors had been either senior military officials or government prosecutors.

During the South Korean presidential transition, the incoming government's policy toward North Korea remained unclear. But change was in the air. That became apparent with President Kim's inaugural address on February 24. In a dramatic pronouncement, the president acknowledged that "no allied country can be greater than one nation" and said he was willing to meet Kim Il Sung "any time and any place."[56] Its implication that ties with Pyongyang were more important than those with the United States set off a firestorm of conservative criticism. While Han Wan Sang's hand was clear— he had led the team that worked on the text for over a month—the president-elect was also deeply involved, frequently attending drafting sessions. Almost immediately, a private emissary from the North visited Han to tell him that Pyongyang had been favorably impressed.[57]

A second initiative undertaken by the new government was to approve the release of Lee In Mo, a North Korean war correspondent and guerilla captured during the Korean War. Lee had been imprisoned for steadfastly refusing to do the one thing—renounce communism—that could win him a return ticket to the North. Though released from jail in 1989, his unconditional repatriation to North Korea had been considered but rejected by the previous government. After being held in captivity for almost four decades, the elderly Lee was hospitalized in February 1993, prompting the North Korean Red Cross Society bitterly to denounce the South's treatment of him and to urge his transfer to "our side."[58]

Meeting with President Kim over breakfast shortly after the inauguration, Han Wan Sang asked him to make another bold gesture: unconditionally release Lee. Such a move made sense because it would be hard for South Korea to explain to the world why Lee had not been allowed to go home to die, and also because it fit into Han's "sunshine" strategy.[59] A week later, Seoul announced that the seventy-six-year-old Lee would be returned to North Korea unconditionally, characterizing its move as a "courageous political decision."[60]

But the new government in Seoul recognized that without a diplomatic solution to the nuclear problem its emerging policy of reconciliation stood little chance of success. After the inauguration, Deputy Prime Minister Han mused in a television interview that a North-South summit could occur by the end of the year, once Team Spirit was over and the nuclear issue resolved. Yet such a solution would be impossible without the active participation of the United States.[61]

As Seoul began its policy review, it dispatched a veteran diplomat, Gong Ro Myung, to Washington for discussions beginning March 8. Ambassador Gong was ideally suited for the mission. Viewed by the Americans as well informed, he had a sophisticated English vocabulary, honed by regular reading of the *New York Times*. After serving as his country's first ambassador to the Soviet Union, Gong had spent the past year as head of its delegation to the Joint

Nuclear Control Commission charged with negotiating a verification regime for the Denuclearization Declaration. That experience had given him a keen understanding of North Korea's behavior born of frequent face-to-face contacts.

After consulting with the new president and foreign minister, Gong came to Washington armed with three ideas. One was fairly mundane, to propose another session of the Joint Nuclear Control Commission. The second was new, to kill two birds with one stone by allowing the IAEA to carry out not only its own inspections but also inspections under the North-South inspection regime, on the dubious premise that Pyongyang would prefer the agency to South Korea. The third idea, familiar but controversial, was that the United States should agree to North Korea's persistent requests for another high-level meeting like the Kanter-Kim session. That might help forestall any rash action by Pyongyang, including withdrawal from the NPT. "Let them bask in glory so we can pump them to do the right thing," Gong told the Americans.

Seoul's envoy was under no illusions. He understood there would be strong reticence in Washington to another high-level session with the North Koreans, but thought it worthwhile putting the idea on the table.[62] Gong met with all the key players in the new administration: Anthony Lake, Under Secretary of State Peter Tarnoff, Assistant Secretary for East Asia William Clark, and Assistant Secretary for Political-Military Affairs Robert Gallucci. Most listened politely while telling him that the United States was reviewing its policy. But Assistant Secretary Clark pointed out that the North Koreans were still signaling a commitment to work with the IAEA. Agreeing to a U.S.–North Korean meeting would send the wrong signal to Pyongyang and detract from the objective of achieving the IAEA inspection. As Gong would later recall, "Everyone was working on the March 25 deadline," the one-month period given to Pyongyang to comply with the IAEA's wishes.

In fact, Pyongyang seemed to have a different timetable. On March 8, as Gong was meeting with American officials, Kim Jong Il issued "Order No. 0034 of the Supreme Military Commander." Denouncing Team Spirit as a "nuclear war game preliminary to invasion of North Korea," he ordered the people and the military to enter a state of semiwar and to be fully prepared for battle. Pyongyang had increased the alert status of its military forces before in response to Team Spirit, although the last time it had used the term "semiwar" was in 1983. The announcement made no mention of the dispute with the IAEA.[63]

The next day, 100,000 workers, students, and citizens, as well as top members of the North Korean leadership, attended a huge rally in Pyongyang. Afterward, participants marched in a parade carrying banners proclaiming, "Let Us Unite around the Supreme Commander." A dusk-to-dawn blackout was ordered. Radio Moscow reported, "Even the torchlight on the *Juche*-Thought Tower was turned off." (*Juche* is the North Korean doctrine of "self-reliance" that Kim Il Sung built into the dominant political credo of his total-itarian state.) Pyongyang also stopped issuing visas to foreigners and began jamming Korean language broadcasts of Radio Japan, a step it had never taken before.[64]

Although the situation appeared to be deteriorating, Washington and Seoul remained calm. Ambassador William Clark sent a memorandum on the sub-ject to the newly confirmed secretary of state, Warren Christopher. Christo-pher had had a long and distinguished career in and outside government, including service as deputy attorney general in the Johnson administration and deputy secretary of state in the Carter administration. He was no stranger to crisis, having negotiated the January 1981 release of the fifty-two American hostages in Iran. The memorandum from Clark told him that the declaration denouncing the Team Spirit exercise was fairly typical. There was, he added "very little reason for serious concern" since the move did not represent an actual increase in the military threat.

On his way home from Washington, Ambassador Gong stopped in Tokyo to consult with the Japanese government. Getting off the airplane at Narita airport, he was met by his country's ambassador to Japan, a courtesy normally reserved for a visiting South Korean foreign minister or president. A puzzled Gong asked, "Why are you here?" His friend replied, "North Korea has with-drawn from the NPT."[65]

2

An Extremely Peculiar Nation

March–May 1993

Late in the evening of Thursday, March 11, 1993, the wire services ran a story that dominated the news the following day: North Korea had announced its intention to withdraw from the Nuclear Non-Proliferation Treaty, becoming the first country ever to make such a move. Catching the story on *CNN Headline News*, Daniel Poneman first called the White House Situation Room to confirm its accuracy, then alerted National Security Adviser Tony Lake at home.

The next morning—at his desk early to prepare a memorandum for the president—Poneman scanned the diplomatic traffic to make sure President Bill Clinton received the latest word on North Korea. The North Koreans had released their statement on Friday, March 12, local time, giving Asian and European governments the first shots at commenting on the stories before Washington awoke that day. From the wire services and the State Department's reporting of those initial reactions, it was clear that American diplomacy was already paying at least one dividend. The official comments—remarkably similar in tone and substance—declared that the North Korean withdrawal from the NPT was unacceptable and that Pyongyang must fully implement its safeguards obligations to the International Atomic Energy Agency.

North Korea's pronouncement—its first authoritative response to the March 25 IAEA deadline for special inspections—was a bombshell.[1] After years of trying to bring Pyongyang into the international nonproliferation regime, months of trying to get it to implement its nuclear safeguards agreement, and weeks of trying to resolve the discrepancies in its initial plutonium declaration, the North appeared ready to bolt. Left unchecked, Pyongyang's withdrawal would present a grave security threat to the world and weaken the NPT's important bulwark against the spread of nuclear weapons.

The announcement set off a frenzy of activity. One hundred and forty countries issued statements denouncing Pyongyang's intended withdrawal. Secretary of State Warren Christopher hoped the North Koreans would rescind their withdrawal; President Clinton told reporters that he was "very concerned and very discouraged."[2] In Seoul, newly appointed government ministers plunged into emergency meetings, placing the South Korean military on "Watch Con 3," a high state of alert issued after border incidents or during special events, such as the 1988 Seoul Olympics.[3] The Japanese government urged the North to reverse course. Even the Japanese Socialist Party, with a history of sympathy for Pyongyang, called the move "extremely regrettable."[4]

Beijing's reaction was typically cryptic. The Foreign Ministry supported a nuclear-free peninsula (thus it opposed the North's program) but also advocated a negotiated solution to the crisis.[5] At the same time, China expressed profound skepticism that Pyongyang could build such weapons, perhaps to deflect American pressure to react more forcefully. Having relied heavily on expatriates trained abroad to build its own bomb, the Chinese could well ask how North Korea could match that feat unaided. Nevertheless, Beijing was taking no chances; it tightened controls on exports to North Korea that might help in building nuclear weapons.[6]

In Vienna, the IAEA Secretariat quickly held an emergency session. Director General Hans Blix scheduled a special meeting of the Board of Governors for March 18 to discuss the situation. Afterward, he immediately sent a telex to the North informing it that Pyongyang's safeguards obligations would remain in place until the withdrawal became effective.[7] Under the terms of the NPT, that would occur three months later.

The press shared the sense of crisis. A *New York Times* editorial cautioned that Pyongyang "was flirting with diplomatic suicide and scaring a lot of people."[8] Another *Times* article highlighted one expert's warning: "Now that one country has pulled out of the treaty, others obviously can begin to think about it."[9]

American policymakers faced pressures from all sides. North Korea's sudden move, whatever the motives behind it, catapulted the nuclear issue to front and center on the Clinton administration's foreign policy agenda only two months into its term. The withdrawal threatened not only the nonproliferation regime but also the security of the United States and its allies in Northeast Asia: South Korea and Japan. Congress was also concerned. Under these difficult circumstances, the Clinton administration began to forge a strategy that focused on building a global coalition in opposition to Pyong-yang's move. But now it also had to face the question that the Bush adminis-tration had deferred: whether to negotiate directly with North Korea.

A Slap in the Face

Although the North had mentioned the possibility of withdrawal during pri-vate exchanges with the IAEA, Pyongyang's announcement came as a surprise. The United States expected "business as usual" would resume once Team Spirit ended, especially since a treaty withdrawal before Kim Il Sung's April 15 birthday would tarnish North Korea's international image. Others believed that Pyongyang would not renounce the treaty because that would kill any possibility for better relations with Washington.

In Seoul, President Kim Young Sam was shocked by the news. Foreign Min-ister Han Sung Joo confessed that the possibility of NPT withdrawal the day after Seoul decided to release Lee In Mo had never been considered.[10] Conser-vatives moved quickly to undercut moderates, calling the move a "slap in the face."[11] Their main target was Deputy Prime Minister Han Wan Sang, the architect of Seoul's sunshine policy and Lee's release.

South Korean decisionmakers also worried how Washington would respond. Testifying before a U.S. congressional committee in 1991, Han Sung Joo, then a professor, was struck by the willingness of the American wit-nesses—think-tank experts and former U.S. officials—to advocate a preemp-tive strike against North Korea. His fears were resurrected in 1993 when Americans visiting Seoul at the time of the North's announcement hinted that pressures could grow in Washington to launch such an attack.[12] One of the visitors, Leslie Gelb, a *New York Times* columnist who was skeptical about engagement with North Korea, wrote that the "two Northern Kims" (father and son) saw nuclear weapons as indispensable to their survival.[13] Preventing precipitous American reactions became a key diplomatic priority for Seoul.

In Washington, Assistant Secretary of State William Clark—the State De-partment's lead official for East Asian affairs—hastily convened an interagency meeting on March 12 to plot the next moves. Kent Harrington—the U.S. gov-ernment's senior intelligence official on East Asia—kicked off the discussion by noting that North Korea's withdrawal was only the fourth such high-level "government statement," and the first since North Koreans had axed two American soldiers to death in the Demilitarized Zone in 1976. (One tool in the obscure art of trying to understand Pyongyang was to look at the author-itativeness of its public pronouncements. "Government statements" were the most authoritative ones.) Foreign visas, Harrington added, had been revoked only twice before, most recently in 1983 when a Russian fighter shot down Korean Air Lines flight 007, killing all the passengers and crew of a plane that had strayed off course en route from the United States to South Korea.

The situation was indeed dangerous, but Air Force Major General Gary Curtin reassured the group that there were no signs of unusual military moves among Pyongyang's million-man army, much of which was deployed along the 38th parallel dividing the two Koreas, within striking distance of Seoul. The meeting then turned to decisions on next steps. All present agreed that Washington would send a message to its diplomatic posts stressing the need for North Korea to return to full compliance with international nonproliferation norms. Ambassador Clark suggested two additional steps. The United States would launch consultations at the UN Security Council to condemn North Korea's move. Further, the United States would communicate directly with Pyongyang through the secret Beijing channel, in order to keep the door open to a negotiated solution to the mounting crisis.

Officials were concerned that the crisis could quickly escalate to involve military actions, given the potentially explosive mix of rising political tensions and a major military exercise—Team Spirit—in progress. But on March 19 Seoul announced the conclusion of the exercise and the departure of American troops.[14] In turn, the North Koreans proclaimed an end to the "semiwar" state, the first time they had ever publicly transmitted such an order. Propaganda attacks on Team Spirit declined, whereas before they had kept up well into April when the demobilization phase was completed.[15] Pyongyang's actions suggested that it, too, wished to ease military tensions.

Following up on Assistant Secretary Clark's suggestion, Washington also set up a secret meeting with North Korean diplomats in Beijing on March 19, urging them to reverse course. The North Koreans rejected the request.[16] Although this discouraged the Americans, Seoul saw Pyongyang's readiness to talk during Team Spirit and the rapid reply as evidence that the North might be in a bargaining mode. Despite the rebuff, the continued availability of the Beijing channel allowed North Korea "to keep hope alive," observed one Japanese official.

That same day, South Korea sent Lee In Mo home to North Korea. Some ministers wanted to cancel his return. A frustrated, angry, and embarrassed President Kim—previously in favor of unconditional release—stayed on the sidelines, a posture he would often adopt when searching for an expedient way out of difficult situations. Nevertheless, the government concluded that it could not reverse course, in part because the move had already been announced, and in part because the new regime wanted to show North Korea that it was "serious, consistent, predictable and rational." A wheelchair-bound

Lee, met by his family at the DMZ, flew to Pyongyang for a hero's welcome.[17] Though the gesture was intended to calm the situation, Pyongyang predictably portrayed it as a triumph of the North's will, further undermining the position of moderates like Deputy Prime Minister Han.[18]

While the initial burst of cables and consultations were clear on the objective of full North Korean compliance with nonproliferation norms, policymakers were far less clear about *how* North Korea could be persuaded to reverse course. "The bomb from Pyongyang denuded the landscape," observed a South Korean official at the time, adding that the "whole foundation was shaky." The day after the North Korean announcement, Secretary Christopher wrote President Clinton that the United States was working with others to put pressure on Pyongyang to reverse its decision. Many U.S. officials also considered whether direct diplomatic contacts with the North might be necessary. But how could they defend the nonproliferation regime while negotiating with a government that seemed bent on undermining it? Assistant Secretary Clark told Seoul's ambassador, "We do not want to take any steps that would be seen as rewarding their behavior," a view that echoed the policy of the first Bush administration and anticipated that of the second. Could the United States negotiate directly with the North without falling into that trap?

Devising a game plan to respond to the North Korean challenge fell to the Deputies Committee. Ranking just below the cabinet-level Principals Committee in the newly reorganized NSC decisionmaking structure, on March 18 the committee met in the White House Situation Room to discuss North Korea for the first time. Chaired by Deputy National Security Adviser Sandy Berger and including representatives from the Department of State, the Department of Defense, the Joint Chiefs of Staff, the Arms Control and Disarmament Agency, and the intelligence community, the group needed a strategy that could yield a solution before the North's withdrawal became effective. As specified in the NPT, that deadline was ninety days after North Korea's notification.[19] The meeting began a process that would consider both carrots (such as direct U.S.–North Korean talks) and sticks (such as sanctions) and would involve consultations with regional allies—South Korea and Japan—as well as with other important players such as China.

The first task was to build an international coalition opposing North Korea's actions. Statements from around the world had condemned Pyongyang. As the deputies met in Washington, the IAEA Board of Governors convened in Vienna, ready to refer the nuclear issue to the UN Security Council if North Korea missed the March 25 deadline for compliance with its request for special inspections. Unofficial consultations had already started among permanent members of the Security Council, where Britain and France, as "nonproliferation hawks" and staunch defenders of the international nonproliferation regime, wanted to seek a UN condemnation. But China—concerned that such a move might provoke Pyongyang—blocked American efforts to secure such a statement. It refused even to consider the matter.

Beijing quickly emerged as a crucial factor in American strategy. Taken by surprise when North Korea made its March 12 pronouncement, Chinese diplomats had been trying to persuade Pyongyang to accept the IAEA's inspections. But the Foreign Ministry also told J. Stapleton Roy, the U.S. ambassador to China, that it opposed "pressure or coercion." These mixed signals reflected Beijing's dilemma. China feared that nuclear weapons in North Korea might trigger an arms race that could destabilize Asia. But China also feared that economic sanctions might trigger the collapse of the North Korean regime, causing a flood of refugees into its northeastern provinces. Beijing seemed happy to let the United States take the lead in trying to thread that needle. Its diplomats told South Korea that promoting dialogue between Pyongyang and Washington presented the best way out of the crisis since "the final leverage is with the United States."[20]

Keeping the China factor in mind, the Deputies Committee sought to build pressure on North Korea by securing wide multilateral support. With the announced end of Team Spirit on March 19—an important firebreak that would allow the United States to pursue its diplomacy in a less tense atmosphere—Washington hoped to secure the IAEA board's support for a strong response to the North Korean nuclear threat, and then take the issue to the UN Security Council. In both Vienna and New York, Washington sought to build the greatest possible consensus in order to influence Beijing while securing condemnation of Pyongyang.

Diplomatic skirmishing broke out almost immediately. A few days after the deputies met, the IAEA Board of Governors unanimously passed a resolution reaffirming the March 25 deadline. But the board also allowed China to block reporting the measure to the Security Council—where it would have triggered continued discussions—even though the resolution could have been approved without Beijing's support. Discretion seemed the better part of diplomatic valor; it was more important to keep China on board than to send the issue immediately to the Security Council. Nevertheless, the stage was set for a confrontation at the next IAEA meeting on March 31. If North Korea had not accepted special inspections by then, the matter would have to go to New York.[21]

Not surprisingly, the deadline came and went without action by Pyongyang. On the eve of the March 31 session, Beijing warned the Americans that the North could escalate the crisis by breaking off all contact with the IAEA if the issue were referred to New York.[22] Nevertheless, on April 1, the board found North Korea in noncompliance with its safeguards obligations and reported the matter to the Security Council, this time in spite of Chinese and Libyan "no" votes. The Chinese bitterly charged the result had been "improvised merely as a justification for referral of the matter to the Security Council."[23] The *Washington Post* saw the vote as a "watershed event" in the changing priorities of arms control in the 1990s.[24]

With action in the Security Council imminent, Washington had to decide what to do there. At the extremes, the Clinton administration could have concentrated on seeking a negotiated solution with Pyongyang or sought immediate sanctions against the North. Neither course appeared attractive. And given Pyongyang's economic isolation from the world, it was unclear whether sanctions would have any tangible impact unless full cooperation could be secured from China (supplier of fuel and food) and Japan (source of hundreds of millions of dollars of cash sent by North Korean sympathizers living in that country). Even if sanctions were applied, would they persuade the North to change course, simply push it further into its shell, or cause it to lash out? The North could make a bad situation worse by withdrawing from the United Nations, accelerating its nuclear program, staging military provocations along the DMZ, or renewing terrorist acts. Later that spring, U.S. intelligence analysts warned the White House that Pyongyang might view sanctions as an act of war and react violently.[25] Indeed, the North had made public statements to that effect.

The administration steered a middle course. That meant a strategy of gradual escalation that would seek to build a coalition, increase pressure on North Korea, and, hopefully, draw China into its ranks. The process would start with expressions of support for the IAEA and calls for North Korean compliance, and then shift to the enactment of sanctions by degrees. A previous 1992 Security Council resolution imposing sanctions against Libya was seen as a model for the first concrete step. While that resolution cut off military exports first, a North Korea resolution would first seek to cut off its missile sales abroad.

In spite of China's intransigence in Vienna, the U.S. Mission to the United Nations, known as USUN, thought that Beijing could be persuaded to take that step. History was on Washington's side. Since 1989 China had either gone along with the consensus of the five permanent members of the Security Council, the so-called P-5, or abstained on key issues considered by the Security Council. Moreover, it had not used the veto since 1972, even acquiescing in sanctions against Iraq, Libya, and Yugoslavia. But North Korea was different. China's deep historic ties to that hermetic nation would force it to balance the diminishing benefits of that relationship against the potential adverse impact of a veto on the growing benefits of its evolving relationships with the United States, Japan, and South Korea. Gradual escalation bought time for Beijing to threaten to veto Security Council resolutions as leverage to soften language and slow multilateral coercive measures in order to promote its preferred outcome, a diplomatic solution.

America's key regional allies—South Korea and Japan—also favored gradual escalation. Tokyo was concerned about how Pyongyang might react to strong pressure in view of its dire political and economic situation. Speaking to the press a few days after the North's March 12 announcement, Chief Cabinet Secretary Yohei Kono said that Japan would support sanctions if efforts failed to persuade the North to rejoin the NPT in the three months left before its withdrawal took effect.[26] Indeed, the government began contingency planning for sanctions just in case. At the same time, the Japanese told the Americans that they should be "firm but flexible," a subtle reminder to give diplomacy a chance.

For the South Koreans, gradual escalation neatly dovetailed with their own emerging escalation ladder designed, in part, to head off American military action. The first step would be talks with the North. Just before Foreign Minister Han visited the United States in late March, President Kim wrote President Clinton to ask him "not to close the window of dialogue with North Korea." Han raised the issue repeatedly in Washington.[27] The second step would be the gradual escalation of sanctions, as agreed by Han and Christopher during a meeting in the secretary's suite at the State Department. Speaking to reporters afterward, Assistant Foreign Minister Sin Ki Pok summarized Seoul's view: "Sanctions exclude military action. But sanctions are unavoidable when diplomatic efforts [are] not enough."[28] Later that month, gradual escalation was enshrined as a common approach at a meeting of U.S., South Korean, and Japanese diplomats in New York.

Interestingly, North Korea's own signals reinforced the growing consensus in favor of gradual escalation. Ever since the March 12 announcement, Pyongyang's diplomats had worked feverishly, but unsuccessfully, to stave off international condemnation in Europe, Africa, and Asia. Against this bleak backdrop, the North hammered away at Washington's "coercive nuclear inspection agitation" but highlighted earlier hints that negotiations were possible. On March 18—the day of the deputies' session—North Korea's deputy UN ambassador in New York, Ho Jong, added substance to these hints by citing four conditions for reversing the NPT decision: permanent cancellation of Team Spirit, opening of U.S. "nuclear military bases" in South Korea to inspection, a guarantee that Washington would not launch a nuclear attack on North

Korea, and restoration of IAEA impartiality. North Korean diplomats in other countries echoed Ho's statement, a sign that they were acting under orders and that Pyongyang might be willing to seek a negotiated solution to the crisis.[29]

The curtain on the first act of Washington's strategy of gradual escalation went up at the Security Council on April 2, the day after the IAEA approved its resolution and referred the matter to the United Nations. As expected, Beijing resisted, prompting an American diplomat to comment, "There is an important difference between too much pressure and the Chinese position, which was no pressure."

With the other permanent members solidly behind the United States, some well-chosen compromises and a briefing by Director General Blix did the trick, opening the way toward a statement by the president of the Security Council on April 8. The pronouncement did not call on Pyongyang to reverse its decision or to comply with its safeguards obligations but only expressed concern and welcomed all efforts to resolve the situation. Trying to quell publicity, China even nixed the idea of a formal meeting to issue the statement. Nevertheless, gradual escalation had begun.

Remember Iraq

Pyongyang's March 12 announcement naturally prompted questions in Washington, Seoul, and Tokyo, as well as throughout the international community, not only about why North Korea took such a step but also about the rationality of its leadership. The North, observed Admiral Makoto Sakuma, a senior Japanese military officer, is "an extremely peculiar nation."[30] The challenge facing the international community, said another Japanese official, was to make North Korea "sane again." As Foreign Minister Han told an audience in Seoul, however, "From the North's perspective, the move had an element of rationality and calculation."[31]

Ample evidence supported Han's view. Kim Jong Il had been the day-to-day manager of the North's government and was deeply involved in using the nuclear weapons program to ensure Pyongyang's security and bolster its diplomacy. But the heir apparent's attempts to improve relations with the United States and South Korea had made only limited progress. Since September, dialogue with the South had stalled. Moreover, Washington had repeatedly rebuffed Pyongyang's efforts to meet again. The rescheduling of Team Spirit was a personal setback for Kim, who had taken credit for its suspension the previous year. Finally, the North appeared to have been caught flat-footed by the IAEA's use of American spy satellites, and its military was particularly resistant to international inspections that could yield further evidence of North

Korean cheating on its safeguards obligations. According to one South Korean, the sharing of intelligence told Pyongyang, "You can run but you can't hide."[32] At best, the impending confrontation could prove embarrassing. At worst, from Pyongyang's perspective, it could directly threaten North Korea's national security.

The recent example of Iraq loomed large in the minds of North Korea's leaders. Pyongyang had closely studied U.S. military operations during Desert Storm, but also the broader political implications of the Gulf War, concluding that Saddam Hussein may have maintained his grip on power, but Iraq had lost its independence of action because of measures taken by the international community. For the North Koreans, such a fate would be intolerable, perhaps fatal. They vowed never to let the United States turn their country into another Iraq. Yet that was precisely the danger Pyongyang perceived, presenting Kim Jong Il with his first major foreign policy crisis since assuming most of his father's responsibilities.[33]

The timing of the crisis was particularly inopportune, crystallizing just as the leadership transition appeared to be entering its final stage. At the Party Plenum in December 1992, many of Kim Jong Il's confederates had been promoted into important jobs.[34] Just before the March 12 announcement, he replaced his father as chairman of the key National Defense Commission, "the highest DPRK organ for military guidance," completing a process that had begun in 1990 when Kim was named first vice chairman.[35] Kim Il Sung's routine birthday celebration in April evolved into an extraordinary tribute to his choice of his son, the "Dear Leader," as his successor.[36] The heir apparent now needed only to accede to the elder Kim's titles as general secretary of the Korean Worker's Party and president of the republic in order to complete the leadership transition.

In spite of the outward trappings, some observers doubted that Kim Jong Il's control of the military was complete. Though he had steadily advanced in its hierarchy while placing his supporters in key positions, Kim had never had a truly military career. Moreover, the policies he seemed to be supporting— normalization with the United States and piecemeal changes in the North's economic system—may have provoked deep skepticism among senior officers. Yet support by the military was critical precisely because of the dreadful condition of the economy and the global ideological assault on socialism.

The passage of the IAEA resolution on February 26, essentially an ultimatum, left Kim Jong Il with few options, all risky. On one hand, he could do nothing and let the IAEA process play out, probably bringing an escalation of international pressure, including sanctions. On the other hand, the younger Kim could try to find a way to submit to the agency's demands for special inspections. Aside from the immediate risk of disclosing further North Korean safeguards violations, acquiescence could open the door for the IAEA to make escalating demands for inspections, including at military sites. It might also have represented a serious setback for Kim, perhaps damaging the succession process. The danger of political emasculation—turning North Korea into another Iraq—was too great.

Another alternative was to rearrange the chessboard, hopefully in North Korea's favor. According to later accounts, the idea of withdrawing from the NPT was advanced by the Ministry of Foreign Affairs and championed by Kang Sok Ju, the first vice foreign minister. Neither was thought of as a bastion of hard line sentiment within the North Korean system. On the contrary, Kang was believed to belong to a group of Foreign Ministry officials who were relatively more pragmatic. Nevertheless, in a political system where currying favor with the two Kims translated into influence and power (or at least survival), the ministry may have advanced the idea of NPT withdrawal in response to the wishes of Kim Jong Il, who may have been looking for a way out of an increasingly difficult situation.[37]

The Foreign Ministry also had its own motives, chiefly to reassert control over dealings with the United States. It had never been happy with Kim Yong Sun's leadership role from his perch as head of the Korean Worker's Party International Department. Since his stewardship had produced few results, by autumn 1992 responsibility had shifted to the Ministry of Foreign Affairs. In December, Kim Yong Sun was promoted, taken off the American account, and put in charge of North-South dialogue. Later he would claim that he had opposed the North's withdrawal from the NPT. That implied the decision was not simply handed down but perhaps discussed within the small coterie of North Korean decisionmakers.[38]

All of this must have required some soul-searching. In the months before its March 12 announcement, North Korea's leadership, as always, appeared defiant when faced by outside pressure but was also trying carefully to feel its way through a difficult situation. Only two months before the announcement, Kim Il Sung seemed to be promoting better relations with the United States and South Korea. As the situation deteriorated, it became harder to do that and also maintain North Korea's dignity and sovereignty. Periods of public silence at key moments suggested the leaders were grappling with tough problems.[39]

At some point, perhaps in early February, Kim Jong Il may have decided that withdrawal from the NPT would allow Pyongyang to avoid the fate suffered by the Saddam Hussein regime after the Gulf War. The move carried a certain amount of risk; if the California-educated South Korean foreign minister worried about the odds that the United States might take precipitous action, the threat must have seemed even more real to North Koreans locked in fifty years of deadly struggle with Washington. One defector later reported that Kim Jong Il virtually lived in a command bunker in March 1993.[40]

Having freed itself from the NPT, Pyongyang could ramp up its nuclear efforts and set up a win-win situation for itself. That course would either bring North Korea access to the ultimate weapon or greatly strengthen its bargaining position with foreign governments seeking to stop it, or both. Pyongyang could use such leverage to promote its objective of regime survival, perhaps by obtaining security assurances or other benefits.

As North Korea felt its way through the political fog created by the March 12 announcement, its posture—measured but defiant—was consistent with this strategy. In a rare press conference, First Vice Foreign Minister Kang warned that referring the issue to the UN Security Council could cause "grave consequences." At the same time, Pyongyang punctiliously followed the procedures for withdrawing from the NPT, justifying its move as necessary to protect "supreme national interests," mirroring the withdrawal provisions in Article X of the NPT. The North's announcement, claiming that its position would remain unchanged "until the United States stops its nuclear threats against our country and until the IAEA returns to its principles of independence and impartiality," implied negotiations might be possible.[41] Finally, North Korea's military posture seemed robust enough to defend against possible surprise attack and sanctions enforcement, but not for offensive action.

The announced withdrawal presented Washington with a fundamental question of whether or not to negotiate with the North. Once the focus shifted to negotiation, Pyongyang's tactics, while extreme and at times clumsy, would force the international community to take the North's agenda into account. More specifically, the North was setting the stage to negotiate with the United States on a package that would secure the greatest benefits on the easiest terms possible. Part of that package would be to get Washington to loosen its stranglehold on Pyongyang, seen as blocking international economic assistance and better political relations.

On the domestic front, generating an external threat was a classic tool for suppressing dissent, demanding sacrifices, and consolidating power. Kim Jong Il could have created a crisis to shore up his position, bolster his credentials with the military, and provide justification for the deteriorating economy. The military focus of the declaration of a "semiwar" state on March 8 included an exhortation to increase economic production. The announcement that Pyongyang intended to withdraw from the NPT was also accompanied by a call to increase socialist economic production. In short, Kim Jong Il may have used the NPT announcement to assert his authority over conservatives throughout the party, the government, and the military.

All of this assumes that the North Koreans would be open to a negotiated solution. But another widely held theory was that the North was committed irrevocably to obtaining nuclear weapons to guarantee its future security. By withdrawing from the treaty Pyongyang had removed the last legal constraint on its program. According to this theory, Pyongyang planned to deceive the IAEA and continue its nuclear weapons program, gaining time and even benefits by temporarily accepting inspections. When it became clear the North had vastly underestimated the IAEA's technical prowess and could not escape the charges of deception, Pyongyang took the most logical course of action, announcing its withdrawal from the NPT. If this were the case, the prognosis for a diplomatic solution to the crisis was quite bleak.

Pyongyang's progress in obtaining plutonium reinforced this school of thought. R. James Woolsey, the newly appointed director of the Central Intelligence Agency, testified before Congress in late February that Pyongyang could have already manufactured enough nuclear material to produce at least one nuclear bomb.[42] A month later, South Korea's head of intelligence, Kim Deok, told the National Assembly that the North had already extracted up to 22 kilograms of plutonium, which would allow it to build one to three nuclear weapons by 1994 or 1995. Reportedly, South Korean intelligence even suggested that the two Kims had considered conducting a nuclear test but decided against it.[43]

North Korea's ballistic missile program compounded outside concerns about its nuclear intentions. With their crude guidance systems, the North's long-range missiles were so wildly inaccurate that they only made good weapons if tipped with nuclear warheads. Even worse, North Korea was a major exporter of ballistic missiles and technology to the world's most dangerous regimes, many located in the volatile Middle East. The threat was keenly felt by Tokyo as it watched the North develop and prepare to test a new missile able to reach western Japan.[44] Nerves became even more frayed following the early April discovery of eight Russian rocket scientists teaching in the North in spite of government restrictions on their travel.

The theory that North Korea was committed irrevocably to acquiring nuclear weapons depended on a dubious premise, that North Korea was on autopilot. As one State Department analyst noted at the time, "Pyongyang has pegged its survival for the past thirty years on its ability to keep its options open and to adapt to the changing international scene." If building the bomb would ensure survival, then so be it. If building the bomb would ensure regime destruction, then Pyongyang would have no choice but to pursue other options that might also include diplomacy.

Outside of the narrow leadership circles of North Korea, indeed perhaps outside of Kim Il Sung and Kim Jong Il themselves, no one really knew which theory was correct. Meeting in New York City ten days after the March 12 announcement, representatives from the United States, South Korea, and Japan agreed that they could not determine whether the North was using the NPT walkout as a high-risk bargaining tactic or as a means of protecting its nuclear weapons program. The only responsible policy, U.S. officials concluded, would be to design a strategy that would be equally effective whether facing an unstoppable North Korean nuclear weapons program or one that Pyongyang would trade away for a price.

We May Not Succeed but We Can't Not Try

On April 7—the day before the Security Council issued its presidential statement—the Deputies Committee convened again. Three weeks earlier, the deputies had focused on building an international coalition that would include a strategy of gradual escalation. Now they faced a more difficult question: whether to open a dialogue with North Korea. The Bush administration had refused to hold such a dialogue after problems emerged with the IAEA, but it was hard to see how the current impasse could be surmounted without talks between North Korea and the United States, given America's interests and influence in the region. Indeed, gradual escalation of pressure aimed to increase the chances that dialogue would succeed. As one former Bush official observed, "The North Koreans do not respond to pressure. But without pressure they do not respond."[45]

Nevertheless, some still doubted the North was serious about a diplomatic solution and worried that starting talks might appear to be caving in to blackmail. The deputies also struggled to analyze the smoke signals rising from the North. Only the previous day, Pyongyang's media had asserted that the nuclear issue was a problem "that should be resolved through negotiation between the DPRK and the United States." But it also attacked the United Nations by invoking memories of the Korean War, warning that "unpredictable consequences" could result if the Security Council took action.[46]

That uncertainty cautioned the deputies against immediate dialogue. One option—to use a private intermediary—would later play a key role in resolving the crisis. But for the moment, it was shelved. Instead, they decided to ask China to act as midwife, in effect giving Beijing a greater stake in a successful outcome. In the meantime, the deputies agreed to hold off on sanctions, a decision that made sense since a presidential statement was expected at the United Nations the very next day. It would be customary to allow North Korea some time to comply before the UN took any further steps. If the dialogue with Pyongyang never got off the ground, the administration could press for sanctions and China would lack any justification for delaying further Security Council action.

In any dialogue with North Korea, U.S. objectives would be straightforward. Tightly focused on security issues, Washington would demand that Pyongyang meet its nonproliferation obligations by returning to the NPT, complying with its IAEA obligations, and implementing the Denuclearization Declaration reached with Seoul. This became the constant U.S. refrain throughout the crisis. Until these issues were resolved, Washington would not discuss improving its nonexistent political relations with Pyongyang or providing North Korea with economic incentives. The Clinton administration's plan essentially replicated the Bush administration's plan. One American who worked for both presidents recalled, "The first meeting between Kanter and Kim in 1992 was the seed of all of this."[47]

The bureaucratic cleavages in the Clinton administration also resembled those in the Bush administration. Whereas the State Department focused on preserving the nonproliferation regime, the Office of the Secretary of Defense (OSD) concentrated on preventing any further accumulation of plutonium by Pyongyang. Since the NPT did not ban reprocessing, the Defense Department focused on the North-South Denuclearization Declaration and a credible bilateral inspection regime to verify it. But Defense wanted more. Speaking at the April 7 deputies' meeting, Frank Wisner, the under secretary of defense for policy, argued that Washington needed an assurance that the entire nuclear program would be dismantled, a step not envisaged by the NPT, international safeguards, or the denuclearization agreement. A month later, a Defense Department task force run by Ashton Carter, the new assistant secretary of defense for international security programs, concluded that the United States should also seek the removal of all plutonium and spent fuel from North Korea.[48]

What would Washington offer North Korea in return? Those ideas were less well developed; it was always easier to decide on demands than on inducements. One option was a statement, modeled after the security assurance recently given to the newly independent state of Ukraine, that the United States did not intend to attack the North with nuclear weapons. Another was a more explicit statement that there were no U.S. nuclear weapons in South Korea. Still another—putting Team Spirit on the negotiating table—was opposed by the Joint Chiefs of Staff, even though there was no funding budgeted for the 1994 exercise and they were considering making the exercise a biennial rather than annual event. Ending the meeting, the deputies asked an interagency working group to write a detailed game plan for talks with the North.

Seoul had also concluded that direct talks between the United States and North Korea were imperative. After Foreign Minister Han returned from Washington, President Kim's close aides advised him that such talks were needed to resolve the crisis.[49] Moreover, the South believed that a window of opportunity was opening. International pressure would intensify as the June 12 deadline for the North's withdrawal from the NPT neared, forcing Pyongyang to act in order to keep the situation from getting out of control. China would then be in a tough spot but also would have more leverage over Pyongyang by virtue of its veto power at the Security Council. While the prognosis for dialogue was still uncertain, Foreign Minister Han told the Americans, "We may not succeed but we can't not try."

Coincidentally, the secret U.S. initiative was set in motion in Beijing on April 15, Kim Il Sung's birthday. Ambassador Stapleton ("Stape") Roy went to see Tang Jiaxun, the new Chinese vice foreign minister. A career bureaucrat and protégé of Foreign Minister Qian Qichen, Tang was a Japan expert. Though new to the Korean issue, he had just visited Pyongyang. Meeting in the diplomatic reception rooms of the Chinese Foreign Ministry, then a dingy 1960s' style building located in north central Beijing, Roy gave Tang the American proposal for dialogue with North Korea. That same day, the State Department spokesman publicly signaled that Washington did not rule out the possibility of a high-level meeting with Pyongyang.[50]

While Tang was noncommittal, one Chinese official said, "This is what we have been waiting for." But who would make the next move? The Americans felt they had done enough in bringing the message to the Chinese. The North Koreans asserted that they had done enough by signaling a willingness to talk through their media. The Chinese handled the matter in their typically murky manner. After asking the Japanese whether Washington was serious—the answer was yes—they officially rejected the role of go-between but "informally" passed the proposal to the North Koreans. Although Beijing wanted to avoid being caught in the middle of the dispute, it still wanted to play a positive role in attempting to end the deepening nuclear impasse.

The Chinese reaffirmed this a week later when South Korean Foreign Minister Han met Foreign Minister Qian in Bangkok. In close touch with the Americans, Han mirrored Ambassador Roy's message to show that the two allies were working together. He left the meeting encouraged; the Chinese confirmed they were telling the North what they were hearing from the

United States and South Korea.[51] Significantly, Qian also accelerated his visit to Seoul from midsummer to late May. The subtle move was intended to send a signal to Pyongyang: it would allow one more meeting before the North's withdrawal from the NPT became effective on June 12.

A few days later, the North Korean Foreign Ministry responded to the U.S. initiative, welcoming the State Department's remarks in a brief public statement, free of polemics. Prior to its announcement, Pyongyang had condemned international terrorism in response to the assassination of the South African communist Chris Hani, a gesture probably aimed at satisfying a long-standing American prerequisite for better relations.[52] Reinforcing that message, a North Korean visiting California said that Pyongyang might allow access to the suspected nuclear sites if the negotiations were not a "one-way street."[53]

The last act in the play came at the end of the month when North Korean diplomats formally proposed talks at another Beijing channel meeting. In spite of all the previous signaling in public and private, they seemed surprised when the Americans agreed on the spot. But the Americans also refused to set a date. That would have to wait until the next milestone in the strategy of gradual escalation: the passage by the UN Security Council of a resolution on North Korea. It would also have to wait until after the upcoming IAEA inspection in the North, now scheduled for mid-May.

Continuity of Safeguards

Since discoveries by the IAEA had precipitated the crisis, Washington believed, and Pyongyang probably understood, that the agency would have to play some role in resolving the nuclear problem. The extent of that role was a key question that would have to be resolved as part of the unfolding diplomatic struggle over the next eighteen months. Washington's objective was to strengthen the IAEA's role as the international community's nuclear watchdog. North Korea would try to weaken the IAEA's role since it viewed the agency as Washington's pawn. Indeed, Pyongyang consistently sought to remove that pawn from the chessboard so it could concentrate on the United States.

North Korea's reaction to the March 31 Board of Governors' resolution had been predictably negative but also included some intriguing hints.[54] Aside from asserting that it intended to fulfill its safeguards obligations and to solve problems "by means of negotiation," North Korea noted that the IAEA was ignoring the Israeli and South African nuclear weapons programs, thereby exposing the international community's "double standard." At the same time, Pyongyang praised South Africa's public admission that it had a program.

Could North Korea be toying with the idea of doing the same? Some specu-lated that Pyongyang might be inching back toward more cooperation with the IAEA.[55]

These hints were not lost on Hans Blix, the urbane director general of the IAEA. Blix had spent his professional life as a law professor and a Swedish diplomat, becoming Foreign Minister in 1978. His work on disarmament issues and the challenges presented by the peaceful uses of nuclear energy made him uniquely qualified to head the IAEA. His main task during sixteen years in office would be to steer the agency through the dangerous post–cold war waters of nonproliferation, including the need to confront countries such as Iraq and North Korea, bent on acquiring nuclear weapons in violation of their own treaty commitments as well as global norms.

Blix had been grappling with a number of challenges. First, he needed to clear up the inconsistencies in Pyongyang's declaration on plutonium produc-tion, if necessary by using special inspections. Second, he had to ensure that the IAEA could monitor the shutdown of North Korea's 5 megawatt reactor planned for early May. The fuel rods to be unloaded contained plutonium that might be diverted for illicit uses. They also contained critical information on the North's nuclear past that might be destroyed. Third, Blix had to consider what to do if North Korea withdrew from the NPT. Would it still adhere to a limited inspection arrangement predating the 1992 safeguards agreement?

But his most pressing challenge was to make sure that IAEA monitoring devices at the Yongbyon nuclear facilities—including cameras at the reactor—would continue to function. These eyes and ears of the agency would stop working without new batteries and film. If that happened, North Korea might be able to divert nuclear material without detection by the agency. In view of this urgent task, after the March 31 board session, the director general met with the North Korean ambassador to unveil a new idea, that of conducting a limited inspection to perform maintenance on the monitoring equipment at Yongbyon. In a telex to Pyongyang, he proposed an inspection to maintain "the continuity of safeguards information." In effect, Blix had moved to delink what promised to be difficult haggling over the full gamut of Pyongyang's safeguards obligations from this immediate priority of keeping track of the plutonium at Yongbyon.

Blix had not created a new type of inspection entirely out of whole cloth. The term "continuity of safeguards information" was in the standard IAEA safeguards agreement, but it had never been used as the sole basis for an inspection. In the agency's lexicon, aside from "special inspections" there were "ad hoc" inspections to verify the characteristics of a facility and "regular inspections" to provide assurance against the diversion of nuclear material.

Since the uninterrupted operation of monitoring equipment fell into the IAEA's purview of assuring that nuclear material had not been diverted, "continuity of safeguards inspections" seemed a plausible option.

While the new device was designed to break the ice with Pyongyang and to reassure the international community that the nuclear program remained frozen, it also set the stage for a continuing struggle between the United States, the IAEA, and North Korea. Since no one really knew where "continuity of safeguards" inspections ended and "regular and ad hoc" inspections began, the IAEA tried to use the former as a back door to the latter. North Korea naturally resisted.[56]

The IAEA director general's proposal was well timed. "We have never rejected it," responded North Korea's atomic energy minister, Choi Hak Gun.[57] As the United States and North Korea inched toward dialogue in late April, Pyongyang asked the IAEA to send inspectors and proposed a meeting in Vienna to discuss safeguards.[58] A month after the March 12 announcement, both sides seemed ready to renew limited cooperation.

Although the signs were encouraging, Minister Choi also set off alarm bells in Washington by asserting that there might be problems with the IAEA observing the much anticipated unloading of the reactor fuel rods. Without proper international supervision, the spent fuel containing plutonium might be diverted, or North Korea could destroy valuable historical information contained in those rods. But a few days later, Pyongyang informed Blix that refueling would not take place owing to the need for technical and practical preparation.[59] Reflecting on these developments, a Principals' Committee meeting on May 6 decided that the IAEA presence at reloading was important enough to be a precondition for U.S.–North Korean talks. North Korea's breach of that precondition would soon bring the two countries to the brink of war.

The four-day inspection began on May 10. The North Koreans browbeat the IAEA team about their requests for special inspections. Then two of the three members experienced stomach problems. When the third began to feel ill, concerns mounted that the inspectors might not be able to finish their work. In the end, they rallied sufficiently to ensure that the monitoring equipment at key nuclear facilities continued to function. Moreover, after indicating that unloading would not take place before Pyongyang was scheduled to withdraw from the NPT in mid-June, the North allowed the agency to install a new device at the reactor that would help monitor operations when the rods were unloaded. After the inspection was completed, the North Koreans asked the IAEA to manufacture special baskets to store the unloaded rods.[60]

Why was Pyongyang so uncharacteristically cooperative? The most obvious explanation was that it did not want the results of the inspection to hinder upcoming talks with the United States. Indeed, the North may have intended the positive outcome to pave the way for those discussions. The inspection did not provide any definitive clues to what Pyongyang would do on June 12 or afterward. But the North Koreans had not created any technical barriers that would prevent the IAEA from continuing to conduct inspections whether or not they withdrew from the NPT. That suggested a third possible scenario: North Korea might withdraw from the treaty as a bargaining ploy while taking whatever steps were necessary to keep the situation from spiraling out of control. Modulating its cooperation with IAEA inspections could be a valuable spigot for Pyongyang to shape the political environment.

Soon the Security Council would act against Pyongyang's nuclear defiance, effectively ending the thaw that had begun to develop between North Korea and the IAEA. That danger had been understood, but the Americans had viewed a UN resolution as an indispensable component of the strategy of gradual escalation. The long hoped-for consultations in Vienna were first stalled by the North as the resolution was about to be considered and then postponed once it passed on May 11.[61] Yet all hope was not lost. According to the North Koreans, a "good" atmosphere was expected to prevail—perhaps a reference to upcoming talks with the United States—and maybe then a date could be set for consultations.[62]

Still, Blix remained anxious. The prospect of continued IAEA inspections even if Pyongyang withdrew from the NPT now seemed uncertain. During a May visit to Washington, a pessimistic Blix told Assistant Secretary of Defense Ash Carter that he expected the North would let its NPT obligations lapse. A few weeks later, as the U.S.–North Korean negotiations commenced, his worst fears seemed to be confirmed. Pyongyang's ambassador in Vienna told Blix that his country would withdraw from the NPT and no longer adhere to the safeguards agreement.[63]

Rice Cake to Rice Cake

By May, the Clinton administration stood on the threshold of talks with North Korea. In the few months since the March 12 announcement, Washington had begun to forge a multilateral coalition in opposition to Pyongyang through its own diplomatic efforts, including those at the United Nations, and in close consultations with South Korea and Japan. Beijing was in Washington's diplomatic crosshairs, although gaining its support would be difficult. The ground had also been prepared for dialogue with Pyongyang, which was now waiting to hear from the United States about when talks could begin.

But before that could happen, Washington wanted to put one more multilateral building block in place, a UN resolution that would increase the pressure on Pyongyang and demonstrate that it could not count on a Chinese veto. In New York, the Chinese took a more constructive stance this time—perhaps because of the impending U.S.–North Korean dialogue—even saying publicly that their abstention on the proposed resolution did not reflect opposition to the will of the international community.[64] Passed on May 11, UN Resolution 825 called on Pyongyang to meet its nonproliferation obligations and urged "all member states" to "facilitate a solution." It cleared the way for America's dialogue with North Korea to begin.

In the meantime, Washington had been moving to put the other pieces of the dialogue puzzle in place. Restarting North-South talks as a visible sign of Seoul's participation in a joint effort to engage Pyongyang remained crucial. But the South was hesitant, with some officials worrying that North Korea's talks with the United States would steal the show. Some feared Pyongyang might use talks with Seoul to generate propaganda or to escape pressure if the American dialogue faltered. Others argued for moving in tandem with Washington. Still others believed North-South talks could pay off only after U.S.–North Korean discussions showed progress. The result of this welter of divergent views was bureaucratic gridlock.[65]

Seoul vacillated even though clues mounted that President Kim's inaugural speech and the release of Lee In Mo had indeed created a positive momentum in Pyongyang. Immediately after the March 12 announcement, South Korea's intelligence chief publicly alluded to hints from Pyongyang that there would be a breakthrough in inter-Korean relations in the next month.[66] He may have been referring to secret contacts between the two Koreas in Beijing during which the North stated that "something good" would happen in late April. Kim Jong Il himself reportedly informed a visitor that talks between the two Koreas would begin after discussions with Washington had been set up. Reinforcing his statement, North Korea's press stopped personal attacks on President Kim and limited negative comments to individual cabinet members rather than the whole government.

The signals reached a crescendo in early April when North Korea's premier, Kang Song San, welcomed President Kim's inaugural offer and unveiled a new proposal for national reunification authored by Kim Il Sung. It was familiar in substance but moderate in tone. Contrary to standard practice, no rallies were held in support of the new missive nor was it sent to sympathizers in the South, probably to avoid aggravating Seoul.[67] Speaking to a visitor a few weeks later, one North Korean official observed, "Once there is a positive response to the plan . . . we hope and expect North-South talks can resume." Traveling home through Seoul, the visitor passed the message to the South Koreans.[68]

As always, these signals were open to varying, often contradictory, interpretations. South Korean conservatives were skeptical. But so were moderates, given what they viewed as "insincere" behavior by North Korea after the 1992 talks failed to reach a bilateral inspection regime for the Denuclearization Declaration. Whether the North Koreans were "sincere" or not was important but indecipherable. A proposal was now clearly in the works.[69]

Domestic pressures also were building to resume dialogue. Polls showed 40 percent of the public thought the pace of talks with Pyongyang was too slow, almost double the number since the North's spy ring was exposed in late 1992.[70] The business community lobbied "hard and heavy" for talks, according to one government official.[71] With Pyongyang's encouragement, trade contacts had continued in spite of the March 12 announcement. Companies still pushed for a relaxation of trade restrictions and made new deals even though the government was unlikely to approve them under the current circumstances.[72]

Finally, Washington had made it clear that North-South dialogue had to be part of the unfolding diplomatic strategy. While the previous South Korean president, Roh Tae Woo, had been leery of U.S. engagement with Pyongyang—a view acknowledged in the U.S. position that inter-Korean dialogue was the primary means of resolving problems on the peninsula—President Kim seemed less suspicious. But Washington knew that managing Seoul was a tricky business. The South Koreans had to be seen as taking a strong role in resolving differences on the peninsula and Washington had to support them. On top of that, the Pentagon believed the North-South Denuclearization Declaration's ban on reprocessing, uranium enrichment, and associated facilities was the only viable hope for stopping the North's nuclear program. In late April, Under Secretary of State Peter Tarnoff told President Kim in no uncertain terms that the South should reengage the North.

As a final vote on the May 11 Security Council resolution approached and Washington's own dialogue with Pyongyang seemed ready to begin, South Korea could delay no longer. In a May 3 meeting with his ministers, President Kim decided to propose the resumption of inter-Korean talks after Washington's discussions with the North commenced.[73] While Pyongyang might reject the proposal, a South Korean official observed that Seoul "does not have much to lose."

Having secured the South's participation, Washington now had to finalize its negotiating position. Some rumblings from officials in the Department of Defense suggested that dealing with the North's threatening ballistic missile program—its deployment at home and export abroad—should be made a key priority for the upcoming talks. But that view was rejected by the Deputies Committee, on the grounds that linking other matters to the nuclear agenda would only delay resolution of the most critical issue and give North Korea more bargaining leverage than it deserved.

Meeting on May 6, the deputies settled on an approach that sought to persuade the North to meet its existing NPT and IAEA obligations in return for the suspension of the 1994 Team Spirit exercise (already on the chopping block for military reasons unrelated to the North Korean nuclear issue) and a rehash of familiar positions. That meant the United States would be prepared to repeat existing security assurances that applied to all NPT parties in good standing under the treaty, reaffirm President Roh's statement that there were no nuclear weapons deployed in the South, and offer trial inspections of American bases on the peninsula.

New inducements would be put on the table only after Pyongyang implemented the North-South Denuclearization Declaration, a tangible demonstration of Seoul's central role in the diplomatic process. In return, Washington would permanently end Team Spirit and agree to a nuclear-free zone on the peninsula similar to that established by the Latin American Treaty of Tlatelolco. But the deputies were careful not to offer any carrots beyond those in the security realm. Better political and economic relations would have to wait until after the nuclear issue was resolved.

Finally, the administration chose Robert L. Gallucci, the assistant secretary of state for political-military affairs, as its lead negotiator. Trained as an academic, the New York–born civil servant was a veteran of almost twenty years in the Arms Control and Disarmament Agency and the State Department. His career had focused on nuclear nonproliferation. Tapped by the Bush administration to help set up the UN Special Commission, the organization charged with inspecting Iraq after the first Gulf War, he had led a team that seized Iraqi documents and refused to relinquish them to Saddam Hussein's henchmen during a standoff in a Baghdad parking lot. Gallucci's next assignment was to establish programs to cope with the proliferation dangers posed by the Soviet Union's collapse. Then Secretary of State James A. Baker III promoted him to the position of assistant secretary of state for political-military affairs, a job he kept even after the Clinton administration assumed office. Gallucci had a long friendship with Tony Lake, the new national security adviser, who had been his boss on the policy planning staff in the Carter State Department.

Despite this experience, Gallucci had a relatively low bureaucratic profile. He reported to two under secretaries at the State Department and rarely saw Warren Christopher. Riding back to his office with a colleague after briefing Congress, Gallucci discovered that neither one had ever discussed North Korea with the secretary. That remained true for most of 1993 as the crisis simmered.[74] Gallucci's choice of Tom Hubbard, a deputy assistant secretary of state in the East Asia Bureau, as his de facto deputy minimized sniping from inside the department. Nicknamed "the tank" by the North Koreans because of his stocky build and fierce concentration during negotiations, Hubbard would play a key role in formulating and implementing policy. But Gallucci's weak bureaucratic position would hamper his ability to influence policy throughout the first year of the crisis.

Even more important, it threatened to derail negotiations even before they had begun. Gallucci's profile was so low that his appointment came as a complete surprise to the North Koreans. With talks imminent, the main channel of communication between the two governments had shifted to New York, where the North Korean Mission to the United Nations was located. Logistically, the shift made a great deal of sense. If necessary, U.S. officials could hop on a plane from Washington and be in New York in a little over an hour. The New York Mission was also home to Ho Jong, who had emerged as a barometer of North Korea's views and would play the role of point man in secret negotiations with Washington.

In mid-May, a few weeks before the U.S.–North Korean negotiations were expected to begin, a "New York channel" meeting was held between State Department official Charles Kartman and Kim Jong Su, the number-two man in Pyongyang's UN Mission. The North Koreans, always sticklers for details, said they wanted to call the upcoming negotiations "high-level talks," mirroring the session with Kanter in 1992. The American diplomats broke the news that Robert Gallucci, not Under Secretary Tarnoff, would be the negotiator, so the upcoming talks could not be called "high-level." Turning to his colleague, Kim asked, "Should we leave?" The quick reply was, "No." Both agreed to call the negotiations "policy-level talks."[75]

North Korea also seemed to be preparing for the talks. Ever since March 12, Pyongyang's demands had focused largely on removing the American nuclear threat. Once it became clear the United States would talk, the North added to and refined those demands. Speaking to the National Council of Churches in Washington, D.C., on May 27, Ho Jong asserted that Washington had to remove the "nuclear umbrella" from South Korea. (The nuclear umbrella comprised U.S. security assurances to its treaty allies that it would deter conventional aggression by their adversaries in part by reserving the right to employ nuclear weapons if necessary.) The North previously had told the United States that it did not care about the umbrella.[76]

Visitors to Pyongyang that spring were treated to encouraging hints. Kim Jong Il reportedly told a guest that the IAEA could visit the two waste sites if the North Koreans could visit American bases in the South. He also wanted to establish diplomatic relations with Washington and would be willing to end missile exports in return for economic assistance.[77] In early May, another North Korean, meeting a former American official in Pyongyang, did not rule out inspections but added, "We cannot agree to hundreds of inspections at once."[78] A few days later, Kim Yong Sun—who met Kanter in 1992—quoted an old Korean proverb to a visitor: "Sword to sword, rice cake to rice cake. It is now time to throw away the sword and hold up the rice cake."[79] It may have been the right time to negotiate, but there was no guarantee that North Korea would take the escape route it seemed to be preparing.

Whether testing Pyongyang through dialogue was the best approach remained open to debate. On the eve of the talks, Gallucci told the Senate Foreign Relations Committee that the United States was "prepared to respond to North Korean concerns with appropriate actions if the North agrees to meet our objectives."[80] His staff predicted that Pyongyang would suspend its withdrawal from the NPT, buying time for a negotiated solution. On the other hand, skeptics like Director of Central Intelligence R. James Woolsey thought the North was playing for time to complete its nuclear weapons.[81] As the talks commenced, the *Far Eastern Economic Review* asked the question that was on everyone's mind: "Will it or won't it withdraw from the NPT"?[82]

3

No Sitting President
Would Allow North Korea
to Acquire Nuclear Weapons

June–August 1993

O N June 2, ten days before Pyongyang's withdrawal from the Nuclear
Non-Proliferation Treaty would take effect, American and North
Korean negotiators gathered in New York City. Senior diplomats from the two
countries had not met since January 1992. The discussions were held in the
same location, the top floor conference room of the American Mission to the
United Nations, with its panoramic view of the United Nations, the East River,
and the Queens skyline beyond.

The U.S. delegation was led by Robert Gallucci and included representatives from all the major bureaucratic players: the National Security Council,
the Office of the Secretary of Defense, the Joint Chiefs of Staff, and the Arms
Control and Disarmament Agency. Few of the Americans had ever met a
North Korean. That was certainly true for Gallucci. Before the talks started, he
had to be coached by his interpreter on how to pronounce the North Korean
chief negotiator's name properly.[1]

Only three delegation members qualified as Korea experts. The most senior
was Charles ("Chuck") Kartman, the director of the State Department's Office
of Korean Affairs, who had served in Seoul. C. Kenneth Quinones worked for
Kartman. Fluent in Korean, he had been the first American official to meet
Kim Il Sung. Robert Carlin, the department's chief North Korea watcher, had
spent twenty years analyzing Pyongyang. A controversial figure in the intelligence community because of his view that negotiations could be productive,
Carlin had a habit of grilling North Koreans at academic conferences for
information. One "victim" would later describe him as "relentlessly friendly."[2]

Still, Gallucci suffered from no lack of advice on how to deal with the North. Seoul prescribed heaping spoonfuls of diplomatic castor oil, but most Americans knew enough to be cautious, given the spotty record of inter-Korean talks, which often degenerated into "did not, did too" exercises. The representative from the Joint Chiefs of Staff fell back on past experiences, presenting Gallucci with *How Communists Negotiate*, a book written by the U.S. negotiator of the armistice that ended the Korean War.[3] Its tone reflected a cartoon-like image of the "commies" typical of the 1950s. According to Gallucci, the message was "If they act nasty, they are nasty, but if they act nice, they are sneaky."

Inexperience with the North Koreans also led the U.S. delegation to tend to view them as two-dimensional figures. Sitting across from grown men wearing pins with pictures of Kim Il Sung in their suit lapels reinforced the perception of the North Korean regime as a cult. One U.S. official remarked on an odd inverse relationship between the size of the pins and the rank of his counterparts: the more important the delegation member, the smaller his pin.

The North Koreans suffered from similar problems. A European expert who studied French, First Vice Foreign Minister Kang Sok Ju—their negotiator— was a short, stocky man who displayed a mixture of earthiness, bluster, and unexpected candor. He had a penchant for folksy metaphors and malapropisms. At the March 12 press conference announcing the decision to withdraw from the NPT, Kang accused the United States of trying to "inspect and expose all of our military sites," proclaiming, "do you think we can take off our pants?" During the talks, whenever uncomfortable with a U.S. position, Kang would assert that he felt like he was standing in his underwear. When the going got tougher still, he would blurt out, "You want to strip me naked." Kang was a dogged negotiator, able to repeat the party line ad nauseam to make his point.[4]

Other delegation members had varying degrees of experience with Americans. A gregarious man who often played good cop to Kang's bad cop, Ambassador Kim Gye Gwan had met with Americans once before, in the 1992 session with Under Secretary Arnold Kanter. Ho Jong, the deputy ambassador at the United Nations, and Li Gun from the Foreign Ministry had spent their recent careers focusing on the United States. Although mixing with Americans could prove dangerous to their futures, it was part of their job, so Ho and Li spent coffee breaks trying to gather information or floating trial balloons with the U.S. delegation.[5]

The North Koreans also seemed to find the Americans perplexing. Baffled by Gallucci's informality, they wondered whether his habit of slouching in his chair and cracking jokes were signs of disrespect. "Who is this Gallucci person?" they often asked. One confided that his delegation viewed the presence of a U.S. military representative at the talks (a routine occurrence) as a veiled threat. When Kanter met Kim in 1992, none was present.[6]

The first day of negotiations began early in the morning and lasted seven hours. The main players—Gallucci, Kang, and their senior aides—were arrayed around a long rectangular table. The other delegation members sat behind them. The North Koreans appeared tense.[7]

Kang took the floor first; it was diplomatic custom to allow the visiting delegation to make the opening statement. Not surprisingly, he portrayed his country as the injured party, having made all the right moves—joining the NPT, signing its safeguards agreement, and accepting inspections—only to be treated by the International Atomic Energy Agency in a "high-handed manner." (He conveniently glossed over North Korea's six-year delay in concluding a safeguards agreement with the agency.) "We were as humble or obedient as sheep," Kang asserted. But "we got no benefits, nothing so much as a *nunkkop*," a not very elegant Korean expression referring to the dried mucous discharge from the eye.[8]

Kang accused the United States of acting behind the scenes to put pressure on North Korea. Washington slowed reconciliation between the two Koreas, instigated the holding of Team Spirit, and prompted the IAEA to request special inspections. The United States had followed "the policy of a strong man against a weak man." Expressing shock, Kang added, "This was flabbergasting to us . . . a great insult and interference . . . [you are] just waiting for North Korea to die." Since staying in the NPT posed a grave threat to the North's political system, his country would never return to the treaty again. His claim that the NPT posed such a threat reflected a theme he would return to again and again throughout the New York meeting. "We are not East Germany, we will not collapse," Kang repeated as the negotiations unfolded. The North Koreans were well aware of speculation since the collapse of the Soviet Union and its East European satellites that they would be next.[9]

Now, according to the chief delegate, his country faced an important decision: whether to use its reactors to produce nuclear weapons or electricity. Kang said Pyongyang had the "capability" to build such weapons, but going that route made little sense since the United States had a large nuclear arsenal. "We make one, two, three or four but what is the use," he shrugged. His government's decision, however, hinged on the outcome of this meeting. Switching to English for emphasis, Kang proposed a deal. If the United States stopped threatening North Korea, his country would commit itself never to manufacture nuclear weapons.

The American experts recognized Kang's remarks as a distinct departure from Kim Il Sung's previous statements. The North Korean leader invariably told visitors that his country did not have the capability, desire, or need to build nuclear weapons, prompting South Korean wags sarcastically to dub his mantra "the three nothings."[10] Kang was now upping the ante, boasting of the North's capabilities while dangling a pledge to refrain from pursuing them.

After a long morning, the two delegations broke a few hours for lunch. Once they returned to the negotiating table, the North Koreans made two new proposals, neither raised by them in the months after the March 12 statement. If America agreed not to "strangle" the North or pose a nuclear threat, Pyongyang would pledge never to manufacture nuclear weapons. Instead of returning to the NPT, however, it would move forward with Seoul in implementing the dormant Denuclearization Declaration. Kang explained, "We are still fearful of nuclear weapons in South Korea and are concerned about their moves to develop nuclear arms." Moreover, the new idea could form the basis for a nuclear-free zone in Northeast Asia. Kang would later whisper to Gallucci that expanding the accord would curb Japanese efforts to acquire nuclear weapons.

The North Koreans also resurrected an old trial balloon, a trade of their threatening gas-graphite moderated nuclear technology for less threatening light-water reactor technology. The idea had some merit; while their current gas-graphite facilities would allow Pyongyang to accumulate bomb-making material relatively quickly, the light-water reactor fuel rods were harder to divert to that purpose and more easily safeguarded. Moreover, since North Korea could not build those rods itself, it would have to depend on outside suppliers for the necessary materials. That would give the United States more control over the North's nuclear program.

Most of the Americans were unfamiliar with the North's interest in light-water reactors, which dated back to at least 1985, when it had signed the NPT at the Soviet Union's urging. Although Pyongyang was to receive Russian light-water reactors in return, the deal was never consummated since the North Koreans did not implement their IAEA safeguards agreement. In 1992 the North resurrected the light-water reactor idea with a vengeance, first raising it with Hans Blix during his May visit, then asserting in public that the two Koreas should cooperate on nuclear technology if suspicions about the North's program were eliminated. They also probed the United States in the Beijing channel. In July, North Korea's vice premier Kim Tal Hyun, a reformer who read the *New York Times,* raised the point once more during a highly publicized visit to Seoul.[11]

Throughout the first day, Gallucci tried to strike a balance. At lunch, he elaborated on the American plan for a two-stage diplomatic solution to the crisis. But he made it clear that there were limits to what Washington could tolerate if talks were to continue. In particular, North Korea had to allow the IAEA to monitor unloading of the 5-megawatt reactor.

In a private conversation, Gallucci responded to Kang's explicit threats, calmly observing that if the North withdrew from the NPT, the international community would have to take its own steps, a thinly veiled reference to sanctions. A bristling Kang called sanctions a "declaration of war," which would prompt Pyongyang to make public a document already prepared declaring its ability to build nuclear weapons. North Korea would then proceed to extract enough plutonium from its spent fuel rods to build one or two weapons. Gallucci replied, "No sitting president of the United States would allow North Korea to acquire nuclear weapons." He did not need to spell out the "or else." His meaning was understood.

At the end of the day, the Americans felt discouraged. Gallucci told anxiously waiting reporters that there had been no "significant progress"; in fact, the gap between the two sides seemed to be growing, not narrowing.[12] North Korea's proposal to substitute the inter-Korean denuclearization agreement for the NPT seemed designed to stall the discussions, by moving the nuclear issue back into those unproductive sessions, or to defuse international pressure by giving the appearance of flexibility. The Americans' objective was somehow to nudge the North Koreans back toward full NPT compliance, or at least to buy time while a more enduring solution was sought. And it had to be done without making any substantive concessions. Under the shadow of the ticking clock, that was a tall order.

Meeting for dinner at Godfather's Restaurant on Second Avenue, some of the Americans began to bat around new approaches that might find resonance with Pyongyang but would cost Washington nothing. What if the United States simply agreed to restate its existing international obligations from the UN Charter, such as an affirmation to refrain from the use of force, in a joint statement with North Korea? Beyond a willingness to issue such a statement— a move well within the mandate of UN Resolution 825, which called on all nations to contribute to resolving the crisis—Washington would be giving away nothing new. The North Koreans, on the other hand, could tout the statement as meeting their fundamental concerns.[13]

Korea watchers on the U.S. delegation also had discerned a strange disconnect between the signals Pyongyang had been sending after its March 12 announcement and the position Kang was taking in New York. Pyongyang had hinted many times that it would be willing to rejoin the NPT under the right conditions. Now Kang was saying that was impossible. The delegation set about culling ammunition out of those pronouncements to use the next time Kang refused to consider such a step.[14]

A day off from the talks did little to ease tensions. Press speculation that Pyongyang was preparing to withdraw from the NPT increased after Japan's ambassador to the United Nations confirmed reports that North Korea had ordered all foreigners to leave the country by June 15.[15] In fact, the South Koreans speculated that the North may have been preparing for a large influx of foreigners attending a Non-Aligned Movement conference in Pyongyang later that month. It had taken similar steps when hosting meetings with Seoul's prime minister in the past. But the move provided more grist for the media mill enveloping the negotiations.

Pyongyang did its best to pour gasoline on the fire. In response to Gallucci's veiled threats, its UN ambassador warned the president of the Security Council that sanctions "would bring about destructive results," adding, "I hope there won't be any repetition of June 25 forty-three years ago." That was the day the North Koreans came streaming across the 38th parallel to launch the Korean War.[16] The situation once again seemed grave. Later that week, Japan's vice foreign minister, Kunihiko Saito, told Walter Mondale, the newly appointed U.S. ambassador in Tokyo, that the New York talks were the "only hope" for avoiding a crisis.

When the negotiators reconvened on Friday, the Americans tried their new approach. Gallucci told the North Koreans that the United States would be willing to provide assurances based on selected principles in the UN Charter. In return, North Korea would have to remain in the NPT and implement nuclear safeguards. When Kang insisted once again that remaining in the NPT was impossible, Gallucci reminded him that North Korea had already said it could stay in the agreement under certain conditions. Kang seemed startled; he noticed the American interpreter reading from a xeroxed copy of a Korean language newspaper. A colleague whispered to him that Gallucci was repeating the official North Korean position from *Rodong Sinmun*, the party newspaper.[17]

For the rest of the day, Kang insisted that rejoining the NPT was impossible, stubbornly reiterating Pyongyang's willingness to brave all consequences, even economic sanctions. At one point, after a dramatic pause, he announced that he would quote from *Gone with the Wind*. All the Americans held their breath, wondering whether Kang would exclaim "Frankly, my dear . . ." and walk out. Instead Kang slowly said in English, "The dogs bark, but the caravan moves on," apparently meaning that nothing would stop Pyongyang.

The North Koreans were not walking out. Rather, Kang merely seemed to be saying that North Korea intended to go its own way. He looked pleased by his ability to draw this literary allusion. As the session ended, Kang emphasized in English that he would report Gallucci's remarks to Pyongyang.

Coming out of the American Mission, Kang told reporters that the "meeting did not fail," that his country was determined to escape the impasse, and that there would be at least two more sessions before the June 12 deadline. Later that day, his delegation canceled its airplane reservations for a flight home.[18] On this occasion—and on many in the future—the travel plans of the North Koreans would provide valuable clues to their intentions.

Though the Americans did not yet know it, their proposal had marked an important turning point. Afterward, the North Koreans no longer talked about withdrawing from the NPT, but rather about the circumstances under which Pyongyang could remain in the treaty. The U.S. diplomatic artifice allowed the two sides to begin to edge away from the brink.[19]

After a weekend recess, more progress occurred on June 7. At the North's request, Ken Quinones met two members of its delegation in the coffee shop of the New York Helmsley Hotel on the East Side of Manhattan. One of the two was Li Yong Ho, a perceptive diplomat with an easy manner and a wry smile, but also someone Kang could trust with important missions. He would prove to be a key negotiator in U.S.–North Korean talks in the future.

Reading from a small notebook, Li said Kang had directed him to meet with the Americans "the sooner, the better." Observing that Gallucci seemed willing to address Pyongyang's concerns about Washington's intentions when he referred to principles such as the nonuse of force, Li asked, "Could they be issued publicly as a joint statement?" He did not mention it, but the North had tried unsuccessfully to get a similar document at the 1992 Kanter-Kim meeting. A joint statement with the United States would be a significant political breakthrough, symbolizing that Washington recognized the North as an equal partner.

"Yes," Quinones replied, "provided you do not withdraw from the treaty." Both North Koreans sighed audibly and smiled, cryptically repeating three times that Kang had misunderstood Gallucci.

While Li said the North Koreans would try to get approval from Pyongyang for this approach, the Americans believed the fact that the meeting occurred meant they had already been told to work out a solution. That same day, Ho Jong resumed using language similar to the March 12 withdrawal statement, telling the press that a compromise was possible if the U.S. nuclear threat was removed and IAEA impartiality was restored.[20]

The Quinones-Li meeting had immediate reverberations in Washington. The Deputies Committee had been closely following events in New York, managing—or micromanaging, according to some—the diplomatic dance. Before the negotiations began, the deputies were even consulted about the placement of the U.S. and North Korean flags at the same negotiating table, presumably because of political sensitivities. Once the talks began, Gallucci spent hours daily on the secure telephone talking to them, individually or in conference calls.

Initially, differences appeared to be emerging inside the U.S. government. Pyongyang's suggestion that it might implement the Denuclearization Declaration as a substitute for the NPT threatened to reopen the bureaucratic fault line between the State Department and the Pentagon. While the former saw no reason to soften demands that North Korea rejoin the NPT and implement IAEA safeguards, the latter wanted to pursue Pyongyang's suggestion, which was consistent with its priority of stopping any further production of plutonium. This emerging split promised to create problems at a Deputies Committee meeting scheduled for June 8, the purpose of which was to discuss what to do if Pyongyang withdrew from the treaty.

The American threat of sanctions had not been idle talk. After the first day of negotiations Gallucci told the permanent members of the Security Council, the South Koreans, and the Japanese that it would be time to discuss tough measures if the next session did not go well. When it did not, they all agreed to begin talks on sanctions, knowing that word would get back to Pyongyang and, hopefully, intensify pressure on the North. When the negotiations seemed headed for stalemate after the Friday session, the Americans put China on notice that there would be intense pressure for sanctions if Pyongyang withdrew from the treaty. Meanwhile, Washington put the finishing touches on a strategy of escalating sanctions in case Pyongyang did not relent.

In view of the results of the coffee shop session, however, Washington shifted its attention away from finishing preparations for sanctions to exploiting the opening provided by the North. At the June 8 meeting Under Secretary of State Peter Tarnoff described the North as willing to "suspend its withdrawal" from the NPT. Frank Wisner, a Foreign Service veteran who was under secretary of defense, wanted to make sure what that meant. Sandy Berger added that Pyongyang also had to agree not to take any actions inconsistent with the NPT. It had to maintain the continuity of safeguards, to refrain from reprocessing any spent fuel, and to allow proper supervision by the IAEA of any reloading of the reactor. Anticipating how to deal with the press, the deputies settled on emphasizing that a suspension was an encouraging step but not a solution.

What would Washington do if it proved too difficult to bring the negotiations to a quick conclusion? "Would U.S. interests suffer if the two sides just kept talking?" The deputies concluded that talk was fine if there was progress, but talk just for the sake of talking would only damage the nonproliferation regime. "We should say our patience is not infinite," suggested Wisner.

Two days later, just forty-eight hours before North Korea was slated to withdraw from the NPT, the New York talks resumed. The mood was serious but less tense. Both negotiators exchanged Asian proverbs to imply that more work remained. "A journey of 10,000 miles begins with a single step," Gallucci observed. Kang chimed in, "A spoonful cannot make a full stomach."

While the North Koreans seemed ready to suspend their NPT withdrawal, Gallucci made one last try to persuade them to cancel their withdrawal outright and remain in the treaty. Over lunch, he launched a proposal keyed to Pyongyang's pre–New York signals, telling Kang that the United States would allow a "trial" inspection of an American military base in the South if the North accepted inspection of a site on its territory. (Kim Jong Il himself had supposedly made that suggestion in April.) Washington would also address Pyongyang's concerns about the American nuclear threat by providing it with a negative security assurance, considering a formal nuclear-free zone on the peninsula, and suspending Team Spirit. But Kang was not interested in a permanent deal. Shifting gears once again, work resumed on a joint statement along the lines suggested in the coffee shop meeting.

But Gallucci had a price for consummating that deal. He insisted that if North Korea would not agree to remain in the NPT, it would at least have to make a positive reference to all of its nonproliferation obligations including the NPT, its willingness to accept international inspections, and implementation of the denuclearization agreement. That would leave open the possibility for future discussions on all three issues. After resisting, the North Korean relented. Gallucci himself offered a key compromise. The statement would specify the "impartial" application of safeguards in deference to the North's claims that past IAEA inspection demands were anything but impartial.

After nine hours of talks, the meeting ended in agreement. The short, simple joint document laid out a number of agreed principles, among them an assurance against the threat and use of force (including nuclear weapons), mutual respect for each country's sovereignty, and noninterference in internal affairs. It merely restated obligations that the United States had already undertaken in existing international agreements. The penultimate line was that North Korea "decided unilaterally to suspend for as long as it considers necessary the effectuation of its withdrawal" from the NPT.[21]

Kang had one final request before cabling the document back home for final approval. He wanted the two negotiators to sign the statement. Quickly recognizing that neither Seoul nor Washington wished to give North Korea the added benefit of a joint statement that morphed into a signed agreement, Gallucci quipped, "How about taking a picture we could sign?" The draft statement was sent back to the two capitals and quickly approved.

The next day, the two delegations faced one more hurdle, figuring out how to deal with the scores of reporters waiting for the unveiling of the new document. One wrong word from the North Koreans, particularly any negative comments on special inspections, could ruin the agreement. Kang reassured the Americans: "We will not say we will once and for all exclude any IAEA safeguards in our country." Speaking to the reporters in the courtyard of the U.S. Mission under the watchful eye of an American delegation member, he followed the agreed script.[22]

But the work was not yet completed. At Kang's request, the two chief negotiators held one last private chat. Having insisted throughout the talks that North Korea could not return to the NPT, Kang now asked what Washington was willing to offer if the North agreed to remain in the agreement. In spite of its protestations, Pyongyang was open for business. His next question framed what would become the crux of Washington's dilemma: was the United States more interested in finding out what nuclear activities had been conducted in the past or in preventing future nuclear activities?

Kang's question reflected a concern that the United States would use the NPT and IAEA as tools to dig into North Korea's past record and find fault with it. Gallucci replied that Washington could not put aside concerns about the past. But he added that the United States had no intention to embarrass North Korea and urged Kang to consider a face-saving solution pursued by South Africa and Romania, amending the North's original declaration of plutonium production to admit it had made an error. The two negotiators left the conversation there for the moment.

With the conclusion of the June 11 statement, a day before North Korea's deadline, the crisis subsided. For the Americans, the price seemed modest. True, they had agreed to the first joint document ever between the two countries; the symbolism could not be denied. But it was merely a rehash of principles that the United States had already accepted in other international agreements. Aside from buying time to resolve the nuclear issue through diplomacy, the last-minute inclusion of a principle on the "impartial application of safeguards," which did indeed cause the IAEA discomfort since it implied the agency had not been impartial, opened the door for further discussions about access to the two suspected sites. Understanding this issue was critical. The North Koreans clearly would have liked to avoid it altogether but seemed to be fishing for solutions.

Privately, Gallucci remained troubled; focusing on resolving the past would still allow Pyongyang legally to accumulate plutonium in the future and to transfer it to other NPT members with nuclear aspirations, such as Iran and Libya. While the North-South Denuclearization Declaration banned reprocessing and the possession of plutonium, it did not prohibit operation of gas-graphite reactors from which spent fuel could be easily reprocessed to produce plutonium. In addition, it was unclear how the North could operate its gas-graphite reactors without reprocessing, since their spent fuel could not be stored indefinitely, unlike that from light-water reactors. Moreover, the United States was skeptical that accord would ever come into force. Kang's proposal to build new reactors might help fill these gaps, but to some Americans it appeared to be little more than a request for a $4 billion handout. Balancing two objectives—dealing with the past and the future—would preoccupy U.S. negotiators throughout the crisis.

The New York meeting began an educational process for the Americans, most of whom would remain intimately involved in resolving the crisis. Gradually, they came to understand better how the North Koreans thought and how they might react to various moves and countermoves. One delegation member, perhaps exhibiting symptoms of "Stockholm syndrome," when kidnap victims start to sympathize with the kidnappers, recalled that after listening to Kang, his perspective began to make some sense. Others noticed that the North Koreans were not two dimensional. They had a sense of humor and would use it frequently to get over tense moments.[23]

The Americans also began to develop their own typology about North Korean negotiating behavior. First, "impossible demands" frequently became possible to meet after the North Koreans suddenly took, in their words, a "bold step" to resolve problems they themselves may have created. Sometimes they simply stopped raising an issue; silence often meant consent. Second, positive suggestions early on or accepting language from Pyongyang's proposals kept the North Koreans focused on solutions, short-circuiting their inclination to engage in endless arguments. They rarely raised the ante when the Americans pursued this approach. Third, as in most negotiations, the real work was done in small informal meetings where possible solutions could be explored without the awkwardness of onlookers. Finally, Kang had a variety of ways to signal he was in a negotiating mode, by emphasizing common points, presenting differences in a neutral fashion and speaking "frankly," and often ending meetings on an upbeat note.[24]

The New York talks also reaffirmed the universal proposition that reaching understanding often depends on personal rapport. The two negotiators—a North Korean and a New Yorker—could hardly have been more different. But during lunch on the second day, Kang remarked that Gallucci's surname was Italian, prompting Gallucci to talk about his time in Rome in the mid-1980s. The American referred to the opening of a McDonald's near the fabled Spanish

Steps, which he said spoiled a bit of the classic beauty and ambience of the piazza. Kang looked stunned, confronted by a U.S. official describing something American as less than perfect.[25] Over time, the two seemed to build a relationship based in part on straight talk and informality.

Still, the Americans had much to learn about the North Koreans. Before New York, they had closely followed Pyongyang's signals in order to gauge what it would take to reach an agreement. Reading those signals had helped find the solution recorded on June 11. But even though they deployed enticements the North had mentioned in the months before New York, the Americans were unable to coax Pyongyang to return to permanent membership in the NPT. There may have been any number of explanations for Pyongyang's mixed signals, ranging from a tactic to throw the United States off balance to a negotiating position that was simply evolving over time. Understanding the North's position, particularly without the benefit of constant face-to-face contacts, would remain difficult.

For Pyongyang, New York represented a significant step forward in its effort to engage Washington. It needed to sustain momentum and to avoid the appearance of an early deadlock. But the North Koreans probably were not prepared to reach a deal at any cost. If pressed too hard on special inspections, they likely would have broken the talks off no matter what the consequences. As a U.S. official wryly observed, "If there is one thing the North Koreans know how to respond to, it is a frontal assault."[26]

Kang had carefully explored a solution that would sustain engagement at home and abroad. He staked out a tough position initially, yielding ground slowly. The Americans speculated that this approach would make it easier to sell a deal in Pyongyang where it was politically risky to appear "weak." The North's generally upbeat media treatment of the June 11 statement suggested he had hit the mark. To sustain momentum, Kang had laid the groundwork for more talks, making sure the Americans understood that his country was willing to negotiate over the issue of IAEA impartiality and even hinting cryptically that the request for special inspections might ultimately be accepted. Kang later hailed the June 11 statement as a "turning point in bilateral relations" between the United States and North Korea.

In Washington, the response was mixed. In line with the deputies' discussion, the administration adopted a cautious public posture. President Clinton called the statement "a first but vital step in worldwide non-proliferation."[27] The State Department asked its embassies to tell their host governments that the New York statement was a good interim outcome, far better than the alternative of North Korea's departure from the NPT, an imminent prospect just a few days earlier.

Not everyone agreed. While the *New York Times* applauded, *Washington Post* columnist Lally Weymouth warned that the North would mate a nuclear warhead with a ballistic missile tested in May. She urged the administration to set a "timetable for the North to come into compliance with the NPT, demand Pyongyang to allow the IAEA inspection and meanwhile encourage the UN to impose sanctions."[28] Trying to fend off critics, Gallucci denied that the promises in the statement were concessions, a message echoed by Secretary Warren Christopher traveling in Greece.[29]

Internationally, the reaction was also cautious. Beijing lauded the "preliminary progress" made in the talks.[30] The Japanese had much the same response. On several occasions, Prime Minister Kiichi Miyazawa had asked whether he should stay home or in his office to await reports from New York rather than attend scheduled functions. Once agreement was reached, Tokyo publicly applauded the progress while stressing that "real" problems remained. Privately, the Japanese told the Chinese that if the North believed the United States, Japan, and others were completely satisfied, it was mistaken.

Preparing for the worst, on the day the agreement was concluded, IAEA director general Blix informed the Board of Governors that even if North Korea's safeguards agreement lapsed, it would still be bound by the earlier, more limited inspection agreement reached in 1977. Once the New York talks concluded, he sent a letter to Pyongyang calling the statement a "positive" outcome, but asserting that the North's current safeguards obligations were still in force.[31]

Of all the interested parties, South Korea should have been the most pleased. The June 11 statement vindicated its strategy of encouraging the United States to negotiate. Echoing American and Japanese statements, South Korea's foreign minister Han Sung Joo—on a tour of European capitals—told the French paper *Le Monde* that the suspension of the withdrawal was a "positive gesture" but "does not settle the problem."[32] Trouble was brewing in Seoul, however, providing the first of many tests for the two allies' close relationship in dealing with the nuclear issue.

Alphonse and Gaston

By the time the June 11 statement was issued, Seoul was knee-deep in trying to restart its own dialogue with North Korea. Its effort reflected a delicate consensus achieved inside the government between moderates, conservatives left over from previous military regimes located throughout the bureaucracy, and centrists who swung from supporting one group to the other. As South Korea's effort faltered and Washington's negotiations succeeded, that consensus began to fray, yielding hints that managing the close alliance while trying to reach out diplomatically to North Korea would be difficult.

Launched in late May, almost ten days before the New York meeting, Seoul's diplomatic offensive produced a surprising result. South Korea's request for "contacts between delegations to the high-level talks to discuss the nuclear issues" prompted North Korea's premier Kang Song San to make an entirely new proposal. He wanted to exchange special envoys with the rank of deputy prime minister, who would arrange a summit with the objective of resolving differences between the two countries, including implementation of the Denuclearization Declaration.[33] Keyed to President Kim Young Sam's inaugural address, the fact that the envoys would be deputy prime ministers was no coincidence. Han Wan Sang, a strong advocate of reconciliation with the North, held that rank.[34]

Although Seoul and Washington had anticipated a North Korean initiative, the new "special envoys" proposal caught them off guard. The idea, probably in the works since President Kim's inaugural speech, also seemed keyed to Kim Il Sung's ten-point plan for reunification presented at the April meeting of the Supreme People's Assembly.[35]

The North's motivations remained unclear. The language was conciliatory and the timing—just after Washington and Pyongyang announced they would hold a dialogue—meant it could have been part of a broad, positive diplomatic offensive.[36] Seeking to open a new channel also may have reflected a serious concern in Pyongyang that the previous prime minister talks had become nothing more than public theater. Second, by trying to open this channel on the eve of the New York talks, Pyongyang could have been trying to increase its room for maneuver. If those talks faltered, it could avoid ultimatums and sanctions by stepping up discussions with the South. Third, the proposal may have been a first step by Kim Yong Sun, who had met Under Secretary Kanter in 1992, to regain control of policy toward Washington since he would be a prime candidate for the special envoy job.

Whatever Pyongyang's purpose, the proposal tied Seoul in knots. Suspicion was widespread. The opposition party expressed a "guarded welcome" while the conservative newspaper *Chosun Ilbo* urged the Kim government to be "prudent in responding."[37] The prime minister, too, was cautious, worried that the exchange would bypass his role in North-South relations.[38] After all, the talks between the two countries' prime ministers had been at the center of North-South relations until the crisis erupted. Moderates viewed the proposal as a positive development, but their leading light was hamstrung. Deputy Prime Minister Han Wan Sang could not say "Yes, I would like to go to Pyongyang" lest he appear a willing accomplice to North Korea's plans.[39]

Since Seoul understood that turning down Pyongyang's initiative could have negative consequences at home and in Washington, it parried, triggering an argument over form, dates, and agenda that bordered on farce. Initially, Seoul agreed to discuss the envoy exchange if the nuclear issue remained the top priority. An argument stretched over the next month as the two Koreas exchanged proposals through various channels controlled by the Foreign Ministry and South Korean intelligence in Beijing and New York, trying to gain a tactical advantage. Though agreement seemed to have been finally reached to hold a meeting on June 10, the session never happened. Contrary to customary practice, the North Koreans did not provide the South with a delegate list beforehand.[40] As the diplomatic pas de deux unfolded, the South Koreans conducted daily simulations of how the talks might play out just in case.[41]

An intensifying propaganda war between the two Koreas only made matters worse. In his first major foreign policy speech, delivered on May 24, President Kim Young Sam emphasized a "policy of peaceful coexistence, joint prosperity, and common welfare," prompting the U.S. Embassy to praise his policy as having far more clarity and fewer caveats than previous South Korean regimes. But a week later, President Kim told the press, "I want to make clear that we cannot shake hands with any partner who has nuclear weapons."[42] Kim's comment appealed to conservatives but, from the North Korean perspective, he also appeared to be turning his back on the offer to hold a summit in his inaugural address. Pyongyang immediately accused him of inconsistency, escalating its attacks on South Korean leaders.[43]

Seoul became more flexible after the June 11 New York statement, viewed as a sign that Pyongyang might be serious. The South dropped its insistence that the nuclear issue had to be addressed first, prompting the North to agree to a meeting on June 15. But again the session never took place. Shutting down the night of June 14, the South Korean liaison officer at Panmunjom asked his North Korean counterpart if there was any word on tomorrow's meeting. The reply—a message would be coming in a day or so—caused the South Koreans to abort their trip to avoid being stood up. Subsequently, Pyongyang proposed a session for June 24, eliciting a sense of déjà vu among the South Koreans.[44]

Nevertheless, Seoul decided to try one more time. During a June 22 cabinet meeting, Foreign Minister Han and Deputy Prime Minister Han argued that Seoul should be flexible in responding to the special envoy proposal. That would reinforce New York's positive outcome and demonstrate to the world that the South was making every effort to find a way out of the impasse. They carried the day; a positive message was drafted gently asking North Korea for a meeting on June 24.[45] But Pyongyang rejected the overture. Shortly afterward,

Premier Kang publicly revoked the special envoy proposal, blaming the South's "undue attitude despite our side's month-long patient efforts."[46]

Exactly what motivated Pyongyang's behavior was, of course, open to speculation. Moderates in the South believed that the North may have been serious at first; the special envoy idea tracked with its initial proposal in New York for North-South talks on an inspection regime. Also, Pyongyang would not have agreed to include the nuclear issue in summit talks if it were engaging purely in a propaganda exercise. Nevertheless, the North lost interest once the United States rejected the New York proposal and then exploited the envoy issue to exacerbate differences in the South. While nominally rejecting Seoul's June 22 proposal for talks because it continued to seek preliminary discussion of the nuclear issue, Pyongyang by then had probably decided to abandon the special envoy exchange regardless of Seoul's positions. Conservatives believed the North's initiative had been a cynical ploy from the start.

Whatever Pyongyang's motivation, the U.S. government had urged the South to show flexibility, for example, by persuading Chung Chong Wook, the Blue House national security adviser who was visiting Washington in June, to support the June 22 proposal to reach out to Pyongyang. In any situation, trivialities easily block dialogue when either side is ambivalent. Those obstacles would have been overcome handily if both decided that their best interests were served by dialogue.

Washington's successful talks with North Korea only widened the fissures, both inside South Korea and with its major ally. The Foreign Ministry's initial, positive response to the New York talks was overwhelmed by the spillover of Japanese press criticism into the Korean media.[47] Pervasive but unfounded anxieties about a deal that bypassed inter-Korean dialogue and Seoul's interests affected everyone from President Kim Young Sam to the man on the street. One official caustically remarked that the public reacted to front-page pictures of a smiling Gallucci and Kang emerging from meetings in New York and later in Geneva as if it had caught the United States "committing adultery."[48] Compounding the problem, many South Koreans felt that only they had the necessary experience to deal with Pyongyang.

These feelings seemed irrational to the Americans, who had done everything possible to keep the South well informed, including daily meetings between Gallucci and Seoul's UN ambassador, Yu Chong Ha, as well as close contacts between the State Department and its Washington embassy.[49] That information was passed to the Blue House and President Kim. In turn, Seoul passed Washington its advice.[50] One American remarked, "If we got any closer to them, we would have been brought up on a morals charge."[51]

Nevertheless, divisions in Seoul still posed a major problem. A case in point concerned Lee Dong Bok, an influential conservative with the intelligence service. Assertive and outgoing, often monopolizing conversations with his excellent English, Lee believed that talking to North Korea was a waste of time; South Korean decisionmakers were deluding themselves when they thought they discerned moderation in North Korean policy. Although fired from the delegation to the North-South talks in 1992 over reports that he had tried to sabotage those discussions, Lee had managed to retain his job as a special assistant to the head of South Korean intelligence. His influence flowed from ties with bureaucrats from past military governments, with Prime Minister Hwang In Sung (an old-guard conservative), and with newspapers like the *Chosun Ilbo*. Moderates, who believed that Lee had a history of leaking to the press, suspected he was behind right-wing press attacks on the government.

Following the New York statement, Lee circulated a paper to South Koreans and Americans entitled "Worst Case Scenario for the Next Round of U.S.-North Korea Talks," outlining how Pyongyang might abuse the joint statement for its own purposes. He asserted that the North would use the statement to avoid international sanctions, to extract further concessions from Washington, to convert the talks into a political conference with the United States excluding the South, and to consolidate Kim Jong Il's shaky position. Like American conservatives, Lee thought it best for the United States to set a new deadline for full compliance by North Korea and to threaten sanctions if it were missed.

Problems with the conservatives had a domino effect. The June 11 statement sparked consternation in the Blue House. Some South Koreans feared that the United States was about to normalize relations with North Korea without consulting Seoul, especially since Pyongyang's Korean-language version of the statement conveyed the impression of a quasi-official document.[52] The Foreign Ministry knew otherwise but was hamstrung because Foreign Minister Han was in Europe.

As a result, the skeptics had a clear field with President Kim, who in any case had told visitors during the New York talks that he did not support making concessions to secure a suspension of Pyongyang's NPT withdrawal. Reflecting the advice of skeptics and his own predisposition, Kim recorded an interview with the BBC on June 17, asserting that the United States should not make any further concessions since North Korea was only trying to buy time. The interview, slated for broadcast on June 25, clearly indicated a possible rift between the two allies.[53]

Faced with the prospect of tensions with the United States and a disintegrating domestic consensus, moderates in Seoul (and Washington) tried to steer the Kim government back on course. Two days after the June 11 agreement, Foreign Minister Han dispatched a trusted diplomat to Washington, ostensibly to congratulate the Americans, but really to seek ammunition to deal with the skeptics. Trying to disabuse the South of any notion that the United States was about to normalize relations with Pyongyang, Tom Hubbard told his visitor that the agreement reached in New York was in English, not Korean. Also, the United States had made every effort to avoid the appearance of an official document, rejecting a North Korean request that both sign the statement and insisting on separate press conferences once an agreement was reached.

Upon his own return to Seoul on June 18, Foreign Minister Han met with President Kim, the press, and other officials. His lobbying seemed to have a positive effect. Four days later Kim reversed course, telling the Americans that although some believed Washington had given away too much, he was confident with the process. Thirty-five minutes after his BBC interview was broadcast on June 25, the Foreign Ministry reminded Washington that it was taped before the president had the benefit of a balanced analysis. To reinforce that message, the foreign minister publicly defended the June 11 statement as just repeating the contents of the UN Charter, adding that the use of carrots and sticks was "necessary and right."[54]

Supplementing Han's efforts, Washington used the visits of South Korean "skeptics" to help turn the tide. Before National Security Adviser Chung Chong Wook—one of those skeptics—came to Washington in mid-June, Assistant Secretary Winston Lord told other State Department officials, "We need to help Chung counter criticism from Korean conservatives who are concerned the United States was too forthcoming in its talks with the North." After meeting Tony Lake, Gallucci, and Lord, Chung came away reassured.

Still, President Kim continued to oscillate. He strayed once again on July 2, telling the *New York Times* that the North Koreans were manipulating negotiations with the United States "to buy time to finish their nuclear weapons," a comment that was even more surprising given the imminent visit of President Clinton in a few days.[55] Once again, it was up to Foreign Minister Han to repair the damage, explaining to the *Washington Post* that Kim "had no misgivings about the results of the talks" and that his remarks were intended for domestic critics, not to express unhappiness with the United States.[56]

President Clinton's visit to South Korea, from July 10 to 11, had a calming effect. Emphasizing the U.S. commitment to South Korea's defense, he told troops at the demilitarized zone about his decision to launch an attack on Iraq a few weeks earlier in response to an attempt to assassinate former president

Bush. "It is pointless for them [North Korea] to try to develop nuclear weapons because if they ever used them, it would mean the end of their country," Clinton declared. His comments were intended not just for North Korea but also his South Korean hosts.[57] At a joint press conference, President Kim warmed to the tough message, warning that "appropriate countermeasures" would be taken if North Korea were to make the wrong move.[58] Privately, Clinton told Kim that the May UN resolution laid the foundation for "one with teeth" if that became necessary.

In addition to soothing the South Koreans, the Clinton visit also seemed to establish a good relationship between the two leaders. Building personal rapport, not conducting intellectual discourse, was more President Kim's style. The Blue House went to great lengths; a special Korean-style hut was set up for the two to have a private meal together. Also, extensive research was done to identify Clinton's favorite music.[59] According to the press, the biggest dispute between the two men was deciding on when to go jogging together. In the end, President Kim felt he could trust Clinton to conduct a dialogue with North Korea. Otherwise, according to a Blue House aide, "things could have become a lot worse."[60]

For the moment, serious strains between the two allies were avoided. But events had demonstrated that the bilateral relationship could be extremely volatile as the two countries entered the uncharted, politics-infested waters of dealing with North Korea. While the alliance may have been critical for South Korea, domestic politics and a fragmented government led by a vacillating president created a situation that could change rapidly. Constant American attention would be required.

A Small, not Entirely Satisfactory but Significant Step Forward

On July 14, Americans and North Koreans met in Geneva under more auspicious circumstances than the previous session. Normally, the period between June 25 (the day the Korean War began) and July 27 (the day of the armistice) was filled with mass rallies and polemics against the United States. In New York, however, the North hinted that this year's "Month for the Anti-U.S. Joint Struggle" would be toned down to signal a desire for better relations.[61] Subsequently, there were no reports of rallies, and the annual June 25 editorial in the party newspaper did not even mention the "U.S. imperialists."[62] Pro–North Korean newspapers in Japan had already printed issues with stories critical of American "imperialism," but they never appeared.

In another positive gesture, Pyongyang returned the remains of some American soldiers killed in the Korean War. More than 36,000 GIs were killed in the war, and another 8,000 are unaccounted for, even after four decades. Recovering remains was an emotional quest for the United States. Pyongyang had begun returning them in 1990. After Team Spirit was over, negotiations had quietly resumed and an agreement was reached in June. A senior North Korean officer commented that the agreement was "sure to contribute to the normalization of relations." The remains were returned a few days before the Geneva talks began.[63]

Pyongyang's public statements had also been upbeat. Chief negotiator Kang said on June 18 that the sides "will achieve positive results" by continuing negotiations "in good faith" and "on a fair and equal basis."[64] In spite of President Clinton's tough remarks in Seoul, North Korea's rhetoric toward the United States remained low-key.[65]

The first day's session was held at the American Mission. Located on a hill just up the road from the old League of Nations, the blockhouse-like building had formerly housed U.S.-Soviet arms control negotiations in the heyday of détente. Now the austere first-floor conference room hosted a new post–cold war negotiation, between the United States and a potential nuclear outlaw state. Just as in New York, the five leading members of each delegation were seated around a rectangular table in the middle of the room, with others positioned behind them.

The two chief negotiators fell into a familiar pattern, using their opening statements to fire broadsides at each other. Kang praised the New York agreement, highlighted the North's conciliatory steps since then, and contrasted them with inflammatory statements by "high-ranking Americans." He added that ordinary North Koreans had sent him letters complaining, "I think Kang is such a foolish guy; you don't need to believe these Americans." The irony of referring to the *vox populi* in a notorious police state was not lost on the Americans present. He demanded that the United States take steps to implement the New York statement and secure an apology by Blix for his biased treatment of North Korea. But almost all of these demands were hardly mentioned after the first day.

In his opening remarks, Gallucci urged Kang to get over what President Clinton said during his visit to South Korea. Placing the blame for the crisis squarely on the shoulders of North Korea, he observed that Pyongyang could make things right by beginning talks with the IAEA and South Korea to meet its obligations. Only then, Gallucci added, would Washington be willing to conclude a new statement to show there was no nuclear threat to the North and to eventually move on to discuss better bilateral relations. Throughout his presentation, Kang took notes, frequently nodding or consulting members of his delegation.

After the opening salvos, the two negotiators got down to business. Over lunch, Gallucci tackled the issue that had caused the crisis, discrepancies in the North's plutonium declaration. Again he urged Kang to follow the examples of Romania and South Africa: "North Korea could defuse the whole issue by allowing the IAEA to make a visit" Gallucci suggested.

Kang just laughed and said there was no possibility that North Korea would take similar steps, but he also asked some intriguing questions. Would the IAEA have to drill to take samples at the suspected sites? What would happen if the inconsistencies still remained afterward? Gallucci tried to reassure Kang, but he backed off once again, asserting, "The Army will not allow it. North Korea is not Iraq." However, that afternoon Kang did suggest that his country would agree to seek a solution if the IAEA made a firm commitment not to abuse its authority and the United States demonstrated sensitivity for his country's "prestige."

After eight grueling hours, the talks adjourned. The first day had been rough, but the North Koreans were careful to avoid a breakdown. They did not criticize President Clinton by name but instead referred to "high-level" American officials who had recently made inflammatory remarks. They had also put on the table some positive gestures, including a willingness to allow another IAEA inspection of Yongbyon like the one in May.

Two days later, the negotiations resumed, this time at the North Korean Mission. Pleased to host the Americans on their own turf for the first time ever, Kang Sok Ju called the session "a good harbinger of bright prospects." To celebrate the occasion, he held a special lunch for Gallucci and his senior aides. Although Kang joked that his chefs might not be up to the task, the meal was sumptuous, served on an elegant array of china and silver. The North Koreans handed out a menu engraved with gold print in Korean and English and bordered with pink flowers. Their intent was to impress, but the contrast to the privation in North Korea was stark.[66]

More important, Kang used the special occasion to unveil "bold, new instructions": Pyongyang was ready to trade its existing nuclear program for new light-water reactors. Kang had floated the idea in New York, but it got lost in the shuffle of trying to get North Korea to return to the NPT. Only the day before, Gallucci had mentioned to Kang that Pyongyang should make the switch to the new reactors to erase concerns about its program, but Kang just played dumb. Looking back, the Americans believed the North Koreans already had a proposal in their back pocket. Gallucci may have given Kang the "green light" to spring the proposal in its entirety by suggesting the idea had promise.[67]

After reviewing the history of North Korea's interest in new reactor technology, Kang asserted that pursuing graphite technology was the North's only alternative since it did not require dependence on foreign suppliers of enriched uranium needed to run light-water reactors. Yet North Korea recognized that concerns about its gas graphite technology would never go away until it was replaced.

All North Korea wanted in return, according to Kang, was a guarantee from the United States that the new reactors would be made available. In the meantime, his country would freeze its nuclear activities and allow the IAEA to keep tabs on that freeze. Once the new reactors were in place, North Korea would reaffirm its commitment to the NPT. This process would be accompanied by discussions with the IAEA to resolve the problem of "impartiality" and its return to the safeguards regime.

Over the elaborate lunch, Kang gave credit for the proposal to the leadership of Kim Il Sung, who wanted better relations with the United States. The North Koreans also launched an implicit threat, expressing concern about what would happen if their military gained control of large quantities of spent fuel and perfected the technology for making bombs. In a classic understatement, one North Korean observed, "That could pose great problems for those who favored better relations with the United States." Cooperation on light-water reactors would prevent that from happening.

The American response was positive but cautious. "It strikes me personally that this is exactly the right direction for the political and economic future of North Korea," Gallucci told Kang. Although the proposal seemed to address a significant aim of Washington's negotiating position—it required North Korea to get rid of all dangerous nuclear facilities—some Americans thought the idea was just another negotiating ploy to delay access to the two suspected waste sites that held important clues about Pyongyang's nuclear past. Moreover, even if the proposal were not a ploy, it would be impossible for the United States to approve a multibillion-dollar deal including equipment that, under U.S. law, could only be shipped after, not before, the North complied fully with the NPT.

When Gallucci pointed out that Washington could support acquisition over the long term but Pyongyang first had to address U.S. nonproliferation concerns, Kang surprisingly said he understood. All that was needed now was agreement "in principle" that the United States would provide the technology. Even more surprising, he added that Pyongyang was willing to discuss with the IAEA the possibility of visits to the suspected sites under a different nomenclature than special inspections. Once the North had American support for conversion to the new reactors, all safeguards issues could be worked out, and NPT adherence would not be a problem.

By the end of lunch, the North Koreans seemed ready to sign on the dotted line. They would begin discussions right away with the IAEA and South Korea on implementing safeguards and the Denuclearization Declaration. Once those issues were resolved, the United States would be willing to "explore" ways in which North Korea might obtain new reactors, reflecting the understanding that the provision of technology was a long-term proposition. Since the North Koreans said they probably would not receive further instructions from Pyongyang for a few days, Gallucci promised the press a "substantive" announcement next week.

The Americans, however, were in for a rude awakening: the North Koreans just as suddenly reversed course. When the talks reconvened later that day, Kang now insisted on an American guarantee that it would provide the new reactors to North Korea, not just an expression of willingness to "explore" the possibility. Without such a promise, accepting special inspections would be impossible, according to Kang. In any case, inspections could not take place until after the North had the technology.

As day turned into night, the two negotiators continued to argue. Gallucci repeatedly told Kang that the United States was willing to explore making reactors available only after Pyongyang had satisfied its nonproliferation obligations. Kang responded with the familiar refrain: his country would be embarrassed if the IAEA found discrepancies at the suspected sites. North Korea could not even sit down and talk with the agency until the United States provided its guarantee. But when asked what he meant by such a guarantee, Kang was vague. He was talking so rapidly that his interpreter asked him to slow down.

Frustrations reached new highs. Tempers flared as Gallucci, meeting with Kang and their closest aides, pounded the table. He bluntly told the North Koreans that there would be no more meetings unless Kang agreed to talk to the IAEA and did not rule out visits to the two suspected sites. As the dispute unfolded in a private session, the rest of the American and North Korean delegations waited in the main meeting room. Even there, one informal chat degenerated into a fierce argument over IAEA inspections.

Gallucci gathered his papers to leave, but there was a knock on the door. In walked the wife of a North Korean official carrying a tray of Big Macs from the local McDonald's. For a long moment, no one moved. But the absurdity of the situation broke the impasse as both negotiators laughed, grabbed a hamburger, and ate. With the tension defused, Kang agreed to try to meet Gallucci's request for a session with the IAEA. The long day ended with him bidding good-bye to the Americans at the door, promising that the two delegations would meet again.[68]

After two days, the North Koreans requested another meeting, which was held at the Le Richemond Hotel on the banks of Lake Geneva, away from the prying eyes of the press. The tense three-hour session became known as the "whorehouse meeting" in honor of the hotel's lurid red décor. Gallucci showed up with just Hubbard and his interpreter but was surprised to find a much larger group of North Koreans waiting for him. Perhaps Kang thought there was greater safety in numbers.

"Without a U.S. commitment regarding the new reactors," Kang proclaimed, "it is inconceivable to enter into consultations with the IAEA on special inspections." Gallucci tried once again to get Kang to change his mind, offering a sweetener: discussions on nuclear safety, a subject closely related to the eventual acquisition of new reactors. Kang took one step back, offering to talk about verifying his country's past plutonium production, but only by using methods other than special inspections—such as providing the IAEA with more scientific data.

Once again, tempers flared. After clearing the room of his delegation, except for his deputy, Kim Gye Gwan, and the interpreter, Kang seemed to be genuinely agonizing over how to break the impasse. The North Korean military would "remove the fuel rods and declare to the world they would make bombs," he warned, if consultations with the IAEA did not go well. But Gallucci was equally adamant. Only if North Korea agreed to talk with the IAEA and did not rule out special inspections could the two sides meet again. In a message to Washington that evening, Gallucci reported that Kang seemed "very nervous."

At the final session the next day, also requested by the North Koreans, the two delegations grudgingly codified a small patch of common ground. The United States would be prepared to "support" the introduction of light-water reactors in North Korea, a deliberately ambiguous formulation. In return, the North Koreans agreed to begin consultations with the IAEA on safeguards and with South Korea on bilateral issues, including implementation of the Denuclearization Declaration. Gallucci and Kang would meet again in the next two months. Unlike the New York communiqué, the statement was issued separately by each delegation, reflecting both unhappiness with the Geneva tug of war and sensitivity to South Korean concerns about any more joint documents.

In his parting comments, Gallucci told the North Koreans that he hoped productive discussions with the IAEA and South Korea would begin soon. Vice Minister Kang closed the meeting by observing each side had come away from the talks with responsibilities and obligations. He hoped the United States would move ahead with its agreement to explore providing new reactors to North Korea.

One American delegation member recalled that the July round ended on a "very sour" note.[69] Nevertheless, trying to put the best face on the meetings,

Gallucci told the waiting press that the results were a "small but significant step forward."[70] Secretary of State Christopher sounded even more equivocal, calling Geneva "another small step forward, not entirely a satisfactory step but nevertheless a significant step."[71]

In contrast to its reaction after the New York talks, South Korea seemed relaxed with the results of Geneva. Seoul had taken the added precaution of dispatching experts from home to Geneva to keep close tabs on the talks. After long meetings with the North, the Americans would then brief the South Koreans, often over dinner and drinks. To give them further comfort, Washington added Danny Russel, a political officer from its embassy in Seoul, to the American team. His role was akin to that of a canary in a mine: he would keel over whenever an American suggested a negotiating approach that the South was unlikely to approve.[72] In the end, there was no outpouring of anxiety since, as one South Korean official observed, the "Korean switch was now flipped to complacency." The Blue House was particularly pleased that Geneva seemed to set the stage for inter-Korean dialogue.

Exactly why the July round fell short of an agreement remains unclear. The two protagonists had quickly come to the brink of a major breakthrough, but the North then backed away. Pyongyang may have been motivated by tactics, perhaps to throw the United States off balance by shifting the focus of the negotiations or trying to squeeze additional concessions out of it. This was an approach the North would use on numerous occasions. Alternatively, the North's hesitation when staring a possible solution in the face may have reflected nervousness about agreeing even to discuss special inspections without securing an American promise to provide new reactors. It also could have reflected opposition to the lunchtime agreement in Pyongyang or flak from Kang's own delegation.

In retrospect, while it was not clear at the time, Pyongyang's tabling of its reactor proposal may have represented the first sign that North Korea was willing to abandon its bomb-oriented, gas-graphite nuclear program. The July 1993 reactor proposal clearly formed the basis for the crisis-ending bargain reached a little over a year later. North Korea would meet its nonproliferation obligations and dismantle existing nuclear facilities in return for light-water reactors. At the time, however, that was not at all apparent to any of the American negotiators.

Yet in making the proposal the North Koreans created a precarious tightrope for both negotiators. At the core of the proposal was the sensitive argument over self-reliance versus dependence on the outside world. That issue went to the heart of a decade-long debate between "conservatives" and "realists" in North Korea, carried on in North Korean newspapers and theoretical journals. Accepting the new reactors meant accepting dependence. Shortly before Vice Premier Kim Tal Hyon visited Seoul in July 1992 and asked for assistance in building light-water reactors, an article in the party newspaper sharply attacked the idea of energy dependence. The June 11 Joint Statement may have given the "realists" more ammunition, allowing them to argue that a new situation, a better U.S.–North Korean relationship, was emerging.

Even so, the North Koreans still had to figure out how to square the circle on special inspections. Given what was probably very strong internal opposition to any concessions, special inspections remained a political "third rail." This fact of life in Pyongyang was reflected in the North Korean delegation's almost desperate attempts to get around the problem and its constant quizzing of the Americans on what would happen if the IAEA discovered the North's plutonium declaration was in error.

Kang probably recognized that he had to be careful in proceeding once the new reactor proposal was made. He appeared to have been whittled down to his bottom line after a tough fight and worked hard to extract American concessions. The North Koreans, however, may also have been groping in the dark. When Gallucci repeatedly asked what kind of commitment Kang sought on the new reactors, he refused to be pinned down. He may not have known the answer, but vagueness allowed Kang to avoid any stumbling blocks with the Americans and to protect any final agreement from criticism back home.

In short, North Korea's real intent remained unclear. Certainly, Pyongyang had significant energy problems that new reactors might eventually solve. By July it was clear that the North was not going to meet the goal of its third seven-year plan, scheduled for completion by the end of the year, to generate up to 100 billion kilowatt-hours. Pyongyang had even tried to save power by registering irons and hair dryers in barbershops with power supply organizations.[73] Longtime North Korea watchers pondered whether the reactor proposal was really about energy or something else, including stalling while continuing a nuclear weapons program.

Leaving intentions aside, Gallucci thought the proposal had some merit since it would require Pyongyang to dismantle its entire nuclear infrastructure. But he also had to convince his superiors. Speaking on the phone to Peter Tarnoff and Frank Wisner, two key members of the Deputies Committee, Gallucci tried to explain the advantages of Kang's idea. After a long pause, Wisner asked, "Aren't we talking about millions of dollars?" "No," Gallucci replied, "billions." Wisner told him not to make any commitments.

The mind-boggling cost, combined with Kang's unwillingness to be specific, hamstrung Gallucci. In the end, the American negotiator had gone as far as he could in agreeing to "support" the introduction of new reactors. He was forward-leaning but still vague.

With Geneva over and Washington publicly denying that it would provide reactors or assistance before Pyongyang implemented nuclear safeguards, some officials began to give the idea serious consideration. One was James Laney, a native of Arkansas, the former president of Emory University, and the incoming U.S. ambassador in Seoul. A kindly, solidly built man with a firm handshake, Laney had long-standing ties to Korea. He spoke decent Korean, loved Korean food, and had been a pastor in South Korea, whose elite was heavily Christian. He also had close ties with Southern Democrats—including Al Gore, Jimmy Carter, and Sam Nunn—that would prove useful as the crisis mounted. Although he and Gallucci had never met before, they quickly developed good relations.

During a private lunch with Gallucci, Laney suggested that the United States put together a consortium to build the new reactors using Japanese money earmarked for the North should the two countries normalize diplomatic relations. Laney had been working in Seoul when Japan established ties with South Korea in 1965, when Tokyo provided an $800 million financial windfall to Seoul that helped fuel South Korea's economic miracle in the 1970s.[74] The idea was not entirely new. South Korea had considered forming a consortium in 1992 after the North Koreans expressed interest in new reactors but then dismissed the idea as unrealistic. Now the U.S.–North Korean talks seemed to bring the approach back to life, although Japan experts, such as Tom Hubbard, had to explain to others that Tokyo would be unwilling to foot the entire bill.[75]

Falling short of agreement, the United States and North Korea pursued the only course of action that seemed likely to pave the way for another meeting. For the United States, securing Pyongyang's agreement to talk to the IAEA and South Korea was a stopgap measure that protected the agency's institutional prerogatives and maintained solidarity with a key ally. It also protected the administration's domestic flank by demonstrating further progress in diplomatic efforts to resolve the crisis. Although the Americans anticipated another meeting with the North Koreans by the end of September, in fact, the two delegations would not meet again for almost a year.

4

The Twilight Zone

September–December 1993

A s American negotiators looked forward to a few days off that August, they had reason to be relieved. The talks with the North Koreans did not accomplish as much as some had hoped; the Geneva session had been particularly disappointing. But they had dodged a bullet. North Korea had suspended its withdrawal from the Nuclear Non-Proliferation Treaty and agreed to begin discussions with the International Atomic Energy Agency and South Korea. In return, Washington had given little. The administration's threat to end the negotiations if Pyongyang crossed "red lines," such as failing to allow the IAEA visits to Yongbyon, appeared to be working. So did the threat of sanctions if the dialogue broke down. Potential problems with South Korea had been averted, although it was clear that close consultations would continue to be essential.

The signs from Pyongyang were also encouraging. North Korea's premier Kang Song San said the discussions had laid the foundation for "putting an end to the 40 years of hostile relations."[1] Reinforcing that message, the party newspaper characterized Geneva as "forward looking and productive," emphasizing that the North would "sincerely" try to resolve the nuclear issue through talks. Citing Kang Sok Ju's parting statement that each side had responsibilities, the North pledged to start consultations with the IAEA, although the article said it was "not our position" to discuss special inspections. While some Korea watchers thought this a sign of bad faith, Kang had said the same thing in Geneva, adding that if the agency raised special inspections, the North might respond.[2]

Meeting in early August, the Clinton administration devised an elaborate three-pronged plan for the next round of talks with Pyongyang. The IAEA would suggest near-term steps for the North to solve the problem of past nuclear activities—for example, allowing the agency to conduct an initial survey of two suspect sites—while continuing to pursue a full inspection. Washington would suggest compromises to Seoul to jump-start previously stalled negotiations on inspections for the Denuclearization Declaration. Both talks, in turn, would serve as building blocks for the Gallucci-Kang negotiations expected in late September.

Over the next four months, Washington would find out that maintaining its multilateral coalition by sharing responsibilities with the IAEA and Seoul, while a political necessity, was a practical nightmare. The administration slowly became a hostage to politics in Seoul and Vienna as it maneuvered to reach a diplomatic solution to the crisis. South Korea and the IAEA were ill-equipped for talks with North Korea because of internal political and bureaucratic constraints, past history with North Korea, and the fact they had little in the way of incentives to offer Pyongyang. The North Koreans only made matters worse, grudgingly engaging the two as the price for continued talks with the United States. As a result, American diplomatic strategy quickly bogged down in a multitrack morass, coming under increasing domestic attack. Extricating itself not only took time and effort but also forced the Clinton administration seriously to consider how to use other tools of national power, including military force, to resolve the crisis.

Cinderella Time

From their perch in Vienna, a grim complex of drab buildings outside of the city, IAEA officials had been closely monitoring the U.S–North Korean talks since June. Grateful to Washington for urging Pyongyang to renew discussions with them, they were also nervous. Some thought that when push came to shove, the Americans might cut their own deal, in the process undermining the IAEA's role as the final arbiter of safeguards requirements. After all, the July agreement's reference to the "impartial application" of safeguards implied that the IAEA had been "partial." Determined to defend its institutional integrity and the international nonproliferation regime, the agency was vigilant.

While IAEA bureaucrats agreed that the North Koreans, in spite of what they said, were still legally members of the NPT and bound to implement their safeguards agreement, differences divided the agency. "Safeguards hawks" wanted to expand the IAEA's access to North Korean facilities, both to ensure against cheating and to protect the agency's image, which had suffered because of its failure in pre–Gulf War inspections to uncover Saddam Hussein's ambitious nuclear weapon program.

Others, like Hans Blix, who had extensive diplomatic experience as Swedish foreign minister, were sensitive to those needs but tended to be more politically adept. If a pragmatic, imperfect solution protected the agency's credibility more than a rigid posture that resulted in a North Korea unbounded by either safeguards or the NPT, then so be it. Reinforcing this practical impulse, Blix also had the weighty responsibility of having to answer to his political masters. The IAEA Board of Governors ranged from European representatives, who had little patience with Pyongyang's behavior, to China, motivated by an overriding urge to avoid tensions on the peninsula. But Washington also was a major concern since it was the IAEA's leading supporter and had taken on the burden of tackling the nuclear crisis.[3]

While the agency was sensitive to the fine line between defending its prerogatives and undermining American diplomacy, it tended to err in favor of the former. There were significant pressures, particularly from "safeguards hawks," to seek inspections well beyond the limited activities conducted in May 1993 that more closely approximated the extensive ad hoc and routine inspections provided for in the 1992 safeguards agreement. Pyongyang, however, sought to limit IAEA access to make the opposite point; continued inspections did not derive from safeguards but from U.S.–North Korean talks. The stage was set for a constant battle over how to define "continuity of safeguards."

The dogfight between Vienna and Pyongyang put Washington in a tough spot. The administration's own technical experts believed the agency could ensure that key North Korean facilities (the reactor and reprocessing plant) would remain inoperative if its technical monitoring equipment were serviced regularly. As a result, limited inspections like the May visit seemed to serve near-term American objectives. Stronger political imperatives, however, meant the United States had to tread lightly. True, its views were influential in Vienna, but the United States also had to uphold the IAEA's institutional integrity. While agency threats to declare the continuity of safeguards "broken" were intended to induce Pyongyang to compromise, they were often a double-edged sword, also keenly felt in Washington.

Since the New York meeting in June, the IAEA had been inching along a tightrope, trying to secure expanded inspections and safeguards consultations with North Korea while not derailing American diplomacy. The North Koreans proved uncooperative, asserting that the implementation of the safeguards did not depend on the defunct agreement but on the outcome of U.S.–North Korean discussions.[4] An angry Blix warned the Americans that the next inspection would have to be conducted by the end of July to maintain the continuity of safeguards.

The Geneva meeting appeared to clear the way for the next inspection, but the agency's experience would scar the IAEA's psyche for some time. Problems cropped up almost immediately after the agency backed off some of its more extensive demands. Once the IAEA team arrived in Beijing on its way to Pyongyang, the North Koreans insisted on an inspection with even fewer activities than had been conducted in May. After failing to reach agreement on activities allowed, the inspectors continued on to Yongbyon, arriving the first week of August, hoping the situation could be resolved there. They were told, however, only to change videotapes and batteries, not to conduct other maintenance activities performed during the May visit.

Faced with the potential failure of the inspection, the Clinton administration stepped into the fray. Washington warned that unless Pyongyang cooperated with the IAEA, the United States would break off any further bilateral contacts. IAEA headquarters sent a similar message on August 5.[5] The North Koreans reversed themselves the next day, allowing the inspectors to complete their duties. But Kang also informed Gallucci that agency demands for extensive inspections well beyond what was needed for continuity of safeguards would "be harmful for our third round of talks."

The reaction in Washington and Vienna to the August inspection only highlighted a growing gap between the two. Despite the State Department's public criticism of Pyongyang, Tom Hubbard told a visiting South Korean that the IAEA visit was a moderately positive sign. In Vienna, however, IAEA officials felt humiliated after having compromised on their original demands and sent a team to North Korea only to find no agreement on inspection activities. The team then had to carry out some work under lamentable conditions, sometimes at midnight with flashlights. The outcome itself could have been much worse; the IAEA had found a suspicious broken seal in the reprocessing plant but concluded that nuclear material had not been diverted from the reactor.[6] Nevertheless, in a classic understatement, an IAEA spokesman said, "The overall degree of access granted is still insufficient for the agency to discharge its responsibilities."[7]

The August inspection was only the beginning. With tempers now on a short fuse, problems emerged from the very start in setting up IAEA–North Korean negotiations. Both seemed to have a very different view of the agenda; the IAEA wanted to talk about outstanding safeguards and other issues—a code word for special inspections—while the North Koreans wanted to focus on the agency's "unjustice." Faced with what seemed to be another looming fiasco, Blix warned the Americans that if the North Koreans prevented the agency from raising safeguards issues, he might have to give the Board of Governors a negative report, further straining relations between Washington and Pyongyang.

The IAEA–North Korean talks, held September 1–3 in Pyongyang, accomplished little. From the start, the two staked out diametrically opposed positions. The agency team called for more extensive continuity of safeguards inspections, setting a deadline of September 28, the day IAEA cameras at the reactor and reprocessing plant would run out of film.[8] For good measure, the IAEA also wanted to talk about special inspections. The North Koreans, in turn, insisted on an apology from the agency for touching off the nuclear controversy and preferred to talk about their proposal to acquire new reactor technology, the last topic on the minds of IAEA negotiators.[9] Afterward, Ho Jong complained to the Americans in New York that he had received an "SOS" from Pyongyang about the IAEA team's bad behavior.

The next two days were no better. The tone of the formal sessions was at times tense but not harsh. Informal discussions were measured and calm. The results were dismal, however, relieved only by word from the North Koreans that they were willing to meet again. As a parting shot, before leaving Pyongyang, the agency team told the North Koreans that Blix's report to the September Board of Governors meeting would not be positive.

Vienna and Pyongyang continued their battle by fax during the three-week run-up to the September 28 deadline. The IAEA asserted that it had the right to conduct more extensive ad hoc and routine inspections under the safeguards agreement (which was still in force) and that these inspections were necessary to maintain continuity of safeguards.[10] North Korea's atomic energy minister Choi claimed that, since his country was in a "unique and extraordinary" situation owing to the suspension of its NPT withdrawal, implementation of the safeguards agreement would have to be discussed in further consultations. Pyongyang, however, would let the agency conduct the same activities as it did in August.[11]

As the deadline approached, U.S. officials felt compelled to intervene once more to prevent a breach in the continuity of safeguards. Piggybacking on Blix's threats, Gallucci sent a series of letters to Kang urging North Korea to accept the IAEA position in order to avoid breaking the continuity of safeguards. In Vienna, American diplomats played for time and worked to ensure that the Board of Governors, which met on September 23, tempered its statement on North Korea to prevent Pyongyang from breaking off its dialogue with the IAEA. Nonproliferation hawks such as France were unhappy, but the final statement covered the essential points, urging Pyongyang to hold a second round of consultations and to take the necessary steps to ensure continuity of safeguards.

Inside the IAEA, there were two views on the developing situation. Safeguards hawks believed that the limited May and August inspections already fell below the level necessary to preserve continuity of safeguards. Pragmatists like Blix believed delays past the deadline would strain but not break the continuity of safeguards, recognizing that position would give the United States more time to persuade the North to accept inspections. They were not willing to say when continuity would be broken but seemed to be thinking in weeks, not days. This position, held by the agency's top leadership, won out for the moment.

On September 20, Blix informed the North Koreans that without inspections, "the agency would have to conclude that the area of noncompliance is widening," a step back from asserting that continuity would be broken.[12] Privately, Blix told the United States that the damage could be corrected if the inspections were conducted within weeks. Longer delays might require more inspection activities. Clearly, the consequences of declaring continuity of safeguards broken weighed heavily on Blix. "If I announce that continuity is lost, then what?" he would later ask the South Koreans. One South Korean remarked that Blix felt there was no "Cinderella time." He did not want to turn U.S. policy into a pumpkin by declaring the continuity of safeguards broken.

While the IAEA and North Korea had managed to work out an agreement to hold more talks in early October after the scheduled IAEA General Conference, that too now fell victim to the deteriorating relationship. In what appeared to be a potentially interesting development, the North Koreans had agreed to discuss "inconsistencies and the inspection issue," an allusion to special inspections. But almost immediately after the toned-down September 23 IAEA resolution, Pyongyang began to backtrack. It hammered the final nail in the coffin, seizing on a mistake in a letter to the IAEA General Conference from the UN's secretary general, Boutros Boutros-Ghali, which not only referred to "North Korea" rather than the official "Democratic People's Republic of Korea" but also suggested that it was developing nuclear weapons. Accusing the IAEA of forging the letter, Pyongyang postponed the second round indefinitely.[13]

In the span of ten weeks since the U.S.–North Korean meeting in Geneva, one of the three negotiating tracks had collapsed. Whether North Korea really had any intention of cooperating with the IAEA was unclear. But Vienna also faced limits on how far it could go and on how much it could achieve. The agency had the unprecedented job of coaxing back into the nonproliferation regime a country that viewed it with disdain. Moreover, North Korea wanted to communicate directly with the United States, not its surrogate. The IAEA had little leverage other than the threat to declare the continuity of safeguards broken. Finally, institutional imperatives and a deep commitment to maintaining the integrity of the nonproliferation regime left agency officials little room for flexibility.

The agency decisions—first to set the September deadline and then to let it slide—pushed the limits of that flexibility. The IAEA stuck to the substance of its demands but waffled on the timing, damaging its credibility and probably creating doubts about the strength of its views on substance as well. In early October, the North Koreans, after complaining to the Americans that the IAEA had repeatedly changed the date on which continuity of safeguards would lapse, expressed confusion about how to interpret the latest deadline, now set for October 31.

More important, the IAEA's demand for significantly expanded "continuity of safeguards" inspections placed a new burden on the Clinton administration. Given the need to treat the agency with deference in order to preserve its credibility as the international watchdog for the nonproliferation regime, the administration refused to press the IAEA to accept limited inspections like those conducted in August. The new task was to secure Pyongyang's agreement to expanded inspections; this would take almost eight months to complete.

Bring Kim Il Sung to His Knees

While the IAEA was seeking to renew contacts with Pyongyang after Geneva, the second of the three dramas was playing out on the Korean peninsula. Seoul was also about to renew its effort to restart dialogue with the North. In spite of the Geneva meeting, the South Koreans were still cautious. Their public posture was confident; Deputy Prime Minister Han Wan Sang insisted, "There is no possibility that we will be estranged from resolving the issue of the Korean peninsula even after the high-level talks between the United States and North Korea."[14] Privately, however, Foreign Minister Han Sung Joo told Secretary of State Warren Christopher in July that the only way Pyongyang had any incentive to move forward would be to make North-South talks a prerequisite for better relations with Washington.

The core ministers, meeting in July after Geneva, faced many considerations. For one thing, Washington favored an early resumption of the talks. For another, Seoul could not simply reject North Korea's special envoy proposal made that spring without contradicting President Kim's inaugural statement that he was willing to meet Kim Il Sung. Public opinion remained divided. Some doubted that Pyongyang was serious, while others complained the government's inability to restart dialogue was leaving the field wide open for the United States. The chronic divide also opened between moderates and conservatives. Deputy Prime Minister Han, fond of comparing the North to the ill-fated, dangerous Branch Davidian cult, reasoned that the South must seek workable compromises. Lee Dong Bok, special assistant to South Korea's intelligence chief, on the other hand, argued that compromise had achieved nothing in twenty-three years of talks. Only the imminent threat of sanctions would "bring Kim Il Sung to his knees."

Balancing these different pressures, the Blue House choreographed a two-part plan, keyed to progress on the IAEA–North Korean front. If Pyongyang agreed to an IAEA inspection in August, Seoul would propose talks at the Joint Nuclear Control Commission, originally used to try to negotiate a North-South nuclear inspection regime. If, as expected, the North rejected this pro-posal, Seoul would then fall back to a variation of the plan that would allow both sides to name a special envoy other than the deputy prime minister. Seoul could then appoint a more conservative envoy than Han Wan Sang, such as Blue House chief secretary Park Kwan Yong. The nuclear issue would remain Seoul's top priority, but Pyongyang was expected to focus on arrang-ing a summit to handle all issues outstanding between the two Koreas.

The strategy was set in motion on August 4 after the IAEA inspections began. As expected, the North rejected the South's initial proposal. Soon after-ward, Deputy Prime Minister Han publicly hinted that if the North proposed special envoys again, Seoul would accept.[15] Once consultations between Pyongyang and Vienna were scheduled, South Korean officials recommended to President Kim that Seoul offer to resume dialogue regardless of modalities. While IAEA–North Korean consultations were taking place in early Septem-ber, Prime Minister Hwang In Sung proposed a North-South meeting for Sep-tember 7 to prepare for the exchange of special envoys "appointed by the top leaders of their countries." They would try to settle the nuclear problem first.[16]

Inevitably, as Seoul became more flexible, Pyongyang became more rigid. The North Koreans now set two preconditions for a meeting. First, the South had to demonstrate a willingness to stop "nuclear war exercises," such as Team Spirit. Second, Seoul had to refrain from working with other countries to pur-sue sanctions against the North. While both demands were familiar—they had appeared in Kim Il Sung's April 1993 program for reunification—it was unclear whether this rehash reflected mere polemics or real reluctance to engage Seoul in meaningful talks, mirroring the North's approach with the IAEA. The United States and South Korea did not have long to find out. The North made September 20—the target date for the next U.S.–North Korean meeting in Geneva—the deadline for Seoul to meet these demands.

As the deadline approached, the Kim government worked with Washing-ton to break the impasse. Just before September 20, South Korea signaled that Team Spirit might be suspended if Pyongyang showed a "sincere" attitude in settling the nuclear issue. That was as far as moderates could go since they were under attack by the hard-liners, who had been strengthened by the

North's tough position.[17] Gallucci reinforced that proposal in a letter to Kang, warning that failure to respond positively, combined with a lack of progress with the IAEA, would call into question the North's commitment to further talks with the United States. But the deadline came and went without a response from Pyongyang.

The next week, during talks in the New York channel, there seemed to be a breakthrough. Sitting with Ho Jong in a conference room at the United Nations, Tom Hubbard made a proposal that Washington and Seoul hoped would break the ice. Foreign Minister Han would be willing to meet his North Korean counterpart at the UN General Assembly in early October. Ho nonchalantly responded that this would be impossible since his foreign minister would not be coming to New York. But on September 29, Ho gave Hubbard some good news. Pyongyang had decided to propose a North-South session for October 5 without preconditions. Its concerns could now be addressed at the meeting.

After eight months in office, the Kim government found the stage set for its first face-to-face encounter with North Korea. Previously, representatives from the two Koreas had met in the austere barracks-like structure inside the Demilitarized Zone, a building customarily used by the Neutral Nations Supervisory Committee, one of the bodies established to implement the 1953 armistice that ended the Korean War. By 1993 both had built their own pavilions on the North and South sides of the military demarcation line, respectively. Microphones and, in the case of South Korea, closed-circuit television cameras relayed proceedings back to the capitals. Rumor had it that Kim Il Sung even listened occasionally.

Expectations in South Korea were decidedly low. North Korea's chief delegate, Pak Yong Su, had been participating in North-South talks since 1978 and was seen as an expert in delaying tactics. Vice Unification Minister Song Young Dae, the South's delegate, was also a veteran of North-South talks. The two had met seventeen times since 1984; Song liked to say that he knew what Pak was thinking by just looking into his eyes.

The talks got off to a good start. At the first session, Song came armed with specific proposals, a sign of the South's seriousness. Aside from proposing a timetable for the envoy exchange, to be completed before President Kim went to Washington in late November, Song emphasized that Seoul was flexible on holding Team Spirit provided Pyongyang was sincere in resolving the nuclear issue.[18]

Pak stuck to two key North Korean demands: the envoy exchange would take place only after Pyongyang's preconditions were met, and the summit should resolve a broad range of differences, not just the nuclear issue. But he accepted Seoul's idea that the two sides could appoint special envoys other than the deputy prime ministers, provided they held the same rank.[19] At the end of the session, the South Koreans were encouraged. The atmosphere was good, the focus was on substance not oratory, and the North had not raised any new obstacles. The two agreed to meet again on October 15.

While the talks were off to a good start, Seoul recognized that the only way to secure its demands was to build up its bargaining leverage. The original U.S.–South Korean strategy envisioned trading Team Spirit for North Korea's commitment to remain in the NPT and accept international safeguards. Just before the October 15 session, however, South Korea's core ministers decided that the best way to secure the envoy exchange was to drop the linkage to the nuclear issue. Instead they would tell the North that Team Spirit would be canceled if its special envoy met President Kim in Seoul. The new approach would also have domestic political benefits; it would counter criticism that South Korea had ceded its rightful leadership on an important foreign policy issue to the United States.

Initially, Washington balked at this shift. When the Deputies Committee took up the proposal a few hours after the South Korean ministers met, Gallucci pointed out that Team Spirit had little military utility and no budget. Lieutenant General Mike Ryan from the Joint Chiefs of Staff countered that the exercise might be scaled back, but the United States should stick to its original strategy. Civilian leaders at the Pentagon took the position that cancellation could be announced after a satisfactory third round of U.S.–North Korean talks. Since no conclusion was reached, Washington urged Seoul not to offer to cancel Team Spirit. Without new ammunition, the October 15 North-South meeting made no progress.

A few days later, however, the White House reluctantly agreed to consider suspending Team Spirit if North Korea agreed to the exchange of special envoys and the inspection activities required by the IAEA. In a gesture to those who opposed a shift, the announcement would not be made until after the "satisfactory" conclusion of the next round of U.S.–North Korean talks. Hubbard relayed the new position to Ho Jong in New York.

From Seoul's perspective, the American proposal was a step forward but still fell short. Since the announcement of Team Spirit's demise would come after "satisfactory" U.S.–North Korean talks, cancellation would likely come only after progress on special inspections, a tall order for the North Koreans. Moreover, Seoul wanted an envoy exchange as soon as possible, not after a U.S.–North Korean meeting that might not happen for some time. The core ministers considered a novel solution: concluding a secret memorandum with North Korea suspending Team Spirit when the North's envoy came to Seoul, even if that predated U.S.–North Korean talks. The official pronouncement would be made only after the Americans and North Koreans had met. The October 25 North-South meeting came and went, however, without addressing the issue. More talks were scheduled for November 4.

That session never occurred. The November 4 meeting happened to coincide with annual talks between the American and South Korean defense ministers, the Security Consultative Meeting (SCM), which previously had been used to send tough messages to Pyongyang. This year, the South Koreans, leaving nothing to chance, decided not to mention Team Spirit. But on November 2, Seoul's Defense Minister Kwon Yong Hae warned, "in the event of sanctions, North Korea could perpetrate military provocations. The Defense Ministry will discuss our measure for such provocations at the ROK-U.S. Security Consultative Meeting."[20] Taking what appeared to be a fairly restrained statement of fact as a provocation, Pyongyang canceled the November 4 meeting.[21]

While the South Koreans tried to make the best of a bad situation—characterizing the cancellation as a temporary setback—the North's move did not bode well for the future. The most likely explanation for Pyongyang's behavior was that since it viewed talks with the South as secondary to those with the United States, the South Korean defense minister's statement provided a pretext for the North not to show. Whatever the reason, the second track of America's three-prong diplomatic strategy collapsed. The North Koreans also further undercut the position of pro-dialogue moderates in Seoul while strengthening the hand of conservatives. As a result, South Korea increasingly focused on a tight linkage between its own talks with Pyongyang and U.S.–North Korean discussions as the only way to ensure a successful dialogue, a linkage that would severely complicate future American efforts to resolve the crisis peacefully.

Avoiding the 1992 Trap

North Korea's behavior in the aftermath of the Geneva meeting was puzzling. At first, Pyongyang had seemed willing to implement its obligations. It had tried to take the minimum steps necessary to hold another round of talks with the Americans. But the North was unable, or unwilling, to sustain enough momentum in its dealings with the IAEA or South Korea. When September 20—the target date for the next round of Gallucci-Kang talks—came and went without implementation of the Geneva arrangement, speculation increased about Pyongyang's real intentions.

Was the North serious about solving the nuclear problem? Did hard-liners who would never agree to "trade away" the nuclear weapons program control the policymaking process? Were they just stalling while North Korea continued that program? The fear of stalling became more pronounced as the Geneva arrangement sputtered. President Kim Young Sam, in an interview with the *Washington Post* on October 24, expressed concern that the North was merely playing for time to finish its nuclear program.[22] He said the same thing to Ambassador James Laney, newly arrived in Seoul.

American officials had no conclusive evidence to suggest Pyongyang was accelerating its nuclear weapons program. There were some activities at Yongbyon, such as continued construction of the larger 50-megawatt reactor and the reprocessing plant. But there was no sign the North was about to separate more plutonium or to break out from the self-imposed constraints it had accepted in New York and Geneva. In March 1994, when the IAEA finally returned to Yongbyon, it was surprised to find that a second reprocessing line was almost finished. The North may have been stalling while secretly moving forward with this work, but throughout 1993 it had been consistently willing to allow the agency to visit the plant. Neither the Americans nor the South Koreans—and President Kim said as much in his interview—had any solid evidence that the North was fashioning weapons from plutonium produced in the past at some secret site. Nevertheless, it is a commonplace in intelligence circles that "absence of evidence" is not "evidence of absence." Hence serious concern about possible nuclear activities remained.

Another explanation may account for Pyongyang's behavior. Surveying the scene in the fall of 1993, North Korea may have felt that it had little to show for its two rounds of talks with the United States. It had grudgingly moved forward with the IAEA and South Korea, but past experience with those two interlocutors had been unproductive and neither had much to offer. Pyongyang saw a real danger of becoming bogged down in these talks while the prospect of meeting Gallucci again diminished. On September 12, Gallucci sent Kang a stern letter telling him that failure to satisfy the Geneva requirements placed in jeopardy future U.S.–North Korean meetings. Moreover, South Korean newspapers emphasized that Pyongyang had to comply with the "preconditions" for the September 20 meeting with the United States, a phrase guaranteed to rankle. Government officials said publicly that if these preconditions were not met, sanctions might be sought.[23]

For Pyongyang, this all had a familiar ring. In 1992, after the Kanter-Kim session, the North was told to meet certain conditions before the Americans would hold another session. The North took real steps—ratifying its safeguards agreement with the IAEA, embarking on a lengthy effort to implement that agreement, and negotiating with South Korea on an inspection regime for the Denuclearization Declaration. But these efforts came to naught in North

Korean eyes. The IAEA discovered discrepancies in Pyongyang's initial plutonium declaration and inter-Korean dialogue broke down. As a result, the
United States would not meet with the North again, Team Spirit was rescheduled, and Pyongyang faced the prospect of international sanctions as a result
of its disagreement with the IAEA. North Korea could not abide a reprise of
that situation.

In the immediate aftermath of Geneva, Pyongyang adopted a low-key
posture. The North was clearly unhappy with a number of developments—
public statements by U.S. officials about the threat posed by Pyongyang, as
well as the Ulchi-Focus Lens U.S.–South Korean military exercise that had
been held that summer.[24] But Pyongyang did move forward with the IAEA
inspection in August, held talks with the agency in early September, and
agreed to a second round that would even address past "inconsistencies." On
the North-South front, it sought to arrange a new round of talks.

As the possibility emerged of falling into a "1992 trap," Pyongyang's threats
escalated. Responding to Gallucci's warning that talks might not resume, Kang
reminded him on September 14 that the North's suspension of its NPT withdrawal was based on the continuation of those talks. Turning up the heat,
Kang later wrote that if the prospects for a third round dimmed, the North
would not be able to freeze operations at the 5-megawatt reactor indefinitely.[25]
Pyongyang even sent a letter to the IAEA, the day after publicly condemning
Gallucci's September visit to Seoul and Tokyo, charging it with threatening the
North's "supreme interests," the phrase previously used before its March 12
announcement.[26]

The North also rejected the validity of "preconditions" to another session
with the Americans. Ever since Geneva, Pyongyang had readily acknowledged
its obligations to hold consultations with the IAEA and to resume dialogue
with Seoul but had also emphasized that the United States had its own obligations to meet. According to Kang's post-Geneva press conference, the United
States should take practical steps to abandon its nuclear threat, such as ending
Team Spirit, and should be ready to discuss the introduction of light-water
reactors and "improving relations" at the next round. Washington had never
agreed to scrub Team Spirit, and it is unclear whether the North really
believed that it would do so now. But the prospect of energy assistance and
improved U.S.–North Korean relations may have been sufficient to paper over
any differences. Once that prospect began to fade, Pyongyang feared falling
into the politically untenable position of taking unilateral steps just to secure
another meeting.

That position was particularly unacceptable in view of internal political
realities. North Korea had used the fortieth anniversary of the end of the

Korean War in July to mark what might be the last decade for the eighty-one-year-old Kim Il Sung. Pyongyang also conspicuously highlighted the important role played by the heir apparent, Kim Jong Il. After an absence of eighteen years, his father's younger brother and an earlier contender for leadership—Kim Yong Chu—reappeared, in a move that was widely interpreted as demonstrating universal acceptance of Kim Jong Il's succession. Some analysts believed that at the next Party Congress, expected by the end of the year, he might be named party secretary or president.

Whether that was true or not, Kim Jong Il may have needed to continue building his leadership credentials by demonstrating he could manage relations with the United States. Ideally, he would have wanted to go into the Party Congress with a victory in the form of successful negotiations leading to an improvement in bilateral relations. As that hope faded, the Dear Leader had to appear resolute, unafraid to stand up to the United States, and ready to defy international pressure. That may have meant maintaining the status quo until after the Party Congress, to avoid making concessions that could alienate the old guard in the military and party in any settlement of the nuclear issue. On the other hand, he did not want Washington and Seoul to announce Team Spirit or the United Nations to move forward with sanctions. To keep these competing forces at bay, it made sense for the younger Kim to delay the third round until after the Party Congress while trying to dissuade the parties from abandoning negotiations.

In a nutshell, North Korea's actions may have reflected an attempt to build the strongest bargaining position possible before more talks with the United States. That would have required refocusing on U.S.–North Korean talks in order to extricate itself from the political noose Washington seemed to be tightening through the use of proxies like South Korea, the IAEA, and the United Nations. It may have led to attempts to "psych out" the United States by stalling to see what developed while trying to create rifts between Washington and its close allies, all the time fostering a crisis atmosphere to keep the Americans off balance. The North's threats in September about withdrawing from the NPT filled that prescription and did trigger concern in Washington. Pyongyang may have hoped that any concessions it might subsequently make—however small—would then appear more substantive and dramatic.

A Short Walk Down a Real Long Road

As Indian summer turned into fall, Washington's August optimism evaporated. North Korea's continued foot-dragging on IAEA inspections and North-South talks fell short of its commitments, dimming prospects for another meeting in Geneva by September 20. Subsequently, the collapse of the talks with Vienna and Seoul made it unclear whether Gallucci and Kang would ever meet again.

The U.S. administration had not been standing by idly. Gathering on September 7, just as the process of disintegration was beginning, the deputies decided not to wait out the clock. They would dispatch Gallucci to see Kang—either at the DMZ or overseas—to tell him that Pyongyang's failure to meet its commitments could end the dialogue between the two countries.

Underlying their decision was the nagging feeling that only a face-to-face meeting could guarantee that Pyongyang understood the seriousness of the situation. The correspondence between Gallucci and Kang helped, but there were concerns that reports sent home after meetings in New York were sugar-coated, in part because low-level diplomats might hesitate to break bad news to their superiors. A face-to-face meeting with Kang might also help the Americans better understand any nuances in Pyongyang's position, something they could not glean from letters or sessions in New York. But Seoul objected, fearing that it might be seen as a sign of weakness, and Washington deferred to its ally.

Nevertheless, South Korean moderates shared Washington's concerns. Foreign Minister Han had worried for months about the problems of choreographing the U.S., South Korean, and IAEA channels. The continued harping by hard-liners that U.S.–North Korean talks would drag on without resolving anything also threatened to undermine support for dialogue. Reflecting that concern, a Foreign Ministry official sent to Washington in August urged the United States to present the North an ultimatum at the third round that any further talks would depend on accepting special inspections. But the administration felt that would prove counterproductive.

A previously scheduled trip to Seoul by Gallucci for consultations from September 9 to 13 allowed Foreign Minister Han and Deputy Prime Minister Han Wan Sang—nicknamed "the two Hans" by the Americans—to float another idea. They advanced a "comprehensive approach" that jettisoned the step-by-step strategy and its focus on trading "security for security." The idea was to offer the North a fourth round of talks that could lead to political normalization if it resolved the nuclear issue at the next Gallucci-Kang session. The proposal was designed to appeal to conservatives, who wanted the third round to be the last on the nuclear issue, as well as moderates, who hoped for a dialogue calculated to make cooperation attractive for Pyongyang. Gallucci liked the idea since he had doubts that the step-by-step strategy would work. A new "big package" began to take shape.

The problem was how to jump the hurdles in the way of a third Gallucci-Kang meeting where a "big package" could be discussed. Washington had to rely on a series of coincidental encounters to test the diplomatic waters. In early October, the Americans took advantage of a visit by a senior North Korean diplomat to the UN General Assembly to probe Pyongyang. That official proposed a "small package" to clear the way for the "big package." In return for expanded IAEA inspections, which the agency was demanding again, North Korea wanted an end to Team Spirit, serious discussions on new reactors, or the lifting of some economic sanctions. The proposal to end Team Spirit came at the same time that Seoul was moving toward greater flexibility on that issue. The "small package" built on simultaneous steps had begun to take shape.

The next opportunity to advance Washington's diplomatic agenda came during the October 9–12 visit to North Korea by House member Gary Ackerman (D-N.Y.), chairman of the Subcommittee on East Asia and Pacific Affairs. During an earlier visit to Seoul for President Kim's inauguration in February 1993, Ackerman had told reporters that the United States would not meet with North Korea until it accepted IAEA inspections. Now Ackerman was anxious to see Kim Il Sung.[27] His predecessor on the subcommittee, Stephen Solarz, had the distinction of meeting the elder Kim twice. Moreover, Ackerman's New York constituency had a growing number of Korean Americans, some of whom urged him to make the trip. Though Ackerman originally intended to go in August when the prospects for progress on the nuclear issue seemed good, his departure had been unavoidably delayed for unrelated reasons, placing him in the middle of a growing crisis.[28]

The North Koreans were also clearly interested in a visit by Ackerman. They even complied with his unprecedented request to leave their country through the DMZ, a passage that was sure to garner press attention. The fact that Pyongyang readily agreed to the trip was even more surprising since the last Solarz visit had gone badly. Kim Il Sung had trotted out his standard line that North Korea had neither the intention nor the capability to build nuclear weapons. When Solarz accused Kim of lying, the North Koreans quickly ushered him out of the country.[29]

Ackerman had two objectives. (Contrary to speculation in the South Korean press, he was not carrying a secret message from the Clinton administration.) First, he wanted to make sure Kim Il Sung understood American policy and to dispel any illusion that North Korea might exploit any perceived differences between the executive branch, Congress, and the American people. Second, he wanted to "show them that we were not there to eat their lunch," that Americans were human.[30] He would later tell reporters he went to Pyongyang to "break the ice."[31]

The trip got off to a bumpy start. Just before boarding his flight at New York City's Kennedy Airport, Ackerman discovered that he had forgotten his official passport. The congressman quickly sent for his tourist passport from his local office in nearby Queens. At the time of departure, Ackerman still did not know whether he would see the North Korean leader.[32]

In the event, after three days of pro-forma talks with lower-level functionaries and plenty of sightseeing, the New Yorker was taken to a guesthouse east of the city for a two-hour chat with Kim Il Sung. U.S. intelligence officials had warned him beforehand that Kim was in poor health; North Korean television had shown him on the verge of collapse during festivities that summer.[33] Indeed, in May 1993 the North's media had been forced to dispel rumors of his ill health by reporting on-the-spot guidance Kim had given at a chicken farm, the third such appearance in a single week. In recent years, the North Korean leader had given guidance sparingly.[34]

Speculation on Kim Il Sung's health often bordered on the absurd, prompting Americans to suspect a disinformation campaign by South Korean intelligence. Seoul's press reported that an attendant had to wipe Kim's mouth with a napkin during meals. Also, Kim had become "chronically enraged" after Beijing normalized relations with Seoul, forcing his son to make him go to bed before ten o'clock every night.[35] Even more absurd, other stories talked about programs at the "Kim Il Sung Longevity Research Institute" to prolong his life, including having comedians make him laugh, on the theory that it was good for his health, and giving Kim regular blood transfusions from virgin girls.[36]

When Ackerman met Kim Il Sung, it became clear that the lurid press accounts on the aged leader's health had reflected more speculation than fact. He had developed a large unsightly growth on his neck that the North's press never showed, but American specialists did not consider this to be life threatening. Intelligent, at times witty and charming, Kim Il Sung was also slightly hard of hearing. At the start of the session, he placed his hearing aid on the table and left it there the entire time; his interpreter had to raise his voice to be understood.

Foreign Minister Kim Yong Nam and Vice Minister Kang, as well as a retinue of plainclothes guards and waiters, were present. The two senior officials spoke only when spoken to, standing up and barking out answers to questions. The Great Leader seemed to rely most on Kang, confirming American suspicions that he was more influential than his nominal boss, who was viewed as a figurehead.[37]

"In the past some thought we had horns on our head," Kim remarked casually. The North Korean had an outline of topics to discuss but no briefing book or notes. He had an impressive grasp of a wide range of topics, particularly relations with South Korea and the security situation facing his country. Kim became quite animated when the topic turned to his country's nuclear weapons program. In a booming voice with his right arm thrust in the air for emphasis, the Great Leader repeated: "We do not have the capability to build them, the money to buy them, or the desire or need to have them." According to Kim, the nuclear problem was created by the United States and should be resolved in bilateral talks. But that would be impossible if Team Spirit were held.

One American, seizing a rare opportunity to advance the historical debate over the roles of Stalin and Kim Il Sung in launching the Korean War, somewhat disingenuously asked Kim whether Stalin was surprised when the conflict began. "Why bring Stalin into it?" he replied equally disingenuously. The war was a matter for the Korean people.[38]

While the North Koreans seemed nervous, perhaps because of their experience with Solarz, the Ackerman meeting went off without a hitch. He made sure Kim Il Sung understood the American position but emphasized that current problems could be worked out with goodwill on both sides. Ackerman also made it clear that the American people were united in their views on North Korea. It was fine if Kim said he had no nuclear weapons, no ability to produce them, and no money to pay for them. The American response, however, must be "trust but verify," just as it had been with the Soviet Union.

Ackerman also urged Kim Il Sung to resume North-South dialogue. After presenting the New Yorker with autographed copies of his ten-point unification proposal made last April, the North Korean leader asked Ackerman to give a copy to his South Korean counterpart. He then observed, somewhat mischievously, that President Kim Young Sam seemed to be the only person in the South who had not read it. But Kim Il Sung added that he was willing to meet the South Korean president.

More substantive talks were held separately. Before leaving Washington, Ackerman had asked the State Department to send someone with him who spoke Korean and understood the nuclear issue. Ken Quinones, the North Korea desk officer, was chosen. While he was given strict orders not to negotiate with the North Koreans, Quinones was a captive audience. They gave him new proposals for both the small and big packages, handwritten in English with visible scratch-out changes, to take back to Washington.[39]

The North Koreans had clearly done some fine-tuning on the "small package" since the earlier meeting at the UN General Assembly. They were still willing to agree to expanded IAEA inspections. In return, the suspension of Team Spirit remained an important aim, even though some North Koreans knew there was no money budgeted for next year's exercise. The North's strong feelings against it were reflected in Kim Il Sung's comments. They now wanted to set a date certain for suspension and for the beginning of the next Gallucci-Kang session, as well as to confirm that Washington did not intend to threaten Pyongyang with nuclear weapons. Earlier mention of dropping economic sanctions had disappeared.

As for the "big package," that proposal had also evolved since the near-disastrous July session in Geneva. North Korea would agree to remain a member of the NPT, fully comply with safeguards, and commit itself to implementation of the North-South denuclearization agreement. In return, the United States should conclude a peace agreement, including legally binding assurances on the nonuse of force against the North, take responsibility for providing the North with light-water reactors, fully normalize diplomatic relations, and commit itself to a balanced policy in its relations with the North and South. Moreover, Kang was ready to meet Gallucci once again, either at Panmunjom or in another Asian country.

While only informal, North Korea's proposals gave Washington important clues as to the outline of a potential deal. Elements in Pyongyang may have been inching toward this approach, but in the absence of any early prospect for a third round of talks with the United States, they took advantage of Ackerman's visit to get their proposals on the table. The North's "big package" seemed to accept the idea of special inspections. In spite of Pyongyang's negative public position, its negotiators were still grappling in private with ways of accepting them in fact if not in name. Pyongyang also agreed to rejoin the NPT without mentioning "IAEA impartiality," one of the two conditions it had previously set for resuming those obligations. Other demands, such as reaching a peace treaty with Washington, were new and clearly unacceptable, but the North Koreans told Quinones that counteroffers were welcome.

"It's a short walk down a real long road," Ackerman exclaimed as he stepped over the concrete border marker in the middle of the Panmunjom truce village wearing a baseball cap. He hoped his loose paraphrase of Neil Armstrong's first words on the moon would reflect his status as the first visitor to North Korea to return south via the DMZ.[40]

Unaware of the content of Quinones's talks with the North Koreans, Ackerman told the New York Times that his visit had been long on symbolism but short on substance.[41] Once back in Seoul, Ackerman briefed President Kim, noting Kim Il Sung's offer to hold a summit. But the South Korean was skeptical; he believed the North's overriding goal was to drive a wedge between

Washington and Seoul. While he did not say so, President Kim felt that Ackerman's trip had been counterproductive. "In the end, the only way left will be the UN Security Council and sanctions," Kim concluded. Hard-liners like Lee Dong Bok echoed his tough reaction. As for Quinones, he quietly briefed the South Korean Foreign Ministry on the North Korean proposals, strongly urged that leaks be avoided, and caught an airplane for Washington.[42]

Sticks

In Seoul for the annual meeting with the South Korean defense minister held November 4, Secretary of Defense Les Aspin met with Foreign Minister Han. With the collapse of the North-South talks on everyone's minds, Aspin asked him what he would do if there were neither compliance nor noncompliance with safeguards by North Korea, a kind of "twilight zone." Han replied that the two allies should create their own twilight zone for the North in which they would neither declare war nor go for heavy sanctions. As its noncompliance deepened, "our actions should grow stronger." By the winter of 1993, formulating such a strategy became necessary as the Geneva arrangement unraveled. The plan for holding another U.S.–North Korean meeting in late September had been scrapped as Pyongyang maneuvered to avoid anything but symbolic sessions with the IAEA and South Korea in hopes of satisfying the conditions for more talks with Washington. The two allies would have to consider sticks to compel or punish Pyongyang if it did not comply with their demands.

Success depended on hitting the right diplomatic note. On October 13, the Deputies Committee took a significant step, opting for the comprehensive approach suggested by the two Hans. Meeting with Sandy Berger before the session, Gallucci told him, "So far our position has put all of the North Korean performance up front and all of our performance way at the back end. The North Koreans have noticed." He concluded, "It's not going to work." Many qualities had been imputed to the North Koreans, but no one ever believed them to be dupes at the bargaining table. A comprehensive approach would trade "security for security" but would also include a road map for improved bilateral relations. The deputies forwarded their recommendation to the principals and the president for approval.

The new approach reflected several factors. First, the two Hans' suggestion cleared the path for American officials who felt the step-by-step approach would only involve Washington in drawn-out, inconclusive grappling with North Korea. Contrary to the popular perception in South Korea that Seoul was only the tail on the American dog, South Korean views carried a great deal of weight in Washington. Significantly, only a few hours beforehand a meeting

of key South Korean ministers had decided not to stand in the way of opening diplomatic relations between Washington and Pyongyang—a key component of the new approach—as long as the nuclear issue were solved first.[43]

Second, American decisionmakers were uncertain how long the IAEA
would wait before declaring the continuity of safeguards broken. With
another inspection deadline approaching in late October, IAEA spokesman
David Kyd reiterated publicly a few days earlier, "We are coming upon something of a technical deadline and North Korea has not been responsive at all."[44]
The Americans knew that if the IAEA pulled the trigger it would greatly complicate, if not eliminate, the option for a diplomatic solution.

Third, Washington was concerned about the international community's
diminishing ability to monitor developments at the Yongbyon nuclear facility.
The IAEA's on-site cameras and other monitoring equipment had begun shutting down after the late September deadline passed without action. Using
national technical means such as spy satellites, the Americans were able to discern a great deal about what was happening at Yongbyon, notably that construction was continuing on the North's two larger reactors. But the administration knew that national technical means were not enough.

Fourth, the North Korean proposals made during Ackerman's visit seemed
to offer a reasonable way out of the developing stalemate. Some might question whether they were serious, a negotiating tactic to extract more concessions, or just plain stalling. President Kim Young Sam had dismissed the proposals, in part because they were handwritten, in part because he viewed them
as a mere tactic. But other officials in Seoul believed the hints dropped by the
North Koreans that there was a debate in Pyongyang about what to do next.
They felt that Washington should try to reinforce the position of those officials
who seemed inclined to seek a negotiated solution.

After the deputies' session, negotiations were stepped up in the New York
channel on a "small package" that could clear the way to another Geneva
meeting. Typically, the American delegation—Tom Hubbard, Gary Samore,
and Ken Quinones—would rush to National Airport, catch an early morning
shuttle to New York, and grab a taxi to the U.S. Mission at the United Nations,
then meet the North Koreans. In the beginning, the press tracked the group
down by studying the schedule for the UN conference rooms. Hubbard and
Ho Jong invariably encountered lights, cameras, and questions when they
showed up at the appointed time. As a result, the Australian mission to the UN
was enlisted to reserve rooms for the New York channel meetings in its own
name. This simple ploy worked; the press never figured out what happened,
even speculating about a secret location somewhere else in New York City.[45]

Hubbard and Ho each tried to play their cards to secure the best outcome for their respective sides, not only on substance but also on timing. The United States sought expanded IAEA inspections and the beginning of North-South dialogue up front, holding out the possibility of Team Spirit suspension and announcing a date for the third round later in the process. The North Korean objective was just the opposite: to use the prospect of expanded IAEA inspections and agreement over North-South dialogue to secure Team Spirit suspension and a third round up front. As a result, the negotiations over the small package deal became increasingly complex.

By November, Ho had given some ground, agreeing to allow the IAEA to inspect some additional facilities, but only to discuss the details when the agency team arrived in Pyongyang. With the memory of the August inspection fresh in their minds (the IAEA team had showed up at Yongbyon, only to be surprised at the limited number of activities it would be allowed to conduct), agency officials told the Americans the proposal was a nonstarter. Other important differences also remained, primarily over when Team Spirit cancellation would be announced. Ho insisted that the announcement must precede the third round; Hubbard took the opposite view.

Since the New York talks played out at the same time as the inter-Korean discussions at Panmunjom, the two allies worked together, prompting Ho Jong to complain that Seoul was trying to drive a wedge between Pyongyang and Washington. It was unclear whether he intended the irony of parroting frequent American and South Korean statements about the North's efforts to drive a wedge between them. While a South Korean newspaper observed that Hubbard's commute to New York was not "worthy of a powerful country's official," Deputy Prime Minister Han told him that he slept better after being briefed on the New York meetings.[46] Even President Kim thanked Hubbard when he accompanied Les Aspin to Seoul.

In spite of the push forward in New York, all sides seemed to be entering a "twilight zone." North-South talks scheduled for November 4 had collapsed with the North using the excuse of the South Korean defense minister's "harsh" public remarks. Moreover, a new IAEA deadline had passed on October 31 without inspections to ensure that the agency's technical equipment at the Yongbyon facility continued to operate. While Blix did not declare the continuity of safeguards broken, he warned that, as time went by, "the more safeguards-related data deteriorate, the less assurance safeguards provide." His report to the United Nations bought Washington a little time, but the agency's doomsday clock was ticking. The prospect for higher-level Gallucci-Kang negotiations seemed uncertain at best.

As a result, the Clinton administration followed Foreign Minister Han's advice and sought to create its own "twilight zone" for Pyongyang. With the objective of convincing the North that Washington might suspend dialogue and return to the Security Council for sanctions, it emphasized the omnipresent IAEA deadlines during contacts with Pyongyang. Washington also kept the Security Council churning, informing the P-5 of the difficult situation and assuming that, through press leaks and channels to North Korea via China and others, these pressures would be felt. At the same time, the administration wanted to avoid backing the North into a corner while the possibility of a negotiated solution remained. Hence, while American officials emphasized that Washington's patience was limited, they avoided setting formal deadlines that could be read as ultimatums in Pyongyang.

Walking this fine line proved hard. Public pronouncements sometimes sent mixed signals.[47] In Asia, Secretary Aspin tried to strike a tough posture on sanctions. But he also mused aloud: "Are they appropriate? Would they work? Would they have the desired outcome?" The *New York Times* reported that Aspin thought sanctions might not work.[48] The same problem plagued the administration on the issue of using military force. In another interview, Aspin denied that the United States would take such action against North Korea.[49] But a few days later, President Clinton refused to comment, leaving all options open.[50] Talking to *U.S. News and World Report* the president slightly modified his stance, saying that the United States was not planning any imminent military action, although all options were open.[51]

America's problem in threatening the use of "sticks" was not just public relations. While "sticks" had been considered after North Korea announced its intention to leave the NPT, once it agreed to meet the United States attention in Washington naturally focused on preparing the negotiating track. As the Geneva arrangement unraveled, the administration had to shift gears, not only trying to integrate "carrots" and "sticks" to secure diplomatic progress, but also in preparing to carry out those threats if the North Koreans moved ahead with their nuclear program. This task was all the more difficult since the available "sticks" had inherent limitations.

One stick, sanctions, had been a part of U.S. strategy before the Clinton administration. Repeated studies considered various approaches: limited or comprehensive, implemented gradually or all at once. Gradual escalation might maximize chances of Chinese support and minimize the danger of a violent North Korean reaction. But U.S. government analysts all concluded that the North was unlikely to reverse course because of sanctions. More likely would be a chain reaction: dialogue would end, Pyongyang would accelerate its nuclear program, and Washington would face enormous pressure to use military force. In those circumstances, fear of a U.S. strike might cause North Korea to launch a preemptive attack. Alternatively, with tensions rising, conflict could be touched off by an unintentional incident along the DMZ. Reflecting these concerns, a senior intelligence official told the White House in November that the danger of war was higher than when Pyongyang made its announcement in March, although war was not the only or most imminent response.[52]

International support for sanctions was also lukewarm. The Japanese told Secretary of Defense Aspin, on his way to Seoul, that they would support sanctions, but only after diplomacy had been exhausted. In spite of polls showing 54 percent of the public favored sanctions and 29 percent opposed them, the Japanese government feared that sanctions legislation would be opposed by major coalition partners, particularly the Socialist Party with its long history of sympathy for North Korea.[53] Also, the Foreign Ministry was loath to isolate Pyongyang further and possibly provoke terrorist attacks. Finally, the Japanese public might turn against sanctions and the politicians who had supported them if tensions with North Korea escalated.

The South Koreans gave Secretary Aspin the same message: keep the threat of sanctions prominent but exhaust diplomacy first. A few weeks before Aspin arrived, President Kim told the *Washington Post* that if dialogue failed, "we must resort to sanctions." But he was also concerned that sanctions might induce North Korea's collapse, a nightmare that haunted most South Koreans because of the overwhelming political, economic, and social problems that would result.[54] After Secretary Aspin left Seoul, President Kim and Japan's prime minister Morihiro Hosokawa met and agreed that it was important to "make patient efforts" to solve the problem through dialogue "to every possible extent."[55]

Finally, China was in no mood to support sanctions. From Beijing's perspective, events since June had reaffirmed its view that patient diplomacy worked. Privately, the Chinese urged Washington to avoid "pressuring Pyongyang" and to work toward a negotiated settlement. After all, Kim Il Sung had recently reassured a visiting Chinese official that he had no intention or capability to build nuclear weapons. According to Chinese diplomats, Kim's statement to them, as the North's principal patron, meant more than when he said it to visiting Americans. Visiting Beijing in October, Foreign Minister Han was told that the only way to resolve the nuclear issue was through negotiation.[56]

Washington's other stick, the threat of military force, was an even more delicate matter. The bulk of Pyongyang's million troops were deployed just north of the DMZ, a mere 30 miles from Seoul, which accounted for a quarter of the

South's population and nearly half of its economic output. Thousands of North Korean artillery tubes could unleash a destructive barrage before a single infantryman started to march south. While an article in the *Washington Post* had recently reported on a classified Pentagon study suggesting Pyongyang might win the next Korean War, the accepted wisdom was that the United States and South Korea would ultimately prevail.[57] According to one Pentagon planning document, it might take up to four months of "very high intensity conflict." But since that assessment was based on the assumption that American reinforcements would be on the same scale as those sent to the Persian Gulf—545,000 men—some military officials felt it was optimistic.[58]

General Gary Luck, the commander of U.S. forces in Korea, understood the military situation well. After joining the army in 1960, he rose through a series of increasingly important assignments in Washington, Europe, and East Asia, now reaching the rank of four-star general. Luck had seen his share of combat, serving two tours with special forces in Vietnam and as a senior commander during Desert Storm. Also, Luck had been stationed in South Korea before as the commanding officer of the Second Infantry Division. That experience served him well in his new job, which included a second hat as commander-in-chief of the combined forces command that integrated American and South Korean units. This gave Luck operational control of the South Korean as well as the U.S. military in wartime.

Luck believed that the United States would win another war fought on the Korean peninsula. The real issue was cost. He was fond of saying that "every day you don't fight the war on the Korean peninsula, you win that day." As he would later recall, "Our training got better, our material got better day in and day out while the North atrophied day by day." Pyongyang's equipment was outdated and its economy was deteriorating. It was worthwhile to be patient with the North Koreans, given the gradually shifting military equation.[59]

Visiting Washington that fall, General Luck made the rounds to ensure that Clinton administration officials understood the dangers of military action. At the National Security Council, he told Daniel Poneman that the North Koreans were a formidable foe, strong on the ground and reasonably well modernized, although weaker in the air. Luck described a recent war game that showed the United States and South Korea would win, but with 300,000–750,000 casualties among military personnel. That did not include civilian casualties or measure the enormous economic damage to the South. Luck concluded that this "is not a chess game; it's serious."

One military option that was frequently the subject of public speculation was a preemptive strike against Pyongyang's nuclear facilities. North Korea was a prime focus for an administration about to announce a policy of "counterproliferation" to deal with more countries acquiring weapons of mass destruction.[60] The Pentagon had been studying the requirements for attacking the Yongbyon nuclear facility for some time, including targeting options ranging from individual buildings to the whole installation, relying upon tactical options ranging from cruise missile attacks to commando raids.[61] Making matters more difficult, over 300 antiaircraft guns were located in the vicinity and six new surface-to-air missile bases were under construction. The terrain was hilly, further complicating any attack.[62]

While the United States could conduct a surprise attack and easily wipe out the facility, a second, more ominous scenario was ever present in the minds of senior American decisionmakers. By the end of 1993, North Korea's 5-megawatt reactor had been operating for some time. While arrangements had been made with the IAEA to shut it down for maintenance earlier in the year, the North Koreans subsequently changed their minds. American decisionmakers were concerned that the North Koreans would stop operations without IAEA supervision, unload the 8,000 fuel rods in the reactor into the spent fuel storage pond, and then move them to the reprocessing facility or a secret location, where plutonium would be separated from the rods. Afterward the bomb-making material could be sent to some other unknown location, possibly to fabricate nuclear weapons.

The prospect of North Korea extracting about five bombs' worth of plutonium from the fuel rods created a major challenge for military planners. To head off that possibility without risking a significant release of radiation or the movement of material to unknown locations required timely intelligence, accurate targeting, tight command and control, and pinpoint timing. An attack would have to be launched no sooner than when the North Koreans began to move the spent fuel to the reprocessing plant, but it would have to be executed before they moved the separated nuclear material elsewhere. That, in turn, required enough information to apprise American decisionmakers of these activities in time to allow the military option to be executed successfully. Whether that information would have been available is unclear. But testifying before Congress in 1995, on the subject of a preemptive strike against Yongbyon, Secretary of Defense William J. Perry said, "I can tell you flatly that we know how to do that."[63]

Destroying buildings was one thing, preventing the North Koreans from building nuclear weapons another. One important limitation of a preemptive attack was that it was unlikely to destroy already unaccounted-for plutonium or key bomb-making equipment. The North Koreans were well aware of the historical precedents. In 1981, Israel had launched a successful surprise attack against the Iraqi nuclear installation at Osirak. But Pentagon studies showed that American attacks on the same facilities during the Gulf War were unsuccessful because of advance warning and Iraqi efforts to disperse their program.[64]

Logic suggests that Pyongyang would have certainly moved its plutonium stock and key equipment to other secret locations, quite likely underground, given the North's penchant for tunnel building. Speaking to reporters, Air Force Chief of Staff General Merrill McPeak said, "We can't find nuclear weapons now except by going on a house-to-house search."[65] Even if the locations were known, Pyongyang tended to build tunnel entrances in steep, narrow valleys that faced north, making it difficult to attack them from any direction. And the Americans' best bunker-buster at the time, the GBU-28 bomb, could only penetrate 100 feet of dirt or 20 feet of concrete, a shortcoming Secretary Aspin highlighted in his announcement of the counterproliferation initiative.[66]

Moreover, a preemptive attack could trigger North Korean retaliation ranging from a limited artillery salvo to a full-scale counterattack. One option that concerned decisionmakers was an attack on South Korea's nuclear power plants that could shut down the electricity provided to the South's economy and cause large amounts of radioactive fallout. Government studies showed that North Korea would have problems destroying South Korean reactors with conventional weapons. But nearly all of the South's reactors were located on the coast, exposing them to sea-based attack by Pyongyang's 65,000-man strong special forces. They could attempt to trigger reactor meltdowns, breach containment vessels, and destroy spent fuel storage sites, releasing severe local radiation.[67]

An even more serious concern was that Pyongyang might opt for a full-scale counterattack. Logic seemed to dictate that it would favor a limited response on the assumption that a full-scale attack could end in the destruction of its regime. Indeed, a recent revision to the American war plan called for the destruction of the North Korean regime as an important war objective.[68] The overwhelming majority of American officials, however, believed Pyongyang could well respond to a preemptive strike with a full-scale assault. As General Luck told Poneman during his Washington visit, "If we pull an Osirak, they will be coming south."

Another military option was to send additional American forces to South Korea to deter North Korean aggression and to defeat an attack if necessary. Additional military deployments would have to be carefully calibrated so as to deter, rather than provoke, a North Korean attack. General Luck would often invoke the concept of a seesaw. American and South Korean forces had to be strong enough to maintain the military balance, but not too strong or else Pyongyang would think it was "Desert Storm all over again."[69]

The concept of sending additional forces to Korea prior to hostilities fit in nicely with ongoing revisions to the American war plan based on the experience of the Persian Gulf War. That plan emphasized aggressive counter-offensives. American and South Korean forces would try to slow Pyongyang's ground assault north of Seoul, buy time for reinforcements to pour in, and then repulse the invaders. Allied forces would then cross into North Korea and occupy Pyongyang. At the November 1993 meeting in Seoul between Secretary of Defense Les Aspin and his South Korean counterpart, planners were encouraged to include Flexible Deployment Options (FDO) in their plans. Under this new concept, rather than send reinforcements after a war broke out, as tensions heightened commanders would send reinforcements in advance in order to deter conflict.[70] FDOs, planned modernization programs, and other military measures still unplanned provided the administration with a plethora of "sticks" in dealing with Pyongyang.

The administration was just beginning to embark on a crash course in coercive diplomacy. October 1993, dubbed "Black October" by one senior official, taught the administration about the need to integrate military power with diplomatic strategy.[71] On October 3, American Rangers suffered heavy casualties in an ill-starred mission to capture a Somali warlord. A week later, the USS *Harlan County*, carrying American and Canadian military engineers and trainers, was turned back from Port-au-Prince, Haiti, in spite of a previous agreement with the military junta that the ship could dock.

Tony Lake, President Clinton's national security adviser, would later recall that there was too little debate about whether the administration should use military force in general and specifically in these crises.[72] President Clinton himself seemed ambivalent. In an interview with *Time* magazine published at the end of "Black October," the president observed, "We will be more respected if it's clear that we're making every attempt to blend force with diplomacy." But Clinton also noted, "You may actually lose some political mileage if there is no actual force: if the bombs aren't dropped and people aren't shot and no one dies."[73] Clearly, the marriage of force and diplomacy was part of an ongoing learning process in dealing with Haiti, Bosnia, and North Korea. That fall, such a plan had yet to be formulated for the nuclear crisis.

Coming one right after the other, these setbacks undermined public confidence in the Clinton administration's handling of foreign policy. In September, *New York Times*/CBS News found that 52 percent of Americans approved of President Clinton's handling of foreign affairs.[74] After Somalia, 61 percent of those questioned were uneasy about the president's approach in dealing with a foreign crisis.[75]

As the political spotlight scanned the horizon for other possible failures, Clinton's North Korea policy was a perfect target, particularly since the administration seemed to be caught in its own "twilight zone." Dick Cheney, a possible contender for the Republican presidential nomination, observed, "If you're in North Korea today and you are told by the President of the United States that developing a nuclear weapon is unacceptable, and then you watch the performance in Haiti, you have to wonder whether or not you have to pay any attention to what he says."[76]

Democrats were also critical. Representative Dave McCurdy, a Democrat on the House Armed Services Committee, argued, "If we failed in a confrontation with an African warlord, how can we go toe to toe with Kim Il Sung, who has thrived on brinksmanship for four decades."[77] Recognizing a growing problem, an NSC staff member told his superiors that the administration needed to be clear in its Korea policy and consistent in describing it.[78]

On November 15, the Principals Committee met in the White House Situation Room to grapple with these issues. In their first session on North Korea in six months, the principals reviewed U.S. strategy and finalized preparations for President Kim's visit to Washington slated for the next week. The meeting was attended by Tony Lake, Sandy Berger, Warren Christopher, Les Aspin, General John Shalikashvili (recently appointed to succeed Colin Powell as chairman of the Joint Chiefs of Staff), Leon Fuerth (the vice president's national security adviser), and R. James Woolsey (the director of Central Intelligence).

As their first order of business, the principals endorsed the deputies' recommendation from October 13 to pursue a comprehensive approach toward Pyongyang. While the plan was to secure formal approval at the upcoming Clinton-Kim summit, differences remained. Some wanted to impose tough conditions for allowing the North Koreans to get to a third round of talks with the United States. Knowing that North Korea objected bitterly to Team Spirit, they opposed canceling the exercise before the next U.S.–North Korean meeting, seeing no reason to show flexibility just in order to get Pyongyang to the bargaining table. Indeed, the very name of the exercise had become such a red flag that the Pentagon could trim and shape Team Spirit to almost any dimension and still get a rise out of the North Koreans.

"That's the beautiful thing about it," Les Aspin said with a smile. If the North actually managed to thread this needle to get to the third round, the United States could then afford to be flexible on mixing the security, political, and economic measures in a comprehensive approach during the session.

Other principals saw little point in being flexible in the course of a third round that would never occur if the United States imposed rigid preconditions that North Korea would never meet.

General Shalikashvili presented the Pentagon's assessment of the military situation. The North Koreans had a numerical advantage in manpower and all major weapons, tanks, artillery, and rocket launchers. But the vastly superior training and readiness as well as air superiority of the allied forces offset that advantage.

Lake asked whether it was possible to destroy Yongbyon. Yes, the chairman replied, but he could not guarantee the destruction of plutonium the North was thought already to have, especially since it could be easily moved. Woolsey, the director of Central Intelligence and a former Pentagon official during the Carter administration, added that the location of the material was unknown. Also, heavy air defenses and hilly terrain in the area would make an attack difficult. At best, an attack would set back the nuclear program by some years. Asked how North Korea would react, Shalikashvili replied there would probably be some response across the 38th parallel.

The principals turned to the question of sanctions and how to enforce them. Aware that two officials from the Bush administration—former assistant secretary of defense Stephen Hadley and former under secretary of state Arnold Kanter—would soon release a study recommending a multinational naval exercise off North Korea to show America's determination to enforce sanctions, the principals discussed that possibility and agreed that would be too provocative.[79] Moreover, Pentagon studies had shown that enforcing sanctions with a naval blockade would take, according to one military officer, a "staggering number of ships."[80]

The meeting reconfirmed what everyone knew: the available sticks were less than perfect, there was no evidence to suggest that the administration's initial halting steps at turning up the pressure on Pyongyang were having any effect, and it would take time to define a coherent coercive strategy. As the principals' meeting drew to a close, the intelligence community was tasked to refine its estimates on how sanctions would affect North Korea. The Pentagon was asked to examine whether any additional forces should be sent to Korea or any special military exercises should be considered.

We Got What We Wanted

President Kim had anticipated his visit to Washington for months. As the first freely elected civilian leader of South Korea in thirty years, he did not need the American stamp of approval, in contrast to his military predecessors. But a White House visit would give a strong boost to Kim's policies of democratization and anticorruption. While those policies had made him popular, the South Korean leader knew that continuing his reform program meant taking on vested interests; that would require spending political capital. Building an image as a statesman would help him continue his fight.[81] On top of that, President Kim genuinely admired Bill Clinton; just as Kim was trying to change South Korea, Clinton was "doing his best to change U.S. society." He was looking forward to another face-to-face talk, frequently telling close associates he needed to set the president straight on how to deal with Pyongyang.[82]

While Congressman Ackerman's trip to Pyongyang had given new prominence to the concept of a "package deal," President Kim viewed that approach as a communist tactic and was skeptical about the handwritten proposal given to Ken Quinones.[83] Moreover, unlike his advisers, who seemed inclined to accept diplomatic relations between Washington and Pyongyang as part of that deal, the South Korean leader believed such relations should be severely limited. The idea was further discredited in his eyes when Kim Dae Jung, his bitter foe in the 1992 presidential election, embraced it during a visit to the United States.[84] American press reports highlighted the need for a "comprehensive" deal to solve the nuclear issue, but to President Kim that was no better; in the Korean language, "comprehensive deal" and "package deal" were identical.[85]

President Kim's aversion to a "package deal" was aggravated by two events before he left for Washington. On November 12, Deputy Prime Minister Han and Kim Deok, the South Korean intelligence chief, reportedly told the National Assembly that they supported a package deal, including normalized U.S.–North Korean relations. Their remarks quickly leaked to the press, angering the South Korean leader and prompting the government quickly to deny the reports.[86] Minister Kim and the deputy prime minister also claimed they were misquoted. Although the president appointed a "nuclear ambassador" in the Foreign Ministry to give the appearance that policy was being closely managed, the Korean media had a field day criticizing the government's confusion.[87]

A leak in the *Washington Post* of the Principals Committee's decision to approve the "comprehensive approach" had an even more pronounced effect.[88] Since Seoul had always been nervous that the American security commitment or other South Korean interests could be undermined by negotiations between Washington and Pyongyang, the story touched a raw nerve. The Americans had planned to wait until President Clinton approved the meeting's conclusions before briefing the South Koreans, but the *Post* leak changed all that.[89] The Korean press wrongly concluded that the new policy was to can-cel Team Spirit unconditionally, to accept Pyongyang's offer of a package deal including diplomatic recognition of North Korea, and to relegate North-South talks to a secondary role. Uninformed, the Foreign Ministry was unable to debunk that misinterpretation.

When damage control began a few days later, it was too late. U.S. officials provided briefings in both Seoul and during the Seattle Asia-Pacific Economic Cooperation (APEC) summit, held just before President Kim flew to Wash-ington. Afterward, one South Korean official told the press it was "inconceiv-able that the United States would make a policy switch without us knowing about it."[90] But the Korean media firestorm portrayed the government as a bystander to a major policy shift and the president's summit with Clinton as a briefing on a unilateral American fait accompli.

The Blue House was furious. According to one official, the president's staff were more inclined to believe the *Washington Post* than their own Foreign Ministry.[91] As a result, President Kim decided to assert a more prominent role in his meeting with Clinton, to show that he personally was deciding policy. One close aide recalled: "Above all Kim was a politician. He sometimes said things purely for domestic consumption not realizing that they would also play on the international stage."[92]

The Americans had little or no warning that President Kim was about to switch gears. Months had been spent haggling over the timing of a summit. At one point, South Korea's ambassador Han Seung Soo proposed to Tony Lake that the summit be held on November 16, coinciding with the congressional vote on the North American Free Trade Agreement. Knowing that President Clinton would be working the phone to sway votes, Lake offered November 23 instead. In hushed tones, the ambassador said this was regrettable since the South Korean advance team already was on its way to Washington and that a large block of hotel rooms had been reserved for the South's preferred date. It was an awkward moment, but Lake could not relent. Whether the team was ever in the air is unclear; the Americans suspected it was a negotiating tactic. The next day, the Korean Embassy told the White House that a November 23 summit would be fine.[93]

National Security Council and State Department officials worked with the South Koreans to choreograph agreement on the comprehensive approach. Fly-ing on *Air Force One*, Clinton had reviewed and approved the concept.[94] Subse-quently, Secretary Christopher counseled the president to perform a delicate balancing act with Kim, telling the tough-minded South Korean leader that U.S. patience with Pyongyang was ebbing but also that Washington was pre-pared for constructive dialogue and to work on a comprehensive approach. The day before the summit, Clinton confirmed to the press that a new approach was being considered in close cooperation with "the countries most affected in the region."[95] Lake had told the president that South Korean approval was wired.[96]

Though they did not reach the White House, signs of trouble were brewing. At the APEC summit in Seattle, a few days before Kim arrived in Washington, the South Koreans expressed concern about the controversy over a "package deal" and how it had generated political pressures on their president. Consequently, they told Tom Hubbard that they might have to switch gears and not allow the small package to move forward until the envoy exchange actually happened. That would make Seoul's central role abundantly clear, although it would also up the ante since Hubbard had previously told the North Koreans that they just had to agree to exchange special envoys in the small package itself.[97]

More hints emerged after President Kim arrived in Washington. The day before he met with Clinton, the New York Times cited anonymous South Korean officials who were concerned the United States might be pursuing too conciliatory a policy.[98] At an awards dinner that evening, the South Koreans buttonholed Hubbard and said they were thinking about backing out of the summit press release. Hubbard urged them to let him know if they made a decision but never heard back from them.[99] There were no signs of trouble when President Kim met with Vice President Al Gore the next morning.

Just before the summit with President Clinton, the South Koreans gathered at Blair House, the official guest residence across the street from the White House where Kim was staying. The president was joined by his foreign policy advisers—Foreign Minister Han Sung Joo and the Blue House secretary, Chung Chong Wook—as well as the Blue House chief secretary, Park Kwan Yong, a veteran politician whose influence was growing, though he was not part of Kim's inner circle.

Surprisingly, Yu Chong Ha, the South's ambassador to the United Nations, also attended.[100] A tough and persistent diplomat, Yu's colleagues compared him to a German shepherd. He was fond of saying, "Once you bite into something, you should never release." As vice minister during the previous regime, Yu had demonstrated his persistence by besting the Ministry of Finance over budgetary issues.[101] A rival of Han for the post of foreign minister, Yu was his subordinate but had spent much of 1993 sending secret messages to the Blue House advocating a tougher approach with North Korea. They struck a sympathetic cord, particularly with the chief cabinet secretary Park who, like President Kim, was sensitive to conservative domestic critics. Yu was invited to the session by Park, not by his nominal boss, who was surprised to see him.[102]

The Blair House meeting was short, heated, and decisive. Foreign Minister Han laid out the comprehensive approach agreed to in consultations with the Americans. Ambassador Yu, however, advocated a more aggressive stance for Seoul, including linking the carrots being offered the North, particularly the cancellation of the Team Spirit joint exercise, to progress on North-South inspections. The chief cabinet secretary supported Yu; his main concern was how President Kim's visit would play in domestic politics. Although Kim just listened, Yu's presentation had clearly resonated with him, since it would plainly demonstrate that Seoul was in the driver's seat.[103]

Subsequently, Foreign Minister Han did not even attend the meeting in the Oval Office. The first part of the session was billed as a "one-on-one" with only the national security advisers and interpreters attending. Neither Han nor Secretary Christopher was supposed to participate. As the session was about to begin, however, Christopher strolled into the Oval Office. Not seeing where he went, Han thought the American had gone to the men's room. Once Han realized Christopher had gone in, he just waited outside, in part because he knew the meeting was going to be difficult and there was nothing he could do about it.[104]

The game plan had been to hold a short session on the nuclear issue in the Oval Office, followed by a much longer session on the broad bilateral agenda in the Cabinet Room, but the opposite occurred. The Oval Office meeting began with a resentful President Kim objecting to a new approach on North Korea—the comprehensive package—that, in his view, had been decided by the United States and then briefed to South Korea. Kim repeatedly pointed out that the press was describing this approach using the terms "package deal" and "comprehensive deal," both implying concessions to the North, such as the normalization of relations between Pyongyang and Washington. Putting into play the tough approach advocated by some of his advisers during the Blair House meeting held only a few hours earlier, President Kim argued that Washington and Seoul should "reserve" on whether to cancel Team Spirit even if the North Koreans agreed to IAEA inspections and entered into dialogue with the South. Kim mused over whether the United States and South Korea should cancel Team Spirit only after Pyongyang had demonstrated to the South that it did not have nuclear weapons, which would set the bar even higher.

Clinton, Lake, and Christopher were stunned; summits with allies are carefully staged to avoid surprises. The president defended the comprehensive approach, but it was clear that Kim had made up his mind. Now he appeared not even to be listening. Lake and Christopher tried to intervene, but Kim was adamant. He eventually admitted that the problem with "comprehensive" may have been just one of terminology that misled the media. Lake recalls glancing at his counterpart Chung Chong Wook and never having seen anyone look so stricken.

After Clinton suggested that the national security advisers find another formulation, they discussed synonyms and came up with the convoluted phrase, a "thorough and broad" approach. What seemed to be an interminable session ended as the door to the Oval Office flew open and Lake urgently motioned Poneman to enter. "We had a problem here. What if we dropped the phrase 'comprehensive' approach and called it a 'thorough and broad' approach? Is that OK?" After a quick huddle confirmed that the change was just cosmetic, the two sides reached agreement. "We got what we wanted," Kim told a close aide as he left the Oval Office.[105] Outside, Hubbard seethed when he heard the news, having been blind-sided after weeks of painstaking diplomacy.[106]

As for Kim's demand that Team Spirit cancellation be withheld until the last possible moment, since Hubbard was set to meet Ho Jong the next day, Americans and South Koreans worked into the night to come up with a new formulation for the "small package." During the White House dinner that evening in honor of President Kim, Lake, Poneman, and South Korean national security adviser Chung kept shuttling revised texts back and forth until agreement was reached. Team Spirit would only be canceled after the North's special envoy visited Seoul and held "serious" discussions. What "serious" meant was unclear, but the change certainly raised the hurdle Pyongyang would have to jump. Afterward, Hubbard told Lake that the new arrangement was destined to fail.[107]

In a strained press conference following the summit, Clinton warned North Korea that it risked increased international pressure if it persisted in blocking IAEA inspections but at the same time offered to settle the nuclear issue through a "thorough, broad approach" to security and other challenges. The president also said no decision had been made on whether to cancel Team Spirit.

President Kim, repeating the concerns he had expressed in the Oval Office, observed that since the media had been distorting the meaning of the comprehensive solution, "we have modified the expression into all thorough extensive efforts for the ultimate solution." He also seemed to draw back from using Team Spirit as a bargaining chip, saying that the "matter of suspending" the exercise "should be dealt with on its own."[108]

Afterward Poneman told the press that the thorough and broad approach meant a willingness to discuss "the full array of nuclear and security-related issues with a view towards finding a resolution of the nuclear problem." As for Team Spirit, Seoul and Washington would reconsider holding the exercise "if the North Koreans meet the conditions we have laid out."[109]

For President Kim, his first venture into international diplomacy was a success. The South Korean media hailed the summit as a personal triumph for him. It appeared to reaffirm close U.S.–South Korean ties, enhance his country's international prestige, and bolster his domestic political standing. His close personal relationship with Clinton was reflected in casual shots of the two at the APEC summit and jogging in Washington. One South Korean newspaper observed that Kim Young Sam said "no" to an American president, something previous South Korean leaders had been unable to do.[110] Eight out of ten Koreans thought the trip was productive, and Kim's meeting with Clinton was seen as the most impressive part.[111]

President Kim's diplomatic foray also signaled a more active, personal role in shaping policy toward North Korea. Part of that entailed getting rid of prominent conservatives and moderates. On November 24, the conservative Lee Dong Bok resigned from his government job, a victim of renewed allegations that he had concealed instructions in 1992 that might have led to a breakthrough in North-South talks on family reunions.[112]

A few weeks later, Deputy Prime Minister Han Wan Sang—architect of President Kim's aborted "sunshine policy" and lightning rod for conservatives—also was dismissed. His replacement, Lee Yung Duk, a university president whose family was separated by the Korean War, was known for "his firm maintenance of the South's position to the end" in North-South talks.[113] Lee reaffirmed his conservative credentials when he told reporters that it was about time North Korea respected universal values such as human rights.[114]

The Kim administration would subsequently restructure its formal decisionmaking process to lessen the influence of the Foreign Ministry and to inject greater sensitivity toward domestic politics. Until the summit, a small group of advisers—the foreign minister, national security adviser, deputy prime minister, and head of South Korean intelligence—had been making decisions. After Deputy Prime Minister Han was dismissed, a new body, the Policy Coordinating Group, was established to include chief cabinet secretary Park, who helped engineer the turn of events at the summit, and the prime minister's chief of staff. Both were acutely sensitive to domestic political currents. In short, according to one former senior official, the new body's purpose was to "prevent giving away too much to North Korea."[115] Nevertheless, Foreign Minister Han, now the leading moderate in Kim's cabinet, still wielded enormous influence by virtue of his position, intellect, and frequent access to the president.

If President Kim succeeded in making himself look tough, he also succeeded in making the Clinton administration look weak. After the November 15 principals' meeting, the administration was poised to move forward with the comprehensive approach, based more on "carrots" than "sticks." The day after the summit, the *Washington Post* proclaimed, "South Korean Holds Line on North; President Opposes Concessions until Direct Talks Are Re-opened."[116] Conservative columnist Charles Krauthammer was more to the point, observing that the Clinton-Kim news conference "rang with polite but unmistakable discord." Calling the administration's approach "pathetic," Krauthammer added, "Bill Clinton seems to think he is dealing with some Florida congressman whose NAFTA vote can be bought with a dam and a mess of tomatoes. Kim Il Sung is no Florida pol."[117]

Beyond the immediate political damage, the summit drove home to senior American officials the unpredictability of their South Korean ally. One moment Seoul was complaining the Americans were too weak and the next that they were too aggressive. President Clinton, while puzzled by Kim's behavior, had maintained his composure.[118] But Secretary Christopher—meeting with Gallucci, Hubbard, and others afterward—ordered Hubbard to rebuke the South Koreans.[119] The summit made it clear that dealing effectively with Seoul meant staying in close contact with the Foreign Ministry, the Blue House, and the president himself. Lake began regular conversations with National Security Adviser Chung and instructed Poneman to keep an open channel with his Blue House counterpart.[120]

That lesson was put to good use as talks resumed in the New York channel the next day. There had been signs, beginning just before the Clinton-Kim meeting, that Pyongyang might have new flexibility. First Vice Foreign Minister Kang hinted at the possibility, first mentioned during the Ackerman visit, of accepting international safeguards.[121] After the summit, Pyongyang announced plans to return more remains of Americans missing in action; another sign that it was trying to foster a favorable atmosphere.[122] A Foreign Ministry statement issued on November 30 renewed Pyongyang's threat to withdraw from the NPT but also hinted at the possibility of accepting safeguards.[123]

Ho Jong had clearly been following the press stories about the summit. "What is the difference between the 'comprehensive' and 'broad and thorough' approaches?" he asked, echoing a question on the minds of many other observers. Hubbard explained that the change was only intended to correct misunderstandings in the South Korean press. "If North Korea takes the necessary steps to get to the third round, the door will be open to a wide range of issues, not only with the United States but other nations of the world," Hubbard responded.

As for the new American position, Ho's response was exactly what Hubbard expected. The veteran Foreign Service officer told his North Korean counterpart that Team Spirit would now not be suspended and a date for the third round would not be announced until after the North Korean envoy visited Seoul and engaged in "serious" discussions. Clearly disappointed, Ho complained that the Americans had been "tricked" into giving Seoul control over the pace of U.S.–North Korean talks.

But on December 3, the North Koreans came back with a counterproposal. They would be more flexible on IAEA issues, allowing inspections at all the sites requested by the agency, although there would still be limits on activities at the key facilities, the 5-megawatt reactor, and the reprocessing plant. Pyongyang demanded, however, that Team Spirit suspension be announced when talks to arrange the envoy exchange resumed between the two Koreas, obviously much earlier than the actual visit of the special envoy to Seoul.

Now Vienna got into the act, further complicating Washington's task. At the beginning of December, since months had gone by without an inspection, Blix reported that the safeguards system "could not be said at present to provide any meaningful assurance of the peaceful use of the DPRK's declared nuclear installations and facilities." According to the IAEA "the game is not totally over, but we're close to that." Privately, Blix allowed that his objective was to show that the situation was urgent but could be repaired if the North cooperated soon. A few days later, however, after learning of the December 3 proposal, he reminded the Americans that additional, unspecified activities would be needed at Yongbyon to ensure the continuity of safeguards, presumably since so much time had gone by since the August visit. That imposed another requirement on American negotiators.

The Principals Committee met on December 6 to discuss the latest developments. Keeping in mind that securing continuity of safeguards was the main priority, the options were to accept North Korea's offer, come back with a counterproposal, or reject it. Les Aspin was once again the odd man out, speaking alternatively in favor of either the first or the last option, which were diametrically opposed. This led to a tense exchange with Tony Lake, who was trying to impose more discipline on the decisionmaking process in the wake of Black October. Just at the moment of stalemate, the president entered the Situation Room and stayed for the rest of the meeting.[124]

In the end, the principals came up with a counteroffer. If North Korea accepted the IAEA's requirements, Seoul would announce Team Spirit suspension when working-level South-North talks agreed to the exchange of special envoys. That was sooner than the envoy's arrival in Seoul for "serious discussions," the Clinton-Kim summit position, but later than North Korea's demand that the exercise be suspended when North and South sat down to arrange an exchange. If Pyongyang proved unresponsive, Washington would increase the pressure by stepping up activity in the Security Council.

With the lesson of the recent summit clearly in mind, the principals agreed that President Clinton would need to have a personal chat with the South Korean leader to get him on board. Later that day, Clinton told reporters that he was hopeful something could be worked out with the North but he had to consult with U.S. allies and planned to talk to Kim in the next twenty-four hours.[125]

The next morning, he called Kim. After addressing a number of difficult, but less explosive issues associated with the Uruguay round of multilateral trade negotiations, Clinton asked the South Korean leader to support the U.S. counteroffer. He emphasized the need to use every opportunity for progress since without inspections Washington and Seoul would have to seek sanctions. President Kim deferred any detailed discussion of the proposal to the two national security advisers but told Clinton that the very fact of the presidential call would send a strong signal of U.S.–South Korean solidarity. Lake phoned Blue House secretary Chung with the details, and Gallucci relayed the same message to the South Koreans in Washington.[126]

Although Seoul's immediate reaction to the December 3 proposal had been that it fell short of the summit agreement, the day after the Clinton-Kim conversation, Chung called Lake to tell him that South Korea agreed to the American proposal. President Kim was willing to withstand press criticism about his inconsistency since Clinton had taken the trouble to phone.

Over the next few weeks, as the New York negotiations moved slowly to a conclusion, American officials took a tough stance, to put pressure on the North Koreans while keeping their South Korean allies on board. Secretary of State Christopher warned that North Korea's program would be stopped "by whatever means," while White House chief of staff Thomas "Mac" McLarty asserted that an oil embargo was possible if dialogue failed.[127] Still, the State Department's Korea desk observed in its weekly activities report, "We are heading into Christmas weekend with substantially higher hopes of a breakthrough this year to a third round of formal talks with North Korea."

On December 29, more than two months after negotiations had begun, preliminary agreement was finally reached. The two sides would take four steps on the same as yet unspecified day—dubbed "Super Tuesday" by the Americans in reference to the March date in presidential election years when fifteen states all hold primaries—putting into effect the principle of simultaneous and reciprocal actions. One step would be the beginning of IAEA inspections at the seven sites specified in the September 8 IAEA letter to Pyongyang. On that day, North Korea would also resume talks with South Korea to arrange for the exchange of special envoys. In return, Seoul would announce the cancellation of Team Spirit. Finally, the United States and North

Korea would announce the long-awaited date for the next meeting between Gallucci and Kang.

While the December 29 arrangement represented a step forward, important details remained unresolved. The diplomatic action now shifted to Vienna, where the combustible mix of North Korea and the IAEA were slated to work out the specific activities the agency could conduct during its inspection. The arrangement also left the timing of the special envoy exchange unresolved. For the moment, Hubbard and Ho agreed to disagree. Washington was about to learn that, for the tenacious hagglers from Pyongyang, the relentless pursuit of tactical advantage sometimes had potentially disastrous consequences.

5

A Sea of Fire

January–March 1994

As it entered the New Year, the Clinton administration felt encouraged. Although North Korea and the International Atomic Energy Agency had not met since September and their relationship remained sour, the December 29 agreement allowing the IAEA to return to the Yongbyon nuclear facility seemed to open a new path to renewed talks between Robert Gallucci and Kang Sok Ju. At a January 5 press conference, Under Secretary of State Lynn Davis said, "We are very close to having accomplished those requirements" to begin a third round, and the president highlighted the goal of a nonnuclear Korean peninsula as a key foreign policy objective in his State of the Union speech.[1] Administration officials knew, however, to expect problems at every step of the way.

North Korea also began 1994 on an upbeat note. For decades, Kim Il Sung had delivered an annual New Year's speech that rarely contained initiatives but always provided direction for detailed proposals and propaganda in the months ahead. This year, his twenty-six-minute message, aside from addressing important domestic issues, struck a positive tone about U.S.–North Korean relations, focusing on the New York joint statement. While warning that pressure would result in the collapse of talks, the aging leader added that if the two sides abided by that agreement, the nuclear issue could be resolved in a "fair" manner to both countries. A week later, the party newspaper asserted a solution was "in sight."[2]

At the same time, Kim Il Sung was stridently critical of the South Korean government. Although he stopped short of saying that Pyongyang had given up on Seoul, the North's propaganda attacks on the South's president were disturbing because Pyongyang usually toned down its rhetoric before resuming dialogue with Seoul.[3] The verbal assaults had begun in December after the moderate Kim Yong Sun lost his position as an alternate member of the North Korean Politburo, though he was left in charge of reunification policy. There might be more problems ahead if the move reflected unhappiness with the state of North-South dialogue. On the other hand, his demotion may have been one of the normal ups and downs the two Northern Kims imposed on their minions to keep them off balance.[4]

In South Korea, President Kim Young Sam's New Year's message expressed hope that "the nuclear matter will be resolved this year, so that true peace can come to the Korean peninsula."[5] The same day as the Great Leader's speech, he told the press that he opposed holding a summit just for the sake of having a summit. Kim Il Sung frequently had used the same excuse to rebuff South Korean requests.[6]

The South Korean leader was uneasy. The December agreement signaled that America's dialogue with North Korea was on track, perhaps consigning Seoul again to the back burner. Also, while President Kim publicly claimed that there had been "round-the-clock" contacts with Washington, he feared his close ally would not protect his country's interests in that dialogue, a concern shared by 52 percent of South Koreans polled.[7] Because the president was so incensed by Pyongyang's attacks—brought to his attention by intelligence officials who showed him daily press clippings—Kim's son considered stopping the practice since it might adversely affect his father's health.[8] Kim Il Sung's New Year's speech, respectful of the United States but vituperative toward the South Korean president, further aggravated him.[9]

Imperceptibly at first, the first few months of 1994 marked the beginning of a slow drift into crisis and confrontation. That drift reflected the inexorable failure of an American diplomatic strategy that continued to defer to key partners—the IAEA and South Korea—whose organizational and domestic political interests sometimes led them in directions inimical to the goal of arresting North Korea's unsafeguarded nuclear activities. Pyongyang only made matters worse; its diplomacy skillfully targeted the bonds that united its adversaries, fraying them in order to gain short-term tactical advantage. As a result, the first few months of 1994 dashed hopes for an early resolution of the nuclear issue.

The February Crisis

On January 4, Ho Jong notified the State Department that his government was ready to start talks with the IAEA. State relayed the message to the agency, which in turn contacted the North Korean mission in Vienna. A few days later, Dimitri Perricos sat down with Yun Ho Jin, the senior North Korean official in Vienna responsible for day-to-day contacts with the IAEA. Perricos, the fast-talking director of the agency's safeguards division dealing with North Korea, whose aggressive style was the model for the post-Iraq IAEA bureaucrat, was also a close associate of Hans Blix. The contrast between the soft-spoken Swede and the boisterous Greek could not have been more striking.[10]

Not surprisingly, sparks began to fly almost immediately. While the December 29 agreement with the Americans seemed to ensure North Korean cooperation with the IAEA, Yun initially took a stance based on the tougher position Pyongyang had staked out prior to that arrangement. The North Korean negotiator was willing to accept most of the activities the agency required at most of its nuclear facilities, but agreement on others would have to wait until the team arrived at Yongbyon. Some new activities would be permitted at the reprocessing plant and 5-megawatt reactor, to help compensate for the data lost following the failure of surveillance equipment, but they would also have to be arranged once the inspectors arrived in North Korea. Yun claimed others were unacceptable.[11]

Whether deliberate or not, the North Koreans could not have taken a position more infuriating to the IAEA negotiators. If there was one maxim that Blix and Perricos had taken to heart, it was that "the agency's inspection requirements are not an à la carte menu." All of those activities—including checking broken seals on key equipment found on previous inspections, taking samples, and gamma mapping—were designed to ensure that there had been no diversion of nuclear materials for building nuclear weapons.[12] Sampling would help inspectors find traces of plutonium while gamma mapping would detect changes in radiation levels that could indicate undeclared nuclear activities. In view of the agency's humiliation during the August 1993 inspection, Perricos insisted that agreement had to be reached in Vienna before any IAEA team stepped onto North Korean soil.

At first Yun gave ground, but the negotiations quickly reached an impasse. Initially, he agreed that all inspection activities would be worked out in Vienna and asked the IAEA for a list of tasks. After the IAEA provided a list, the North Koreans accepted more activities. But Yun refused to agree to sampling or gamma mapping, both critical for the IAEA to perform its duties properly.[13]

The cautious optimism that began the New Year quickly faded. The IAEA's expectation that the negotiations would be a mere formality seemed dashed after two weeks.[14] Blix warned the United States that he might soon declare the negotiations had failed, triggering a return of the nuclear issue to the UN Security Council. Ho Jong, in turn, pointed the finger at the IAEA, blaming its excessive demands for jeopardizing the third round of U.S.–North Korean meetings. Faced with the feuding protagonists, Gallucci wrote Kang on January 21 reminding him that the United States would take "other measures" if the continuity of safeguards were broken. Reinforcing his message in public, the State Department warned that Washington would "have to look at alternative means of resolving this dispute" other than another round of U.S.–North Korean talks. Once again, sanctions seemed on the horizon.[15]

As the talks in Vienna teetered on the brink of collapse, an unanticipated event threatened to make a bad situation worse. The press had got wind of a Pentagon recommendation to deploy Patriot antimissile missiles in South Korea. The Patriot, originally built in the 1970s to defend against aircraft, was modified in the 1980s to knock down short-range ballistic missiles. First used in the Gulf War, the missile was hailed by some for its successful defense of Saudi Arabia and Israel against Iraqi missiles. Supporters claimed the Patriot had shot down forty-one out of forty-two ballistic missiles. Critics argued that the intercept rate was lower than 10 percent. The debate over exactly how effective the Patriot had been was still raging when the crisis broke out on the Korean Peninsula.[16]

For General Gary Luck, the commander of American forces in Korea, the requirement for Patriots was obvious. A veteran of the Gulf War, he had experienced the threat of Iraq's short-range SCUD missiles firsthand. Since North Korea also had SCUDs, Luck saw Patriots as an indispensable asset. They would be deployed around airfields and ports in order to protect those facilities from missile attacks. Transporting the Patriots to South Korea before a crisis would also have the added benefit of freeing valuable aircraft to ferry in more equipment and troops during the crisis.

While the Americans had not planned to deploy Patriots in South Korea until 1995, events in Europe allowed General Luck to move more quickly. The collapse of the Soviet Union and the downsizing of American forces in Europe freed the antimissile missiles much sooner than expected. General Luck thought the decision would not be controversial since the Patriot was a "defensive" weapon. Instead, as he would recall, "I was hung out to dry by both the North and the South."[17] American spokesmen would repeatedly emphasize that the Patriot was not an offensive weapon, but its mission of protecting key airfields and ports of entry for much-needed American reinforcements would help make offensive strikes possible.

At their first official meeting in November 1993, General Luck had discussed the possibility of deploying Patriots with General John Shalikashvili, the new chairman of the Joint Chiefs of Staff, who was visiting Seoul. Luck's formal request for deployment was then sent to Washington and proceeded up the chain of command. By the end of December, the request had been endorsed by the Pentagon and was forwarded to the White House for a final decision by President Clinton.

To assist the president in making this decision, both the Deputies and Principals Committees met in rapid succession. The issue was not whether to deploy the Patriots—after the October disaster in Somalia, Washington was strongly inclined to support all requests from field commanders—but when. An immediate deployment would respond positively to General Luck and send a strong signal to both Koreas that Washington's security commitment remained firm. But it would also risk adversely affecting the Vienna negotiations. Deferring deployment until after the talks had played out, probably by the end of February when the next IAEA Board of Governors meeting was scheduled, would avoid that problem. The situation was further complicated by rumors that reporters were already on to the story. The principals agreed that Tony Lake should call his Blue House counterpart to discuss the problem.

Lake spoke to South Korea's national security adviser Chung Chong Wook the morning of January 21. Major deployment decisions in Korea required a complicated minuet. On the one hand, deference had to be accorded the South Korean government. It was, after all, their country. Seoul would absorb the brunt of any conflict on the peninsula and American forces were stationed in Korea at the invitation of its government. On the other hand, as long as the United States posted 37,000 troops in Korea, Washington would insist that they were properly armed and equipped to perform their mission there.

Lake understood the situation was delicate: he told Chung that Washington was consulting, not informing Seoul on the Patriot. But to keep the pressure on, he added that President Clinton was inclined to go ahead. The real question was timing. Chung said he had heard rumors that there might be a *New York Times* story. Both agreed that a low-key public approach would help facilitate the deployment.

When *New York Times* reporter Michael Gordon called the White House, any hope that the missiles could be sent to Korea quietly and quickly evaporated. Lake recognized the inevitable and tried to soften the blow. Emphasizing the importance of defending American forces and friends, he told Gordon that a final decision had not been made but Pyongyang would not deter the United States from sending Patriots to South Korea.[18] The next day—January 26—the article ran on the front page of the *Times* and spread like wildfire to South Korean newspapers.[19]

The leak set off a political firestorm. Conservatives supported the Patriot deployment, the ruling party split, and the opposition naturally was opposed.[20]

Many also suspected the United States had ulterior commercial motives. Washington had been trying to get the South to purchase Patriot in response to the North Korean missile threat for some time. The government had only recently received a letter from Senator Edward Kennedy (Democrat of Massachusetts) asking it to buy the missile, which was built by Raytheon, a Massachusetts-based company.[21] Also, doubts about Patriot's effectiveness resonated with a leak to the newspapers of a recent attempt by the Americans to persuade the South to buy a piece of military equipment that had proven defective. Adding to the indignity, the Americans wanted Seoul to buy that weapon on a commercial basis, not under the usual, less costly foreign military sales program.[22]

Events fueled a growing impression that Washington was spoiling for a military confrontation. The New York Times story was followed in rapid succession by other alarming press reports that the administration intended to send new helicopters to Korea and was considering deploying an aircraft carrier as well. (In fact, the aircraft carrier Independence was returning to its base in Japan as part of a normal rotation in the Indian Ocean, not as part of a new campaign to press Pyongyang.) The New York Times then published the gist of the American war plan, highlighting its objective to seize Pyongyang. Next came a Washington Post story that the Pentagon planned to send 1,000 troops to Korea for Team Spirit if the Vienna talks were not successfully concluded soon.[23]

To top it off, the United States Senate passed two toughly worded, though nonbinding measures, one advocating sanctions and the other urging the president to consider redeploying American nuclear weapons in South Korea.[24] Congressional frustration was growing daily; only a few weeks earlier, Under Secretary Davis had confidently announced the December agreement. Now, speaking on the Senate floor, Robert Dole, a potential Republican presidential candidate, deadpanned, "The North Koreans are having their carrot cake and eating it too."[25] Watching the situation unfold, puzzled North Koreans at the UN Mission asked one American visitor what a "nonbinding" vote meant.

The disturbing tone of events in Washington had an immediate, negative impact in South Korea. Businessmen claimed that exports were being hurt. The public was increasingly concerned that the United States might be leading the South unwillingly into war. That, in turn, threatened to rekindle traditional feelings of resentment against foreign domination, which had previously surfaced in the early 1990s amid rumors that the Bush administration was contemplating an air strike against Yongbyon. Even conservatives complained that the United States was going to force Koreans to fight among themselves. One American official observed: "Goodwill toward the United States sits on a reservoir of resentment that the fate of the country is not in the hands of Koreans."

For President Kim and his government, the Patriot story was a nightmare. It was a political nightmare because the story undercut his claim that Seoul was in constant consultations with Washington. General Luck had been in close contact with the South Korean Ministry of Defense and would later recall, "We didn't plan to sneak them in."[26] Just as in the United States, however, the leak seemed to short-circuit the South's decisionmaking process before the plan could be approved by top-level civilians. As a result, many were taken by surprise, fostering the perception if not the reality that the government had not been fully consulted beforehand.

It was a policy nightmare because the deployment deliberately appeared to challenge North Korea. President Kim feared it might be just the excuse that Pyongyang needed to avoid exchanging special envoys. Washington was about to find out once again that the South liked to talk tough, but rising tensions brought home the realities of confrontation, which Seoul wanted to avoid.

Part of the government's response was to try to calm public anxiety. It correctly pointed out that a final decision had not been made and that the Patriots were part of an old modernization decision made before the nuclear crisis in any case.[27] Seoul also dismissed press reports of escalating tensions.[28] It quickly repatriated two North Korean soldiers rescued from a drifting raft, avoiding an extended propaganda battle over whether they had been held against their will.[29]

Part of South Korea's response was also to equivocate on the timing of the Patriot deployment, making the issue a political football between Washington and Seoul. On January 29, three days after the New York Times story broke, Tony Lake called Chung Chong Wook once again. He explained to his South Korean counterpart that no final decision had been made on Patriot, but the United States would not be deterred from taking the necessary steps to defend its forces and friends. Trying to put the best face on a bad situation, Chung replied that the Times story had provided a psychological boost in Seoul, demonstrating the seriousness of the American commitment to South Korea's security. He added that President Kim much appreciated the missiles, but Chung made it clear that Seoul wanted to defer the deployment. Lake met him halfway, agreeing to delay the final decision for a few weeks. It was becoming painfully obvious that while Seoul saw Patriot as upsetting the delicate diplomatic process under way, Washington saw what might be an endless series of excuses for not moving forward.

As the time for a decision approached, Foreign Minister Han Sung Joo made a quick, unscheduled visit to Washington. Aside from concerns about the delay, American decisionmakers also thought Patriot might trigger the same unpredictable reaction from President Kim as before his November visit to the United States. Han's visit afforded both sides the opportunity to avoid a similar incident and to compare notes on how to deal with the crisis. The minister was able to accomplish three important objectives: to show the South Korean public that Seoul was "doing something" to prevent a crisis, to demonstrate that the two allies were working closely together, and to deflate press reports pointing toward an imminent blowup.

But neither Han nor his American counterparts were able to bridge the gap on Patriot. On February 8, the day before he arrived, the Principals Committee recommended to President Clinton that he approve the deployment, to begin at the end of February, after the next IAEA board meeting but before any further sanctions activity at the Security Council. While they wanted to avoid either handing Pyongyang a convenient excuse to break off negotiations or undermining support for sanctions, the principals also took heed of Secretary William Perry's concerns about the dangers of taking any action in the Security Council without Patriots on the ground. It was also reported that General Luck was eager to avoid flying the missiles in during a crisis, when their effect could be more destabilizing. President Clinton approved the Pentagon's recommendation before Foreign Minister Han's plane touched down at Dulles International Airport.

Try as the administration might, it was unable to budge Han Sung Joo. In a letter received just before he arrived, President Kim warned Clinton that the two allies should avoid heightening tensions with Pyongyang. Vice President Al Gore was particularly forceful with the visiting foreign minister, pressing Han to agree that the Patriot shipment could begin at the end of the month according to the American game plan.[30] In separate sessions, Lake informed Han that the president had approved deployment by the end of February while Secretary Perry told him that Washington had to respond positively to requests from its field commanders. In spite of the full-court press, the South Korean foreign minister stood his ground. At the end of his visit, Han told reporters, "The deployment of Patriot missiles is still in the stage of discussion," and a decision would not be made until after the IAEA meeting in a few weeks.[31]

Warning of War

Pyongyang must have been puzzled by the U.S. plan to deploy the Patriot in the wake of the December agreement. Although the Americans portrayed the missile as "defensive," the North Koreans were suspicious. To them, the massive

American military buildup over six months in preparing for the Gulf War may have appeared as a dress rehearsal for a second Korean War. The Gulf War reinforced a lesson Pyongyang had learned from the first conflict in Korea, that it would have to quickly neutralize available air and naval points of debarkation, in military jargon "PODs," to prevent a similar American buildup; the Patriot was intended to protect those facilities. Whether Pyongyang knew the intricacies of the American war plan was unclear, although the February 6 leak of its broad outline to the *New York Times* was a timely reminder of the role Patriots would play blunting an attack and pushing northward.

Though negative, North Korea was restrained and circumspect about the Patriot deployment, as it often was at an early stage of deliberations in sorting out new developments. On January 28, an unattributed commentary—a less authoritative vehicle than a Foreign Ministry statement—recorded strong opposition to the deployment and appealed to the South Koreans to stage antiwar rallies. At the same time, Pyongyang tempered its criticism by only attacking "conservative" forces in the United States and continued to talk positively of its negotiations with Washington.[32]

Three days later, North Korea's rhetoric against Patriot escalated. A more authoritative Foreign Ministry statement warned that Pyongyang "cannot overlook" the deployment of Patriots but still refrained from issuing an ultimatum. Criticism was reserved for "conservative forces" that were "hurrying" to deploy the missiles in order to achieve military superiority. American statements that the deployment was not provocative were dismissed as "sophistry."[33]

Pyongyang reserved its harshest language to accuse the United States of reneging on its diplomatic promises. Warning Washington not to miscalculate about its eagerness for better relations and accusing the Americans of buying time to prepare for "crushing North Korea," Pyongyang threatened to withdraw from the Nuclear Non-Proliferation Treaty and to resume reprocessing. But it also said action would be taken only if the United States "goes ahead and reverses its promises."[34] Designed to project an image of defiance along with a willingness to pursue a diplomatic solution, the North Korean anger, observed one U.S. government analyst, was tinged with "nervousness and anxiety."

The impression left by Pyongyang's public statement was reinforced by a private—and abstruse—communication received by Gallucci from Kang Sok Ju that same day. Aside from regretting that the United States could not hold a third round of talks, in a new twist Kang said that the North's resumption of "frozen nuclear activities" would take place in phases, starting with refueling the 5-megawatt reactor. By not including withdrawal from the NPT up front, North Korea seemed to be trying to minimize adverse reactions. But the letter also was based on the false premise that the United States had canceled the third round. Some experts felt that meant the North was looking for a diplomatic way out of the budding crisis. All Washington would have to do was reaffirm its willingness to hold the meeting.

As the Clinton administration mulled over how to respond to Kang's letter, Pyongyang raised its rhetoric another notch, tempered once again with a conciliatory gesture. A February 3 article in the party newspaper went beyond the January 31 Foreign Ministry statement, hinting at a possible military confrontation and warning that Pyongyang's threats should be taken seriously. But one day later, Pyongyang media reported remarks by the North Korean ambassador to Moscow—he had played a central role in arranging inter-Korean family exchanges in the 1980s—suggesting that a peaceful resolution of the nuclear issue was still within reach. Publicizing his statement, which stood in stark contrast to the tenor of North Korea's other comments, seemed to be part of a well-calibrated campaign to signal that at least some in Pyongyang were still open to talks.[35]

North Korea's escalating rhetoric was not mere bravado. The Korean People's Army was on a heightened state of alert, normal practice for its winter training cycle that lasted from December to March. But early in 1994, the North also conducted other unusual activities that may have been related to rising tensions. Those activities gave rise to a serious concern; one scenario thought likely to start a second Korean war was for the North Koreans to roll out of their winter training exercises into a surprise attack. Moreover, in early 1994 American intelligence detected what appeared to be either two new ballistic missiles or mockups with longer range than their predecessors. The missile display may have been intended to send a defiant signal to Washington.[36]

Now, the combination of Pyongyang's escalating rhetoric and military moves set off alarm bells inside the United States intelligence community. As a member of the National Intelligence Council—the CIA's main think tank—the national intelligence officer (NIO) for warning, Charlie Allen, was responsible for watching regions where vital American interests and troops faced hostile forces. The NIO kept tabs on a list of "indicators," key measurements of the status of North Korea's military forces as well as the overall political and economic situation in that country. The indicators could be green, orange, or red, reflecting whether an activity in question was normal, a source of concern, or at a level ready for war. If enough indicators "lit up," hostilities might be imminent, prompting the NIO to issue a "warning of war." That did not mean that Pyongyang was about to attack or had even decided to go to war. It did mean North Korea had finished or was in the midst of completing steps that would make it truly ready for war.[37] If hostilities appeared imminent, the NIO would elevate a "warning of war" to a more urgent "warning of attack."

The NIO's job had become more difficult because of recent changes in the North Korean military. The forward deployment of ground forces near South Korea had been increasing for some time, reducing the warning time of any military action. Moreover, some U.S. government analysts took seriously a previous North Korean announcement that 1995 was the year the peninsula would be unified. In view of the increasing tempo and substance of Pyongyang's military exercises, as well as its five-year effort to bolster supplies, they believed the North might be getting ready for that fateful moment.[38]

The convergence of these developments triggered a debate. One school argued that it was now impossible to warn of war since such large numbers of North Korean forces were so close to the 38th parallel.[39] Others went a step further, arguing that Pyongyang was preparing for an attack when its winter training cycle ended in early 1994. Another school disagreed, countering that it was still possible to issue a warning since a number of nonmilitary indicators seemed to demonstrate that Pyongyang was in no position to launch an attack. For example, North Korea's failing economy diminished the prospects of a military strike.[40] By 1994 the debate had become divisive, prompting those who believed that warning was still possible to put their opponents on the spot. Why not issue a warning of war right away if the situation was that bad? The others backed down.[41]

Though somewhat theological, the debate was a concern for American policymakers. The "warning of war" was not supposed to signify that the United States was on the verge of hostilities, but that was precisely how it would look. Equally certain would be the early leak of such a finding to the press, inflaming an already dangerous situation. As a result, the State Department asked that senior administration officials be the first to consider any warning.

These officials had recently received an object lesson in the dangers of injecting intelligence into the political debate, always a risky business. When the intelligence community assessed in November 1993 that there was a better than even chance that North Korea had already produced one or two nuclear weapons, it shed no light but plenty of heat on the subject. The bottom line, of course, was that no one knew whether North Korea possessed nuclear weapons. But by attaching numerical values to the probability—providing what some policymakers called "precision without accuracy"—the intelligence community handed ammunition to critics of administration policy. As they saw it, administration statements that the North "cannot be allowed to have nuclear weapons" were empty rhetoric, since the intelligence community said it might have the bomb already. The net effect was to damage the administration's credibility at a time when it was trying to marshal international efforts to contain the North Korean nuclear threat.

When the warning issue was referred to the National Security Council, Poneman sought guidance from the CIA deputy director for intelligence, Doug McEachin, a blunt-speaking, straight-shooting career official whose judgment and steady temperament made him invaluable at times when others were swayed by the heat of the moment. When Poneman asked MacEachin who had the better side of the warning argument, the latter replied: "Look, the problem here is that the North Koreans are deployed so far forward that almost every indicator is lit up. They could stay that way for years or they could attack tomorrow. But actual preparations for war or an attack get lost in a sea of orange and red dots given North Korean forces massed along the DMZ." The CIA veteran concluded, "The value of the whole warning process is very limited in this circumstance."

In the end, faced by troubling indicators but also significant uncertainties, the NIO came close to issuing a "warning of war" in early 1994. If he had done so, the president could have received recommendations to authorize General Luck to prepare for a conflict that might have drawn the United States, North Korea, and South Korea into a highly volatile cycle of action and reaction. Since the allied war plan from the outset relied heavily on reinforcements from outside the theater, the Americans would have insisted on having those assets on hand, or at a minimum stationed nearby, when hostilities commenced. The North Koreans, in turn, would have been under great pressure to act before the United States could bring its military assets to bear. After all, North Korea had learned the lesson that if Washington was able to mobilize its overwhelming military power, Pyongyang's fate would be sealed.

While the "warning of war" was never issued, Gallucci—in a widely circulated memo—warned his colleagues that "the next crisis could spark an escalatory spiral that will be extremely difficult to stop because neither side will be aware of the other's motivations." Korea watchers would have been hard pressed to determine whether Pyongyang's moves were the beginning of a premeditated attack, a spasmodic response triggered by uncertainties about U.S. intentions, or a bluff designed to get a better deal in resolving the nuclear issue. To avoid that scenario, Gallucci observed, "we will need to work very closely with our Pentagon colleagues . . . to ensure that our military moves support our diplomatic objectives." The administration had dodged a bullet but it might not be so lucky next time.

We Will Respect Him the Most

With only a few weeks left before the IAEA Board of Governors met, time was running out. On February 3, Blix warned the Americans that the next week he might announce that the continuity of safeguards had been broken, returning the issue to the United Nations Security Council and triggering a significant escalation in the crisis. Subsequently, he decided to hold off until the board meeting at the end of the month, but the continuity of safeguards was hanging by a thread. Counselor Yun, the North's chief negotiator, told South Korean television that there was no possibility the two sides would iron out their differences.[42]

Meeting in Washington on February 8, the Principals Committee discussed the Patriot issue but also reaffirmed the need to restart sanctions consultations at the United Nations if the talks in Vienna collapsed. A week earlier, Secretary of Defense Perry publicly warned that the United States would soon decide whether to seek sanctions absent agreement by the time of the IAEA board meeting.[43] U.S. Ambassador to the United Nations Madeleine Albright had already begun briefings for Security Council members, all of whom believed the council should take the matter up again if necessary.[44] Only China remained silent. The prevailing mood in New York was clearly mounting anger at Pyongyang. The Spanish ambassador bluntly warned the North Koreans that they should make any concession necessary to meet IAEA requests.

But even as it prepared to take tough measures, Washington kept diplomacy alive. Responding to Kang's January 31 letter, the United States took its cue from Seoul, which wanted to do everything possible to find a solution before the upcoming board meeting. Gallucci's response denied Kang's false assertion that Washington had canceled the third round and mentioned President Clinton's commitment to building a better relationship between the two countries.

Washington and Seoul, however, remained uneasy about the difficulty of communicating with the North Koreans, either through low-level officials in New York or the exchange of letters between the two negotiators. By 1994 the Gallucci-Kang pen pal relationship seemed to be a wasting asset. In Washington, the letters tended to be homogenized through the interagency process, causing concern that they were becoming stylized exchanges rather than an effective vehicle to explore positions and possible solutions. The same seemed to be happening in Pyongyang. But the letters, along with New York channel meetings, were the only games in town. As a result, more direct communication seemed to make sense. Demonstrating that the North's leaders had rejected direct overtures from Washington would put the United States in the strongest possible position if there were a showdown in the Security Council.

Once again, an unexpected opportunity to communicate directly with the Kim Il Sung government presented itself, this time courtesy of the Reverend Billy Graham, the evangelist. While the minister and the godless communist appeared to have little in common, Kim's mother had exposed him to Christianity as a child.[45] Moreover, the Graham family had long-standing ties to Korea. Before World War II, Billy's wife Ruth—herself the daughter of missionaries in China—had gone to high school in Pyongyang, then known as the "Jerusalem of the East" because of the large number of churches there.[46]

Billy first met Kim Il Sung in 1992. Aside from preaching in Pyongyang's two churches—one Protestant, one Catholic—Graham delivered a message from President Bush.[47] An ecstatic Kim told the *Washington Times* that he felt "spring has set in between the two countries."[48] The family connection was deeper than just with Billy and his wife. Their son Ned visited Pyongyang in 1993 and also met with the Great Leader.[49]

In January 1994, before the crisis heated up, Graham notified the State Department that he would visit North Korea again at the end of the month. Concerned about events on the peninsula, the evangelist spoke to the president, who referred him to the National Security Council staff. Graham's religious mission had earned him friends in many countries. He ranked year in and year out as one of the most admired figures in the world. Continuously approached on matters that brought the spiritual and secular worlds into uneasy contact, Graham needed assistance in dealing with such matters in a way to serve his God without blundering in Caesar's world. He found it in John Akers, an amiable, soft-spoken aide, who ably represented him in a wide array of diplomatic tight spots. Beneath his genial manner, Akers was an individual of keen intelligence and judgment born of his diverse experiences.

To follow up on his conversation with the president, Graham sent Akers to meet with Tony Lake and Dan Poneman. After a briefing on the current situation, Akers asked whether it would be useful for Graham to carry a message to the reclusive North Korean leader. The idea was not entirely unprompted; the North Korean Mission in New York had urged Graham to bring such a message, hinting that a direct presidential contact could produce a North Korean concession on special inspections. There was precedent, as the evangelist had performed the same service for the last administration.

Lake was receptive to the idea, particularly since Reverend Graham's stature guaranteed that he would be able to pierce the many veils protecting Kim Il Sung and reassure the White House that the North Korean leader actually understood the situation confronting him. In order to protect Graham, the president, and the effectiveness of the message, Lake, Akers, and Poneman agreed that the fact and content would remain confidential and that it should only be delivered orally.

Graham called the president again before leaving for Asia. He spoke easily and at length, in the unhurried manner of one who had counseled presidents for decades. After expressing sympathy for the First Lady's travails over White-water, Graham turned to North Korea. The president thanked Graham for carrying the message and wished him a successful journey.

Before departing for Pyongyang from Beijing, Graham was visited on January 27 by the American ambassador to China, Stapleton Roy. The ambassador handed over the president's oral message to be delivered to Kim Il Sung. It expressed Clinton's hope that, as the United States and North Korea entered the New Year, the two countries could make rapid progress in resolving the nuclear issue. That would permit a better bilateral relationship. The message seemed fairly mundane, but American officials felt its significance lay not so much in the content as in the mere fact that Clinton would communicate with the North Korean leader.

Two days later, the North Korean leader warmly received Graham and took his visitor off to the side for a private discussion. The conversation was lengthy and seemed to tire both men. Graham's interpreter, Dr. Stephen Linton, had to repeat and explain Graham's words several times to be sure they were understood. Afterward, sitting down for a long, leisurely lunch, Kim Il Sung asked the evangelist to say grace before the meal, bellowing out "amen" when Graham was done. At first, Graham reminisced about Ruth's days as a student in Pyongyang but then turned to the nuclear question, handing Kim his own letter, which expressed the fervent hope for a peaceful resolution to the crisis.

Without telling the White House, Graham had included the "oral message" from the president in the text of his own letter to avoid any misunderstanding of the president's words, but also to elaborate on Clinton's positive yet terse statement in his own far more conciliatory tone. Knowing how eager Kim was for a summit meeting with Clinton, Graham volunteered his personal view that, if the nuclear crisis were successfully resolved, a meeting might be possible.

In fact, for the Great Leader, securing a meeting with the president of the United States would be akin to finding the holy grail of international politics. He had attempted, unsuccessfully through intermediaries, to set up summits with Presidents Richard Nixon and Jimmy Carter. With the fall of the Soviet Union and the emergence of the United States as the world's sole superpower, a summit with Washington probably became even more attractive. It would signal to the international community that the United States had accepted North Korea. Then other countries, particularly Washington's allies in Seoul and Tokyo, could be expected to fall in line. As for the United States, holding a summit with the man who started the Korean War seemed out of the question. President Carter had raised the idea of meeting Kim Il Sung and the South Korean president in the DMZ. But his brainstorm was scotched in the face of vehement opposition from his own advisers.

The North Korean leader responded at length to Graham, becoming agitated at times, but signaling his own wish to meet President Clinton. After assuring the American evangelist that North Korea did not want to acquire nuclear weapons and promising never to do so, Kim Il Sung plaintively asked why the United States listened to the IAEA and not to North Korea. He urged the Americans to "trust us." As the two men talked, North Korean officials hovered outside the door, hoping to hear the details of their conversation, perhaps so they could report to their superiors afterward.

Returning to the summit proposal, Kim Il Sung asked Graham to play the role of "go-between" between the North Korean and U.S. leaders, since he was close to both men. As an incentive, he would be prepared to sign a document at a summit pledging never to produce nuclear weapons. Lamenting that the cold war was over everywhere except on the Korean Peninsula, the aging North Korean dictator promised that if Clinton helped resolve the nuclear crisis, "we will respect him the most."[50]

Speaking to a Hong Kong press conference after leaving Pyongyang, Graham revealed that he had a confidential message for President Clinton that would be delivered by an associate to the White House. The next day, Akers arrived in Washington, reported on Kim Il Sung's remarks to Lake, and offered his view that the aging North Korean leader seemed eager to show his continued command of the situation and also to resolve the nuclear issue "before he dropped from the twig."[51] In an Oval Office meeting afterward, Lake and Poneman told Clinton that Kim's remarks could be a familiar effort to provide assurances outside the NPT and IAEA safeguards, or they could represent an opening to test whether a negotiated solution was possible. Clinton decided to test whether the Great Leader was serious or not.

To do that, the administration turned to a second unofficial envoy, Ronald Dellums, a longtime member of the House from California who had become chairman of the House Armed Services Committee after Les Aspin moved to the Pentagon. He had planned to go to North Korea at the end of 1993 but abruptly canceled the trip. While President Kim Young Sam believed Graham's approach had been too conciliatory and opposed sending a senior American official, he was comfortable with Dellums going to Pyongyang. Other South Koreans officials, however, felt that the California member of Congress was not the right person since he had no experience dealing with Koreans or the nuclear issue.

At the State Department, Gallucci and Winston Lord, the assistant secretary in charge of Asia and a former ambassador to China, sketched out a possible response to the Great Leader in a memorandum to Secretary Warren Christopher entitled "Mr. Dellums Goes to Pyongyang." The message would reassure North Korea that the United States did not intend to "strangle it," and that Washington preferred a diplomatic solution provided that IAEA safe-guards were part of a solution. Breaking the continuity of safeguards, however, would end the prospects for future dialogue. As for Kim Il Sung's summit suggestion, such a meeting would be possible after a diplomatic solution was implemented and better relations between the two countries were established.

The Principals Committee approved the Dellums mission on February 8, the same day it gave the go-ahead to the Patriot deployment. The hope was that a clear expression of American policy conveyed by Dellums might persuade North Korea to cut a deal with the IAEA before the impending Board of Governors meeting. As for a summit between President Clinton and Kim Il Sung, he was to tell the North Korean leader that it might be possible but not without major progress, beginning with the successful resolution of the nuclear crisis. The same message would also be double-tracked through the New York channel to help ensure that there were no mistakes.

For the next twenty-four hours, Gallucci, Lake, and Poneman struggled over the language of the message Dellums would convey. The approach followed the script in the Gallucci-Lord memo to Christopher. But the key issue was how far forward to lean regarding the possibility of a summit. Should the hint of such a meeting be framed as "yes if" or "not unless" certain conditions were met? As the fine-tuning continued, Dellums's office, prompted by the administration, contacted the North Korean Mission to the United Nations and requested a visit.[52]

Just as suddenly as tensions had mounted over the previous month, they subsided. After five days of silence from the North Koreans, Kang wrote Gallucci on February 12 that the Great Leader was committed to resolving the nuclear issue through dialogue. Kang stated that the IAEA had backed away from its demands and therefore Pyongyang was willing to talk again to the agency. The reference to Kim Il Sung was significant, perhaps as a hint that, at his direct order, the North Koreans had declared the IAEA had backed down. In fact, it had not. But the declaration cleared the way for Pyongyang to resume talks. That same day, a Foreign Ministry statement also signaled a willingness to stand down from confrontation.[53]

On February 15, Counselor Yun Ho Jin visited IAEA headquarters to inform Perricos that all of the agency's inspection requirements had been accepted. "We are satisfied with the outcome," the North Korean told waiting reporters.[54] IAEA spokesman David Kyd said: "There was no explanation. They simply agreed to all the measures."[55]

Why did Pyongyang provoke a crisis and then reverse direction? Even the Chinese were unsure whether the events of February were a setback or just the latest in a series of twists and turns. North Korea may have provoked a crisis to squeeze concessions out of the United States and the IAEA or for some other unknown purpose. Pyongyang may have backed down when it became clear that Washington would not, because of implicit American threats to return to the Security Council, or for fear that the United States might take military action. Kang's letter followed closely on the heels of the February 6 press leak on the details of the American war plan, which may have been sobering. In any case, the North declared victory and moved on. Hard-line statements, in the words of one South Korean official, provided "covering fire to guard their retreat."

A more intriguing explanation has to do with Billy Graham's visit. Since late 1993, there had been growing speculation that Kim Il Sung was unhappy with his son's handling of the nuclear crisis. As a result, he had once again become actively involved in day-to-day management of the issue. This was the view of Chinese officials, but the North Korean leader also gave the same impression to foreign visitors, including Graham. Moreover, North Korea watchers noted that Kim Jong Il, who normally gave "on-the-spot guidance" four to five times a year, had not given any in 1993. In contrast, his father had made numerous pronouncements.[56]

Reinforcing this speculation were rumors that Kim Jong Il was sick or injured. The younger Kim was alleged to have hurt himself in a fall from a horse the previous year. His failure to appear at the February 15 celebration of his birthday rekindled speculation. (In fact, he never appeared at these celebrations.) Lee Ki Taek, the South Korean opposition leader, told reporters that Kim Jong Il had indeed sustained critical injuries. North Korea publicly denied the rumors, and Lee's spokesman later told reporters his comments were "sort of a joke."[57] Nevertheless, Pyongyang was concerned enough to invite a senior official in the Chosen Soren, the organization of North Korean sympathizers in Japan, to meet the younger Kim. The official spent two hours with the Dear Leader and later reported that he looked "very well." To demonstrate his health, Kim even rode a white horse alongside his Japanese visitor's car as he left.[58]

If Kim Il Sung had assumed a more prominent role in policymaking, then Graham's intervention was well timed. Even though Washington did not have a chance to respond to Kim Il Sung's summit proposal, the North Korean leader may have decided to continue down the diplomatic track while awaiting that response. The fact that Kim was cited in Kang's February 12 message to Gallucci as the authority for the North's sudden change of direction could be interpreted as a sign that he was more engaged, perhaps as a result of his meeting with Graham.

With the end of the immediate crisis, the Americans put the North Korean summit proposal on the back burner. Three days after the February 12 message, Hubbard told Ho Jong that President Clinton was committed to resolving the nuclear issue through dialogue. But he made no mention of Kim Il Sung's proposal for a summit. Hubbard suggested he and Ho should start meeting to discuss implementing the December 29 arrangement now that agreement had been reached in Vienna.

Super Tuesday

After North Korea had accepted the IAEA's terms, talks resumed in the New York channel to nail down the small package and clear the way for the next Gallucci-Kang meeting. Optimism, however, quickly gave way to concern. The day after the February 15 agreement, the North Koreans sudden shifted gears once again, telling Blix that the IAEA's inspection would not happen until after Washington agreed to the small package. And even then they might not go through with the inspection, unless the IAEA dropped the nuclear issue from the agenda of the upcoming Board of Governors' meeting.[59]

Pyongyang's continued refusal to exchange special envoys with South Korea before the Gallucci-Kang talks presented an even more serious problem. On February 21, Pyongyang publicly signaled that an "early inspection" by the IAEA would be realized once Washington announced cancellation of Team Spirit and the date for the third round of talks. The North Koreans said they had agreed in December to "affirmatively examine" any South Korean proposal for exchanging envoys. But the statement made no mention of timing, the crux of the whole matter.[60]

Seoul wanted to hold the third round as much as Washington did, but the South Koreans remained adamant about timing. The February 15 agreement had been received in Seoul with relief bordering on jubilation. As a result, the South Korean government considered sidestepping the envoy exchange on the eve of Hubbard's renewed talks in New York. But President Kim and others still clung to the idea that the exchange had to happen before the third round, if only to demonstrate that Seoul was not playing second fiddle to Washington. The government would pare its demands in hopes of securing a quick agreement but was so fixated on the timing of the exchange that, according to one Korean official, it had no idea what to do in the meeting if the North actually agreed to it.[61]

Under these circumstances, Washington had to figure out how much the traffic would bear in three key capitals: Pyongyang, Seoul, and Vienna. As expected, at the first New York meeting held on February 22, timing quickly emerged as the main problem. Ho Jong claimed that holding the envoy exchange first would give the South veto power over U.S.–North Korean talks and could jeopardize the North's willingness to implement the IAEA inspections. The next day, the North Koreans told the press, "We oppose the United States intention to make the issue [the envoy exchange] a precondition for the third round of talks."[62]

As the New York talks resumed, thousands of miles away in Vienna, the IAEA Board of Governors was convening. To avoid creating complications in New York, American diplomats in Vienna had to play for time. First, they succeeded in delaying discussion of the nuclear issue by the IAEA Board of Governors for a few days, until February 23. Then, when it became apparent that agreement would not be reached in time in New York, the board approved an American proposal to buy even more time by convening a special session at the end of the month if the New York talks failed.[63]

Hours after the first session of the special IAEA board meeting ended on February 25, the Americans and North Koreans wrapped up what had been a frustrating week in New York that failed to bridge the gap between their positions on the timing of the envoy exchange. The American team rushed to the airport in the evening to catch one of the last shuttle flights to Washington, only to return the next day after Ho Jong called to say he had received new instructions from Pyongyang. But Ho still would not budge.

Faced with a possible deadlock in the talks and concerned about the wild card of the special IAEA board meeting, Hubbard proposed a diplomatic sleight of hand. The United States would agree to make a unilateral statement asserting that the third round and the cancellation of Team Spirit were "based on the premise" that the envoy exchange would take place beforehand. Ho was delighted since North Korea would not have to explicitly commit itself on the timing issue.[64] After tracking down members of the Deputies Committee and nailing down Seoul's support, Hubbard and Ho announced the agreement around midnight. The new "Super Tuesday" package had greater specificity that built on the December arrangement but still did not resolve all of the key issues.

The February deal required four simultaneous steps to take place on March 1. North Korea would allow the IAEA to complete its inspection. It would also begin working-level meetings with Seoul to arrange the eventual exchange of special envoys. Washington and Pyongyang would announce that the third round would start on March 21. Finally, Seoul would announce the suspension of Team Spirit, and Washington would second the motion. Each side also attached unilateral statements to the agreement making it clear that agreement on the envoy exchange had not been reached. Neither side released the unilateral statements to the public.[65]

Why did the United States and North Korea acquiesce in a deal absent resolution of the envoy exchange issue? Viewed from Washington, after seven long months without inspection Super Tuesday secured its most important objective: getting IAEA inspectors back into North Korea. Otherwise it seemed likely that the agency would have had to take further action at the next Board of Governors meeting, including declaring the continuity of safeguards broken. Given this situation, the United States was willing to move forward with Super Tuesday even without agreement on the timing of the special envoy exchange. If the envoy exchange did not occur, or the inspection were not completed, or if the inspection did not proceed satisfactorily, or if IAEA found out the North was conducting suspicious activities, Washington could cancel the planned Gallucci-Kang session.

Pyongyang probably believed that the Super Tuesday agreement worked to its advantage. Knowing the importance the IAEA inspections held for the Americans, the North Koreans may have yielded on that point while refusing to agree on the envoy exchange. Hence they could focus on the IAEA channel in an effort to marginalize Seoul, soften it up for the eventual working-level talks, and exploit potential tensions between the two allies over the Patriot deployment. Pyongyang may have believed that accepting an imperfect New York agreement hinging on the IAEA inspections would enhance its ability to do all of these things and at the same time keep hope alive for stopping Team Spirit and holding a third round with Gallucci.

Whatever Washington's calculations and Pyongyang's motivations, Seoul felt its interests had been neglected. While the government's public pronouncements were positive, Foreign Minister Han Sung Joo cryptically hinted there were problems with some of the details. Privately, an acutely sensitive President Kim remained concerned about both Pyongyang's efforts to marginalize Seoul and domestic criticism that the United States was deciding an issue fundamental to South Korean security. He urged the Americans to continue to stress the importance of North-South dialogue.

To put his country front and center, the South Korean leader swallowed hard and cooked up his own surprise. In a stunning about-face, President Kim announced on February 25 that he was now willing to meet the Great Leader at a summit provided the nuclear issue was discussed. The initiative, which came as a surprise to the Americans, helped the South Korean recover some lost ground with the public, although one Korean newspaper criticized the government for looking like a "groomsman."[66] The North Koreans ridiculed the proposal, calling Kim a "traitor," a "puppet," and a "political mountebank."[67]

On March 1, the Super Tuesday initiative lurched forward, but faltered. The IAEA inspectors had arrived in Pyongyang that morning, Seoul's announcement that Team Spirit would be suspended was ready to go, and the South had also notified the North it was willing to resume working-level talks that day.

The North, however, suddenly deviated from the script and countered with a proposal for a March 3 North-South meeting, a clear effort to score political points and to emphasize its reluctance to deal with anyone except Washington. Finally, on March 3, Super Tuesday was announced.[68] Kang, in a tough press statement, warned that, contrary to assertions from Washington and Seoul, there were no preconditions in the New York agreement requiring an envoy exchange. He did not, however, rule out such an exchange.[69] Reacting to the statement, the South Korean Foreign Ministry said, "We don't feel the need to say anything about it. We have to wait and see."[70]

Safeguards or Dismantlement First?

The administration had been working for months on a comprehensive strategy for the third round. Despite President Kim's theatrics in the Oval Office during his late November visit to Washington, the change in labeling to "broad and thorough" had no effect on substance. As Washington and Pyongyang moved slowly back onto the path toward another Gallucci-Kang meeting—first through the December New York arrangement, then the February agreement with the IAEA, and finally with Super Tuesday—that work became increasingly urgent.

Formulating a comprehensive approach was a complicated task. The nuclear issue remained the top priority, but such an approach also required moving toward the normalization of bilateral relations by addressing additional nonnuclear demands and by throwing into the mix new nonnuclear incentives. Those demands would focus on Pyongyang's export of ballistic missiles, threatening conventional military forces, large chemical and biological weapons stockpiles, and its deplorable human rights practices. Candidates for incentives included lifting economic sanctions that had been in place since the Korean War, establishing diplomatic relations with Pyongyang and, the biggest wild card of all, providing energy assistance to North Korea. Stitching together a package of nuclear and nonnuclear demands that would be implemented over time required a detailed road map with simultaneous steps to be taken by each side.

By early 1994, an interagency working group of representatives from the State Department, the NSC, the Office of the Secretary of Defense, Joint Chiefs of Staff, the Arms Control and Disarmament Agency (ACDA), and the intelligence community had made progress. The slow, painstaking process involved iteration after iteration as the working group pored over the evolving road map. Two competing options emerged from the deliberations.

The State Department wanted to protect the nonproliferation regime and determine what North Korea had done in the past. For the "safeguards-firsters," the top priorities were that Pyongyang rejoin the NPT and implement nuclear safeguards, including special inspections, up front. In return, the United States would try to address North Korean concerns about the American nuclear threat but also begin a careful process of normalization by establishing diplomatic relations and beginning to lift some economic sanctions. Positive steps would be rewarded; if Pyongyang implemented the North-South denuclearization agreement, dismantled its existing reactor program, or stopped its missile sales, the United States would take more far-reaching steps. These included providing assistance in building light-water reactors, establishing full diplomatic relations, lifting more sanctions, and signing a peace treaty.

The Defense Department's main concern was the stuff of bombs. The "dismantlement-firsters" viewed stopping the threat of more plutonium production for more nuclear weapons as a higher priority than bolstering the nonproliferation regime. They knew that safeguards would not stop that growth since obtaining plutonium could be defended as consistent with activities permitted under the NPT. Instead, dismantlement-firsters focused on freezing and dismantling key nuclear facilities—particularly the reactors and plutonium reprocessing plant—up front. Special inspections were a secondary concern and could be deferred without the risk of adding to North Korea's plutonium stash.

Unlike State, the Defense Department was perfectly willing to pay "more" for "more." Defense was inclined to offer greater incentives sooner, for example, taking North Korean statements about light-water reactors at face value and providing large-scale energy assistance up front. The State Department was not so sure; if the North's demand for new reactors reflected a real desire to improve relations with Washington, it might be accomplished by other means, such as closer political and economic ties. In short, new reactors might be unnecessary. State wanted to offer the North an energy survey, for example, conducted by the International Energy Agency, to determine its electricity needs. (The Paris-based International Energy Agency was established in response to the 1973 oil crisis to encourage cooperation in the development of rational energy programs by its member states.) Then the United States and its allies could consider building an electric grid to help improve power distribution, followed by a power generation project most likely involving non-nuclear energy sources.

The bureaucratic differences also extended to the form of an agreement. The State Department wanted to reach two arrangements, a framework agreement that would lay out the principles of a solution and a more detailed implementing document that would spell out the sequencing of each side's steps. Such an approach had been used to resolve diplomatic problems in the past. The Defense Department thought this approach might be too hard to negotiate. It advocated a unilateral statement of principles by the United States at the beginning of the talks that would go well beyond the nuclear issue, including Washington's desire for a peace treaty, normalization of relations as well as implementation of confidence building measures, and other non-nuclear issues.

Forging a negotiating position was also a multilateral task; it required an understanding of views in Tokyo and Seoul and an ability to cope with differences between the trilateral partners that resulted from them. For example, although South Korea was comfortable with a "safeguards-first" approach, it was in disarray about how far and how fast Washington should go in establishing diplomatic relations with Pyongyang. Foreign Minister Han wanted to use diplomatic relations as an added inducement and worked to establish a consensus in Seoul supporting this position. After all, the idea of cross-recognition of the two Koreas by the United States, China, Russia, and Japan had been an important component of former president Roh Tae Woo's "Nord-politik."[71] But Han's approach angered President Kim, who did not want to be nearly as forthcoming. The issue of normalization continued to be a potential flash point in South Korea and with the United States.[72]

As the March 21 starting date for the third round drew closer, bureaucratic differences in Washington began to narrow. At a Principals Committee meeting on February 23, consensus quickly emerged that the only viable path would be negotiating a framework, pacing key performance milestones along the way, and enabling each side to monitor the other's performance before going further down the road. While the principals harbored no illusions that Pyongyang would punctiliously observe the letter and spirit of a negotiated agreement, they understood that North Korean behavior unconstrained by a written agreement would likely be even more adverse to American interests.

The same Principals Committee meeting also took an important step toward resolving the debate between safeguards-firsters and dismantlement-firsters. All present accepted the political necessity that Pyongyang would need at least to commit itself to accepting special inspections up front, even if their conduct could be deferred, to justify any grant of significant benefits to the North in the first phase of a settlement. This required a concession from the dismantlement-first crowd, who saw no purpose in making special inspections a negotiating priority.

Safeguards-firsters, however, were also beginning to rethink their position. Gallucci, a member of that camp as a State Department official, felt decision-makers in Washington had not really confronted the consequences of their actions, a concern shared by American officials in Seoul. General Luck later observed: "The Yogi Berra rule was in effect back in Washington. Many people thought when you came to a fork in the road, you should take it."[73]

In a blunt March 9 memo to the deputies, Gallucci pointed out that insisting on special inspections up front might bolster domestic and international support, but it could also force the United States to choose between a nuclear North Korea and a second Korean War. Most American analysts thought Pyongyang would not accept special inspections up front. Some believed it would never accept them. If the United States became fixated on this demand, the talks could break down, and a mild sanctions resolution might follow. North Korea would then retaliate by not accepting IAEA inspections, discharging the spent fuel from its reactors, and beginning reprocessing, separating enough plutonium for about five nuclear weapons. The United States would then have to attack Yongbyon before the reprocessing was completed to prevent the plutonium from being moved to an unknown site where it might be used to manufacture nuclear weapons. At best, North Korean retaliation would be limited. At worst, such a strike would trigger an all-out war.

Gallucci concluded that Washington should reconsider its negotiating strategy. While defending a failure to address special inspections immediately could prove difficult, it might be preferable to delay that objective in order to focus on more pressing problems. He argued that if the principals agreed to this approach, Washington should tone down its rhetoric making special inspections the standard for success. If not, then it needed to plan now to deal with this potentially catastrophic chain of events.

Staking out this position placed Gallucci on a collision course with his boss, Under Secretary of State Lynn Davis, an expert on security issues who had held positions at the NSC and the International Institute for Strategic Studies, and had served as a deputy assistant secretary of defense during the Carter administration. She argued that if the administration brought home an agreement without special inspections up front, the criticism would be overwhelming.[74] Only a week before the Gallucci memo, Davis had appeared in front of the Senate Foreign Relations Committee where members from both parties complained that none of the recent commitments by North Korea provided access to the two suspected sites.[75] Gallucci recognized this problem but believed neither domestic politics nor the congressional concerns about uncovering the past should determine policy in light of the potential dangers ahead.

His view prevailed. On March 16, the Principals Committee agreed that the United States should seek to implement special inspections immediately, but would be prepared to fall back to some compromise position. Secretary Perry hinted at a shift in the American approach when he told reporters, "We don't know anything we can do about already built nuclear weapons," but added, "what we can do something about, though . . . is stopping them from building beyond that."[76] This hint, however, soon became swamped by dramatic developments, calling into question whether the third round would be held at all.

The Little Tugboat That Couldn't

Gallucci arrived at Kimpo Airport, just outside Seoul, on March 11. The increased tension could be measured by the press attention. He was invariably met by a horde of reporters. Danny Russel, the U.S. Embassy officer who took part in the Geneva talks and a black belt in *aikido,* was responsible for clearing a path through the waiting throng without precipitating a riot. On one occasion, a reporter running backwards to keep focused on Gallucci raced by mistake straight into a concrete pillar, the first casualty of the North Korean nuclear crisis.[77]

The press problem continued even as the Americans went about their business of meeting with South Korean officials. The standard practice was to give the reporters a photo opportunity. Government officials would open the doors; a stampede of photographers would surge into the room, motor-driven shutters whirring and flashes popping. After about 30 seconds, South Korean officials would shoo the first group out and usher the next one in. Occasionally, this slapstick-like scene was repeated yet a third time, to the amusement of both American and Korean officials, who had no choice but to engage in small talk until the press left the room.[78]

While Gallucci's original objective had been to consult on third-round strategy, ensuring implementation of Super Tuesday had become a more pressing problem. Meeting with a group of South Korean officials the day after arriving, he compared the United States to a tugboat that had to keep pushing two barges—the IAEA and South Korea—toward North Korea in order to make progress. The analogy seemed especially appropriate given the events of the past few weeks.

The air pockets buffeting implementation of Super Tuesday had become more violent. North Korea refused to allow the IAEA inspection team at Yongbyon to take samples and smears or to conduct gamma mapping at the reprocessing plant, the last remaining items agreed to in the February 15 arrangement. To add insult to injury, the North Koreans requested a $300,000 payment before allowing them to take samples at another facility, a demand that was later dropped after IAEA headquarters complained about the "unprecedented charges."[79] Downplaying the problems, IAEA spokesman Hans Meyer claimed, "There is never an inspection where you don't have an argument."[80]

The day Gallucci arrived in Seoul another deadlock had been reached. The problem of sampling at the reprocessing plant had been resolved, but the North Koreans still refused to allow the inspectors to take swipes from the glove box area of the plutonium production line, where seals had been found broken during earlier visits. That entailed wiping surfaces with a clean cloth to detect minute traces of plutonium, which was isolated and handled through rubber gloves in Plexiglas boxes since its particles were toxic if inhaled. Pyongyang claimed that since previous samples from those locations had led to the IAEA assertion that the North's plutonium production declaration was wrong, the agency's demand would have to be discussed with the United States. As delay piled on delay, the chances of finishing the inspection by March 15—the agreed completion date—diminished.[81]

In spite of their mounting problems, the IAEA inspectors made an important but disturbing discovery; North Korea had made surprising progress in completing a second reprocessing line. When finished, the line would double Pyongyang's ability to separate plutonium from the irradiated fuel rods that could be produced by two new reactors under construction. This unsafeguarded production line undermined confidence in North Korea's self-restraint regarding plutonium reprocessing and also smacked of a ploy to build up negotiating leverage. But it also meant that Pyongyang might ramp up its nuclear weapons program rapidly if diplomacy failed.[82]

At Panmunjom, where inter-Korean meetings had resumed on March 3, the situation was also touch-and-go. Determined to make progress, the South tabled a detailed procedural proposal for the envoy exchange that was nearly identical to Pyongyang's position. But North Korean negotiator Pak Yong Su raised the ante: in addition to two old preconditions for agreement—the South had to stop all nuclear exercises and renounce multilateral efforts to secure sanctions—he added two new ones. Pak demanded that Seoul should call off Patriot deployments and withdraw President Kim's 1993 remarks that he would never shake hands with a partner who had nuclear weapons.[83] Hopes in the Blue House for progress quickly turned into disappointment.

At the next Panmunjom session, in spite of heated discussion, there was some forward movement, mainly on procedural issues. Fireworks erupted when Song Young Dae, the South Korean negotiator, insisted that Kim Il Sung retract his recent speech vilifying President Kim Young Sam. While Pak continued to insist that Song meet his four conditions, he tried to coax the South Korean forward. According to the North Korean, instead of a written agreement, Song could simply announce that Seoul was deferring the Patriot deployments. If he did, then remaining differences could be resolved. Song, however, did not take the bait.[84]

The North Korean tactic was obvious: to use the four conditions to control the pace of the talks. They could negotiate over them to delay progress, simplify them when convenient, or never drop them at all. Some South Koreans thought the objective was to hold the special envoy exchange after March 21, the starting date for U.S.–North Korea talks, rendering that deadline useless. Others thought the North did not want to hold the exchange at all. While Song said publicly there had been "no progress," Pyongyang had started to temper its personal attacks on President Kim, a sign that an eventual compromise might be possible.[85]

On March 12, the North Korean delegation adopted what appeared to be a more flexible position, which included dropping the demand that President Kim Young Sam retract his remarks. Agreement was reached on almost all procedural issues. Pyongyang also suggested the quick completion of a communiqué stating that both Koreas would exchange envoys "at an early date."[86] While a step in the right direction, the North Korean formulation still fell short of the U.S.–South Korean position that the envoy exchange had to occur before the third round.

Pyongyang's move was no surprise. Two days earlier, Kang had sent Gallucci a private message telling him that his government would do all it could to reach agreement on the envoy exchange by March 21. But the exchange itself might not take place until April after the third round. Tempering his flexibility with a threat, Kang warned that if Washington continued to insist on the exchange prior to the third round, Pyongyang would neither honor the Super Tuesday agreement nor finish the IAEA inspection. North Korea was drawing its own red line.

As events were coming to a head in Panmunjom, Gallucci was meeting with President Kim Young Sam at the Blue House. The vast, high-ceilinged audience room, paneled in gleaming wood, conveyed a sense of grandeur and prosperity. It was furnished with huge, comfortable armchairs so far apart that visitors had to speak loudly to be heard. The distance also made it impossible for guests to whisper or pass notes to each other. At one session with the president, an American official fell asleep after a long trip across the Pacific and was snoring audibly. But he was so far away from the other Americans that it was impossible to rouse him. The thought of bouncing a pen off their sleeping colleague occurred to more than one member of the U.S. delegation.

The exchange was fairly typical. President Kim complained at length that he was willing to meet Kim Il Sung but the North Koreans spent hours every day personally attacking him. When Kim pointed out that "there could be no solution to the nuclear crisis without North-South dialogue," Gallucci agreed. Both stipulated that if those talks failed, Patriot should be deployed and Team Spirit should also go ahead.

But the picture of allied harmony was not entirely unblemished. The South Korean leader ended on a note that foreshadowed tension between Washington and Seoul in the months ahead: "Time is on our side so we don't need to rush. The North's nuclear card is losing force." For the United States, the opposite was true. If the nuclear threat could not be headed off soon by diplomacy, the use of force might become the only effective option.

At noon, Foreign Minister Han Sung Joo hosted the Americans to a fine lunch atop one of Seoul's best hotels. Ironic toasts were raised to note the first anniversary of the crisis as North Korea had announced its intention to withdraw from the NPT the same day one year earlier. Messengers frequently interrupted the meal, bringing in the latest reports on progress at the North-South talks being held at Panmunjom. But the date for the envoy exchange still remained a problem.[87]

The United States and South Korea had reached a critical moment. In deference to Seoul, Washington had insisted for months on holding the exchange before the third round. But now it had to weigh the possibility that, unless the timing were delayed, North Korea would not complete the inspection and would thereby scuttle the third round. If Washington could smooth the way for the completion of the inspection, it would then be in a stronger position to insist on the envoy exchange to get to a third round. The administration, however, also wanted to avoid damaging its relationship with South Korea.

There was an obvious compromise. Rather than hold the exchange before or after the third round, why not hold it simultaneously? Moreover, because of the time difference between Geneva and Korea—Korea was eight hours ahead of Geneva—the exchange could actually begin before the third round. That seemed like an elegant solution to the Americans. It avoided the appearance of Seoul taking a back seat to Washington and also might satisfy Pyongyang's demands that the exchange not take place before the third round. Furthermore, the South Koreans were well aware of the idea. It had been raised informally with them at a "brainstorming session" during Foreign Minister Han's visit to Washington in late February.

Gallucci's presence in Seoul presented the perfect opportunity to press for simultaneity. Initially, the South Koreans told him simultaneity would make them look like an appendage to the U.S.–North Korean talks. But then, as reports of progress by the IAEA inspectors and the successful North-South meeting came in, the South Koreans seemed flexible. Gallucci quickly cabled Washington, recommending that it try to lock in simultaneity by making the proposal in his reply to Kang's last letter. In the event, Gallucci's March 12 reply said nothing about simultaneity, since Seoul and Washington had not yet reached final agreement inside their governments or with each other. Instead, it assured Kang that progress in North-South contacts opened the way for an exchange before the third round.

From that point on, the situation rapidly deteriorated. On March 14, the agency withdrew its team from North Korea, not just because the inspectors had been hamstrung, but also because the IAEA felt the need to defend its institutional integrity. Angry IAEA officials blamed North Korea's "flimsy, small town lawyer's tricks" for the breakdown. Nearly lost in the rancorous departure was the significant news that the inspectors left believing that no reprocessing had taken place since their last visit in August 1993.[88] Vienna wasted no time; the day after the team left North Korea, agency officials began preparations for a special session of the Board of Governors on March 21 to consider the failed inspection.

With the inspection derailed, Washington tried one last time to secure Seoul's agreement to the simultaneous exchange of envoys. Pyongyang might then allow the inspection to be completed. The South Koreans, focused on the tactics of the diplomatic minuet, agreed to propose a meeting for one day before the third round—good enough in view of the time difference between Geneva and the Korean peninsula—but only if the North Koreans proposed simultaneity. The issue, however, never came up at the next North-South meeting on March 16. Instead, Pak threatened to re-impose the conditions he had withdrawn at the previous session.[89] While another meeting was set for March 19, the South Koreans told Laney afterward that Pyongyang was not in a "deal-making mode."

As prospects for Super Tuesday began to disintegrate and the March 21 IAEA meeting approached, tensions mounted. Just before the inspectors left North Korea, Kang sent Gallucci an ultimatum. Not only would the envoy exchange have to take place after the third round, but if Washington evaded its obligations—canceling Team Spirit and holding the U.S.–North Korean talks—Pyongyang would back out of the North-South meetings and suspend all cooperation with the IAEA and United States. Gallucci had three days to respond.

In no mood to be conciliatory, the administration staked out an equally tough stance. Meeting after the failed March 16 North-South session, the principals decided to lay down some tough markers, particularly that

Pyongyang would still have to complete the inspection and the exchange of envoys before March 21—the date for the third round—and not interfere with the continuity of safeguards. Otherwise, the session would be canceled and Team Spirit might be rescheduled. Publicly, Secretary Christopher warned that other options at the United Nations would be pursued if North Korea continued its stance.[90] Secretary Perry denied that the United States was beefing up naval deployments near Korea. But he also added, "If there was an imminent risk of military activities taking place, we would make use of those warships."[91]

With front-channel diplomacy on the verge of collapse, both the United States and South Korea turned to back-channel contacts. The White House once again contacted Billy Graham. Tony Lake, supported by other senior officials and after consulting his South Korean counterpart, now felt the time might be right to respond to Kim Il Sung's February summit trial balloon.

President Clinton called the evangelist on March 18, the day before the next North-South meeting. "I need your help on Korea," Clinton began. Referring to Graham's earlier efforts, the president added, "I think you did some good." He quickly brought Graham up to date on the diplomatic effort that now stood on the brink of failure. "It would be tragic if we missed this opportunity. Would you be willing to convey a short oral message to Kim Il Sung on the phone?" Graham agreed to help. The president offered to have Poneman send the evangelist suggested points to make with the Great Leader that could "maybe help avoid a train wreck."

But Graham had trouble piercing the veil around the Great Leader. He tried to reach Kim by telephone and also sent a letter to him via the New York channel. Warning that the nuclear issue would be referred to the United Nations and no one could predict what would happen there, the letter said the United States preferred a negotiated solution and better relations with Pyongyang. Moreover, President Clinton thought high-level meetings would then be possible. Graham said he, too, believed a summit could happen. "This could be your finest hour," the evangelist wrote in his letter. But no response came.

Unknown to the Americans, Seoul had also been trying, with the help of the Chinese, to set up secret meetings with North Korea. Some Americans suspected they might even be attempting to arrange a surprise summit since President Kim was slated to visit China at the end of March. Moreover, his ambassador to Beijing had handled the secret negotiations that led to the merger of Kim's opposition party with the ruling party in 1990. Foreign Minister Han disclosed the secret North-South contacts to Jim Laney, and then mentioned them in a letter to Secretary Christopher on March 17. The

Americans found these contacts disturbing. Seoul had not kept Washington fully informed and had engaged in these back-channel communications while sensitive front-channel talks were under way.

Exactly why both back-channel efforts failed to elicit a North Korean response remained unclear, but the March 19 North-South session put the final nail in Super Tuesday's coffin. Neither Washington nor Seoul was optimistic, but the meeting exceeded even the most pessimistic expectations, rupturing after only fifty-five minutes. Pak remarked to his South Korean counterpart: "Mr. Song, your side has to deeply consider the dear price of war. Seoul is not far from here. If war breaks out, it will be a sea of fire. Mr. Song, it will probably be difficult for you to survive." With that, the session abruptly ended, and the North Korean left without shaking hands.[92]

The lurid "sea of fire" imagery stunned everyone. With all hope of progress gone, the Kim government moved quickly to use Pak's threat to its political advantage. Like all meetings at the South's Peace House at the DMZ, this one was transmitted live via closed-circuit television to various ministries, including the National Unification Board and the Blue House. President Kim decided to leak the videotape to South Korean television in an effort to influence public opinion and to put the North on the defensive.[93] That same day, the public saw the unedited version, including Pak's threat, on the evening news.[94]

The collapse of North-South negotiations killed the Super Tuesday accord and the third round of U.S.–North Korean talks. But for the United States, the effort was not a total loss. The IAEA inspectors, making their first visit to Yongbyon since August 1993, provided valuable information that there had been no recent reprocessing, but that the second reprocessing line was closer to completion than anticipated. In return, the United States yielded little. Also, the collapse further strengthened American support in the international community. While Radio Pyongyang had tried to place the onus on the South, the failure of diplomacy was widely viewed as North Korea's fault, bolstering America's position at the United Nations.[95]

The collapse also ended the simmering dispute between Washington and Seoul over Patriot. Since Foreign Minister Han's visit to Washington in early February, the two allies had remained at loggerheads. Following the February 15 agreement, Han had returned to Washington once again. The administration resumed its full-court press. After President Clinton dropped by Han's meeting with Tony Lake, the national security adviser urged the foreign minister to agree to ship the missiles by sea around March 1. That would be less visible and cheaper than an airlift. But Han once again urged delay until after the envoy exchange, hopefully sometime later in March.

Washington became increasingly concerned that rising tensions over Patriot might cause a rift in the alliance just when a premium needed to be placed on military cooperation. Lake's South Korean counterpart warned him that Patriot was causing severe domestic problems, while General Luck concluded that the need for alliance solidarity outweighed the need for Patriot. A week after Foreign Minister Han Sung Joo left Washington, the principals decided not to insist on sending the missiles immediately. All they needed now was a firm commitment to deploy them by a date or an event certain. On March 19, just before the collapse, President Clinton sent the South Korean leader a letter, assuring him of Washington's firm support against aggression and asking for approval of a deployment date. Clinton added that if North Korea failed to implement Super Tuesday conditions, Team Spirit should be rescheduled and Patriot deployments should proceed.

The South Korean leader's March 23 reply reflected a dramatically changed situation. Drawing comfort from the strong American stance toward North Korea, Kim proposed a gradual increase of international pressure on Pyongyang as well as deploying Patriot and rescheduling Team Spirit. The NSC quickly prepared the paperwork for President Clinton to authorize shipment by sea, and by the end of the month the missiles were on a train from their base in Oklahoma to California. The first shipment arrived in South Korea on April 18.[96]

The collapse of Super Tuesday also increased skepticism about America's diplomacy in Korea. While Tony Lake argued that "calm, non-belligerence" was in order, Senator John McCain warned that either North Korea address American concerns or the consequences would "hasten the collapse of that despicable regime."[97] House Democratic leader Richard A. Gephardt joined another critic, Republican Senate minority leader Robert Dole, in suggesting more troops be sent to South Korea.[98]

In Seoul, the collapse of Super Tuesday further divided the body politic. Left-leaning publications and the opposition Democratic Party urged the Kim administration to renew North-South talks, to avoid provocative measures such as sanctions, and to agree to a simultaneous exchange of envoys. Conservative and moderate newspapers, on the other hand, urged the government to heighten its "security and defense posture" to reassure the South Korean people.

President Kim tried to walk a political tightrope. The government said the door would remain open to further talks if North Korea changed its position. To demonstrate his toughness, however, he quickly held a publicized meeting of his security advisers and approved deployment of Patriots.[99] The defense minister testified before the National Assembly in detail about the U.S.–South

Korean war plan, testimony that was widely covered by the South Korean press but branded by the North as evidence that Seoul had never been sincere about dialogue.[100] The South Korean military was placed on a slightly higher state of alert than normal, although the real reason for the move may have been that the South Korean leader was about to leave for China.[101]

But President Kim Young Sam's short-term success in walking his tightrope barely masked growing unhappiness with his inconsistency. Calling Kim's policy a failure, conservative representative Lee Si Ki advocated a strategy of "maximizing strength," implicitly backing a South Korean nuclear option. Representative Chey Jey Moon, chairman of the Foreign Affairs Committee and a more moderate ruling party member, said his committee did not advocate harder or softer policies but rather consistent ones. These pressures inside the party were particularly dangerous to moderates such as Foreign Minister Han and were magnified by the president's declining public support.[102]

Why did Super Tuesday fail? At the time, American negotiators thought both Pyongyang and Seoul were eager enough to resolve the crisis that they would be amenable to the compromises necessary to secure another meeting between Gallucci and Kang. In retrospect it is clear that, despite these aims, the timing of the envoy exchange took on all the baggage of the broader struggle between the two Koreas. The North Koreans kept trying to use the threat of not completing the IAEA inspection and the timing of the envoy exchange to marginalize Seoul and alienate it from Washington. Pyongyang wanted Super Tuesday to fail in order to prove that U.S.–North Korean talks should not be contingent on North-South relations. South Korea's approach was just the opposite. Washington was caught between the two, each bent on winning the tactical struggle between them.

The collapse of Super Tuesday may also have been the first instance of a major North Korean miscalculation during the crisis. Subsequently, Pyongyang would repeatedly overplay its tactical hand without seeming to calculate seriously, much less understand, how its negotiating partner would react. But looking back at the "sea of fire" episode, the North Koreans would later tell the Americans that they never intended the collapse of Super Tuesday to turn into a crisis. Pyongyang had prevented the IAEA from completing the inspection out of anger at Seoul and the need to show that it was tough. But it did not expect Blix to act as quickly as he did after the collapse, convoking a Board of Governors meeting just two days later.[103]

Pak's widely publicized "sea of fire" threat made a bad situation worse by putting Pyongyang on the defensive. A few weeks later, his deputy claimed that the comment did not mean North Korea would start a war.[104] Foreigners visiting Pyongyang were told that since Pak had let his emotions get the better of him, he would be replaced. But the South Korean negotiator would also have to go since his remarks provoked Pak.[105] Even Kim Il Sung got into the act, informing the *Washington Times* on April 19 that the North Korean envoy had said "something which was out of place" and that "actually we don't want any war."[106] Observers who saw a tape of the session believed Pak was indeed speaking extemporaneously.

From the American perspective, Super Tuesday's failure drove home the lesson that the administration could no longer cater to the whims of South Korea and the IAEA. The agreement may have been a natural but complex result of the American "tugboat strategy," pursued ever since the 1993 Geneva meeting to push the IAEA, South Korea, and North Korea together. But in attempting to choreograph the actions of four participants—the United States, South Korea, North Korea, and the IAEA—down to a single twenty-four-hour period, the Clinton administration had taken on a difficult, perhaps impossible task. According to one American official, the episode was the "catharsis" needed to prod Washington into an active leadership role. It would no longer have to push the IAEA and South Korean tugboats but rather tow them toward a solution to the crisis.[107]

The Sword of Damocles

With the collapse of Super Tuesday and what appeared to be an important set-back for U.S. diplomacy, the Principals Committee regrouped on Saturday, March 19. Normally, senior aides attended, but because of sensitivities about press leaks, the meeting was restricted to the principals only. Aside from Patriot, rescheduling the Team Spirit exercise, and reassuring South Korea, the focus was on the next steps after the IAEA board meeting on Monday, which was expected to send the nuclear issue to the Security Council. Once again, the principals turned to a strategy of gradual escalation, particularly since Blix had not found the continuity of safeguards broken and South Korea, Japan, and China wanted to give diplomacy yet another chance. If North Korea made good on a March 14 threat to withdraw from the NPT, Washington would then revisit that approach.

Responding to a White House request, the U.S. Mission to the United Nations (USUN) came up with a game plan. China was again the key. The idea was to secure Beijing's support for the strongest possible measure as soon as possible, both to signal the resolve of the international community while delaying, if not precluding, the moment when a Chinese veto could prevent further multilateral action. USUN believed China would recognize the inevitability of some council response but would want to balance demands that North Korea carry out its nonproliferation obligations with support for diplomatic efforts. Quick action was important to prevent North Korea from arguing that the nuclear issue was no longer an international concern given its dialogue with the United States. On the basis of these recommendations, the principals decided that immediately after the IAEA board meeting ended, USUN would seek a resolution or a presidential statement warning North Korea that time was running out before sanctions.

On Monday the IAEA Board of Governors acted. In the days before the meeting, the United States had prepared a draft resolution calling on North Korea to allow the March inspection to be completed and on the IAEA to report recent developments to the Security Council. That would open the way for the next step in the strategy of gradual escalation. Washington, however, encountered unexpected pockets of resistance. France, a key member of like-minded countries in dealing with Pyongyang called the "core group" and a leading nonproliferation hawk, opposed further diplomacy.[108] This break in the ranks threatened to undermine American efforts to secure broad support and to create the impression of acrimony, an image Washington did not want to project publicly or to the North Koreans.

France's hard-line position reflected frustrations in Paris. The Foreign Ministry and delegation in Vienna were willing to go along with the Americans, but the French Atomic Energy Commission, which played a key role in making nonproliferation policy, expressed a different view. It argued that North Korea's continued flouting of the NPT could set a dangerous precedent for other potential proliferators such as the former Soviet states or Pakistan. Also, the French voiced concern that Washington might opt for a diplomatic solution that would not secure complete North Korean adherence to IAEA obligations, undermining the authority of the agency and the legitimacy of the treaty.

Paris was not shy in staking out these tough positions in public, prompting a war of words with Pyongyang at the height of the February crisis. After the French Foreign Ministry issued a statement that it was time to discuss sanctions, the North Koreans responded with sarcasm, pointing out that a country that possesses nuclear weapons and conducts nuclear tests should not cry out for sanctions against North Korea, "charging it with a nuclear problem." If the French persisted, "we will take necessary measures against them."[109] It was not clear what those measures might be, or whether the French cared.

In the end, American efforts failed to secure France's support but succeeded in recruiting a large number of other cosponsors for the resolution. The lobbying extended beyond Vienna to the capitals of board members. American diplomats visiting key officials invariably found that the South

Koreans had already been there a few days earlier to seek support of the resolution. On the eve of the meeting, the document had seventeen cosponsors out of thirty-five board members. All the core group members signed up, except France.[110]

Kicking off the board meeting the morning of March 21, Director General Blix walked a fine line. He declared that overall, the continuity of safeguards in North Korea had not been broken. But the agency could not conclude whether any nuclear material had been diverted from Yongbyon since it had been prevented from re-establishing continuity of safeguards at the reprocessing plant.[111] In the ensuing debate, Pyongyang's representative claimed his country had done nothing wrong and warned that the agency's technical judgments would jeopardize diplomatic progress, but he stopped short of issuing an ultimatum. Only the Libyan representative came to North Korea's defense while the Chinese accentuated the positive, arguing that the board should not create an atmosphere filled with "the smell of gunpowder." Defending the proposed resolution, the United Kingdom said the authors had tried to be objective but also to reflect the director general's report and the gravity of the situation. The final tally was twenty-five countries in favor, with only Libya voting "no." Five countries abstained, including China, and four did not vote.[112]

The big surprise was China's abstention, a sharp departure from its past practice of consistently voting *against* IAEA resolutions on North Korea. The United States had asked Beijing to persuade Pyongyang to act responsively after the IAEA inspectors left North Korea on March 14. But the Chinese gave only a cryptic response; one official quoted a poem stating that, "at the end of the mountain and the river, one may not know whether the road lies, then suddenly, one finds a new village with willows and flowers." Leaving the Chinese Foreign Ministry, American diplomats encountered glum-looking North Koreans, perhaps an encouraging sign of things to come. China told the United States it would abstain only on the eve of the IAEA vote.

For months there had been a string of vague and not so vague indications that China was active behind the scenes. Before the December agreement in New York, the Chinese had encouraged the North Koreans to settle the IAEA inspection issue. In January there were unconfirmed reports that they had invited Kim Il Sung to visit Beijing sometime in 1994. During the February crisis, the Chinese had urged the IAEA and Washington to compromise and passed messages from the United States to Pyongyang. Afterward, Vice Premier Zhu Rongji, visiting Tokyo, told the Japanese that China welcomed the February 15 agreement and would continue to try to play a positive role.

China's activity was underpinned by successful efforts to improve relations with both Seoul and Pyongyang. The first-ever meeting of the Chinese and South Korean leaders took place at the November 1993 Asia-Pacific Economic Cooperation summit, to be followed by President Kim's visit to Beijing, slated for the end of the month. Beijing tactfully used those better ties to prod Pyongyang, prompting a former Chinese official to bluntly observe, "North Korea now recognizes that China is its only friend and it needs China for survival."[113] In January 1994, party secretary Hwang Jang Yop went to Beijing and met with President Jiang in what was almost certainly an effort to mend bilateral relations.

The collapse of "Super Tuesday" may have persuaded China that its coaxing had not done the trick. The escalating rhetoric from Washington, Pyongyang, and Seoul, combined with the Patriot deployment and the possible rescheduling of Team Spirit, threatened to create instability on its border and to complicate an already rocky relationship with the United States. Secretary Christopher's first visit to Beijing a week earlier had been a disaster because of differences over China's treatment of political dissidents. As a result, Beijing may have concluded that it had no choice but to distance itself from Pyongyang at the IAEA, signaling the North Koreans that they did not have a Chinese blank check. On the eve of his own visit to Beijing, Foreign Minister Han said that China's vote in Vienna had sent a strong message to North Korea.[114]

Naturally, Washington saw Beijing's shift as vindicating its patient diplomacy. For the past year, the administration had been subjected to periodic attacks, not only for coddling the North but also for not putting enough pressure on Beijing. Two months earlier, in a *Wall Street Journal* article entitled "Korea, Clinton's Missile Crisis," Karen Elliot House claimed the evidence did not support China's assertion that it was playing a constructive role. "China," she argued, "must shut down its overland border with the North."[115] Secretary Christopher, reading the piece before leaving for a meeting with the Chinese foreign minister, asked his Asia experts whether the administration should lean harder on Beijing. But he and his colleagues decided to stay the course; now American diplomacy appeared to be making progress.

After the vote in Vienna, the diplomatic action quickly shifted to the United Nations. The debate there took place against a backdrop of growing tensions and mounting North Korean threats. Faced with the cancellation of the third round, the Patriot deployment, the rescheduling of Team Spirit, and the beginning of deliberations at the Security Council, the North Korean Foreign Ministry issued a warning that Pyongyang might withdraw from the NPT.[116]

Consultations among the P-5 members moved quickly. The British, French, and Russians supported the draft American resolution mirroring the one approved in Vienna but also added that the council would "consider further action" if necessary, a hint that sanctions might be in the offing. In anticipation of a Chinese assault to water down the resolution, the nonproliferation hawks toughened it up. For example, the French added a deadline of "one month" for the IAEA to report back to the Security Council. Outside the council meetings, the North Koreans prowled the corridors, threatening British and French diplomats that they would withdraw from the NPT if the UN acted.

While Washington had been preoccupied with China, there were new signs that Russia was dissatisfied. As talks at the Security Council continued, Thomas Pickering, the American ambassador to Russia, visited the Foreign Ministry. An extraordinarily gifted diplomat of indomitable intelligence and energy, Pickering had already served as ambassador to El Salvador, Israel, Nigeria, India, and the United Nations before arriving in Moscow. As the American envoy slipped into his limousine for the short ride to the Foreign Ministry, he had an inkling that something was up. Japanese newspapers, reporting on Russian foreign minister Andrei Kozyrev's visit to Tokyo, said that he might propose a multilateral meeting on Korea. After arriving, Pickering asked Deputy Foreign Minister Aleksandr Panov if those reports were true; he did not get a straight answer.

The next morning, Panov explained. Russia would support the American proposal in the Security Council but would also call for an international conference on Korea. Such a conference, according to the Russians, would create an umbrella for movement toward a comprehensive solution, including North Korea's adherence to NPT obligations and international guarantees that the two Koreas would be denuclearized. Both Koreas, China, Japan, the United States, representatives of the UN secretary general, and the director general of the IAEA would attend. Panov gave Pickering a letter from Foreign Minister Kozyrev to Warren Christopher laying out the proposal but also lobbing a diplomatic grenade. There would be no time for Washington to comment on the Russian move since it would be unveiled at a news conference that afternoon.

How did U.S.-Russian coordination go off the rails? Even though Moscow had generally supported Washington's policy on the peninsula, the Russians had long been frustrated by their secondary role. Hidden beneath their support was a yearning to regain influence on the peninsula that had been lost as the Soviet Union had disintegrated. Nowhere was this lost influence more apparent than in Russia's now uneasy relationship with North Korea. Pyongyang had made it clear that it preferred to deal directly with Washington, in part because, as the North Koreans pointed out tongue in cheek, the

Russian position was the same as that of the United States. Only that January, President Clinton and Boris Yeltsin had issued a joint statement calling on North Korea to honor its safeguards agreement with the IAEA.[117] With the collapse of Super Tuesday, Moscow now saw an opportunity to step into the limelight.

American diplomats thought the Russian idea was hastily conceived. In part, the Yeltsin government may have been reacting to critics who claimed it was unable to come up with initiatives independent of Washington. Proposing conferences was a tried and true modus operandi; the Korean conference was the third such proposal following similar initiatives on Bosnia and the Middle East.[118] Moreover, the Yeltsin government seemed just as interested in public relations as in substance, since it planned to announce the new plan before getting reactions from prospective participants. One Russian official told the Americans that, like fireworks, the Korea proposal would fade away after blazing for only a few moments.

The immediate problem was to prevent the unexpected move from undermining U.S. efforts at the United Nations or damaging relations with Russia. The proposal called into question a recent agreement between Christopher and Kozyrev, reached in the wake of Russia's surprise Middle East initiative, to consult more closely in the future. Moscow insisted on going ahead with its announcement in spite of Pickering's request for a delay to allow Washington to respond. The State Department's public response welcomed any initiative that might settle the nuclear issue but also suggested the proposal might allow the North to evade its nonproliferation responsibilities or delay action at the Security Council. Russia viewed the carefully hedged statement as a vote of no confidence.[119]

Although Washington and Moscow seemed on the verge of confrontation, cooler heads prevailed. Even before Kozyrev's first letter had been answered, a second one arrived. Reminding Christopher that Moscow had reacted favorably to the draft UN Security Council resolution despite no prior consultation, Kozyrev expressed anger that his country's proposal had been dismissed out of hand. But Christopher's response, in a letter dispatched to Moscow that same day, had a soothing effect. He gently chided Kozyrev for not allowing time for consultations, called the whole incident a misunderstanding, and added that Washington was open to any forum as long as it was useful. Mollified, the Russians cryptically, and sheepishly, admitted that the timing of the announcement could not be stopped.

Other key diplomatic players echoed Washington's lukewarm reaction to the idea of an international conference. China politely pointed out that the time was not ripe for such an initiative. While Japan thought a multilateral conference was not a good idea, it hesitated to say so publicly for fear of making Russia lose "face." South Korea believed the proposal would only prove to be an unhelpful distraction from ongoing UN Security Council discussions.

It fell to Pyongyang to drive the final nail into the coffin. Russia seemed to be trying to secure North Korean support. In spite of previous attempts to extricate itself from a 1961 treaty committing Moscow to come to North Korea's aid in case of an unprovoked attack, Deputy Foreign Minister Panov seemed to reverse course on March 29, saying Russia would consider rendering assistance.[120] But two days later, the North's Foreign Ministry called the conference a complication, reflecting concerns that it would be an unnecessary diversion from attempts to engage Washington and could turn into another forum where the North would come under attack.[121] The Russian effort ebbed, but only for the moment.

While Washington worked with Moscow, deliberations at the Security Council moved toward a climax. Blix briefed the council on March 24, setting the stage for final consideration of Washington's proposal. Appearing on CNN that evening, he compared North Korea's behavior during the March inspection to the conduct of a patient who says, "You can check my arms and legs but not my heart."[122]

At the Security Council meeting the next day, China put its cards on the table. The normal procedure was for the five permanent members—the United States, China, Russia, Britain, and France—to agree to a draft and then to present it to the whole council. Since China was unwilling to engage in discussions, the American draft was forwarded without its support. This had been done in the past, most recently during the Gulf War. Whereas Beijing had previously warned that it did not want the nuclear issue brought before the council, it now gave the green light. Ambassador Li Zhaoxing said he could not support the American proposal for a Security Council resolution but would consider supporting a statement by the council's president, which would carry less weight while still putting the council on record.

The main battle was waged over the "further action" clause in the American draft. Beijing thought it smacked of sanctions. Washington viewed the clause as essential for precisely that reason. It was supported by the nonproliferation hawks—British ambassador Sir David Hannay and French permanent representative Jean-Bernard Mérimée—who hammered away at Chinese diplomats. Threatening to use their veto, the Chinese argued that regardless of whether the disputed clause was included or not, the "sword of Damocles" would always be there.

As the spectacle unfolded, New Zealand's permanent representative, Colin Keating, stepped in to suggest a compromise: why not substitute "further

Security Council consideration will take place if necessary." The formulation was less definite but still left the door open to future efforts by the council. Busily taking notes, receptive Chinese diplomats asked Keating to repeat his idea.[123]

Recognizing that deliberations had reached a critical moment, USUN sent a cable to Washington that evening identifying three options. The first was a resolution with "further action," which could trigger a veto or Chinese abstention, signaling North Korea that the P-5 was split and, in fact, that there would be no further council action. Second, the administration could accept a presidential statement with New Zealand's compromise language. If China agreed, that would send a unanimous message. A statement might appear weaker than a resolution, but that would be offset by the benefit of having China accede to the Security Council's authority. Third, Washington could conduct protracted negotiations with Beijing, but that only made sense if it believed the Chinese would change their position.

Washington had good reason to doubt China's threats to veto a resolution. After deliberations at the United Nations had concluded for the day, President Kim Young Sam talked to Clinton for thirty minutes. Just back from talks with China's leaders, Kim said that Beijing was unlikely to exercise a veto, a message echoed by Foreign Minister Han Sung Joo, who was in Washington meeting with Secretary Christopher. Han also sensed the Chinese were now ready to become more actively involved in bringing about a diplomatic solution.[124] But whether China would abstain on a resolution remained unclear. On the other hand, if China's support could be gained, perhaps for a presidential statement, that prospect seemed attractive given the possibility that it would signal greater diplomatic efforts from Beijing to resolve the crisis.

The next day, Christopher dispatched Gallucci to New York to wrap up the negotiations. After meeting with the permanent representatives of Britain, France, and Russia to make sure of their support, he called Christopher for final instructions before confronting the Chinese. Given Washington's patient efforts to hook Beijing, the secretary gave him the green light to seek a presidential statement with the New Zealand compromise. Gallucci then quickly reached agreement with the Chinese. On March 31, the statement, with unanimous support, was issued during the 3,357th meeting of the Security Council.[125]

While the *Washington Post* frowned ("UN Bows to China, Issues Mild Call to N. Korea to Permit Nuclear Check"), the final language in the presidential statement was almost the same as in the draft resolution.[126] The United States had sacrificed the quest for an immediate resolution with greater legal and diplomatic weight, but probably lacking Beijing's support, in favor of a less weighty, but substantially identical statement with China's support. The stage was set for another diplomatic offensive against North Korea, hopefully with Beijing's participation. If that effort failed, Washington would be in a good position to move toward sanctions with China on board.

Surprisingly, North Korea also remained open to more talks. Following a tried and true pattern, as the United Nations deliberated, the North's threats escalated. At Panmunjom, one North Korean officer told the Americans: "This will not be a situation like the Iraq war. We will not give you time to collect troops around Korea to attack us. We will not attack the South first but if it is clear you are going to attack, then we will attack." Just before the Security Council acted, Pyongyang launched an authoritative attack on Patriot, warning that America's "pressure-bound machinations" would drive the North out of the NPT.[127]

Pyongyang backed up its rhetoric with action. It stepped up exercises of both offensive and defensive forces and tested a secure communications network used in national emergencies.[128] The North also mobilized its population, staging a mass rally against Patriot and the first conference of party cells (the smallest organization unit in the ruling Korean Worker's Party) ever held.[129] Covered extensively by the media, Pyongyang convoked as many as 100,000 members to rally support and to ensure discipline.[130] Lee In Mo, the resistance fighter released in March 1993, was trotted out and touted as the "incarnation of faith and will."[131]

In the final analysis, however, experienced North Korea watchers thought they recognized a familiar pattern. Pyongyang's rhetoric more often followed rather than preceded crisis-provoking incidents. Past acts—such as the seizing of the *Pueblo* or the 1976 incident in the DMZ when two American soldiers were axed to death—had not been foreshadowed by threatening rhetoric. Pyongyang's recent pronouncements were not mere political theater—the North had backed them up with military moves and mobilization of its population—but those moves fell far short of preparations for armed conflict.

Moreover, Pyongyang's authoritative public pronouncements, which the North Koreans often used to warn when they were prepared to act, still displayed a modicum of restraint. They had begun to criticize administration officials but continued to refer in neutral terms to President Clinton. The March 28 Foreign Ministry statement, while condemning Patriot, intimated that the North still had a lingering interest in pursuing dialogue with the United States.[132] Even as Pyongyang's campaign reached a fever pitch, it still balanced its harshest attacks with an indirect appeal for talks in the guise of a KCNA news report claiming that foreign leaders in Malaysia, Congo, and Senegal had called for a peaceful resolution of the crisis.[133]

After all was said and done, Pyongyang's reaction to the Security Council statement signaled more negotiations were at hand. Responding to a March 28 message from Gallucci that the completion of the March IAEA inspection was needed to reschedule U.S.–North Korean talks, Kang seemed willing to restart discussions with the agency.[134] Citing an old proverb, one North Korean in New York told a visitor, "An Asian answers his door always and welcomes a friendly visitor, but does not go knocking himself on strange doors."

6

Ending History

April–May 1994

A PRIL in Washington brought warming breezes and cherry blossoms around the Tidal Basin. Joggers shed a layer as they headed past the Jefferson Memorial, crossed Independence Avenue, and headed up the grassy swail toward the one of the last fine stands of American elms along the Eastern Seaboard. A few hundred yards away, masons were laying stones for the new Korean War Memorial, forming the final point of a triangle with the Lincoln and Vietnam Memorials.

The American Battle Monument Commission was determined to finish the memorial in time for the forty-second anniversary of the armistice ending the Korean War, to be commemorated by a visit by South Korea's president Kim Young-sam the following summer. The core of the memorial would be nineteen life-sized bronze figures of poncho-shrouded GIs, stomping up an anonymous ridge on the mountainous peninsula. Five yards away, the ghostly faces of nineteen other GIs etched from Korean War photographs into highly polished stone mingled with the reflection of the nineteen bronze soldiers, their numbers joined to symbolize the 38th parallel that divided Korea into two nations, so deeply at odds.

Surveying the diplomatic landscape, the *New York Times* observed, "North Korea is bristling like a porcupine caught in a trap. But it may be looking for a way out."[1] Willing to give the North one more chance, particularly since Seoul and Tokyo remained interested in a diplomatic solution, Washington came up with another proposal akin to Super Tuesday, which it hoped could be implemented before Director General Hans Blix reported to the Security

162

Council in early May. Under the new plan, if North Korea agreed to complete the inspections necessary for continuity of safeguards and resumed North-South dialogue, Washington would reschedule U.S.–North Korean talks and "resuspend" Team Spirit.

The new diplomatic offensive would require progress on several fronts. Washington would have to nudge Beijing to be active; after supporting the Security Council statement, the Chinese had already contacted the North Koreans. The administration also needed to secure Seoul's agreement to a new proposal to break the North-South impasse, seen by the Americans as the main reason that Super Tuesday failed, and to encourage the International Atomic Energy Agency to seek completion of the March inspection. In addition, Washington would prepare for more Security Council discussions and more enhancements of its military forces in Korea.

In public, the administration maintained a firm, measured posture but also one that explained U.S. national interests. If the American people and other nations were to be asked to join together in imposing sanctions against North Korea, with the risk of war this implied, it could not be over the parsing of esoteric distinctions between "routine and ad hoc" inspections versus "continuity" inspections. Secretary of Defense William Perry explained that the dangers in standing up to the North now would be compounded in a few years when it might start producing bombs "at a rate of a dozen a year."[2] Speaking on television on April 5, President Bill Clinton observed, "I am determined to put the pressure on but I do not believe it serves any useful purpose to inflame the situation with rhetoric."[3]

Washington, Seoul, and Vienna shared a sense, however, that the margins for a peaceful solution were narrowing. With the events of early 1994, the United States and South Korea seemed on shaky diplomatic ground. Moreover, both felt the domestic political heat for pursuing policies that, for better or worse, appeared to be unsuccessful. One more diplomatic failure could propel them down the path of applying "sticks" to the North. Making matters even more complicated, Blix and the IAEA had moved ever closer, seemingly asymptotically, to the fateful declaration that North Korea had destroyed the "continuity of safeguards."

There also must have been a chill in Pyongyang. While Kim Il Sung had espoused peaceful aims to Billy Graham, his government had backed itself into a corner. It had pushed the IAEA to the breaking point and driven the United States and South Korea together—rather than apart—by overplaying its hand with the "sea of fire" threat. The last vestiges of Seoul's resistance to the Patriot deployment and rescheduling of Team Spirit, now slated for November, had been swept away. The North also must have felt a deepening sense of isolation; attempts to keep others, particularly China, from swinging behind American policy were failing. While Beijing would neither explicitly abandon its North Korean friends nor publicly "gang up" on them, it also did not seem inclined to step into the breach to defend its former ally.

Exactly how these developments played out in the murky world of North Korea was unclear. In hindsight, there may have been a drift in Pyongyang toward a tougher approach as the March crisis mounted. The same North Korean statement that hinted at new talks with the IAEA also warned ominously that Washington had given Pyongyang no choice but to conduct unspecified "peaceful nuclear activities," hitherto frozen to promote dialogue with the United States. These comments were not seen at the time as alarming; they came just before an early April meeting of the North Korean leadership characterized by mild rhetoric, no mention of the nuclear issue, and no sign of putting the country on a wartime footing.

In fact, trouble was brewing in the hermit kingdom. Two weeks later, Pyongyang notified the United States that it had decided to resume the long-awaited unloading and refueling of the 5-megawatt reactor. The move did not necessarily mean a break if North Korea cooperated with the IAEA, but it soon became clear that Pyongyang had other priorities, placing it on a collision course with Washington. While the administration still tried to keep a crack in the door open for a last-minute solution, its emphasis had clearly shifted to sanctions, enhanced deterrence, and preparation for the use of military force if necessary.

Putting Humpty Dumpty Back Together

The events of early 1994 convinced the Clinton administration that North Korea required more careful handling. Coordinating military and diplomatic efforts had proved especially difficult. Up until March, the Pentagon had resisted any measure that would limit its autonomy and excluded the State Department and other agencies from military planning. According to Under Secretary of Defense Walt Slocombe, since the United States needed to keep military equipment and material flowing into South Korea to prepare for the worst, a low public profile was essential to avoid political distractions or interference. The administration could not waste time debating each and every deployment needed to protect its 37,000 troops in the South. That was an important lesson of the Patriot experience.[4]

In fact, a steady stream of military moves had already begun, making better integration with the rest of the administration's strategy critical. Besides Patriot, planning for Team Spirit was set to resume. Other less publicized steps included the deployment of new Apache attack helicopters in mid-March as part of a planned modernization program, although their dispatch had been accelerated because of the crisis.[5] By the end of the month, aircraft spare parts and maintenance crews were being sent to South Korea and Japan.[6] Steps were also taken to allow for a second Patriot battalion and the rapid insertion of weapons designed to target North Korean artillery. On April 18, Assistant Secretary of Defense Edward ("Ted") Warner testified in Congress that the United States would deploy one brigade of new military equipment to the peninsula by the summer of 1994.[7]

Given the quickening pace of events, more than ever the administration needed a senior interagency group to manage Korea policy across the board. In the year since the crisis began, Gallucci had served as its point man in name and deed. As assistant secretary of state for political-military affairs, however, he still had far-flung responsibilities ranging from negotiations to provide U.S. military forces with access to bases overseas to the whole panoply of non-proliferation, arms control, and export control issues. That made it impossible to concentrate exclusively on the confrontation with North Korea.

Without better crisis management, observed Jim Laney, the U.S. ambassador in Seoul, the United States would remain caught between dealing with the burgeoning nuclear program and maintaining peace and deterrence. Neither goal should be sacrificed, but in Laney's judgment Washington seemed hell-bent on achieving the former without paying enough attention to the latter. In pursuing that course of action, he thought the administration was drifting toward disaster. Kim Il Sung seemed equally determined not to let the United States build up a force of 500,000 troops south of his border, as had happened in the Gulf. As Laney would later tell a seminar at Georgetown University, "We were moving like some Greek tragedy to some sort of inexorable collision."[8]

Washington, said the ambassador, needed to take two steps to correct this problem. First, it should appoint a new, less visible official other than Gallucci to be available for discreet contacts with Pyongyang. Gallucci himself had become a bargaining chip, able to meet the North Koreans only when they had fulfilled certain conditions. That problem reinforced an important drawback in American diplomacy: the haphazard communications with Pyongyang, often through unofficial intermediaries. Likening the situation to "sending up smoke signals in the wind," Laney called for an "open line" to the North.[9] Though his idea seemed more important after the collapse of Super Tuesday, it received little support inside the administration.[10]

Laney's second recommendation—that a full-time policy czar be appointed to deal with the crisis—gained more traction. A similar view was taking hold elsewhere in the bureaucracy. In February, Assistant Secretary of Defense Ash Carter sent a memo to Dan Poneman at the NSC recommending the creation of a special interagency process to develop a strategy on North Korea, arguing, "We don't want this on the same agenda or timeline as steel dumping." Agreeing that the bureaucracy was not focusing on first-order issues, Poneman urged his boss Tony Lake to ensure that Gallucci had enough support from the principals to manage the interagency process as the situation in Korea became more acute.

Separately, Laney pitched the idea of a Korea policy czar to officials in the State Department. When his pleas went unanswered, the ambassador turned to his old friend Sam Nunn. During a meeting at a waffle house off the interstate highway in eastern Georgia, Laney laid out his reasoning to an already concerned Nunn. The Democratic senator from Georgia arranged for him to see Mac McLarty, the White House chief of staff. "For god's sake put somebody in charge of Korea policy because the downside is too big," Laney urged McLarty.[11] This time, Laney connected. After receiving a call from the White House, Secretary Warren Christopher summoned Gallucci and asked him to figure out how to improve the coordination and coherence of U.S. policy.

Gallucci quickly reviewed a number of models, settling on the one Winston Lord used to manage China policy. It had the unique feature of an assistant secretary (Lord) chairing a special meeting attended by higher-ranking under secretaries. Since the model would undercut the existing Deputies Committee chaired by Sandy Berger, he knew the National Security Council would have to sign off on the idea. Tony Lake agreed, stipulating that Poneman would act as Gallucci's deputy. On April 6, Lake issued a directive establishing the Senior Steering Group on Korea (SSK) to coordinate the daily diplomatic, congressional, and public affairs activities and ensure their consistency with military and intelligence operations.[12]

To ensure such consistency the administration had to make one more adjustment. With Lake's backing and the approval of the Pentagon's top brass, Gallucci and Poneman were invited to attend regular Pentagon meetings on Korea. Chaired by Under Secretary of Defense Walt Slocombe, these sessions discussed military plans for building up American forces in Korea if the diplomatic situation deteriorated, the execution of the American war plan, and options for launching a military attack against the Yongbyon nuclear facilities.

This new arrangement had two important benefits. First, it fostered the dissemination of information important to coherent decisionmaking. Gallucci would pass on what he learned to his immediate superior, Under Secretary of State Peter Tarnoff, and the secretary of state, while Poneman would report back to Lake and Berger. Second, the meetings reassured Pentagon officials who suspected, in the words of one officer, that State would not "play hardball with North Korea." That reassurance would serve the administration well as tensions mounted and as it sought a diplomatic solution with Pyongyang.[13]

One of the first tasks of the SSK was to run the administration's new diplomatic offensive. Americans working on the North Korea issue often felt like the plate-spinner on the *Ed Sullivan Show* of the 1960s. They would dash madly from one spinning pole to another as each plate began to wobble, shoring up U.S. diplomacy before key relationships came crashing to the ground. (Of course, some china always shattered in both the Sullivan and SSK versions.) In addition to the usual channels—dealing with South Korea, Japan, the IAEA, and the international community—volunteers to serve as go-betweens invariably popped up. In April, for instance, Egypt suggested that President Hosni Mubarak could convey a message to Kim Il Sung; the administration was cool to the idea.

Nowhere was the diplomatic challenge greater than with South Korea, which was central to American strategy. The "sea of fire" remarks had rattled the government in Seoul, prompting a visit by Foreign Minister Han Sung Joo to Washington to coordinate Patriot deployments and the rescheduling of the Team Spirit military exercise. Christopher and Perry reassured him by underlining America's commitment to South Korean security; a commitment amply demonstrated by the arrival in Pusan of three Patriot missile batteries and eighty-four Stinger antiaircraft missiles to defend them.[14]

The administration believed that the key to reconstituting Super Tuesday was to resolve the impasse over the timing of inter-Korean dialogue, persuading Seoul to accept the idea of simultaneity. Ironically, as the Americans regrouped, the mood in Seoul had now swung to dropping the condition altogether. A strong conservative backlash after the "sea of fire" threat had given way to strong interest in catalyzing U.S.–North Korean talks as a way of avoiding economic sanctions. While the Kim government initially denied public hints that it was moving toward "de-linkage" of the North-South and U.S.–North Korean tracks, a ministerial meeting on April 8 revealed a developing consensus precisely in support of that position. A final decision was slated for April 14, the day before Gallucci was slated to arrive in Seoul for consultations.[15]

From the U.S. perspective, changing the timing or form of inter-Korean dialogue was one thing, but de-linkage could undermine its negotiating position and cause substantial political damage. Inter-Korean dialogue and implementation of the Denuclearization Declaration had been an essential part of U.S. policy dating back to the Bush administration. Without either as part of an integrated approach, it would appear as though Seoul were not actively involved in resolving the nuclear issue, a sure-fire prescription for causing domestic political problems in South Korea. The declaration also banned reprocessing and related facilities. Although the prospect of swapping North Korea's nuclear facilities for new reactors could resolve this problem, that was by no means even close to a done deal.

On April 11, National Security Adviser Tony Lake took a break from dealing with the problems in Bosnia to call his counterpart, Chung Chong Wook. Lake emphasized that the two allies needed to consult *before* South Korea announced any change in its position in order to present a united front to the world. Chung responded that Seoul would take American views into account before the April 14 decision, but the issue had become politically volatile in Korea and his government wanted to act before Gallucci arrived. Though Chung did not say so explicitly, it was important that the Koreans appear to be the masters of their own fate.

Seoul's pending decision triggered a debate in Washington. Under Secretary of State Lynn Davis and some in the Defense Department and the Arms Control and Disarmament Agency believed a change in the timing of the envoy exchange would signal weakness to Pyongyang. Gallucci and State's East Asia Bureau argued that the United States should be flexible and work with Seoul to develop tactics for presenting the idea to the North. That would avoid the appearance of a breach between the two allies and unceremoniously dumping the Denuclearization Declaration. While Secretary Christopher approved that position, it was left for the NSC to resolve the bureaucratic differences. When Poneman raised the issue, Sandy Berger objected to dropping the linkage because of concern that Seoul would balk. Once he learned that dropping the linkage was the South's own idea, he quickly relented.

The "de-linkage story" appeared in the Korean press the day Gallucci arrived in Seoul, making his task of ensuring alliance solidarity even more delicate. Evidently, a disgruntled member of the ruling party had leaked to a few select newspapers that the government had decided to give up on special envoys as a precondition for further U.S.–North Korean talks to embarrass the government. The public reaction was mixed; some newspapers claimed the new approach corrected a "wrong-headed policy" while others asserted that Seoul "threw in the towel."[16] One positive side effect was that the disclosure effectively preempted the risk that Gallucci, who would arrive later that day, would be viewed as dictating South Korean policy.

In spite of the leak, Gallucci's two days of meetings ended well. Ironically, he initially pushed for at least one North-South contact before a U.S.–North Korean meeting, a position he thought unwise before the collapse of Super Tuesday. The South Koreans, who had previously clung to that view, now wanted to drop the exchange altogether since they worried it might block a settlement of the nuclear issue or result in another humiliating rebuff by Pyongyang. The two compromised; a meeting could take place on the first day of the third round, but they would be prepared to drop the linkage between the envoy exchange and the third round completely. That position was to be encased in the new Super Tuesday scheme to take place on May 2, the IAEA deadline for completing the March inspection. On that day, the inspections would begin and a May 18 starting date for the third round would be announced (leaving enough time for the completion of the IAEA activities), as would the suspension of Team Spirit.

Gallucci left Seoul on April 19. It proved to be an eventful day. Not only had the Patriot missiles begun to arrive in South Korea, a development noted by the North's media, but Gallucci received a message from Kang Sok Ju replying to a letter sent three weeks ago, an unusual delay given the fast pace of events on the peninsula.[17] Now it became apparent why; the letter contained a bombshell. Pyongyang had decided to unload the fuel rods containing bomb-making material from its reactor.

Creating an Incident?

Kim Il Sung celebrated his eighty-second and last birthday on April 15, the same day that Gallucci arrived in Seoul. The modest ceremonies may have reflected Pyongyang's sinking economy, but that did not stop the North Koreans from inviting CNN, some foreign press, and the *Washington Times*. The Great Leader seemed to have his own personal charm offensive in mind, launched the day after his birthday at a palace outside Pyongyang. To visiting reporters, Kim appeared not to have a care in the world, claiming that any concerns created by the "sea of fire" threat were exaggerated.[18] He wanted better relations with the United States and held out the prospect for cooperation with IAEA inspectors. "We are keeping no secrets, except some military ones," Kim Il Sung proclaimed.[19]

But some reporters were not willing to take his statement at face value. Pressed by Mike Chinoy from CNN, Kim replied forcefully: "The world is calling on our country to show the nuclear weapons we don't have. I have had just about enough." He added: "We will never have nuclear weapons, I promise you. Who can we use them against?"[20] Responding to the North Korean leader's comment, Secretary Perry observed that it was "very moderate, very conciliatory" and he was "anxious to follow up on it."[21]

Yet Kim Il Sung's reassuring remarks had a very short half-life. North Korea's actions on April 19 threatened to further escalate tensions. On the theory that the best defense is a good offense, Kang's letter claimed that Washington had not been sincerely pursuing further talks and had driven the situation to the brink of war by deploying new weapons in the South and promoting a resolution against the North at the United Nations. Then came the kicker. He declared that North Korea had decided to defuel its 5-megawatt reactor because the provision of the new reactors seemed to be a distant prospect. Kang also cited "technical" reasons for ending the freeze.

Kang reassured Gallucci that the IAEA could be present to verify that none of the unloaded fuel rods containing plutonium would be diverted so they could be used to build nuclear weapons. He did not, however, say that the agency would be able verify the exact locations of certain key rods in the reactor core as they were removed. Such data were critical, although not the only source of information, to calculating how much plutonium might have been extracted in the past, the issue that started the crisis in the first place.[22] That was one reason why the United States had made IAEA presence during any unloading operations an important condition for dialogue with Pyongyang ever since 1993.

The North Koreans must have understood this. As early as February 1993, the IAEA had informed Pyongyang about the proper procedures for unloading the reactor, including the selecting, segregating, and securing of specific fuel rods—some 300 out of 8,000—to determine how much plutonium had been produced in the past. The agency reminded Pyongyang of these requirements in early 1994 when the North Koreans shut down their reactor for a short time. With the North's approval, the agency had even begun procuring special baskets that would be needed for sampling the rods.

All parties—the United States, North Korea, South Korea, and the IAEA—understood a still more ominous implication if the North carried through on its defueling threat: it would bring Pyongyang one major step closer to building five or so new nuclear weapons. The irradiated rods containing plutonium could be removed from the reactor, then chopped up and dissolved in a solution that would separate out the plutonium from the waste material in the rods at the reprocessing plant, also located at Yongbyon. The separated plutonium could be used to build nuclear weapons. Whether the North Koreans were capable of taking the last step was unclear, but unloading the rods would make more material available if they decided to do so.

Why did Pyongyang announce its defueling decision on April 19? There may have been plausible technical reasons to perform overdue maintenance at the reactor, but not to unload *all* the rods. They had been in the reactor for a relatively long time, since the unloading scheduled for early 1993 never took place. Moreover, the North Koreans had been operating the reactor in such a way that put additional stress on the rods, causing a number of them to fail. The North, however, had removed these failed rods during a short shutdown in early 1994. All of this was confirmed by the IAEA, although the failures were not characterized as a major threat to safety or continued use of the reactor. In addition, the reactor's gas cooling system—which prevented the fuel rods from overheating and causing a meltdown—may have failed in April. That could have justified a shutdown but once again was no reason to disgorge the entire load.[23]

More important, Kang Sok Ju's letter blamed North Korea's actions on a deteriorating political situation. Pyongyang's diplomacy of the preceding months had backfired, as the international coalition opposed to North Korea's nuclear ambitions strengthened and Beijing's support of the UN presidential statement was secured. Finally, Kim Il Sung's personal diplomacy with Billy Graham had not produced a summit or another meeting with Gallucci. All of this was taking place against the backdrop of a growing U.S. military buildup that appeared to be a prelude to the execution of the war plan.

Faced with perhaps the worst external political and military environment in recent memory, North Korea may have decided to rearrange the diplomatic chessboard yet again. According to C. Turner Joy, the U.S. negotiator of the armistice ending the Korean War, this was the last option short of military action that the North Koreans resorted to in diplomatic extremis.[24] This meant taking precipitous action that would *both* force the adversary to react *and* increase Pyongyang's bargaining leverage by presenting a fait accompli that the other side would need to pay a higher diplomatic price to reverse.

Refueling the reactor seemed to fit the bill. In his very first meeting with Kang in June 1993, Gallucci made it clear that refueling without proper supervision by the IAEA was a red line for the United States. Hence Pyongyang's move would require a cover story, both to avoid undermining the little remaining political support North Korea retained in China and not to invite a military strike from the United States. So the North Koreans cloaked their motives in defensive rhetoric, insisting that they were *forced* to defuel the 5-megawatt reactor because of safety concerns and because the United States had no intention of reaching a diplomatic solution.

North Korea's move also may have resulted from shifting internal politics. Kang's promise in June 1993 not to unload the reactor made political sense. From his Foreign Ministry perch, the North Korean negotiator did not have operational control of Yongbyon, but his pledge, presumably approved by a higher authority, gave him a measure of control. The breakdown of the scheduled third round and the sudden escalation of tension in early 1994 may have reignited the debate over whether to unload. During talks in February leading to the Super Tuesday agreement, the North Koreans pressed Tom Hubbard to hold the third round in mid-March rather than April for "technical reasons." Hubbard speculated that Pyongyang might be planning to unload the reactor in April. If there was a debate, Kang lost. The April 19 letter may have represented the most that could be salvaged from that defeat.

Exactly who won the internal battle in Pyongyang was also unclear. The shift may have been related to Kang Sok Ju's rival—Party Secretary Kim Yong Sun—from whom he wrested control of American policy and who was making a political comeback. Renewed efforts to replace the armistice agreement with a new, more permanent peace arrangement reinforced this speculation. Kim had raised this issue during his session with Arnold Kanter in 1992, but Kang had set it aside. A week after the April 19 letter was sent, however, the North Koreans began a new diplomatic offensive, highlighted by authoritative Foreign Ministry statements that the Korean People's Army had withdrawn from the Military Armistice Commission. Pushing the issue back to center stage may have been part of a negotiating ploy, but some American analysts believed it was a distraction Kang probably did not welcome.[25]

Alternatively, the shift could have reflected pressures from other elements inside the North Korean leadership. In the past, Kang had alluded to problems with the reactor operators because they were pressing to unload and refuel the reactor. If those statements were not just a negotiating tactic, the deteriorating external environment as well as continued technical problems with the reactor may have allowed the defense industrial bureaucracy and supporters in the military to make a strong case that now was the right time to act.

Whatever the reason for the North's move, the required response was clear. On April 28, Gallucci wrote Kang tabling the new Super Tuesday proposal but also warning that satisfactory arrangements would have to be made with the IAEA if the North unloaded the reactor rods.[26] Four days later, Kang told Gallucci that unloading would begin on May 4, adding that the IAEA might be allowed to select and segregate fuel rods after the "process of a package solution was under way." This reference to progress in U.S.–North Korean negotiations seemed to hint at a possible compromise. Gallucci replied the same day, warning Kang that if the North unloaded the reactor without IAEA inspectors present, Washington would conclude Pyongyang no longer wished to resolve the nuclear confrontation through dialogue.

What would the North Koreans do next? As in February, Pyongyang might push matters to the brink and then reach a bargain with Washington that would resolve the problem, clearing the way for a third round. But there was always a nagging concern that the North Koreans might go for broke, unload the reactor, destroy evidence in the fuel rods come what may, then regroup for the next phase of the confrontation. The lesson of the February crisis may have been that North Korea could push the nuclear issue to the breaking point for bargaining purposes. But it was also true that Pyongyang could just as easily miscalculate in its quest for tactical advantage, as it may have done with the collapse of Super Tuesday. Unfortunately, miscalculation could bring the peninsula to the edge of armed conflict or perhaps beyond, unleashing untold devastation upon its inhabitants.

Fair Warning

The Principals Committee met in the White House Situation Room on May 7. At a previous White House session in November, Tony Lake had mused, "If I were the North Koreans and I wanted to jerk our chains, I would defuel the 5-megawatt reactor." It was cold comfort that his prediction seemed to be coming true. Yet a whiff of ambiguity still hung in the air. Three days after the date the North Koreans had said defueling would begin, no word had arrived on whether it had actually started. The Chinese were confident it would be delayed, but the Americans took Kang's statements at face value. As a matter of policy, it would have been reckless to *assume* he was bluffing.

The main topic on the agenda was how defueling would affect Washington's willingness to pursue another Gallucci-Kang meeting. In the end, while refusing to meet might have been emotionally satisfying, the principals decided it could be counterproductive. Pulling the plug on U.S.–North Korean talks before Pyongyang broke continuity of safeguards might hand the North Koreans an easy excuse to continue to flout the nuclear nonproliferation regime. Giving every opportunity for negotiations to work—provided North Korea completed the March inspection activities and allowed the IAEA to separate the necessary fuel rods—would place Washington in the strongest possible position to galvanize international support for sanctions if its efforts failed.

Under these trying circumstances, close cooperation between Washington and the IAEA was imperative, but the agency had staked out a position that many in the U.S. government saw as a prescription for failure. The IAEA wanted not only to select and segregate rods but also to measure them, since that was standard operating procedure for countries with safeguards agreements. The problem was that North Korea believed its IAEA agreement was not in force. Moreover, Pyongyang's technicians knew that such measurements might provide valuable information on their nuclear past, perhaps even substituting for the conduct of special inspections, the issue that had precipitated the crisis. On top of that, the agency was demanding to conduct new activities to complete the March inspection, seemingly contradicting the U.S.

position that all Pyongyang had to do was complete the old ones.[27] The negative North Korean response on both counts was predictable.[28]

The IAEA, however, showed some tactical finesse. Vienna quickly realized that piling on would not only jeopardize its chance to safeguard the unloaded reactor core but also hand the North Koreans fodder for their propaganda mill. The agency did not want to appear so rigid that it would be accused of undermining Washington's policy but was also concerned that the United States might sacrifice too much. The IAEA was willing to "suspend history" but preferred a showdown to "ending history," according to one official.[29] In agency parlance, "suspending history" meant *preserving but not analyzing* data necessary to measure past activities. "Ending history" meant *destroying* data necessary to measure past activities. This guiding principle resulted in a new proposal: to insist on selection and segregation immediately but defer measurements until after progress in U.S.–North Korean talks. The agency also would drop its request for new activities to complete the March inspection.[30]

That stance resulted in some progress. The good news was that the Americans secured the North's agreement to go ahead with the March inspection. The bad news was that after some signs that Pyongyang's position on unloading might be evolving, the North backtracked: only observation, not segregation of rods, would be allowed.[31] With the May 4 deadline looming, Blix added another facet to his position, proposing that unloading be delayed until the two sides could meet. On May 6, the North Koreans agreed to hold consultations but also made it clear that unloading would proceed unless the IAEA accepted their terms.

The unfolding dispute naturally fueled concern in other capitals, particularly Beijing, which had become more active in seeking a diplomatic solution since the March 31 statement of the UN Security Council. Reflecting its nervousness, China had urged the United States to proceed quickly to the third round without preconditions while telling Pyongyang that the time was ripe for progress. In a rare move, Beijing even floated its own solution to the defueling crisis, coming perilously close to the role of mediator, which it had studiously avoided. Rather than select and segregate a few fuel rods, why not mark all the rods according to their exact location in the reactor core and store them in discrete containers? While more expensive and certainly inconvenient, Chinese experts had concluded this would preserve the option of conducting measurements later on, perhaps after U.S.–North Korean talks made further progress.[32]

But no solution could be adopted without IAEA inspectors in place; whether to send them remained an open question for Hans Blix, who worried that such a move could confer legitimacy on North Korean activities designed to destroy historical data. If he refused, however, the IAEA would miss a chance to safeguard about five nuclear weapons' worth of plutonium in the rods. A refusal, even on the sound principle that the receiving state may not define the scope of an inspection, would also allow North Korea to claim that it had invited the IAEA to observe the unloading but the agency had turned down the offer. Pyongyang would then be in a better position to defend itself at the UN Security Council: how could the international community penalize it for the IAEA's own decision not to send inspectors to Yongbyon? However disingenuous, the argument could complicate American diplomacy.

For the principals who met on May 7, the best course of action was a "fair warning" approach: rather than assume that witnessing misconduct somehow made the IAEA complicit in the act, the agency should view the unloading as the irreplaceable "eyes and ears" of the international community. That approach, combined with completion of the March inspection activities required by the UN Security Council, would position the IAEA in a way that would sustain the broadest political support and give strong momentum to further Security Council action. Blix came around to this viewpoint and asked the North Koreans to let the inspectors' visit go ahead.

Pyongyang was in no mood to wait. On May 12, Kang privately informed Gallucci that unloading had begun without the inspectors present, although he claimed the possibility to separate the key fuel rods was being preserved. According to one North Korean diplomat, it would take two months to unload, leaving ample time for the United States and North Korea to strike a deal and afterward for the IAEA to select and measure the rods. A foreign ministry statement followed, announcing the unloading and linking "measurement" of the rods to progress in the talks.[33] Three days later, the inspectors left Vienna for North Korea.[34]

Going to War with a Second-Rate Country

Confirmed as secretary of defense in March, William Perry was a master at translating complex situations into a series of simple propositions whose logic drew one inexorably to an incontestable conclusion. He had played an increasing role in the formulation of policy toward Pyongyang. The new defense secretary also assumed a central role as a soft-spoken communicator who could integrate military and diplomatic considerations into the most persuasive articulation of the president's policy. Perry was no stranger to the nuclear crisis; he had been deputy defense secretary under Les Aspin during the first year of the administration. As a young man, the new defense secretary had served in the Army of Occupation in Japan and was well acquainted with the gruesome realities of war.

On May 3—the day before Pyongyang was expected to begin defueling—the secretary gave a major address to the Asia Society. He explained that North Korea had an easy way to convince the world of Kim Il Sung's assertion that his country had no nuclear weapons: by fulfilling Pyongyang's commitments to the IAEA, allowing inspections to proceed, and implementing the North-South accord to denuclearize the peninsula. The United States sought not endless discussions but "certifiable compliance." Otherwise, the United Nations might have to consider appropriate steps, including sanctions.

Perry also acknowledged that equating sanctions with a declaration of war might merely reflect overheated rhetoric on North Korea's part, but as secretary of defense, he was responsible for ensuring "the adequate readiness of U.S. military forces in the face of such threats. . . . Our forces have been, are, and will be ready to meet any contingency." Perry detailed recent American and South Korean military moves: the deployment of Patriot missiles (by this time all operational in theater), an increase in intelligence assets to watch the North more closely, and the deployment of new AH-64 Apache helicopters and Bradley fighting vehicles to replace older models. Absent progress on the nuclear issue, the Team Spirit military exercise would be held in November. Perry concluded:

> We must understand that every course of action we could take has consequences. Acquiescing now to an active North Korean nuclear program would invite a future crisis. Taking military action now would invite an immediate crisis. Even the course we've chosen—a course which combines diplomacy with military preparedness—is not entirely free of risk. It is possible that North Korea could misperceive these efforts as provocations. We must face that possibility, comparing that risk to the far greater risk of letting North Korea develop the capability of producing a nuclear arsenal or the risk inherent in not maintaining the readiness of our forces.[35]

Although the secretary focused on military preparedness on the peninsula, he did not mention an open secret at the Pentagon: the United States could not fight a war in Korea without Japan.[36] Bases in that country would be critical to support forces on the Korean Peninsula, since American troops stationed in and around Japan would be involved in a conflict. While the 1960 Mutual Defense Treaty provided for prior consultations if the United States wanted to use those bases, Prime Minister Eisaku Sato affirmed in 1969 that since Japan's security would be seriously affected by an attack on South Korea, it would respond "positively and promptly" to any request.[37] American requirements even extended to civilian airports and seaports. One U.S. official recalled, "We were going to turn Narita [Tokyo's international airport] into a big military staging ground."[38]

American planning contemplated Japanese help in contingencies—for example, in blockading the North—that ran smack up against the constitutional principle of collective "self-defense" imposed on Tokyo after World War II. The possibility of expanded participation in American regional military operations increased in the 1960s, as Japan's economy grew and its forces became more capable. The leak of the secret "Three Arrows" study in 1965, which concluded that operations with the United States were the best way of defending Japan in case of another Korean conflict, created a backlash among the Japanese public. That blocked any governmental hopes to loosen the constitutional restraints on expanded military operations.[39] Only a decade later, once U.S. forces were withdrawn from the Pacific after the Vietnam War, did it seem unavoidable that Japan would have to take more responsibility for its own defense. A set of U.S.-Japanese defense guidelines issued in 1978 emphasized territorial defense but also mentioned cooperation in providing for "peace and stability of the Far East."[40]

Exactly what that phrase meant became the subject of deep soul-searching by both sides. Japan's inability to deploy units to the Persian Gulf to help fight the 1991 war against Iraq because of insufficient domestic support starkly illustrated the limitations on alliance cooperation. After that failure, Japanese officials showed renewed interest in becoming part of "collective defense" efforts. In 1992 Japan passed a law allowing its forces to participate in United Nations peacekeeping operations, albeit with strict restrictions. Japanese decisionmakers and the public were gradually coming to understand that in the post–cold war world, Tokyo needed to play an expanded military role. Still, according to Nobuo Ishihara, the former vice chief cabinet secretary, "At that time, the government did have almost no preparations for the emergency on the Korean Peninsula."[41]

Faced with a potential crisis in Korea, the Pentagon and the Japanese Defense Agency (so named after World War II when Japan's defense organization was downgraded from a ministry) launched secret discussions in 1993 on "contingency planning." Essentially, the Pentagon gave the Japanese a list of everything they had to do, such as provide logistical support, handle casualties, carry out search and rescue operations, conduct minesweeping, support an economic blockade, and oversee base security. One American participant characterized it as "payback time" for all the United States had done for Japan after World War II.[42] These talks were supplemented by weekly contacts between Tokyo's highest-ranking military officer and the commander of U.S. forces in Japan, Air Force General Richard Myers, as well as their staffs. Americans and Japanese also conducted joint war games—staff exercises not involving actual forces—covering various scenarios for a conflict on the peninsula.[43]

The Japanese knew how important it was to stand shoulder-to-shoulder with the United States in addressing what might also be a grave threat to their own national security. Tokyo's internal studies had highlighted the possibility of North Korean attacks using chemical or biological weapons or attempts to destroy the twenty-five nuclear reactors along the Sea of Japan, vulnerable to North Korean commando operations and missile attacks.[44] Such attacks would untie Japan's hands, allowing the government to take any and all measures to ensure the defense of its territory. Until then, the government could not even evacuate its thousands of civilians on the peninsula in case of a conflict.[45]

Recognizing this problem, Prime Minister Morihiro Hosokawa's government began to devise ways to remove Japan from its legal straightjacket. Temporary emergency legislation was prepared for the Diet allowing, among other things, logistical support for and participation in a naval blockade of North Korea, an activity both the Defense Agency and the Ministry of Foreign Affairs had concluded would be unconstitutional.[46] Consulted informally, members of the Diet seemed supportive. However, the subject was still extremely sensitive; after all, 70 percent of the Japanese public was opposed to the use of American bases in Japan for the defense of South Korea even in the event of a North Korean attack.[47]

Other potential difficulties remained as well, one being how to meet America's request for over 1,900 items to support military operations. Japan faced no constraint in providing nonlethal equipment such as ambulances, beds, and warehouses, but ammunition was out of bounds. Civilian industries might be able to help with various repair activities, just as they had during the Korean War, except that now they might not know enough about sophisticated new military equipment.[48]

As the crisis heightened in April, Secretary Perry decided that he needed personally to assess the state of readiness of American forces in Northeast Asia. At his first stop in Seoul, Perry raised some unpleasant realities and was reminded of some as well. He asked Foreign Minister Han Sung Joo what South Korea would do if diplomacy failed and sanctions proved ineffective. Han did not answer. Perry warned President Kim that sanctions might be accompanied by measures to bolster the joint U.S.–South Korean military posture. Summing up his philosophy, he told the South Korean minister of defense, "We will not initiate war. We will not provoke a war. But we should not invite a war" through lack of preparation.

At his next stop in Tokyo, Secretary Perry confirmed that Japan was prepared to support America's military preparations and discussed help for the U.S. interdiction of North Korean shipping if the United Nations imposed sanctions. He reassured the head of the Japanese Defense Agency, Kazuo Aichi, that Washington would take no steps without consulting Tokyo first. Aichi, in turn, reassured him that Japan was preparing special legislation that would allow it to respond to military contingencies related to the Korean Peninsula. Tokyo's cooperation added a critical piece to the military planning puzzle that Washington was assembling.

After his visit to the Far East, Perry gathered all the four-star generals and admirals in the American military, including commanders-in-chief of the unified and regional commands, in a secure Pentagon conference room, "the tank," to review the steps needed to carry out the plan for a second Korean War. Some measures had already been taken. Further moves would include deploying troops and transport from other commands, sending aircraft carriers and land-based aircraft closer to the peninsula, and injecting massive reinforcements of ground forces. The opinion was unanimous. With a green light from the president, the war plan could be implemented.[49]

Secretary Perry, General John Shalikashvili, and General Luck presented the findings of the "tank" session to the president and his senior advisers in the Cabinet Room on May 19. Clinton and Vice President Gore had been updated periodically on the developing military situation, but this briefing would prove critical in shaping policy in the tense days ahead.[50] On entering the room, the president, looking forward to the nearing commemoration of the fiftieth anniversary of the D-Day invasion of Normandy, asked whether any of the veterans planned to parachute at the ceremonies. "I sure hope they [Congress] pass the health care plan first," cracked Shalikashvili, amid laughter.

Perry then took the floor. Summarizing the conventional military balance at the Demilitarized Zone, he noted that North Korea's rhetoric had become "increasingly obnoxious" of late, including repetition of its slogan that Korea would be reunified by 1995 and the March 19 threat to engulf the South in a "sea of fire." The on-again-off-again nature of the third round reminded Perry of the *Peanuts* comic strip in which Lucy kept pulling the football away before Charlie Brown had a chance to kick it. Meanwhile, North Korea's dangerous export practices raised the prospect of a rampant proliferator selling a matched set of ballistic missiles with nuclear warheads. The issue of whether

North Korea might sell completed nuclear weapons to a country like Iran or Libya was "not merely an academic one" to Perry.

The secretary of defense said that American forces could strike the Yong-byon facility and set the North Korean nuclear program back by years. The downside risk, however, was that this action would certainly spark a violent reaction, perhaps even a general war. He judged that South Korea and Japan would probably not support such a strike. Perry continued that "hard sanctions," such as an economic embargo requiring interdictions at sea, were more likely to provoke a violent reaction than "soft sanctions," such as restricting financial remittances from overseas, particularly from North Korean sympathizers in Japan.

Perry was determined to ensure that American force levels in Korea were adequate to the level of risk in theater. He did not wish to witness a reprise of Task Force Smith, the first U.S. Army unit sent to South Korea after the North's attack in 1950. Named after its commander, Lieutenant Colonel Charles B. ("Bud") Smith, it consisted of some 400 soldiers from the American 24th Infantry Division stationed in Japan. Task Force Smith was overrun in its first battle, in part because it underestimated the North Koreans, not only shocking the American Far East Command but also the Joint Chiefs in Washington.

The secretary worried that the North Koreans could miscalculate in two ways. They could judge the United States too weak and seek to take advantage of that. Or they could interpret the firm steps Washington authorized to reinforce its presence in Korea as a provocation. The North Koreans were like adolescents with guns. He concluded that the United States needed to punch a hole in their mindset.

Shalikashvili then took over, describing the balance of forces on the peninsula. No doubt the North Koreans outnumbered allied forces. He recited the two-to-one advantage enjoyed by North Korea in tanks, airframes, and other key indicators. South Korea had serious deficiencies, particularly in the face of massive North Korean artillery batteries arrayed just 24 miles from Seoul. Vice President Gore asked whether the South had sufficient counterbattery radar; Shalikashvili said no. On the other hand, Seoul's troops were better fed, trained, and equipped and in better physical condition.

But unlike some in the intelligence community, Shalikashvili did not find strong enough indicators in the North to issue a warning of war. Training and other activities were proceeding at about normal levels. If war were to occur, the United States and South Korea would win, but it would be costly. Computer projections showed 30,000 American casualties and 450,000 South Korean casualties, but these numbers might be too low; the killed-in-action numbers would likely be higher since the battlefield was far more lethal than during the Korean War in the 1950s. He did not mention Pentagon estimates that another Korean war would kill or wound 1 million civilians, cost more than $60 billion, devastate the South Korean economy to the tune of at least $1 trillion, cause an Asian recession, and adversely effect the rest of the global economy. When asked by the president at a different briefing whether the United States would win the war, General Luck replied, "Yes, but at the cost of a million and a trillion."[51]

Shalikashvili also pointed out that a Korean conflict would have important implications for the global U.S. force posture. It would require substantial reinforcements, including 400,000 troops, carrier battle groups, and fighter squadrons, not to mention marine amphibious units and reserve call-ups. Still, that would not significantly affect the nation's Haiti operation or enforcing the no-fly zone against Iraq. Referring to worries that planning "major regional contingencies" risked diverting too many fighting assets, one participant noted, "There will always be some SOB who tries to take advantage" of U.S. focus in one theater by making trouble in another. Shalikashvili added that Saddam Hussein was too weak to try to make a military move at the moment.

General Luck, recently arrived from Seoul, then took the floor, noting dryly that dealing with a war zone in Korea was better than dealing with the press corps in Washington. Luck reported that he had been working hard to persuade the South Koreans to take prudent steps to shore up their position in relation to the North, for example, through the purchase and deployment of counterbattery radar to help defend Seoul. But turning the South Koreans, Luck concluded, was like trying to turn a battleship.

The military leaders agreed that Washington had to remain in lockstep with South Korea on dealing with the nuclear issue, particularly since the North continued to try to drive a wedge between the two allies. Inevitably, the task grew more difficult the more tension mounted, as South Korea would absorb the brunt of any assault from the North. Since Secretary Perry's return from Seoul, a secure telephone line had been set up for direct consultations with South Korea's defense minister Lee Byong Tae. Perry had called Lee for the first time that very day, telling him that the two allies needed to increase U.S.–South Korean military readiness if the nuclear issue returned to the UN Security Council for action. General Luck and his staff at U.S. Forces Korea had worked closely with the South Korean Joint Chiefs on developing those plans.[52]

After the May 19 briefing, the administration was ready to move forward with whatever steps were needed to deter and, if necessary, fight a second Korean War. Don Oberdorfer, former *Washington Post* reporter, would later observe that such a war "would be by far the gravest crisis of Clinton's sixteen-month presidency, overwhelming nearly everything else he had planned or dreamed of doing at home or abroad."[53] The administration's preparations brought that home to the president and his foreign policy advisers.

Throughout 1993, some officers at the Pentagon had wanted to play "hard-ball" with Pyongyang. General Luck was more cautious; he had to live with the North's threat and America's South Korean allies every day. The process initiated by Perry that spring, however, led the U.S. military to a consensus on the best strategy to move forward. A strong posture was essential, but diplomacy had to be open to an agreement that achieved American objectives while avoiding, in the words of one officer, "going to war with a second-rate country that was falling apart anyway."[54]

A Needle in a Haystack

Stepping off the Beijing-to-Pyongyang flight, Ollie Heinonen, a soft-spoken Finnish national who headed the IAEA inspection team, got to work immediately. Heinonen was in a tight spot; he arrived on May 19, just as the Korean Peninsula teetered at the brink of crisis. He reported to Vienna that the inspectors were well received. The North Korean technicians were providing information about the fuel discharge operations, and only a small percentage of the 8,000 fuel rods had been removed. They had not yet come close to unloading the rods the agency wanted to separate for eventual measurement.

But Heinonen also relayed disturbing news. He discovered that Pyongyang's unloading of the spent fuel was proceeding at twice the expected rate since it had two, not just one, machine to discharge the fuel. Earlier in the year, Secretary Perry had predicted defueling could take three months, a judgment that U.S. intelligence reiterated a few days before unloading started. The North Koreans themselves had told the Americans that the campaign would take two months. Now it looked as though the rods would be removed in a matter of weeks. That would not have mattered if they were being unloaded carefully to preserve information on their location in the reactor core. But Pyongyang's technicians were literally dumping the rods into storage baskets (perhaps deliberately), making it impossible to reconstruct where each one had been situated. In short, the North Koreans were moving more quickly than anticipated, not only to unload the rods but also in a manner guaranteed to destroy the historical information needed for any scheme on the table, including the Chinese compromise proposal.[55]

The same day Heinonen arrived in North Korea, Blix, faced with the imminent loss of history, offered to send Dimitri Perricos to Pyongyang for discussions on how and when to segregate the fuel rods for future measurements. The agency's public pronouncements sounded both upbeat and ominous: "As of today, it still seems possible to implement the required safeguards measures." Should the DPRK continue the discharge operation without these measures, it would result in "irreparable loss of the agency's ability to verify whether all nuclear material subjected to safeguards in the DPRK is in fact under safeguards and that no such material has been diverted."[56]

One day later, the Principals Committee met again at the White House. While unloading had created a dilemma for the IAEA over whether to send inspectors to Yongbyon to observe that process, the IAEA inspection now under way to complete the March activities presented the Clinton administration with its own dilemma: whether to schedule the next meeting between Gallucci and Kang. A few weeks earlier, the principals had decided to schedule the meeting if North Korea completed the March inspection activities and preserved historical information in the fuel rods. While the North was on the road to satisfying the first condition and had not yet broken the second condition, as a practical matter, its method of unloading meant the issue would soon be referred back to the Security Council. How could the United States offer another round of talks in the face of such egregious North Korean conduct?

This question took on added salience since President Clinton's foreign policy was under attack for weakness and inconsistency. On May 17, Ted Koppel, host of ABC's *Nightline*, asserted that "this administration is becoming notorious for making [threats] against countries all over the world, making threats and then backing down." A majority of Americans thought President Bush had done a better job on foreign policy, and only 13 percent felt Clinton had a clear approach.[57] Furthermore, Republicans and Democrats alike wanted a tougher stance on Korea. Appearing on television together, Senator Robert Dole and Democratic majority leader George Mitchell called for sanctions.[58] Jim Hoagland, a columnist for the *Washington Post*, warned, "Serious consideration must now be given to how America would prepare for and fight a second Korean war."[59]

As the crisis deepened, the president spent more time on Korea. He remained open to ideas from any quarter, tearing op-ed articles out of his news clips and sending them to the NSC staff with questions and comments. The uninitiated found it hard to decipher southpaw Clinton's loopy backhanded writing. Help came from his assistant, Nancy Hernreich, who neatly printed the translation beneath. When Richard Perle, a conservative foreign policy strategist, opined in the May 3 *Wall Street Journal* that with or without international inspections, the North Koreans would not give up their nuclear weapons, Clinton asked, "What's the answer?"[60] (The reply was that the United States did not know North Korean intentions with certainty, so it should test whether they might give them up diplomatically before resorting to harsher measures.) The president also asked about a May 19 *New York Times* op-ed piece by Donald Gregg, the former ambassador to South Korea under the Bush administration, titled "Offer Korea a Carrot."[61] The NSC staff told him that the United States had already made clear the carrots available to North Korea.

The Principals Committee meeting on May 20 began with Gallucci's terse update; 1,400 of the 8,000 rods had now been removed, and Blix was dispatching more inspectors to help the team at Yongbyon. Did continuing to pursue the third round of Gallucci-Kang talks still make sense? Also, what were the political consequences in view of the administration's statements that it would not move forward unless the North allowed satisfactory inspections and stopped obstructing activities at the reactor? In the end, the principals reached the same consensus as at the last session: negotiations should continue. Going the extra diplomatic mile seemed to make sense, in part because North Korea had not yet diverted any fuel or destroyed history and was allowing the IAEA to complete the March inspection, but also because it would strengthen the U.S. hand if the time came to take tougher steps. Anticipating the principals' conclusion, just before the meeting Secretary Perry told reporters that, so far, the North was only guilty of a "technical violation."[62]

The administration also decided to reach out to Pyongyang again, this time through Sam Nunn, a highly respected national security authority and chairman of the Senate Armed Services Committee. Nunn had visited Seoul in early 1994 along with Senator Richard Lugar of Indiana, a senior Republican on the Senate Foreign Relations Committee. The two had teamed up on a number of important foreign policy and defense issues, demonstrating that bipartisanship was still possible in an era of increasing political rancor on Capitol Hill. Their flagship achievement had been the Nunn-Lugar program of assistance to the states of the former Soviet Union, to help dismantle, destroy, and secure that country's far-flung nuclear weapons infrastructure and intercontinental-missile delivery systems.

During his birthday celebration in April, Kim Il Sung had evidently extended an invitation to Senators Nunn and Carl Levin, another Democrat on the Armed Services Committee, to visit North Korea. Nunn got wind of it when told by Jim Laney, who visited Washington on May 10. Still concerned about the administration's inability to communicate directly with the North's leaders, Laney discussed the idea with Perry, Lake, and Gallucci, all of whom reacted positively. Nunn agreed to carry a message from President Clinton if it would help, but wanted Senator Lugar to join him.[63]

An April 26 letter from the chairman of the Supreme People's Assembly to Vice President Al Gore, in his capacity as president of the Senate, provided additional cover. No one viewed the assembly as a meaningful body, so a letter inviting a delegation of legislators to Pyongyang was interpreted as simply another line of communication the North was trying to open with Washington.[64] After the principals gave the go-ahead, Vice President Gore responded, proposing that Nunn and Lugar visit Pyongyang on May 25 to meet Kim Il Sung. The purpose of the trip would be to "exchange views on how we can expedite resolution of the nuclear issue, and from there open a new era for the Korean peninsula by moving toward more normal relations, both political and economic, between our two nations."

But time stood still for no intermediary, official or otherwise, as the defueling campaign rapidly forced the issue. A New York channel meeting three days later ended in a tenuous agreement to hold the next Gallucci-Kang meeting in early June but without resolving the spent fuel problem. The North Koreans threatened to escalate the crisis dramatically by expelling IAEA inspectors and disabling the agency's monitoring equipment—enabling Pyongyang to divert nuclear material with impunity—if the third round were canceled. Briefing the Security Council afterwards, Gallucci glanced at the Chinese ambassador and warned "those with influence" to persuade Pyongyang not to preclude further IAEA historical analysis. Otherwise, the third round would be scuttled and the UN Security Council would have to consider sanctions.

The last remaining hopes for a diplomatic solution gradually began to melt away. First, the Nunn-Lugar visit ran aground. Just before they were scheduled to leave for Pyongyang, Gallucci and Poneman spent ninety minutes with the two senators going over points that the administration would like Kim Il Sung to understand. The message was clear: the United States was serious about normalizing relations with the North, would not walk away from the nuclear problem, and could not be split from its allies. Kim should understand that he could open or close the door to future cooperation but could not keep haggling over minutiae.

On May 25, Nunn and Lugar arrived in their Senate offices, bags packed, fully briefed, and ready to go. Out at Andrews Air Force Base, their pilot and copilot reviewed the flight plan: a 12:15 PM take-off, refueling in Alaska, and then a landing in Pyongyang. Should North Korea fail to grant them landing rights, the two senators would land in Japan and switch to a smaller, non-U.S. plane. Then came word from North Korea. While Pyongyang "agreed in principle" to the visit, the "shortness" of notification made it impossible to receive the senators so soon. Could they come around June 10? Gallucci called them to break the news. According to Lugar, "Things sort of fell apart immediately thereafter."[65]

The next day American and North Korean diplomats met again in New York but failed to reach agreement on a date for the third round after the Americans refused to drop the condition that the North allow separation and segregation of the discharged fuel rods. The two sides agreed to meet again after talks with the IAEA were concluded on May 27.

All hope for a diplomatic solution now focused on Dimitri Perricos, who arrived in Pyongyang just before the Nunn-Lugar trip was canceled. He immediately consulted with his colleague, Ollie Heinonen, and then cabled their boss, Hans Blix: "We are still OK but the North is getting awfully close to hitting the select fuel."

But his talks proved futile. The North's proposed compromise, similar to that advanced by the Chinese, was dubbed the "needle in the haystack" approach by the acerbic Greek. The random dumping of fuel rods into baskets made it impossible to determine where they had been located in the reactor core, a key data point for extracting historical information. Perricos reported to Blix on May 27 that the negotiations had failed, prompting him to inform the UN secretary general that the opportunity to separate the critical rods would be "lost within days."[66]

Save the Past but Lose the Future?

With the failure of the Pyongyang talks and the loss of historical information imminent, the principals convened on May 27 to discuss sanctions against North Korea. Little had changed since the earlier discussions; a spectrum of measures remained available, including a comprehensive economic embargo, which would be implemented gradually or rapidly. But now, with North Korea's deliberate flouting of the international community's demands, the principals needed to begin laying the groundwork for the imposition of sanctions.

Their review exposed some serious dilemmas. No one present thought sanctions would induce North Korea to comply with its nonproliferation obligations, or to curtail or reveal its nuclear activities. Indeed, there was a clear danger that sanctions over past production of perhaps one or two bombs' worth of plutonium could lead North Korea to separate enough additional plutonium to produce about five more. The principals also could not simply ignore Pyongyang's assertion that it would view sanctions as an act of war, particularly if an embargo were enforced militarily. If sanctions were not imposed, however, the credibility of the nonproliferation regime and of long-standing U.S. policy would be badly compromised. In the end, they supported the imposition of sanctions as the least bad option, although they would continue to grapple with its broader implications.

For now, the principals agreed to begin stepping up pressure on North Korea. First, Secretary Christopher would urge China's foreign minister Qian Qichen to lean on Pyongyang before defueling led to a train wreck between North Korea and the Security Council. Immediately after the White House meeting, Christopher tried unsuccessfully to call his Chinese counterpart twice. Evidently, the only equipment available for Qian to hold an official conversation with a translator was located in the Foreign Ministry, but the minister had left the building. Press reports speculated that there might have been an ongoing session of the Politburo on Korea, and rumors circulated about a possible rift between Qian and President Jiang. The president wanted to show support for Pyongyang's brinksmanship, while Qian was said to be concerned about the potentially destabilizing effect of a harsh American reaction against North Korea as well as the possibility of jeopardizing relations with South Korea and Japan. Whether true or not, the rumors captured the dilemma facing Chinese leaders.

Although Christopher failed to talk to Qian, a letter with his message was delivered. The secretary warned that the third round was close to being lost and with it the possibility of normalized relations between the United States and North Korea. If Blix found that the basis for determining the operating history of the reactor was destroyed, the United States would have no choice but to seek "prompt adoption of a resolution establishing appropriate economic sanctions." Beijing passed the message to Pyongyang but offered little beyond counseling patience once again.

A second step approved by the principals was for the State Department to draft a presidential statement for discussion at the Security Council condemning the North's recent moves, widely understood to be the last step before seeking sanctions. When the draft was tabled soon afterward, the Chinese resisted, arguing that the North Koreans had assured them there was still plenty of time to work out an arrangement, but that excuse was wearing thin. Two days into the debate, Rick Inderfurth, the deputy U.S. representative, reported that over half of the rods had been removed and discharge was continuing at 360 rods a day, the fastest rate since May 4. Everyone knew North Korea had already begun unloading rods critical to determining the past. Finally, the Chinese gave in and the Security Council issued a statement on May 30 urging North Korea to proceed with the discharge in a manner that preserved the possibility of measurements. It also called for immediate consultations between Vienna and Pyongyang.[67]

The day after their May 27 session, the principals convened once again. With tensions rising and the emphasis now on day-to-day tactical decisions, they took a step back to continue considering the effect of sanctions and whether they would defend the virtue but defeat the purposes of the Nuclear Non-Proliferation Treaty. "It is crazy that we should go to war to save the past if we lose the future," argued one principal. That view reflected the concern that sanctions might simply make a bad situation worse, provoking a hostile Pyongyang to continue to refuse to disclose its past while simultaneously unshackling its capabilities to move into serial production of un-safeguarded plutonium. Others saw the "past-versus-present" dichotomy less starkly: past and present objectives were mutually reinforcing, not inconsistent. The North's possession of "a few" nuclear weapons perhaps produced in the past was still unacceptable. Pyongyang's violation of safeguards, moreover, provided a firm legal basis for U.S. actions.

In grappling with this dilemma, the principals came up with a face-saving way out for the North Koreans, dubbed the "Rudolf Hess option" after the flight of the high-ranking Nazi to England during World War II in an ill-fated attempt to negotiate a separate peace. As long as the North Koreans had spent fuel in their possession, there would be one nightmare after another. Under the Rudolf Hess option, the United States would send a special envoy to Beijing to enlist its help in securing a North Korean pledge to send the spent fuel to China. If Pyongyang agreed, Washington would hold off on international sanctions, and Gallucci would meet Kang to work on a diplomatic solution. Gallucci and Poneman were asked to work with Perry to draft a secret message for the Chinese. In the meantime, the principals agreed to proceed down the sanctions track; they asked the Deputies Committee to develop recommendations within forty-eight hours.

Following the session, the NSC staff reported the results to the president. As usual, Clinton used his pen to propel himself through the text, heavily lining passages and noting key points with asterisks. The memo explained that the United States had secured a strong and unanimous Security Council statement and that Christopher had written the Chinese foreign minister seeking Beijing's intervention with North Korea. The principals recommended that the United States proceed with sanctions. Despite the risks, the United States could not allow North Korea to flout its nonproliferation obligations. Nor could it reverse four decades of nonproliferation policy by countenancing one or two bombs' worth of plutonium already separated in North Korea, in exchange for a promise to keep five more bombs' worth under safeguards. At the same time, the Rudolf Hess option would be further developed. "Not bad," the president noted in the margin.

The Deputies Committee gathered on June 1 to flesh out sanctions strategy. The meeting revealed new splits over how they should be phased. Some continued to support gradual escalation—the previous U.S. approach—since it would increase pressure steadily on Pyongyang, secure Chinese support, and reduce the chances of an unpredictable North Korean reaction. But a new concern emerged that it might not be politically feasible to go repeatedly to the Security Council to obtain increasingly restrictive resolutions. Others favored passing a strong resolution right away but stopping short of a total economic embargo. A compromise option would seek a single resolution that would include discrete triggers so the level of sanction would increase if North Korea committed further transgressions.

The administration was also split over what Pyongyang would have to do once sanctions were enacted in order to secure relief from their restrictions. (Such a provision would be built into the UN resolution.) One option would lift sanctions only if the IAEA declared North Korea in full compliance with its safeguards obligations. By keying sanctions relief to the resolution of the safeguards violations that caused the crisis in the first place, the international community would condemn Pyongyang's past behavior and set a precedent that others could not escape their nonproliferation obligations without penalty. But the "dismantlement-firsters" wanted to see tangible progress on constraining the more urgent threat posed by Pyongyang's ability to accumulate plutonium—for example, by having North Korea ship its spent fuel out of the country—before granting sanctions relief. As usual, a third option combined elements of both positions. The meeting ended with Berger asking Gallucci, Poneman, Lieutenant General Wesley Clark, and the Pentagon's Walt Slocombe to draft options for the president.

As Washington deliberated over sanctions, it was now clear that the Korean Peninsula was heading into a full-scale crisis. Nerves in the region were on edge. North Korea test-fired an antiship missile in the Sea of Japan the day after the May 30 Security Council statement was issued. Japanese officials played down the test as routine, but some experts saw it as a veiled threat against Tokyo not to support sanctions. At home, Senator Nunn warned Pyongyang that "playing this game has very dangerous consequences."[68] Vice President Gore sought to reassure America's allies and deter its adversaries, saying the "United States of America is committed to the security of South Korea and we will not flinch on that and the North Koreans ought to understand that."[69]

President Clinton was also closely following the situation. Before leaving for Europe, he spoke to President Kim on the telephone, reaffirming the need for the two allies to work closely together. In England, after meeting Prime

Minister John Major, President Clinton tried to strike a balanced note, telling reporters that the North could avoid international sanctions only if it complied with inspections of its nuclear program. But he also said, "I do not want a lot of saber rattling over this, or war talk."[70] Once arrived in Rome, the presidential party kept the pressure on Washington for real-time updates to press guidance, since Korea was the subject of the first question at every press conference.

On June 2, IAEA director general Hans Blix finally pulled the plug. He had tried up until the very last minute to reach agreement, exchanging a flurry of faxes with the North Koreans. It was no use. Blix informed the secretary general that "the limited ability . . . to select and segregate rods had now been lost since all important parts of the core had been discharged." But he also held out hope that the history of Pyongyang's program could be determined by other means if North Korea provided "full cooperation."[71]

Whether North Korea had ever been interested in pulling back from the brink no longer mattered. In retrospect, the weight of evidence seemed to suggest that Pyongyang may have decided in early 1994 to defuel, in response to the Patriot deployment, the collapse of Super Tuesday, or both. The Foreign Ministry may have objected to the move because of the potentially negative impact on diplomacy with the United States. Others may have argued that defueling could not be delayed, particularly since the possibility of a diplomatic solution seemed distant. Moreover, defueling would destroy historical information, helping to further obfuscate the North's nuclear past, and might even put Pyongyang in a stronger negotiating position with Washington. The unloaded rods could serve as important leverage in upcoming talks.

Once a decision was made, the Foreign Ministry had to make the best of a bad situation. Its job was to do everything possible to keep the United States off balance, to limit the potential adverse consequences of defueling, and somehow to get Washington back to the negotiating table. That helped explain the curiously contradictory signals coming from Pyongyang throughout the defueling crisis, accepting talks with the IAEA and holding open the possibility of resolving the problem in the context of a package deal with the United States as unloading continued. Even after the Perricos mission failed, while the party newspaper said there would be no compromise, the Foreign Ministry spokesman portrayed the talks in a positive light. At the same time, unloading accelerated as the North Koreans threw more personnel into the campaign.[72] Since unloading would bring the peninsula to the brink of war, the whole episode reinforced the theory that Pyongyang was perfectly capable of miscalculating in seeking tactical advantage.

The next day, as Blix and Perricos briefed the Security Council in New York, the State Department announced that the third round of U.S.–North Korean talks had been canceled. In Rome, the president said the United Nations would now address the question of sanctions.[73] Back in Washington, the National Security Council staff circulated a draft decision memorandum on sanctions strategy to the rest of the government. The memorandum asked for final views within twenty-four hours.

7 At the Brink

June 3–June 14, 1994

I N unloading its 5-megawatt reactor, North Korea destroyed historical information in the spent fuel rods. Washington responded by canceling talks with Pyongyang and now pressed the United Nations to impose sanctions on the North. With grim determination, Pentagon planners stepped up their efforts to develop options to augment allied military forces in the region, recognizing that the need for deterrence and perhaps defense would spike along with tensions over the nuclear crisis. Explaining the nuclear threat to a concerned public and building an international consensus behind a strong and unified response would now become as urgent as it was essential.

The task would be difficult. North Korea's defueling had elicited howls of protest about the "failure" of American diplomacy. In the *New York Times*, William Safire growled that the United States had to decide "whether to continue the protracted runaround, hoping vainly that Kim Il Sung wants to be bought off, or to enforce international law, which would require the credible threat of war."[1] In the *Washington Post*, Charles Krauthammer was even more acerbic, asserting that the administration's "self-delusion" on North Korea had reached "pathological levels."[2]

This shrill chorus missed a vitally important point: the North had also backed itself into a corner. Just as Pyongyang's effort to intimidate the South with its "sea of fire" comments had backfired, driving the trilateral allies closer together than at any time in the crisis, so its blatantly defiant defueling campaign unified the international community in its willingness to act collectively against Pyongyang. That was not a preordained result, but rather a product of the administration's year-long effort to define defueling as a "red line" in its diplomacy with the North, its regional allies, the permanent members of the Security Council, and the world. Whether North Korea's defueling was the product of delusion or desperation, in crossing that line it essentially dared the United States to cut off dialogue and to refer the nuclear issue to the Security Council for punitive action.

In accepting the dare, U.S. officials knew it would be hard to coordinate positions with their allies and to establish clear understandings with the international community regarding the consequences of such a North Korean action. The path ahead was strewn with obstacles and would twist and turn through unknown terrain. There would be setbacks, pitfalls, and a need to improvise in the face of unexpected actions by unexpected actors. But Washington's painstaking diplomacy had readied it for this moment.

In one sense, the high degree of international consensus on the nuclear question complicated the search for a solution to the crisis by narrowing the scope for further diplomacy. Pyongyang's slash-and-burn tactics had deprived the North of any protective allies. Having snapped the lifeline of talks with the United States, it was hard to imagine—much less secure—a graceful way out of its growing predicament. This worried the president and his national security team. While Washington tried to build an escape hatch for North Korea into its sanctions resolution and considered last-ditch diplomatic missions, devising a successful endgame continued to bedevil the Americans.

Managing the North Korean crisis felt like playing a multitiered chess game on overlapping boards. It required dealing with the North, the South, China, Japan, the International Atomic Energy Agency, the United Nations, the non-aligned movement, Congress, the press, and others. Critical issues included sanctions, military strategy and, ominously, the threat of a rash North Korean action to seize and extract plutonium from the spent fuel rods left corroding in the pool at Yongbyon. The situation had grown so complex that the National Security Council staff—which confined most memos going to the Oval Office to one or two pages—took nine single-spaced pages to lay out the strategy and options for the president. Clinton devoured the detail; the memo came back, as usual, with his familiar heavy lining.

Building an International Coalition

The weekend of June 3 brought summer to Washington. With the IAEA verdict in, South Korean and Japanese officials had flown in to meet with Gallucci. The main topic was sanctions. Some sessions were held at the State Department, others at Roosevelt Hall, home of the National War College. The college was located at Fort McNair overlooking the Potomac River, where the diplomats were safe from the prying eyes of reporters.[3] There, an enormous map hanging in the main stairwell proclaims, "Everything changes with geography." That awkward aphorism may have weighed on South Korean and Japanese diplomats confronting the threat of a nuclear-armed North Korea.

Trilateral cooperation had been the cornerstone of American strategy for dealing with North Korea. In the aftermath of the reactor unloading, securing support from Seoul and Tokyo would be the first act in the unfolding drama of building a multilateral coalition supporting sanctions. Once that foundation was established, the partners could fan out to persuade the permanent members of the UN Security Council to come on board. Proliferation hawks like Britain and France could be counted on, but Russia was unpredictable and China would be a tough sell. Cutting Pyongyang off from its diplomatic lifeline to third world countries, some of which were members of the Security Council, would also be important. But for now, the most pressing task was building firm trilateral support for what would come next.

With the mounting crisis, Japan had become even more critical. According to one Japanese diplomat, until 1994 Tokyo was riding in the back seat of a car driven by Washington and Seoul.[4] With the events that spring, it moved up front. But the timing could not have been worse from the Japanese perspective. In the span of six months, from January to June, it had been ruled by three different governments, two coalitions with substantial participation by the Socialist Party (which had close ties with North Korea), and one that commanded only a minority in the Diet. Despite press speculation to the contrary, however, the Japanese government was determined to support the United States.

That support was crucial not only politically but also because Tokyo had close economic ties with Pyongyang. Although bilateral trade had been declining since the early 1990s, Japan was still the North's second largest trading partner after China. Indeed, Pyongyang's economic ties with Japan were in some ways even more important since they did more to link North Korea to the outside world. It had imported the beginnings of a modern clothing-assembly industry, much of its heavy machinery, and sizable quantities of agricultural chemicals from Japan.

The critical conduit for capital, technology, and expertise ran through the Chosen Soren, an organization of 600,000 pro-Pyongyang Koreans living in Japan that made substantial but poorly monitored cash contributions to North Korea (in the range of $200 million to $600 million a year). By 1994 its cash remittances were shrinking as the recession, publicity on Pyongyang's human rights violations, and the aging of the generation most devoted to the

North took their toll. After years of dramatic growth, the Chosen Soren's clothing-assembly joint ventures in North Korea faced grave difficulties in maintaining production levels, the result of a crumbling infrastructure, scarce access to raw materials, and chronic problems with the government. In short, the Chosen Soren's aid to the North might be vulnerable to sanctions.

Japan had been studying the possibility of sanctions since early 1993 but only took them seriously after President Clinton discussed the matter twice with Prime Minister Morihiro Hosokawa. The American president first raised the issue of cutting off Chosen Soren remittances at the November 1993 Asia-Pacific Economic Cooperation summit. Then in February 1994, as the crisis with the IAEA escalated, Clinton raised sanctions again.[5] The Cabinet Office promptly launched studies by different government agencies, with the Foreign Ministry pulling all of the work together.[6]

Quietly, the government also began to test procedures that might be used to implement sanctions. In February, the Cabinet Office called in officials from the Ministry of Finance and asked them to strengthen customs checks on boats leaving Nigata port for North Korea, believed to carry contraband and hard currency.[7] Aside from helping to perfect sanctions procedures, the checks would also gauge the Chosen Soren's reaction since Tokyo was concerned the organization could turn violent if events with North Korea spun out of control. But the Chosen Soren seemed barely to notice the test run.[8]

By the end of March, Prime Minister Hosokawa had told the Diet that Tokyo would "respond as far as it can under the constitution and within the scope of its laws."[9] But the Japanese Defense Agency was seeking every means to work around as many limitations as possible. Existing laws and regulations also may have limited the government's ability to enforce absolute measures such as prohibiting travel, trade, and the transfer of funds. But it could use the weapon of "administrative guidance" that would bring to bear the weight of public exposure and bureaucratic displeasure in forcing the compliance of the business community.

Above all, the government needed to build public support for sanctions. Previous efforts to rouse the populace had fizzled. A deliberate leak to the press in June 1993 of information on a Nodong missile test the previous month did little to stimulate public concern. Still, opinion polls showed at least a base of support for sanctions. By October 1993, 54 percent of the Japanese supported sanctions against North Korea, although that figure dropped to 49 percent by the end of the year.[10] The government, however, remained cautious, in part because the strong Socialist Party traditionally had opposed sanctions. Just before leaving office on April 8, Prime Minister Hosokawa told President Kim that he did not want to increase public anxiety.

The issue of sanctions figured prominently in discussions leading to the formation of a new government. When the Shinseito Party succeeded in forging a governmental platform calling for Japan to abide by Security Council sanctions and to prepare for possible emergencies, it effectively drove the Socialists out of the coalition. This resulted in the formation of a minority government led by former foreign minister Tsutomu Hata, which lasted just long enough to lend support to American efforts at a critical moment. [11]

In Seoul, the equation was less complicated. Despite past vacillations, the government responded to the crisis with firmness, a reflection of public opinion. Six in ten citizens already supported sanctions. [12] The business community lined up behind the Kim government and had substantial leverage to bring to bear on the North. Trade between major conglomerates and Pyongyang had reached about $200 million over the past year, small potatoes for the South but an increasing share of the North's shrinking economy. Moreover, South Korean firms were the only companies providing credit to Pyongyang, again in amounts that were small in absolute terms but significant to the North.

As the trilateral partners met in Washington, President Kim Young Sam told his prime minister to take "all necessary steps" to support sanctions. On June 3, the government unilaterally suspended trade and banned civilian companies from contacting North Koreans in third countries, a common method for doing business with Pyongyang. Hard-liners felt vindicated while even opposition politicians such as Kim Dae Jung were willing to support sanctions. [13] Still, many officials, particularly in the Ministry of Foreign Affairs, saw sanctions as a tactic designed to promote dialogue, not to preclude it. For that reason, the South sought limits on their implementation to prevent tensions from escalating too sharply. [14]

At the end of the Washington meeting, Gallucci ventured out of the State Department to read a joint statement, which concluded: "The situation demands that the international community, through the UN Security Council, urgently consider an appropriate response, including sanctions." [15] The partners had reached broad agreement on a two-phased approach. The first would include "soft measures" such as a ban on development assistance as well as on sports, cultural, and scientific exchanges; an arms embargo; and a drawdown of diplomatic ties between Pyongyang and other countries. The second phase, after a pause to allow the North to react to the first resolution, would include "hard" sanctions such as an embargo on trade and financial transactions.

The statement did not address an issue that was on everyone's mind: what would happen if China or Russia blocked UN sanctions? In fact, the allies had discussed cobbling together a coalition in support of sanctions if that happened. Tokyo seemed to be the weak link in the chain, having warned Washington it would be difficult to move forward without the imprimatur of the UN Security Council. But a senior official conceded that this position was largely a "smoke screen." Japan had imposed its own sanctions against the North before, for example, after the 1983 Rangoon bombing that killed four South Korean cabinet officials. By June, Prime Minister Hata was ready to give the go-ahead for non-UN sanctions if necessary.[16]

But the best course of action was to secure Security Council support, and that required a concerted diplomatic offensive in order to court Moscow and Beijing. Even as the noose was tightening, however, a slipknot was being tied in Moscow, as it prepared to resurrect the idea of an international conference as a last opportunity to resolve the nuclear confrontation. As the defueling crisis mounted, Foreign Minister Andrei Kozyrev had quietly refloated the proposal with Warren Christopher. But after the May 30 Security Council statement, Kozyrev informed his American counterpart that Russia intended to act; Moscow's diplomats then tabled a UN resolution and proposed a conference without referring to sanctions, confirming Washington's fears. Now the Americans had to prevent this toothless idea from undermining the campaign to press Pyongyang without so alienating Moscow that it would veto sanctions.

Washington and Seoul worked hand in hand lining up Russian support. President Kim Young Sam called Clinton on May 30 just before the South Korean departed for Moscow. He seemed in buoyant spirits. After agreeing that the time was right to move forward with sanctions—allowing perhaps one more warning to Pyongyang—Kim said he would tell President Boris Yeltsin that patience had its limits. Looking at overall strategy, Clinton observed that they would need to work hard together to get Chinese support for sanctions. That, along with firm Russian and Japanese backing, meant there could still be a peaceful solution to the crisis. Slated to visit Europe, the American president assured Kim that he would be available to talk day or night. The South Korean leader ended on an upbeat note, telling Clinton that he was very encouraged by the call.[17]

President Kim's visit to Moscow proved an important first step in marshaling a P-5 consensus. Over a long dinner at President Yeltsin's country retreat, Kim secured a promise for sanctions support. Yeltsin also reconfirmed an earlier statement by Foreign Minister Kozyrev to Christopher, that the article in the 1961 military assistance treaty between the Soviet Union and North Korea stipulating automatic intervention in case of war was "de facto dead."[18] If Pyongyang was to be truly isolated, it had to understand there was no hope of military support from at least one of its former major allies, Russia.

In a rare moment of seamless cooperation, Clinton and Kim seemed to "triangulate" Yeltsin into backing down. Clinton followed up the Kim-Yeltsin dinner with calls to both of them on June 3, after the South Korean leader had left Russia and after Yeltsin had referred again at a June 2 press conference to a possible international conference. In his call to Yeltsin, Clinton reinforced Kim's message, urging him not to reward Pyongyang's efforts to string along the international community. Yeltsin agreed; the two leaders would instruct their foreign ministers to work out the details. Back in Seoul on June 9, President Kim and Clinton talked again for almost an hour, reaffirming their opposition to a conference that would *precede* (and possibly derail) Security Council sanctions.

Similarly, the patient, brick-by-brick diplomacy with China, the other potential opponent of sanctions, began to yield results. China faced a dilemma. On one hand, it opposed a nuclear-armed North Korea and did not want to favor an old, declining friend over its burgeoning relations with the United States, South Korea, and Japan. On the other hand, China was genuinely concerned that if pressed, Pyongyang might lash out, provoking armed conflict, or it might collapse, creating an unstable situation and unleashing a flood of refugees. Furthermore, Beijing traditionally opposed sanctions, although it had voted for such measures against Iraq in 1990. On top of all this, the choice between unpalatable options could open leadership rifts at home.

Indeed, China had come a long way from the traditional Maoist view that the spread of nuclear weapons to third world states was a good way to counteract the hegemonic ambitions of the United States. Beginning with an exchange of toasts between Ronald Reagan and Zhao Ziyang at a White House dinner in 1985, China had begun to move, fitfully, toward cooperation in combating nuclear weapons proliferation. In 1992 it acceded to the Non-Proliferation Treaty. American and Chinese diplomats began a stilted, but mutually useful, dialogue on nonproliferation that shared the premise that the introduction of nuclear weapons in regions bordering China—South Asia and Korea—would be destabilizing.

Informed by these evolving interests and perspectives, China played a nuanced—but ultimately helpful—role. Publicly, Beijing would neither abandon its North Korean friends nor openly "gang up" on them. During most of the crisis, the government issued mostly Delphic utterances, to the effect that China would play a "positive" role in dealing with the nuclear crisis. That was why its refusal to block the May 30 Security Council statement was highly significant—and must have sent a worrying signal to Pyongyang. Even after the statement, Chinese officials maintained a public profile of skepticism toward sanctions, continuing to emphasize the search for dialogue.

Beijing, however, had begun to show flexibility. Visiting Tokyo and Seoul on June 1–3, Vice Foreign Minister Tang Jiaxun was heavily lobbied on the nuclear issue. His Tokyo hosts were pleased to hear him announce priorities—a Korean Peninsula that was stable, secure, and free of nuclear weapons—that mirrored the U.S. position. But the Japanese were even more pleased when the Chinese admitted in hushed tones their exasperation. Speaking in fluent Japanese, one senior Chinese diplomat intoned, "China will not cover North Korea's ass." That same week, influential think-tankers in Beijing told the U.S. Embassy that China would abstain on a "limited" sanctions resolution.

China's growing alienation from Pyongyang was telegraphed in other ways. On June 4, the Hong Kong newspaper *Da Gong Bao*—considered a voice of the mainland government—suggested that Beijing would cut off oil and food aid to North Korea if the Security Council imposed sanctions. American officials assumed this reflected not a formal decision by the Chinese leadership to abandon North Korea but a warning to Pyongyang: China might not stand in the way of the international community in either passing or enforcing sanctions. The article reinforced a growing view in Washington that if it played its cards right, China would abstain on a UN Security Council sanctions resolution.[19]

As with the Russians, Washington and Seoul coordinated their efforts. On June 8, Foreign Minister Han Sung Joo flew from New York to Beijing to secure China's support.[20] Over breakfast with Foreign Minister Qian Qichen, it became clear to Han that his Chinese counterpart was more accepting of the fact that dialogue alone would not resolve the nuclear crisis. Not once did Han's hosts say they opposed sanctions. Instead, they were more interested in the details of a possible resolution, a subtle sign that Beijing's views were moving in the right direction.[21]

The diplomatic campaign even extended to the Non-Aligned Movement (NAM), members of which held Security Council seats and had been actively lobbied by Pyongyang. Months earlier, the trilateral partners had failed to prevent a NAM meeting, chaired by Indonesia, from issuing a statement that failed to acknowledge that Pyongyang had not lived up to its nonproliferation obligations. Afterward, North Korea had continued to lobby hard; in March it sent nine missions to NAM capitals and in early April dispatched a vice foreign minister to meet with Indonesian President Suharto.[22] But the United States was active as well: its diplomats persuaded a key Indonesian official to travel to Vienna to see Director General Hans Blix after the collapse of Super Tuesday. They also nudged President Suharto to write to Kim Il Sung, urging North Korea to return to full compliance with the NPT and its safeguards provisions.

American diplomacy paid off at the June NAM meeting in Cairo. In the chair once again, Indonesia drafted language calling for the peaceful resolution of the nuclear issue and North Korean cooperation with the IAEA. The North objected, managing to get the draft referred to a subcommittee run by an African country friendly to Pyongyang. Not surprisingly, the disputed language was not in the new draft forwarded by that group. Indonesia promptly presented the North with an ultimatum: accept the original draft and the IAEA language or the NAM would go ahead anyway. Since the Indonesians had overwhelming support, the North Koreans caved.

The Clinton administration had reason to be pleased with its coalition building. Pyongyang's isolation was now complete. Secretary Christopher expressed optimism on the NBC *Today* show that the Security Council would agree on "a very effective sanctions regime." Deployment of Patriot and other military improvements in Korea enabled Christopher to respond evenly to North Korean threats the day before that sanctions meant war. The United States, he said, would not be intimidated.[23]

Domestic support also seemed strong. On the ABC *Nightline* show, Senators John McCain (R-Az.) and Bob Kerrey (D-Neb.) displayed bipartisan agreement that resolving the nuclear crisis warranted running the risk of war. McCain underlined the urgency of the situation, asking whether

> it is better to act now, while the nuclear weapons program is still in an embryonic stage, or is it better to wait two or three or four years when you are facing an enemy with nuclear weapons and the means to deliver them as far away as Japan? I think the answer is we have to act now.[24]

McCain's characterization of the nuclear program as "embryonic" struck some American officials as strange since U.S. information suggested Pyongyang was only a few years away from producing large quantities of plutonium. But the administration was not about to quibble, focused as it was on marshaling support from all quarters. Meanwhile, unfolding events in the South would soon disrupt the steady march to sanctions. Not in South Korea, but the Deep South—Georgia, to be specific.

Plains Speaking

Jimmy Carter, the fortieth president of the United States, was no stranger to Korea, nuclear weapons, or personal diplomacy. As president, he almost single-handedly tried to reduce American ground forces stationed in Korea but was forced to abandon the idea. His interest in personal diplomacy manifested itself in another scheme: to set up a meeting between himself, Kim Il Sung, and Park Chung Hee, the South's leader, in the Demilitarized Zone after the 1978 Camp David summit. That proposal nearly caused a revolt among American officials, who were convinced it would flop.[25] But Carter's grasp of nuclear technology was genuine—a product of his education as a nuclear engineer and a submariner in the service of the father of the nuclear navy, the legendary Admiral Hyman S. Rickover—as was his distaste for nuclear weapons.

Carter's term in office and his activities afterward struck a positive chord with the North Koreans. Kim Il Sung had called Carter a "man of justice" and tried to contact him at the beginning of his administration. After leaving office in 1981 and embarking on a career of mediating international crises, he received yearly invitations at the Carter Center to visit North Korea. The Bush administration dissuaded the former president from accepting the first such invitation. Another year, only his staff went. In February 1993, Carter was invited again, but Secretary Christopher urged him not to go until after the nuclear issue was resolved. Subsequently, the North Koreans renewed the invitation three times, but they were declined each time.

The events of spring 1994 convinced Jimmy Carter something had to be done. In May, Jim Laney—the U.S. ambassador in Seoul and the former president of Emory University where the Carter Center was located—had flown to Atlanta after setting the Nunn-Lugar visit in motion. He urged Carter, an old friend, to get involved. Laney's philosophy was, "You flush as many birds as you can and hope you get one."[26] The former president was struck in particular by Laney's concern that there was no way to communicate directly with Kim Il Sung, "the only one who could make decisions to alleviate the crisis and avoid another Korean war," according to Carter.[27] After their meeting, Carter called President Clinton on June 1 to express his concern. Soon Gallucci was dispatched to brief the former president.

Gallucci was unaware of President Carter's conversation with Jim Laney as he headed for Plains. In his presentation to the former president, he emphasized the administration's strong concern that North Korea not reprocess, a concern heightened by the reactor unloading that brought them one step closer to doing so. Gallucci also covered the roots of the current crisis, the "broad and thorough approach," and what would happen if Pyongyang did not return to the negotiations.

The former president asked how the Clinton administration could oppose reprocessing if it was a legitimate activity for any NPT member. This struck Gallucci as ironic; in April 1977, Carter decided to discontinue the U.S. reprocessing program as a major pillar of a new nonproliferation policy, insisting that the separation of plutonium from spent nuclear fuel was illegitimate in any but the most advanced nuclear economies, and unwise even then. At that time Washington even discouraged its nuclear-armed allies—Britain and France—from plutonium reprocessing. The administration opposed all such activity in Asia, sparking a major diplomatic flap when President Carter tried, unsuccessfully, to muscle the Japanese out of their own reprocessing efforts. Gallucci remembered this period well. He had helped formulate and implement the Carter policy as a young official in the State Department.

Carter was right, Gallucci responded: reprocessing was allowed under the terms of the NPT, although the Denuclearization Declaration signed by North and South Korea prohibited it. But he also reminded Carter of the long-standing policy initiated by the Georgian's administration to prevent the spread of reprocessing technology, to discourage even advanced industrialized states from reprocessing, and to stop such activities by states of proliferation concern—including North Korea—whether they were NPT members or not. Differences over this issue would later emerge as a key irritant between the administration and Carter during his visit to Pyongyang.

In addition to two large bags of peanuts, Gallucci carried away the clear impression that Jimmy Carter viewed the meeting as an opportunity to see if he could help end the growing confrontation. Carter's perception that the U.S. position toward the North was too rigid seemed to convince him that he had a role to play. Back in Washington, Gallucci called Deputy National Security Adviser Sandy Berger with a terse message: "I am sure that President Carter wants to go to North Korea." Sure enough, on June 6 the Georgia Democrat called Vice President Al Gore to report that Pyongyang had reconfirmed his standing invitation with assurances that it came from Kim Il Sung. He wanted to accept the invitation. The next day, Gallucci sent an eyes-only memo to Berger about his three-hour meeting in Plains, guessing that the former president would not wait long before taking the initiative, and not knowing that he already had.

President Carter's volunteerism unleashed an intense but brief debate inside the administration. From the outset, officials had been concerned that the North Koreans might act foolishly from miscalculation based on misperception. The regime was so insular that there was no clear sense that an accurate picture of reality—or the dire straits it faced—was fully conveyed to the North Korean leader. To the contrary, invariably totalitarian dictators seemed to be briefed by courtiers and sycophants who shrank from telling truth to power. For this reason, both the Bush and Clinton administrations had used congressional leaders and private citizens to communicate with top North Korean leaders.

In that spirit, the offer was especially timely, coming after the aborted Nunn-Lugar trip and in the midst of an escalating crisis. But some officials (especially those who had worked for Carter in the past) worried that the strong-willed former president would freelance when he disagreed with U.S. policy. That could undermine the administration at the very moment it had succeeded in mobilizing the international community to act collectively against Pyongyang. On the other hand, policymakers nursed a nagging concern that while the course to increasing pressure on the North was clear, the exit strategy leading to its compliance with global nonproliferation norms was far less so. A visit from Carter just might help Pyongyang find a way to climb back from the precipice.

These dueling considerations split the administration. While Vice President Gore was inclined to approve the trip, Secretary Christopher thought it was a bad idea. Gore called *Air Force One* to discuss the issue—as the president's party was en route to France for the fiftieth anniversary of the Normandy invasion—and convinced Tony Lake that Carter should go. Though not enthusiastic, Lake could not exclude the possibility that a face-to-face meeting with Kim Il Sung might actually accomplish something. When he briefed the president on the situation, Clinton decided to approve the trip.[28]

Both Carter and the administration were happy to keep up the pretense that he was traveling as a private citizen. In a note to the White House on June 8, Carter confirmed that he would be visiting Korea representing the Carter Center, not the government. Though subsequent events highlighted the former president's differences with U.S. policy, at this point he said that he would be glad to carry any message—in any capacity, official or unofficial—from President Clinton to Kim Il Sung. That same day, he wrote North Korean foreign minister Kim Yong Nam, making clear that his trip would be unofficial, but with the full knowledge and approval of the U.S. government. On June 9, the Carter Center announced the visit, once more emphasizing that the former president would visit Pyongyang as a private citizen.[29]

These repeated assertions were viewed skeptically on both sides of the DMZ. When Carter contemplated a visit in 1993, the South Koreans believed Pyongyang would be incapable of seeing him as anything other than a personal emissary, in a gesture of conciliation showing deference and respect from the sitting U.S. president. At first, the South Koreans believed the new initiative was a coordinated effort between the White House and Carter but soon learned that Washington had initially been just as surprised.

Coordinated or not, President Kim Young Sam thought the visit was a bad idea that once again would relegate Seoul to a bit part in its own national drama. Moreover, his political enemy, Kim Dae Jung, had recently made a similar proposal that Carter help resolve the nuclear standoff. That was the kiss of death for any idea as far as the South Korean leader was concerned.

Upon learning of the impending Carter visit to North Korea, President Kim immediately called President Clinton, ostensibly to talk about his trip to Russia, but also to tell him the Carter trip was a mistake, particularly since support for sanctions was growing. Kim hinted that Carter had a different agenda from that of Washington and Seoul. Clinton did not address Kim's concerns directly but reassured him that the United States would do nothing without closely consulting its ally. While Kim could barely contain himself, telling the press that "Kim Il Sung is likely to utilize Carter's visit as a tactic of dialogue and smile towards the West," Seoul avoided public hints that it opposed the trip.[30]

The Gathering Storm

On June 10—in his weekly memorandum to the president—Bill Perry wrote that the United States must look ahead to the endgame of the nuclear crisis and warned against limiting American options, either in terms of military preparations or preemption. Noting that Pyongyang already devoted massive resources to its military, Perry mused that forcing it to invest more might break the bank. This raised the question of whether the United States should seek to hasten the regime's end, which in turn depended on whether sudden or gradual change was riskier. While Perry conceded that necessity forced urgent focus on the nuclear problem, the United States also needed to be clear in its ultimate purpose. Was this narrow focus enough or was Washington also seeking to hasten the end of the North Korean regime? This issue would return to the fore eight years later when another Bush administration considered its policy toward North Korea.

The question was far from academic. That morning, the Principals Committee met to consider a military buildup in South Korea and sanctions against Pyongyang. Exit strategy was also an important concern: the "Rudolf Hess option" and now the new factor of President Carter were in play. In considering the military options, the president had to consider not only the Korean situation but also the implications for force deployments around the world, for the "bottom-up" review of America's post–cold war defense policy, for reserve call-ups, and for the evacuation of U.S. citizens from South Korea. Tougher still, he would need to decide how to phase a military buildup in order to ensure the physical capability to enforce the sanctions, while signaling the North that any aggressive military action by it would be foolish, or

Two generations of dictators: Kim Jong Il and Kim Il Sung, shown here in 1982. Kim Il Sung had led North Korea since the nation's inception but by 1994 was nearing the end of his long life and reign. Even as power steadily grew in the hands of his heir apparent, questions persisted over whether the younger Kim's reportedly sybaritic ways would weaken and ultimate destroy his hope of succession. (*Chosun-ui Yonggwang*, Pyongyang)

Hans Blix, director general of the International Atomic Energy Agency. Chagrined by the revelation after the 1991 Gulf War that Saddam Hussein had a far more extensive nuclear weapons program than the IAEA had detected, Blix was determined not to allow North Korea to slip out of its international safeguards obligations. (Reuters/CORBIS)

Left: South Korean foreign minister Han Sung Joo. The soft-spoken former academic kept a steady eye on the strategic aims of a stable Korean Peninsula free of nuclear weapons. His efforts helped resolve the crisis, but cost him his job. (Reuters/Corbis)

Right: U.S. ambassador James Laney, a former president of Emory University with longstanding ties to Korea, played a critical role in bridging the views of Seoul and Washington. In his younger days, he had been a missionary in South Korea. (LaGrange College)

A women's unit of the Korean People's Army marches in formation. The bulk of North Korea's 1 million troops were deployed menacingly near the border with South Korea, greatly outnumbering the combined South Korean and U.S. forces defending the South. U.S. military planners were confident that their forces—better trained, fed, and equipped—would prevail in any conflict, but the costs would be high. (AP)

After the tragic deaths of eighteen American soldiers in Somalia in October 1993, U.S. military commanders and political leaders alike were determined to ensure that U.S. forces were fully equipped to deter and defend against military attack. The American desire to deploy batteries of the Patriot missile air defense system in South Korea became the symbol of U.S. determination to deter Pyongyang and defend Seoul. (CORBIS)

Secretary of Defense William Perry, a veteran of the U.S. Army of Occupation in Japan, played a critical role in both forging and articulating U.S. policy. He was determined to strengthen U.S. and South Korean forces in South Korea to deter any ill-considered military moves by the North. (AFP/CORBIS)

U.S. president Bill Clinton and South Korean president Kim Young Sam jogging around the White House track. Only through frequent consultations at the presidential level were the two allies able to manage the rising tensions of the North Korean nuclear crisis without destroying their half-century-old alliance. (Clinton Presidential Library)

Vice President Al Gore and President Bill Clinton, accompanied by national security officials Anthony Lake and Samuel Berger, receive a Pentagon briefing on Korean military options, May 19, 1994. The briefing confirmed that allied forces in Korea were ready for war, should diplomacy fail. (The White House)

President and Mrs. Carter admire a gift presented by North Korean president Kim Il Sung in June 1994. The former president's intervention in the crisis created headaches for the White House but provided the missing link to a solution: a face-saving path of retreat for Pyongyang. (The Carter Center)

National security officials in the reception area separating the Cabinet Room and the Oval Office watching former president Jimmy Carter being interviewed on CNN. Left to right: Director of Central Intelligence James Woolsey, Robert Gallucci, Daniel Poneman, Vice President Al Gore, Secretary of Defense William Perry, National Security Adviser to the Vice President Leon Fuerth, Chairman of the Joint Chiefs of Staff John Shalikashvili, Secretary of State Warren Christopher, National Security Council staffer Stanley Roth (partially hidden), and U.S. Permanent Representative to the United Nations Madeleine Albright. (The White House)

Vice President Al Gore had supported Jimmy Carter's visit to North Korea. When Carter publicly strayed from administration policy, Gore attempted to bridge the gap, literally, as he consulted with the former president on one phone line and national security adviser Anthony Lake on another. (Tipper Gore)

President Bill Clinton responded to Jimmy Carter's June 16, 1994, interview by issuing an official statement outlining the terms under which the United States would resume talks with North Korea. Here, Daniel Poneman and Robert Gallucci consult with Vice President Al Gore, while Anthony Lake and Clinton work on the president's remarks to be delivered in the White House Briefing Room. (The White House)

Relations between Washington and Seoul were stretched to breaking point in the weeks leading up to the signing of the Agreed Framework. In October, President Bill Clinton called President Kim Young Sam to reassure his ally during the final phase of the negotiations. (The White House)

Joel Wit, who directed U.S. efforts to implement the Agreed Framework, and a North Korean official stand inside the 5-megawatt reactor at Yongbyon. Under the accord, Americans and North Koreans worked together to ensure that the nuclear facility was shut down and the spent fuel rods were safely and securely stored.

North Korean Vice Foreign Minister Kim Gye Gwan often showed flexibility when chief negotiator Kang Sok Ju showed none. Even if part of a planned good cop/bad cop routine, he handled his role with diplomatic skill, and would return to the scene as the North's chief negotiator when the crisis resurfaced a decade later. (Reuters/CORBIS)

In both Geneva and Kuala Lumpur, State Department officials Thomas Hubbard (left) and Gary Samore (right) used informal sessions to explore possible solutions with their North Korean counterparts at key moments when the formal talks reached an impasse. At times they abandoned subtlety for bluntness—Samore rejecting "Berlin Kim's" shopping spree for Western reactors, and Hubbard insisting on the safe and prompt return of downed American pilot Bobby Hall. (Left: U.S. Army photo by SSG Douglas Mitchell; right: International Institute for Security Studies)

American evangelist Billy Graham, accompanied by his interpreter, Stephen Linton, meeting with Kim Il Sung. The White House welcomed Graham's offer to communicate with the North Korean leader without risk that aides and bureaucrats in Pyongyang would alter or distort the message. (Russ Busby, reprinted by permission of the Billy Graham Evangelistic Association)

North Koreans mourning the death of Kim Il Sung. Kim's sudden demise, just three weeks after his fateful meeting with former president Jimmy Carter, brought renewed uncertainty to the peninsula. But when negotiations resumed a month later, they moved swiftly toward a conclusion. (Haruyoshi Yamaguchi/CORBIS SYGMA)

The unveiling of the haunting Korean War Veterans Memorial marked the forty-second anniversary of the armistice. Presidents Bill Clinton and Kim Young Sam visited the memorial a month after the Kuala Lumpur accords averted another near crisis with the North. (Markowitz Jeffrey/CORBIS SYGMA)

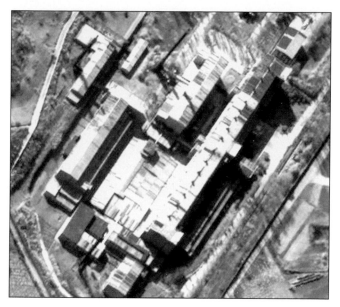

Overhead imagery of the reprocessing facility at Yongbyon, where the North Koreans secretly separated the plutonium that analysts feared had been fashioned into one or two nuclear weapons. (DigitalGlobe)

The two sites suspected of containing wastes that could help unlock the mystery of how much plutonium North Korea had separated can be seen in this image. "Building 500" is the isolated rectangular building to the right of the reprocessing complex, while the buried waste site is located south of the Kuryong River in the foliated area to the north of the road leading from those facilities to the 5-megawatt reactor in the upper right of the photograph. (DigitalGlobe)

The steam plume rising from the cooling tower shows that the 5-megawatt reactor was operating when this photograph was taken. The 8,000 spent fuel rods removed from the reactor in mid-1994 contained enough plutonium for approximately five nuclear weapons. (DigitalGlobe)

Under the Agreed Framework, the North stopped building this 50-megawatt reactor, which would have generated enough plutonium for up to ten bombs a year. (DigitalGlobe)

even suicidal. The buildup also would have to be deliberately paced so as not to trigger the very military response it aimed to deter.

General John Shalikashvili and Perry reviewed the military posture. The president had already approved sending an advance party of 250 men to set up a headquarters operation that would manage the smooth inflow of the rest of the deployment. The next steps would be more far-reaching. Working with General Luck, Perry and Shalikashvili prepared three options for the president. The first involved sending up to 2,000 military personnel, not combat troops but those needed to prepare for the large-scale deployments to follow. The Pentagon wanted all this to take place *before* UN sanctions entered into force. The second option included 10,000 troops, squadrons of front-line aircraft to be based near Korea, and another carrier battle group for the region. The third option, to be put in place before any enforceable sanctions were imposed, included over 50,000 troops, 400 aircraft, and over 50 ships, as well as multiple rocket launchers and Patriot batteries. It would also require a reserve call-up and the deployment of additional carrier battle groups around Korea to deter and interdict would-be sanction-busters.[31]

In Perry's philosophy of the plus-up, the stronger and more vigorous the U.S. military posture, the more effective the deterrent. Since the North Koreans appeared to be viewing the imposition of UN sanctions as a highly provocative move, it was vital to ensure that the military buildup *preceded* the imposition of enforced sanctions. Indeed, the *faster* the United States deployed additional military assets, the more stabilizing would be the effect against North Korea.

Timing was critical. Ideally, the president would snap his fingers and deploy the full buildup instantaneously. In practice, it would take some time. In these circumstances, the North would have an incentive to lash out against the South before the allied forces were prepared to do battle.

South Korea, General Luck reported, was taking a different view. Its military was reluctant to allow a rapid buildup of U.S. forces on the peninsula. Moreover, American military planners and Ambassador Laney agreed that the tens of thousands of U.S. civilians living in South Korea should be evacuated before the imposition of enforced sanctions against North Korea. An evacuation on that scale could cause panic in the South and possibly provoke an irrational act by the North.[32] The principals, keenly aware of history throughout the discussion, recalled that lack of political resolve and capability were the critical mistakes leading to war in 1950 and should not be repeated.

As the pacing and content of a military buildup were debated, the president entered the Situation Room, accompanied by Vice President Gore and Counselor David Gergen. Secretary Perry and General Shalikashvili told Clinton that they would likely propose significantly increasing troop strength in Korea. A deployment on that scale would have to be accompanied by a reserve call-up, an evacuation of U.S. civilians from the South, and a presidential speech to the nation. Recalling 1950, Perry urged that U.S. actions be designed to persuade North Korea that it would lose any military conflict without provoking an attack. While all agreed that success would depend on maintaining strong international support and the president was willing to contact various leaders, he and Gore worried that sanctions might only provoke North Korea without compelling it to come clean with the IAEA. Even if the North Koreans were inclined to accede to U.S. demands under the threat or reality of sanctions, they might not grasp that opportunity without also being provided with a life preserver.

How Many Times Have You Visited North Korea?

June 10 was also the day Jimmy Carter arrived in Washington for official briefings before his trip. He had already consulted others, including the Rockefeller Foundation, where former U.S. official Tom Graham expressed concern that many experts failed to understand what was happening in North Korea.[33] Tony Namkung—the scion of a prominent Korean family who had settled in the United States and had been visiting the North since 1990—argued in a briefing paper for Carter that the United States could either steer North Korea to make peace or mistakenly send a message that would further isolate and destabilize "an already paranoid, dangerous and extremely suspicious military power." He added that Koreans favored mediation as a face-saving way of negotiating, an observation that may have fit in nicely with Carter's own view of his upcoming trip.[34]

Talk of an emissary at the principals' meeting that day naturally brought the conversation around to President Carter. Recalling his policy blunder in proposing a U.S. troop withdrawal from Korea early in his own presidential administration, they agreed that he was not the right person for the job, that he might stray from U.S. policy, mixing signals at a time when clarity and consistency were of vital importance. Of course, this hand-wringing was beside the point: the decision to let Carter travel had already been made. Nevertheless, two nagging concerns led the principals to conclude that the risks of the Carter trip were worth running. First was the chronic problem of assuring that Kim Il Sung—isolated and surrounded by his heir apparent and associated minions in his hermit kingdom—received a clear and direct rendering of the U.S. position. That is why the administration had been willing on repeated occasions—

with Billy Graham, Ron Dellums, Sam Nunn, and Richard Lugar—to encourage eminent Americans to speak directly with Kim Il Sung.

The second concern was one the president kept raising: the lack of a clear path to allow North Korea to inch back from the brink. A coercive step in the form of sanctions was shaping up, but without any clear exit strategy allowing the North a face-saving means to comply with its international obligations. The visit of a former president might provide them with just such an avenue of retreat.

Three hours after the principals' meeting concluded, Lake, Gallucci, and Poneman rode to National Airport for a 3:15 PM meeting with Jimmy Carter, to be followed by a briefing at the State Department. It was the only time Carter and his former aide could meet, as the former president was flying in to Washington and Lake was leaving town that same afternoon. The session was tense and terse. Lake, who had run Carter's State Department transition team in 1977, delivered the principals' concerns: that both Koreas should understand he was traveling in a private capacity only and would not carry a message from Clinton. Nor was he authorized to negotiate on behalf of the U.S. government. His value added was to elicit Kim Il Sung's real objectives, and to see if he understood that Washington wanted a peaceful resolution of the crisis as well as better relations with the North. Moreover, Lake wanted it made clear to Kim that North Korea should not mistake prudent defensive measures as provocative.

"We want you fully briefed," Lake concluded, "so that you can accurately describe the U.S. position."[35] While the former president had always indicated he would be traveling as a private citizen, he seemed to chafe at these limits. Carter clearly viewed his own role far more expansively than as a messenger between Washington and Pyongyang.

At the State Department, Deputy Secretary of Defense John Deutch—who had served in Carter's Department of Energy—and a number of Korea experts waited in Gallucci's office to brief the former president. Former presidents rarely wander the halls of the State Department; Jimmy and Rosalyn Carter turned heads as they made toward Gallucci's office. In the anteroom, Gallucci's loyal and able secretary was so excited that as the former first couple entered, she rose and said, "Welcome, Mr. President. Welcome, Mrs. Mondale." The briefing in Gallucci's office did not proceed more smoothly.

The topics included the ins and outs of the NPT, the North's nuclear program, and the respective roles of Kim Il Sung and Kim Jong Il in calling the shots in Pyongyang. Tensions soon surfaced as President Carter expressed his firmly held opinions. "How many times have you visited North Korea?" he would ask each expert. "None" was the common reply, reinforcing Carter's skepticism toward their ability to understand the North Korean mind-set. He doubted the opinions of anyone who had not been to North Korea or had not talked to its officials directly. During one pause in the briefing, a tray of Pepsi Colas was brought in, but since Carter was from Atlanta, home of Coca Cola, he and his entire party politely declined. It was another awkward moment in an awkward meeting.

Not surprisingly, the former president was especially skeptical about sanctions. In the midst of President Bush's effort to build a coalition against Iraq after its 1990 invasion of Kuwait, Carter wrote Security Council members asking them not to support the UN resolution authorizing the use of force to eject Iraq.[36] Many considered such actions, seeking openly to subvert an incumbent president's foreign policy by directly communicating with foreign governments, to be inappropriate. But it was certainly indicative of Carter's determination once he seized a policy bit in his teeth. His bottom line on sanctions against North Korea was clear: anyone who thought Pyongyang would see a UN Security Council vote as a warning and only react once sanctions were implemented was mistaken.

That evening, President Carter and his wife had dinner with the South Korean ambassador, who extended a private invitation for them to meet President Kim Young Sam on their way to Pyongyang. The South Koreans may have been skeptical about Carter's trip, but they intended to let him know their views in no uncertain terms. Carter certainly understood that a stopover both before and after his visit to the North was essential to mollify the South. Two days later, on June 12, the former first couple boarded a Delta Airlines flight for Seoul.[37]

The Osirak Option

On June 14, the principals prepared to convene again. In the four short days since their last meeting, the international situation had continued to shift. Multilateral support of sanctions was growing, most conspicuously in Beijing, where a visit by North Korea's chief of staff Choe Kwang ended on June 10 amid a public display of friendship that may have masked China's real intentions. There were rumors that Choe had been subjected to criticism in a private meeting with President Jiang Zemin, who asked that his message be relayed to Kim Il Sung and Kim Jong Il.[38]

Reinforcing these rumors, the same day Choe left Beijing, China's vice foreign minister Tang held an extraordinary meeting with the North Korean ambassador. Signaling that China's patience had run out, Tang said Beijing's role was "limited" in resolving the sanctions issue. (Washington was informed of the meeting the next day.) The implication was that Pyongyang should not assume Beijing would veto Security Council sanctions. Tang's message was reinforced by more stories in Hong Kong newspapers, known to reflect Beijing's thinking, implying that China was likely to abstain on limited sanctions and that it might not support Pyongyang if hostilities erupted (notwithstanding the 1961 Mutual Friendship Treaty committing China to come to North Korea's defense).

While China seemed to be moving in the right direction, progress with Russia was slow. On June 13, President Clinton asked Boris Yeltsin once again not to allow Russia's proposed international conference to delay the enforcement of North Korea's obligations. Once again, Yeltsin insisted that the conference should be on an "equal level" to the UN resolution, although he conceded that it should be a carrot to induce North Korean compliance, not an excuse for delaying the resolution. Happy to give up the point of form (equal level) to win the point of substance (sequencing), Clinton agreed. Nevertheless, Foreign Minister Kozyrev subsequently told Christopher that the conference should be held at the same time sanctions were imposed, not after Pyongyang complied with its obligations.

Presidential diplomacy was also needed to ensure firm trilateral support. A June 9 *New York Times* story asserting that Japan was having second thoughts about sanctions triggered a phone call four days later from President Clinton to Japanese prime minister Tsutomu Hata. Coincidentally, the call was put through as the coffee was being served at the Clintons' first state dinner, held in honor of the visiting emperor of Japan. Clinton was scheduled to take the call not in the Oval Office but rather in the Treaty Room on the second floor of the White House, once the Cabinet Room, before presidential staff offices were moved to the West Wing in 1902. Now the Treaty Room served as the president's office in the executive mansion.

The president was clearly enjoying himself, and it took several minutes to pull him away from his guests. As Clinton ascended the tiny elevator to the living quarters of the White House, he began crooning "The Tennessee Waltz." But the phone call was brisk and business-like. Clinton told Hata he had just bid farewell to the emperor and his wife. After complaining that the press reports about Japan's reluctance to enforce sanctions were wrong, Hata reaffirmed that he was fully behind the American campaign. He agreed that the Russian proposal for an international conference should not delay the passage of a sanctions resolution.[39] Hata was clear and crisp and his points dovetailed precisely with the American position, dispelling any concerns that Japan might be drifting.

But the progress in coalition building was overshadowed by the news out of Vienna. On June 10, after the principals had last met, the IAEA Board of Governors approved its own sanctions against the North. Largely a symbolic move, the cutoff was limited to the "nonmedical assistance" portion of the agency's small $250,000 technical assistance program to Pyongyang. Though the U.S. government had supported the sanctions, when the president learned of the IAEA's action, he snapped, "Why the hell did they do that?" He was concerned about further painting Pyongyang into a corner when what it needed was an escape hatch.

Pyongyang's response three days later threatened to trigger a major escalation of the crisis. North Korea announced its intention to withdraw from the IAEA, an unprecedented move that occasioned serious international concern. Even more disturbing was a threat by North Korean diplomats in Vienna to expel IAEA inspectors from Yongbyon, bringing Pyongyang a step closer to building a nuclear weapon in weeks. Without inspectors on site, the international community would not know what was going on at Yongbyon. Pyongyang then seemed to back off slightly, saying, "The agency's inspectors now will have nothing to do any further in our country."[40] But Gallucci warned that expulsion would be a "very, very serious development," calling into question "the peaceful nature of the program."[41]

Coming a day after this startling move, the June 14 principals' meeting accelerated American preparations for a military buildup, sanctions, and last-ditch diplomatic efforts to resolve the confrontation. But there was now a new focus, the "Osirak option." Named after a 1981 Israeli strike against Iraq's nuclear reactor, the plan contemplated a preemptive attack on Yongbyon. Aside from the complex policy issues surrounding such an attack was the possibility that it could become a political football, as soon became apparent in an op-ed article by former Bush officials Brent Scowcroft and Arnold Kanter advocating such a strike unless the North allowed the IAEA continuous, unfettered monitoring to ensure that no further reprocessing took place.[42] There was no need for an immediate decision, but the principals agreed that such a strike could be unleashed only *after* U.S. reinforcements were in place. South Korea would also have to be consulted.

Logically, there were three military possibilities for attacking Yongbyon. The United States could just destroy the reprocessing facility. Or it could take out the reprocessing plant plus other nuclear facilities at Yongbyon, primarily the 5-megawatt reactor and the spent fuel storage pool. The third option would be to destroy all of those nuclear facilities and remove key North Korean military assets, in order to degrade Pyongyang's ability to retaliate. All three presumed some sort of violent reaction was possible or likely.

Taking out just the reprocessing plant would set back the nuclear program for some period, minimize the risk of releasing a radioactive cloud, and seemed least likely to provoke a general war. Of course, there was no guarantee that the one or two bombs' worth of plutonium that North Korea may have already produced—each perhaps the size of a soda can as President Clinton would later describe it—were present at the reprocessing plant.[43] To the contrary, it was inconceivable that the North would leave any separated plutonium in such an obvious target for attack. At best, the attack might delay the problem without eliminating it while risking a conventional war in Korea. It was not at all clear that America's regional allies would support this option.

Destroying all the nuclear installations at Yongbyon would constitute a more severe blow to North Korea's ambitions, setting back the program an even longer period, but would increase all of the risks from the single-plant attack, including those of a radioactive release and a general war. If one accepted that this option posed a much greater risk of war, an argument could be made that the United States should take the opportunity of the attack to broaden the target list significantly. The purpose would be to degrade the North's ability to lash out in retaliation. But such a broad strike would likely produce greater international opposition to the U.S. action.[44]

The principals also quickly agreed on a draft UN sanctions resolution. This was surprising since the previous consensus supporting gradual escalation had broken down, resulting in what appeared to be stark bureaucratic differences. The safeguard-firsters now favored a single resolution authorizing a broad array of sanctions, with the "relief mechanism" triggered by North Korean compliance with its IAEA safeguards obligations. The dismantlement-firsters favored a phased approach spreading ever-increasing sanctions across three separate resolutions, with a relief mechanism focused on steps that would physically reduce North Korean access to plutonium, such as freezing and dismantling the nuclear facilities at Yongbyon.

In the end, the principals agreed to a single resolution imposing sanctions in two phases, in part to avoid the danger that after the first resolution passed, pressures for further action would dissipate. The first phase would go into effect thirty days after the resolution was approved unless North Korea agreed to meet its safeguards obligations and was cooperating fully with the IAEA. It banned any trade that could contribute to North Korea's nuclear activities, North Korean exports and imports of any materials related to weapons of mass destruction or conventional weapons, flights to and from the North except regular commercial flights and humanitarian missions, and economic and development assistance. The resolution also urged other countries to reduce their diplomatic ties with North Korea.

The Security Council would "urgently meet" to impose phase two sanctions if North Korea took additional steps in defiance of the international community, such as withdrawing from the NPT, resuming reprocessing, or further obstructing safeguards activities. Then a freeze on financial assets and a ban on remittances would be imposed. Under the American plan, an international conference on Korea would be held only if Pyongyang agreed to meet its safeguards obligations and was cooperating fully with the IAEA. The draft resolution was quickly sent to Tokyo and Seoul for their approval, while Ambassador Madeleine Albright told reporters the first draft might be distributed in "the next few days."[45]

Although the sanctions resolution built in an exit strategy for Pyongyang, the principals worked on finalizing the additional escape hatch provided by the Rudolf Hess option, to be executed before the UN acted. Once in Beijing, the U.S. envoy would offer to suspend efforts to secure sanctions and to renew negotiations if North Korea met stiff conditions. The most important was that Pyongyang would have to transfer its spent fuel immediately out of the country, but it would also have to refrain from refueling the 5-megawatt reactor and not undertake any reprocessing. Lake asked Gallucci to prepare a memorandum recommending that the president launch this initiative before the military buildup began, but not before he first consulted with President Kim Young Sam.

The following morning, after Tokyo and Seoul approved the proposed sanctions resolution, Ambassador Albright began consultations at the United Nations. While the permanent members divided as expected—Britain and France were supportive while China warned about dire consequences—Russia provided the only surprise. Angry that the Americans had moved forward on their own resolution rather than working together on a joint proposal, Ambassador Yuli Vorontsov gave Albright a competing draft that only warned of sanctions without specifying a date certain for their imposition. The lingering proposal for the international conference that President Clinton and Secretary Christopher thought they had dealt with remained a thorn in the U.S. side.

While the crisis was escalating, faint signs began to appear that North Korea might be looking for a way out of its predicament. On June 15, the day consultations began at the United Nations, Selig Harrison came to Tom Hubbard's office on the sixth floor of the State Department with a curious tale. A senior fellow at the Carnegie Endowment for International Peace, a former *Washington Post* reporter, and a strong proponent of better relations with North Korea, Harrison had been visiting Pyongyang since 1972 and had just been there a week earlier to meet with Kim Il Sung. Harrison painted a picture that was disturbing yet encouraging. The Great Leader seemed to think relations with the United States were not so bad; Kim was either posturing or badly misinformed. The elder Kim once again proposed to swap Pyongyang's nuclear program for new reactors, implying that only a commitment to a deal was sufficient to trade away parts of the program, including the reprocessing plant. That may have meant a softening of the North's July 1993 demand for reactors up front.[46]

Moreover, since he returned to the United States, the North Koreans had told Harrison that the IAEA inspectors could remain at Yongbyon "as long as they behaved themselves." Because the North's ambassadors in Thailand and Paris had made similar statements on June 15, they may have been reflecting official guidance sent out by Pyongyang, signaling a further retreat from threats made a few days earlier.

Harrison's story confirmed the view of some Americans that North Korea may have decided in early June that engagement with Washington should remain the centerpiece of its policy. On June 3, the North had issued a rare statement by Kang Sok Ju—usually trotted out when talks seemed dead-locked—including a new offer, later repeated to Harrison, to dismantle its reprocessing plant. Also included was an intriguing hint that "all questions in which the United States might be interested" could be addressed and "even more complicated problems than measurement of the spent fuel rods could be worked out."[47]

For some, Kang's hint reinforced signs that Pyongyang was still trying to find a solution to the vexing problem of special inspections. When a third round seemed imminent in March 1994, a key North Korean ambassador in Asia said that access to the two waste sites was possible if the IAEA could show that they were nuclear-related and as long as the North was not pressed too hard early in negotiations. Pyongyang's diplomats in New York also were con-sidering a proposal by private Americans to form a joint scientific team that might take samples at the two sites. These rumblings were, at best, a signal rather than a fully formed policy. But the North appeared to be searching for a way to step back from its previous insistence that the two sites could "never be opened."

Still, as always, the North's signals were mixed. Kang also implied that Pyongyang was on the verge of reprocessing. On June 7, with sanctions loom-ing larger on the horizon, the North Koreans issued another message dismiss-ing Gallucci's allegation—that they had destroyed the possibility of future measurement of the fuel—as a pretext for special inspections. A quasi-official organ used to map out its position on inter-Korean issues declared: "Sanctions are war, period and there is no mercy in war." Previously, the North had only asserted that sanctions were a "declaration of war."[48]

In the end, Harrison's tale had little impact on U.S. policy. Coming just after the reactor-unloading episode when Pyongyang held out hope for a diplomatic solution that never materialized, there seemed good reason to be skeptical. Also, events were moving quickly, and Harrison had relayed his tale to officials not directly involved in deliberations at the White House. It would take time to digest his story. Finally, some officials were skeptical of Harrison precisely because he had been a strong advocate of accommodation with North Korea. Months later, after a crisis was averted and a diplomatic solution had been reached, it became clear that Pyongyang had been serious.

In the Eye of the Hurricane

Jimmy Carter's plane touched down at Seoul's Kimpo airport at 4:00 PM on June 13. Carter planned to stay for two days, long enough to meet Ambassador Laney, General Luck, and South Korean officials before crossing into the North. He landed just as Pyongyang announced it was going to withdraw from the IAEA and threatened to kick out the agency's inspectors. Secretary of State Christopher called to tell the former president that "the outcome of the whole crisis could depend on what happens to the inspectors."[49]

When Hans Blix had declared the North Koreans had destroyed historical information a few weeks earlier, the mood in Seoul was one of concern, not crisis. The public was used to the North's brinksmanship and confident that allied forces could deter an attack. General Luck conveyed a sense of quiet confidence. So did President Kim, who reassured his people that the United States was prepared for all contingencies. Kim also chaired the first National Security Council meeting in his sixteen-month-old administration to show a seriousness of purpose.[50]

The government seemed sober about the future. The director of intelligence testified to the National Assembly that "it now appears their [North Koreans'] ultimate goal is to develop nuclear weapons and they are now employing delaying tactics to earn time."[51] Privately, President Kim told his ministers that coordination with Washington was good, that he was determined to do something now to resolve the crisis, and that sanctions were the only available option under the circumstances.

As the crisis accelerated, unease began to spread. Rumors of shortages became common; members of the National Assembly began receiving phone calls from constituents asking if they should stockpile supplies. The mayor of Seoul was said to be considering emergency measures. Indeed, one of the largest noodle makers reported that it had increased production by 30 percent because of growing demand.[52] The financial markets were also jittery: the

Seoul stock market fell almost 4 percent during Carter's stay.[53] Government officials blamed the press, noting the arrival of a CNN team reminiscent of those that covered the Gulf War, a worrying sign.[54]

The government sought to reassure the public and to prepare for the worst, while not provoking the North Koreans to do the worst. The day President Carter arrived, the South conducted an exercise to check the mobilization status of over 6 million reservists for civil defense. Two days later, when he crossed the DMZ, it held another previously scheduled, nation-wide civil defense exercise, which took on new meaning under the circumstances. The Ministry of Defense also tried to reassure the public, beginning with daily press briefings.[55] It admitted that the North Korean Army had reached its highest state of readiness since 1990. The North had not made any belligerent moves, proclaiming over loud speakers at the DMZ that it neither had the intention nor the capability to build nuclear weapons. Only a small number of the hundreds of "warning" indicators pointed toward a war, but the South was on its guard nevertheless for a sudden provocation that might lead to a limited conflict or all-out war.[56]

Recognizing that trying times might lie ahead, the government sought to bolster a broad political consensus in favor of a tough approach. Hard-liners needed little convincing and also hinted publicly that South Korea might reconsider adhering to the North-South Denuclearization Declaration, a conservative pet peeve that had just as much to do with protecting Seoul's nuclear options as limiting Pyongyang's. The domestic debate over this issue had flared up before, usually when Pyongyang appeared to be veering away from dialogue.[57] The opposition party, traditionally in favor of a softer line, offered conditional support for UN sanctions following a May 28 meeting with President Kim.[58] Reports that the opposition might try to score political points by greeting Carter at the airport triggered the U.S. Embassy to discourage them from doing so. Kim Dae Jung, who claimed some credit for having initially suggested the Carter mission, also agreed not to meet the former president.

Jim Laney and his staff watched these developments closely. Embassy Seoul bore the responsibility not only to report accurately to Washington the mood in South Korea but also to ensure the safe evacuation of thousands of Americans living in Korea if hostilities seemed imminent. All U.S. embassies had plans to conduct noncombatant evacuation operations, or NEOs. Typically, the document gathered dust in a locked filing cabinet, but on the volatile Korean Peninsula it was an integral part of the American war plan.[59]

The deputy chief of the U.S. Mission in Seoul, Charles Kartman, was responsible for the embassy's evacuation planning. After participating in the 1993 New York meeting with North Korea, he had left for Seoul to become the number-two official in the embassy. Calm and analytical, Kartman started his Foreign Service career as a Japan expert but had done two tours of duty in Seoul and one as the director of the State Department's Korea desk, giving him a keen understanding of that country. When he arrived in Seoul, Kartman found a twenty-year-old NEO designed to evacuate Americans on the same aircraft that brought in troops once the second Korean War had begun. He concluded the plan was unworkable.

For one thing, South Korea had changed a great deal over the past two decades since the plan had last been updated. The number of Americans living in the South had grown significantly, ranging from 80,000 to 100,000 by the early 1990s. Most were located in Seoul, which had been transformed by the South Korean economic miracle into a crowded metropolis; its few exit routes were clogged with traffic. Trying to reach embarkation points would be a nightmare, especially if Seoul was under artillery attack, or if South Koreans were rushing to leave the country when the exodus of foreigners became apparent.

Kartman had been working for months with the U.S. military to develop a new NEO. Now nearly complete, the plan aimed to save lives by quickly getting Americans out of the range of North Korean artillery. Initially, it was expected that a large number of military dependents, Department of Defense civilians, and their families, as well as other U.S. citizens, would leave using regular commercial transportation. Washington had a number of administrative procedures at its disposal to encourage an orderly exodus. That would greatly lessen the burden on the NEO. Once the State Department asked the Pentagon for assistance, the remaining citizens would be evacuated in ten days.[60]

An NEO would be executed in a straightforward manner. U.S. citizens would be warned of an impending evacuation through the mass media or a "warden system" using organizations such as the Chamber of Commerce to get out the word. Trains would be provided by the government to move the Americans south to embarkation points, such as the port of Pusan, where they would be transported by air or sea to Japan. The small distance from the peninsula would make it possible to set up a shuttle with short turnaround times. The evacuees could then make their way to commercial airports and their final destination. If North Korea attacked airfields in the South, the Americans would evacuate by sea.[61]

Tokyo's cooperation was obviously critical. The State Department and the Gaimusho—Japan's Foreign Ministry—worked together; a joint committee was formed in Seoul to ensure that the plan was ready, while Tokyo put the finishing touches on preparations for receiving the Americans. One potential hurdle was the worldwide U.S. policy of not committing to evacuating foreign nationals of other countries. But in Korea, perhaps because of the presence of the multinational UN Command, "everyone understood we were going to take care of everybody," according to one American. That applied not only to thousands of Japanese but also to hundreds of Westerners. By mid-June, foreign embassies in Seoul were transfixed by the question of whether it was time to evacuate their nationals.[62]

The new NEO was a vast improvement over its predecessor, but Embassy Seoul still worried that tensions might climb to the point of igniting a "spontaneous evacuation" as concerned foreigners voted with their feet, either moving south or leaving the country on their own accord. Initially, the numbers might be small, but mounting tensions could generate widespread panic. Even without an announcement of imminent hostilities, the perception of impending conflict would send a torrent of people streaming to the airports. That, in turn, would generate great pressure on the embassy to announce an NEO and to make available all means of transportation, including charter aircraft, to help civilians leave the country.

By the time President Carter touched down at Kimpo Airport, there were signs that a spontaneous evacuation was about to begin. Some foreign companies had already ordered dependents of their employees to leave the country, issued advisories permitting travel to Korea only under urgent circumstances, or begun to review evacuation plans. At the Seoul Foreign School, a number of parents elected to withdraw their children immediately and send them home. Embassies had started to book seats on airplanes leaving South Korea just in case. They began calling Chuck Kartman daily to make sure he was still in the country. The week of June 13, Embassy Seoul received abnormally large numbers of phone calls from Americans registering their Korean residence and inquiring about evacuation plans.

But it was unclear whether Washington fully understood the powerful dynamic that might be set off by rising tensions. One assumption underlying the original NEO was recognition that an American evacuation would send a strong signal that war might be imminent. It could cause North Korea to heighten the readiness of its troops or, at worst, to launch a preemptive attack. It could start a panic in South Korea with thousands of locals streaming to the airports. In short, the NEO itself could become part of an "action-reaction" cycle that would make matters worse. That, in part, explained the original plan to delay evacuation until the very last minute when military reinforcements began streaming into South Korea. But the old plan would no longer save American lives under the new circumstances.

Embassy Seoul had tried to alert Washington to the problem. It warned that the risks of disorderly evacuation were so great that a request to authorize an evacuation might take place much earlier in an unfolding crisis than under the old plan. The response, according to one embassy official, was "not a one hundred percent yes but a pretty clear indication that they understood the problem and would do their best."[63] The State Department set up a special task force run by William Breer, one of the most senior and well-respected East Asia specialists in the Foreign Service. His job was to monitor the status of preparations for evacuations and to send regular reports to Under Secretary of State Peter Tarnoff.

As the pace of events accelerated and the principals moved toward making key decisions, Laney and Luck grew increasingly concerned. The principals—thousands of miles from Seoul—might act on what the two Americans viewed as the dubious assumption that a well-orchestrated strategy of escalating military and diplomatic steps was possible. Yet decisions taken in the White House Situation Room could cause panic among foreign civilians in Korea, forcing Laney to announce an evacuation. That, in turn, could cause a stampede of South Korean citizens and trigger a precipitous North Korean response.[64]

The situation came to a head just before the June 16 principals' meeting when General Luck called Laney to set up an urgent meeting. The American commander had learned that the president was about to decide on sending more troops to Korea. He quickly drove to Laney's residence since a session at the embassy might attract attention. There, the two drafted a rare joint message to Washington, arguing that the administration was about to make decisions that affected the safety of thousands of Americans without taking the proper precautions. They strongly recommended that no further steps be taken without consulting them first. Aside from making sure Washington understood how high the stakes had become, the two officials hoped to slow the pace of decision-making and give diplomacy more time to work.[65]

Exactly how much time remained was unclear. General Luck's staff viewed the whereabouts of his Labrador "Bud" as an important indicator of how serious the crisis was, given their commander's close attachment to the animal. If it disappeared (and presumably had been evacuated), they would know the situation was serious.[66] But Ambassador Laney was taking no chances; he told his visiting daughter and grandchildren to leave the country.[67] The embassy also began drafting a message requesting Washington's approval for an NEO just in case.[68]

All of this did not escape the notice of the South Korean government. It had two channels of communication with Americans involved in evacuation planning: U.S. Forces Korea and Embassy Seoul. In the military-to-military channel, the two allies had cooperated closely, for example, in ensuring that trains were available to transport American civilians south to embarkation points.[69] As a general principle, the embassy did not involve the South Koreans in evacuation planning since protecting American citizens was viewed as a purely U.S. prerogative. At least one senior embassy official, however, attempted to keep his contacts in the Foreign Ministry informed.[70]

The South became increasingly suspicious when the U.S. military conducted a regularly scheduled NEO exercise on June 6 to check preparedness for an evacuation in case of an emergency. Of course, Pyongyang labeled the exercise another example of preparations for "a northward invasion."[71] The Blue House expressed alarm: "They could not understand that American preparations were not proof that it was going to happen," according to one South Korean. "People remembered Vietnam. It was the same thing with the helicopters on top of the U.S. Embassy."[72]

South Korean concerns were magnified by the impending tough measures the Americans were preparing to take. Seoul had been on board for sanctions; President Kim himself had supported them in hopes that they might bring the North back to the negotiating table on favorable terms. The South Koreans were also very well aware of Washington's plans for a military buildup before sanctions were imposed. General Luck and his staff, working closely with the South Korean Ministry of Defense, had played a key role in formulating the options for those steps. The ministry had naturally kept the Blue House informed. Foreign Minister Han Sung Joo was also well aware of the joint planning.[73]

As the possibility of conflict loomed larger, the consequences of a tough strategy began to sink in. South Koreans grew increasingly suspicious that the Americans were seriously exploring military options that, despite the close consultations, were not being fully shared with their Asian allies. As one American official stationed in Seoul recalled, the South Koreans "were not prepared to be sacrificed on the altar of nonproliferation."[74] Relating his interpretations of these events in his memoirs years later, President Kim Young Sam intimated that the United States was about to evacuate its citizens and, indeed, to ignite a conflict with North Korea, without even consulting its close ally. He claimed that he stopped Washington through timely interventions with Ambassador Laney and President Clinton.

The South Korean leader's story is wrong on a number of counts. First, the Americans were not on the verge of announcing an evacuation, although they did give the Blue House the details of such a step if it were to become necessary. Indeed, following the Luck-Laney cable, Washington asked Laney to return home so he could more effectively communicate his concerns to the principals. If an evacuation were imminent, Washington would have insisted that he remain at his post. Second, the South Korean government was well aware of the military steps the United States was taking and the options being considered at the White House for further deployments. Third, there is no official record of any phone conversations at this time during which President Kim expressed to President Clinton his urgent concerns about an evacuation or an imminent war.

The one issue that may not have been fully discussed between the political leaders of the United States and South Korea was the possibility of a preemptive strike against the Yongbyon nuclear facility if North Korea expelled the IAEA inspectors. Both in Washington and in Seoul, there had been rumblings in the past about a preemptive attack; certainly the Pentagon had thoroughly studied the option. The first formal interagency discussion of such an attack, however, did not take place until the principals' meeting on June 14, prompted by the North's withdrawal from the IAEA and its threat to expel the inspectors. It was clear to everyone at that meeting that a preemptive strike could not be executed without full consultation with the South Korean leaders, which was expected to produce agreement between the two allies on how to proceed. Talk of an attack subsided only two days later after Jimmy Carter reported a renewed willingness by the North to resume and even expand the freeze of its nuclear activities. From that moment, there was no urgent need for serious consultations with Seoul on a military strike.

On June 16 Washington time, senior U.S. officials converged on the West Wing of the White House to meet with the president. Their main task was to help make a fateful decision on the number of additional troops to send to South Korea, and to deliberate further on the "Osirak option." A U.S. force buildup would almost certainly start the countdown to the evacuation of foreign nationals from South Korea. All of these steps would take place against the background of a multilateral effort to impose sanctions on North Korea. As one American diplomat on the scene later recalled, on a scale of one to ten with ten close to panic, the situation in Seoul was "a six and rapidly moving in the wrong direction."[75]

8

We Liked You Starting from Then

June 15–30, 1994

L<small>ATE</small> in the morning of June 15 in Seoul, President Jimmy Carter, his wife, their aides, and a Secret Service detail crossed the heavily fortified border dividing the two Koreas. Carter later recalled that the crossing was "a bizarre and disturbing experience." His wife, Rosalyn, was particularly uneasy about visiting the "hermit kingdom."[1] The next day, President Clinton was slated to decide how many additional troops to send to South Korea. Still, before Carter had left Seoul, a nervous President Kim had handed him a diplomatic trump card to play: a proposal that the leaders of North and South meet without any preconditions.

Carter spent the next two hours speeding along a nearly deserted four-lane highway, the only one in a country conspicuous for the absence of motorized transportation. After arriving in Pyongyang and lunching with his delegation, the former president met Foreign Minister Kim Yong Nam at the Mansudae Assembly Hall, part of the sprawling complex that housed the Supreme People's Assembly. A longtime apparatchik and relative of Kim Il Sung by marriage, the foreign minister was predictably dogmatic, launching into a canned presentation attacking Seoul and the IAEA. But Kim also recalled President Carter's plan to withdraw American troops from South Korea, adding, "We liked you starting from then."

Concerned about Washington's response if Pyongyang kicked the IAEA inspectors out of Yongbyon, Carter asked Kim what his government intended to do. The foreign minister would only repeat vague language from an earlier government statement that the inspectors had nothing further to do in his country. Discussions with the nuclear experts the next day would address the matter.

That evening, the foreign minister hosted a lavish banquet for President Carter. An all-female rock band with frilly dresses and electric guitars improbably sang "Oh Susannah," "My Darling Clementine," and local favorites such as "My Country Is the Best." In his toast, the former president urged the North Koreans to address the nuclear issue, prompting Kim Yong Nam to respond harshly: sanctions would equal a declaration of war. The North Koreans and Americans momentarily froze in a motionless tableau, chopsticks and glasses suspended in midair as each guest took in this defiant gesture.[2] Though it would have been uncharacteristic for the North Koreans to show flexibility right away, President Carter was distressed. The foreign minister had not given the Americans any basis to believe that he understood what was going on. While other North Koreans were probing Carter's aides about what they had to do to meet Washington's concerns—a potentially positive sign—the visit seemed in jeopardy.

Early the next morning, a concerned Jimmy Carter woke up his wife and Marion Creekmore, a former State Department official who was now a close adviser, for a two-hour walk in the garden adjoining the official guesthouse where they were staying. As floodlights illuminated the trio, they discussed how to ensure that the former president's visit did not end in failure. They mulled over the possibility that the foreign minister's hard-line stance was part of a "good-cop, bad-cop" routine with Kim Il Sung slated to play the role of "good cop" the next day. But what if all the North Koreans were "bad cops"? President Carter decided to dispatch Creekmore to the DMZ—the only place where he could communicate securely with Washington—with a message asking President Clinton to authorize him to propose that the two sides move quickly to Gallucci-Kang talks. Creekmore would only send the message as a last-ditch measure if the meeting with the Great Leader went badly, leading Carter to fear that the United States and North Korea were heading for armed conflict.[3]

As Creekmore headed south, Ambassador Laney, tipped off by the U.S. liaison officer at the DMZ that the former diplomat was en route, dispatched embassy officer Danny Russel north. Meeting that evening in a bunker near the command post for U.S rapid reaction troops at the DMZ, Creekmore showed Russel the draft letter. Whether or not he explained it would be sent only if the meeting with Kim Il Sung failed is unclear. But a stunned Russel told him that nothing the former president had heard during his meeting with the foreign minister, a "scarecrow" according to Russel, was newsworthy.

Moreover, if President Carter went on record claiming it was time to resume negotiations on the basis of anything less than a clear commitment from Kim Il Sung himself, he would completely discredit himself.

Concerned that Creekmore might go ahead anyway, Russel then made a secure phone call to his boss in Seoul. Laney had the same reaction to the potentially disastrous proposal. "Don't do this," he begged Creekmore, asking him to tell the former president not to make a move until after he met with Kim Il Sung. In any case, Creekmore returned to Pyongyang following a phone call from Dick Christenson, a Foreign Service officer who was acting as the former president's interpreter with the North Koreans. Carter's meetings were already under way, and, as hoped, Kim Il Sung's role in the unfolding drama had proved to be "good cop" rather than "bad cop."[4]

That morning at Pyongyang's Kumsunsang Palace, Kim Il Sung greeted Jimmy Carter with a big smile; the former president flashed his familiar grin. Bow-legged with age, Kim shambled with him into an ornate meeting room. Like other visitors, Carter found Kim to be "vigorous, alert, intelligent and remarkably familiar with the issues."[5] The North Korean appeared genuinely happy to see Carter, recalling previous attempts to contact the Georgian in the late 1970s through intermediaries such as Marshall Tito and Anwar Sadat.

The two men seemed to develop a quick rapport. President Carter explained that he was there as a private citizen but with the knowledge and support of the Clinton administration. Although the two countries had different political systems, that should not be an obstacle to friendship. This assertion, repeated by Carter throughout the talks, appeared to reassure the North Koreans, worried above all about the preservation of their political power.

Getting to the crux of the matter, the former president emphasized that the IAEA should be permitted to maintain constant and unbroken surveillance of the fuel rods, but the international community was not sure whether North Korea intended to allow this. Calling the American effort to seek sanctions a serious mistake, he concluded that they might not in themselves hurt North Korea, but they would drive a wedge between Pyongyang and the rest of the world. President Carter believed misunderstanding had caused the crisis, since the United States and North Korea had no easy way to communicate.

Puffing slowly on a cigarette, Kim occasionally nodded as Carter spoke or asked for clarification of key points. When Carter assured him that there were no U.S. nuclear weapons present in South Korea and that Washington was prepared to enter into a process that would ensure the peninsula was free of them permanently, the Great Leader said, "That is good." Kim Il Sung agreed that creating trust was critical. Repeating his standard disclaimer that North Korea could not make and did not need nuclear weapons, a frustrated Kim added that no one believed him even though he was the president of his country. Pyongyang was ready to dismantle its graphite-moderated reactors if the United States would help it get new light-water reactors.

After recalling the history of his country's efforts to secure new reactors, Kim turned to the central issue: "We must have a way to live. We need electricity and if we cannot fulfill our electric power needs, our economic development efforts will be harmed." Kim also pledged that if North Korea received new reactors, it would return to the NPT, and there would be no more problems with transparency, implying that special inspections might be possible. The North Korean leader recalled having given the same message to Representative Gary Ackerman, Billy Graham, William Taylor, and Selig Harrison.

These different elements, Kim continued, could be part of an agreement between the United States and North Korea that could be signed in Pyongyang by President Clinton and himself. (Perhaps Kim was thinking of the earlier efforts by Billy Graham to arrange a Kim-Clinton summit.) But recognizing that a visit by Clinton might be too difficult to arrange, he allowed, "Perhaps you could come in his place."

All of this was interesting, but President Carter's immediate concern was whether the IAEA inspectors would be allowed to stay at Yongbyon. He did not know it, but that same day the North Koreans had told the inspectors it would be "illegal" for them to stay once their visas expired on June 22.[6] After not getting an answer from the foreign minister, Carter asked Kim Il Sung point blank whether he would agree to allow the inspectors to remain in place.

Although the North Korean leader had a firm grasp of the "big picture," he did not seem to know significant details. Surprisingly, earlier his staff had to explain to him the current status of the U.S. sanctions drive. At first, Kim Il Sung did not understand Carter's request. He also seemed wary of giving away something important. But Kang Sok Ju—the North's chief negotiator, who was also present—urged him to agree, explaining that the decision had already been made to allow them to stay. Kim turned to Carter and agreed to his request, prompting the former president to reciprocate. He promised to recommend to Washington that it support Pyongyang's request for new reactors and quickly convene another round of U.S.–North Korean talks.

After lunch, Carter met separately with Vice Minister Kang to confirm the results of the morning meeting. While his American colleagues knew of Kang's role as Gallucci's counterpart, none had ever met him before. They found Kang forceful and confident, but also cautious. His presence seemed to eclipse that of most others, including his nominal boss, the foreign minister. Only Kang spoke to Kim Il Sung in a direct and assured manner.

As Kang related the long history of negotiations with the United States,

Carter listened politely. The North Korean official vigorously defended North Korea's decision to unload the fuel rods. Waving a piece of paper in the air, Kang claimed it contained his country's proposal to analyze the fuel rods, a proposal that had never been given a fair hearing by the IAEA or the United States.[7] That was, of course, untrue. Attempting to turn up the pressure, Kang (flatly contradicting what he had just told Kim Il Sung) asserted that when President Carter arrived, a decision had already been made to expel the IAEA inspectors and disconnect the surveillance equipment because America was pursuing sanctions. While he reconfirmed that Kim Il Sung and Carter had reached agreement on that issue, he complained that news reports indicated that Gallucci and Ambassador Albright were still staying up late into the night preparing sanctions.

"All the people in this country and our military are gearing up now to respond to those sanctions. If sanctions pass, all the work you have done here will go down the drain." (Carter concluded from Kang's remark and others like it that Pyongyang would have launched its own preemptive strike if sanctions were enacted while the United States was engaging in a major military buildup.) Responding to Kang's threat, Carter said that he had not been able to contact Washington to explain his agreement with the Great Leader. After he did, the former president planned to go on television and was willing to say that the sanctions resolution should be withdrawn because of that agreement.[8] Conveniently, the same CNN team that had covered Kim Il Sung's birthday in April had been allowed to return with Carter, the only one approved out of 300 news organizations that had applied.

When Kang seemed to back away from other commitments made by Kim Il Sung earlier that day, the Georgian did not hesitate to push back. For example, when Kang asserted that special inspections of the two sites were unthinkable, Carter pointed out that he was contradicting the Great Leader. Kang quickly retreated, allowing that full transparency was possible, but only after both sides had more confidence in each other. In his view, that level of confidence would be demonstrated if, among other things, Washington supported the acquisition of new reactors by the North.

The discussion then turned to the 8,000 fuel rods still sitting in the spent fuel pond. Kang asserted that the fuel might need to be reprocessed after three months because of corrosion, yielding about five bombs' worth of separated plutonium. President Carter responded that reprocessing was fine as long as it took place under IAEA safeguards, prompting a surprised Kang to exclaim "Really?" Aside from the fact that this baldly contradicted American policy, his State Department interpreter whispered to Carter that this would cause a problem with Seoul since the United States had consistently discouraged

South Korea from reprocessing. Indeed, reprocessing was proscribed any-where on the peninsula under the terms of the North-South Denucleariza-tion Declaration.[9]

By the end of the day, the former president believed he had achieved a breakthrough. His session with Kim Il Sung had produced a public commit-ment to keep the IAEA inspectors in place, locking in a decision the North had already made. The North's main demand—the provision of new reactors and a pledge not to launch a nuclear attack against Pyongyang in return for meet-ing its nonproliferation obligations—seemed eminently doable to the former president. Carter felt he needed to nail down this tenuous arrangement some-how since, as the discussion with Kang indicated, it might quickly crumble once the bureaucrats got back into the action.

Lacking the diplomatic credentials to reach agreement on Washington's behalf, President Carter resorted to another device, using statements to the media to present a fait accompli to both sides. As the meeting with Kang drew to a close, Carter reemphasized that he planned to go on CNN, prompting the North Korean to remind him to be sure to say that Pyongyang had agreed to keep the inspectors in place. Nervous that Carter might have something up his sleeve, Kang wanted to see his text before he went on the air and then asked him to delay the interview for a day. Instead, the former president tried to get Kang to appear with him. The North Korean demurred.

Didn't You Tell Him Not to Go on CNN?

As Jimmy Carter was finishing dinner in Pyongyang, across the international date line, in Washington, the Principals Committee was gathering in the Cab-inet Room of the West Wing. Just a few weeks earlier, the president had met in this room with all of the four-star commanders of the unified and regional commands, to discuss the war plan for Korea. Now Clinton had to decide whether to authorize executing the first phase of that plan.

Before the meeting, the president had reviewed the pros and cons of the "Osirak option." That morning, Secretary Christopher and Gallucci had breakfasted with Secretary Perry, Under Secretary Slocombe, and General Shalikashvili at the Pentagon to discuss the military options and to forge a common recommendation to the president. Now the State Department rep-resentatives joined the rest of the principals as Perry and Shalikashvili began to lay out the options, ranging from a modest deployment of 2,000 troops to a full-scale deployment of 50,000 troops.

At one point in his presentation, Perry observed that whatever the United States did to enhance its presence in order to deal with the North Koreans' reaction to sanctions might be regarded by them as provocative. It was easy to see how the United States and the North could end up taking steps aimed at defending against each other that would only prompt additional steps by the other side in response. Perry said that unchecked, such a cycle of measures and countermeasures could lead to war. He referred to Barbara Tuchman's analysis in the *Guns of August*, and the way in which the events of 1914 seemed to escape the control of European leaders and led inexorably to world war.

The meeting was already in its second hour when the president's steward stepped softly into the Cabinet Room and announced that former President Carter was on the telephone from Pyongyang. President Clinton slowly began to move his chair away from the table to take the call when the steward quickly added that Carter wanted to talk to Bob Gallucci. Somewhat sheepishly, Gallucci then left the room to take the call. Picking up the receiver, he recognized President Carter's distinctive voice, telling him about Kim Il Sung's willingness to leave the inspectors in place. Carter asked what he thought about the offer in exchange for resuming talks and no sanctions. "It doesn't matter what I think," Gallucci replied, noting that President Clinton and his national security team were meeting in the next room.

Carter asked that someone call him back when President Clinton had decided what to do. Gallucci replied that since Washington could not call Pyongyang, it would be better if Carter called back instead. Almost as an afterthought, the former president ended the conversation by saying he planned to go on CNN momentarily.

After nearly twenty minutes on the phone, Gallucci returned to the meeting and did his best to transmit Carter's message. But before anyone commented on the substance, Tony Lake queried, "You did tell him not to go on CNN, didn't you?" "No," Gallucci replied, adding that Carter would not have listened even if he did. Secretary Christopher—sitting next to Gallucci—asked if he had even tried. Once again, the answer was no. It was not a good moment for Gallucci. A chilly silence was broken only by someone's suggestion that they adjourn to watch Carter on television.

The former president announced on CNN that Kim Il Sung had promised not to expel the IAEA inspectors and to keep their surveillance equipment in place. Carter said that North Korea was also willing to discard its old reactors in exchange for new ones. Moreover, "transparency" (not further defined) was possible if the two countries pursued negotiations. After implying that talks involving Christopher or even the president would be helpful, Carter asserted that the administration was mistaken in pursuing sanctions, starting a running debate that would escalate over the next few days. His meetings had resulted in a "very important and positive step toward alleviation of this crisis." President Carter concluded that what happened next was up to the Clinton administration.[10]

While Carter seemed to have secured a commitment from Pyongyang to leave the inspectors and equipment in place for the moment, there was little that was new from his discussions. His tone was critical, particularly on sanctions, but tolerant of North Korea. There was no mention of North Korea forgoing reprocessing or producing more plutonium to build bombs. Carter even asserted that Pyongyang's withdrawal from the IAEA was no cause for alarm. After all, forty other countries were also not members.

"What we have is nothing new," one official concluded. "The problem is that North Korea now has a former president as its spokesperson." Poneman argued against portraying old North Korean positions as new ones just because Carter restated them. The president agreed. The only useful comments suggested that North Korea would accept continued IAEA inspections to allow the agency to keep track of its spent fuel. But the interview certainly was not binding on the North, nor had Pyongyang endorsed his statements. President Carter was trying to use the press to box in both sides.

How should the United States respond, without making Carter appear like an official emissary? President Clinton mused aloud that the current situation reminded him of the Cuban missile crisis, when President Kennedy received two letters from Soviet leader Nikita Khrushchev. One was a conciliatory message that opened the path to a Soviet agreement to withdraw its nuclear-tipped ballistic missiles from Cuba, the other a harsh and unbending note. Following that example, Clinton told his advisers "the best approach diplomatically and psychologically" was to view the Carter interview in the light most favorable to American interests and then to put the burden on the North Koreans—and perhaps President Carter—to contradict the administration interpretation.

Practically speaking, a U.S. statement responding to the day's developments would serve the same purpose as instructions, without giving the impression that the former president was an emissary. Washington should simply pocket the good elements in the CNN interview. A message could be sent to Pyongyang later through diplomatic channels to confirm that interpretation. If the gambit failed, a sanctions resolution with substantial international support was ready to go.

No one at the principals' meeting supported returning to negotiations merely on the basis of North Korea's renewed pledge—even if implemented— to allow limited IAEA inspections. Defueling had destroyed historical information. In order to return to negotiations, North Korea would need to do more than restore the fiction of the status quo ante when that past could no longer be reconstituted. It would have to take an additional step. But what?

After some discussion, Stanley Roth, NSC senior director for Asian affairs, hit on a solution: the United States should insist that North Korea *not refuel* the 5-megawatt reactor as a condition for another round of negotiations. The Pentagon had advocated this approach during Roth's tenure as a senior Defense Department official before joining the NSC staff. But others had resisted since the proposal went far beyond IAEA requirements, which permit research reactor operations. It therefore might have given North Korea an easy pretext to refuse IAEA compliance and garner significant multilateral support in doing so. Now that Pyongyang had crossed a clear American red line, raising the bar appeared to be exactly the right thing to do, and the principals quickly agreed to the new proposal.[11]

Lake asked Gallucci, Poneman, and Leon Fuerth, the vice president's national security adviser, to draft the necessary language. The statement they hammered out was delivered by the president in the White House briefing room:

> Today there have been reports that the North Koreans, in discussion with President Carter, may have offered new steps to resolve the international community's concerns, saying that International Atomic Energy Agency inspectors and monitoring equipment would be left in place and that North Korea desires to replace its present nuclear program with a new light-water reactor technology that is more resistant to nuclear proliferation. If North Korea means by this, also, that it is willing to freeze its nuclear program while talks take place, this could be a promising development.
>
> If today's developments mean that North Korea is genuinely and verifiably prepared to freeze its nuclear program while talks go on—and we hope that is the case—then we would be willing to resume high-level talks. In the meantime, we will pursue our consultations on sanctions at the United Nations.[12]

In response to a question, Clinton reinforced this last point by noting that "Ambassador Albright continued today pursuing our consultations on sanctions with the non-permanent members of the Security Council and we are proceeding and we're just going to watch developments."[13]

After the president departed, Gallucci was left behind to fill in the details. He welcomed the "indications given to President Carter that North Korea desires to find a constructive solution to the very serious issues between North Korea and the international community." The first question from the back of the briefing room was "Didn't you try to talk President Carter out of going on CNN to describe his deal?" After a pause, Gallucci responded that he did not. With that simple but true answer, speculation about a Carter-Clinton split was momentarily quashed.[14] Tony Lake would later observe that Gallucci was a "lucky son of a bitch."[15]

Gallucci then noted that the United States would be prepared to go to a third round of negotiations if the North confirmed through diplomatic channels that it would not refuel the reactor or reprocess the spent fuel. It also had to permit the IAEA to maintain the continuity of safeguards. When asked whether this might not be a tactic by the North Koreans to buy time, Gallucci replied: "I'm well past myself trying to interpret the motivations of North Korea. And what I tell you is, we will look at what they say and what they are prepared to do and we'll act on that basis."[16]

Gallucci trod carefully on the question of whether the United States had "raised the bar," the traditional kiss-of-death to any new public proposal. The North Koreans would notice instantly that this was precisely what the United States had done. On the other hand, for Gallucci to rub North Korean noses in that new condition publicly could squander the opportunity to convert the Carter trip into a diplomatic opening. Thus when Gallucci was asked point-blank whether the U.S. demand for a freeze on all North Korean nuclear activities was an "additional condition," he somewhat obliquely responded that North Korea had

> undercut the basis [for negotiations] in such a way that we were forced to return the issue to the UN Security Council, while telling [the North Koreans] that it was always possible and it must always be possible to reestablish the basis for a dialogue. What I was doing was describing to you a way in which the dialogue could be reconvened . . . a way that draws from the message we received today but not in such a way that I could say that it was part of the message and therefore something we wished to follow up through diplomatic contacts.[17]

By admitting that the offer to restart the dialogue was not drawn from the message conveyed by President Carter, Gallucci essentially confirmed that the bar had been raised. Before the United States would agree to more talks, Pyongyang would need to respond positively through diplomatic channels, not through Jimmy Carter.

Gallucci used another question to provide a rationale for the new U.S. demand, while clarifying *how* the United States had raised the bar: "We have had a basis for dialogue which assured that not a single additional gram of plutonium would be *separated*. It is our intent if we resume that dialogue now, that there not be a single additional gram of plutonium *produced*. That's what happens when you don't refuel the reactor" (emphasis added).[18]

The American response had put the ball back in North Korea's court. The *earlier* basis for negotiations required that the North not *separate* additional plutonium. That would allow Pyongyang to continue *producing* more pluto-nium—as operating the 5-megawatt reactor would shower more uranium-238 with neutrons in order to produce more bomb-usable plutonium-239—*so long as it did not separate the plutonium out of the resulting spent fuel.* Now the United States was insisting that there could be neither plutonium separa-tion nor production—hence the need to keep the 5-megawatt reactor idle.

That Young Man Used to Work for Me

Whether Washington and Seoul liked it or not, there was a new diplomatic player on the block. Jimmy Carter's foray had already caused strains in the alliance. Early in the morning Seoul time—just before Gallucci's press confer-ence—Secretary Christopher had called Foreign Minister Han to tell him that since Carter's meetings could be interpreted as either the basis for progress or further delaying tactics, the United States would continue working on sanc-tions until more information was available. South Korean officials then woke up President Kim, literally briefing him on the run at a jogging track. "This was very awkward," one recalled in a classic understatement.[19]

The South Korean president felt vindicated; he had been concerned from the very beginning that President Carter's trip would undermine the strategy of turning up the heat on North Korea. Now, the CNN interview caused him and others in Seoul to take umbrage at what they believed was an apparent fait accompli from Pyongyang. The interview also reignited President Kim's fear of being sidelined, prompting him to try—unsuccessfully—to get Washington to mention North-South talks in Gallucci's statement.

Recognizing the consequences of an unhappy Kim, the Americans moved to head off any further problems, subsequently explaining that they had to respond quickly to President Carter to prevent him from boxing them in. That had some resonance in Seoul. For good measure, the White House installed a secure telephone line in the Blue House to allow confidential communication between the two presidents.[20] (The line failed the first time President Kim tried to use it.)

Having assuaged the South Koreans, the White House had to make sure that Carter understood its response to his interview and took no further actions that contradicted American policy. Someone other than Gallucci would be needed for what was likely to be a tough conversation. National Security Adviser Tony Lake was the logical choice.

Phone contact was reestablished just before dawn Pyongyang time. Sitting on the edge of his bed, the former president heard Lake describe the adminis-tration's new position and pushed back hard. Carter argued that prohibiting refueling and reprocessing could be a nonstarter for Pyongyang, not to mention that he would have to back-pedal after having already told Kim Il Sung and Kang that reprocessing was allowed under the NPT. Carter also objected to the continuing U.S. drive for sanctions. The whole discussion, presumably monitored by the North Koreans, was very chilly. Afterward, President Carter appeared taken aback by the conversation with Lake, ruefully recalling that "that young man used to work for me when he was a young pup."[21]

Later that day, Jimmy Carter went back to the diplomatic drawing board during a three-hour cruise down the Taedong River with Kim Il Sung. As Carter and Kim took a special lift to the top deck, the other Americans talked with their counterparts down below. Aware that the emerging agreement was still fragile, the Americans made a point of telling their hosts that the arrangement would collapse immediately if Pyongyang failed to keep even the smallest promise. Kang seemed to understand that skeptics on both sides would seize any opportunity to ruin things.

Heeding Washington's concerns, Carter made some midcourse corrections while advancing his own personal diplomacy. On reprocessing, he now said that it was a "theoretical" possibility under the NPT but was probably a deal breaker for the United States. Moreover, Pyongyang did not have to reprocess the spent fuel; it could just bury the rods. While the North Koreans understood and probably had been listening to Carter's conversation with Lake, they did not agree on the spot. "What if we give up reprocessing but don't get the light-water reactors? We will get nothing," one asked.

All the same, President Carter was able to secure two new understandings. First, he and Kim agreed on establishing U.S.–North Korean teams to recover the remains of Americans killed in the Korean War.[22] Second, Kim Il Sung agreed to an inter-Korean summit. This was an about-face from their meeting of the previous day, during which the North Korean leader complained that Seoul had resisted exchanging special envoys and stepped in to thwart the nuclear talks just as the United States and North Korea were making progress. Now Kim Il Sung admitted that the lack of progress was the fault of both sides. Recalling President Kim Young Sam's inaugural offer to meet "anytime, anyplace," Kim Il Sung said he accepted without preconditions and asked Carter to relay the message. He even gave an intriguing preview of summit topics, including the possibility of pulling back ground forces from the DMZ, the likely flashpoint for any North-South confrontation.

Exactly why Kim Il Sung agreed to meet the South Korean leader after his government had carried on six months of excoriating attacks on him was unclear. He had come close to a summit with President Roh Tae Woo in 1992

and also seemed open to the idea during meetings dating back to the Ackerman visit in October 1993. The elder Kim may have realized that his days were
numbered and wanted to smooth the path for his son's succession, or he may
have been acting on impulse. In any case, the move gave instant credibility to
President Carter's diplomatic mission in the eyes of the South Koreans when
the summit commitment was revealed in Seoul the next day.

Just as he was taking two steps forward, however, Jimmy Carter moved one
step back. On the boat, the CNN crew filmed him erroneously telling Kim Il
Sung that the United States sanctions effort had stopped as a result of their
talks the previous day.[23] Once again his remarks elicited a swift response, this
time from Dee Dee Myers, the White House press secretary, who immediately
reaffirmed in a June 18 statement that U.S. policy remained unchanged and
that "we are continuing to consult on a sanctions resolution at the UN Security Council." An irritated President Clinton delivered the same message a few
hours later.[24]

Early the next morning, as Carter's motorcade left Pyongyang, the administration was already under attack because of the former president's personal
diplomacy. On June 18, a *New York Times* headline read: "U.S. Shift on Korea:
Clinton Retreating from a Showdown."[25] The negative press, suggesting weakness and vacillation in the face of imminent sanctions, may have been
inevitable in view of the White House decision to downplay in public the fact
that it had raised the bar for the North to secure further negotiations. But the
stakes were too high and the margin of maneuver too constrained to allow
administration chest thumping at the expense of the North Koreans, especially given the long track record of their self-defeating reactions whenever
their pride was affronted. Despite the negative headline, the *Times* at least
allowed the administration its say, quoting Tony Lake's insistence that "as the
President said yesterday, our policy has not changed one iota."

Waiting at Panmunjom, Ambassador Laney had talked to Washington just
before President Carter arrived. His instructions—bound to anger the former
president—were to tell Carter to back off talk about sanctions and to focus on
the steps North Korea had to take to secure another meeting with Gallucci.
Moreover, since President Clinton would be unavailable for a few days, Carter
would have to speak either to Vice President Gore or National Security Adviser
Lake about his trip. Finally, it was suggested that Carter should return home to
Plains, and come to Washington in a week or two. That was not the kind of
reception expected by someone who believed he had helped stop a second
Korean War. After posing for scores of cameramen, an angry President Carter
headed for Seoul and then on to the ambassador's residence.[26]

Two hours later, Jimmy Carter talked to Vice President Gore, a key supporter of his trip. The situation was sufficiently complex—and tense—that Gore asked whether Carter objected to having notes made of the telephone conversation. To make sure there were no misunderstandings, Gore explained that it was not enough for North Korea to say that it was continuing the freeze in order to return to the negotiating table. The United States needed three North Korean commitments before restarting the dialogue: no reprocessing of plutonium from spent fuel, no restarting of the 5-megawatt reactor, and the continued presence of IAEA inspectors at Yongbyon.

Carter asserted that Pyongyang's nuclear activity had stopped and that the North Koreans had a right under the NPT to reprocess plutonium. Gore responded that North Korea was not in the situation of a normal NPT party, that it was out of compliance and was launching a major plutonium production program. It could not be considered "entitled" to reprocess under the NPT.

Switching to the other "hot button" issue, sanctions, Gore stated that Washington had *not* stopped efforts to pass a Security Council resolution. "It was unfortunate that CNN picked up your comment on that point," the vice president told him. In his own defense, Carter reported that before leaving Pyongyang, he had made it clear to the North Koreans that the United States had not withdrawn the sanctions resolution, but the agreement with Kim Il Sung would form the basis for an end to punitive action and the beginning of negotiations. Moreover, according to Carter, the conditions he had expressed to the North were the same as those Lake had briefed to him. That sparked another disagreement over Carter's failure to press the point that no reprocessing was essential to the resumption of talks.

"How long does the United States expect North Korea to stop reprocessing? Just during the U.S.-DPRK talks or forever?" asked the former president. Carter asserted that North Korea would never give up reprocessing forever absent getting another source of energy to replace its reactors. Gore broke off from Carter to check with Lake. With a phone in each hand, the vice president served as the go-between to confirm from the national security adviser to the former president that the no-reprocessing condition just applied to the duration of talks. Since Carter was convinced the North would not reprocess during the talks, that seemed to patch up the difference for the moment. The discussion ended in agreement that the former president should make a short stop in Washington after all, but over the weekend, to brief administration officials firsthand. The conversation had been long and impassioned; the discussion had reverberated throughout the ambassador's residence.[27]

President Carter had better luck with the South Koreans. His next stop was lunch with President Kim Young Sam at the Blue House, where he unveiled the offer from Kim Il Sung to meet the South Korean leader "at any time, anywhere, without conditions at an early date." (There had been public discussion of a freeze but the press had not caught wind of the secret summit proposal.) Kim, who had grudgingly met Carter only a few days earlier, was ecstatic. Having once told a close aide that a good politician should be able to seize opportunities quickly, he immediately accepted Kim Il Sung's offer. He seemed on the threshold of realizing a long-standing dream, to be the first leader of South Korea to meet with his North Korean counterpart. As a test of Pyongyang's sincerity, President Kim (with Carter's agreement) instructed his press secretary to announce immediately that North Korea had agreed to a summit meeting. Pyongyang's response would show whether the proposal was serious or not.[28]

Having concluded his diplomatic mission, President Jimmy Carter left Seoul bound for Portland, Oregon, that afternoon, but not before delivering a stinging rebuke of the Clinton administration. Speaking to reporters, he asserted that sanctions against North Korea were doomed to failure and would only be "a personal insult to their so-called Great Leader . . . branding him as a liar and a criminal." The statement, along with the prospect of the first inter-Korean summit ever, made front-page news back home.[29]

Welcome Back, Carter?

On Sunday, June 19, a small group of officials gathered in Tony Lake's West Wing office, awaiting President Carter: Gallucci, Poneman, Assistant Secretary of State for East Asia Winston Lord, and Deputy National Security Adviser Sandy Berger. While many in the administration felt Carter's claiming credit for the diplomatic breakthrough and his sanctions bashing had gone too far, this session was intended to mend fences. Moreover, this was the first chance to get Carter's direct impressions on his meetings in Pyongyang.

Just before the session began, President Carter stiffly entered the office, "the tension . . . so thick, you could cut the atmosphere with a knife." The national security adviser warily tried to put Carter at ease. The two agreed to put all differences behind them and to move forward without mutual recrimination. Carter sat on the sofa and began to read his trip report verbatim. In it, Carter bore in on his disagreement with the administration over Lake's "instructions" concerning plutonium reprocessing. Though perhaps unintentional, the draft also left the impression with some in the room that the North was a more sympathetic interlocutor than South Korea, and that the highly decorated commander of U.S. Forces Korea, General Luck, quailed before the prospect of military conflict. Lake insisted on the spot on corrections dealing

with his own interactions with Carter and with the former president's assessment of General Luck's views.

Carter only made matters worse when he informed those present: "I only
intend to distribute this report to the president, the vice president, the secretary of state, secretary of defense . . . and my mailing list of supporters." The
half-hour-old agreement between Lake and Carter to put differences aside
looked doomed even before the meeting ended. Trying to avert a renewed
press squall that could damage U.S. policy, Poneman suggested that the report
be shared only with the president and cabinet members, but not the mailing
list. Dismissing the suggestion, Carter took a phone call from President Clinton congratulating him for his accomplishment, while Poneman and Carter
aide Marion Creekmore repaired to an adjacent office to iron out the problems in the report.[30]

Whatever progress had been made in closing the breach between Jimmy
Carter and the administration that morning, the former president's public
tack was still troubling. Briefing the press afterward, Gallucci emphasized that
the administration welcomed Carter's efforts and planned to follow up on
them immediately.[31] But back at his hotel, the former president continued to
complain to the press that U.S. policy on Korea had been misguided. Returning to a major concern, Carter added that sanctions "would be a direct cause
of potential war."[32]

The Clinton team had to deal not only with Carter but also with the political firestorm ignited by his trip. Some observers came to his defense. Donald
Gregg, who had been President Bush's ambassador in Seoul, wrote in the
Washington Post that the administration had been too focused on the "IAEA's
nuclear agenda." Carter's visit may have helped by "broadening the dialogue
between Washington and Pyongyang" to include economic issues.[33]

But the predominant reaction was harsh, and the criticism was bipartisan.
While Carter was in Pyongyang, President Clinton had talked to Newt Gin-
grich, the Republican leader in the House of Representatives, and urged him
to show caution until it was understood whether or not this was a useful
opening. Once the former president returned, the attacks began. Lee Hamilton (Democrat of Indiana), the chairman of the House Foreign Affairs Committee, disagreed with Carter's assessment that the crisis was resolved: "The
fundamentals have not changed. . . . North Korea is still not living up to its
commitments."[34] The generally supportive *New York Times* also said that
Carter erred on sanctions and was premature in declaring the crisis over.[35]

Republicans were blunter. Former secretary of state Lawrence Eagleburger
said he was "horrified" to hear President Carter "taking the word of this mur-
derer who runs North Korea," caustically adding, "I really wish he'd stayed
home."[36] Columnist Charles Krauthammer evoked the spirit of Chamberlain

at Munich, disparaging "people convinced that all that stands between war and peace is their dining with a dictator."[37]

In an attempt to firm up its base of support and to chart the road ahead, the administration convened a bipartisan meeting of experts at the White House on June 20. They held in the Roosevelt Room in the West Wing, across from the Oval Office. The turnout showed how seriously the administration was taking the Korea issue. Virtually the entire national security team was present, including the president, vice president, Lake, Berger, Christopher, and Perry.

The experts in the room were a who's who of the think-tank world and academia. Bush administration officials included former under secretary of state Arnold Kanter, former ambassadors to South Korea Donald Gregg and James Lilley, and former assistant secretary of state for East Asia and Pacific Affairs, Richard Solomon. Robert Scalapino, the dean of America's academic experts on Asia, was also present. Rounding out the cast were Selig Harrison, Janne Nolan of the Brookings Institution, Leonard ("Sandy") Spector, an expert on nonproliferation at the Carnegie Endowment, and Alan Romberg, a former State Department official who was now affiliated with the U.S. Institute for Peace.

Lake opened the session: "We had been making progress on the future, but ran aground on the shoals of the past. When Jimmy Carter called the vice president, we believed it would be useful to get better information directly from the North Korean leadership, and to convey our views directly to them." Christopher explained that the administration would be going through the New York channel to confirm the North Koreans' commitment to the freeze as Washington had described it.

Clinton and Gore entered after the meeting had already begun. They both stayed for forty-five minutes. Gore walked the group through the logic of the administration's military approach, to enhance American capabilities sufficiently to deter the North without provoking an attack before the augmentation was complete. The experts' responses highlighted continuing differences over how to deal with Pyongyang. A skeptical Jim Lilley appeared unconvinced by the vice president's description of the military option, questioning whether Kim Il Sung had in fact gotten the message. Professor Scalapino disagreed, arguing that Pyongyang clearly understood.

Another question raised was whether a negotiated settlement was still possible. Don Gregg thought it was; Harrison added that the Carter mission had produced a tremendous diplomatic opportunity. The United States should seize the moment to make a deal based on the new reactor project. Lake reminded him that Americans still needed to find out if the North Korean offer was real. Arnold Kanter also doubted that the light-water reactors were "the holy grail." They could be a red herring or a multibillion-dollar face-saver. To secure a nonnuclear peninsula, he stressed, required not just a freeze but dis-mantlement of North Korea's nuclear facilities. That meant not giving up on the past and reviving the North-South Denuclearization Declaration. Perhaps the United States should offer to buy or transfer the North's spent fuel out of the country, he said.[38]

As the discussion wore on, it became clear that no meeting could repair the political damage. While the session had been scheduled before Carter's trip, coming on the heels of what the press had characterized as a "retreat," it was viewed as a forum for a confused administration to look for guidance. That also seemed to be the perception of the public, which was less opposed to negotiations than concerned about how the whole episode had been handled. A *Newsweek* poll found 68 percent of the American public in favor of resum-ing talks with North Korea and only 28 percent opposed. But when asked about President Clinton's handling of North Korea, the majority disapproved by 42 percent to 31 percent, with the remainder having no opinion.[39]

I Was Glad He Went

As the swirl of publicity continued, the administration turned to the serious business of ascertaining whether the apparent opening reported by President Carter could be converted into a genuine diplomatic breakthrough. Late in the evening of June 20, Gallucci sent a letter to Kang that sought to nail down North Korea's acceptance of the administration's expanded definition of nuclear freeze:

> My government has received the message that former President Carter has conveyed at the request of President Kim Il Sung regarding the DPRK's willingness to return to full compliance with the NPT and IAEA safeguards and its desire to replace its gas graphite reactors and related technology with light-water reactors as part of an overall settlement of the nuclear issue. . . . Former President Carter has also conveyed Presi-dent Kim's assurances that the DPRK will permit IAEA inspectors and IAEA surveillance equipment to remain in place at the nuclear sites at Yongbyon and will freeze the major elements of the DPRK's nuclear pro-gram while US-DPRK talks are under way. On the basis of these assur-ances, we understand that your willingness to freeze the nuclear pro-gram means that the DPRK will not refuel the 5-MW reactor nor reprocess spent fuel while U.S.-DPRK talks continue. We also assume that the DPRK will permit IAEA inspections necessary to maintain con-tinuity of safeguards at the declared nuclear sites.

The letter concluded that upon receipt of North Korea's confirmation, the United States would be willing to hold talks in Geneva as early as July 6.

Pyongyang responded just two days later. The letter was from Kang, and it stated that Kim Il Sung had made a "momentous proposal aimed at breaking the current DPRK-USA impasse and resolving the nuclear issue at its root once and for all." This was a rhetorical device the North had used on many occasions to signal a change in its position. Then came the key passage:

> In this connection, we would liked to make it clear that we are willing, within the framework of the DPRK-USA confidence-building process and also of our proposed package solution to the nuclear issue, to fully implement the Nuclear Non-Proliferation Treaty and the safeguards agreement with the International Atomic Energy Agency (IAEA), to replace the existing graphite-moderated reactors with light-water reactors and to freeze the major elements of our nuclear program while the DPRK-USA talks go under way.
>
> For the immediate future, we would like to assure you that, for the sake of the third round of the DPRK-USA talks, we are prepared neither to reload the five-megawatt experimental reactor with new fuel nor to reprocess the spent fuel, and to permit the inspections for the continuity of safeguards including the maintenance of the presence of IAEA inspectors and of the Agency's surveillance equipment in place at the Yongbyon nuclear facilities. Issues at that stage will be subject to the discussion at the third round of talks.

Kang went on to express no objection to the proposed July 6 date for the third round but suggested a meeting two days later "for the convenience of air route connections."

Reading the letter as it came over a fax machine in the Old Executive Office Building, Poneman was struck by its unprecedented nature. Never before during the North Korean nuclear crisis had Pyongyang simply accepted the key U.S. demands without reservation or counteroffer. American officials had become accustomed to the incessant haggling common in dealing with the North Koreans. Where were the customary polemics and shrill accusations? This straightforward letter simply *acquiesced* to the U.S. conditions for a resumption of the bilateral dialogue. Poneman took the message across West Executive Avenue and up the stairs to the national security adviser's suite, where he told Berger the good news.

President Clinton soon appeared in the White House briefing room to announce, "This afternoon we have received formal confirmation from North Korea that it will freeze the major elements of its nuclear program while a new round of talks between our nations proceeds." The United States would inform North Korea of its readiness "to go forward with a new round of talks in Geneva early next month," during which the United States would suspend its efforts to pursue UN Security Council sanctions.[40]

Ironically, the president's announcement came only hours after Secretary Christopher and Russian foreign minister Kozyrev, meeting in Brussels, finally reached closure on a UN sanctions resolution. The United States made one last concession, agreeing to hold the Russian-proposed, international conference before sanctions automatically kicked in.[41]

The president also took the opportunity to further mend fences with Carter. Before the briefing, he had called the former president to tell him about the North Korean response. Subsequently, Clinton told the press that the Carter trip had provided a chance to send a direct message to the Great Leader, something he had been trying to do for some time. "I was glad he went and I thought it was a trip worth taking."[42]

In an earlier Oval Office session, Clinton explained his thinking to his staff: "Look, I knew I was going to take some heat for letting Carter go there. But I also knew we needed to give the North Koreans an escape hatch, some way to climb down without losing face. I figured if they could say to themselves that a former president had come to their country, it would allow them to do that." Whether Clinton was considering a summit with Kim Il Sung was unclear, although Secretary Christopher publicly hinted that it might be possible if the North Koreans started behaving in a way that justified such a meeting.[43]

That same day, Pyongyang accepted Seoul's proposal to hold a meeting to prepare for the summit. Unlike previous excruciating exchanges, the message from North Korean premier Kang Song San agreed to the South's offer without modification.[44]

Clinton and President Kim Young Sam talked that evening. The American president told his counterpart that the day's events were not a solution, but created an opportunity to solve the nuclear problem. The two presidents would have to work together closely in the days to come. President Kim admitted that he had doubts about the Carter trip but now viewed it as a positive development. Kim added that 93 percent of his countrymen supported the summit and 60 percent thought it could help resolve the nuclear issue.[45]

In North Korea, the IAEA inspectors' visas were extended and new ones issued to another team about to replace the old group. The agency was told that its inspectors could stay at the Yongbyon nuclear facility for as long as it wanted.[46]

On June 24, a New York channel meeting formalized the agreement to resume U.S.–North Korean negotiations on July 8. A week later, President

Jimmy Carter wrote Gallucci with some observations and suggestions, including his view that it was excessive to demand that North Korea not conduct any reprocessing. The crisis was not over, but the prospect of imminent military confrontation now receded as the diplomatic track reopened. Time would tell whether that reopening would lead to a successful resolution of the crisis or to another series of marches and countermarches, dangers and disappointments.

For Want of a Nail

Memories fade quickly, especially where conflicts are averted rather than endured, but it is important to recall that during the fateful month of June 1994, six out of ten Americans surveyed thought that U.S. vital interests were at stake in North Korea, a far higher figure than for any other international situation at that time.[47] For the past year, the United States had been holding out two paths to North Korea. The path of compliance with international rules against the spread of nuclear weapons held some promise for improved political and economic relations with the outside world. The path of defiance would bring only hardship and increased isolation to North Korea. U.S. efforts to resolve the crisis through diplomacy reflected its preference for the first path, but the administration realized that North Korea was unlikely to take that path without the credible threat that Washington would take the second path.

By its own actions in defueling the 5-megawatt reactor without cooperating with IAEA inspectors on preserving the history of the rods, North Korea had abandoned the path toward negotiated settlement in favor of the path toward confrontation. Although the U.S. government had not sought the confrontation, it did not shrink from it once Pyongyang crossed that red line. American officials had quickly locked in critical allied support from Seoul and Tokyo to proceed toward sanctions and had worked the diplomatic angles in Beijing and Moscow to the point where Pyongyang had good reason to doubt that either of its erstwhile backers would save it from the impact of such sanctions. At the same time, the Pentagon was firming up options for the president to reinforce the 37,000 U.S. troops in Korea with a package that would add tens of thousands of ground forces and back them up with significant additions to sea- and air-based assets in theater.

Though fraught with danger and uncertainty, the U.S. decision to move toward the imposition of UN Security Council sanctions was the right thing to do. The red lines had been clearly expressed by Gallucci since the June 1993 meeting in New York; unquestionably the North Koreans understood them. Had the Americans faltered in moving toward sanctions, it would have undermined the credibility of any subsequent U.S. position while reducing, if not eliminating, the effective threat of coercive action. The North Koreans would quickly have seized the tactical advantage, continued probing for weakness in allied positions, and undertaken further steps in its nuclear program to, at a minimum, enhance its bargaining leverage and, at most, secure a nuclear weapons arsenal.

The United States was also correct in its policy to precede any move to enforced sanctions with military measures to deter any North Korean aggression. The North Koreans had asserted that they would consider such a move an act of war. Given the stakes for both the Koreans and the Americans on the peninsula, it would have been irresponsible simply to assume Pyongyang was bluffing. The packages of reinforcement under consideration for deployment to South Korea were intended to constitute a decisive show of force that would deter any foolhardy military strike from the North.

The one missing element in the strategy, as the president kept saying with increasing frustration during the weeks when the crisis continued its upward spiral, was an escape hatch for the North Koreans to return to the path of compliance without what they would have viewed as an unacceptable loss of face. In other words, if Pyongyang wanted to climb back from the brink, the United States and its allies needed to offer them an opening to do so without embarrassment.

Enter Jimmy Carter. He was not the first volunteer to intercede with the North, nor the first that the administration accepted. But the timing of Carter's intervention, combined with the unique status enjoyed by a former American president, created a new opportunity. No one viewed the former president as the ideal envoy (witness the heated debate among the principals as to whether his trip to Pyongyang should be approved). Carter had his own agenda and could be very difficult to deal with, much less control. Perhaps most important, his antipathy to the use of force, as demonstrated by his actions in the run-up to the Gulf War, was inconsistent with the U.S. policy toward North Korea throughout the crisis. Finally, Carter was bad news politically to an administration seeking to govern from the center and to avoid being labeled "liberal" or viewed as "subcontracting" its foreign policy to the former president.

At the same time, Carter brought a number of critical assets to the diplomatic arena: a commitment to and track record of dispute resolution, a doggedness in the quest of any goal upon which he set his sights, and the unique status and stature of a former president of the United States. He knew it. The North Koreans knew it. President Clinton knew it. That rare combination allowed Carter to do something no one else had done: to give the North Koreans the opportunity to retreat from their overplayed hand and accede to *increased* American negotiating demands *without appearing to knuckle under pressure from the U.S. government.* The gambit worked; Pyongyang this time seized the opportunity to escape the looming confrontation and scrambled back to the path toward compliance and negotiation.

This is not to suggest in retrospect that the whole Carter involvement was smoothly planned, cleanly executed, and without rancor and recrimination. But at the strategic level—of advancing core U.S. national security interests— the Carter intervention worked in the same sense as what screenwriters call a "plot point" in a movie, when an unexpected event disrupts the plot and spins it into a different direction. In Carter's case, the plot spun away from the road to conflict toward the road to agreement.

Both sides in the intense administration debate over whether to let Carter go to North Korea turned out to be correct. Carter *was* a difficult messenger who attempted to redirect and, in fact, weaken U.S. policy. This was politically costly to the administration. At the same time, Carter *did* provide what turned out to be a successful exit ramp to allow the North Koreans to give in to the substance of American demands on how to escape from the looming UN Security Council sanctions and military buildup. By seizing on Kim Il Sung's acceptance of the Carter proposal, the administration was able to secure a North Korean agreement to greater restrictions on their nuclear program than had ever been accepted. This put the United States in a better position to resume negotiations on that issue.

Any assessment of Carter's role must consider what might have happened had he *not* gone to North Korea. First, it is virtually certain that on June 16 the president would have authorized the largest proposed buildup, sending 50,000 more Americans to defend South Korea. That was the recommendation of his senior military advisers—Secretary Perry and General Shalikashvili—and none of the other principals had either the credentials or any apparent inclination to argue for anything less. The president would have gone on television to explain to the nation why American troops were being deployed to the distant Korean Peninsula, and why the specter of nuclear weapons' proliferation there justified the most forceful American response. He would have had to have ordered a limited call-up of the reserves.

At the United Nations, Security Council members would most likely have come to an agreement on a phased sanctions resolution, which would have ratcheted up the pressure on North Korea. Pyongyang would surely have reacted, but how? The best (but least likely) reaction would have been to acquiesce to American demands to refreeze the nuclear program and come into full compliance with its nonproliferation obligations. No one predicted such a North Korean reaction. The best *plausible* outcome from sanctions would have been increased pressure on Pyongyang to the point that it would have returned to the negotiating table.

A more likely North Korean reaction would have been to lash back at the United States and its allies, perhaps by kicking out the inspectors and blinding the international community as to the status of its nuclear program. The next obvious step would have been to move toward reprocessing of the 8,000 spent fuel rods to obtain the five bombs' worth of plutonium they contained.

Had North Korea taken either of those steps, the option Secretary Perry had decided not to recommend to the president—a military strike against Yongbyon—would have returned to the forefront. Recall that Secretary Perry's decision *against* recommending such an action had been based upon the continued viability of a negotiating path leading to an outcome supportive of U.S. and allied security objectives. The closure of that path would likely have led him to recommend at least that the president consider that option. Beyond that point speculation becomes difficult. All knew that a military strike against Yongbyon carried with it the risk of triggering a general war in Korea. An enhanced U.S.–ROK defensive posture, bolstered by additional troops and armament, *might* have deterred a frontal assault from North Korea. But few present during the 1994 crisis doubted that the North Korean leadership would feel compelled to undertake some form of violent retaliation, whether instigating some incident along the DMZ, lobbing artillery shells at Seoul, or staging commando attacks with special forces and fifth columnists somewhere deep in South Korea. Once events had reached that stage, it would become difficult for political leaders on either side to control the pace of the escalation of hostilities.

Given those stakes, it is obvious that before deciding whether or not to launch a military attack against Yongbyon, President Clinton would have consulted closely with President Kim Young Sam. That would have pitted the South Korean leader's antipathy toward the Kim Il Sung regime and its nuclear activities against his understandable anxiety about starting a war that could result in the destruction of Seoul and the deaths of hundreds of thousands of Korean citizens. The South Korean reaction to the "sea of fire" speech suggests the Kim Young Sam government likely would have opposed a military strike against Yongbyon. If that had been the case, it would have left President Clinton on the horns of a harsh dilemma: whether to sit idly by, watching North Korea separate and hide forever five bombs' worth of plutonium, or to proceed against Yongbyon and possibly destroy the U.S.-ROK alliance at the very moment it might need to defend the South against an attack by the North.

That dilemma would have thrust the United States, and indeed all of Asia, into a full-blown crisis. South Korea, China, and Japan would have been forced to confront their worst nightmare: the imminent prospect of a major war in Asia, which would have dashed all of their hopes for growth, stability, and security throughout the region. Under those circumstances it would be virtually impossible to predict what might happen. Perhaps the "spontaneous" evacuation feared by Ambassador Laney would have erupted in Seoul, throwing the South Korean government and population into a panic that could have greatly complicated allied military planning.

Pressure would have continued to build for some diplomatic solution to avert the horrors of war. The Chinese leadership—as the indispensable source of food and fuel to the Kim Il Sung regime—could have given North Korea an ultimatum to halt all nuclear activity at Yongbyon and invite IAEA inspectors back to verify the accounting of all weapon-usable material at the facility. The United States could have found some other interlocutor—perhaps returning to Senators Nunn and Lugar, or resorting to the Rudolf Hess option—to help arrive at such a result. Or, just possibly, the imminent specter (or warning) of a military strike against Yongbyon may have led the North to blink and refreeze its program along with some negotiating proposal to cloak its retreat in the guise of a diplomatic offensive. All of these possibilities are so remote from the actual events of June 1994 as to make assignments of probabilities a bootless exercise.

North Korea also could have taken steps to ratchet up the pressure without crossing the red lines tied to a possible American attack on Yongbyon. For instance, it might have undertaken unusual movements or exercises of its conventional forces, or launched another Nodong missile into the Sea of Japan. How the United States, its allies, China, Russia, and the UN Security Council would have reacted—and interacted—to such North Korean steps is also impossible to assess with confidence.

How close did we come to war? We will never know, because the crisis was averted before it reached that stage. It does seem clear that, but for the Carter mission, the two sides would have been launched onto a collision course driven by Pyongyang's nuclear outlawry and the American determination to stop it, by force of arms if necessary. A straight-line assessment of that course would have ended in an attack upon Yongbyon and, possibly, war. But, as just mentioned, the universal recognition that war would have killed hundreds of thousands while shattering the Asian economic miracle and political evolution would have led to intense efforts to find another solution.

We conclude that without President Carter, war would have been more likely, but not inevitable. Thus in the annals of the perennial debate between those who believe large social forces lead history in an inexorable arc through time and those who believe in the decisive role of individuals—or even mere chance—the North Korean experience supports the latter school of thought, in a sense reminiscent of the old English folk tune:

> For want of a nail, the shoe was lost,
> For want of the shoe, the horse was lost,
> For want of the horse, the rider was lost,
> For want of the rider, the battle was lost,
> For want of the battle, the kingdom was lost,
> And all for the want of a horseshoe nail!

Hard problems seldom yield to easy or cost-free solutions, as anyone who has suffered painful side effects from a medical treatment aimed at curing a graver ill can attest. President Carter, despite all the difficulties his involvement created for the administration, did provide a way for the North Koreans to return to the path of compliance with global nonproliferation norms. Perhaps the administration could have found another gambit to resolve the crisis in a manner that blocked North Korean access to more plutonium without triggering a land war in Asia. Perhaps not. Given the national security benefits provided by the accord that eventually resolved the nuclear problem that fall, we conclude that the results of the Carter mission justified both the risks and the costs it entailed. The next question would be whether the United States could convert that strategic opening into a concrete solution to the nuclear challenge. To answer that question, the parties would soon return to Geneva.

9

Sailing to an
Uncertain Destination

July–August 1994

Having stepped back from the brink, Washington turned its attention once again to negotiations with North Korea. Before Blix had declared history to have been lost in early June, the Senior Steering Group on Korea had produced a draft game plan to resolve the nuclear confrontation. The task, in Sandy Berger's metaphor, was to decide what cards were in the deck, that is, what specific steps could be taken to address security, political, and economic issues dividing North Korea from the international community. The administration then needed to decide how to shuffle the deck, interweaving the various steps by North Korea, the United States, South Korea, Japan, and others. Finally, the administration had to decide on tactics, or in what order to play the cards.

In shaping up an administration position, the debate between safeguards-firsters and dismantlement-firsters continued, with the latter group prevailing to the extent that the administration now planned to seek an immediate freeze on Pyongyang's construction of new reactors and the dismantlement of existing nuclear facilities. The Pentagon continued to favor starting big, offering substantial inducements up front in exchange for big steps by the North. While wanting to take only modest steps in exchange for full implementation of safeguards, the State Department recognized that in order to win major concessions from Pyongyang, Washington would need to give something, too. In late May, it agreed to move the first steps toward the establishment of diplomatic relations much higher in the deck. This would start with opening a low-level liaison office—an approach that had been taken in China—and eventually conclude with an exchange of ambassadors. Playing higher-value security cards, such as canceling Team Spirit permanently, would have to wait until the North played its own higher-value security cards.

By the time the Principals Committee met on June 30 to discuss the strategy for the long-awaited third round, there were so many diplomatic, military, and intelligence balls in the air that prior to the meeting the National Security Council staff prepared a checklist of twenty-five tasks that needed urgent attention. The principals went to work as public attention reached a new high. An NBC poll released a few weeks earlier found 46 percent of Americans viewed North Korea as the biggest foreign policy challenge facing the United States.[1]

For American decisionmakers, the most urgent issue was what to do with the 8,000 fuel rods North Korea had unloaded from the 5-megawatt reactor. The danger was that Pyongyang could invoke a plausible scientific justification—the rods would corrode over time in the cooling pond water, leaking radioactivity—and claim that it needed to reprocess the fuel and separate out the plutonium. How long it would take before the corrosion reached the danger point was unclear. The North Koreans had told Selig Harrison two months. American estimates were anywhere from two to six months. In either case, time was short.

In spite of the proffered technical rationale and the fact that the Nuclear Non-Proliferation Treaty did not proscribe plutonium separation under safeguards, the principals decided that reprocessing by North Korea was unacceptable. Legalities aside, further separation would give North Korea more material to build nuclear weapons. They preferred to have the rods shipped to another country. But since removal could take years, the United States first would send experts to Yongbyon to adjust the water chemistry of the storage pond, slowing the rods' deterioration. Storing the fuel in North Korea without reprocessing but under safeguards was another option that the government needed to study.

The principals also approved a proposal for a two-stage diplomatic solution to the crisis. By the end of six months, North Korea would have to meet its international nonproliferation obligations as well as new demands to freeze all reactor construction, ship the spent fuel abroad, and stop ballistic missile exports, a key proliferation threat beyond the immediate nuclear concerns.

But Washington's inducements fell short of the "big bang" approach proposed by Pentagon. Rather than provide immediate assistance in acquiring new reactors, Washington would first discuss multilateral energy aid, followed by an international commitment to provide such technology. In the first stage the United States did plan to provide "nonnuclear" energy assistance, including an analysis of whether the North's needs could be better met through means other than nuclear power. In addition to opening liaison offices in each other's capitals, other early incentives included the lifting of some economic sanctions and an assurance that the United States would not launch a nuclear attack against Pyongyang.

U.S. demands in the second stage of a settlement would require even more far-reaching steps by North Korea. They included reducing conventional military forces, adhering to international agreements controlling the spread of ballistic missiles, banning the possession of chemical weapons, and improving human rights conditions. In return, reactors would be provided, additional economic sanctions lifted, ambassadors exchanged, and visits by senior government officials held. Whether that meant a summit between President Clinton and Kim Il Sung was not addressed.

Since much of the game plan required a multilateral effort, the United States had to work closely with potential partners. Before the Carter visit to Pyongyang, South Korea and Japan seemed wary of participating in a new reactor project. In May Gallucci told them that the United States could not provide the North with new reactors owing to legal restrictions, but it could put together an international effort. "Why should our taxpayers provide funding for North Korean reactors when they continue to fire missiles at Japan?" asked a senior Japanese diplomat.[2] But with the agreement on a North-South summit, the South began to sing a different tune. Foreign Minister Han Sung Joo told Ambassador Jim Laney that the new project could be a big piece of a package offered the North at that meeting.

The multilateral effort also promised to extend to other countries, particularly in dealing with Pyongyang's spent fuel. U.S. and British experts met just before the third round. Visiting London, Under Secretary of State Lynn Davis was told that all it would take to seal a bargain was a call from President Clinton to Prime Minister Tony Blair. France was more cautious, noting that its reprocessing facility best suited to handling the spent fuel had been shut down. Beijing hesitated for political reasons, allowing that it did not want to "jump on this boat and sail to an unknown destination." Russia asked for details on compensation.

Finally, the administration took steps to ensure that the upcoming negotiations were well coordinated with other U.S. activities in and around Korea. The Principals Committee asked the Senior Steering Group on Korea to review planned military moves in the region, knowing that Pyongyang was particularly sensitive about the movements of U.S. aircraft carriers. A schedule of military exercises for the next five months was sent to the NSC, but those movements, even when anticipated, would later cause diplomatic ructions with Pyongyang.

On the domestic front, lowering public expectations was seen as important in plying the largely uncharted waters of negotiations with North Korea. Before leaving for Europe, Gallucci admitted that recent events did not suggest "one can have a week in Geneva and kind of walk out with the issue solved."[3] Privately, he believed the administration had a better chance of resolving the crisis since Pyongyang had blinked in June, recalling that Kang Sok Ju's letter had accepted word for word the U.S. conditions for more talks. Still, one U.S. official later observed, "Nobody was under the illusion they would stop being North Koreans."[4]

In that context, the U.S. intelligence community remained split as to what would happen next. Many analysts continued to believe the North had no intention of bargaining away its nuclear weapons program. For example, the Defense Intelligence Agency thought Pyongyang would continue a covert program no matter what agreement it signed.[5] In contrast, the State Department's intelligence bureau, staffed by analysts who thought a diplomatic solution was possible, held a cautiously optimistic prognosis, concluding that Pyongyang still wanted a deal to justify better ties with Washington and to ensure a smooth leadership transition. It predicted that the North would not require the immediate provision of new reactors, but Washington would have to demonstrate it was serious about supporting their introduction.

The signs from North Korea seemed positive. Pyongyang had acclaimed Kim Il Sung's proposals to Jimmy Carter, which were meant to reach a "fundamental solution" to the crisis and even hinted that special inspections might be resolved. Also, it toned down the June 25 commemoration of the anniversary of the outbreak of the Korean War for the third year in a row, although internal propaganda highlighted U.S. atrocities and a recent Japanese crackdown on the Chosen Soren.[6] The North's radio warned that U.S. military deployments could hamper the talks, but a more authoritative press article acknowledged those in Washington "who support dialogue and negotiations to resolve the nuclear issue."[7]

Having shot the rapids of the June crisis, the Clinton administration was ready to restart negotiations. The year since the last Gallucci-Kang meeting had been dominated by the diplomatic tug-of-war in New York, the resort to private citizens to communicate with the North's leadership in the absence of a sustained government-to-government dialogue, cooperation and conflict with Seoul, a complex relationship with the IAEA, and tensions bringing Washington and Pyongyang close to armed conflict. The administration had assembled a multilateral coalition in support of its policy. The U.S. military posture had been strengthened to put pressure on Pyongyang, to deter attack and, if necessary, to execute its war plan. Yet American attempts to negotiate a diplomatic solution had repeatedly stumbled over rocks in Pyongyang, Seoul, and Vienna.

The June crisis created a window of opportunity. Pyongyang seemed to have learned from its experience, having come closer to a military conflict than its leadership probably expected or wished. It now approached negotiations with new vigor, demanding a high price for abandoning its nuclear weapons program but also offering important compromises. Having learned the pitfalls of depending too much on third parties, the administration would take the bull by the horns and doggedly pursue a solution through direct talks with North Korea. That required a new strategy in dealing with Seoul and Vienna, one that would depend more upon American leadership, even though sometimes straining relationships with important partners. That leadership would be severely tested as it tried to forge a consensus around offering Pyongyang a new relationship with the international community. It would also be tested by the death of Kim Il Sung, whose demise created new uncertainties, making Washington's task all the more difficult.

The Third Round

The third round convened on July 8 at the North Korean diplomatic compound, just outside the old section of the city and near the banks of Lake Geneva. Arriving in the days beforehand, Gallucci and Kang had sounded optimistic notes.[8] Now they once again faced each other across the negotiating table, flanked by their senior aides.

Little mention was made of the past year, although Kang said that unexpected developments had resulted in a "strained situation." But the "historic and significant" Kim-Carter meeting had made the third round possible. He added that both countries were at a "decision point" that could only be navigated if the two negotiated in good faith.

As always, the two chief negotiators spent much of the three-hour morning session making their formal presentations. Trying to sound upbeat, Gallucci observed: "We have an historic opportunity to substitute the open hostility and mutual distrust that has characterized the United States-North Korea relationship in the past for the peace, trade and security benefits of a more normal political and economic relationship." He refuted the standard North Korean complaint, asserting that the United States did not intend to strangle Pyongyang. Instead, Washington "hoped to open the door to North Korea's full participation in the international community." That would be impossible, however, unless it adhered to common standards of behavior.

After making it clear that a nuclear freeze was essential for talks to continue, Gallucci added, "The best way to demonstrate Kim Il Sung's statements that he has no desire for a nuclear weapons program is the removal of the spent fuel from your country." He offered to work together on removal, starting with sending U.S. experts to Yongbyon to extend the lifetime of the fuel in the storage pond.

Kang naturally focused on topics near and dear to North Korea: the early introduction of light-water reactors, diplomatic normalization since "the United States and North Korea have the most hostile relations in the world," assurances that Washington would not use force against North Korea, and the "impartial application" of the International Atomic Energy Agency's safeguards. Gallucci responded that Washington was prepared for detailed talks on the new reactors provided North Korea met its nonproliferation obligations. The United States was also ready to provide a formal assurance that it would not use nuclear weapons against Pyongyang. As for the "impartial application" of safeguards, the agency had always acted in an impartial manner and surely would continue to do so.

The key issue remained what it would take for Pyongyang to dismantle its plutonium production program and adhere to its nonproliferation obligations. Kang answered: "If the United States takes real steps to secure the provision of LWR [light-water reactors] to North Korea, the two sides can get a fundamental resolution of the nuclear issue."

At lunch and throughout the afternoon, Kang stressed repeatedly that he wanted a firm guarantee from the United States, "an intergovernmental agreement," to provide financing and construction of new reactors. They would replace existing reactors as well as those Pyongyang had planned to build in order to generate 2,000 megawatts of electricity by the year 2000. Indeed, Kang pointed out that the Supreme People's Assembly had recently mandated an increase in the number of indigenously produced reactors to meet that objective since hopes to acquire new ones from outside North Korea had faded.

Pyongyang's technology of choice was Russian. Their reactors could become operational in as little as five years; production of the equipment had already started in 1985 for the now-canceled project. Moreover, Kang expected Russian technology to cost only half as much as Western technology. But the North Koreans did not entirely trust Moscow, which is why they wanted American financing, possibly paid for from U.S. economic assistance to Russia or arranged through an international consortium. As for Seoul's reactors, Kang dismissed them as "politically unacceptable."

Aside from the push for new reactors, the North tabled its own road map that would allow its nuclear program to grow for years while requiring the

United States to make important concessions up front. If Washington guaranteed the provision of the new reactors by the end of August, the 5-megawatt reactor would still be refueled and the spent fuel rods reprocessed, albeit under IAEA supervision. When the first new reactor was completed—years down the road—North Korea would freeze the operating reactor and the two larger units, scheduled to be in operation. Even further down the road, when the second new reactor was completed, the North would dismantle all of the old reactors. For good measure, Kang demanded that the IAEA retract its request for special inspections.

"That plan is not even remotely possible," Gallucci announced and then proceeded to describe an "alternative vision of the future": the road map approved by the principals on June 30. That vision included the political, economic, security, and energy tracks on which the United States was prepared to move if Pyongyang took simultaneous steps. But all of this was based on North Korea's performance up front, especially early, demonstrable steps to deal with its spent fuel.

This was the first time the North Koreans had heard the details of the American approach. Kang scribbled furiously throughout Gallucci's presentation, commenting frequently that he found his ideas "greatly interesting." The North Koreans seemed visibly intrigued with the prospect of early diplomatic relations between Washington and Pyongyang.

Ending the session, Kang said he would respond to Gallucci's proposals the next day. But before the meeting adjourned, he made a positive gesture, expressing an interest in U.S. spent fuel experts visiting Yongbyon. "We should work together in this area," Kang announced. Moreover, he was willing to examine all options for dealing with the fuel, including its sale after reprocessing, long-term storage in North Korea, and shipment out of the country.

That evening the Americans alerted Washington that North Korea might be ready to strike a deal. The atmospherics had been good. The North Koreans also were in a bargaining mode, using the small Gallucci-Kang lunch, the afternoon delegation meeting, and the cocktail hour to explore compromises. They had been surprisingly candid, admitting that Pyongyang did not want to ship the spent fuel abroad because it did not trust the United States to fulfill its end of the deal without keeping leverage until the bitter end. Finally, though it may have been a small thing, the Americans noticed that in contrast to the previous summer's session when Kang visibly squirmed every time special inspections were mentioned, this time he did not show any discomfort.

On substance, the North Koreans seemed open to key U.S. demands, willing to return to the NPT and to accept full IAEA safeguards, although not yet willing to accept special inspections. They had even said that implementation of the Denuclearization Declaration with South Korea might be part of the package at some unspecified future date. Kang also agreed to work together to extend the life of the spent fuel in the storage pond and to explore the different long-term options for what to do with it.

To be sure, important differences remained. Each side had front-loaded its road map with demands while leaving important inducements until the end of the process. This reflected both standard negotiating tactics and political realities in Washington and Pyongyang. Asking the other side to take the most important steps first was much easier to sell internally than volunteering to take important steps oneself. It also was an effort by both countries to maintain enough leverage until reaching the very end of the road map to ensure that any agreement was fully implemented. A successful negotiation would need to find some point in between the two extremes that would be acceptable to both sides.

The demand for new reactors, particularly for reactors backed by what appeared to be a legally binding guarantee, seemed to be the most serious problem. The North Koreans were still vague about what they really wanted, at times speaking of a legally binding obligation but then suggesting they might be willing to accept a less binding "political" assurance. Since a legal guarantee was out of the question, the task ahead would be to structure an appropriate political commitment. Although that might fall short of meeting the North's requirements, the stronger the commitment, the greater the likelihood that Pyongyang would modify its road map to accommodate U.S. concerns. As a first step, the Americans decided to probe what type of commitment the North had in mind and what it would be willing to offer in return.

A second problem was weaning the North Koreans from their existing gas-graphite nuclear program. Proposals to replace that power would strengthen the U.S. negotiating position seeking to freeze and dismantle those facilities. One approach would be to refine ideas to provide energy to substitute for the 250 megawatts of power generation the North would lose by canceling the two reactors under construction and by freezing the operating 5-megawatt reactor, which provided some heating for the surrounding district. Interim conventional energy supplies seemed even more important as a bridge to the future, since the new reactors would take years to complete. The administration had already considered options, such as helping North Korea upgrade its electrical transmission lines, but would now need to study the issue further.

Finally, more work had to be done on a plan for dealing with the spent fuel. The United States needed a concrete proposal to extend the lifetime of the fuel in the cooling pond since Kang had agreed to a cooperative effort. As for sending the fuel out of the country, while the North Koreans said they needed it for leverage, the Americans nevertheless felt a detailed shipping plan would help counter that argument. Washington also needed to flesh out the details of safeguarded storage since the North had mentioned this alternative over cocktails.

All in all, the first day of talks had been promising. Delegation members went to sleep encouraged that a diplomatic solution might be in reach. Early the next morning, Gallucci was awakened by a phone call from the South Korean foreign minister. Kim Il Sung was dead.

Singing the Song of a Bystander

On July 9 at 0100 Greenwich Mean Time, Pyongyang radio asked its listeners to stay tuned for a "special broadcast." Two hours later, North Korea announced Kim Il Sung's death due to "heavy mental strains" followed by a "heart shock."[9] Ironically, the Great Leader had died before the long-awaited third round even began in Geneva. The announcement had probably been delayed to help prepare whatever public face North Korea would present to the world, to take security precautions, and to ensure that all the Central Committee members, including the Dear Leader, were present in Pyongyang. In any case, none of the North Koreans in Geneva seemed to know that the Great Leader had died before the negotiations began; when they found out, they appeared to be genuinely shocked and saddened. While there were no signs of panic, disorder, or police activity, the people in North Korea also appeared stunned and distraught, as was evident from television coverage showing thousands in Pyongyang bowing before a large statue of Kim outside the parliament building.[10]

The Great Leader's death also provoked strong reactions in South Korea. A television announcer broke the news with a shaking voice. Television and radio stations carried nonstop programming as people gathered around the giant screen at Seoul's main rail station.[11] For some, his demise dashed hopes for the coming summit. Slamming his fist into the dashboard, one taxi driver exclaimed, "I can't believe he died now when things were working out."[12] Others were jubilant; an elderly man observed, "When Kim Il Sung was alive, change was unimaginable." Peace was impossible while the man who started the Korean War was still alive.[13] Kim Dae Jung told his American contacts that he was concerned because of the question of power succession and instability in the North.

Kim Il Sung's sudden death raised suspicions that it had been caused by foul play. Almost immediately after the announcement, governments intensified their intelligence gathering to figure out what was happening. Japanese aircraft scrambled and flew near the Korean Peninsula to discern whether there were any unusual military movements. Ground stations in Japan monitored North Korean radio to see if they could pick up any clues. All sought evidence that Kim Il Sung's death might have been caused by something other than natural causes, an assassination or a coup staged by pro–Kim Jong Il forces or by anti-Kim conspirators.[14]

Seoul was also suspicious; the timing of Kim's death, just before the Geneva talks and the inter-Korean summit, seemed to be an unlikely coincidence. Only a few months earlier, South Korean intelligence reported that there had been a clash between father and son over the nuclear crisis and the failing economy.[15] Interestingly, information from China and Japan indicated that Kim senior did not die of natural causes.[16] Some officials even believed television pictures of the dead leader showed something unusual on the back of his head, leading to suggestions that he may have died from a fall.[17]

Speculation was given a boost when Robert Gates, the former director of central intelligence, told an American television audience that there was "some small chance" Kim's death was not caused by a heart attack.[18] But administration officials publicly dismissed such assertions.[19] Talking on the phone a few days later, Tony Lake and his South Korean counterpart agreed that there was no credible information to support a conclusion that the North Korean leader had died an unnatural death.

President Kim Young Sam had his own theory. Though President Carter said the Great Leader looked healthy, Kim remembered that his own father had also been fine into his eighties and then suddenly deteriorated. The same thing might have happened to Kim Il Sung. Beyond the hazards of old age, President Kim believed that the stress of preparing for the upcoming summit contributed to his demise: he had died of worry that he would have to confront Kim Young Sam.[20]

Kim Il Sung's death raised new questions for Washington and Seoul. Would there be continuity in North Korean policy now that he had suddenly passed from the scene? On the day before the announcement, the Geneva talks opened to a promising start, and the first-ever North-South summit was on the horizon. For the first time in months, South Korea was actively on board. Now everything was uncertain, including how to proceed in resolving the nuclear issue and how Kim Il Sung's death would affect future cooperation between the two allies.

But the greatest uncertainty had to do with his son and likely successor, Kim Jong Il. While most U.S. and South Korean experts believed the junior Kim had no real competition, they also felt that he would have difficulties governing. Reports of his drinking, womanizing, and health problems, combined with lukewarm support from the military, meant that Kim Jong Il might have to adopt tougher policies to assuage hard-liners or would be unable to make compromises to resolve the crisis. Others believed he had already been in charge of the nuclear issue for some time and would continue down the same path. As for his personal behavior, one U.S. government expert saw it as no different from that of any other "princeling."[21]

The second issue was whether the regime itself would outlast Kim Il Sung. His death magnified North Korea's severe economic problems and the possibility of political instability. A South Korean intelligence official recalled: "There was an assumption that while Kim was alive, there was very little possibility of collapse." After he died, a "theory of early collapse" emerged.[22] Most former South Korean intelligence officials thought Kim Jong Il and his regime would last three years at most.[23] The U.S. Defense Intelligence Agency concluded that his survival depended on managing "a surge of popular protests and demands" for reforms, a curious and profoundly mistaken prediction regarding a society in which popular protests and demands had been—and remain—unknown. The agency did not rule out a coup against him since he "is less respected by the military than his father."[24]

In spite of their long-standing relationships with Pyongyang, Russia and China also were uncertain about the future of North Korea. The Chinese had the distinction of being notified of the Great Leader's death before the announcement, but they knew little about Kim Jong Il and were apprehensive about his future. So were the Russians, who had not met him in ten years. Both felt that Kim would be quickly named to the top government and party posts, president and general secretary, and that his succession would have little effect on the North's approach to the nuclear issue. Some Russians, however, believed there would be an inevitable fight for power with the "old guard" later on if their interests were not satisfied.

Seoul and Washington reacted differently to this bizarre turn of events. In the United States, Kim Il Sung's death raised concerns about whether the commitments that followed his meetings with former President Jimmy Carter and the new sense of momentum in Geneva would survive. Immediately following the announcement of Kim's death, the Geneva talks recessed at North Korea's request. But the Americans stayed focused. In spite of doubts about the future, Washington's priority was to handle his departure so as to advance American objectives in resolving the crisis.

For the South Koreans, dealing with Kim's death was more difficult. Beforehand, conservatives were critical about the North-South summit, but the public had been optimistic. Leading the South's furious preparations, President Kim read everything he could find about Kim Il Sung and talked to many people who had met him. The emerging game plan was to discuss issues of war and peace, but also specific problems such as family reunions, economic assistance, and new reactors. South Korean officials believed that a breakthrough might be in the offing; if Kim Il Sung were ready to withdraw from political life and wanted to make final preparations for his son's succession, he might be willing to issue "on-the-spot guidance" to reach a comprehensive deal. His death dashed these expectations.[25]

Instead, it opened a political Pandora's box. Public opinion reversed; in a telephone poll taken immediately afterward, 50 percent called the late Kim a "dictator" and 36 percent a "war criminal" for having started the Korean War.[26] In addition President Kim Young Sam felt that Kim Jong Il was not only ill—he looked thin and pale in television pictures taken immediately after his father death—but weak and maybe even mentally impaired.[27] The president's aides tried, but failed, to expand his information from which to judge the heir apparent by introducing him to people who had met Kim Jong Il.[28] Nevertheless, the South Korean leader concluded Kim Jong Il would not last long.

The divergent perspectives in Washington and Seoul immediately became apparent over the issue of expressing condolences after Kim Il Sung's death. Normally, after a leader dies other governments express condolences and send a representative if a state funeral is held. The death of Kim Il Sung presented a more complicated problem given his role in starting the Korean War and the fifty years of hostility between North Korea and the United States and South Korea. The decision on how to respond was complicated further by the fact that his death occurred just as the three countries seemed to be moving toward a diplomatic solution to a crisis that had almost spiraled out of control only a few weeks earlier.

President Clinton—in Naples, Italy, for the G-7 summit—was given the news of Kim's death at 5:30 AM, while American officials spent the night on the phone plotting a course of action. The State Department Operations Center tracked down Sandy Berger and Dan Poneman in Washington, Tony Lake in Italy with the president, Bob Gallucci and Tom Hubbard in Geneva, Winston Lord in Seoul, and Jim Laney in Ireland. As various conference call participants were being located, those already on the line speculated how the Great Leader met his demise; during one pause while the State Department operator was patching in another line, Berger suggested that the missing bloody glove matching the one that had recently been reported from the O. J. Simpson trial might be found behind Kim Il Sung's residence.

Once assembled, the participants turned to the business at hand, focusing on keeping the Geneva talks on track. Gallucci brought up concerns about issuing a condolence expressed to him by Foreign Minister Han Sung Joo.[29] But, on the theory that the United States had no quarrel with the North

Korean people, the conference call participants agreed to express condolences only to them, not to the government, striking a balance aimed at acknowledging sensibilities on both sides of the 38th parallel.

Afterward, Poneman drafted the message and dictated it over the phone to Tony Lake's assistant, Neal Wolin, who was with the presidential party in Naples. President Clinton issued a statement the same day expressing sympathy for the North Korean people.[30] As one U.S. official recalled, "This was one of the most critical moments in North Korean history. It was an opportunity for the United States to do something that was relatively minor but would be seen by North Korea as a tremendously important symbolic action."[31]

The Americans also accepted a North Korean invitation for Gallucci to pay a condolence call at their Geneva mission. There was considerable debate within the U.S. delegation over whether he should sign the condolence book and what he would write. The main concern was the inevitability that his inscription would be leaked to the South Korean press, which was swarming over every possible angle of the story. In the end, the Americans agreed that he would sign the book with the purposely ambiguous inscription, "Words cannot express the feeling of sympathy I have for the Korean people."

But Gallucci had to think fast once he arrived at the mission. The North Koreans instructed him to enter the main room, bow in front of the dead Kim's picture, and then sign the condolence book. When he approached the picture and saw all the cameras focused on him, Gallucci had an instant vision of how he would look bowing before a picture of the deceased Great Leader. It reminded him of the actor David Niven, who played the British ambassador in the epic *55 Days at Peking*, which told the story of foreigners under siege during the Boxer Rebellion. The image of Niven, kicking aside a pillow he was to kneel on before the Chinese empress, flashed through Gallucci's mind. He paused before the picture and then turned to sign the condolence book, skipping the bow.

The visit was not all public relations. Before he left the mission, the North Koreans told Gallucci that talks could resume after the mourning period, that there would be no change in their negotiating position, and even hinted at further compromises, including freezing of the nuclear program once the reactor guarantee was received. That evening, Gallucci reassured reporters that the "course set by President Kim Il Sung will be pursued by the new government." Talks would resume in the "coming weeks."[32]

While the administration seemed to be successfully navigating a tricky diplomatic situation, it was less successful in mollifying domestic critics. Senate Republican leader and presidential hopeful Bob Dole said that perhaps Clinton had "forgotten that Kim Il Sung was responsible for the war that caused the loss of more than 54,000 American lives."[33] To make sure it was on firm ground, the administration had done some historical research. One American hyperbolically recalled that the researchers were "able to find every expression of condolence that had ever been issued for dictators going back to Genghis Khan. Every time someone had died, normal practice was to issue some form of condolence."[34] Nevertheless, having made its point in Geneva, Washington instructed all U.S. diplomatic posts not to sign North Korean condolence books.

In contrast to the straightforward American approach, the South Korean government initially adopted a "wait-and-see" attitude. At the time Kim Il Sung's death was announced, key cabinet officials were meeting to prepare for the summit. They immediately went to the Blue House to see President Kim, who interrupted a luncheon to go into emergency session.

He made two quick decisions. While the situation appeared calm, South Korean troops were placed on a higher state of alert just in case tensions rose along the DMZ. Second, President Kim decided that the government should use the Korean word *ashipta* to describe its position on the North Korean leader's death.[35] Roughly meaning "he will be missed," *ashipta* was a notch above "too bad" but less personal than "regret." Some officials wanted to be more forward leaning, but according to one cabinet member, "considering the national sentiment, the expression was probably the best that could have been done." South Korean government statements stuck carefully to this script.[36]

South Korean moderates struggled to sustain this approach in the face of growing domestic turbulence. In spite of Pyongyang's cancellation of the summit on July 11, a radio broadcast the next day quoted Yasser Arafat—who had been close to the Great Leader—as saying Kim Jong Il planned to continue North-South talks. Also, a journalist just back from the North reported that Kim Yong Sun, the official in charge of inter-Korean relations, planned to go to Panmunjom after the Great Leader's funeral to discuss details of the summit schedule. Responding to these positive indicators, Foreign Minister Han expressed a reasonable reaction: "We sincerely hope that the new leadership in Pyongyang will keep alive the recently created momentum for dialogue, resolve the nuclear issue and pursue peaceful coexistence and prosperity between North and South Korea."[37]

The drift toward a tougher stance, however, had already started. Many South Koreans, including President Kim, felt that Kim Jong Il was no Kim Il Sung. Therefore concessions made in negotiations with Pyongyang would have to be reconsidered. Chief among these was the agreement to hold a summit in the North without securing a return visit to Seoul by the North Korean leader.[38] At the very least, the two sides might have to renegotiate the venue for an initial meeting.

Then, on July 12, Lee Bu Young, a rising opposition star in the National Assembly, ignited a political firestorm by suggesting that the Foreign Ministry study whether to express condolences to the North Koreans. His remarks provoked an angry counterattack by a conservative member of the ruling party who, far from viewing the Kim administration as too harsh toward the North, argued that the government was too moderate in its criticisms of Kim Il Sung, to the point of misleading the South Korean people into underestimating his perfidy. Newspapers called talk of a condolence delegation "totally ridiculous."[39] The opposition disavowed Lee's remarks, while he protested that his statement had been misinterpreted. A senior South Korean moderate observed that the "ultraconservatives were trying hard to poison the atmosphere for a summit." They were unwittingly aided by leftist groups, who added fuel to the fire by advocating a more forthcoming "condolence" policy.[40]

Since President Kim did not want to expose himself to further conservative attacks, his government shifted toward their position. After forbidding visits to North Korea to pay respects to Kim Il Sung, a long-standing policy in any case, two individuals were arrested on their way to Panmunjom by taxi.[41] During a police crackdown on student "dissidents," they discovered pro–North Korean materials, including a secret shrine where mourners could pay tribute to the Great Leader.[42] These raids were accompanied by claims that the students were receiving faxes from Pyongyang ordering them to make condolence visits to the North. Opinion polls showed a large majority of South Koreans were fed up with extremist students and were particularly disturbed by any contacts they may have had with Pyongyang.[43]

To further demonstrate its conservative credentials, on the day of Kim Il Sung's funeral, Seoul released documents given to President Kim during his June visit to Moscow, proving beyond a shadow of doubt the Great Leader's responsibility for starting the Korean War. The release had already been delayed once in view of the upcoming summit. But with the meeting now unlikely and the more pressing need to counteract those people who wanted to eulogize Kim Il Sung, the Blue House insisted on moving forward over the objections of the Foreign Ministry, which did not want to make the chances of a summit even more remote.[44] Prime Minister Lee Yung Duk followed the release with a harsh public statement that Kim Il Sung did not deserve condolences since he started the war.[45]

In shifting toward a tougher approach, the government also took steps that threatened to derail American efforts to resolve the nuclear standoff. At the end of July, South Korean intelligence unveiled two defectors. One of them, Kang Myong Do, the son-in-law of the North Korean premier, claimed Pyongyang had already built five nuclear weapons. His statement surprised the Foreign Ministry, but provoked an angry protest from Washington since it both lacked credibility and seemed to call talks with the North into question. A back-pedaling Blue House told the press his assertion was based on hearsay, since Kang had no real evidence.

Talking over the newly installed secure phone line between the White House and the Blue House, Tony Lake told National Security Adviser Chung Chong Wook that he appreciated the disclaimer but that it merely begged the question of why the press conference was held in the first place. Chung replied that there had been no malice intended by the South Korean intelligence services and Kang had been reprimanded for his remarks. The incident may not have been staged, but there was clearly pressure on the defectors to come up with negative comments about North Korea. The result may have been spontaneous, although one South Korean official observed that Kang Myong Do had been "led to it."[46]

In three short weeks, South Korea had moved from a "wait-and-see" attitude to a much tougher policy toward the North. President Kim had followed his tried-and-true approach when confronted by political turmoil: hold his counsel until public opinion could be gauged and then stake out the position most likely to bolster his standing. As conservatives stepped into the void and mounted their attack, shaping the public debate, and left-wing students aggravated the situation, the government moved to a tougher stance. Because the conservative view appealed to his natural inclinations, President Kim seemed (in the eyes of many South Korean moderates) to enjoy the momentary popularity from being "tough" with Pyongyang.[47]

At the same time, the seemingly slow succession in the North increased the uncertainty between the two Koreas. Naturally, Kim Il Sung's death triggered speculation about when Kim Jong Il would assume his father's official titles: general secretary of the Korean Worker's Party and president. The majority view was that he would be anointed with one or both titles after his father's funeral on July 19. The signs were already present. Pyongyang had begun to portray the "Dear Leader's" achievements as almost equal to those of his father. The order of ranking of those present at the funeral had Kim Jong Il at the top of the list. One broadcast in late July even referred to him for the first time as "Great Leader." The normally reclusive Kim also stepped up meetings with foreigners, perhaps in an attempt to bolster his image as the new head of state.[48]

As time went by and Kim Jong Il did not formally assume either leadership position, speculation in South Korea mounted that something might be wrong. After the funeral, the North Korean Workers' Party newspaper warned against "the slightest attempt to damage" Kim Il Sung's accomplishments, implying that there were some opponents to his son's elevation. Also, a radio commentary on party leadership atypically failed to mention Kim Jong Il.[49] Finally, Kim did not show up for the July 27 celebrations of the end of the Korean War. In fact, he never attended such events, but his failure to appear confirmed President Kim's view that his new counterpart would not last. The South Korean president, known as a skillful orator, could not understand why Kim Jong Il did not take advantage of opportunities to speak in public.[50]

The North Koreans also seemed increasingly ambivalent about a summit. Miffed by South Korea's failure to voice condolences, they seemed bent on matching the hostile behavior of their hard-line counterparts in Seoul. The North Koreans invited South Korean "mourners" to visit Pyongyang, prompting the Kim administration to reiterate its ban on travel to the North. Once Seoul launched the student crackdown, viewed as a calculated slap in the North's face, Pyongyang's rhetoric escalated. After the Russian war documents were released, Vice Marshal Kim Kwang Jin accused Seoul of "bestial barbarism" for placing its troops on alert and arresting "patriots" who expressed condolences. [51]

But there were signs that other North Koreans were trying to keep matters from getting too far out of hand. At Kim Il Sung's memorial service, Foreign Minister Kim Yong Nam, in a speech that must have been authorized by Kim Jong Il, implicitly praised the Great Leader's decision to hold the summit. Moreover, the only response to the South Korean media's frequent use of the harsh terms "war crimes" and "war criminal" in connection with the Great Leader was a broadcast merely accusing Seoul of "distorting past history."[52]

In late July, Kim Jong Il himself reportedly told Pak Bo Hi, a South Korean publisher affiliated with the Unification Church, that he had to rein in North Koreans who wanted a sharper response to the South's ban on condolence visits and the publication of the Russian materials. Reinforcing what seemed to be a sympathetic stance was the increasing identification of the new leader in the official media with inter-Korean dialogue that he was said to have guided since the early 1970s. But the issue of Seoul's reaction to Kim Il Sung's death was too important to ignore. Kim also told Pak that the South should somehow indicate that it regretted the Great Leader's death before a date could be set for the summit.[53]

In fact, the North Koreans once again seemed to be turning their entire attention to the U.S.–North Korean talks. Kim Jong Il told Pak that he was very satisfied with those talks. An authoritative statement by the Foreign Ministry on July 25 noted that a package deal with the Americans was now in sight. After a deal was reached, a "decisively favorable phase" would open in North-South relations.[54] Washington had quickly reestablished contact with

Pyongyang through the New York channel following Kim Il Sung's funeral, leading to an announcement that talks would resume on August 5.[55]

Did Washington's condolences help keep North Korea on track? The North's gratitude was apparent. Its delegation in Geneva had been visibly moved by the U.S. reaction. Pyongyang's media gave prominence to the American stance. The first private communication from the new regime on July 16 expressed thanks from the "supreme leadership" to President Clinton and Gallucci. While the new regime may have set its course on a diplomatic solution no matter what, the talks may have been delayed with unpredictable consequences if condolences had not been offered. A Chinese official compared the U.S. approach to that of a famous Chinese general who was known for creating good outcomes out of dangerous situations through wisdom and wile. In fact, when the talks resumed, Kang told Gallucci over one of the small lunches where the wash of propaganda often slipped away that the U.S. message of condolences had significantly softened Pyongyang to Washington's demands. Sure enough, the North Koreans maintained their negotiating flexibility first displayed at the one-day July meeting with the Americans.

A related question is whether the delay in the North-South summit could have been avoided. That would have required behavior from both Koreas that may have been politically impossible for either. Conservative sentiment, President Kim Young Sam's political instincts, and the Seoul government's unwillingness to risk appearing too sympathetic to the North meant that taking the high road was not in the cards. Pyongyang, on the other hand, would not ignore even the slightest hint of insult from Seoul at such a sensitive moment. To the North, the South's inability to express condolences and its subsequent actions constituted more than sufficient grounds to take actions that would only encourage events to spiral out of control.

A contributing factor may have been a strong degree of mistrust and misperception. Later during the August round of talks with the United States, the North Korean delegation seemed convinced that President Kim Young Sam personally authorized South Korean newspapers to call Kim Il Sung a "war criminal." They asserted that "hell would freeze over" before there was a summit with him. While the Americans pointed out that President Kim did not edit the newspapers, and in fact the media printed extremely critical stories about him too, the North Koreans remained adamant. They knew that nothing could have been printed in their party newspaper without the express approval of Kim Il Sung.

The chronic paucity of intelligence about North Korea gave policymakers no choice but to base decisions on fragmentary information. The Americans tried to interpret events in Pyongyang but avoided the pitfall of shaping policy around certainty, given the great uncertainties. President Kim Young Sam, on the other hand, filtered incomplete information through the lens of his own strong views. In fact, Kim Jong Il only began to assume the formal leadership positions of his father in 1997, at the end of a three-year mourning period. The different American and South Korean views on post–Kim Il Sung North Korea added one more complication to an already testy relationship. The gap in perceptions became such a problem that the two allies conducted a secret study later in 1994 to try to arrive at some joint conclusion about the future of North Korea.[56]

The tensions created by Kim Il Sung's death came at a critical juncture. Upset that the Americans had ignored their advice on condolences, Seoul claimed such moderation would only embolden hard-liners in Pyongyang. From the South's point of view, Washington did not sufficiently consider uncertainties in Pyongyang. On July 14, President Kim told Clinton "we should be prudent and patient." But to the Americans, Kim seemed mis-guided. Clinton responded that Washington could not delay resolving the nuclear problem in light of the continued threat to remove the spent fuel from Yongbyon, allegedly for safety reasons. It was time, he concluded, to address the new reactor project squarely.[57] Summing up, a South Korean official recalled: "We were clumsy and the Americans were too hasty."[58]

The indefinite delay of the summit, along with the rise of conservative sen-timent in the South, presented a tough challenge for the United States and South Korea as talks with North Korea resumed. South Korean moderates pre-dicted that conservatives would "sing the song of a bystander." That meant Seoul would renew complaints about its exclusion from the diplomatic track, insist that a solution could not be left to Washington alone, and assert that the United States was too generous and too gullible. The sensible cure for this problem was for the two allies to forge a strong common position that held promise for progress without excessive accommodation to the North. But in the supercharged political atmosphere after Kim Il Sung's demise, that advice was easier said than done.

Homework

A great deal of work remained before the Geneva talks could resume. The July meeting had highlighted the light-water reactor project, offsetting North Korea's conventional energy losses, and dealing with the spent fuel as impor-tant tasks. The reactor issue was the most complex. Since the United States would supply neither the new reactors nor the financing, it required foreign commitments to build them, a U.S. guarantee for the project to persuade

Pyongyang to drop its existing nuclear program, and financing for the multi-billion-dollar effort. In any case, Pyongyang preferred Russian assistance, even though Seoul was a promising source of technology and financing.

Meeting on July 15, the principals began to tackle the remaining work. A quickly discarded option was to transport to North Korea one of two unfinished State of Washington Public Power Supply System reactors halted in mid-construction. These units were known as the "whoops reactors," a double entendre referring both to the utility acronym, WPPSS, and to the fact that the cancellation of the reactor project after the Three Mile Island nuclear accident occasioned the largest municipal bond default in American history. Ever since then, the desperate owners had sought some alternative use for the reactors to recover at least part of their investment. The State Department made discreet inquiries, but the option was found to be impractical. Since the principals did not express a preference for either South Korean or Russian reactors, they asked Gallucci to prepare a viable reactor package.

The most immediate problem was developing an American guarantee that North Korea would receive its new reactors. The job was given to the State Department's Office of the Legal Adviser. At the Geneva meeting, the North Koreans seemed unsure whether they wanted a legally binding guarantee. From the American perspective, such a guarantee posed enormous problems. It would obligate the United States to vouch for the performance of whoever contracted to deliver the reactors. If the reactors were not delivered, Washington would have to arrange for the construction. But the president could not make such a financial commitment on behalf of the United States without the approval of Congress.

Under the best of circumstances, this would have been a tall order, but circumstances in Congress were far from ideal. The day the principals met, the Senate unanimously approved a Republican-sponsored amendment to the Foreign Assistance Act. The amendment barred aid to North Korea unless the president certified that it did not possess nuclear arms, had halted its nuclear program, had come into full compliance with both the Non-Proliferation Treaty and its IAEA safeguards agreement, and did not export plutonium or missiles. While the administration managed to deflect the amendment since meeting this standard would have been impossible, the message was clear. Congress was in no mood to provide *any* financial support, let alone funding for a multibillion-dollar project.[59]

The alternative seemed to be what one State Department lawyer called a "beefed-up" political guarantee that would need no congressional approval but, hopefully, suitably impress the North Koreans. One lawyer suggested language that the president would "use the full powers" of his office to deliver the new reactors. The phrase sounded impressive to the untrained ear, but to lawyers it just highlighted the fact that the president was not committing the U.S. government beyond the scope of his constitutional powers. It underlined that the guarantee did not commit the Congress and that the president could not deliver a project without congressional approval. Different historical models were consulted, ranging from the 1940 North Atlantic Charter signed by Franklin Roosevelt and Winston Churchill to a 1979 letter from President Carter to the Israelis and Egyptians pledging to set up a peacekeeping force in the Sinai if the Security Council failed to do so.[60]

Any guarantee would not be worth the paper it was written on, however, unless backed by financial and technical commitments from other countries. Not surprisingly, the White House was hesitant to let the president climb out on a limb without such backing. Consequently, in late July Gallucci left for a round-the-world tour of Seoul, Tokyo, Beijing, and Moscow to secure the necessary support to make it possible for President Clinton to provide North Korea with a beefed-up reactor guarantee.

South Korea was his first stop. A week before Gallucci arrived, Foreign Minister Han told Ambassador Laney that his government was prepared to fund the project if South Korean companies played a major role. Conversely, it would not provide funding if Russia built the reactors. President Kim Young Sam reaffirmed that message; he saw the reactor project as the beginning of broader North-South economic cooperation. While the South Korean option seemed to be financially and technically feasible, the problem of its "political viability" remained. Privately, officials admitted that it would be hard to insulate the project against the ups and downs of inter-Korean politics.

The Americans came up with a gambit to help persuade Pyongyang to accept a project dominated by South Korea. The United States would propose a project that appeared to be multilateral but, in reality, drew almost totally from the South Korean model. The reactor project would be given an American veneer, not only by providing Pyongyang with a political guarantee from the president of the United States, but also by appointing an American company as the prime contractor. South Korean subcontractors would do the real work; they would build South Korean reactors. After Gallucci departed, the Blue House told the U.S. Embassy that President Kim liked the new approach.

In spite of the initial meeting of minds, there were signs of more problems ahead. South Korean officials echoed President Kim's feeling that the Americans might be too impatient, expressed in his earlier conversation with President Clinton. They questioned whether the North was exaggerating the immediate safety problems of continuing to store the spent fuel as a way of pressing Washington to reach a quick deal. In fact, the Americans agreed with the South Koreans that though the fuel was corroding, the North *was* exaggerating the urgency of reprocessing from a safety perspective. But doubts in Seoul about Washington's ability to negotiate with the North remained.

In addition, the issue of linkage between the inter-Korean and U.S.–North Korean talks once again was beginning to rear its ugly head. Expressing concern that Pyongyang would seek to move forward rapidly with the United States rather than reschedule the summit, President Kim warned Gallucci that if that track went too far without progress in North-South talks, it would not be in the two allies' best interests. With the collapse of Super Tuesday still fresh in their memories, the Americans argued that explicit linkage was not the right approach. But they conceded that any agreement with the North would have to include a commitment to restart inter-Korean dialogue and perhaps even to implement the Denuclearization Declaration between the two Koreas.

In Tokyo, Foreign Minister Yohei Kono let Gallucci know that if negotiations produced results, Japan "would not just applaud from the sidelines." Tokyo had been willing to commit billions of dollars to North Korea once the two normalized political relations, but that seemed unlikely to happen any time soon. Now the Foreign Ministry was considering participation in a multilateral consortium as a way around this roadblock, provided Gallucci could recruit other members to give it political cover at home. (That would demonstrate Japan was not just being called on to bankroll American diplomacy.) But the powerful Ministry of International Trade and Industry remained skeptical. Finally, the Japanese had not decided whether to support the South Korean or Russian reactor model. For the moment, Tokyo was willing to provide some financial support for an initial feasibility study or a survey of the North's energy needs.

The third stop on the trip was Beijing. While China was not likely to be a key player on the reactor project, its political support remained critical. Beijing also could help in other ways, perhaps providing Pyongyang with electricity, constructing power plants, or improving the transport of coal. Of course, it was likely to be hampered by practical limitations. For example, connecting the North Korean and Chinese power grids would be technically complicated. Moreover, the Chinese region bordering the North suffered from its own electricity shortages. China might provide trains to help carry coal to North Korean power plants, but this was also uncertain since Beijing had its own transportation problems. Finally, Beijing might agree to allow Pyongyang to ship its spent fuel rods to China.

The Beijing talks yielded no tangible results. Aside from predictably nudging Gallucci to be more accommodating toward Pyongyang, the Chinese did not rule out helping build power plants, but only if someone else paid for them. As for spent fuel, Beijing's experts concluded that there were no technical obstacles to accepting the North's rods. But officials were unwilling make any commitments until the course of U.S.–North Korean negotiations became clear.

The last leg of the trip was Russia, the other main contender for the reactor project. Before Kim Il Sung died, President Boris Yeltsin was ready to announce that Moscow would provide reactors to the North Koreans if it received financing for the project. On July 15, Foreign Minister Andrei Kozyrev told the *Itar-Tass* news agency that Russia's technology was "maybe the most advanced in the world," although he admitted that this is a "colossal order and it is linked to a huge amount of finance. It is exactly this financing issue that we are discussing with our foreign partners to get them to help in this project."[61]

The key bureaucratic player was the Ministry of Atomic Energy, Minatom. Once the ultimate symbol of cold war Soviet might, the Russian nuclear complex could no longer count on ample state subsidies. Minatom felt a strong sense of entitlement to run the project, as the Russian government had earlier bowed to U.S. pressure to cancel its own light-water reactor contract with North Korea. It was only fair that, if the deal were back on, the Russians should be restored to their rightful place as the principal reactor supplier. The sale, potentially worth billions of dollars, would represent a major windfall for Minatom, helping it fund activities across the board, ranging from advanced research and development at its design institutes to reactor and fuel cycle operations.

Minatom officials told Gallucci that they would like to provide North Korea with reactors based on a new design, the NP-500, which incorporated the latest safety features. Russia also offered to train the North Koreans to operate the reactors and to help them set up an independent nuclear regulatory authority in order to ensure their safe operation. But the Russian proposal had serious drawbacks. The prototype under construction was not yet completed, making it hard to imagine that any country would be willing to finance a reactor that might or might not be technically viable. While labor costs were likely to be cheaper, Moscow could provide no financing for the project. It may have been politically acceptable to the North Koreans, but it was neither financially nor technically viable.

Complicating matters further, the Russian government was not of one mind. Some Foreign Ministry officials agreed with Gallucci that the two countries had to maintain a common front, without being sidetracked into commercial squabbles over profiting from the reactor sale. Minatom had exactly the opposite idea; it saw the new project not as a solution to a political problem but as a commercial opportunity. Other Russian officials worried that the atomic energy bureaucracy, with its long-standing ties to North Korea, would encourage Pyongyang to hold out for a Russian reactor.

One way out of this bureaucratic thicket was to find an alternative role for Moscow in lieu of providing the reactor model. Gallucci tried to highlight what Russia might contribute; while it had little experience with North Korea's type of spent fuel, Minatom was interested in reprocessing the rods. Washington was already planning to build storage facilities for Russian pluto-nium; adding a little North Korean plutonium should not pose a problem and would significantly reduce the proliferation risk compared with leaving the material in the North. At best, however, the commercial gain—on the order of tens of millions of dollars—would fall far short of the jackpot Minatom had hoped for in winning the reactor contract. Its frustration would remain a con-tinuing problem for U.S.-Russian cooperation.

Gallucci's whirlwind trip emphasized to key foreign officials that the United States meant business, highlighted the remaining uncertainties and clarified the Clinton administration's options. Before a Deputies Committee meeting on July 28, Gallucci sent a message from Moscow to Sandy Berger. He recommended that the committee approve a simple, lean political guarantee that a reactor project would be provided to North Korea contingent upon Pyongyang meeting its nonproliferation obligations. This would be an essen-tial element of the U.S. position.

For a variety of reasons, the American delegation leaned toward the South Korean model, with some participation for Russian companies. Seoul and Tokyo would provide most of the funding, acting through a board consisting of themselves, the United States, China, and Russia. Gallucci came up with a name for the new organization, the Korean Energy Development Organiza-tion, or KEDO, which sounded like the Japanese martial art *aikido* he had been practicing with his son. (The name would ultimately be the Korean Peninsula Energy Development Organization, but the acronym KEDO stuck.)

Gallucci also urged Washington to finish its preparations on other critical issues. By the end of July, an interagency group run by the Arms Control and Disarmament Agency had fleshed out a proposal to slow the corrosion of the North Korean rods and ship them out at a cost of $70 million, a small price to pay given the danger. The Department of Energy had put together a $17 mil-lion package of conventional energy assistance consisting of portable boilers, electric generators, or an emergency coal supply to be used if the 5-megawatt reactor were shut down. Longer-term cooperation would seek to optimize the use of North Korea's current resources rather than build new capacity, first by authorizing a Chinese firm to reexport $1.5 million in American computer

equipment to the North that would help minimize the blackouts and brown-
outs in Pyongyang.

Three days after the deputies met, the Principals Committee conducted a
final review of American preparations. In addition to the usual participants,
Leon Panetta, the director of the Office of Management and Budget, and
David Gergen, counselor to the president, attended. The discussion quickly
focused on the presidential guarantee for Pyongyang.

Just back in town, Gallucci reported that the best approach he could propose
would be a political guarantee backed up by written commitments from South
Korea and Japan to provide funding for the project. If Pyongyang refused, the
principals would need to consider whether to offer a legally binding guarantee.

A spirited discussion ensued, with some arguing that a North Korean
demand for a legal guarantee could be considered blackmail, at once triggering the need for, while undermining the prospect of, congressional approval.
Others—worried about the risk of offering a multibillion-dollar guarantee if
there were any doubts that the United States could deliver—proposed a quick
"small deal" to get the spent fuel shipped out while continuing to pursue a big
deal that would include a guarantee. Still others argued that any deal would
have to solve the nuclear problem for good. While all understood that proliferation risks would persist as long as the North had a nuclear energy program,
the American negotiating position did address both Pyongyang's nuclear past
and future. Some thought that the reactor guarantee would be a bargain well
worth taking to Congress if necessary. After all, the Camp David accord had
cost the United States $10 billion to $15 billion and there were no American
troops in the Middle East. In Korea, there were 37,000 GIs already deployed in
defense of the South.

By the end of the meeting, Gallucci was given the green light to propose a
politically binding, presidential guarantee. It would essentially promise only a
"good-faith effort" to bring about the light-water reactor project. It would also
explicitly state that if the original project failed, Washington would still be on
the hook to provide the North with new reactors, "subject to the approval of
the U.S. Congress." Even this guarantee would only be offered after Seoul and
Tokyo backed it up with their own written commitments. If they did not, the
issue would have to be reconsidered by the principals.

The Lion's Share of Work Is before Us

Gallucci and Kang Sok Ju met again in Geneva a month after Kim Il Sung
died. Talking to reporters at the State Department before leaving for Europe,
Gallucci repeated that he was "expecting continuity in the North Korean

approach because Kang had told him so shortly after Kim's death." In addition, their negotiating team remained unchanged since the Great Leader died, another positive sign.[62] Privately, however, the Americans still harbored doubts about whether the new North Korean regime was strong enough to make the necessary compromises, particularly on shipping the spent fuel out of the country and forgoing reprocessing.

The first day of talks on August 5 lasted more than eight hours. In his opening statement, Gallucci emphasized that the positive vision of future relations between the two countries he described in July remained within reach if they could work together to resolve concerns over the nuclear program. Invoking one of Kang's most familiar metaphors—he often complained that American demands would leave him naked—Gallucci said, "Let's discuss nakedness: neither of us wishes to be."

The American negotiator had a new ace in the hole, the promise of a presidential guarantee for the new reactor project. "We are prepared to provide a letter from the president of the United States of America committing that the full powers of the presidency would be used to facilitate arrangements for the financing and construction in North Korea of a light-water reactor project," Gallucci announced. If the reactors were not finished for reasons beyond the control of North Korea, the president would use those powers, subject to approval by Congress, to arrange for its completion.

But he added that "a commitment of this magnitude" could only be made if Pyongyang accepted Washington's July 8 road map. That meant confirming its NPT membership, agreeing to comply with IAEA safeguards, including acceptance of special inspections, and confirming its commitment to the Denuclearization Declaration. The nuclear program would have to be frozen; the 5-megawatt reactor could not be refueled, construction of the two larger reactors would stop, and Pyongyang could not separate plutonium from the spent fuel in the storage pond. That fuel would have to be shipped out of the country as soon as technically possible. Finally, North Korea would have to agree to dismantle its whole program, to begin at the same time as construction of the light-water reactors.

Gallucci, Poneman, and Hubbard hoped to make progress with a smaller group of North Koreans over lunch. Choosing a secluded villa converted into a restaurant, the Americans settled into a corner table by a trellis in the courtyard with their North Korean counterparts. Bees droned among the flowering vines. Kang told the Americans how President Clinton's condolences and Gallucci's visit to the Geneva mission had allowed him to secure more negotiating authority in Pyongyang. Gallucci sought to exploit an apparent moment of

North Korean flexibility. Pointing to a nearby tree, he told Kang, "I am going out on a limb. I need a positive Korean response."

But if Kang had more negotiating authority, he did not deploy it that first day over lunch. Turning to an important American priority, Gallucci emphasized that shipment of the spent fuel to another country was essential if Pyongyang wanted a reactor guarantee. Kang stiffened as he told Gallucci, "Don't raise the question of spent fuel shipment again." He added that people in Pyongyang "nearly beat me up" in July since they viewed that proposal as an infringement of sovereignty. At the end of the meal, the American negotiator gave Kang a draft presidential letter with the American road map attached. The message was clear: if Kang wanted the guarantee, he would have to do better than the North Korean road map proposed in July.

Gallucci revealed the rest of the American position that afternoon. He told the North Koreans that the new reactor project would need to be multinational since it cost too much for any one country to support on its own. The United States would lead a consortium, but South Korea would play the main role. Recognizing North Korea's sensitivity about Seoul's involvement, Gallucci added that an American company would be the prime contractor with overall responsibility for supervising the project and providing some key reactor components. Russia might chip in fuel-enrichment services.

To compensate for the continued shutdown of the 5-megawatt reactor, Gallucci said his side would provide conventional energy to North Korea before winter. An extensive multimillion-dollar feasibility study and energy survey would also be conducted to identify requirements to upgrade and improve the North's electrical grid and provide interim power until the new reactors were completed. For this purpose, the United Nations Development Program might give $2.5 million worth of computer equipment, designed in the United States and manufactured in China. Gallucci pressed the point, urging the North Koreans to consider conventional energy alternatives to the nuclear plants, offering cooperation in building coal-fired or hydroelectric plants to replace the power displaced from the 50-megawatt and 200-megawatt plants under construction.

The logic of his case was compelling. Building new nuclear reactors made little sense in energy terms. Tying such large units into the small North Korean transmission network would create a serious imbalance in the distribution of power around the grid, raising serious risks of blackouts and other disruptions. But no matter how hard Gallucci pressed the North Koreans, no matter how compelling the logic, they declined. It was clear that they were not driven principally by a desire to find the least costly, most efficient solution to their energy problem, but apparently by the political benefits available only from a nuclear project.

On the critical issue of shutting down the 5-megawatt reactor, Kang also resisted, repeatedly citing the need to provide heat to the local population. Frustrated, Gallucci resorted to humor as he often did, to try and break the impasse. "Mr. Kang," he said, "I can understand your concern for the residents' plight in the harsh North Korean winter. We will supply you with truckloads of long johns, one for every resident, so you can freeze the reactor." Both sides agreed to continue to discuss the matter.

Theatrics aside, the North Koreans seemed intrigued. They had hoped for a new U.S. proposal; when the meeting schedule was set for the talks, they had insisted that no sessions be held on the second day, presumably to give themselves time to formulate a response. Initially, Kang did what any experienced diplomat would do: stick to his approved script but try to find out more details. In the plenary session, he complained that the presidential guarantee was only a promise. Privately, he conceded that the North Koreans took great notice when Gallucci mentioned the guarantee but were concerned that it was not legally binding. One North Korean asked what would happen if a Republican president took office.

At the end of the meeting, Kang asked for a two-day recess to relay the new proposals to Pyongyang and obtain new instructions. While the North Koreans said that they might now need to adjust their position, the Americans suspected they had come to Geneva with fallback positions already in their back pocket and needed to modify them in view of the new proposal. To keep the pressure on, the American delegation expressed disappointment at what seemed to be the North's lack of an immediate response. Gallucci chided Kang, saying that he felt as if he only got an "E for effort."[63]

When the two delegations reconvened on Monday, it became clear why the North Koreans had asked for two days to formulate their response: the beefed-up presidential guarantee had broken free a series of major North Korean concessions. During a marathon session lasting almost nine hours, Kang said Pyongyang had some qualms that the assurance was not legally binding, but it was "an important starting point." The North Koreans welcomed the American willingness to take "full and ultimate" responsibility for the provision of new reactors as a positive development.

In return, Kang was willing to accelerate implementation of key provisions in his road map. First, once the presidential guarantee was received, construction of its two larger reactors would be frozen. They would be dismantled later when the new reactors began to operate. The original North Korean road map provided for a freeze only when it received the new reactors, many years in the future. "This is an enormous political loss and sacrifice on our part," Kang proclaimed "because it will mean changing our self-reliant economic policy." To compensate for the lost energy, those reactors would have produced until the new reactors began operating, Kang asked for 500,000 tons of heavy fuel oil to be delivered annually.

Second, Kang agreed to help the United States "save face" on the spent fuel issue. It would be stored at Yongbyon and a U.S. team of experts could provide assistance in preventing corrosion so that it would not need to be reprocessed. Reinforcing that pledge, construction at the reprocessing plant would be halted and the plant would be shut down once the presidential letter was received. Decommissioning could take place later, tied to progress on the reactor project. According to Kang, nothing would be left inside except "rust and cobwebs."

Third, the North Koreans accepted Gallucci's proposal for a multilateral reactor project. They would only deal with the United States as the leader of the group and still had qualms about Seoul's role. Kang predicted that the South would use the project as a "horse of Troy" to drive a wedge between Washington and Pyongyang. The other North Koreans looked puzzled, apparently mystified by his classical allusion. But Kang did not reject South Korea's role, expressing confidence in the American president's assurance.

By the end of the day, the North Koreans had moved closer to the U.S. position, although major stumbling blocks remained. They continued to refuse to ship the spent fuel out of their country and also wanted to refuel and operate the 5-megawatt reactor. Their excuse was that the reactor provided research opportunities for the North's nuclear physicists, employment for thousands, and a hedge against the possibility that Washington would not complete the new reactors. "We can take off our pants but not our underwear," Kang insisted, returning to his favorite metaphor. But since the North's position clearly implied an increase in its plutonium inventory, Gallucci bluntly told him, "The world would not accept an agreement that left North Korea with some 30 kilograms of plutonium in the spent fuel and the production of more in the operating reactor."

Kang also failed to address special inspections. During a private lunch, he seemed to suggest that they would be possible once the two countries had built mutual trust. That was the implication of Pyongyang's statements after the Carter visit. After Gallucci explained that they would be necessary for any nuclear cooperation, Kang shifted gears. Asserting that it was "the will of our supreme leadership to reject special inspections," his arguments became increasingly shrill and doctrinaire as the day wore on.

Gallucci warned Kang that if he was saying special inspections were impossible, contrary to what Kim Il Sung had told Jimmy Carter, then no settlement could take place. Kang also invoked Carter, claiming to have a tape recording of him telling Kim Il Sung that the past could be left unaccounted for until the new reactor project was completed. The two sides had reached a similar point during the July 1993 Geneva meeting. Then, the stalemate almost resulted in a collapse of the talks. Now, they agreed to disagree and adjourned.

In spite of the remaining obstacles, the negotiations that day had made rapid, significant, and unexpected progress. Gallucci told the BBC that they were "particularly productive and interesting."[64] But the American delegation warned Washington that the threat to restart the reactor was, in itself, particularly serious since that would effectively end the freeze and the negotiations. Problems with the spent fuel only aggravated the situation. Given these potential roadblocks, the U.S. delegation floated a new idea: to freeze the amount of plutonium in North Korea by either allowing it to refuel its reactor or keep the spent fuel in storage, but not both. At this stage, however, Washington was not ready to budge.

The North Koreans' rigidity on special inspections was also disturbing. They still did not seem to understand that these inspections were necessary for Pyongyang to come into full compliance with its nonproliferation obligations and that no state would provide new reactors until then. Nevertheless, one U.S. delegation member discerned what he thought was a glimmer of hope. In the past, the North's position was "never," with a hint of "not until" tacked on. Now, the North Koreans seemed to be saying "not until," indicating that the phasing of implementation could be critical to reaching agreement.

With all of these difficult issues still unresolved, the Americans concluded that the nuclear problem could not be resolved during the current round of talks. That evening, they provided the North Koreans with a new document, incorporating the day's discussions, which was intended to form the basis for an interim arrangement until further talks could be held. The Agreed Minute, the detailed road map for the solution of the nuclear problem that Gallucci had initially provided Kang, was set aside for the moment as too ambitious. The North Koreans agreed to respond quickly.

Over the next few days, Tom Hubbard and Kim Gye Gwan, the number-two officials on each delegation, worked to finalize the interim "Agreed Statement." The single most contentious issue was whether Pyongyang would commit itself to implementing full-scope safeguards, which would have also meant accepting special inspections. While Kim gave in, Kang, in his role as "bad cop," tried unsuccessfully to resurrect the phrase "impartial" application of safeguards that had been used in the July 1993 statement. He acquiesced, however, after Gallucci refused to make any changes.

The other major issue was North-South dialogue. The North predictably groused at its mention. When reminded by Gallucci that implementation of the Denuclearization Declaration was an important objective for Washington, Kang said that trying to discuss inter-Korean issues in a meeting between the United States and North Korea only complicated matters. He added: "A total freeze on our nuclear activity including reprocessing will automatically fulfill the North-South declaration." Of course, the Denuclearization Declaration also included a ban on uranium enrichment activities whereas the freeze on activities at Yongbyon did not, a point Kang failed to address in his comment.

Recognizing that Seoul was unlikely to be satisfied with this solution, the Americans pressed the point. The U.S. draft for the Agreed Statement proposed that in order "to help secure peace in Korea, the Democratic People's Republic of Korea would remain prepared to resume North-South dialogue and implement the North-South Denuclearization Declaration." But Kim Gye Gwan objected, claiming that the political climate in Pyongyang would simply not tolerate a reference to North-South dialogue. The final language only referred to Pyongyang's willingness to implement the Denuclearization Declaration. The Agreed Statement was released shortly after midnight, August 12. "The direction of our path has been determined," Kang told Gallucci. Speaking to the press after the document's release, both praised the accord, with Kang describing it in glowing terms and comparing it to the 1993 joint statement reached in New York.

For the Clinton administration, the Agreed Statement represented the first tangible diplomatic result from its dealings with Pyongyang. North Korea would immediately give up reprocessing, the reprocessing facility, and two larger reactors under construction, as well as shift from its existing reactors to the less dangerous light-water reactors. Pyongyang had agreed to unqualified language on safeguards, on remaining in the NPT, and on implementing the Denuclearization Declaration. It had also accepted the concept of a presidential assurance that fell short of a legally binding document. Finally, the option of removing the spent fuel had been preserved. All this had been achieved despite the difficult circumstances arising from the June crisis and the death of Kim Il Sung.

While the Agreed Statement did not say so, the North Koreans seemed ready to accept South Korean participation in the reactor project, another important accomplishment. In the press conference afterward, the first question for Kang was whether the North would accept reactors from the South. He artfully finessed the issue: "Both North and South Korea have deeply rooted mistrust. We have reached an initial agreement with regard to the provision of light-water reactors that the United States will undertake full responsibility for the provision of light-water reactors. Therefore, I think which country or countries may be the vendor of light-water reactors, I think that is the business and the responsibility of the United States."[65]

The agreement also addressed other steps in the normalization of relations that had been approved at the June 30 principals' meeting and by the trilateral partners. The statement announced that the United States and North Korea were prepared to establish diplomatic relations, a development that was given top billing in the New York Times the next day.[66] Not the subject of extensive discussion, the Americans suspected this provision meant more to Pyongyang than it was willing to admit. One North Korean asked, "Could Gallucci really deliver on something like that?" Not surprisingly, President Kim was unhappy with the news. The United States also agreed to reduce "barriers to trade and investment," by beginning to eliminate restrictions in the Trading with the Enemy Act that had been in effect since the Korean War.

The reaction in Washington to the Agreed Statement was muted, in part because the agreement was reached during the dog days of August, in part because it did not tackle the controversial issue of special inspections. Brent Scowcroft, President Bush's national security adviser, said that the document was "a cautious step forward if everything in it is implemented," adding that "it's important to implement everything that needs to be implemented on the North Korean side before we start giving away things."[67] Senator John McCain allowed that the agreement "has some promising aspects to it." But he also feared the inspectors might not get access to the nuclear waste sites and wanted the North to destroy rather than seal its reprocessing plant.[68]

The August meeting proved once again that negotiations could produce results. The North had moved with unusual speed into bargaining mode. Its delegation had apparently come to Geneva with much, if not all, of the key August 8 proposals to freeze construction and reprocessing, suggesting that Pyongyang had decided on a more forward-leaning approach during the hiatus occasioned by Kim Il Sung's funeral. Once it decided how to integrate this proposal with the presidential guarantee, the North made an important gesture, breaching the sacred principle of reciprocity by offering concrete steps for "a piece of paper." Differences remained, but most of the work now focused on phasing and sequencing. One American observed that the North Koreans kept saying that they could not be expected to take all the steps requested by the United States "at this time," very different from saying they could not take them at all.

In terms of the art of negotiation, North Korean behavior reaffirmed the view that putting something positive on the table early paid dividends. It kept the North looking ahead to benefits it might achieve if negotiations made progress, rescuing its negotiators from their own tendency to become bogged down on tactical points that might balloon into nonnegotiable matters of "dignity." It forestalled the North's inclination to move slowly in negotiations, fighting fiercely before abandoning each rhetorical redoubt to the next fall-back position. The American tactic may have also given the North Korean delegation ammunition to use with Pyongyang in arguing for a more flexible approach.

As always, the reasons for Pyongyang's actions were open to interpretation. To some, its concessions reflected weakness after Kim Il Sung's death. Others felt they were a response to Washington's gesture in expressing condolences to the North Korean people. Still others saw their moves as the continuation of an altered strategic direction, courtesy of the events in June when an isolated Pyongyang, faced with economic sanctions and military force, charted a new course following Jimmy Carter's fortuitous appearance on the scene.

In spite of progress made in Geneva, the diplomatic situation was still precarious. Uncertainties surfaced almost immediately when Gallucci insisted publicly that the North Koreans had accepted special inspections and Kang denied accepting or even talking about them. But the North Korean negotiator also hedged, adding that their implementation "could depend on how much the partiality of the IAEA officials will be redressed."[69] In a subsequent interview, Kang was even more forthcoming, saying that special inspections "will be resolved as mutual confidence improves," the same approach enunciated after President Carter's visit.[70] These statements were not entirely positive—a fact emphasized by the Western press—but neither were they entirely negative. Evidence supported either a glass "half full" or "half empty" interpretation.

Ultimately, the Agreed Statement represented only an outline of the kind that would be needed to resolve the crisis. The Americans had given the North a similar, more detailed document in Geneva, called the Agreed Minute, but set it aside under the pressure of time. That draft, which posited simultaneous steps by each side in phases, would later serve as the basis for a final agreement. In his post-Geneva press conference, Kang acknowledged that the two countries had a "long way to go" and that many "complicated" and "sensitive" issues would be raised.[71] An anonymous White House official admitted, "progress has been made but the lion's share of work is before us."[72]

Before parting, Gallucci and Kang agreed to resume talks in Geneva on September 23. In July 1993, they had made a similar pledge, only to have their meeting delayed for almost a year. This time, the Americans left nothing to chance. They suggested, and the North accepted, meetings of experts in the weeks ahead to discuss the reactor project, spent fuel, and diplomatic relations. In theory, these sessions were to establish a firmer basis for the final push in the fall. In reality, the talks, combined with intensifying bickering between the two Koreas, would cast doubt on whether a solution was possible.

Anxiety Attacks

Five days after the Geneva talks ended, President Clinton telephoned Kim Young Sam. Beneath the customary exchange of pleasantries, the South Korean leader's anxiety was palpable. Only a few days earlier, his top foreign policy advisers had previewed for the Americans their lukewarm reaction to the Agreed Statement. Now Kim told Clinton that any assistance to the North should depend on complete transparency and on Pyongyang accepting South Korea's reactors. Also, Kim pointed out, the Agreed Statement made no mention of North-South dialogue, an important South Korean concern. Salting his conversation with comments on the North's instability and unpredictability, the president observed that Kim Jong Il had not been seen in public for some time and repeated his admonition that it was not prudent to rush toward an agreement. He concluded that the two allies had to work together closely in the future given uncertainties about events in North Korea.

Clinton tried to reassure Kim. "The Agreed Statement was a good beginning," he countered, tallying up the pluses, including important nonproliferation commitments that could open an opportunity to eliminate the nuclear threat and to move toward normal relations. In addition, Pyongyang appeared willing to accept South Korean reactors and even made reference to the Denuclearization Declaration. But Clinton agreed that the two leaders had to be cautious given events in Pyongyang. Ending the conversation, Kim welcomed an offer by Clinton to send Gallucci to Seoul.

Although the Blue House portrayed the conversation in a positive light, President Kim admitted to the press that he told Clinton: "Excessive progress is being made in U.S.–North Korean talks despite the unstable North Korean situation."[73] Only the opposition was enthusiastic. During a reception given in his honor, Kim Dae Jung praised the accord as a landmark agreement that must be followed by a North-South summit, an endorsement that in itself discredited the proposal in the eyes of the government.[74]

President Kim's reaction reflected a divided and anxious public. A slight majority in South Korea felt that the United States valued reaching an agreement more than guaranteeing nuclear transparency. Respondents split almost evenly on the establishment of liaison offices; some felt it would isolate Seoul whereas others felt it would help inter-Korean relations. Almost 60 percent viewed cooperation between Washington and Seoul as unsatisfactory although acceptable.[75] Fueling the political fire, the press slammed the United

States for rushing after a deal and President Kim for promising to pay for the reactors without first gaining concessions from the North.[76]

Just as important, President Kim remained skeptical about the situation in North Korea. Cracks in the succession façade—imagined or real—seemed to be appearing. An unattributed North Korean radio roundtable, often a vehicle for airing differing leadership views, admitted that even when the successor is "designated in a timely manner, it does not mean that the question of the leader's successor is completely solved." Signs of renewed debate over issues that Kim Il Sung had settled in favor of his son began to appear. For example, the younger Kim's push for emphasis on light industry had been enshrined in a Party Plenum decision in December 1993. Yet in late August another radio discussion show emphasized the importance of heavy industry and did not mention the plenum.[77]

Adding to President Kim's skepticism, Pyongyang's economic deterioration seemed to be accelerating. One sign of its possible demise was a North Korean request at the end of the Geneva talks for 2.5 million tons of wheat because of a food shortage, a request that was repeated to a businessman visiting Pyongyang at the same time. In the debate shaping up in Washington and Seoul about North Korea's future—some concluded that Kim Jong Il was secure in the short term while others believed that the North might collapse soon—President Kim fell firmly in the latter camp.[78] On August 18 he told the ruling party's Executive Committee, "We must prepare for an abrupt reunification," a stark contrast to Kim's 1994 New Year's speech when he said no one knew when reunification would come.[79]

The president's concern resonated through an odd episode in Pyongyang on the night of August 19. Antigovernment leaflets showing pictures of the defectors who had made a splash at the July press conference were found in a compound where most foreigners lived, at a nearby hospital, and at another location. The inflammatory captions pointed out that "even North Korea's elite are fleeing to the ROK," and "why are even the well-dressed and well-fed elite fleeing from the North. Disillusioned with the Kim father-to-son succession, they have decided to leave hopeless North Korea." The names of other defectors were also listed on the leaflets. During the week after they were found, several diplomatic missions received nightly phone calls in English claiming that Kim Jong Il had died.[80]

Most assumed that South Korean intelligence was responsible for these activities. Even the North Korean elite might not have access to sophisticated printing, photographs, and reports in the South's media. Furthermore, the two Koreas had a long-standing propaganda war using balloons on autopilot to release leaflets over their destinations.[81] Balloons had been used for the same purpose in the 1950s when the Central Intelligence Agency and the U.S. Air Force released propaganda leaflets over Eastern Europe and the Soviet Union.[82] It was still puzzling, however, why South Korea would use leaflets that clearly pointed the finger back at Seoul. They may have been distributed by someone else and in some other way, but a wall surrounded the diplomatic compound and its gates were under constant surveillance. While the North Koreans opted publicly for the balloon theory, two days after the incident was reported, all the guards at the compound were changed.

President Kim cited the leaflets as another sign that North Korea was in trouble. At a dinner for ruling party lawmakers he remarked, "Various significant moves are going on in North Korea," citing the scattering of the leaflets as an act "aimed at a precise effect."[83] Others disagreed; after a briefing by South Korean intelligence, Representative Sin Sang U, chairman of the National Assembly Intelligence Committee, said: "There is no need to over-interpret that Kim Jong Il's regime will crumble based on events such as anti-Kim leaflets being scattered in the diplomatic quarter of Pyongyang."[84]

President Kim's reaction to the events in Geneva also reflected a decline in his political fortunes over the previous months. Despite some progress, the president's program of domestic reform was seen as a vindictive effort to punish political enemies. One former supporter and subsequent political victim coined a phrase that stuck to the president: "He boiled the hunting dog that caught the rabbit." Buffeted by scandals, including accusations that he sold out the country's rice farmers in the Uruguay Round of international trade talks, his administration was increasingly blamed for disorganization and inconsistency in its policy toward Pyongyang. All of these problems manifested themselves in a key electoral loss in a conservative bastion in early August, which threatened to reignite ruling party factionalism. As a result, the president needed to show conservatives in his party that he was even more sensitive to their view that North Korea was an intractable security problem.

While President Kim used the death of Kim Il Sung to demonstrate that he could be tough with Pyongyang, it became clear that a hard-line approach ran the risk of alienating the United States. It might also lock Seoul into an embittered refusal to resume dialogue with Pyongyang and undermine support for Kim Young Sam's government. With strong encouragement from moderates, the president used the August 15 holiday celebrated by both Koreas as the end of Japanese colonial rule to lay out his view of reunification, which included a "joint development program" with the new reactor project as the first step. In return, the North had to guarantee the "transparency of its nuclear activities" and implement the Denuclearization Declaration. No mention was made of Geneva or the United States.[85]

More moderate in tone than the public debate over the past month, President Kim's speech nevertheless implicitly criticized the Pyongyang regime, focusing on the values of freedom, democracy, and human rights as the foundation for reunification, and was aimed at a South Korean audience. It also reflected long-standing anxieties about being sidelined in negotiations with Pyongyang, appearing to be subordinate to Washington, and retaining some control over the pace of improvement in U.S.–North Korean relations. His initiative received broad political and media support. President Kim's telephone conversation with Clinton after his speech was designed to achieve the same political objectives. Subsequent statements by government officials repeated the president's pronouncement.[86]

National Security Adviser Chung Chong Wook also had made it clear to Lake that the Blue House was concerned about the rapid pace of U.S.–North Korean efforts to establish diplomatic relations. Reflecting that anxiety, the South tried to scuttle an American plan to send two teams to North Korea to discuss establishing diplomatic liaison offices and dealing with the spent fuel. Seoul insisted that the two teams be combined into one, a proposal designed to derail the liaison office talks since it was unclear whether the spent fuel experts would be allowed to visit North Korea.

Efforts to calm the situation foundered. Foreign Minister Han's moderate views came under strong attack when he suggested that Seoul cared more about the substance of steps to ensure transparency than about "special inspections" per se.[87] A similar statement by Han a year earlier had received little notice. Now only the opposition party applauded. The next day, President Kim and the Blue House publicly disavowed Han's pronouncement and confirmed there had been no change in Seoul's policy.[88] Observing that the two allies might be in for difficult times because of President Kim's focus on domestic politics and the public's hypersensitivity, the U.S. Embassy predicted that Washington's ability to coordinate strategy with Seoul could become more difficult in the face of what appeared to be the South's growing inflexibility.

Washington did its best to try to steer Seoul back on course. President Clinton tactfully congratulated Kim on his August 15 speech. But Winston Lord, the State Department's senior Asia expert, summoned a South Korean Embassy official to object that its aggressive tone toward the North could not have come at a worse time, on the heels of what appeared to be the still fragile compromise in Geneva. The North would view Seoul's harping on nuclear transparency as confirming its worst expectations, that the reactor project was a "horse of Troy" (as Kang had claimed), which Seoul would use for its own political purposes. For good measure, Lord rejected South Korea's proposal to combine the liaison office and spent fuel teams, suggesting that diplomatic relations were not a reward for North Korea. Liaison offices were a means to communicate more directly.

Just as Washington feared, Seoul's pronouncements triggered an escalating, harsh reaction from Pyongyang. Five days after the August 15 speech, the Foreign Ministry blamed Seoul for getting in the way of the Geneva talks.[89] The North then followed up, telling the Americans in the New York channel that the South Korean reactor was unacceptable. An August 27 letter from Kang to Gallucci said it was "inconceivable" that the North would accept Seoul's reactors. A media commentary that same day did not go as far, only falsely claiming that "the issue of South Korean model was never even considered" in Geneva. (Some thought this late, light response suggested that Pyongyang was treading softly to avoid endangering the chance for better relations with the United States.)[90]

To back up its public statements, the North Koreans ostentatiously searched for another reactor. They contacted potential German suppliers. Moscow also still seemed in the running; a high-level Russian official confirmed to the press that Pyongyang had firmly maintained its position of wanting a Russian model reactor.[91] The North Koreans may have been interested in a non-Korean reactor, but they may also have intended to throw Seoul off balance. If that was their objective, they succeeded. Japanese newspapers speculated a German reactor might be a logical alternative, while Seoul's newspapers cited those reports as evidence that Tokyo might withdraw its support from the South Korean model.[92]

The Senior Steering Group on Korea met at the end of August to assess the situation. The U.S. game plan for the weeks before the next Geneva session— to build on the Agreed Statement by putting together an international coalition in support of the South Korean reactor model—now seemed in jeopardy. To recover its footing, the administration intended to use the upcoming expert meetings to reinforce the message that the United States, as guarantor of the new project, saw the South Korean reactors as the only model that was politically, technically, and financially viable. Second, Washington would have to nail down Seoul's commitment to the project in spite of its growing reluctance to allow Washington's talks with Pyongyang to move ahead.

Berlin Kim

Against a background of increasing rancor between the two Koreas, delegations from the United States and North Korea convened in Berlin on September 12 for four days of experts' talks. Berlin seemed an unlikely location; the

North requested the German capital since the national airline, Air Koryo, had a direct connection from Pyongyang and its large mission in Berlin could house the delegation. Of course, Washington suspected an ulterior motive. Sure enough, on the eve of the talks, a North Korean spokesman claimed they were being convened in Berlin to affirm his country's intention to ask for German reactors.[93]

Held in Pyongyang's former East German Embassy, part of which was leased out to a women's health club to help pay expenses, the talks were difficult and unproductive. Gary Samore, a veteran of negotiations with the North in New York and Geneva, headed the U.S. delegation. After a stint at the Lawrence Livermore National Laboratory working on nuclear proliferation, Samore had joined the State Department in 1987, serving on the staff of Ambassador Richard Kennedy, the State Department's point person on nuclear nonproliferation during the presidencies of Ronald Reagan and George H. W. Bush. Samore later went on to serve with Gallucci, before moving to the NSC as Poneman's deputy and then successor. His delegation included other veterans from the Geneva talks and experts on nuclear energy from the Department of Energy.

In contrast, the North Korean delegation included only one junior Foreign Ministry official who had been in Geneva. The rest, mostly technical experts, were new faces. Chief among them was Kim Jong U, the head of the delegation. At age fifty-one, Kim bragged he had reached vice-ministerial rank twelve years earlier. At the Committee for External Economic Affairs, he was one of the spark plugs of North Korea's tentative efforts to open up its economy to the outside world, including the Rajin-Sonbong free-trade zone, which was supposed to draw foreign investment. Outsiders viewed Kim as an intelligent, widely traveled, sophisticated pragmatist. He cut an odd figure; like many North Koreans, he wore platform shoes and dyed his hair jet black, but unlike others sported an ostentatious Rolex watch.[94]

Kim Jong U had a long-standing interest in acquiring light-water reactors for his country. He had negotiated the 1985 reactor contract with the Soviet Union and told the Americans he was in charge of Pyongyang's "Light-Water Reactor Task Force." One remembered that his "personal behavior was so offensive and his demands so outrageous that it was almost comic."[95] Dismissive of the Agreed Statement, Kim had come to Berlin to rewrite that agreement. "Those Foreign Ministry guys," Kim said contemptuously, "didn't know what they were doing."[96]

The battle lines were drawn from the outset. Both Washington and Pyongyang had agreed before Berlin that the agenda would include a briefing by the U.S. Department of Energy on its plan for dealing with the spent fuel. At the first session, Kim refused to listen, but acquiesced when Samore threatened to cancel the talks. As American experts spoke, the North Korean delegation sat silently, not taking notes.

Kim Jong U had his own views on the proposed new reactor project. He declared that Pyongyang would select the reactor; the South Korean model was out of the question as was the Russian reactor, since North Korea now had serious reservations about its safety. He had in mind American reactors—Germany, France, or Japan could provide some of the critical nonnuclear components—and hundreds of kilometers of power lines to connect them to Pyongyang and Hamhung, another North Korean city. According to Kim's estimate, the total cost of the project was a little over $4 billion. The United States would provide financing, but if that was a problem, it should talk to Germany or France. Indeed, according to Kim Jong U, the North Koreans were already having technical discussions with private German firms.

As for the presidential assurance, he seemed to think it was not worth the paper on which it was written. During the first day of talks, a State Department lawyer told the North Koreans that if American companies were to provide technology or equipment for the new reactors, Pyongyang would have to meet its safeguards obligations as well as sign on to an agreement for peaceful nuclear cooperation. He added that Congress could block such an agreement. Asking what good was a presidential assurance if the project would still be subject to these legal constraints, Kim suggested American laws should not apply to North Korea. Samore told him that was unrealistic.

Over the next two days, Kim Jong U added new demands. For example, he wanted the United States to compensate North Korea not only for research and development on its own reactors but also for its existing and partly built reactors as well as those it had planned to build. That would mean billions of dollars in compensation for the seventeen reactors North Korea said it hoped to complete by 2001. Kim suggested the money could be deducted from the new reactor project. Or the United States could provide North Korea with annual heavy fuel oil shipments three times the size of its original request in Geneva.

Early on, the Americans decided not to take Kim seriously. Aside from his substantive flights of fancy, he was irked to be negotiating with Samore, who was younger and not even an economist. In contrast, Kim was civil to David Brown, the white-haired State Department director of Korean affairs who was an economist. Aware that there were different levels of respect in the Korean language, Samore would jokingly ask his interpreter whether his North Korean counterpart was referring to him as a gravedigger or a janitor. In spite of the insults, he decided that the best way to deal with Kim was to be polite. Samore's standard response to unrealistic proposals was that they would have to be referred to Washington, a tactic that infuriated the North Korean more, especially since he claimed to have the authority to make decisions on his own.

Still, the Berlin talks were not a total failure. Samore unveiled that KEDO would be responsible for all financial, technical, and administrative matters related to the reactor project. It would hire an American prime contractor and South Korean subcontractors. Samore emphasized that Seoul's participation would be critical since no other government was willing to commit the funds and other resources to make the project work. The United States would be the leading member of the new organization, but other countries would be invited to join. Surprisingly, Kim thought KEDO was a good idea as long as the United States played the main role.

The session also gave the American delegation a chance to pitch its arguments to the mute but furiously scribbling scribes sitting on either side of Kim, and to cull useful tidbits of information from the North Korean negotiators. At one reception, a North Korean expert told the Americans that Pyongyang wanted 500,000 metric tons of heavy fuel oil to replace supplies it no longer received from Russia. Almost half would be used by a thermal power plant at the eastern port of Sonbong. When asked why North Korea did not want coal, a possibility the United States had raised with China, he replied it was not in short supply and, besides, the North Koreans were unimpressed by inferior-quality Chinese coal.

On the other hand, the U.S. technical experts sometimes strayed into dangerous diplomatic territory. One American from the Department of Energy mistakenly extolled the virtues of a U.S.-designed reactor in a paper given to the North Koreans. The South Koreans, who met with the Americans every evening after the talks, were furious at what they viewed as a move to secure the reactor contract for a U.S. company.[97]

As the Berlin meeting drew to a close, the futility of Kim Jong U's bluster became apparent. U.S.–North Korean meetings had typically produced a final document. At lunch on the second day, Kim gave Samore a detailed draft that recorded U.S. agreement to a number of unreasonable demands, including his reactor proposals. Samore warned Kim that his proposal would be a nonstarter for Washington. He did not say that he would also recommend that it be rejected. Sure enough, the next day Samore received instructions to tell Kim that "it is inappropriate to determine the issues you have raised in your document" until further talks were held in Geneva.

The North Korean was upset but not ready to yield. He proposed a new document outlining areas of agreement and disagreement. Once again, Samore told Kim he needed to consult Washington but did not think his proposal was acceptable. That evening, the two agreed that a short statement might list the topics they had discussed. When Kim tried to include his reactor proposal and compensation as well as characterizing the talks as "serious and constructive," Samore warned him Washington would not accept his proposal. Instead he suggested that the talks be described as "full and frank." Nevertheless, Kim insisted that Samore relay his ideas back to Washington.

Once again, Washington's instructions were exactly what Samore had told Kim they would be. In the end, the North Korean was forced to accept an anodyne statement. The final document, issued on September 15, only mentioned that the two sides had discussed reactors, conventional energy, and spent fuel. The talks had been "full and frank."

The Berlin meeting failed to achieve Washington's most important objective: to move North Korea closer to accepting South Korean reactors. When asked by reporters about those reactors, Kim Jong U replied they were still under development, would not become operational until 1995 in South Korea, and would not even be tested in North Korea until 1998. "The father hasn't even been born; it's a mistake to speculate about the offspring," according to Kim. On the other hand, Seoul's participation in KEDO was fine by him if it would pay for reactors manufactured by the United States, Germany, France, and Japan.[98] That prompted the State Department to warn the Germans and French to cease contacts with the North Koreans unless they were willing to pay for the new reactors, which they were not.

While the meeting created uncertainty about the prospects for the upcoming Geneva talks, Kim Jong U's performance also managed the impressive feat of simultaneously destroying his credibility with the Americans and his fellow North Koreans, who came to dismiss "Berlin Kim" and his strange ways. But he may have correctly calculated that he had little to lose in trying to extract more concessions from the United States. If he succeeded, Berlin Kim would undoubtedly gain favor with his country's leadership and best his Foreign Ministry rivals. Kim Jong U would appear once again after the Agreed Framework was signed in October, this time in a negotiation with Samore on the light-water reactor contract that threatened to bring the two countries back to the brink of war.

Teammates

In spite of the fractious Berlin talks and the escalating inter-Korean rhetoric, South Korean reactors remained at the core of Washington's strategy. Before the last Geneva meeting, the principals had decided that they would need written funding assurances from the trilateral partners before President Clinton could sign a guarantee for the North Koreans. While commitments to cover the total cost would have been nice, the United States was willing to accept assurances that 70 to 80 percent of the money would be available. The feeling was that any shortfall would eventually be made up by Japan and South Korea, which would have already made a substantial commitment, or by other countries. In any case, time was short.[99] Gallucci packed his bags yet again for Seoul and Tokyo.

Seoul's support would make or break the reactor project. In early September, a few weeks before Gallucci left for Asia, Foreign Minister Han Sung Joo came to Washington. His mission was to start negotiating an assurance, to calm fears in the Blue House and the public that the two allies were out of step, and to slow the U.S.–North Korean talks by establishing tighter control over Washington. An American draft of a presidential assurance, presented to Han by Secretary Christopher, made no mention of the Korean model or of the need for nuclear transparency, both key South Korean conditions. The draft also stipulated that Seoul would have to provide funding even if its reactors were not chosen, a reflection of U.S. concerns that financing still would be needed if the deal collapsed because of inter-Korean squabbling. When Han told Gallucci that any assurance would have to be conditioned on the supply of the Korean model and the transparency of the North's nuclear past, the American readily agreed.

Foreign Minister Han had tougher sledding in trying to slow U.S.–North Korean talks. His argument that the two allies should establish a loose "parallelism" between North-South talks and the Geneva negotiations—the administration was moving too quickly with North Korea in view of its escalating attacks on Seoul and the political situation in South Korea—fell on deaf ears. Too many U.S. officials had lived through past attempts at establishing linkage. In a forty-five-minute meeting in the West Wing, Tony Lake used the analogy of riding a bicycle: it would topple unless the United States and South Korea kept pedaling. President Clinton dropped by Lake's office to tell Han: "We need South Korean leadership. It is better to move quickly. Let's keep going."[100]

Talking to the press in the State Department lobby, Han said: "We have confirmed the . . . importance of parallel involvement in North-South relations on the one hand and the U.S.–North Korean dialogue on the other." Standing by his side, Christopher sounded a different note, that Washington's relations with Pyongyang could not "take shape" and the nuclear issue "finally be resolved" without direct dialogue between North and South.[101] In fact, the secretary's effort to tread a fine line satisfied neither Seoul nor Pyongyang. Immediately afterward, Kang sent a sharp letter of protest to Gallucci complaining about reports of linkage. Seoul also was left feeling uneasy about the American position.

In the weeks before Gallucci's trip, there had also been progress with Tokyo. During the August meeting in Geneva, the Foreign Ministry had secured formal approval for providing reactors through an international consortium.[102] Tokyo also threw its support behind the South Korean reactor; the Russian reactor was technically unproven, and Japan believed that throwing in its lot with the South would allow the two of them to form a stronger common front with respect to the United States if necessary. But when Japanese officials visited Seoul to discuss the new reactors, the South Koreans were loath to divulge details of their thinking, perhaps a vestige of historical distrust but also a reflection of the fear that Japan might try to steal the project.

Still, Japan hesitated to provide the necessary reactor assurance on time. A week before Gallucci left for Asia, the visiting Japanese deputy foreign minister warned him that Tokyo might need assurances first from North Korea that it was serious about resolving the nuclear issue. Gallucci told him that he had it wrong, that Washington would first have to demonstrate that it was serious about meeting the North's energy requirements before it could secure such an assurance. To keep the pressure on, he alluded to a growing consensus in Washington that Japan should finance the entire cost of the project remaining after the South Korean contribution.

When Gallucci arrived in Tokyo a week later, the Japanese told him they recognized the need for a significant contribution to the package for North Korea. Vice Minister Kunihiko Saito volunteered that Japan was ready to participate in an international framework "if the safety of the reactors is assured and if the United States is prepared to play a key role." Foreign Minister Kono was even more positive: "We want to be supportive. I will consult the Prime Minister directly. . . . We do not have negotiations, but rather work as teammates." One American recalled, "They could have been using our talking points. I thought to myself: so this is why we have spent hundreds of hours consulting with the Japanese."

The talks did not yield a specific financial commitment, but they did end with an informal understanding that Tokyo would contribute funds covering about 20 percent of the reactor's cost. For good measure, Kono told Gallucci that Prime Minister Tomiichi Murayama was willing to provide a written assurance that Japan would help finance the reactor project and also some funds for nonnuclear energy. In return, Tokyo wanted the North to meet its nonproliferation commitments and to dismantle its existing nuclear program.

Far more difficult was the issue of security assurances. In exchange for giving up its nuclear program, North Korea wanted assurance that the United States would not attack it with nuclear weapons. The Americans were willing to provide such an assurance, as they had earlier done as part of the arrangement to persuade Ukraine to give up the nuclear weapons left on its soil in the aftermath of the breakup of the Soviet Union. But Washington needed to consult Seoul and Tokyo, existing beneficiaries of U.S. security assurances, to avoid any implication that somehow the proposal would dilute the American commitments already in place.

On September 12, the Americans had a surprisingly tough session on this subject with Shunji Yanai, director general of the powerful Foreign Policy Bureau in the Ministry of Foreign Affairs, who laid out Japan's problems. Yanai was concerned that the proposed security assurance for Pyongyang would adversely affect his country's security. Specifically, Tokyo worried that the draft omitted the precondition that North Korea had to be an NPT member "in good standing" and that it would not apply if the assured party attacked another state "with or in alliance with" a nuclear weapon state. These omissions could be construed by Pyongyang to assert legal protection against U.S. nuclear attack, even if it continued to defy the NPT and even if it attacked Japan in alliance with Russia or China.

The Americans were taken aback at how concerned the Japanese were over these highly unlikely events. Gallucci told Yanai that the United States had simply tried to formulate a negative security assurance along the lines of that given to Ukraine and reassured his Japanese hosts that the U.S. security commitment to Japan was unshakable. But the episode underlined the depth of feeling over the importance of the American security commitment to Japan. Under the shelter of the U.S. nuclear umbrella—the ultimate deterrent against any adversary—Japan had emerged from the ashes of destruction in 1945 to grow into the world's second largest economy. Political and constitutional constraints had limited Japan to modest defense expenditures for half a century, but any erosion in the U.S. security commitment could undermine Tokyo's confidence in its own security, potentially sparking political as well as economic instability. In retrospect, the U.S. delegation should have anticipated these concerns.

The situation in Seoul was more delicate. Gallucci landed in a politically charged atmosphere, aggravated by a press leak that the United States had requested South Korean funding no matter whose reactors were built. That made it look as though Washington might use those funds to help build an American model, leaving it open to charges of high-handedness and insensitivity.[103]

Complicating matters further were considerable crosscurrents inside the Kim regime. The government had said publicly that it would not provide aid for the new reactors unless North Korea met several conditions. But it had also moved from the conceptual stage to active planning. The Korean Electric Power Company (KEPCO)—which as Seoul's sole utility company would be in charge of the project—held talks with Combustion Engineering, an American firm that had designed the "Korean standard" reactor and whose participation was essential to the light-water reactor project. One former South Korean official recalled that KEPCO "did not hide its enthusiasm" for reasons of pride and nationalism, not to mention profits.[104]

As always, the key to doing business in Seoul was President Kim. On September 16, Gallucci, Laney, and Poneman traveled to the Blue House. Kim seemed in no hurry to discuss the letter of assurance or to conclude negotiations with the North. "It has been three months and there is still no formal transition to the rule of Kim Jong Il," the president intoned, adding his well-worn bromide, "Time is on our side." Gallucci echoed points made by President Clinton, Lake, and Christopher to Foreign Minister Han the week before: the allies needed to keep the negotiations moving, and insisting on specific linkages was a recipe for stalemate. He assured President Kim that Washington was pressing Pyongyang to engage the South.

This last point elicited the South Korean leader's skepticism. "They have a hundred agreements and abide by none of them," he replied. Moreover, Kim continued to be deeply offended by North Korea's personal "slanders" of him. Gallucci struggled to convince the president: "In one week we are supposed to play the LWR card." He argued that managing the pace of the negotiations was fine to ensure that the allies obtained a good bargain. But Gallucci also warned that excessively mechanical linkages were imprudent and could lead straight back to the Security Council, with all that implied.

Finally, President Kim agreed to send the letter of assurance to President Clinton. But his attitude reinforced a point made by other South Korean officials, that it would be difficult to support the reactor project if Washington moved too quickly to establish diplomatic relations with Pyongyang.

While Gallucci pressed on in his meetings, the main brunt of the work fell on Foreign Minister Han. From his perspective, the project was not only an important tool to improve North-South dialogue, but if Seoul played its cards right, the money would go to its companies. Moreover, with eventual reunification in mind, the tremendous gulf in prosperity between the two Koreas could at least be mitigated through the new reactor project. That could at least dampen the tremendous burden the South would need to bear in absorbing the North, a key concern in light of the recent difficulties that West Germany had suffered in subsidizing the integration of the East into a unified nation. Still, Han met strong resistance from cabinet colleagues, the Blue House, the National Assembly, and the conservative press.[105]

In spite of the charged atmosphere, Gallucci and Han were successful. South Korean drafts of the proposed assurance—much scaled back from the initial American proposal—invariably included chest-thumping rhetoric and gratuitous restatements of long-held conditions for providing the reactors. Gallucci argued for the clearest possible statement of Korean support and the greatest possible financial commitment. To help cope with the sensitive atmosphere in Seoul, the government requested a letter from President Clinton to Kim that would trigger the kind of letter Washington wanted. The Americans agreed; Gallucci handed over the draft Clinton letter to President Kim Young Sam during their meeting.

One final question needed a response: how much money would South Korea provide? The issue was so delicate that it was handled by Han himself, telling Gallucci and Poneman in a private meeting that Seoul would provide the "lion's share" of the financing. Late the next day, the foreign minister gave Ambassador Laney a letter stating that South Korea was willing to finance "around 70 percent" of the work. Han, working with KEPCO, came up with a figure that was large enough to ensure the Korean model was built and small enough to see that most of the contribution went to South Korean companies.

The letter also reflected other South Korean concerns. Financing would be provided only if the reactors were "of the type currently under construction in the Republic of Korea." Support would be provided only if Pyongyang fulfilled its nonproliferation obligations, "including those related to special inspections."

The reaction in Seoul to news of President Kim's pledge was mixed. The government tried to put a positive spin on the press reports, emphasizing that the reactors would only be financed under certain conditions, including that they were the South Korean model.[106] While the opposition party was supportive of the Kim Young Sam government on this issue, the ruling party was critical. Representative Ahn Moo Hyuk, a former NSP director, warned that nuclear transparency was the sine qua non for assistance and that "the South Korean people will never bear a financial burden for decisions made by Pyongyang and Washington without government participation."[107]

All in all, Gallucci's trip had been a success. In a note to Secretary Christopher penned on the long flight home, he labeled Seoul's commitment to provide a specific percentage of the financing as a "new and welcome wrinkle." Prime Minister Murayama's letter pledging to play a role in the reactor project, without specifying a funding percentage, arrived in Washington at the same time as Gallucci did. Although the combination of these two commitments fell short of full funding, it was enough to allow President Clinton to sign the reactor guarantee for the North Koreans.

The South Koreans intended to keep the extent of their financial commitment secret. They had not even told their Japanese "teammate" the exact amount. When Tokyo requested a copy of President Kim's assurance, Seoul instructed its embassy in Washington to issue a modified letter without the "about 70 percent" language. The South's diplomats refused to vary the text of the letter, reasoning that honesty was the best approach if Seoul wanted Japan to make a substantial financial contribution. But the Blue House insisted and the embassy finally did as it was told. By that time, an American official had already informally passed the Japanese a copy of President Kim's complete letter.[108]

10

Progress Usually Comes at the Eleventh Hour

September–October 1994

THE Principals Committee gathered in the White House before the negotiating team's departure for Geneva in late September. Worrisome posturing by the two Koreas colored the atmosphere of the session. South Korean foreign minister Han Sung Joo had come to Washington earlier that month to express his government's continuing concern about the pace of negotiations with the North: it was too fast, with Washington willing to exchange liaison offices with Pyongyang before any comparable progress was made in improving inter-Korean relations. After all, President Kim was being asked to invest in a deal that would address Washington's concerns about the nuclear program but not Seoul's concerns about Pyongyang's hostility. Kim's popularity, as well as domestic support in the South for a deal, could suffer. At the same time, "Berlin Kim" had put on the table new and tougher positions. If this was the beginning of the endgame, it was far from clear how the game would end.

While the principals needed to provide Gallucci with negotiating instructions, the first order of business was to calibrate the U.S. military posture. The push to deploy more forces to Korea had subsided after the June crisis; the existing posture seemed adequate and the North's military deployments routine. But the need to negotiate from strength and to hedge against a breakdown in the talks led the principals to renew efforts to persuade Seoul to accept more counterbattery radar for pinpointing North Korean artillery near the Demilitarized Zone. "If the talks crater in October, we could accelerate deployment," Secretary of Defense William Perry noted. The principals agreed to the proposal and to resume a military buildup if the Geneva talks collapsed.

Gallucci then gave his assessment of the diplomatic situation relating to the unexpected developments in Berlin: "North Korea thought its role was to choose a [reactor] vendor and ours was to write a check." Important differences remained between the U.S. and North Korean positions. One was that Washington wanted the spent fuel shipped out of North Korea and the 5-megawatt reactor not refueled or restarted. The North had taken a small step toward the Americans by agreeing to store the fuel and forgo plutonium separation but refused to ship the fuel out or to freeze the reactor.[1]

The participants considered once again the "no net increase" of plutonium approach, under which North Korea would be allowed either to restart the 5-megawatt reactor or keep the spent fuel in storage, but not both. The North Koreans themselves had offered at one point to sell any extracted plutonium to the Americans. Interestingly, this idea would have resulted in the removal of the weapons-usable material from their clutches. Unfortunately, allowing Pyongyang to reprocess would bring it one step closer to building nuclear weapons and would reduce warning time for those watching the North's bomb program. While the principals remained intrigued, for now the U.S. delegation would keep this possibility under wraps.

The principals also reaffirmed the main provisions of the U.S. negotiating position. Washington would remain flexible on the timing of special inspections, the highest profile issue but the least important in terms of stopping North Korea from producing more weapons. But it would insist that the reprocessing plant and the two large reactors then under construction—capable of producing enough plutonium to build dozens of bombs each year—be shut down and dismantled.[2] Gallucci was authorized to explore the permutations of a comprehensive settlement on these topics. As for Seoul's concern that the administration was rushing the negotiations, particularly the establishment of diplomatic ties with Pyongyang, most agreed that the American track should not slow down but rather the North-South track should speed up.

The twenty-nine days from September 23 to October 21 were marked by intensive negotiation between the Americans and North Koreans in Geneva, consultation and confrontation between Seoul and Washington, and adjustments in both capitals to the course of the negotiations. Ultimately, differences were reconciled and an agreement ending the immediate crisis, the Agreed Framework, would emerge.

If We Wanted to Go to War with You, We Wouldn't Need Any Preparations

On the eve of the Geneva talks, Washington seemed ready for what it hoped would be the last round of negotiations. Once again, unanticipated events threatened to upset those careful preparations. Just before the talks resumed, Admiral Ron Zlatapor, the commander of the U.S. Pacific Fleet, told the military newspaper *Stars and Stripes* that the presence of the aircraft carrier *Kitty Hawk* in Northeast Asia would show North Korea that as in the recent American intervention in Haiti, "strong military power will back up diplomacy."[3] In fact, the *Kitty Hawk*'s patrol was nothing out of the ordinary; it had been scheduled for some time and took place after routine exercises were completed. Admiral Zlatapor's remarks were the result, according to one senior officer, of "some unilateral chest thumping," when "speaking softly and carrying a big stick" would have been better.[4]

When negotiations began thousands of miles away in Geneva, the North Koreans naturally wanted to talk about Admiral Zlatapor's comments first. For Pyongyang, the movement of aircraft carriers was a sensitive topic since they knew that those ships, by virtue of their ability to augment U.S. air power, would play a key role in executing the American war plan. Moreover, the United States had a history of using aircraft carriers to threaten Pyongyang. The same *Kitty Hawk* was moved off the North's shores during the 1976 confrontation following the axe murders of two American soldiers in the DMZ. As one North Korean would later tell the Americans, "We know your ships sail around . . . but you should not say anything about it. It makes our people suspicious, especially the military."

Before the two delegations sat down, it was customary for Gallucci and Kang Sok Ju to have coffee and chat informally, if not entirely comfortably. On this occasion, Kang gave him a "heads up" that he would have to begin his formal remarks by expressing unhappiness with the admiral's comments and the presence of American warships in the East Sea. The Americans would have to understand that it was simply inappropriate for this to be happening during negotiations in Geneva. Ready with a response, Gallucci replied, "North Korea would have to understand that the deployment and the admiral's remarks reflected reality," the tense relationship between Washington and Pyongyang. But the fact that Kang gave Gallucci advanced notice indicated that the North Korean did not want the Zlatopor issue to derail the talks.[5]

Minutes later, the delegations took their seats and the fireworks began. Kang and Gallucci launched into lengthier versions of their private remarks. Kang accused the American negotiator of extending "one hand in friendship while holding a pistol in the other." Gallucci rejected his accusation, asserting that the United States would operate as necessary to defend its security and that of its allies. That said, the word went out from the Pentagon to the Pacific Fleet in Hawaii that everyone was to "shut up."[6]

The North Koreans also seemed to want to put the incident behind them.

Pyongyang's public reaction was threatening but low key. Anger over the *Kitty Hawk* incident continued to pop up in its media, however, and Kang often used the specter of U.S. aggression as a foil. Whenever Gallucci resisted his demands, Kang would blame him for stalling so the United States could get ready for war. At one point, Gallucci looked him in the eye, and said, "If we wanted to go to war with you, we wouldn't need any preparations." Kang seemed at a loss for words.[7]

Aside from the confrontation over the *Kitty Hawk*, the initial session fell into a familiar pattern as the main battle lines were drawn for what could be the final negotiating session between the two sides. Gallucci marched through his presentation first, expressing unhappiness with Berlin Kim's effort to reopen issues the Americans considered settled and to raise new demands. On a more positive note, he reported that the South had agreed to play a central role in the proposed light-water reactor project, but the United States would lead KEDO in deference to North Korean concerns.

As for the panoply of other issues, the United States repeated five demands. First, the North had to freeze its plutonium production program, including the 5-megawatt reactor, once it received President Clinton's assurance. Washington would provide coal or oil to offset electricity that the reactor might have produced. Second, the spent fuel had to be shipped out of North Korea right away. The United States was willing to provide Pyongyang with assistance to achieve that objective. Third, the North had to dismantle all frozen facilities as it converted to the new reactors. Fourth, the North must acknowledge its membership in the Nuclear Non-Proliferation Treaty and implement nuclear safeguards, including special inspections. Washington was flexible on the timing of inspections, but they had to be completed before any new nuclear technology could be provided. Finally, Pyongyang had to improve ties with Seoul and, in particular, implement the Denuclearization Declaration.

Kang's response was entirely predictable. He zeroed in on the American president's assurance, pointing out that it was a "big and bold" concession for North Korea to take those first "concrete" steps in return for only a promise. But Kang would later ask Gallucci if he had the signed presidential letter with him, a sure sign that the North Koreans were hooked. On special inspections, Kang said that it was "inconceivable" to talk about them before trust was built between North Korea and the United States. That would only follow the construction of the new reactors. "Shipping the spent fuel from the research reactor out of the country is unimaginable," according to Kang. As for the 5-megawatt reactor, he boldly asserted that it would have to be restarted in order to give the United States some incentive to complete construction of the new reactors. Finally, Kang called the North-South Denuclearization

Declaration irrelevant in light of these discussions and Seoul's negative actions after the death of Kim Il Sung. Rounding out his presentation, he repeated his old claim that the new reactor project would be a "horse of Troy" if the South played a central role.

On the basis of past experience, the Americans hoped more progress could be made outside of plenary meetings. Over lunch, it was agreed that the separate talks between Tom Hubbard and Kim Gye Gwan that had resulted in the Agreed Statement would resume immediately. But even before those talks began, Kang reversed himself on a key issue. That evening, he told Gallucci that Pyongyang could tolerate South Korea's role in the reactor project if it did not have to deal directly with Seoul and could work with the United States as "chairman of the board of KEDO." While the first day had been long and difficult, Kang's cocktail concession was an important step forward.

The next day—a Saturday—Tom Hubbard and Kim Gye Gwan held the first of what would be many negotiating sessions. Closeted with their small teams, the two spent hours pouring over the longer "Agreed Minute" produced for the August meeting but set aside as too ambitious. They came up with a new joint document that highlighted major differences, cleared away some underbrush, and made progress on some nonnuclear issues. Interestingly, it did not include any of Berlin Kim's demands, which North Korea discarded after the first day of talks.

One immediate result was that North Korea softened its position on requirements for the normalization of relations with the United States. A draft given to the Americans before the meeting had demanded that Washington agree to the "full-scale" reduction by year-end of U.S. economic sanctions in place since the Korean War. Pyongyang had also wanted to establish diplomatic relations at the ambassadorial level "in the near future." Now it was willing to accept more modest steps, in tune with the American position. In the near term, relations would be established through opening liaison offices, a lower form of representation than exchanging ambassadors. As noted, the Americans took the same approach when ties were first restored with the People's Republic of China. Trade barriers only had to be "reduced."

On Monday, the two chief negotiators met again, ostensibly to go over the Hubbard-Kim draft. But Kang laid out a new proposal for a resolution of the nuclear issue, keyed to four stages in the light-water reactor project. The proposal was not entirely a surprise; two days earlier, he told the press that he had the idea of a stage-by-stage freeze. The North's media reported Kang's remarks, signaling that Pyongyang had already approved the new position. He had probably come to Geneva with it in his briefcase.

Kang's plan was a step in the right direction. If the United States would provide the presidential assurance and some form of energy assistance up front, North Korea would freeze the two nuclear reactors under construction, and the spent fuel from the research reactor would be stored under the surveillance of the International Atomic Energy Agency. But Kang continued to insist that the 5-megawatt reactor would be restarted. Moreover, only when the new reactors became operational—perhaps a decade down the road—would the North consider shutting down the operating reactor, rejoining the NPT, shipping the spent fuel to another country, implementing special inspections, and dismantling its nuclear facilities. In short, in spite of the plan's promising elements, Pyongyang would still not take a number of key moves until sometime in the distant future.

"It is absolutely inconceivable" to ship the spent fuel out or implement special inspections before then, Kang asserted. Gallucci countered by suggesting that the United States might be willing to begin shipments of heavy fuel oil immediately to North Korea if it agreed to shut down the 5-megawatt reactor right away. He also resurrected the idea of putting aside explicit mention of the politically charged issue of special inspections in favor of having the North "voluntarily" embrace full transparency. But Kang showed no interest.

Frustrated by Gallucci's response, the North Korean negotiator attempted to force him to choose between uncovering the North's nuclear past or ending its present activities. He had used the same tactic in the summer of 1993. "If the United States is so interested in learning about North Korea's nuclear past, Pyongyang would be happy to take up the matter with the IAEA immediately," Kang offered. The North would provide scientific evidence in support of its declaration on how much plutonium had been produced in the past, disproving the need for special inspections. The kicker was the discussion could take years; in the meantime North Korea's plutonium production would proceed unhindered.

But Kang's effort to whipsaw the Americans failed just as it had failed the previous summer. Instead, Gallucci embraced the idea of beginning immediately to settle the safeguards issue while dismissing any thought that he would accept no limits on the North's present program. The session ended as both sides agreed to meet again the next day after consulting with their superiors at home.

Regrouping that evening, some Americans felt the September 26 meeting may have convinced Kang that the United States would not give up on special inspections. Others saw his staged freeze proposal as significant. Robert Carlin, who had observed the North for two decades, recognized a familiar pattern. By making its proposal, Pyongyang now could move, however grudgingly, toward compromises by tinkering with each stage of the freeze. Still, it would never flaunt flexibility. If anything, fundamental change was often covered in a veil of inconsistency, to keep the negotiating partner and potential opponents back home off balance.[8] The change was not readily apparent that evening, however; the Americans warned the Chinese ambassador in Geneva that the North's new position could destroy any basis for dialogue.

At first, the events of the next day seemed to confirm the view that the negotiations were faltering. Kang picked up that morning where he had left off the previous day, announcing that North Korea would resume its peaceful nuclear activities—a clear reference to restarting the 5-megawatt reactor—and begin a "long and intense" process of convincing the IAEA that special inspections were unnecessary.

Gallucci quickly countered that the talks appeared to have reached a stalemate over special inspections. Recognizing the consequences of leaving Geneva without agreement, he suggested an interim arrangement that would preserve the freeze, allowing the two countries to resume talks in the future. But if the North reloaded the 5-megawatt reactor or began reprocessing, that would spell disaster.

Then, out of the blue, Kang hinted at a major concession. Expressing his "personal view," diplomatic doubletalk for a position that his government had likely already approved, Kang said North Korea would agree to cooperate with the IAEA after a "considerable amount" of the nonessential parts of the new reactors were in place and when essential components were shipped. That was much sooner than his previous position, which had delayed cooperation with the IAEA until after the new reactors were operating. No sooner had he let the cat out of the bag than Kang tried to put it back in. Pyongyang would never allow access to the two suspected sites, but it would provide new information that would help clarify the past. The U.S. delegation left the meeting believing it had reached a deadlock.

Anticipating the next day's session could be the last, the Americans drafted a farewell statement for Gallucci. It expressed a willingness to meet again in the future but warned the North not to do anything, like restarting the 5-megawatt reactor, that would prevent further talks. But the statement was never issued; Washington told the delegation to continue to plug away. If no movement appeared possible in the next few days, Gallucci was instructed to seek agreement that both sides would return to their capitals, reconvening in Geneva the following Wednesday to resume discussions.

On September 28, the Gallucci-Kang session again seemed to produce slow, almost imperceptible forward movement. The sixth day of meetings began with Gallucci hinting that a contract for the new reactors could be signed before the North had complied with its safeguards agreement, a shift from his original position that compliance had to come first. But significant deliveries of a reactor's nuclear components could not be made, for legal and political reasons, before the safeguards issue was resolved.

His North Korean counterpart immediately seized upon the opening, asking if the United States would be willing to deliver "eight out of ten" components for the new project before Pyongyang satisfied the IAEA. Gallucci responded that he could imagine only completing initial construction work on the site, enough to demonstrate the consortium's commitment to the project. Kang said that was far too little; if he agreed to such an arrangement he "would be immediately shot."

As the discussion proceeded, it became clear that two issues had to be resolved in order to reach final agreement. The first was exactly how far construction of the new reactors could go before the North would have to implement IAEA safeguards fully. The second was whether resolution of that issue would require special inspections. Negotiation was possible on the first, according to Gallucci, but Pyongyang would have to accept special inspections and any other measures the IAEA needed to satisfy its concerns about the nuclear past. Kang insisted that such a demand would end any further discussions, but by the end of the session, he agreed to discuss the issue of the two suspected sites with the IAEA.

The two negotiators also touched on other differences; some appeared open to resolution, and others not. The North Koreans remained firm on the need to restart the 5-megawatt reactor and the Americans just as firm that it could not be restarted. But even on that score, pushing the limits of his instructions, Gallucci floated the idea that the spent fuel might be shipped out somewhat later in association with a continued freeze on the reactor. That same day, meeting with the Russian foreign minister in Washington, Secretary Warren Christopher cautioned the press against predicting that the talks would fail, adding, "Progress usually comes at the eleventh hour."[9]

A statement out of Pyongyang, however, dampened the glimmer of hope in Geneva. The North's military, in a rare pronouncement, sharply escalated its rhetoric. It mounted a full frontal assault on the Geneva talks, presenting them in uniformly negative terms. Rather than tiptoe around the inspection issue like the Foreign Ministry, the statement asserted: "Our People's Army, which has the mission of protecting the country's sovereignty, can never allow any attempt to open up military facilities through special inspections."[10]

Although the Western press interpreted the statement as another sign that a negotiated solution was hopeless, it could have been a reflection of leadership differences coming to a head, or North Korea's own brand of "gunboat diplomacy" aimed at forcing a better deal. Just a few days earlier, Secretary

Perry had publicly warned that Washington could destroy North Korea's reprocessing plant if necessary, while Senator Sam Nunn repeated Admiral Zlatapor's caution that the display of American power in Haiti should serve as a good lesson for North Korea.[11]

Uncertain where the talks were heading, Gallucci received Kang at the U.S. Mission the next day. In a tense two-hour meeting, both agreed that there was little more to say without consulting their home capitals. But when Gallucci suggested an adjournment, Kang pointed repeatedly to his problems with the North Korean military. If talks adjourned without agreement, he expected Pyongyang to restart the 5-megawatt reactor and perhaps even to reprocess plutonium from the spent fuel at Yongbyon. Kang asserted that the only possible deal would have North Korea consider demonstrating its nuclear transparency after it had received the majority of the new reactor equipment. There could be no prior commitment to accept special inspections.

Then, as had happened before, after staking out a hard-line position, the North Korean followed with what might be a significant concession. If the Americans accepted the delay and uncertainty on special inspections, Pyongyang might reconsider its previously unalterable position on restarting the 5-megawatt research reactor. He suggested that the two chief negotiators take a few days off while others continued talks to consider how to build on his new idea. Gallucci agreed; though he planned to go back to Washington, Kang would remain in Geneva. On Friday, September 30, after a week of tough sledding, Gallucci left for the United States.

Slightly Good News

Hours after the talks recessed in Geneva, Secretary of State Warren Christopher and South Korean foreign minister Han Sung Joo met privately in New York City. Both were in town for the annual session of the UN General Assembly. Before leaving Seoul for New York, Han had told reporters that "if the current situation continues, the talks will collapse." As Han and Christopher posed together for press photos, Christopher sounded a more hopeful note, cautioning reporters that it was premature to conclude the outlook in Geneva was "bleak" because the third round was "still in an interim stage."

American and Korean officials milled about the South Korean's suite at the Waldorf Astoria Hotel. The star attraction was Tom Hubbard, fresh from Geneva, who was there to give Christopher and Han a firsthand account of the negotiations.[12] Hubbard described the mood in Geneva as much less upbeat than in August, in part because of the *Kitty Hawk* incident, although by the end of the week, the North Koreans seemed more willing to bargain. The good news was that they seemed ready to accept South Korean reactors through KEDO. Aside from convincing Pyongyang to ship out its spent fuel and not to restart the 5-megawatt reactor, the toughest issue remained clearing up uncertainties about the North's nuclear past.

Han reported that the Chinese believed the North was eager for an agreement; its rigidity in Geneva was only a tactic. Under these circumstances, he wondered whether it might not be best to break off talks for several weeks, after which South Korea expected Kim Jong Il would be anointed as the supreme leader. Hubbard effectively quashed the idea by describing Kang's vehement assertion that any suspension in the talks would immediately lead to a decision to reload the reactor and reprocess the spent fuel. Kang had only mentioned Kim Jong Il once recently but frequently referred to the military and its skepticism over talks with Washington. The image of a negotiator under pressure from his hard-liners at home was a natural one for Kang to try to exploit, but it still might have contained an element of truth.

Well aware that there would be an important Principals Committee meeting in a few days, Han wanted to know what the United States planned to do next. Christopher was noncommittal; on the one hand, the United States could show flexibility on issues such as the spent fuel, allowing the North to store it under international surveillance. On the other hand, it was possible that North Korea might soften its position. "Perhaps we should just sit tight and see if the North blinks," he concluded.

"Our feeling back home is that because we have made our going-into-Geneva positions very public, any backsliding would also be quite public," Han cautioned. Christopher agreed there would be a political cost. But Han hastened to add: "There are decisions that are unpopular but reasonable." He hoped the outcome in Geneva would be both reasonable and politically tenable.

Han did not mention that only a few days earlier in Seoul, the National Assembly's Foreign Affairs and National Unification Committee had reaffirmed tough conditions—full disclosure of the nuclear past, restarting North-South talks, and a central South Korean role in the reactor project—for a settlement. The public reaffirmation, endorsed by members from both the ruling and opposition parties, highlighted South Korea's fragile political situation.

On October 3, the principals convened at the White House. In anticipation of what was likely to be a critical meeting, some members of the Deputies Committee also attended in the back row of chairs against the wall of the Situation Room. As usual, the session began with a military update. In spite of the Defense Ministry's threats in opposition to special inspections, Pyongyang's military activities appeared at or below normal levels. While he was satisfied with the preparedness of U.S. forces, General John Shalikashvili remained concerned about Seoul's unwillingness to buy more counterbattery radars to help deal with North Korean artillery. The Pentagon planned to press the South on that and other readiness issues at the upcoming defense ministerial talks.

But the main topic of discussion was Geneva and how to deal with the critical issue of deferring special inspections. Before the collapse of Super Tuesday in March, the principals had agreed not to insist on immediate action regarding special inspections. Now the North's hint that such measures might be implemented at a certain point in the construction of the new reactors crystallized further thinking on the subject. With strong support from Secretary Perry, and on the condition that both Seoul and Tokyo would back such a move, Gallucci was authorized to offer that special inspections could be deferred until just before key nuclear components of the reactor were delivered. Someone suggested that might be five years away.

This was a critical moment in the evolution of the American negotiating position. While U.S. decisionmakers had earlier considered the delay of special inspections, whether any thought that delay would take years remains unclear. Certainly, earlier papers prepared for senior decisionmakers had only viewed the delay in terms of months. The South Koreans had focused on those papers—shared by the administration with their government—and were also thinking in those terms. But as a result of the North Korean proposal, the administration had to address this issue directly. The principals' decision might be important in helping break the deadlock in Geneva—and in securing a freeze on the more important threat of plutonium production—but it was bound to cause problems with South Korea and inadequately prepared American domestic constituencies.

As for other important differences between Washington and Pyongyang, the principals reconsidered permitting the restarting of the 5-megawatt reactor in exchange for simultaneous shipment of the spent fuel out of the country. But some preferred to see a breakdown in the negotiations and a return to the UN Security Council rather than to make the concession of allowing Pyongyang to restart the reactor, even if that persuaded the North to ship out the spent fuel right away. The compromise proposal was shelved: the principals decided that the spent fuel should be placed in canisters immediately, but they were willing to show some flexibility on the timing of shipping it out of the North.

Reflecting uncertainty about how events would unfold once Gallucci returned to Geneva, Ambassador Madeleine Albright was instructed to renew quiet discussions in the Security Council on a sanctions resolution. One participant observed that "sanctions will do damn little," but the consensus was the same as four months earlier. Such a resolution might not stop the North Korean nuclear program but would be an essential move if negotiations failed.

That same day, Secretary Christopher met with China's foreign minister Qian Qichen at Foggy Bottom. The agenda covered a wide range of concerns, from the human rights situation in China to American policy toward Taiwan, with North Korea a top priority. Mindful of the precarious situation in Geneva, Christopher asked Qian to exercise "maximum influence" with North Korea to be flexible in meeting Washington's concerns and to prevent a return to the Security Council. While Qian informed Christopher that the Chinese leaders had told North Korean vice president Li Jong Ok, who recently visited Beijing, that they hoped the Geneva talks would make progress, he seemed content to repeat the standard line. Washington should be patient, and Beijing's influence with North Korea was diminishing.

In fact, the signals from working-level talks in Geneva, which continued while Gallucci was in Washington, had been positive. Gary Samore, fresh from his aggravating experience with Berlin Kim, met with a new counterpart, Li Yong Ho, who had attended the coffee shop meeting in June 1993 that helped secure the suspension of Pyongyang's withdrawal from the NPT. He would later be Samore's counterpart in wrapping up negotiations to supply the new reactors to Pyongyang.

Working in English and trading drafts back and forth, the two focused on identifying what had been agreed so far, what remained to be done, and which issues they could handle at their level, leaving the more important ones for their bosses. Some progress was made; a long discussion produced a 2003 "target date" rather than a "deadline" for the delivery of the first new reactor, after the Americans explained that nine years might not be enough. They also discovered that a prospective pledge that the United States would not attack North Korea with nuclear weapons (the so-called negative security assurance) could be managed at the working level. The key issues of special inspections and the 5-megawatt reactor, however, were left for Gallucci and Kang. Still, one American reported back to Washington, "There are compromises galore floating around."

There were also ample "social occasions" for the two sides to send signals and to probe. At one point, the two delegations talked over coffee for forty-five minutes; at another, they spent two hours eating pizza and drinking beer. The North Koreans asked whether Gallucci would return with more flexibility, prompting the Americans to reply, "If Kang had gone back to Pyongyang would he have returned with more or less flexibility?" The answer was more flexibility, of course. "Then why didn't he go back?" The North Koreans laughed.

On October 4, the day after the principals met, Gallucci flew back to Geneva via New York, where he briefed Foreign Minister Han. Sitting in Han's suite at the hotel, Gallucci explained that the principals were still adamant that the 5-megawatt reactor not be restarted. But they had also decided that the spent fuel did not have to be removed from North Korea immediately and were flexible on the timing of special inspections. When Han asked whether Kang's "80 percent" formulation was acceptable, Gallucci replied that experts would have to look at how much of the plant might be delivered short of key nuclear components. In any case, the United States would need to whittle down North Korea's demands.[13]

An important question remained in both their minds: what would North Korea do next? Han speculated that the North might be trying to squeeze concessions out of the United States. Or they might not have clear instructions if decisionmaking in Pyongyang remained uncertain, a potential cause for concern in the wake of Berlin Kim's performance. Finally, the threat of reloading the 5-megawatt reactor might be real, because of hard-line influence in Pyongyang. While the Chinese thought the North Korean threat was tactical, Han thought it was real. The speculation was interesting but, as always when talking about North Korea's intentions, the meeting ended without any firm conclusion.

The 75 Percent Solution

Arriving at the Geneva airport the next morning, Gallucci told the waiting press that the United States was ready to make a "very serious energetic effort" to reach a negotiated settlement.[14] But back in Washington, Secretary Perry warned, "Talking isn't the same as agreeing."[15] The public impression was the talks were not going well. A few days earlier, the Washington Post had reported senior American officials were "worried that a stalemate . . . could soon propel the two countries towards a more tense relationship."[16] Time magazine was even blunter, observing that Pyongyang's tough-guy attitude and brazen attempts to extract concessions had forced Washington to call for a recess.[17]

The next day—October 6—would prove critical in shaping a diplomatic solution to the nuclear crisis. Kang spoke first; it was impossible to accept the American position that the new reactor project could take place only after safeguards were imposed. The military already believed the project was a trick to get Pyongyang to reveal military sites. But the North Korean negotiator quickly added that he did not agree with that view, implying that there were differences in Pyongyang on this issue, and went on to describe what he called a new position. Kang would be willing to "take all steps necessary to implement

IAEA safeguards" after 70 to 80 percent of the new reactor components had been delivered. If the IAEA still wanted to visit the two suspected sites, the North could "make a decision in that respect."

Gallucci asked a point-blank question: would Pyongyang accept special inspections once 70 percent of the new reactor components had been delivered? "This is a crucial moment for North Korea," Kang observed. He could not say whether access would be granted but suggested that by then Pyongyang would no longer find it "inconvenient."

From the American perspective, establishing the principle that there would be a point in time when the North would accept international inspections was fine, even if it might take longer than Gallucci had initially proposed. But a deal that would require the commitment of billions of dollars would also require more than vague references to "transparency." Speaking bluntly, Gallucci told the North Koreans he needed an absolutely unambiguous commitment to accept safeguards, including special inspections. Otherwise, there was no point in pinning down the exact time at which North Korea would resolve concerns about its past nuclear activities.

Riding back to the U.S. Mission, the American delegation was divided over whether Kang's offer was genuine. Danny Russel, the "South Korean handler," and Bob Carlin were confident of a breakthrough. "Do you realize what just happened? They gave in." But the others were skeptical. They had heard these false starts before. Moreover, all of the Americans suffered from the occupational hazard of tuning out as Kang went on and on in dogmatic Stalinist-style pronouncements. While the debate continued over lunch, the afternoon would provide an opportunity to test whether the offer was serious.[18]

Meetings resumed after lunch. Since the talks had reached a sensitive point, only the two negotiators and their top aides attended the session, held in one of the smaller rooms at the mission. The atmosphere was tense. The sole subject of debate for the next three hours was whether the North would accept special inspections and when that would happen during the construction of the new reactors.

Making it clear that his flexibility on the timing of special inspections depended on the clarity of North Korea's commitment to accept them, Gallucci held out the possibility that clarification could come sometime between the completion of substantial portions of civil construction and the delivery of sensitive nuclear components. Those components were subject to export controls approved by the multilateral Nuclear Suppliers Group and its "trigger list." Under the group's guidelines, the export of these components "triggered" the need for international safeguards. They could not be delivered without them. In addition, some components not controlled by the suppliers group were subject to U.S. export controls. They also could not be delivered unless safeguards were in place. The American concluded that 75 percent of the reactor components could be delivered before North Korea had to comply with its safeguards agreement. That meant a delay of as much as five years in implementing special inspections.

Kang still insisted that he could only accept safeguards after the delivery of the sensitive nuclear components. After some heated discussion and a short break, he backed off. It might be possible to move forward before sensitive nuclear components were received, but Pyongyang would have to get others that were subject to American export controls. On that basis, Gallucci was willing to take another look at exactly what could and could not be provided before safeguards were in place.

While Kang seemed to be gradually giving way, his position on inspections was still not good enough. The United States did not need a specific reference to special inspections, which it understood was a sensitive issue for the North. But it did need an unambiguous commitment to accept whatever measures the IAEA felt were necessary to clarify the past and put safeguards into place. Indeed, Gallucci had already spoken to the agency's director general Hans Blix on this point. Blix preferred not to specify special inspections in the agreement. Instead, he opted for language that left to the agency the decision on what steps the North would have to take in order to come into compliance with its safeguards agreement. This was consistent with the long-standing IAEA position that it is inappropriate for the inspected party to pick and choose what particular measures would or would not be required by the agency in order for the party to fulfill its safeguards obligations.

After more back and forth over assurances on special inspections—Kang was willing to offer a private assurance but not a public one—the North finally yielded. The accord would state that North Korea would come into full compliance with its safeguards obligations, including all steps that may be required by the IAEA, following consultations with the agency to clarify past nuclear activities. Kang would also provide a more explicit private assurance that such steps included allowing the IAEA access to sites and information necessary to resolve questions about the past. Moreover, he agreed not to contradict any public U.S. assertions that the language meant North Korea had accepted special inspections.

Reporting to Washington that night, the U.S. delegation characterized the "ad ref" language as the most clear-cut statement to date of Pyongyang's willingness to accept all steps required by the IAEA, including special inspections. ("Ad ref," short for "ad referendum," described language that was agreed by negotiators, subject to approval by the leadership back home.) Still, the agreement could fall apart if differences over how much of the reactor project should be completed before safeguards were imposed were not resolved.

For Robert Carlin, the State Department's chief North Korea watcher, the signs of capitulation were now obvious. Pyongyang had taken time to edge toward this major concession, perhaps because of continued internal rivalries. The intensity of opposition to this move was reflected in the Defense Ministry statement issued the previous week. It was almost certainly too risky for Kang to go out on a limb and table this proposal on his own authority. The position may have represented a significant assertion of authority by the new leader in Pyongyang over hard-liners who had been applying the brakes to the negotiations.

Having abandoned the core of their negotiating position, there appeared to be little holding the North Koreans back from compromising on other points, including freezing the operation of the 5-megawatt reactor. There had been similar instances in the past, for example, during the brief upswing in relations at the end of 1991 into 1992, when Pyongyang demonstrated surprising flexibility in trying to nudge forward rapprochement with South Korea, Japan, and the United States. What motivated the North Koreans now—a pressing need to focus on economic issues or to demonstrate the success of the new leadership—was unclear. It was useless to speculate. Carlin, an advocate of solving differences between the two countries through diplomacy, predicted that negotiations would not be easy, but they would be successful. North Korea had decided to make a deal with the United States.[19]

None of Us Will Survive This

That evening, Gallucci met with senior South Korean and Japanese diplomats. Both allies had kept close tabs on the talks; the South Koreans sent a special delegation from Seoul while the Japanese used diplomats stationed at their UN mission in Geneva. Consultations had taken place daily.[20]

All business, Gallucci focused on the North Korean concession that would allow access to the two suspect sites, the issue that had started the nuclear crisis in the first place. The proposed trade-off would be on the timing of that access; it would come at some as yet to be precisely determined point in the delivery of the first reactor. As he had done many times before, Gallucci asked for a quick response from Seoul and Tokyo, this time on the new formula that was beginning to take shape in the talks with the North Koreans.

For the South Koreans, the turn of events posed a serious dilemma. Composed of professional diplomats, some of the best and the brightest in their Foreign Ministry, the delegation was in a tough spot. That summer, it had worked closely with the Americans. But there had been clashes. After Kim Il Sung's death, for example, the South Koreans, acting on instructions from Seoul, urged Gallucci not to visit the North's mission to deliver condolences. He went anyway, believing it essential to the atmosphere of negotiation. Now an even more serious confrontation was looming.[21]

No one was in a more difficult position than Jang Jai Ryong. A slight, courtly career diplomat who was the head of the Bureau for North American Affairs in the Foreign Ministry, Jang was also the chief of the South Korean delegation in Geneva. Foreign Minister Han had entrusted him with many important missions in the past, including discreet contacts with the Americans. The soft-spoken professional had replaced the South Korean "nuclear ambassador" Kim Sam Hoon, who had been removed earlier that summer because of his gruff attitude toward the relentless hordes of South Korean newspapermen covering the talks. Ambassador Kim had also lost credibility with the Americans; his stock had gone downhill since the contentious Kim-Clinton summit he had helped arrange.[22]

Jang had achieved better relations with both the press and the Americans. But he also had to deal with the Blue House. President Kim had told Jang's predecessor that South Korea must be firm on principle but flexible on tactics, a bromide that was unclear except to the professional diplomats who understood that their leader was not flexible on special inspections. Some also understood that the American position was moving in a different direction even before Gallucci's briefing. But given the prevailing atmosphere in Seoul, they decided simply to report the facts rather than their own interpretations.[23]

The morning after the October 6 briefing, it was clear something was wrong; Jang asked Gallucci to call Foreign Minister Han immediately. The American negotiator and South Korean academic-turned-minister had worked together closely over the past year and had built up a healthy respect for each other. Han and other South Koreans had even given Gallucci an endearing nickname, "the Italian soldier." Their positive relationship made the conversation that followed even more difficult.

"None of us will survive this," Han warned. He told Gallucci that postponing resolution of North Korea's nuclear past for five years after providing Pyongyang with billions of dollars in construction and equipment for the new reactors would be a political disaster for the South Korean government. The National Assembly would not support financing the new reactor project, and the foreign minister doubted the IAEA would go along. Underlining his strong dissent, Han also questioned whether the deal violated the public and private U.S.–South Korean commitment to a "broad and thorough" settlement of the nuclear issue.

Gallucci urged Han not to focus solely on the timing of special inspections but to take into account the whole package that North Korea now seemed ready to accept. First, Pyongyang had agreed to full IAEA access to the two suspect sites. Second, all of North Korea's nuclear activities would be frozen, including construction work on the reprocessing facility and two more reactors. Third, the entire nuclear program would be dismantled after the question of past nuclear activity was resolved. Finally, IAEA acceptance was not in question since Director General Blix had been supportive.

The American negotiator reminded Han that the two countries had agreed before to be flexible on the timing of special inspections. The more urgent problem was stopping North Korea from churning out plutonium for a growing nuclear weapons stockpile. The foreign minister responded that he had anticipated a postponement of only one or two years. "Five years and 75 percent of the investment in the first reactor was simply too much." The conversation ended with Gallucci asking him to consider the settlement as a whole and predicting that flexibility on the timing of inspections would be critical if Washington and Seoul wanted to bring the negotiations to a successful conclusion.

In contrast to the South Koreans, the Japanese were reserved but supportive. After the briefing the night before, Ambassador Kojiro Takano, the head of Japan's mission in Geneva, had immediately asked Tokyo for instructions and received a response the next day. Meeting with Gallucci, Takano noted, with typical Japanese tact, that the arrangement put off implementation of safeguards "a little too long" but the formulation was acceptable since critical reactor components would be held hostage to resolution of the safeguards issue. Nevertheless, the North's commitment to accept special inspections had to be as clear as possible. The proposed language, which was still somewhat vague, would be sufficient as long as North Korea did not contradict any public assertions that it had accepted special inspections.

With Japanese support secured, the rest of the day was spent consulting with the South Koreans while treading water with the North Koreans. That evening, after telling Jang he took Foreign Minister Han's message "very seriously," Gallucci gave him a copy of the draft language on the timing of inspections he intended to pass to Kang the next day. Stressing that the language was ad ref, Gallucci cautioned Jang that unless Seoul had suggestions, he could see no other way to get the North to acquiesce to international safeguards.

In addition to the language already accepted by the North, a new sentence would be added, specifying exactly when Pyongyang would have to come into full compliance. That point in time was when a significant portion of the new reactor project was completed, but before the delivery of components controlled by the Nuclear Suppliers Group guidelines. The significant portion would be defined in a confidential minute. Ending the session, Gallucci urged the South Koreans to consider the formula in the context of the overall settlement on the nuclear issue.

Sandwiched between meetings with the South Koreans, a brief session with the North Koreans reaffirmed that an orderly fallback was under way in Pyongyang. While Gallucci emphasized that there could be no deal if North Korea restarted its reactor, Kang delivered another concession, this time on monitoring of the reprocessing facility once it was frozen. At first, the North Koreans had insisted that the IAEA would only be allowed to check the seals on the doors to the facility. The United States, on the other hand, wanted the agency to have a free hand, occasionally going inside. After hinting at some flexibility on October 6, the North now said it would accept whatever access the agency needed. Moreover, Kang ended the session by promising to consider American positions across the board once agreement was reached on the timing of safeguards. The Americans knew that depended on resolving differences with Seoul, differences that were about to become public, plunging the bilateral relationship into crisis.

A Half-Baked Compromise

Since the death of Kim Il Sung, President Kim Young Sam had been warning the Americans not to move too quickly in reaching an agreement with Pyongyang. As tension between the two allies increased all summer, some worried that Kim would go off on a tangent just as he had during the Washington summit in November 1993. Nevertheless, Seoul had managed to pledge its support for the new reactors, albeit conditioned on the full and immediate transparency of Pyongyang's nuclear past.

At the same time, the South Korean president continued to harbor serious concerns. Kim Jong Il had not taken over his father's positions and had disappeared from public view since July 20, only to resurface in mid-October. North Korean leaders at one point even asked the people to pray for his good health, prompting speculation that it was anything but good.[24] That only reinforced President Kim's inclination not to rush into any deals.

The South Korean leader also doubted the Americans' ability to handle Pyongyang, and his willingness to "borrow the brains of others," well informed or not, only made matters worse. In early September, a clergyman told Kim that he had met the U.S. delegation to the liaison office talks in the Beijing airport on its way to Pyongyang and none of them knew anything about North Korea. (In fact, Lynn Turk, the head of the team, was an old Korea hand who contributed insightful analysis of the crisis to U.S. decisionmakers.) Kim also readily believed the same minister when he said he knew the Great Leader well and that North Korea was about to collapse. As a result, the president's advisers had to spend a great deal of time and energy keeping him on course, not always successfully.

The supercharged political atmosphere in Seoul reinforced the president's doubts. Aside from the swirling debate over the nuclear crisis, his archrival Kim Dae Jung was actively promoting the need for greater North-South dialogue and courting politicians in the ruling party, preparing for the 1995 local elections. The result was an equal and opposite reaction on the part of President Kim.[25]

Once he learned about the developments in Geneva, the president boiled over. On Saturday, October 8, the *New York Times* ran an interview with him under the eye-catching headline "South Korean President Lashes Out at U.S." Kim had apparently granted the hour-long interview soon after receiving a briefing on events in Geneva. In the past, he had unwisely given interviews to the media after receiving bad news, always with embarrassing results. This occasion proved no exception.

President Kim took the opportunity to express his views on the ignorance, naïveté, and penchant for concession of the Americans. It was time for toughness, not compromise, with a North Korea so close to total economic collapse. Repeating a refrain that had been ringing in American ears for months, Kim proclaimed, "We should not make any concessions in the future. . . . Time is on our side." Another complaint was Washington's failure to draw on the South's experience in dealing with North Korea: "The problem is we think we know North Korea better than anyone. They are not sincere." Skeptical that anything useful would come from the talks, he concluded: "If the United States wants to settle with a half-baked compromise and the media wants to describe it as a good agreement, they can, but I think it will bring more danger and peril." The whole interview was particularly jarring since in a luncheon "bull session" with the press that same day, Kim had referred to "firm cooperation" with Washington on the nuclear issue.[26] Seoul's unhappiness was duly relayed through diplomatic channels.

At the heart of the matter were three problems, in President Kim's eyes. First, the prospective deal with the North would require South Korea to pay for substantial construction on the nuclear power reactor project before achieving "transparency." The South's concessions would have to be made now by President Kim, while the North's would only come years later and benefit his successor. The American argument, that the threat to security coming from the North's nuclear weapons program would be neutralized, lacked political salience in Seoul. Second, President Kim's worst nightmare appeared to be coming true. In spite of his repeated warnings, his closest ally seemed bent on improving ties with North Korea, including establishing diplomatic relations, regardless of how Pyongyang treated Seoul. Third, the South Korean leader's continued counsel for patience, based on his assessment that North Korea was about to collapse, was being ignored

Yet as so often happened in the past, President Kim realized almost immediately that he had made a serious mistake. He was nothing if not a realistic politician. Worried about the subsequent headlines, the president called Foreign Minister Han, who happened to be on his way to a gathering of foreign ambassadors outside of Seoul, to find out the exact English wording of the article. Scheduled to sing and play the harmonica for the foreign ambassadors, Han instead left for Seoul early the next day.[27]

The Americans did not take long to react. An unhappy Warren Christopher telephoned Foreign Minister Han from England where it was 2:00 AM. Evidently, he had been awakened by a call from an angry Bill Clinton. In addition, Tony Lake spoke to South Korea's national security adviser, Chung Chong Wook, bluntly expressing his unhappiness about "the naïve and half-baked" attack on President Clinton. Lake added that if Seoul insisted on sitting back and waiting for concessions from the North, it risked being blamed for any failure in the talks. South Korea now needed to make clear publicly that it still supported negotiations. Chung replied that the president's remarks reflected genuine concerns in Seoul, but he understood the need for "fence-mending."

In Geneva, Gallucci learned about President Kim's remarks as he and the other Americans were having breakfast in a small restaurant in the basement of their hotel. They were interrupted by a long-distance phone call from Ambassador James Laney who read the interview to Gallucci. The other Americans watched their boss's face slowly turn red.[28]

Han himself called Gallucci, their second tough conversation in as many days. Initially, the focus was on the provision of significant reactor components before special inspections, which Han called a virtual "Maginot Line" for South Korea. He asked Gallucci not to turn over to the North a list of those components and suggested that any list should not include a major conventional power station component, the turbine generator. Coming as close to an ultimatum as an ally could, the foreign minister warned that if the United States went ahead anyway, it would "have to count South Korea out." If there was a silver lining in what he said, it was the implication that Seoul was now trying to figure out what could be delivered before inspections. Pressed by Gallucci, Han conceded that it might be possible to change the minds of his colleagues if the Americans were able to negotiate a satisfactory resolution of the other pending issues.

The discussion of substance was difficult enough, but the conversation also marked the first time the two had spoken since President Kim's interview. The soft-spoken foreign minister tried to preempt the inevitable American reaction, saying the interview was unfortunate. But Gallucci told Han that Kim's remarks were an unacceptable public expression of mistrust of President Clinton and an attack on his negotiator. He promised to report Han's message to Washington but declined to say how he would proceed in the afternoon meeting with Kang. There had been other tense exchanges between the two men, and there would be at least one more. None, however, tested the close working relationship they shared more than this one.

Ironically, there was a chance that problems with Seoul might actually benefit the Americans. While some were concerned about how it would affect the alliance, others felt that the South Koreans had, in the words of one American, "cut their own throats." Washington could use Kim's interview to step up pressure on Seoul.[29]

The sudden difficulties with South Korea also seemed to work to the American's advantage in talks with the North Koreans. Responding to the Blue House's heartburn, they decided only to tell Kang that the details regarding the delivery of components and the timing of inspections would have to wait until the shape of the final settlement became clear. When Gallucci followed that script in the afternoon, a disappointed Kang hinted at another major concession. If the United States agreed that reconciliation of the past would be necessary only after a significant portion of the first reactor was delivered, Pyongyang would forgo refueling and restarting the 5-megawatt reactor.

But Kang also sought to turn President Kim's October 8 interview into another argument in support of his pitch on the timing of special inspections. He raised the "horse of Troy" analogy again, even relating that his foreign minister had called to complain that the South wanted the talks to fail. The implication was plain. Now more than ever, the North needed to receive a substantial portion of the reactor project before satisfying the IAEA, lest the South pull the plug on it for political or other reasons.

That evening, the American delegation recommended, and Washington approved, a package to break the back of the remaining differences. Noting that the proposal would be "politically difficult for the Republic of Korea to swallow," the delegation argued that the deal shaping up was in the national security interests of the United States and its allies. In consideration of Seoul's position, the Americans would not include turbine generators in the list of components to be delivered before special inspections. But they would revisit that issue if necessary.

The delegation also planned to press ahead on other remaining issues: permanently freezing and dismantling the 5-megawatt reactor, shipping out the spent fuel at the earliest possible moment, securing a concrete commitment to dismantle all of North Korea's gas-graphite nuclear facilities, and agreeing to implement the North-South Denuclearization Declaration. Progress on all of those fronts might cushion the blow in Seoul of the proposed delay in special inspections.

Over the next two days—October 10 and 11—the two delegations spent fifteen hours in seemingly endless meetings. In spite of Seoul's objections, Gallucci put on the table the U.S. proposal for how much of the reactor project would be delivered before IAEA safeguards were in place. As expected, Kang balked, arguing that the turbines and other nonnuclear components had to be included. He also sweetened the pot, offering to freeze the 5-megawatt reactor and provide Washington with a written commitment that safeguards—including special inspections—would be implemented once a significant portion of the reactors had been delivered. Continuing to use Seoul's intransigence to his advantage, Gallucci still argued that he could not include the nonnuclear components until all other outstanding issues were resolved.

The talks produced important progress on two of those issues. Dealing with North Korea's spent fuel had been an important American priority for months. The North Koreans had initially insisted they could never ship it out of the country, the Americans that it had to be shipped out right away. Then the North Koreans conceded that the fuel would not be reprocessed and could be placed in interim storage, implying that shipment out of the country would take place at some point. American flexibility was encouraged further when Pyongyang agreed not to restart the 5-megawatt reactor, and not to produce additional spent fuel containing more plutonium. The solution, agreed to by Gallucci and Kang, after two days of haggling, was to begin shipment out of the country when the delivery of key components for the first reactor began and to finish when the reactor was completed.

On the second issue—dismantlement of North Korea's nuclear facilities— the North Koreans passionately rejected the American view that they should proceed in parallel with the construction of the new reactors. The argument heated up as Gallucci insisted that it was unacceptable for the North to retain its existing program while the new one reached completion. Kang, on the other hand, argued that the existing facilities needed to be retained as insurance in case the new project was never finished. But he gradually gave ground. By the end of October 11, the two negotiators reached agreement that dismantlement would begin when the first reactor was completed and finished when the second came on line.

The two days of negotiations, while producing more progress, had proved grueling and frustrating for both sides, though occasionally relieved by humor. At one point, Kang resurrected the idea that one of the two new reactors should be provided by a country other than South Korea. Gallucci dismissed the proposal but suggested Pyongyang could find an alternate supplier for a third reactor. The North Koreans, by now familiar with Gallucci's brand of humor, broke out in laughter at this suggestion.[30]

On October 12, Ho Jong—late of the North's mission to the United Nations and now a key member of its delegation—told reporters that the negotiations had achieved "in some parts a little progress." The Americans realized, however, that, despite the progress in Geneva, the road to an agreement led through Seoul.[31]

I'll Be a Statesman

With the exception of left-wing journals, South Koreans supported President Kim's tough position in the New York Times interview. While this reaffirmation appealed to the politician in Kim at a time when he had been under intense criticism for his policies, his government faced the specter of a major confrontation with its closest ally. Consequently, South Korea began a slow retreat. The Blue House trotted out the usual excuse when President Kim strayed; his remarks were supposed to be off the record. One official admitted that the New York Times story was embarrassing but asserted that other negative comments had been reported out of context. While admitting that Kim's views accurately reflected concerns about the negotiations, members of the ruling party told the U.S. Embassy that there was broader support among the public for the American position than the media's reaction had indicated.

After a weekend of constant consultation, Foreign Minister Han agreed that Jim Laney should speak directly with the president. Late in the afternoon of October 12, the ambassador arrived at the back gate of the presidential compound. At the request of the government, Laney had taken to slipping unnoticed into the Blue House to keep his visits beyond the prying eyes of the press. His objective was to secure Kim's support for the U.S. position in Geneva.[32]

The meeting was difficult. Both men were concerned about the possible deterioration of relations between the two allies. Laney spent most of the ninety-minute session reassuring Kim of the American commitment to South Korea. The gently persuasive former president of Emory University pointed out the tough steps taken by Washington over the past year to modernize its military forces in the South. He observed that those moves reduced the likelihood of North Korean adventurism and were a clear signal that the United States had no intention of betraying South Korea at the DMZ or, pointedly, in Geneva.

President Kim, despite acknowledging shared goals with President Clinton, focused on domestic politics. There were specific promises made to the people from which he could not retreat. As a result, it would be difficult, perhaps impossible, for him to agree to what was being proposed at Geneva. Ending the session, Laney could only express confidence in Kim's ability as a leader and statesman to do what was necessary for his country. There was clearly a gap in perspectives.

The American ambassador continued the diplomatic push. Following his meeting with President Kim, he had dinner with Foreign Minister Han, and the two spent much of the night on the telephone. Han carried on a continuing dialogue with the president to convince him of the need to support the agreement. By the next day, President Kim, in the words of his foreign minister, was ready to "do the right thing" although it would be politically costly. Han predicted he would lose his job in the ensuing furor. The foreign minister was right on both counts.

Early the next morning, the South Korean leader finally gave in. According to Han, the president was "prepared to be a statesman" and would support the Geneva accord. But he had one condition, a phone call from President Clinton that Kim would rely on to defend his last-minute change in policy.

Following up quickly on the breakthrough, Secretary Christopher called Han from Jerusalem for a ten-minute phone chat. That gave the foreign minister an opportunity to emphasize the importance of the two countries standing together and to press for a phone conversation between the two presidents before any agreement was announced in Geneva. Han also made it clear that there should be no eleventh-hour concessions that would make the deal unacceptable to the Korean people. Christopher reassured him, adding that both now had the challenge of selling the agreement to a skeptical public.

That same day, President Clinton called the South Korean leader. Well aware of Clinton's anger, Kim came on the line with a disingenuous opening that seemed designed to be disarming: "I am very delighted to listen to you!" Right off the bat, Clinton focused on the *Times* debacle. "I'm glad we can put that unfortunate incident behind us," he told Kim. But he also added that the two countries should resolve their differences in private and not let anything divide them. The reproach was implicit in the president's comments.

Clinton laid out the case for moving forward. The American negotiators had done everything possible to keep South Korea informed and to reflect its views. Now that they were close to a deal that would dismantle the North's nuclear program, it was crucial that allied solidarity be maintained. Clinton observed that the draft Geneva accord was firm in upholding the principles that the two allies had embraced and flexible in the timing of specific elements of the agreement while providing an opportunity to ensure compliance at each stage of the game. He concluded by offering to send Secretary of Defense Perry and Gallucci to Seoul to consult on any agreement reached in Geneva.

Fresh out of excuses, President Kim volunteered that the *New York Times* interview was an "indirect conversation" and suggested that Clinton look at his more recent, positive CNN interview. The South Korean leader then returned to his favorite refrain: how could he deal with his critics if the Geneva agreement failed to provide for transparency and North-South dialogue? President Clinton said that he had critics also but then went on to review the virtues of the Geneva accord that was being negotiated.

Observing that "it is important to calm public opinion," Kim pressed Clinton to give a press conference that would show America's commitment to its alliance with South Korea, after which he would follow with his own. After all, "press support was very critical." The upcoming visit by Secretary of Defense Perry would also be helpful. It was important for both Clinton and Perry to reaffirm American support for the alliance.

While President Kim seemed to be on board, he still expressed misgivings. The South Korean leader was unclear about his own role in selling the Geneva accord, saying that after his deputy prime minister talked to the press, he would decide when to talk to the public. "I don't believe North Korea will carry out the Agreed Framework," Kim added. "I would not trust them despite the agreement."

But the roller-coaster ride was not over yet. Just as South Korea had quickly reversed itself and closed ranks with the United States on the emerging Geneva accord, though making it clear that the Americans should not negotiate any last-minute compromises, the ground shifted again. A conservative member of the ruling party leaked the contents of the draft accord to the press. His purpose was to discredit the negotiations and to drive a wedge between the two allies.

Foreign Minister Han called Jim Laney and Gallucci again to tell them that the United States should now quickly finish the Geneva accord because of the leak rather than wait for any further consultations. Han expected more leaks concerning negative aspects of the deal, which would provide ammunition for hard-liners and make it harder for President Kim to defend it. He predicted that President Kim would be under increasing pressure to demonstrate that Seoul was a full partner in the negotiations by insisting on changes that would force the Americans back to the negotiating table. Frustrated by the South's behavior, some Americans interpreted Han Sung Joo's admonition as a signal that his president wanted to distance himself from the Geneva deal, using the excuse that it had been presented as a fait accompli. But that cynical view evaporated as Seoul began to defend the emerging accord.[33]

In fact, the Americans were poised for the endgame. The evening of October 14, the U.S. delegation warned Washington that they would reach closure on a deal with the North Koreans soon. Decisions had to be made on how quickly to wrap up the negotiations. One option—to approve the agreement quickly, as Seoul had requested—might not leave much time for consultations with Congress but would minimize the risk that either side would return to the table and reopen the text. A more deliberative approach would be to initial the ad ref text, adjourn for consultations at home, and then return to Geneva to sign the agreement. That might allow more time for consultations but would also give Seoul or Pyongyang a chance to reopen the text. In the end, the Americans decided on the first approach because of concerns over backsliding in Seoul. In retrospect, that decision may have been unwise in light of the criticism leveled at the administration from the Republican-dominated Congress elected a month later, including the charge that the Framework had been sprung on Capitol Hill without adequate consultation.

On October 15, a tumultuous week after President Kim's interview with the *New York Times*, South Korea publicly signaled its acceptance of the imminent agreement in a public statement by Deputy Prime Minister Lee Hong Koo, a leading moderate. But the support appeared lukewarm, clearly reflecting Seoul's ambivalence. At a secret meeting between government ministers and key members of the ruling party, the tide was turned in favor of the accord only when moderates, such as the chairman of the Foreign Affairs Committee, Rha Woong Bae, highlighted the positive aspects of the agreement.[34] Even after the government signaled its approval, the public sniping continued. One legislator called the Geneva accord "tantamount to giving up."

While differences seemed to be papered over, the dispute had seriously undermined trust between the Clinton administration and President Kim Young Sam's government. That problem would rear its ugly head repeatedly in the future during the struggle to implement the Framework, leading in the spring of 1995 to another serious crisis in U.S.–South Korean relations. Further complicating matters, in the wake of the dispute over the timing of special inspections, the statement of support by Deputy Prime Minister Lee argued that the accord would improve the atmosphere for inter-Korean relations. That issue, which had caused so many headaches in the past, was about to provide the final test for the United States and South Korea in ending the nuclear crisis.

Not the Last Act of This Play

As Seoul and Washington were inching toward the endgame, the American delegation was still trying to produce an agreement with the North Koreans. A grueling thirteen hours of talks on October 13 and 14, led by Tom Hubbard and Kim Gye Gwan, resolved many of the remaining textual problems as the North Koreans were more accommodating than at any point in the past. Following the second day of talks, the delegation notified Washington that it expected an agreement soon, prompting Assistant Secretary of State Winston Lord to announce: "We believe we're on the edge of a possibly major agreement."[35] Gallucci was concerned when he heard the public prediction in light of the North's penchant for eleventh-hour antics.

His fears proved well founded. The next day began on a positive note as the two sides quickly wrapped up some of their remaining differences. Gallucci and Kang agreed that Pyongyang would be provided with turbine generators before safeguards inspection issues were resolved. But they did so only after more concessions were wrung from Kang, including a ban on new graphite-moderated facilities. It made little sense to freeze and dismantle existing facilities unless Pyongyang was prohibited from building new ones. Even more significant, the North Koreans finally agreed to end operation of their 5-megawatt reactor, a key American demand since July.

That, in turn, opened the way for resolving the dispute over the provision of alternate energy. Initially, the North Koreans had repeated Berlin Kim's demand for 1.8 million tons of oil annually, beginning simultaneously with the freeze, but they quickly fell back. Washington had held out the notion of providing some energy immediately—coal or oil—but only if the North agreed to freeze the 5-megawatt reactor. Moreover, Washington wanted the Paris-based International Energy Agency to conduct a survey in the North to make sure the assistance was well used, a demand that was rejected because of suspicions of spying. In the end, when Pyongyang agreed to freeze the 5-megawatt reactor, Washington agreed to provide oil immediately. After consulting the Department of Energy, the delegation decided to meet Kang's August request for annual deliveries of 500,000 tons.[36]

As was so often the case, having solved one problem, the delegation found another had moved front and center. This time the issue was whether to include language in the accord committing Pyongyang and Seoul to resume dialogue. Critical to alliance relations and a constant sticking point since the crisis began in 1993, the issue of North-South dialogue had resulted in the collapse of Super Tuesday and brought the United States and North Korea close to armed hostilities. The prospect of an inter-Korean summit seemed to have solved the problem. But with Kim Il Sung's death, the bickering quickly reemerged.

Anxious to break the deadlock, in late September President Kim Young Sam extended an invitation to Jimmy Carter to visit Seoul to see if he could jump-start inter-Korean relations. In a curious role reversal, Kim now actively courted Carter while the North Koreans seemed wary, telling the former president that he would be welcome to visit Pyongyang again at an "appropriate time."[37] Their failure to provide Carter with an ironclad guarantee that he would see Kim Jong Il was, in part, the reason that the Georgian informed the White House in early October that he would not be going to North Korea. Nevertheless, the State Department had no doubt that Carter would change his mind if the U.S.–North Korean negotiations broke down.

The issue of inter-Korean relations had periodically popped up in the talks themselves. Initially, Washington had insisted that the North Koreans restart dialogue with the South on implementation of the Denuclearization Declaration within three months but gradually scaled back this demand. The North Koreans seemed willing to implement the declaration without any language on timing. But they were adamant about not accepting language that would commit them to resume inter-Korean dialogue. One North Korean explained that aside from the usual complaints about Seoul's behavior after Kim Il Sung's death, reengagement would have to wait until the North could balance the South's diplomatic successes, normalization of relations with Beijing and Moscow, with its own. That could only be accomplished through an improved relationship with the United States.

Certainly, Seoul had made its views well known. The day before the October 15 meeting, President Kim told Clinton that the emerging accord should mention inter-Korean dialogue. To reinforce his message, the South Koreans in Geneva warned the Americans of the absolute need for language on inter-Korean dialogue in order for Seoul to support the agreement. Foreign Minister Han would also call Gallucci as the haggling over North-South dialogue unfolded to emphasize the same point.

When the issue moved front and center on October 15, the Americans were ready. The two sides quickly agreed that North Korea "will consistently take steps to implement" the Denuclearization Declaration. But Kang asserted that meeting the U.S. demand that North Korea take steps "at an early date" to resume dialogue was "inconceivable." When Gallucci insisted that such a commitment was essential, an infuriated Kang announced the topic was closed. He never wanted to hear the words "inter-Korean dialogue" spoken again. After this warning was translated with appropriate feeling, there was silence for a few moments, only to be broken by Gallucci's reply: the subject of North-South dialogue could not be closed, and there was every reason to refer to it in the agreement.

The American interpreter hesitated before translating the offending language, but once he was done, Kang quickly rose to his feet. With some flair, he slammed his briefing book shut and looked around at his colleagues. Quickly picking up on his signal, the other thirteen North Koreans followed his example. They were all standing, glaring at the seated Americans who stared back, not quite sure what to do next. Some began to close their books, but Gallucci indicated that they should all stay in their places. He opened a bottle of water, poured a glass, and waited for Kang's next move.[38]

It was a tense moment, but not without humor. Kang could not walk out of a meeting he was hosting. Where would he go? How could he abandon his own mission to the Americans? Kang continued to stand until his anger subsided and his predicament sank in. Eventually, he sat down and opened his briefing book. His delegation followed suit. While a few meaningless exchanges followed, the session ended with Kang and Gallucci agreeing to meet alone later that day to discuss what to do next.

The American delegation already knew what to do next. The following day, a Sunday, would be the last opportunity for reaching agreement. Absent success, they would call for a break in the negotiations so both sides could return home to consult their governments. This was a tactic that had worked before; confronted with the prospect of the Americans leaving Geneva, Kang frequently backed down. But if the North Koreans were serious this time—and that was always possible—they hoped the rest of the Framework would be preserved in the meantime. The Americans returned to the U.S. Mission and took advantage of the fall day to play softball and touch football on the lawn.[39]

Late that afternoon, the U.S. team was invited back to the North Korean mission to celebrate the successful conclusion of the negotiations. This was a stunning and confusing message; earlier in the day, most thought they were at an impasse that might not be bridged. A few thought that this represented the final concession in what had been a number of conciliatory moves over the preceding days as the North drove toward a much-needed agreement. In any event, all hurried back to the hotel to get ready for the unusual evening session.

The U.S. delegation arrived at the North Korean Mission to find the gates open, a mob of reporters in the courtyard, a red carpet rolled down the steps, and all their counterparts outside to greet them with smiles and enthusiasm. The contrast with the earlier somber mood was striking. Once inside, the Americans found large bouquets of flowers everywhere and champagne in buckets, being readied for celebratory toasts. While the two delegations mixed, chatting over cookies and tea before sitting down for the formal meeting, nothing of substance was exchanged. The Americans were not quite sure how they had overcome an apparently insurmountable obstacle to agreement while playing ball all afternoon.

Once seated, Gallucci leaned over to Tom Hubbard: "Do you have any idea what is going on?" he whispered, wondering if there had been some hint that the North had accepted the U.S. language. Hubbard said that he had not heard anything. At first, the North Korean and the New Yorker talked about the next steps before signing the new accord. Hoping the situation would clarify itself, Gallucci stalled, observing that he would go back to Washington for consultations and then return with the president's letter of assurance. But when he could wait no longer and asked Kang to confirm that he had accepted the U.S. position on inter-Korean dialogue, the North Korean expressed profound shock. "There is no place in a U.S.–North Korean agreement for mention of inter-Korean relations." Kang warned, "if Pyongyang learned of Washington's insistence . . . it would see the whole Framework as a trap." He threatened to return home if Gallucci persisted.

The U.S. negotiator also professed to be shocked. Why had Kang asked the Americans to this session to discuss signing the agreement if he was unprepared to accept their language? Kang calmly observed that the only remaining obstacle to an agreement had been the American language on inter-Korean dialogue. Since that language was unacceptable, they could now finalize their talks.

By now, an exasperated Gallucci said that as far as he was concerned, the session was over unless the North Koreans had something new to say. He would be available to meet the next day, a Sunday, but if the impasse continued, the talks should be suspended. Tongue in cheek, Gallucci added that perhaps dialogue would resume after a period of improved inter-Korean relations that would permit inclusion of the kind of language the American delegation sought.

Kang was just as tough; he saw no reason to continue discussions since the North's position would not change. Moreover, if he returned to Pyongyang without an agreement in hand, the nuclear freeze would be over. North Korea's concessions had been made to respond to concerns raised by the United States, not to satisfy Kim Young Sam. Once again, Gallucci offered to stay in Geneva another day, but Kang dug his heels in. "If the United States was prepared to sacrifice talks to one sentence on North-South dialogue, then the reactor project was lost and there was no reason for further meetings."

Glancing at the champagne and flowers, Kang complained that this surprising development put him in a very difficult position. Reflecting what appeared to be genuine frustration, he threatened to tell the press that the talks had failed because the Americans had insisted on the resumption of inter-Korean dialogue. Gallucci warned him not to do that, ending the session on an unhappy note.

The U.S. delegation returned to its cars, telling the assembled reporters that it had nothing to report. Kang did not speak to the waiting press, but Ho Jong told them that because of the "abnormal position" raised by the United States, "I cannot say that we made any progress today."[40]

It had been a long day. Twice, the North Koreans had tried theatrics to get an agreement that avoided mention of inter-Korean dialogue. As they departed, the Americans thought they saw genuine disappointment on the faces of their counterparts. The North's stubborn resistance came as no surprise, particularly for longtime Korea watchers who knew the subject was more important to them than many others, including better relations with Washington or the new reactor project. The Americans speculated that the North Koreans would have to exert considerable effort to get any compromise accepted in Pyongyang, particularly since inter-Korean relations were the province of the party, not the Foreign Ministry.

The report sent to Washington that night gave credit to North Korea for taking the talks to the brink of failure, if indeed it was brinkmanship that Pyongyang was engaged in. Adding to the suspense, the Americans knew the North Koreans had airplane reservations for a flight out of Geneva the next day. The U.S. team would remain through Sunday, but absent a request for another meeting would return to the States the next day. Back in Washington, Under Secretary of Defense Walt Slocombe, reporting to his boss Bill Perry, observed that "today's breakdown was not the last act of this play." He was right.

Much to the surprise of some delegation members, the North Koreans telephoned early Sunday morning to request a meeting with Danny Russel, the Embassy Seoul officer who they knew was responsible for inter-Korean relations. Once again, they sent Li Yong Ho on a sensitive mission to see Russel and Gary Samore at the Le Richemond hotel in downtown Geneva.

Meeting in the hotel parlor, the men spent hours haggling over different formulations. There were three key issues, not just whether the accord could include language on inter-Korean dialogue, but also the timing of when dialogue would commence and whether it would become a precondition for provision of the new reactor project. Assuming the North Koreans called to find some way out of the impasse, Russel gradually pushed them back, securing—to his surprise—a commitment from the North Koreans to resume dialogue once the Geneva accord was concluded. Ending the session, Li asked if Gallucci would meet Kang right away.

Thinking the problem had been solved, Gallucci and Hubbard, accompanied by Russel, once again trudged over to the North Korean mission. But when they arrived, they learned that the North Koreans had backtracked again. Nevertheless, Kang now seemed willing to accept a reference in the text, although he wanted a qualification in the confidential minute that dialogue had nothing to do with the new reactor project. But Gallucci would accept nothing less than an unambiguous public commitment by the North. With a show of indignation, Kang asserted that the discussion had "come to resemble North-South dialogue itself," an allusion to the endless arguments over minutiae that characterized those meetings. Once again, a session ended with Gallucci telling Kang that he would be available for talks the next day, Monday, but planned to return to Washington on Tuesday.

Once again, the North Koreans called to request another meeting. Monday, October 17, was marked by intense discussions, not between Gallucci and Kang, but between their key aides. The North Koreans proposed a number of formulations that they hoped would meet the U.S. demands. The Americans tried to be as flexible and as creative as possible while preserving the principle that inter-Korean dialogue was essential. At one point, a frustrated Tom Hubbard bounced a pencil off a table, accidentally ricocheting the small projectile toward his counterpart, Kim Gye Gwan, who cringed. The American diplomat was too angry to apologize.[41]

Finally, a camel of a sentence emerged, ambiguous and poorly constructed. It read: "The DPRK will engage in North-South dialogue, as this Agreed Framework will help create an atmosphere that promotes such dialogue." Whether "as" meant "at the same time" or "because" was unclear. But the words seemed to commit the North to talk to the South in the same time frame as the construction of the new reactors.

That evening, as the Americans headed to their favorite Italian restaurant, the deal was clinched when Ho Jong called Tom Hubbard to tell him that the North could accept the language. Both had played a critical role in the final negotiation. Hubbard made it clear to Ho that the American interpretation of the ambiguous sentence was that dialogue had to happen. "We agree. We understand it. We'll do it but not right away," said Ho. When Hubbard asked what Ho meant by "not right away," the conversation trailed off.[42]

For Gallucci and the Americans, this final exercise was a painful reminder of the kabuki dance that the two Koreas had been conducting for decades. Unlike other parts of the Geneva accord describing actions that would be taken, or when they would be taken, the debate over inter-Korean dialogue was all about symbolism. Seoul wanted Pyongyang to acknowledge in its bilateral agreement with the United States that it also had to deal bilaterally with South Korea. Seoul would not allow the North to close a deal with Washington, in which it would receive substantial benefits underwritten by the South, while simultaneously ignoring the South. It also would not allow the United States to solve the nuclear issue while ignoring the division of the peninsula that was Seoul's primary concern. But forty years of intermittent negotiations marked by acts of hostility seemed unlikely to give way to one sentence in an accord between the United States and North Korea.

Could Pyongyang actually be forced to the table with Seoul against its wishes? Of course not, but in the short term the South Korean government was driven by the need to present a supportable agreement to the National Assembly, the press, and its people. The North Korean negotiators seemed driven by the need to deliver a document to Pyongyang that did not compromise their ideological and political position denying the equality of the South. Over the longer term, if a serious and sustained dialogue failed to materialize, responsibility could be fixed on the North so that it could be found "in violation" of the Framework.

But the combination of the blow-up over the timing of special inspections and the conclusion of ambiguous language on North-South dialogue left lingering doubts in Seoul, whether justified or not, about Washington's willingness to drive a hard bargain when it came to advancing South Korean priorities. One member of the South Korean delegation in Geneva who was a strong supporter of the emerging agreement bitterly recalled that "the Americans were prepared to negotiate anything" to secure an end to the North's nuclear program.[43] Months later, these feelings would return to haunt Washington as the crisis was renewed over the terms of the contract between KEDO and North Korea to build the new reactors.

With agreement on North-South language, the Framework was complete. Gallucci planned to go back to Washington and then return in four days to sign the accord. But the campaign to sell the Framework began immediately, as he called key members of the American media to explain the deal and scheduled a session with the sizable international press corps following the talks. At midnight, Gallucci announced to the gathered faithful and skeptical that an agreement had been reached. The crisis that had started in March 1993 with North Korea's announcement of its intention to withdraw from the NPT had been contained, at least for now.[44]

Gallucci of Geneva

Early in the morning of October 18, Gallucci and Ralph Earle—a senior official of the Arms Control and Disarmament Agency who had recently joined the delegation in Geneva—flew home. After landing at Washington's Dulles Airport, they were met by White House staff and agents from the State Department's Diplomatic Security unit, who hurried them through customs to a waiting car. Gallucci had a busy day ahead of him: a principals' meeting, a session with the president, and a critical press conference where both would present the Agreed Framework to the media.

The two travelers found themselves being whisked along the Dulles Access Road, into the District of Columbia, and over to Pennsylvania Avenue. On the way, the bar of flashing blue and red lights on the roof of their car blew off, giving Gallucci and Earle the rare opportunity of seeing how quickly Washington drivers could respond to four feet of metal and glass bouncing their way at high speed. It was going to be an exciting day.

When the American negotiator entered the small, wood-paneled White House Situation Room, already filled by the president's senior national security and foreign policy advisers, Tony Lake greeted him: "Gallucci of Geneva has returned!" While the mood was upbeat, there was still some serious business to be conducted. Some principals remained concerned about the failure of the Geneva accord to mandate that Pyongyang ship out of North Korea the spent fuel that would be produced by the new reactors years in the future. No one urged rejection of the accord on those grounds. But they all agreed that the KEDO contract with North Korea for supplying the new reactors should prevent Pyongyang from diverting that fuel for weapons purposes. The Pentagon committed to pay for the storage of the existing fuel while the Energy Department accepted responsibility for placing it in storage canisters so that reprocessing and plutonium separation could be avoided.

Lake concluded the meeting by putting the Agreed Framework on the table for approval: "Going once, going twice . . . congratulations, Bob." The press conference later that day would be a crucial threshold test for the accord. But with the principals' approval, the way was paved for Gallucci to return to Geneva the next day to sign the deal.

Of course, President Clinton, not the principals, made the final decision. The memo from Deputy Staff Secretary Todd Stern to the president seeking formal approval provided an elegant précis of the complicated Agreed Framework. It reduced the essential elements described by the NSC memorandum on the accord to a five-by-seven-inch summary: it would freeze and lead to the dismantlement of North Korea's nuclear program, bring Pyongyang into compliance with nonproliferation obligations, promote stability on the peninsula, commit the United States to oversee the construction of the two new reactors financed largely by South Korea and Japan, and provide interim energy to Pyongyang. It would require the president to approve a letter of assurance to North Korea. Marked with Clinton's unmistakable, fat-nibbed Mont Blanc, the memo came back with a thickly underlined "OK."

The signing ceremony took place in Geneva on October 21. The plan was to present Kang with President Clinton's letter of assurance in a private meeting followed by a public ceremony to sign the accord. Arriving at the North Korean mission at 3:30 PM, the Americans were greeted by the twelve-member North Korean delegation all lined up, each shaking the hands of the arriving Americans as they were shown into the hall. The meeting before the signing ceremony was short and the ceremony itself shorter still.

Kang seemed happy to receive the signed presidential assurance. Indeed, some U.S. delegation members thought he was shaking as it was handed over. After all, this was the first time North Korea had received an official commitment from the president of the United States.[45] But for a moment, Kang also appeared upset. The letter did not have Bill Clinton's title on it. The Americans were perplexed, particularly since it was on White House stationery. Which Bill Clinton did he think the assurance was from? Kang calmed down, but the episode only pointed out that the North Koreans were sticklers for the formalities.[46] Years later, visiting Pyongyang to prepare for Secretary of State Madeleine Albright's visit, Tom Hubbard spent hours with North Korean officials checking and rechecking to make sure that everyone's title was correct.[47]

The official ceremony began at 4:30 PM and was held in the Culture Hall normally used for film screenings and other events. Over 100 reporters were allowed to take pictures of the two delegations lined up behind the chief negotiators as they signed the document.[48] In a social hour that followed, those Americans who had not previously sampled Korean "snake liquor" from a bottle containing a dead adder had their chance to seize the moment. At the end of the gathering, someone noticed a table in the room littered with almost full glasses of snake liquor.

Now that the agreement was signed, one task remained: dealing with the press. As the Americans left the North Korean mission, one press wag who had followed the talks for a year and a half asked, as he had after every session, "So, Ambassador Gallucci, was there any progress at today's meeting?"[49]

Two hours later, Gallucci briefed a standing-room-only crowd of reporters at the U.S. mission. Many of the questions focused on the failure to secure special inspections before the North received any benefits. He carefully explained that Washington's priority was to stop North Korea's capacity to produce hundreds of kilograms of plutonium in the next five years, giving it the ability to build tens of nuclear weapons. What had happened in the past was important but not urgent, since it did not present the same threat. Reflecting his frustration, Gallucci added, "Ladies and gentlemen, if we had gone at that issue and . . . I was standing in front of you saying 'and by God, we're going to find out whether they actually have sixty grams or six kilograms (of plutonium)' . . . and then I told you 'but unfortunately, they're going to be producing 100–200 kilograms of plutonium under safeguards,' I certainly hope you wouldn't be thanking me."[50]

It was an energetic defense of an agreement whose virtues were many, but fell short of what some apparently thought possible: the overarching criticism would be that it gave too much and got too little. While the American negotiators believed they had succeeded beyond what anyone could have hoped for when the talks started in June 1993, they would soon realize that the task of securing support at home and abroad for the agreement was going to be more difficult than anyone had anticipated.

11

What Does Not Kill Me
Makes Me Stronger

October 1994–July 1995

As the American negotiators packed their bags and checked out of their Geneva hotel in October 1994, they felt drained yet exhilarated. The road from the threatened Nuclear Non-Proliferation Treaty walkout to the Agreed Framework had been long and arduous. Over the past eighteen months, they had overcome numerous obstacles in the negotiations with the North; survived the intense, sometimes strained collaboration with Seoul and the International Atomic Energy Agency; and marshaled and sustained an often unwieldy international coalition in opposition to the nuclear challenge, all under close and often critical scrutiny at home.

Now the results seemed to make it all worthwhile. North Korea's plutonium production program would be halted and its facilities placed under monitoring by the IAEA. The 5-megawatt reactor—from which the original plutonium had been drawn—would be permanently shut down. Construction of the two larger reactors would cease. The reprocessing facility would be closed and sealed. The United States would assist in the canning of the spent fuel already in the storage pond, providing solid assurance that the international community could monitor the plutonium. Eventually the whole program would be dismantled. In short, North Korea would be prevented from accumulating a large stockpile of plutonium that could be turned into a growing nuclear weapons arsenal and might even be exported to other countries.

In exchange, the North Koreans would receive two light-water reactors and 500,000 tons of heavy fuel oil per year. The United States was tagged to cover modest organizational costs for getting KEDO up and running plus the costs of the heavy fuel oil that, at current prices, would amount to roughly $50 million per year. The estimated $4 billion price tag for the two reactors would be covered in large part by contributions from South Korea and Japan.

From the standpoint of American taxpayers, the arrangement left them a good deal safer at a relatively small cost, *even if the North Koreans eventually broke the freeze or did not dismantle their nuclear program.* In other words, the Agreed Framework did not deprive the United States of any future options. One way to think of the U.S. contribution to the Agreed Framework was as term insurance; for a small yearly premium, the United States avoided an increment of tens of new bombs' worth of plutonium being separated in North Korea over the same twelve-month period. Eventually, the insurance policy would no longer be needed once the North Koreans dismantled their production program, allowed inspections, and became members in good standing of the Nuclear Non-Proliferation Treaty. And, obviously, if the North broke the terms of the Agreed Framework, the United States would stop paying its yearly premium.

The Clinton administration understood that winning public acceptance— as well as securing the support or at least acquiescence of key constituencies— would be critical to the successful implementation of the Agreed Framework. After all, the accord was not a treaty or an armistice that ended hostilities, nor was it a self-executing solution. Rather, as its name indicated, it was simply a "framework" for subsequent actions. The United States would need to take some of those actions and make certain contributions to ensure its terms were carried out. As those actions were taken, they would help establish the confidence and predictability that would enable North Koreans, South Koreans, Japanese, Americans, and others to take additional steps toward cooperation, edging warily back from the brink of conflict.

The stakes were high and well understood; the American people viewed the threat of nuclear proliferation in North Korea as the top foreign policy risk facing the nation. They and Congress had every right to expect a clear explanation of the issue, and a clear U.S. policy to advance the national objectives of a safe and secure Korean Peninsula, free of nuclear weapons. But the subject was complicated, the location remote, the North Koreans secretive and unsympathetic. The task of persuasion would be as difficult as it was essential to sustaining the support the Geneva accord would need to succeed. The public would be hearing not only from the administration, but also from the press, academic experts, and former officials. The president and his advisers would need to address each constituency.

In parallel, the United States needed to persuade the international community to support the Agreed Framework. It was one thing to sustain a high degree of multilateral support in the face of an imminent nuclear threat from North Korea. Unfortunately, perhaps inevitably, that cohesion could begin to splinter once the North Korean program was frozen and posed less of a threat. That splintering would only be exacerbated once the task turned to the establishment of KEDO, and the funding of its obligations under the Agreed Framework.

In spite of these potential difficulties, Washington believed that selling the Geneva accord would be possible, given what appeared to be the clear benefits of the agreement. Only ten weeks earlier, the Agreed Statement seemed to be well received by both Republicans and Democrats alike. In retrospect, that may have been a misleading impression, the result of reaching an arrangement during the dog days of summer when many opinionmakers were on vacation. More significant, the statement did not address the critical timing of special inspections. So if the members of the negotiating team expected to be greeted by a strong degree of bipartisan approval, they were mistaken.

Indeed, the job of selling and implementing the Agreed Framework added more tiers to the chessboard, and new players moved toward the center of the boards: the U.S. Congress, KEDO and the governments considering participating in that organization, federal budget officials, and others. Meanwhile the original players—North Korea, trilateral partners, and permanent members of the Security Council—continued to make their own moves. By the following spring, the atmosphere was once again clouded with uncertainty.

"Clinton Approves Plan to Give Aid to North Korea"

The Clinton administration considered four steps critical to selling the Framework. First, broad themes supporting the accord had to be disseminated widely through television, speeches, and other media. Second, the administration needed to secure the support of Congress, through meetings with key legislators and staff as well as through hearings on Capitol Hill. Third, briefings needed to be conducted for journalists, academic experts, opinionmakers, and members of Congress. Fourth, a "white paper" (as the British describe comprehensive government policy documents) had to be prepared to explain the details of the accord in support of all these efforts.

The press rollout began even before signing. After the October 18 principals' meeting authorizing Gallucci to sign the agreement, his next stop was the Oval Office to prepare the president for a hurried press conference. The president would make the "big picture" case, followed by Gallucci, who would offer a detailed explanation and take questions from reporters. CNN would cover the event live, giving the administration an important opportunity to make its case from the start of what was likely to be a media feeding frenzy.

The president opened the press conference by announcing that his chief foreign policy advisers had just unanimously endorsed the Framework. He was instructing Ambassador Gallucci to return to Geneva to sign an accord that Clinton characterized as "good for the United States, good for our allies, and good for the safety of the entire world."[1] Gallucci then stepped to the microphone. Since the delegations in Geneva had agreed not to publicize all of the accord's provisions until it was signed, he had the difficult task of providing enough information to portray the deal positively without betraying that understanding. Gallucci ran through provisions linking special inspections to the delivery of the first new reactor, the dismantlement of facilities to the construction of the second reactor, and the securing and shipping out of the spent fuel to the building of both reactors.[2] After watching his performance on television in Geneva, one North Korean told Hubbard that he was happy with the attention but nervous that Gallucci made the deal look too good for the United States. Pyongyang might conclude that the accord must not be good enough for it to sign.

That may have been the North Korean reaction, but clearly the packed audience of reporters included skeptics. Some were quick to ask how long the world would have to wait to find out whether North Korea had cheated in the past. Gallucci responded that it had originally rejected special inspections but now agreed to accept them and whatever else the IAEA may require. "The radioactive waste sites are not going anywhere," he added, also acknowledging that inspections might not come until five years into the construction of the new reactors.[3]

Others asked whether the deal would reward the North for doing what it was supposed to do anyway, implying that the world was essentially being blackmailed, and that other dictators would be encouraged to build nuclear weapons, heartened to learn that crime pays. The North, Gallucci countered, went far beyond what was required to meet its nonproliferation obligations by sacrificing all of its gas-graphite reactors and reprocessing plant. Absent the accord, North Korea could have been fully compliant with its NPT obligations while accumulating hundreds of kilograms of plutonium. It seemed preferable to persuade the North to give up its dangerous program, which was designed for nuclear weapons production, in exchange for new reactors that were not. By the end of the press conference, it was clear that the Agreed Framework would not be given a free ride by the media.[4]

The next morning, Washington awoke to a mixed reaction from the major dailies. Editorials in the *New York Times* and the *Washington Post* would be a bell-weather for the prospects of selling the Framework. The *Times* gave it full marks as a "breakthrough," noting, "Diplomacy with North Korea has scored a resounding triumph."[5] While finding "some very big flaws," the *Post* was conditionally upbeat: "If it works out, the accord just announced . . . marks a gigantic political breakthrough. It could end the specter of a rogue state going nuclear, challenging an American supported regional order and provoking others to go nuclear as well."[6]

The slant of the news stories was harsher. The headline in the *Times* read "Clinton Approves Plan to Give Aid to North Koreans," portraying the deal as a foreign aid program aimed at one of the least sympathetic countries on earth.[7] The *Post* lumped together elements of the accord favorable to Pyongyang as "concessions."[8] The stories did not address the risks of nuclear weapons in the last armed frontier of the cold war, the costs of a second Korean War, and the role of the Agreed Framework in averting both without releasing clouds of radioactive debris over a bombed Yongbyon facility. That was yesterday's news.

Pundits leaped into the fray. Columnist William Safire said the deal showed Clinton could "hypnotize himself into fervently believing that any deal at all . . . 'is a very good deal indeed,'" and quoted former secretary of defense James Schlesinger as complaining, "While it was not unconditional surrender, it was a negotiated surrender."[9] Former Reagan secretary of defense Caspar Weinberger wrote in *Forbes* that the deal was "monstrously wrong."[10]

A few voices of support emerged in support of the accord. Jessica Tuchman Matthews—a Council on Foreign Relations fellow and former official in Democratic administrations—wrote that if the agreement was carried out, "it will be the most important single foreign policy feat of the Clinton Administration to date."[11]

In retrospect, the administration clearly erred in supposing that the agreement's advantages would be quickly appreciated. But the complex accord did not lend itself to a bumper-sticker public relations campaign, prompting Gallucci to complain to the State Department press corps, "I'm still reading stories that misstate the terms or language of the agreement."[12] Playing catch-up ball after the October 21 signing, the administration prepared a white paper explaining that Washington did not "walk away from a material violation of the NPT" but focused on the greater danger that Pyongyang might accumulate plutonium to build nuclear weapons or to export at a handsome profit. Explaining that the United States achieved "more than we thought possible," the white paper pointed out that the Geneva accord had frozen North

Korea's nuclear program immediately while the steps Washington had to take initially were "modest by comparison." On verification, the paper continued, "This is not an agreement that relies on trust" but rather on the IAEA and national technical means.[13]

Senior U.S. officials took to the airwaves to make their case but, as the old saying goes, "You only get one chance to make a first impression." The *Washington Post* headline citing U.S. "concessions" set the administration back in a way that was difficult to reverse. The administration was caught in the trap that Gallucci had warned about in early 1994; if priorities shifted away from dealing with the "past" immediately, then rhetoric about special inspections had to be toned down. Yet Washington never really made that shift. The United States kept the focus on the past during the negotiations even after the principals had decided it was more important to protect the future in order to keep the heat on the North and faith with the South.

The reaction from Congress was no better. Republican Robert Dole, the Senate majority leader, sarcastically commented that the accord "shows it is always possible to get an agreement when you give enough away."[14] Senator John McCain accused the president and Gallucci of appeasement and of going back on their promise that special inspections would be the top priority.[15] Some Republicans avoided Gallucci's efforts to brief them. Some administration officials suspected they preferred to remain uninformed on the details so they could maintain what one official labeled a "carefully modulated degree of rhetorical criticism."

Democrats had little to say; none came out immediately in support of the accord. The few who did speak publicly were not helpful. Senator John Glenn, who had built his Senate career as an ardent opponent of nuclear proliferation, told the *Wall Street Journal,* "I think the worst thing a great power can do is bluff, get caught in the bluff and not be willing to back it up."[16]

Congressional resistance had been anticipated. That was one key factor in the principals' decision to structure the presidential guarantee to the North in a manner that would not require congressional approval. It was also reflected in arrangements for initial fuel oil deliveries without seeking new authorities from Congress.[17] The same day that Gallucci explained that to the press, Deputy Secretary of Defense John Deutch notified the White House that the Pentagon was ready to fund the initial oil deliveries, repeating that congressional approval was not needed.

But when Senator McCain and others came out swinging, the intensity of their reaction caught the administration flat-footed. It may have been lulled into false confidence by the relatively positive reaction to the Agreed Statement two months earlier. But with only two weeks before the midterm elections and the control of Congress hanging in the balance, an agreement that conferred *any* benefits to Pyongyang was too attractive a target to pass up for Republicans already attacking the Clinton foreign policy for weakness.

The stunning Democratic defeat in the November 4 election—resulting in a loss of control of both Houses—only aggravated the problem. A week later, President Kim Young Sam asked Secretary Warren Christopher during a visit to Seoul how the Republican victory would affect U.S. support for the accord. The question may not have been entirely academic; the South Korean leader still may have harbored hopes that the victory would force the administration to reconsider the terms of the agreement. Christopher told Kim that U.S. foreign policy would continue to have bipartisan support. But he later recalled: "I found myself in the awkward position of trying to rally support in a foreign country on a tough and controversial issue just as our political coalition at home was falling apart."[18]

The GOP victory, however, may have had one silver lining. Though it did shift Republican critics into powerful positions in Congress, intensifying the struggle between the executive and legislative branches, they now had to assume greater responsibility for their actions. If Republicans refused to fund implementation of the Geneva accord, they would bear the blame if it collapsed and the nuclear crisis reemerged. The election also highlighted the role of centrists like Democratic senator Sam Nunn and Republican Richard Lugar, who had worked together closely on foreign policy issues and would now push to smooth the edges of proposals made by hard-liners. In a phone call to Lugar after the election, Nunn quipped: "If you think we were joined in the hip during the last three years, we're going to have to be joined at the neck for the next two."[19]

Recognizing the importance of the "responsible center," the White House gave Gallucci and Poneman, both of whom had worked for President George Bush, the job of reaching out to Republicans. In fact, after the Carter trip to Pyongyang, former Bush official Brent Scowcroft advised the White House not to pick and choose among former presidents to brief. It was an excellent suggestion. By then, Richard Nixon had passed away and Ronald Reagan's staff declined the offer though formal word had yet to emerge about his Alzheimer's disease. But both Presidents Bush and Gerald Ford graciously accepted.

Already that summer—before the Geneva accord was completed—Gallucci and Poneman had flown to Kennebunkport to brief President Bush on the state of play in Korea. The former president listened closely, raised questions about a number of critical issues, and offered useful guidance on how to manage key nations bordering North Korea. Shortly after the midterm elections, they flew to Houston to brief their former boss again, this time about the newly completed Geneva accord. President Bush invited his two visitors to join him for lunch at a local pizzeria, before returning to his office to finish the conversation. At the end of the meeting, Bush concluded: "Well, I can't vouch for all the details . . . but I am not going to give you boys any difficulty in public."

The same drill was followed with President Ford. When Poneman had traveled to Aspen to see him that summer, Ford's antipathy toward Kim Il Sung was intense, rooted in his experience as a young member of Congress: "You know, as a first-term Congressman, I supported Truman's call for U.S. support for a United Nations police action to go to war in Korea." It had been difficult for Ford to buck his party elders as well as many of his constituents, who were skeptical about entering the Korean conflict, but he drew inspiration and guidance from his senior Michigan colleague, Senator Arthur Vandenburg, a Republican who was deeply committed to the view that "politics stops at the water's edge." Later, as a member of the House Appropriations Committee, which was responsible for financing the armistice ending the war in Korea, Ford had visited Korea and would never forget "the half-dead, emaciated American POWs as they came streaming across the 38th parallel. That's when I realized how evil Kim Il Sung was." Ford turned to the present with an admonition: "I will support you if I think you are maintaining a strong posture against North Korea. But if you weaken your policy, I will oppose it."

After the Agreed Framework was completed, Poneman visited Ford again, this time in his Palm Springs office. Slated to be the main speaker at the Korea Society's annual dinner, Ford could use that forum, if he chose, to unleash an assault on the Geneva accord, jeopardizing congressional and international support. Poneman emphasized the freeze on the North's plutonium program, the continuous monitoring by the IAEA, and the certain cessation of benefits if the North was caught cheating. In his speech, Ford expressed serious concerns but acknowledged that the Geneva accord contained points that would enable the United States to halt its cooperation if necessary. Though no ringing endorsement, his careful remarks at least signaled a measure of acceptance.

Through the last months of 1994, Gallucci and Poneman met with a "who's who" of Republican experts on foreign policy: Colin Powell, James Baker, Lawrence Eagleburger, Brent Scowcroft, Arnold Kanter, James Schlesinger, Caspar Weinberger, Henry Kissinger, and Paul Wolfowitz. As Gallucci recalled, "If we could neutralize possible opponents, that would have been good. If we could have got a Republican with credibility in security issues to speak out in favor, that would have been great." In the end, the result seemed to be grudging neutrality at best; supporting the Framework would have been tantamount to "Republican suicide."[20] None embraced it; some refrained from direct attacks.[21] Powell pledged neither to speak in favor of nor to denounce the accord. Kissinger—who was joined in the briefing by his colleague at that time, L. Paul Bremer—took the same tack but also pointed out that Pyongyang would have backed down if Washington had taken a tougher stance. Still others—Weinberger, Eagleburger, and Wolfowitz—remained adamantly opposed.[22]

So was former secretary of state James Baker who, always tactically astute, advised Gallucci to change his presentation. Gallucci's standard pitch cited three options: negotiate a settlement, take military action to stop the program (which could have precipitated a war), or sanction the North (which would not have halted Pyongyang's plutonium production program). Baker warned Gallucci that framing the choice as one between war and peace would only expose the administration to charges of appeasement. Rather, he argued the accord should be portrayed as the result of a tough policy, including sanctions and a military buildup. (This was not only sound advice; it was true.) Publicly, however, the former secretary of state attacked the agreement as "a complete and abrupt flip-flop in American policy towards North Korea."[23]

While the critics were often vocal, they failed to advance a better alternative. Senator McCain was willing to accept the consequences of a tough approach, including armed conflict. But most seemed to believe that North Korea could have just been faced down. Writing about a couple in a restaurant who were harassed by someone at another table, author Norah Ephron observed they had four options. They could appeal to the management, attempt to reason with the ruffians, start a fistfight, or walk over to them, look them straight in the eye, and point at the door. The last approach was the "Gary Cooper option," named after the epitome of the "strong silent type" in American movies. Everyone liked that option for dealing with rogues in restaurants or in foreign affairs. Of course, when Gary Cooper did it, the bad guy sheepishly shuffled off stage left, but real life was different. Lacking a better solution, critics faulted the balance of concessions and obligations, or fired broadsides at Washington's weakness. But none in a position of responsibility pressed for wholesale changes, even had they thought of any, lest they precipitate the collapse of the Framework.

Grudging acquiescence, however, was not enough to put the Geneva accord on firm political footing. One U.S. official wrote that its long-term prospects were uncertain "unless the administration can get Democrats and some Republicans to support the agreement publicly and on the record." Somehow, moderate Republicans who were hanging back and Democratic members who were nervous about an accord hinging on North Korean compliance had to be nudged forward to positions of open support.

The administration's problem became clear at the first hearings held on December 1. Leading off a public session in the Senate, Charles Robb, the Democratic chairman of the Foreign Relations Subcommittee on Asia, opened with a critical statement, followed by Republican Frank Murkowski, who accused U.S. negotiators of giving up "virtually on every front."[24] Other Republicans chimed in with criticisms on everything from special inspections to the fact that the agreement was not a treaty. More sympathetic members remained silent. Gallucci, as the main witness, launched a vigorous defense, but with no help from Democrats or Republicans—it seemed that the critics had greater numbers and support.[25]

That same day, a closed session with the Senate Select Committee on Intelligence—beyond the range of the microphones and whirring cameras—went better. Once again, Gallucci was the main witness, accompanied by representatives from the intelligence community who said the agreement could be monitored. This time, Democrat John Glenn (despite his earlier criticism) and Republican John Warner were supportive. John Chaffee, a moderate Republican from Rhode Island, seemed to be in favor. Senator Arlen Specter, another moderate Republican known for his legal acumen, was curious as to why the agreement was not a treaty but also was willing to listen.

As the year ended, recognizing that its sales campaign had not succeeded, the Deputies Committee made three key decisions. Debating whether to give critics a difficult take-it-or-leave-it choice by presenting Congress with a single funding package or to seek less contentious, case-by-case approvals, it decided on a modified "big-bang" approach. The Agreed Framework was a major commitment, based on a broad national security rationale; it made much more sense to make a straightforward case in support of the whole approach than to try to gain congressional support in piecemeal fashion. Only the Department of Energy's funding request to store the spent fuel would be presented separately. More important, to minimize any negative congressional response, the deputies decided to cap funding at up to $30 million for KEDO, far below the estimated cost of U.S. obligations to the organization. The assumption that oil deliveries, expected to cost $50 million per year, could be paid for using foreign contributions would prove false, later forcing KEDO to go into debt.

Finally, the Deputies Committee also agreed on a new strategy targeting the responsible center of the political spectrum. The plan was to win over leading Democratic security experts, such as Senators Nunn, Carl Levin, and Glenn, and moderate Republicans, such as Senator Mark Hatfield, chairman of the

Senate Appropriations Committee, and Senator William Cohen on the Armed Services Committee. To that end, the new year would begin with a round of testimony in Congress, by William Perry and Warren Christopher before the Senate Foreign Relations Committee and the secretary of defense and General Gary Luck in front of the Armed Services Committee. Senator Levin, a member of that committee, had counseled the administration that strong military support would go a long way in dampening the ardor of those who wished to play politics with the Geneva accord.

Not One Centime

While building a multilateral coalition in support of U.S. policy had been critical throughout the eighteen months of the crisis, it was even more critical in helping to get implementation of the Framework off the ground. At the core of the Geneva accord were its provisions for freezing and eventually dismantling North Korea's gas-graphite nuclear facilities as well as for returning Pyongyang to full compliance with its safeguards agreement. That made the view of IAEA head Hans Blix decisive in selling the agreement to the international community and the Security Council.

From the outset, the Clinton administration had worked closely with the IAEA. To be sure, Washington had occasionally, and gently, urged restraint in the agency's dealings with Pyongyang. As a member of the IAEA Board of Governors, the United States certainly had an appropriate say in guiding the agency with respect to its dealings with Pyongyang, and in advising how best to advance the agency's central objectives. But Washington had been careful not to tread too heavily on the IAEA's prerogative as the arbiter of nonproliferation norms. At the time of the June crisis, when Blix had reacted sternly to North Korea's removal of fuel from its 5-megawatt reactor, he had the full backing of the U.S. government. In turn, the Clinton administration now looked for IAEA support of the diplomatic solution emerging from the Geneva negotiations.

As those talks unfolded, the Americans kept Blix well informed. That effort was facilitated by a good relationship between the Swede and Ambassador John Ritch, the U.S. representative to the UN agencies in Vienna, who also was a member of the Geneva delegation. The intense consultations even allowed Blix to play an informal role in shaping the accord's language on how to resolve the discrepancies in the North's initial plutonium declaration. Washington recognized that Blix may have preferred to see Pyongyang comply completely *and* immediately with its safeguards obligations but hoped that he was enough of a pragmatist to accept the current accord in the absence of better alternatives. After all, the former foreign minister had shown subtlety and restraint in navigating the political waters surrounding the Korean issue. That was clear in his willingness to sustain "continuity of safeguards" inspections, which kept the IAEA in the game for almost eighteen months, even though North Korea refused to grant the greater degree of access the agency wanted.

Blix rose to the challenge. He understood that the accord would grant the expanded access to North Korean facilities that the IAEA had been seeking for some time, since it would have to monitor the installations frozen under the Framework. Although the agency could not conduct immediate special inspections, Blix knew that a delay would damage the IAEA and the nonproliferation regime less than an unfettered plutonium production program in a North Korea that had successfully renounced the NPT. In the best of all worlds, that trade-off would never be made, but in October 1994 there was no better choice. At the same time, he was careful to point out that the agreement had to be fully implemented, and that it did not supersede the existing safeguards agreement, which remained valid and also had to be implemented.

Just before the Framework was reached, Blix traveled to New York and Washington for consultations with the Security Council and the U.S. government. Secretary Christopher told him that the United States wanted a new Security Council mandate for the agency to monitor a nuclear freeze in North Korea. Blix, in turn, expressed his public support for the emerging accord. Subsequently, he worked with Ambassador Ritch to formulate the Security Council mandate that would enable the IAEA to do its job. The agency secretariat also began mapping out the requirements for monitoring the freeze in preparation for its own talks with Pyongyang.

The key battleground for securing multilateral support was at the UN Security Council, not only to lay the legal foundation for IAEA action, but also to serve notice that the Framework was widely accepted. In the spring of 1993 Washington had used the authority conferred by UN Security Council Resolution 825 to justify negotiations with Pyongyang. Since then, the United States had assiduously maintained the council's imprimatur in marshaling the international coalition against the North's breach of nuclear rules. Now with an agreement in the offing, Ambassador Madeleine Albright would be seeking its support for the accord.

Problems quickly emerged with France and Russia, reflecting an undercurrent of unhappiness with the Framework in spite of the past sixteen months of painstaking consultation. A stickler for the nonproliferation orthodoxy, Paris was concerned that North Korea would not have to comply with safeguards right away, that the IAEA would be asked to conduct inspections beyond the scope of its mandate to ensure facilities were frozen, and that the NPT's integrity would be compromised just before the 1995 review conference. Our government will not contribute "one centime," to the new reactors, a French official testily blurted out. This asperity struck some Americans as disingenuous and even hypocritical, as France had been the nation most willing to sell facilities, equipment, and technology for the production of weapon-usable materials to such sensitive destinations as Pakistan and South Korea.

In Moscow, the complaints were similar, but the motivations more complex. The Russians claimed the Geneva accord undermined the NPT by setting a bad precedent for countries like Ukraine, which had inherited nuclear weapons but had been persuaded to return its arsenals to Russia. Moscow, however, still nursed a grudge. Having given in to U.S. pressures to cancel its reactor project in 1985, it now found Washington on the verge of ensuring the supply of a *replacement* model. Minatom—the Russian atomic energy ministry—had been waging a guerilla war in the press against the American-based South Korean reactor, a campaign that was seconded by the Foreign Ministry. During a September visit to Pyongyang, Deputy Foreign Minister Aleksandr Panov tried to thaw bilateral relations and reportedly discussed the reactor project.[26]

Beijing was less negative. Unlike Russia, China welcomed the Agreed Framework, behaving, according to one U.S. official, like a "smiling dragon." But Beijing insisted that it would only support Security Council action if North Korea approved its content, not a simple task given the North's track record of opposing any UN involvement in the nuclear issue.

The challenge for the United States was to sew these divergent perspectives into a Security Council mandate approving the Agreed Framework. The French and Russians might push for language demanding immediate compliance with the NPT, triggering considerations of "face" that would likely complicate dealing with North Korea and China without actually advancing the date such compliance would be achieved. The North might press its own unsupportable pet peeves, such as an endorsement of a new peace arrangement to replace the decades-old armistice. Seeking the middle ground, Ambassador Albright recommended a statement or resolution that welcomed the accord and North Korea's decision to remain in the NPT, as well as its willingness to freeze the nuclear program and to implement safeguards. The United States would also request that the IAEA monitor the freeze, verify full compliance with safeguards at the appropriate time, and keep the Security Council informed about its activities.

While these objectives seemed straightforward, a two-week debate ensued. Once again, Hans Blix played a critical role, reassuring nonproliferation hawks during his October 28 briefing of the Security Council and urging the council to act quickly so the IAEA could get on with monitoring the freeze. Still, Russia and France submitted amendments that pressed for quicker North Korean compliance with its obligations and insisted that the council not directly "welcome" the Geneva accord. In addition to lobbying by Ambassador Albright and her colleagues in Washington, American diplomats in Paris and Moscow went to work in emphasizing the need to support Blix without delay. Of course, Pyongyang did not like the draft resolution either.

At the end of the day, the November 4 Security Council statement differed little from the initial American draft. The United States managed to address concerns over saving the NPT in theory (by cooling positive references to the Agreed Framework) while securing the support needed to save the treaty in practice (by calling for full implementation that would bring North Korea back into compliance). Only tactical concessions were made to France and Russia. For example, the final statement "notes with satisfaction," rather than "welcoming" the Geneva accord. Only a few minor suggestions from Pyongyang were accepted. Through patient diplomacy, Washington had secured Beijing's support as well. Most important, the statement included the provisions necessary for the IAEA to monitor the nuclear freeze.[27]

Over the next month, the IAEA and North Korea moved forward quickly. A week after the UN statement, the IAEA Board of Governors authorized the negotiation of an arrangement to implement the freeze. Blix supervised preparation of a "going-in position," with no nonnegotiable demands and with flexibility built in to allow steady progress.[28] An IAEA delegation arrived in Pyongyang on November 22, just after its inspectors had for the first time visited the inside of the two new reactors under construction.[29] Agreement was reached on almost all the key issues, followed by the dispatch from Vienna of more inspectors to begin implementation. Once they arrived, the freeze was put into place.

Who Will Screw the Last Screw into the LWR?

The reactions in South Korea and Japan to the Agreed Framework seemed positive, though marred by some discordant notes. Despite his October outburst in the *New York Times*, President Kim Young Sam grudgingly endorsed the agreement and promised to fund the new reactors. Yet Washington worried that Kim would not follow through with his pledge. President Clinton called him the night before the October 21 signing to emphasize that both had critics but both would need to sell the deal as in their mutual interest. Clinton exhorted Kim to "look at it as a whole. We need to persuade our publics. We need your support. I know that North-South dialogue is important. . . . We'll help you with strong public statements."

As feared, the South Korean leader did little to defend the Geneva accord in the court of public opinion. President Kim had myriad problems. He was distracted by local events, including the collapse of one of Seoul's bridges. But he also remained ambivalent about the Framework, as his government was still smarting from withering criticism for disorganization, inconsistency, and the appearance of having been forced to acquiesce. The South Korean leader was well aware that public opinion polls showed the voters nearly evenly split over the accord, with most convinced the United States had presented their country with a fait accompli.[30]

While President Kim hung back, Foreign Minister Han Sung Joo emerged as the chief advocate for the new accord. "The agreement is a major cornerstone for fundamentally resolving the North Korea nuclear issue and also for maintaining peace and stability on the Korean Peninsula," Han commented on October 18, keying his remarks to those in Washington.[31] Two weeks later, he conceded that the agreement was "somewhat unsatisfactory" but insisted that "the goal of our policy is reflected" and that Seoul should be ready to pay its share of the new reactor project.[32] On that score, Han was on firm ground; although most of the public felt it had been presented with a fait accompli, three-quarters supported paying for the project.[33]

President Kim would later tell Christopher that he knew how to "transform disasters into blessings." In fact, before Christopher arrived for an early November visit, South Korea seemed to recognize that the Geneva accord was irreversible and was already thinking about implementation. The government began to consider how to meet its multibillion-dollar commitment, and a committee headed by a senior Foreign Ministry official was established to plan the new reactor project. The group also gave moderates an opening to push for new initiatives to revive inter-Korean dialogue.[34]

Playing up the potentially positive impact of the accord on North-South relations was a theme that had political resonance in Seoul. On those rare occasions when he did talk about the Agreed Framework, President Kim emphasized the North's promise to reopen talks with the South and Seoul's central role in the provision of the new reactors.[35] Moderates used this sentiment in support of a committee formed to plan the reactor project and to push a new initiative, launched by President Kim in early November, to lift some economic sanctions. The government expected Pyongyang's reaction to be lukewarm (and it was). But the business community welcomed the decision.

Moreover, according to President Kim's calculations, 74 percent of South Koreans favored his initiative.

Bearing in mind that Washington could not persuade its own skeptics to back the Agreed Framework without Seoul's support, Secretary of State Christopher landed at Kimpo Airport on November 9, where he found deeper problems awaiting him.[36] "There remains an underlying fear that the U.S. will prematurely withdraw its security shield in the wake of the agreement," Ambassador James Laney warned. "After nearly five decades of zero-sum competition with the North," he added, "many South Koreans also have difficulty believing any agreement that is good for Pyongyang can also be good for them." Pundits were already predicting that the United States would play the two Koreas off against each other and perpetuate a divided peninsula. Secretary Perry had reaffirmed Washington's commitment to the alliance during a brief stopover on October 21.[37] Christopher knew he would have to reinforce that message.

The secretary's task was complicated by a mistake in President Clinton's weekly radio address just before he arrived. The ink was barely dry on the Agreed Framework when already certain formulas had become so rigid that any variation from orthodoxy caused great disruption. A passage drafted by the National Security Council staff for the weekly radio address acknowledged that Seoul would bear the lion's share of the new reactor costs while Japan would make some contribution to oil shipments. Not surprisingly, this awkward formula succumbed to the pencil of a word-counting White House speechwriter, who condensed the phrasing to state that both countries would support the light-water reactors and alternative energy supplies.

The South Koreans inferred that the United States had foisted a new burden upon them, paying for oil, without their consent.[38] When urgently called by distraught South Korean diplomats to protest this overreaching, Poneman tried to reassure them that the wording in the radio address was inartful but did *not* reflect a new request for Seoul to fund oil deliveries. It did no good. On November 9, the pro-government *Seoul Sinmun* expressed an "uneasy feeling" about Christopher's visit because it might be aimed at "giving us additional burdens."[39]

On the surface, Secretary Christopher's visit seemed to go well. Aside from using his public statements to explain the Geneva agreement's significance and framing it in the context of a strong alliance, Christopher privately nudged President Kim to become more active in promoting the arrangement.[40] After he left, one conservative politician who tried to scuttle the accord told the Americans that he now supported the Framework. Nevertheless, there remained a steady drumbeat of conservative criticism from South Korean officials and pundits that reverberated in the American press and on Capitol Hill. Moreover, in selling the accord, the South had emphasized that it would lead to better relations with Pyongyang, an assertion yet to be proved. Foreign Minister Han told Christopher before he left that a breakthrough in North-South talks was now essential for the reactor project and Seoul's ability to fund it.

Though delicate, the situation in Tokyo was less precarious. The government welcomed the agreement, but major newspapers expressed mixed feelings. Over breakfast with Ambassador Mondale, Vice Foreign Minister Kunihiko Saito said that the reaction "had not been too bad." Privately though, Foreign Minister Yohei Kono told Secretary Perry he was worried about the delay in the implementation of safeguards. Moreover, the Foreign Ministry would have its hands full managing Japan's role in implementing the Framework. There was no plan for structuring Japan's participation in KEDO or in the new reactor project. The ministry also had to cope with the powerful Finance Ministry, public opinion, and the different political parties in Japan's coalition government. Close trilateral cooperation would help deal with these powerful, often competing forces.

But the most sensitive issue was money. Many Diet members wondered why Japan had to help pay, particularly after the billions of dollars it had contributed to America's Gulf War effort. Disagreements inside the government spilled over into the public. While the Foreign Ministry sought multilateral participation in KEDO to help strengthen its argument for a financial contribution, the Ministry of Finance took a tougher position. On October 25, Finance Minister Masayoshi Takemura told the Diet that contributions to KEDO by European countries would be a "prerequisite" for Japan's participation. The ministry also wanted to limit the size of Japan's contribution, telling the press that funding on the order of 30 percent of the money required by the consortium was "out of the question at present."[41]

Yet this was precisely the demand Washington was making. Responding to the U.S. request, in November Vice Foreign Minister Saito told Gallucci that Japan was willing to be the second main funder, but not the *sole* second funder. In addition, efforts to woo Congress by emphasizing Japan's large financial role backfired in Tokyo, where officials sensitive to the charge of "checkbook diplomacy" feared a loss of public support. Making matters worse, Washington was unresponsive to Japanese requests that it also fund the reactor project to help persuade their public to do the same. The Americans knew that would be an almost impossible sell on Capitol Hill.

American diplomacy had to find a way to accommodate the concerns of its two close allies, since close trilateral cooperation remained essential for implementation of the Geneva accord. In some cases, it failed. The administration had intended to issue a statement by the three leaders at the Asia Pacific Economic Cooperation summit in Jakarta, to be held in November, expressing support of the accord and unveiling a plan for financing the new reactors. But when the summit rolled around, the plan fell through, as Japan refused to sign off on a statement that it would be the sole second funder. A more general statement was also scrapped for fear that the press would insist on an answer to the question of financing responsibility beyond the degree of consensus—or comfort level—of the three allies.

Nevertheless, the APEC meeting provided the first face-to-face opportunity for the three leaders to talk about the Geneva accord. Clinton, Kim, and Murayama reaffirmed the need to cooperate closely on implementation. "There must be no daylight between us," Clinton emphasized. While President Kim trotted out his concerns about Pyongyang cheating on its commitments, Clinton countered that the best way to encourage implementation was to insist on compliance while fulfilling our own commitments in good faith. Pyongyang would then have no excuse to renege. That was why, while the press was delving into extraordinary detail—"to the point of wanting to know who will screw the last screw into the LWR"—it was so important for the leaders to make it clear they would see the Geneva accord through to its completion.

The United States had greater success in establishing KEDO. A series of trilateral skull sessions culminated in a KEDO charter in January 1995 that addressed key issues such as decisionmaking, financial resources, and internal organization. That was followed by a meeting of interested states and a formal signing by the partners in March. Australia, New Zealand, and Canada became the first new members. Seldom had a new international organization been set up more quickly.

The process had been painful at times, as differing perspectives often clashed. Japan was interested in recruiting as many members of KEDO as possible to provide political cover at home for its financing of the reactor project. South Korea wanted to ensure its central role in KEDO, and to prevent American domination of the organization. Washington wanted to structure an organization that would effectively implement the Geneva accord, accommodate the concerns of its two partners, and also be an acceptable partner for North Korea. These divergent objectives forced Washington to conduct a difficult balancing act.

The question of KEDO's decisionmaking structure was a case in point. Whereas Japan needed additional members, Seoul would have concentrated decisionmaking authority in the three partners, in effect deterring other countries from joining since they would have too little say in the organization's operations. At the November APEC summit, Secretary Christopher told Foreign Minister Yohei Kono that including other members would only complicate matters. But later the United States supported Japan, in part because it hoped to secure international funding for KEDO projects where shortfalls were anticipated. The prime example was KEDO heavy fuel oil shipments to Pyongyang since Washington had committed to pay only a share of the estimated $50 million annual cost.

American diplomats tried to reconcile the conflicting goals of concentrated decisionmaking and broad participation in the new KEDO charter. It was a difficult challenge. One State Department lawyer recalled trying to extract a structure out of four or five organizational charters spread out over his desk, each laced with notes and scribbles.[42] In the end, the partners agreed to establish a trilateral executive board with decisionmaking authority, advisory committees comprised of other governments and keyed to each of the organization's projects (such as the light-water reactors and the heavy fuel oil), and an annual general conference. But neither the committees nor the conference were granted a decisive role in KEDO's management or activities.

Washington also had to reconcile Seoul's drive to embellish its role in KEDO with the need for an organization that could work with Pyongyang. An early casualty of this balancing act was the plan for a U.S. company to be the prime contractor for the new reactors. Washington stepped aside in deference to Seoul's insistence as the principal project funder on selecting the prime. Instead, the United States settled for agreement that an American firm could play a supporting role as "program coordinator," monitoring the project and advising KEDO's management. Even then, Seoul objected to the possibility that a large U.S. company, such as Bechtel, might be chosen since it could siphon off choice contracts for itself.

The two allies clashed on other issues. The South tried to limit the powers of the executive director in charge of KEDO—slated to be an American—and insisted on using the term "Korean standard reactor" in the charter, which clearly meant the *South* Korean model. That would send a not so subtle signal to Pyongyang and foreclose any possibility that Seoul might still be edged out of providing the reactor. At a trilateral meeting in December 1994, Gallucci traded one demand for the other, agreeing to include the Korean reactor formulation in the charter in return for preserving the authority of the executive director. Balancing Seoul's demands and Pyongyang's concerns would become centrally important in the spring of 1995, when working out a reactor supply contract acceptable to the two Koreas almost led to a renewed military confrontation between Washington and North Korea.

While the trilateral partners managed to bridge their differences, their success had unintended negative consequences for the future. Having established KEDO, the partners tried to recruit new members and to raise money. But the response was disappointing. By the end of 1995, KEDO had to resort to deficit financing in order to deliver the oil required by the Geneva accord. Rhetorical support was easily obtained, but short memories and recognition that new members would have limited say in KEDO quickly obscured the sense of crisis over the nuclear issue. Government purse strings tightened. Australia provided a significant contribution, but modest funds from others barely put a dent in the new organization's budgetary requirements.

Europe seemed the most likely source of large-scale funding, but pitching KEDO across the Atlantic seemed harder than selling it to the U.S. Congress. Only the European style was different; passive resistance as opposed to outright hostility. At one point, President Clinton raised KEDO in a phone call with Chancellor Helmut Kohl of Germany, followed up with a letter, and when Kohl did not respond, sent another message before the 1995 G-7 summit. But there was still no answer. Clinton raised KEDO with Kohl again at the summit. Bonn eventually agreed to a one-time contribution of $1 million, but by now it was clear that limited access to KEDO decisionmaking posed a problem. Faced with harsh realities, just a year after KEDO was formed Washington and Tokyo persuaded Seoul to revise the organization's charter. That opened the way for the European Union to join the Executive Board in 1997 and an annual multimillion-dollar contribution to the implementation of the Agreed Framework.

Home before Christmas

Returning home from a San Francisco meeting with South Korea and Japan on December 17, American officials were pleased with the constructive talks. Then came disturbing news: a U.S. helicopter had been shot down over North Korea. Speaking on CNN, White House chief of staff Leon Panetta called the situation "ominous." Bill Perry responded bluntly: "We want them returned."[43] Although this was not the first time a U.S. helicopter had been shot down over the North, the incident threatened to derail an agreement that was still in its infancy.

Until December, implementation had been progressing well. On October 29, Kang Sok Ju informed Gallucci that the nuclear program had been frozen. Pyongyang made good progress in talks with the International Atomic Energy Agency, with U.S. experts on storing the plutonium-laden spent fuel rods, and with the State Department on establishing liaison offices. The Kim Jong Il regime had given Kang's delegation a special banquet at a restaurant on the banks of the Taedong River in Pyongyang. The dinner was significant since the top military brass attended, implicitly signaling its approval of the Agreed Framework. It also exceeded gestures conferred by Kim Il Sung for past accomplishments; in 1990 he had shown his personal endorsement simply by "receiving" North Korean negotiators after the first inter-Korean prime ministerial talks.

Coincidentally, the day the American helicopter was shot down, Representative Bill Richardson, a six-term Democrat from New Mexico, arrived on a regular flight from Beijing at Pyongyang's Sunan Airport. A graduate of Tufts University's Fletcher School of Law and Diplomacy, Richardson took to politics after hearing Senator Hubert Humphrey speak about public service, moved to New Mexico, and was elected to Congress in 1982. In 1994 Richardson was at the beginning of a career as a congressional diplomat, working to free hostages and prisoners around the world. Three years later, he would be appointed UN ambassador, en route to becoming secretary of energy before returning to elective politics as governor of New Mexico.

Emerging from his airplane, Richardson was instantly engulfed in a diplomatic crisis. Asked by a Chinese reporter what he thought about the downing of the helicopter, a surprised Richardson was whisked away before he could say anything. In his car, the North Koreans told him the incident was under investigation, but apparently had occurred after the helicopter strayed 5 kilometers inside their territory. One pilot, Bobby Hall, survived the crash, but the other, David Hilemon, was dead. The initial report on Pyongyang radio did not suggest the helicopter was on a belligerent mission or that the intrusion was deliberate. It did not even mention the United States. The low-key reaction seemed to imply that the North wanted to resolve the incident quickly.[44]

Confronted with a delicate situation, Richardson and his State Department escort, Dick Christenson, decided to go ahead with their meetings. (Christenson had accompanied Jimmy Carter to Pyongyang just six months before.) But they would now try to secure the release of Hall and the return of Hilemon's remains while staying in close telephone contact with Washington. That task was complicated by the fact that, because of economic sanctions in place since the 1950s, phone calls could be placed from Pyongyang to the United States but not the other way. As a result, Richardson's phone bill ran into thousands of dollars.[45]

Making the rounds in Pyongyang, the New Mexico Democrat encountered a strange disconnect. North Korean legislators pressed for visits to the United States. Economic officials wanted American investment. None seemed to understand the implications of the helicopter incident except to wonder why the United States would launch such a deliberate provocation so soon after the Geneva accord was signed. The foreign minister told Richardson that until the military completed its investigation of the incident, he was powerless to do anything.

In spite of what seemed to be an improving U.S.-North Korean relationship, it quickly became clear that resolving this incident would prove more complicated than past episodes. Intelligence analysts in Washington noted that on the second day of the 1977 downing of a U.S. helicopter, Pyongyang issued an authoritative statement signaling its intention to settle the matter by terming the episode an "unhappy incident" resulting from errors by American personnel. This time, no such statement was made.[46]

For three days, Richardson tried a variety of arguments on the Foreign Ministry. He pointed out the irony that survivors of the 1977 incident were returned quickly, but now, with improved relations, it was taking longer. Richardson even threatened not to leave the North until his demands were satisfied. In the end, though he did not see or talk to Hall, Richardson did secure the release of Hilemon's body, which he escorted across the Demilitarized Zone on December 22. Washington welcomed this "humanitarian" gesture and sent a letter to Pyongyang expressing regret for the incident, attributing it to a navigational error. The North, in turn, said that Hall was in good health, and when the investigation was completed "a step will be taken according to the relevant legal procedures of our army."[47]

Christmas came and went without Hall's release. Then Kang requested that Washington send another envoy to Pyongyang. Tom Hubbard was dispatched, flying to Osan Air Force Base on an old Boeing 707 that in better days had served the President of the United States as *Air Force One*, then on to Pyongyang by car. At first, he had to endure lengthy demands. Displaying photographs and a map illustrating that the incursion was an accident, Hubbard warned against making the American pilot a hostage to gain concessions. He had his own demand, to see Hall and Kang right away.

That evening, Hubbard placed the first of many calls to Tony Lake, the president's national security adviser. Furious that Hubbard had not seen Hall or Kang, Lake bluntly—and in full expectation that the North would be eavesdropping—asserted that this incident proved the United States could not have any faith in North Korea and that the Agreed Framework was threatened by this behavior.[48]

Beginning the next day, the talks moved rapidly to a conclusion. The North Koreans presented a draft proposal for a solution riddled with unacceptable demands, calling on Washington to apologize for espionage, to engage in direct military talks with the North (a clear dig at Seoul), and to ask Seoul to return long-term North Korean prisoners. Pyongyang had made similar demands in a 1963 helicopter incident and after the seizure of the USS *Pueblo* in 1968. Hubbard responded that the United States would only express regret for the incident and that any military-to-military talks would take place in an "appropriate forum," a diplomatic way of sidestepping that demand.

Ultimately, the deal was sealed along the lines of the American proposal. During a late night dinner with Kang outside Pyongyang, Hubbard called Washington and secured its approval. Kang then rushed off, saying he would take the document to Kim Jong Il. The North's final go-ahead was given the morning of December 30 (after Hubbard had overheard the North Koreans totaling up his phone bill and the drivers talking about how they would need snow tires for the upcoming trip to Panmunjom).[49]

The whole affair, though harrowing, provided important insights into dealing with North Korea. First, it shed light on how decisions were made in Pyongyang. In the past, the conventional wisdom was that decisionmaking was monolithic, which was an oversimplification. There were serious differences in the leadership leading at times to inconsistency or paralysis. Now commentators moved to the other extreme. Jim Mann, a well-respected journalist, wrote in the *Los Angeles Times* that "the helicopter incident underscored just how shaky the North Korean leadership is," implying that the recent succession process had left the government paralyzed. According to Mann, that did not bode well for cooperation in implementing the Agreed Framework. The actual situation was probably somewhere in between.[50]

Rather than move quickly to resolve the incident, it may have made sense from Kim Jong Il's perspective to move deliberately, particularly since he was in a testing period in which others were consistently evaluating his performance. The helicopter intrusion was logically the province of the military, at least initially, and the Korean People's Army was in no mood to be cooperative. It was unhappy with the Agreed Framework, the *Kitty Hawk* incident, and the public threats American officials had made at that time. Given the military's dominant stature in society, it would have been neither wise nor necessary for the Foreign Ministry to attempt to preempt it in handling the intrusion. The North Korean leadership may also have seen other benefits to moving deliberately if it could demonstrate that the situation on the peninsula was still dangerous and nobody should take Pyongyang for granted.

In spite of press speculation, there was no evidence that the military was trying to undermine the Geneva accord. Rather, it was probably trying to use the helicopter incident to advance its own agenda with Washington. That agenda included demands for direct U.S.–North Korean military talks and for replacing the decades-old armistice with a permanent peace treaty to prevent such incidents. These themes, prevalent in the North's media, had been given lip service in Geneva by the Foreign Ministry–dominated delegation but then were quickly dropped.

Once it became clear that nothing more was to be gained and something might be lost (the prospect of better relations with the United States), the North Koreans moved quickly. Indeed, the Foreign Ministry seemed to use Hubbard's presence to bring the matter to a head after the military had found no basis to contradict the American version of events. Whether deliberate or not, the timing was fortuitous. Hall was not released by Christmas, maybe to make the point that Pyongyang would not succumb to pressure. But he was set free before Congress reconvened in January, when an unresolved incident would have, as Richardson warned, created significant problems. Senator John McCain did complain about Richardson's phone bill (which seemed odd) and the "gymnastics" the North made the administration go through to secure Hall's release. But the fact that the release had already happened took the wind out of his sails.[51]

The helicopter incident did not affect the implementation of the Geneva accord, though it did threaten the administration's ability to build domestic support for it. Perhaps the most important lesson for the future was that the Agreed Framework would not erase the residue of five decades of cold war confrontation overnight. Washington, Seoul, and Pyongyang now had the more difficult task of managing a new era of cooperation and confrontation.

The reservoir of experience gained from the nuclear crisis was also important, helping Washington secure an acceptable outcome without apologizing or falsely confessing to espionage, something it had done before to secure the return of American personnel. Putting to use his previous experience with North Koreans, Tom Hubbard made a strong initial presentation, drew clear "red lines," refused to negotiate matters unrelated to Hall, such as establishing U.S.–North Korean military talks, and pointed to the downsides of letting the incident drag on. Unlike some South Koreans, who sought to box the North into the smallest corner possible, Hubbard pushed them to middle ground where they realized the incident could be resolved on acceptable terms. In turn, the North dropped demands that crossed U.S. "red lines" and moved directly to the practical task of drafting a joint statement. The outcome was acceptable to both sides.

Tom Hubbard never saw Bobby Hall until they reached the DMZ, and then only for a moment. Hall followed him across the demarcation line, carrying a shopping bag of Christmas cookies made for the American serviceman but confiscated from Hubbard when he entered the North. As he crossed the line,

Hall was engulfed by a group of American military officials and whisked away. Told there was a telephone call for him, Hubbard retreated to a nearby bunker where he found himself talking to the president of the United States, who typically asked a stream of questions about the situation in North Korea.[52]

Hubbard and Hall met later in Seoul and traveled on the retired *Air Force One* back to Hall's home state, Florida. Four years later, American visitors would see the original copy of the "Hubbard Understanding" displayed alongside other trophies, including Washington's apology for the *Pueblo* incident, in Pyongyang's Korean War museum.[53]

Almost Slipping on Heavy Fuel Oil

While the Bobby Hall incident had threatened the administration's drive to build domestic support for the Geneva accord, its resolution cleared the way to move forward on Capitol Hill. The Deputies Committee had decided in December to redouble administration efforts on the Hill. The centerpiece of that campaign would be a rare joint appearance of the secretaries of state and defense before the Senate Foreign Relations Committee. Bill Perry would also testify before the Armed Services Committee, supported by General Luck. It was hoped that the combination of those appearances, the lobbying of centrist Republicans and Democrats, and modest funding requests for implementation would carry the day.

Testimony by Perry and Christopher went ahead on January 24–26. Christopher told the Foreign Relations Committee, "Some critics . . . have said we negotiated with no sticks in our hand. Let me assure them and the public that the Patriot missiles, the Apache helicopters and the Bradley fighting vehicles that we sent to Korea were not armed with carrots."[54]

Perry struck a similar theme; he had seriously considered "going in and taking out the reactor" but decided instead on sanctions combined with augmenting military strength, an approach that brought Pyongyang to the negotiating table. Perry was particularly effective in laying out the adverse political, military, and budgetary consequences of a continuing crisis on the peninsula.[55] As the deputies had agreed, the secretary of state affirmed that the U.S. financial commitment to the Agreed Framework would be limited to no more than $30 million per year for the funding of KEDO and its projects. Designed to ease the path toward putting the Geneva accord on firmer political footing, the United States would later regret this pledge as it became clear that international financial support for the new organization would fall short of its expectations.[56]

In contrast to the December hearings, the January sessions showed that the critics had been stymied, if not converted, and support from the political center was growing. In spite of his stance against the accord, Senator McCain admitted, "I do not think Congress should seek to overturn the agreement," especially since he expected North Korea to renege.[57]

Another critic, Senator Frank Murkowski, was also muted. Only seven weeks earlier, before the Bobby Hall incident, he and Democratic senator Paul Simon had the rare distinction of visiting Pyongyang. Whether the North Koreans grasped the intricacies of American politics was unclear, but some did understand that Congress might cause problems for the accord. Both were given the red carpet treatment. They also stopped in Seoul, where General Luck made his support for the Framework clear. Accordingly, Murkowski toned down his rhetoric, telling the press that he did not anticipate "any efforts to scuttle" the arrangement.[58]

Moderates were more positive. After helping the administration shape its strategy, Senator Levin now endorsed the agreement. Sam Nunn and Joseph Lieberman—centrist Democrats who were members of the Senate Armed Services Committee—were favorably inclined.[59] On the Foreign Relations Committee, Republican Richard Lugar, in his characteristically measured fashion, commented, "This is a reasonable agreement." Nancy Kassebaum, his colleague from the same side of the aisle, also was positive.[60] California Democrat Diane Feinstein, like many Americans of her generation, had lost a close friend in the Korean War. Initially ill disposed toward the accord, she came to see its advantages.[61]

Just as the dust began to settle in Congress, however, a new problem erupted. Under the Agreed Framework, the United States was to provide for the delivery to North Korea of "heavy oil for heating and electricity generation," specifically, 500,000 tons a year that helped seal the freeze on the North's plutonium production program. Heavy fuel oil (called HFO) offered the added advantage that it could not be used to power North Korea's tanks or aircraft. As long as that was the case, some U.S. officials did not care what Pyongyang used the oil for, but the Pentagon had insisted on specifying proper uses in the Agreed Framework. That led to some challenging unintended consequences.

Shortly after the first delivery to the Sonbong Thermoelectric Power Generating Station in January, Washington learned that North Korea may have been diverting some of the oil to steel plants in violation of the Geneva accord.[62] If the reports were true, the move seemed unlikely to advance any military objective. Nevertheless, with skepticism toward the accord running high, the concern could reignite congressional dissatisfaction and threaten funding for implementation. That danger was highlighted by an angry exchange of letters over the HFO issue between Mitch McConnell, the Republican chairman of a key Senate appropriations subcommittee, and Secretary Christopher, who told Congress that Pyongyang was in compliance with the arrangement.[63]

On this occasion, however, there were no differences between the executive and legislative branches: both agreed that any cheating must stop. Gallucci pledged that the United States would not provide heavy oil to North Korea until it could ensure that fuel was not diverted. Poneman and NSC senior director for intelligence George Tenet agreed to keep Congress fully informed through weekly reports.

To respond to the heavy fuel oil diversion, Washington moved on two fronts. First, an interagency group formulated monitoring measures to ensure that no further diversions would take place. The group quickly realized that success would require an on-site presence at plants where the heavy oil would be used, specifically common industrial instruments (preferably sealed to prevent tampering) that would record fuel flows, power generation, and smokestack emissions. Copies of the data produced by the instruments would then be forwarded to KEDO. While the administration planned to seek all three, any one would be adequate. But the big question was whether a closed society like North Korea would agree to such measures.

What followed was an extraordinary exchange of letters in which Bob Gallucci and Kang Sok Ju tried to resolve the potentially lethal problem of North Korea cheating on an agreement on which the ink was barely dry. Right away, Gallucci made it crystal clear that Pyongyang would have to live up to the Geneva accord. Kang first admitted that some heavy oil had been openly "transloaded" into rail cars for temporary storage and then acknowledged that some at Sonbong may have been transported to another enterprise. But "50,000 tons of heavy oil delivered by your side is being used clearly and exclusively by the Sonbong Thermal Power Plant only," the North Korean added. Nevertheless, he offered to let U.S. officials "verify our disposition of your heavy oil, whenever they come to our country aboard oil tankers in the future." Agreement was quickly reached on talks to work out a system of verification on the sidelines of an upcoming meeting on the new reactor project. But those discussions were delayed as the North was focused on solving one problem at a time.[64]

Once the reactor impasse was broken in June, the two countries began discussions on "cooperative measures" for monitoring the heavy fuel oil, a diplomatic reference to on-site equipment to track the use and disposition of the oil. Working on behalf of KEDO, a team led by Foreign Service veteran James Pierce arrived in Pyongyang. The talks took place in a building adjacent to

Kim Il Sung square, in the heart of Pyongyang where mass demonstrations and military parades were held. Since it was a week and a day before the anniversary of the start of the Korean War, the party-faithful were already rehearsing for celebrations that would mark the North's "victory." The fact that talks with the United States were taking place within earshot of thousands of goose-stepping Koreans shouting anti-American slogans cast a surreal air over the proceedings.

Still, the talks went well. The chief negotiator, Li Tae Gun, the managing director of Pyongyang's oil-importing agency, had one main interest, a steady and reliable supply of fuel oil. He wanted the United States to agree to a schedule of deliveries (the Geneva agreement only specified 100,000 tons between October and December 1995) and the early delivery of 40,000 metric tons by mid-July. While the Americans had anticipated his demands, Pierce could not respond positively since KEDO, still struggling through its infancy, would be in charge of those deliveries. He could only parry Li's requests, reinforced by phone conversations with Gallucci, probably monitored by the North Koreans, in which his boss said that the issue was nonnegotiable.

Discussions over on-site monitoring, however, achieved a quick breakthrough. Li ruled out two of the three methods suggested by the Americans but agreed to allow the measurement of fuel flows at designated power plants, the best approach from Washington's perspective. The North Koreans also agreed to transport the team to the Sonbong plant to work out the details. After unsuccessfully trying to pry several thousand dollars from the Americans, claiming they would have to pay for a helicopter flight because of bad weather, the group boarded a train for a twenty-hour trip to Sonbong. The last half-hour was spent riding in a mint condition 1987 Cadillac, oddly out of place in that remote corner of North Korea.[65]

At the plant, the Americans met with a chilly reception, especially when it became clear they wanted to examine every nook and cranny. The only hitch, however, came when they proposed a satellite up-link to transmit data back to KEDO headquarters in New York City. Some North Koreans liked the idea, seeing it as a way to get a free piece of high-tech equipment, but in the end it was rejected as too intrusive. A fax would have to do. Otherwise, the North agreed to all of the measures the delegation wanted.[66]

As the Americans returned to Pyongyang and packed their bags for Beijing, the issue of a delivery schedule still hung fire. In what was becoming standard operating procedure, Li called Pierce in the very early morning hours, the day he was to depart, to ask for more talks. Two hours of discussions proved fruitless. In the car to the airport, Li made some "happy to glad" changes in the proposed text, but Pierce still could not accept his proposal. Remarkably, the

North Korean tried again just as they cleared passport control. As Pierce climbed the stairs to the plane, he glanced back at a dejected Li, clearly not looking forward to telling his superiors that he had failed to secure an agreement on a delivery schedule.[67] Nevertheless, U.S. technicians returned two months later to install the on-site monitoring equipment.

With a showdown over cheating averted, Congress took only limited steps to show its displeasure with the Agreed Framework. Aside from canceling the emergency authority under which the Defense Department funded the first oil delivery, the House held up the administration's first budget request, the provision of $10 million to fund the storage of the plutonium-laced fuel at Yongbyon. The request was finally approved in May 1995 after Pyongyang suggested that it might find its own solution to the problem, a not so subtle reference to the possibility of Washington losing track of North Korea's plutonium stocks.

When the administration's budget proposal for $22 million in implementation funding hit the Hill, the new Republican chairman of the House Appropriations Committee, Robert Livingston, blocked it. Though convinced that the Agreed Framework was worthwhile, he told Gallucci that he could not approve taxpayer dollars to support light-water reactor construction in North Korea because his constituents would not understand why the United States was giving reactors to a country that posed a nuclear proliferation threat. The administration budget proposal was subsequently amended and approved, with all the funding confined to oil deliveries and setting up KEDO. Nevertheless, Congress attached a number of certification requirements that the administration had to meet every year if subsequent funding were to be approved.

In negotiating a successful solution to the potential problem of oil diversion, Washington had once again not only averted another crisis, but also learned more about Pyongyang's behavior. The incident did show that North Korea, in a pinch, was willing to look for ways to stretch the limits of or evade the terms of agreements. That did not come as a surprise to any of the Americans who had experience in dealing with the North Koreans or, for that matter, any of the others who had been engaged in trying to resolve the nuclear crisis for almost two years.

But it also demonstrated the North's ability to turn on a dime and to take surprising steps to resolve potential problems that might undercut its broader interests. North Korea permitted an unprecedented degree of intrusive monitoring in what would normally be considered an area of prime national security, its power generation system. That meant if there was something North Korea wanted badly enough—and in 1995 Pyongyang needed fuel oil because of its growing economic problems—it was capable of taking steps that under other circumstances would have been rejected out of hand. Second, despite failing to agree on a written record of the negotiations, the North honored its commitment to allow installation of the monitoring equipment. Again, if North Korea put a high enough premium on obtaining something, then the implementation of the transaction tended to fall into place relatively smoothly, even if all the details were not resolved on paper.

Finally, the "nonnegotiable demands" for a written schedule of oil deliveries reinforced previous lessons American negotiators had learned from dealing with Pyongyang. As untrusting negotiators who were willing to edge up to the brink in order to find the other side's bottom line, the North Koreans often would go too far for their own good, as in this case. The Americans had leveled with them from the start when they said the North Korean demand was impossible to meet.

In the months since the signing of the Agreed Framework, the administration had weathered the political storm—but at a significant cost. It had voluntarily locked itself into a limit on American funding of up to $30 million per year. That move would soon prove to be a handicap, as U.S. efforts to raise funds from other countries for KEDO heavy fuel oil deliveries fell far short of what was needed to make up the difference between the U.S. contribution and the total cost of fuel obligated under the Framework. Moreover, in spite of growing deficit funding for KEDO, the administration remained leery of seeking more appropriated U.S. funds given its initial experience with the Hill. Funding requests within the announced limit, while usually approved, always triggered a struggle.

In short, while the administration managed to muddle through, it never succeeded in putting the agreement on the kind of long-term political footing that would make yearly skirmishes unnecessary. Rather than winning the war with its domestic opponents, a hard-fought political truce was established. As time would tell, over the next decade that truce would have its ups and downs. It would eventually break down with the election of a Republican administration skeptical about the 1994 accord and new revelations regarding Pyongyang's nuclear program.

Back to the Brink?

While implementation of the Agreed Framework required a range of technical talks between the United States and North Korea, these discussions quickly revealed that the most difficult issue would be the negotiation of a supply contract for the provision of the light-water reactor project. Talks began in

November 1994 in Beijing. The Agreed Framework committed the United States to using its "best efforts" to conclude the contract within six months, that is, by April 21, 1995. This would have been a tall order in the best of circumstances, but the diametrically opposed perspectives in Pyongyang and Seoul quickly hobbled the discussions.

Newly appointed foreign minister Gong Ro Myung used his first visit to Washington in February 1995 to tell Secretary Christopher that South Korea's "central role" in the new reactor project must "be spelled out for all the world to see" for the sake of its "national prestige."[68] For South Korea, that meant any agreement on the new project had to include the magic words "Korean standard model" when describing the origin of the new reactors.

Gong, who had come to Washington as a special envoy of the new government just before Pyongyang announced its intention to withdraw from the NPT, had spent most of the crisis as Seoul's ambassador to Japan. He was recalled at the end of 1994 when President Kim finally fired Foreign Minister Han, who had seen the handwriting on the wall during the October blow-up between Washington and Seoul. Before going to the president's office for their final official meeting, Han told an assistant to separate his own books from the others in his office. He knew that once asked to resign, he would no longer be able to return to his office or to pick up his personal property. President Kim offered Han the job of ambassador to the United States, but he declined, preferring to return to academia.[69]

North Korea had no intention of doing what Gong wanted. From its perspective, Pyongyang knew that Seoul would play a central role in the new reactor project, in providing technology and funding. But to have that role advertised in neon lights was too much to bear without sacrificing its own "national prestige" and losing points in the continuing game of one-upmanship with South Korea. Pyongyang's objective was to play up Washington's role and play down the appearance of dependence on Seoul.

With negotiating positions so polarized, there appeared little room for compromise between North and South. As talks progressed from November into the new year, between an American delegation on behalf of the fledgling KEDO and the North, it became clear that Pyongyang had essentially just one card to play in opposition to Seoul's implacable insistence on openly naming the Korean standard reactor. That card was to renew the threat of breaking the nuclear freeze it had formally accepted under the terms of the Agreed Framework. In February Gallucci already estimated the odds at 60 percent that the North would do just that. Everyone understood that a broken freeze would immediately plunge the fragile accord into crisis, raising the specter of a return to sanctions and military confrontation.

Normally, with so much at stake the United States would be inclined to grab the steering wheel to manage the crisis. But by early 1995, American policymakers were bending over backwards to assuage South Korean feelings that Seoul had been insufficiently involved in the Agreed Framework. In that spirit, Washington was deferring as much as possible to Seoul's preferences—and leadership—in dealing with the North. Moreover, since the new reactor project would ultimately be the responsibility of the multilateral KEDO, which was established in March, the Americans were even more sensitive to views in Seoul and Tokyo. Chafing at the dismally narrow options to resolve the reemerging North-South confrontation, President Clinton showed his unease by commenting on a memo outlining the next steps in U.S. strategy: "OK, but let's discuss." Gallucci apprised Jimmy Carter of the deteriorating situation, while Poneman conveyed the same message to President Gerald Ford and Brent Scowcroft.

The irony in the new crisis was that there was essentially no disagreement among North Korea, South Korea, and the United States on the substance of the approach to the reactor project. Pyongyang was ready to accept the reality of a South Korean reactor model as the one provided to North Korea. But the appearance of that reality—anathema to the North, nirvana to the South—nearly brought the peninsula to armed confrontation. As American officials prepared to leave for Berlin to negotiate the light-water reactor issue with the North, a Principals Committee meeting on March 17 confirmed that—if the North broke the freeze—the United States would work with its allies and return to the UN Security Council for the imposition of sanctions. Everyone knew that also meant resurrecting the military option, including the dispatch of more American forces to the Korean Peninsula and Asia. Before the meeting ended, Lake asked William Perry and John Shalikashvili to dust off those plans for review.

Meanwhile, in Berlin, the difficult task of resolving the reactor-naming issue fell to the pragmatic and resourceful Gary Samore who, once again, had to face Berlin Kim Jong U. Samore repeatedly explained that the South Korean model was the obvious choice since Seoul was bearing the lion's share of the financing. While Russia was an obvious alternative in view of its contract to provide reactors to North Korea in the 1980s, it could not give away reactors for free. But the South Koreans had no intention of providing financing for, or of living downwind from, reactors designed by the parties responsible for the Chernobyl nuclear accident. When the North Koreans expressed interest in American-designed reactors, Samore countered that Pyongyang would benefit from those designs since the South Korean model was based on U.S. technology. He also explained that Seoul would never hand over responsibility to an

American supplier. In short, only the South Korean version of the American Combustion Engineering Model-80, conveniently dubbed the Korean Standard Nuclear Plant, would do.

Berlin Kim pushed back hard. Indeed, the more the substantive differences over the reactor project narrowed, the more the political breach widened, by focusing on questions of image and pride. From the North's perspective, Seoul's preference for an openly advertised South Korean reactor model for the KEDO light-water reactor project would deeply wound its sense of self-reliance. To accept technical assistance from the South would be an admission of weakness and inferiority; hence the attraction to the implausible "shopping spree" approach to reactor selection. In a society where questions of "face" often dominate political discourse, the reactor-naming issue was quintessentially insoluble precisely because it was all about face.

For good measure, Kim Jong U also pressed for a $500 million package to upgrade North Korea's electricity grid to accommodate the two light-water reactors, a request the Americans flatly denied. The irony of the request was not lost on the Americans, who had told the North Koreans during the 1994 negotiations that their electricity needs could far better be met by smaller fossil-fired plants than the large light-water reactors Pyongyang sought.[70]

Berlin Kim thrashed and blustered, often telling Samore that it was impossible even to report the American position to Pyongyang. Samore and his colleagues came up with a number of alternative formulations to achieve the substantive outcome desired by Seoul (South Korean leadership in the reactor project) without rubbing Pyongyang's nose in it publicly. The problem was that the South Korean position seemed to be guided by an obsession with wordplay and domestic politics rather than genuine security considerations. Seoul rejected any negotiating flexibility on the point, and out of deference to its ally, the American delegation allowed the March talks to end without making any progress.

An April 1 letter from Kang to Gallucci was more explicit than the bluster in Berlin. He threatened—absent a supply agreement by April 21—to "unfreeze such a part of our nuclear program as is necessary to save our face in the eyes of the world, and to continue the necessary negotiations during the unfreeze period. We wish your side to understand this." Faced by the possible resumption of operations at Yongbyon, the Pentagon group that coordinated military and diplomatic policy was reactivated. Chaired by Under Secretary of Defense for Policy Walt Slocombe, it included Gallucci, Poneman, Senior Director for Asian Affairs Stanley Roth of the NSC, Deputy Director of Central Intelligence Douglas McEachin, Lieutenant General Howell Estes, and Lieutenant General Wesley Clark. Having actively worked together before in the spring of 1994, the group now proceeded once again to consider American options.

The United States had several alternatives if North Korea ended the nuclear freeze. The main assumption was that the United States would move back to the phased approach to sanctions it had pursued at the time of the June 1994 crisis. This would ensure that appropriate military enhancements to allied forces in the region were paced in accordance with increasing diplomatic and economic pressure from the prospect, then the implementation, of sanctions. The key question was whether the military enhancements would be more likely to deter or to provoke an attack by North Korea. Alternatively, the North might respond to the threat of sanctions by removing the spent fuel from the pond. If they did so, then reprocessing could separate enough plutonium for one bomb within six weeks, for three to four bombs within four months.

Since that was unacceptable, the Pentagon group considered once again the option of attacking the Yongbyon nuclear facility in the event that reprocessing operations were confirmed. Before the president made any final decision on bombing Yongbyon, the administration would need to consult with Seoul and Tokyo, plan for the contingency of civilian evacuation, and carefully evaluate the optimal moment for an attack. Moreover, as a strike at Yongbyon could trigger a general war in Korea, the group assumed that it would be preceded by the deployment of the full complement of military reinforcements that the Pentagon had planned in June 1994. But how should the pacing of the deployments be calibrated?

Two schools of thought emerged. One held that additional forces and equipment should flow seamlessly into position within two months. The rationale was that once the United States had visibly committed to reinforcing its forces, there was every incentive to complete the deployment quickly so as to minimize the window between alerting the enemy and achieving a position that would most effectively deter North Korean aggression. The other school of thought favored a phased approach to flowing in forces, on the grounds that too rapid an introduction could be counterproductive, provoking rather than deterring a North Korean attack. Moreover, flowing the full augmentation in at once could lose South Korean support, cost a great deal, and be difficult to sustain over time.

Meanwhile, Samore returned to Berlin to mount a final push to complete the reactor supply contract by the April 21 deadline. During U.S.–South Korean consultations in preparation for the meeting, Seoul continued to reject any flexibility on the reactor name. Berlin Kim was also back, persisting in his truculent negotiating style, at one point threatening that if the United States did not table a new position, the North Koreans would leave at 3:30 PM the next day. (When Poneman asked CIA official Doug McEachin if the U.S. intelligence community thought the increasingly overwrought rhetoric in Berlin could be discounted as falling within the range considered "normal," he received a simple reply: yes.)

As rigor mortis set into the two Koreas' bargaining positions, the Clinton administration struggled to find a way to bridge the gap. The Principals Committee met no less than four times in April to discuss the reactor negotiations. Some participants placed highest priority on maintaining allied solidarity, preferring to "tough it out" in support of the South on the reactor-naming issue than risk a split with their ally. Lake pressed the point: "Is that a strategy to stick with our ally come what may, or a tactic to induce flexibility?" He added: "If it is not a strategy, and the tactic is wrong, then you will end up with no Agreed Framework, no Security Council sanctions, a military buildup sine die, restart of the 5-megawatt reactor, and an unconstrained nuclear program in North Korea."

Others feared that slavish support for South Korea would jeopardize the nuclear freeze and IAEA inspections, lead to a needless military confrontation, and leave Washington with a pathetically weak case for sanctions at the Security Council: disagreement over a name. Allied solidarity, commented one principal, had to run both ways: "If we are to stay arm in arm with South Korea, why do we do what they want to do and not what we want to do?" Gallucci was even more direct: "This is not about substance. We are not talking about a real concession. It is about President Kim wanting to create a political crisis to help him in the upcoming elections and we should not let him do that."

Despite its growing concern, however, the administration continued to adhere to Seoul's position. As the talks appeared doomed to miss the April 21 deadline, the Americans began to consider elevating the discussions from the technical to the political level, perhaps returning to Geneva. Though Seoul and Tokyo were uncomfortable with the idea, the Americans argued that neither the UN Security Council nor the American people would understand risking a war over a label that experts had failed to define and politicians failed to approve.

After months of dealing with exasperating Korean haggling on both sides of the 38th parallel, Under Secretary Slocombe took refuge in a whimsical draft for Gallucci to send to Kang:

> The present impasse arises because of your side's stubborn refusal to acknowledge in writing what you have repeatedly admitted understanding, that the light-water reactor will be based on Ulchin 3 and 4 with the ROK putting up most of the money and naturally assuming the leading

role. April 21 is a target not a deadline. The interests of peace—and the survival of your inefficient regime—depend on a solution. Thus our generous offer of political level talks. You have responded with a demand that we first concede all the points at issue. Such arrogance would ill become a nation better able to handle its affairs than yours. As a final gesture of magnanimity, the United States would overlook your presumptuous and impertinent reply and renew our offer to meet in Geneva, if and only if the freeze is scrupulously observed. If, instead of negotiations, you insist on precipitating a wholly unnecessary crisis, then the consequences will rest with you and not with

Your obedient servant

R. Gallucci

On April 20, the Berlin talks collapsed without reaching agreement. That same day, the principals agreed that Gallucci would write to Kang proposing that the two sides meet in Geneva to resolve the impasse, provided that Pyongyang maintain the nuclear freeze. Secretary Christopher would call Foreign Minister Gong to explain that since the Berlin talks had reached an impasse, the United States must offer the North an opportunity to meet Gallucci as a prelude to gaining support for Security Council sanctions. The principals also agreed that the United States would proceed with the letter to the North two hours after the Christopher call, even if Seoul objected. Gallucci then sent the letter.

Suggesting an internal struggle over a matter of such urgency, Pyongyang took nearly three weeks to respond. Finally, on May 10, a Kang letter arrived. He steered clear of polemics but insisted that he could not leave Pyongyang. Kang accepted the proposal for higher-level talks, agreed that they would focus on the Agreed Framework, and affirmed that North Korea would maintain the freeze during the discussions. Since Kang could not travel, he proposed that his deputy in Geneva, Ambassador Kim Gye Gwan, lead a delegation.

While there was some speculation that Kang might need to stay home because of uncertainties surrounding the succession, Poneman urged his bosses to accept the proposal and to hold meetings in Asia rather than send lower-level officials to Geneva and tacitly downgrade that channel. Pyongyang quickly agreed to an administration offer to send Tom Hubbard—Gallucci's deputy in Geneva—to meet Kim in Kuala Lumpur. The two deputies had often been able to resolve nettlesome issues that Gallucci and Kang had been forced to set to one side during the 1994 negotiations, offering a glimmer of hope that the intractable reactor problem might finally be resolved.

The Kuala Lumpur talks were a marathon session, beginning on May 16 and lasting over three weeks. As much as anything, their protracted nature reflected the difficulties between the Americans and South Koreans, as Seoul rejected a series of formulations that would achieve the substance of its objectives but allow Pyongyang to save face. One participant recalled the essence of the impasse:

> We were trapped in a zero-sum game over words in which neither Korean side would settle for anything less than wording that would make the other Korean side gag. The substance of the words was irrelevant—it was simply a matter of humiliating the other side. For that reason, compromise—by definition—was out of the question because if the other Korea could live with the language, it wasn't offensive enough. The definition of victory was that the other side was angry.[71]

Kuala Lumpur descended into a monotonous pattern. The Americans would meet with the North Koreans to explore a formula to describe the reactor project. Afterward the Americans would brief the South Koreans on what had transpired, field their objections, then brief the Japanese, then report to Washington. Presently fresh instructions would emerge from Washington, and Hubbard would, once more, begin the round robin of negotiations and consultations.

At one point during a particularly long gap in the negotiations, Washington insisted that a number of the U.S. officials—including Steve Aoki from NSC and Danny Russel from the State Department—remain in Kuala Lumpur, lest by pulling up stakes and returning home the Americans would signal to the world that the talks had "failed" and thereby plunge Korea back into a crisis potentially as grave as that of the year before. Aoki, Russel, and the others quickly dubbed themselves "the hostages."[72]

Finally, three weeks into the talks, Hubbard exclaimed in exasperation: "We have spent all this time arguing over whether we will call them American (as the North Koreans demanded) or Korean standard reactors (as the South Koreans demand). Why don't we agree not to call them anything?" As a rare flicker of relief passed across Kim Gye Gwan's eyes, Gary Samore quickly suggested that the parties find a technical term that could apply only to the originally U.S. technology that the South Koreans call the Korean standard reactor. That turned out to be "two pressurized light-water reactors with two coolant loops." The new turn of phrase became the basis of the U.S. agreement with the North Koreans regarding the description of the reactor.[73]

The next week was spent persuading the South Koreans that they could accept it. This was no mean feat, as the best language the Americans were able to extract from Pyongyang specified that KEDO would select "the advanced version of U.S.-origin design," falling far short of South Korean demands.

From Seoul's perspective, that phrase in the final description accepted by the Democratic People's Republic of Korea and the United States constituted a fatal flaw. So did the failure to mention South Korea at all. During a break from the grueling talks, a South Korean diplomat essentially confirmed what everyone already knew: Seoul could never accept a formula that Pyongyang could accept. Compromise was impossible. But so was war, over such a frivolous issue of verbal gymnastics. The implication was clear; the Americans would need to cut a deal according to its best lights without obtaining permission from a government in Seoul that was hopelessly fixated on form over substance. On June 7, in response to such a U.S. proposal, Pyongyang accepted the structure of a deal whereby KEDO and North Korea would conclude a supplier agreement that did not mention South Korea. KEDO would announce separately that it had selected South Korea to supply the reactors.[74]

Seoul was furious at this sleight of hand. President Clinton tried to contain the South Korean backlash to the Kuala Lumpur deal by calling Kim Young Sam on June 8. Clinton explained that the North Koreans had accepted the substance of the South Korean leading role in the Kuala Lumpur accords. While Kim thanked Clinton for his explanation, he said he was astounded by the North Korean announcement on the reactor type. As Kim went on, he became more and more agitated. South Korea had adopted American advice on flexibility, and now the United States had sold out the South despite its firm resolve on the subject of the naming of the reactor.

As President Kim reeled through his complaints, Poneman, who was taking notes on the other extension in the Oval Office, scrawled page after page of talking points in response and handed them to the president. Clinton emphasized that the text of the Kuala Lumpur accords made clear that the reactor would be the South Korean model. Moreover, South Korea would choose the (presumably South Korean) prime contractor, which would have the central role in designing and manufacturing the reactor. Afterward, comparing notes with the American interpreter downstairs in the Situation Room, Poneman learned that President Kim's interpreter had significantly softened the edge of the South Korean president's anger in translating his words into English. The South Korean interpreter may have been assisted by the egalitarianism of the English language, as President Kim apparently addressed President Clinton in the second-person pronoun form reserved not for honored equals, but rather for social inferiors.

The next day Gallucci and Assistant Secretary of State for East Asia Winston Lord flew to Seoul to persuade the South Koreans to accept the Kuala Lumpur deal. By June 12, Seoul was back on board, albeit grumpily, and President Clinton wrote President Kim to emphasize that South Korea's central role in the light-water project was clearly spelled out in the Kuala Lumpur accords and would ultimately "contribute significantly" to the joint U.S.-ROK efforts to resolve the North Korean nuclear issue.

The stage was now set for coordinated announcements in Kuala Lumpur, Seoul, and Washington on June 13. In Kuala Lumpur, Hubbard and Kim Gye Gwan released a joint U.S.-DPRK statement specifying that the light-water reactor project "will consist of two pressurized light water reactors with two coolant loops and a generating capacity of approximately 1,000MW(e) each. The reactor model, selected by KEDO, will be the advanced version of U.S.-origin design and technology currently under production."[75] In Seoul, Gallucci was joined by his South Korean and Japanese counterparts—Ambassadors Choi Dong Jin and Tetsuya Endo, respectively—in announcing that the KEDO executive board meeting had concluded that the light-water reactor project to be provided to the DPRK would consist of two reactors of the South Korean standard nuclear plant model.[76] Gallucci added that a South Korean prime contractor for the project was also selected. At the White House, the president issued a statement welcoming both the Kuala Lumpur and Seoul decisions as critical steps to keep North Korea's dangerous nuclear facilities frozen.[77]

On June 17, having seen polls showing that 62 percent of his people supported the Kuala Lumpur accords, President Kim responded by reiterating the key elements of the agreement (those ensuring South Korea's central role) and expressing his appreciation for Clinton's unremitting efforts to resolve the North Korean nuclear issue. He also urged the American leader to help renew North-South dialogue. But President Kim's domestic political position continued to slip. In the much-anticipated June 1995 elections—the first democratic local and provincial elections in thirty-four years—President Kim's party took a beating, losing the mayoralty in Seoul as well as a number of other significant mayoral and gubernatorial elections.

Even that could not sour the mood at the much-anticipated trip of President Kim to Washington one month later. His July 27 visit to the White House could not have contrasted more starkly with the blow-up in the Oval Office twenty months earlier. The nuclear crisis had been contained, the leading South Korean role in the reactor project assured, and the desire for a state visit satisfied. It was late on a sweltering summer morning and, after reviewing the honor guard to the strains of "Ruffles and Flourishes" on the South Lawn, the American and Korean delegations repaired to the Diplomatic Reception Room for iced tea and orange juice. The two presidents did not linger, but rather sauntered down the West colonnade to the Oval Office, where they continued to converse through interpreters. Nancy Hernreich, the president's assistant, paged an urgent summons and in short order the aides for the two presidents arrived. Fortunately, this time there had been no surprises in the Oval Office.

Clinton expressed satisfaction that the combined efforts of the two allies had contained the North Korean nuclear threat. As for Kim, he returned to his standard litany: the North was unstable, with barely enough food for many to have more than one meal a day, and its energy production was low. He questioned Kim Jong Il's hold on power, noting that one year after his father's death there had been no formal assumption of power by the son. Under the elder Kim, orders from above were followed; the chain of command was no longer so solid. Perhaps it was a question of incapability or corruption. After all, President Kim continued, Kim Jong Il was known to sleep by day, rise at 11:00 PM, and drink all night long, often in the company of women. How long could this continue? (In the event, Kim Jong Il has been able to survive as leader of his country for nine years and counting as this book goes to press.)

When asked by President Clinton his view of how this would all turn out, the South Korean replied that North Korea was a doomed nation, already in its terminal phase. If that were the case, Clinton replied, the United States and South Korea needed to work together to manage the transition, lest the process of reunification be even more difficult and expensive than in Germany. "We need to manage the outcome so that it is best for the Republic of Korea, while maintaining security in the peninsula," Clinton asserted.

Kim agreed with Clinton: the key challenge would be to manage the North's transition gradually, prolonging the regime in order to avoid an overnight collapse. The two presidents also agreed on the need for close trilateral cooperation in managing the transition. When Clinton and Kim joined their full delegations shortly after noon in the Cabinet Room, the South Korean took the opportunity to "sincerely welcome" the Kuala Lumpur agreement, which reaffirmed his country's central role in the new reactor project. South Korea, he announced, supported the accord and would do whatever it could to implement it. The newly pacified South Korean president even publicly thanked Hubbard—so recently vilified for his role in the Kuala Lumpur negotiations—for his effort on behalf of the Korean people.

In a warm note of thanks to President Clinton, Kim expressed his belief that the visit reaffirmed the "blood" alliance between their two countries. Reading this message, and reflecting on the arduous, often painful, but ultimately successful U.S.-South Korean cooperation in confronting the nuclear threat, one of the American negotiators recalled a maxim from Nietzsche's *Twilight of the Idols*: "What does not kill me makes me stronger."

12

The Land of Counterpane

ALMOST eight years to the day after the signing of the 1994 Agreed Framework, Assistant Secretary of State for East Asia and Pacific Affairs James Kelly landed in Pyongyang. Soon he would face the North Koreans across the negotiating table, the first senior U.S. official to do so since the inauguration of President George W. Bush in January 2001. Kelly carried a brief containing a serious indictment: American intelligence had discovered a secret program to produce highly enriched uranium for nuclear weapons, quite apart from the plutonium production program that the Agreed Framework had frozen. Kelly's visit triggered a cascade of events resulting in the collapse of the accord and a new crisis over North Korea's nuclear program.

What transformed the hope of October 1994 into the disappointment of October 2002? The Agreed Framework did not end the ups and downs characteristic of North-South relations since the 1953 armistice. Cold war–like flare-ups continued—such as the intrusion of a South Korean spy submarine in South Korean waters in 1996 and the sinking of a North Korean naval vessel in a short, sharp exchange in 2002. At the same time, President Kim Dae Jung initiated a "Sunshine Policy" promising a historic opening to the North and became the first South Korean leader to visit North Korea. Each development—good or bad—can be viewed prismatically, broken into wavelengths that shed different colors depending on the angle of observation. For example, the same Sunshine Policy that refracted into the inspiring image of Kim Dae Jung traveling to Oslo to receive the Nobel Peace Prize, upon further refraction generated the sordid image of a summit facilitated through hundreds of millions of dollars passed secretly to the Kim Jong Il regime.[1]

The same could be said for implementation of the Geneva accord. Through most of the 1990s, heavy fuel oil flowed and the new reactor project moved forward. But funding shortages sometimes slowed the movement of oil to an ooze. The reactor project also fell behind schedule, a victim of slowdowns caused by North Korea's continued hostility toward Seoul, South Korea's frosty relationship with Pyongyang before the election of Kim Dae Jung, and other impediments that sprung up with regularity.

Despite the problems—missile tests, famine in the North, incidents at sea—on balance the Agreed Framework contributed to stability in Korea and in Asia throughout that period. The Yongbyon facilities remained frozen under seals and under continuous surveillance by inspectors from the International Atomic Energy Agency. No more plutonium was being generated or separated in North Korea. The eventual dismantlement of these facilities remained a plausible if distant prospect.

As is now known, North Korea was actually playing a far different game, one utterly incompatible with the Agreed Framework and all it represented. It began (perhaps only Kim Jong Il knows the precise moment) when the regime ramped up its secret program to produce highly enriched uranium. Though less urgent—since Pyongyang's plutonium production program was much more advanced—an enriched-uranium weapon program was more *dangerous*, in that the technology required to assemble a working uranium bomb was far easier to master than that required to build a plutonium bomb.[2]

The decade following the signing of the 1994 accord traced a complete arc—from crisis to concord and back again to crisis. Although this book has concentrated on the first North Korean nuclear crisis, it would be incomplete if it failed to draw lessons from that experience and from the benefits of hindsight in order to shed light on current events. This requires a brief review of events since 1994, followed by some reflections on the past and how they may apply to the future.

A Bumpy Road

The Clinton administration's policy toward North Korea after the signing of the Agreed Framework could be characterized as a cold peace. While the administration continued to implement the accord, from the outset its efforts were hamstrung by problems in Washington and Seoul as well as with North Korea. Hence it was impossible to put the framework on a firm and lasting political footing.

In the United States, congressional skepticism toward the Framework translated into a chronic battle by the administration to secure the few tens of millions of dollars needed to support the heavy fuel oil shipments owed by KEDO to North Korea. (Critics of the Agreed Framework might fairly be said to have adopted the posture of a picador, not matador—wounding but never going in for the kill.) At the same time, once the 1994 crisis had passed the international mood quickly shifted from galvanized anxiety to lethargic apathy, leaving the administration struggling in vain to raise significant funding for KEDO from countries beyond South Korea and Japan.

Until the 1998 presidential elections in South Korea, the government there adopted a relatively aggressive posture toward North Korea—and Washington. President Kim Young Sam appeared to nurse a continuing grudge over the belief that he had been slighted during the Geneva negotiations, despite the central role Seoul was to play in the reactor project. Pyongyang, still nursing a grudge about Kim's failure to issue condolences after the Great Leader's death, irritated the South Korean leader even further by its seeming indifference to restarting North-South talks. This slight led Seoul to oppose increased U.S.–North Korean engagement without some improvement in inter-Korean relations. Recognizing that its ally's sensibilities had been wounded, Washington showed substantial deference to Seoul, an inclination that was reinforced by a return to State's Bureau of East Asian and Pacific Affairs as the U.S. bureaucratic focus for implementing North Korea policy. Only when the new regime of President Kim Dae Jung took office in 1998 did the Clinton administration find a more cooperative South Korean partner.

Of course, North Korea did much to aggravate the situation. Its public pledges to support the Agreed Framework seemed but a mask over the old cold war attitudes. While the freeze on the plutonium production program held fast under international monitoring, other North Korean moves provoked serious concern, particularly the trail of ballistic missile–related exports to South Asia and the Middle East. Closer to home, in September 1996, the South Korean Navy captured a North Korean spy submarine in South Korean waters, only stiffening President Kim Young Sam's tough approach toward Pyongyang and setting back implementation several months just when momentum was starting to build.[3] As the decade continued, North Korea was struck by famine—the fatal consequence of bad weather piled on top of disastrous agricultural policies—which perhaps distracted it from pursuing any broader strategic agenda of economic reform or engagement with the outside world.

Even without the problems with Congress, Pyongyang, and Seoul, it would have been immensely challenging to carry out a complex, multibillion-dollar construction project in a country as lacking in resources and infrastructure as North Korea. Anticipating the inevitable difficulties in completing the reactors by 2003, the U.S. negotiators had insisted on characterizing that year as a "target" not a deadline. That caution quickly proved to be justified, as a six-month delay in negotiating the new reactor supply arrangements delayed inking the governing contract until December 1995. Haggling among the KEDO executive board members—the United States, South Korea, Japan, and the European Union—on issues such as determining the overall cost and financing of the project and rules for the procurement of reactor equipment—also took its toll. It soon became clear that even coming close to the 2003 target would be difficult.

Viewing these myriad difficulties, some have speculated that the United States never really intended to implement the Agreed Framework or to build the new reactors. Since American officials expected North Korea to collapse under the weight of its bankrupt economy and political system, so the argument goes, the United States would want to move forward slowly in anticipation of the inevitable demise of the North Korean regime. KEDO would then be relieved of the need to build the new reactors.[4] The possibility that regime change might spare KEDO the need to complete the reactors probably occurred to some officials in Washington, Seoul, and Tokyo. But that consideration never received backing as U.S. policy during the extensive senior-level meetings that formulated negotiating positions leading to the Agreed Framework. The better explanation for the delays in implementation is mundane rather than Machiavellian: the United States and its partners faced too many practical difficultie, while the Agreed Framework suffered from chronically unsteady political support.

In the summer of 1998, the uneasy truce threatened to break down altogether. A front-page *New York Times* story reported that the U.S. intelligence community had discovered a secret underground reactor and reprocessing plant at a place called Kumchang-ri near the North's border with China. If true, the installation would have violated the 1994 agreement.[5] As the validity of the report and its potential consequences were being analyzed, bad news struck again. North Korea shocked Japan, the United States, and the international community by launching a three-stage "space-launch vehicle." Ostensibly dedicated to lofting a satellite into orbit, it looked to all the world like a prototype of a possible delivery vehicle for a nuclear weapon that could eventually bring the United States into range. The Japanese reacted intensely to the discovery that the North had sent the rocket hurtling over their country, exposing their helplessness in the face of Pyongyang's ballistic missile threat.[6]

Perry Redux

Scrambling to avoid the imminent collapse of U.S. political support for engagement with the North, in November 1998 President Clinton—under congressional mandate—appointed former Secretary of Defense William Perry as coordinator for U.S. policy toward North Korea.[7] Aside from giving renewed high-level focus to engagement, Secretary Perry's job was to undertake a comprehensive policy review. As part of that process, he not only consulted with Seoul, Tokyo, and Beijing, but also visited Pyongyang in May 1999.[8] Just before Perry arrived, a team of U.S. experts inspected Kumchang-ri and found no evidence of a covert nuclear facility. Knowing that the Americans would find nothing probably gave the North Koreans adequate incentive to allow the visit in the first place, but Pyongyang's actions were at least consistent with the theory that the North Koreans wished to avoid undermining the future of the Agreed Framework by allowing the Kumchang-ri issue to fester. In September, North Korea announced a moratorium on long-range missile tests for the duration of the U.S.–North Korean talks.[9]

Secretary Perry's October 1999 report to the president proposed a two-path strategy. The first path presented "a new, comprehensive and integrated approach" that called for negotiating "the complete and verifiable cessation" of North Korea's missile and nuclear weapons programs. The second path proposed that Washington, Seoul, and Tokyo act jointly to contain the threat presented by North Korea, should negotiations prove unsuccessful.[10] Reaffirming the essence of the administration's approach to engaging North Korea, the Perry exercise restored the semblance of domestic and international support that had been established in the wake of the 1994 agreement. The value of the exercise derived in part from the high degree of bipartisan support Secretary Perry enjoyed in the national security community, as well as from the process of consultation he engaged in with the U.S. Congress and with the key countries involved in dealing with North Korea.

The Clinton administration followed Perry's advice and spent much of the next year trying to resolve its concerns over North Korea's ballistic missile development and exports, the most visible manifestation of continued problems with Pyongyang. But administration officials also became concerned about reports of North Korean interest in technology related to the production of highly enriched uranium, which, like plutonium, could be used to build nuclear weapons. Troubling evidence also surfaced that North Korea might have conducted more conventional explosive testing related to the development of a nuclear weapon design.

The administration developed two initiatives to "smoke out" suspicious nuclear activities. First, it proposed "nuclear transparency talks," designed to install a bilateral inspection regime that would build on the positive experience of the Kumchang-ri visit; this led to preliminary talks with the North Koreans in 2000. In a second, more far-reaching initiative, the administration proposed revising the 1994 Agreed Framework by substituting conventional power plants for one of the two planned nuclear reactors. Since conventional stations could be built quicker, the quid pro quo for North Korea's earlier receipt of fresh electricity supplies would be accelerating Pyongyang's acceptance of full compliance with its IAEA safeguards obligations. Meeting those obligations would require inspections that would help get to the bottom of Pyongyang's suspicious nuclear activities dating back to 1989. This initiative ran into a brick wall in Seoul, which wished to avoid rocking the boat with Pyongyang at a time when President Kim Dae Jung was struggling to get the Sunshine Policy off the ground.

At the same time, Washington was considering an even more far-reaching initiative to transform the U.S.–North Korean relationship. The theory held that as Pyongyang became more invested in better relations with Washington, the administration would be able to secure much more progress in addressing persistent U.S. concerns. This approach gathered momentum during the second half of 2000, when Vice Marshal Jo Myong Rok, director general of the General Political Bureau of the Korean People's Army and one of Kim Jong Il's closest advisers, visited Washington for talks with President Clinton and Secretary of State Madeleine Albright. The visit produced a joint communiqué that put U.S.–North Korean relations on a positive footing.[11] In turn, Secretary of State Madeline Albright and Ambassador Wendy Sherman visited Pyongyang and met with Kim Jong Il.[12] Against the background of thawing political relations, U.S. and North Korean officials began to make progress on an agreement that would have committed Pyongyang to terminate its missile exports and drastically constrain its indigenous deployments of these dangerous weapons.

The last piece of this puzzle—first raised by the North Koreans during Vice Marshal Jo's trip to Washington—was the possibility of a visit by President Clinton to North Korea. The prospect of a presidential summit might have clinched a verifiable deal on ballistic missiles, provided momentum for dealing with U.S. nuclear concerns, and opened new paths for bilateral cooperation. The idea of a summit had arisen as early as 1994, though at that time such a meeting was inconceivable in light of North Korea's confrontation over the nuclear issue. By 2000 the conditions had begun to ripen. But President Clinton never made it to Pyongyang. Last-minute North Korean foot-dragging over the terms of a possible missile deal cast doubt over whether an agreement could be reached in time for a summit. Moreover, President Clinton decided to focus on peacemaking in the Middle East during the waning months of his administration. Finally, the enervating effects of the national preoccupation with the vote count for president in Florida put an end to any hopes for a summit. As Secretary Albright later reported, the United States extended an invitation to Kim Jong Il to visit the United States, but he declined.[13]

"You Don't Know What You've Got 'Til It's Gone"

The inauguration of George W. Bush ended any early prospect that the president of the United States might visit Pyongyang. Bush harbored deep hostility toward Kim Jong Il and was skeptical about dealing with the North Korean regime. The new administration quickly divided into factions, pitting hard-liners (opposed to the Agreed Framework and eager to transform America's role in the world) against moderates (skeptical about North Korea, yet viewing engagement as the least bad option in dealing with Pyongyang). The tension quickly burst its traces when, the day before President Kim Dae Jung's March 2001 visit to meet President George W. Bush, Secretary of State Colin Powell suggested that Korea policy would continue broadly to follow that of the Clinton administration. The White House quickly slapped him down, and a chastened Powell admitted that he had leaned "too far forward in his skis."[14]

Compounding bureaucratic rivalry were new tensions arising in the bilateral relationship with Seoul stemming from White House uncertainties about the Agreed Framework and hostility toward Kim Jong Il, which in turn threatened the foundations of South Korea's Sunshine Policy. The stage was set for the two presidents to have an unhappy meeting, and they did. The bilateral relationship between Seoul and Washington remained frosty throughout Kim Dae Jung's remaining time in office.

Meanwhile, the Bush administration conducted an internal review of U.S. policy toward North Korea. The results, announced in a statement by the president on June 6, 2001, represented a bureaucratic compromise. Rather than scrap the Agreed Framework, the president called for its "improved implementation," while directing his national security team "to undertake serious discussions with North Korea on a broad agenda to include: improved implementation of the Agreed Framework relating to North Korea's nuclear activities; verifiable constraints on North Korea's missile programs and a ban on its missile exports; and a less threatening conventional military posture." The president talked of "a comprehensive approach to North Korea which will seek to encourage progress toward North-South reconciliation, peace on the Korean peninsula, a constructive relationship with the United States, and greater stability in the region." The statement hinted that positive North Korean actions would be met by expanded U.S. efforts "to help the North Korean people, ease sanctions, and take other political steps."[15] The administration suggested that it was charting a tougher course than its predecessor, but the formal elements of the new policy were consistent with the objectives of the Clinton administration. State Department spokesmen publicly emphasized a willingness to meet "anywhere, anytime," without preconditions, but for reasons that remain obscure, Pyongyang never responded formally to the U.S. offer.

The prospects for successful bilateral diplomacy between Washington and Pyongyang worsened that autumn, as skepticism about the North Korean regime deepened following the September 11 terrorist attack in the United States. Pyongyang attempted some positive moves following the tragedy. On September 12, North Korea issued a public statement of regret and voiced opposition to all forms of terrorism. Subsequently, it passed a private message through Swedish diplomats stationed in Pyongyang expressing condolences, taken by some as a sign of its willingness to cooperate in fighting terrorism and its interest in renewed contacts.[16] The North also signed several international protocols dealing with terrorism.[17] Still, the prospect for resumed U.S.–North Korean talks failed to materialize.

The negative trend in U.S.–North Korean relations took a still sharper turn for the worse in January 2002, when President Bush identified North Korea, Iran, and Iraq as members of an "axis of evil." The president asserted the right to take preemptive military action rather than sit and wait for an adversary to attack the United States or its allies with weapons of mass destruction.[18] Subsequently, newspapers reported that the possible use of nuclear weapons was contemplated in a major Korean contingency outlined in a secret Pentagon review of the American nuclear force posture.[19] By the summer of that year, however, the hot rhetoric from the State of the Union address had been milled through the interagency review process. The result appeared to be a less confrontational approach, one that concluded that engagement with North Korea would be worthwhile, but only *after* Pyongyang had met all of Washington's concerns.

This "bold approach" would offer Pyongyang the prospect of transforming its relations with Washington and the world from isolation and hostility to cooperation and engagement, provided that North Korea definitively resolved the proliferation and other major concerns about its conduct. Assistant Secretary James Kelly was slated to visit North Korea to present that approach in July 2002, when the naval clash in South Korean waters led to a postponement of the American diplomat's visit.

Even as the tensions on the peninsula gradually eased and Secretary Kelly's visit to Pyongyang was rescheduled, evidence was accumulating that North

Korea was engaged in major clandestine uranium-enrichment activities. As mentioned earlier, disturbing signs of such activity began to appear toward the end of the Clinton administration, evidence that was certainly well known to Bush administration officials when they took office. The administration decided to take action in October 2002 because of the scale of equipment procurement the North Koreans had reached in their activities. According to the Central Intelligence Agency, in 2001 North Korea purchased large quantities of materials needed to build a facility for the production of highly enriched uranium, although U.S. intelligence estimates seemed to be uncertain as to its status and location.[20] The administration's bottom line, however, was clear: until the North Korean enrichment facilities had been verifiably dismantled, Washington would not proceed with its bold approach.

Secretary Kelly carried that message to Pyongyang in October 2002. Whatever happened there—U.S. officials claim that the North Koreans admitted to having the secret program while the latter deny any such admission—the session triggered a chain of events leading to the collapse of the 1994 agreement. In November, the United States persuaded its KEDO partners to suspend heavy fuel oil deliveries to North Korea, on the grounds that the secret enrichment effort violated Pyongyang's obligations under the Agreed Framework. True, the Framework did not explicitly refer to uranium enrichment, much less prohibit it. It did, however, explicitly reaffirm North Korea's commitment to the North-South Denuclearization Declaration (which did ban uranium enrichment on the Korean Peninsula) and the Nuclear Non-Proliferation Treaty (which banned the development of nuclear weapons, the clear aim of a clandestine uranium-enrichment program). Thus the program was clearly inconsistent with North Korea's commitments under the Agreed Framework.

Having lost its supply of heavy fuel oil and its access to direct discussions with Washington, in late December 2002 North Korea began a series of provocative steps to rearrange the diplomatic chessboard just as it had done so many times in the earlier crisis. It expelled IAEA inspectors monitoring the nuclear freeze, reloaded and restarted the 5-megawatt reactor, formally withdrew from the Nuclear Non-Proliferation Treaty, and probably began to reprocess the spent fuel that had been re-canned and stored under IAEA monitoring ever since the Agreed Framework.

The political foundations underpinning the 1994 agreement in *both* the United States and North Korea disintegrated. As 2003 opened, with the Agreed Framework moribund, Washington embarked on a course of multilateral diplomacy with South Korea, Japan, China, and Russia, aiming to bring enough diplomatic pressure to bear that Pyongyang would abandon its nuclear weapons efforts. Departing from its 1994 approach, the United States refused to engage North Korea directly in bilateral talks and prompted China to play an unusually active diplomatic role. Stepping into the fray, Beijing attempted to jump-start talks between the United States and North Korea by hosting a first round of trilateral talks in April. The discussions took place against the backdrop of continued North Korean theatrics; Pyongyang's representative at the first round was reported to have threatened to export nuclear materials and to conduct a nuclear test. All the while, Pyongyang repeatedly asserted that it had separated the plutonium from the 8,000 spent fuel rods stored at Yongbyon.

China hosted an inconclusive round of six-party talks in August 2003, this time also including representatives from South Korea, Japan, and Russia. At the time of this writing, another round was expected in early 2004. Where the road will lead is unclear. The good news is that various among the six players have suggested most if not all of the elements of a potential deal: the freeze and dismantlement of North Korea's nuclear program under international monitoring; the institution of a bilateral or multilateral inspection regime to increase the transparency of the North Korean nuclear program; the containment, accounting, and control over fissile materials the North Koreans possess; the provision of some form of security assurance to Pyongyang; the resumption of assistance in the form of providing "replacement energy"; and perhaps other benefits. Further good news is that the protagonists have all expressed a continued willingness to find a diplomatic solution. The less encouraging news is that the parties—either individually or multilaterally—do not necessarily share the same interest in concluding a deal, nor do they seem to have succeeded in designing, much less agreeing on, a "road map" to take them from the current situation to the desired end state. This may be the challenge for the future.

Premises, Premises: The Case for Engagement

That challenge cannot be faced squarely without taking into account the lessons of previous American efforts to combat Pyongyang's quest for nuclear weapons. The first step is to establish a degree of consensus on the "lessons learned." At the level of objectives, for example, it is a universal belief that the Korean Peninsula should remain stable, secure, and free of nuclear weapons. To that end, broad international consensus supports the position that North Korea should adhere fully to applicable nonproliferation norms: the Nuclear Non-Proliferation Treaty, IAEA safeguards, and the North-South Denuclearization Declaration. At the same time, all agree that North Korea is armed, desperate, and dangerous, and that a war in Korea would likely result in massive destruction and loss of life that would not only devastate the peninsula but also destabilize the entire Asian region.

Consensus also exists as to the character of the Pyongyang regime. Kim Jong Il is a totalitarian dictator. His regime has failed miserably at meeting even the minimum physical needs of its people, much less their dreams and aspirations. Worse than having failed, it has not even tried. The hunger and inhuman conditions this despot inflicts on his people are an abomination. Regrettably, it is also clear that the regime has proved itself extremely durable, utilizing the traditional Stalinist tactics of propaganda, intimidation, and brute force to perpetuate itself for half a century despite its miserable record.

When it comes to assessing North Korea's relations with the outside world, few would dispute that North Koreans lie and cheat when it suits their purposes. (The same was true of the Soviet Union.) Pyongyang's admission in 2002 that it had lied for years in denying the abduction of Japanese citizens provided a striking example of that long tradition of mendacity. The only novelty was that the lie was confessed.

Consensus starts to break down, however, when it comes to assessing North Korea's plans and objectives. What does the regime want, and what price is it willing to pay to get it? Some believe that the North Korean leaders are absolutely determined to obtain nuclear weapons as quickly as possible, no matter what. Others believe that Pyongyang views its nuclear program as a bargaining chip, to be used to extract maximum advantage from the outside world, but then (at least potentially) to be curtailed, or perhaps even abandoned, if the price is right. Still others believe that Pyongyang may not have irrevocably decided whether or not to trade away its nuclear option. Perhaps the North Koreans intend to keep advancing their nuclear efforts on the theory that over time they will gain *both* military advantage and bargaining strength, so that they end up either holding a nuclear arsenal, or driving up the price of a deal to give it up.

Consensus also breaks down when it comes to deciding how to respond to the North Korean threat in a manner that optimizes these shared objectives and mitigates the risks of both nuclear weapons and conventional war. In medicine, agreement on the diagnosis of a condition is useful but not always sufficient for forging consensus on the appropriate prescription for its treatment. In policy, however, agreement on the diagnosis of the Pyongyang regime (an evil tyranny) has failed to produce consensus over the appropriate U.S. policy prescription.

This should not come as a surprise. American foreign policy has venerable yet conflicting traditions of value-based idealism (exemplified by Woodrow

Wilson's dogged and ultimately self-defeating quest in support of U.S. membership in the League of Nations) and interest-based realism (exemplified by Nixon's opening to China and arms control agreements with the Soviet Union). Idealists recoil at the notion of engaging directly with North Korea and believe that any agreement is useless anyway since the North Koreans are inveterate cheaters. Realists proceed stoically while probing whether some agreement with North Korea can advance U.S. interests, recognizing that no such agreement can succeed if based on Pyongyang's word; the provisions of any accord must be reliably, independently, and continuously verified.

If the same *diagnosis* produces such radically different responses, the divisions over the *prognosis* of the North Korean nuclear program compound the disagreement over the appropriate policy prescription. If North Korea is hell-bent on developing nuclear weapons, negotiations will be of no avail. They will simply buy Pyongyang time to complete its crash nuclear effort. Under this view, the better course would be confrontation *now*, because delay only benefits Pyongyang. Those who believe that Pyongyang can be persuaded to relinquish—or at least defer—its nuclear weapons program favor diplomatic efforts to solve the problem, especially in light of the likely consequences of war in Korea. Those who believe North Korea's leaders may be playing for time while they preserve both options favor dealing with the nuclear question as a matter of intrinsic urgency. They advocate positions that present North Korea with a stark choice between the consequences of defying, versus complying with, nuclear nonproliferation norms.

Can these different premises be reconciled in one coherent policy? The Clinton administration saw the North Korean regime as a failure and a menace to its neighbors and its own people. It remained agnostic regarding the ultimate objectives of the nuclear program in North Korea. This agnosticism was justified by the facts or, rather, by the lack of facts regarding North Korea: the information was so poor that it was simply impossible to know Pyongyang's bottom line with certainty. For starters, North Korean decisionmakers may themselves not yet know their bottom line, or are keeping options open, or may change their strategic aims. Moreover, although totalitarian, the Pyongyang regime is not an immutable monolith. The North Korean elite holds competing views regarding objectives, strategies, and tactics, all of which may vary over time. North Korean statements may reflect a papered-over difference, a trial balloon, or internal advocacy. They cannot be taken at face value, if one can discern their face value behind the propaganda and stilted rhetoric. Similarly, North Korean actions also give rise to different interpretations, even among longtime watchers of their behavior.

Given the obscurity of the North Korean decisionmaking process, it is unwise to base U.S. policy on a particular assumption about what the Pyong-yang leadership "really" wants. Washington needs to hedge against each possi-ble objective. The only sensible policy, if attainable, would be one that would succeed regardless of whether Pyongyang is going all out for the bomb, hag-gling over the price, or preserving more than one option.

In short, American policy should be geared to *U.S.* objectives not *North Korean* objectives. There, all ambiguity disappears, as the U.S. objective is clear: to avoid having nuclear weapons in the hands of North Koreans. Given the tremendous devastation and loss of American and Korean lives that would accompany war in Korea, U.S. and allied interests would best be served if that goal could be attained through diplomacy, as every U.S. president has agreed.

Given the horrendous consequences of a North Korea uncontested in its quest for nuclear weapons, the Clinton administration believed that *if there were a chance* Pyongyang could be induced to abandon or defer its program, then U.S. interests *demanded* that it test that proposition. However loathsome the Pyongyang regime, that proposition could not fairly be tested absent direct negotiations with the North Koreans. No other nation—not allies like South Korea and Japan nor other powers such as China—had either precisely the same interests or ability to shape outcomes as the United States.

Looking Ahead by Looking Back

What is to be done? Broadly speaking, four kinds of options are available to address the North Korean nuclear program: military action, containment, negotiation, or regime change. In 1994 the military option on the table was an attack on the Yongbyon facilities. A direct hit on the spent-fuel pond would have had a good chance of eliminating the five bombs' worth of plutonium as a proliferation threat. It is virtually inconceivable, however, that the North Koreans would have kept the one to two bombs' worth of plutonium they might already have separated in the same place, vulnerable to the same attack. American military leaders thought North Korea would probably respond vio-lently to a U.S. strike, raising the serious prospect of a general war on the peninsula that would have cost hundreds of thousands of lives.

Containment as a policy option has a venerable history from the cold war, when it described the effort by the United States and its allies to deter and, if necessary, defend against Soviet expansion through a combination of conventional military alliances and a robust nuclear threat. The limitation on containment is that it does not seek to deny an adversary the possession of nuclear weapons. In that sense containment is a weaker or perhaps a fallback position, once denial of access to the weapons is no longer an option. During the cold war the United States used its nuclear arsenal to deter a Soviet *attack* and worked with its allies to impose multilateral export controls that contained Soviet access to advanced military technology. But the U.S. policy of containment never sought to block the Soviet Union from *building* or *possessing* its own nuclear arsenal. It was too late for that.

In 1994, however, it was not too late to try to deny North Korea access to significant quantities of plutonium beyond the one to two bombs' worth that might have been separated in 1989. So containment held little appeal to U.S. policymakers and was not considered as a serious option; it would have seemed needlessly defeatist. If the United States had a shot at *preventing* Pyongyang's acquisition of nuclear weapons, why settle for merely containing it, which would imply at least tacit acquiescence to North Korea's continuing nuclear activities without taking the initiative to stop them? Indeed, the authors of this book do not recall anyone in the policy community, either in or out of government, ever advocating such a course.

The third option, negotiation, has in one sense been the most attractive. It offers the possibility of achieving more than containment (in that North Korea would be precluded from obtaining any additional quantities of separated plutonium) *without* running the risks inherent in the military option. In another sense, it has been the least attractive option. Unlike containment and military attack, negotiation requires the active participation and, ultimately, cooperation of the North Koreans. Given the difficulties of negotiating any agreement with Pyongyang, this seems a tall order.

In considering whether to seek a negotiated settlement of the nuclear question, no one has harbored any illusions about the nature of the North Korean regime. No one would have relied on trust to hold the North Koreans to their promises. The question has been whether the immorality of the Pyongyang regime and its untrustworthy character should dissuade the Americans from seeking a negotiated settlement with such a regime. Constitutionally, the president is invested with the duty and authority to carry out the foreign policy of the United States in the service of the preambular goal to "provide for the common defense" of the American people. Historically, presidents have repeatedly concluded that they need at times to negotiate with despots— including some who are friendly to the United States—in order to fulfill that constitutional duty.

The president does not have the luxury of dealing only with honorable interlocutors. North Korea had a rampant plutonium production program. Ignoring it was unacceptable to our national security interests. Attacking it militarily presented huge risks. To paraphrase Winston Churchill, negotiation was the worst option, except all the alternatives.

Of course, the United States is not forced to make simple either-or choices among attack, contain, or negotiate. In practice these approaches invariably are mixed or sequenced in a variety of ways. The Clinton administration chose to attempt negotiations in the first instance, to offer the North Koreans an opportunity to comply voluntarily with international nonproliferation norms. *At the same time*, the United States maintained and, indeed, strengthened its military posture on the Korean Peninsula and in the region to deter any North Korean military assault, and to signal that more coercive measures would be taken if Pyongyang refused the offer of a negotiated settlement. That message was reinforced by the continuing threat to seek UN Security Council sanctions against North Korea if it crossed any of the red lines set forth by the U.S. government.

Resort to UN Security Council sanctions, however, was not an *independent* option. Although the possibility of sanctions was central to U.S. policy, no one thought that exercising that option would have induced North Korea to surrender its nuclear program. Rather, the sanctions were intended *either* to bring sufficient pressure to bear to induce North Korea to freeze its nuclear activities and return to the negotiating table or to serve as a justification for tougher coercive actions—including military measures—down the road, should North Korea choose to defy the UN Security Council. Thus the sanctions track was a potential element of the military and negotiating tracks, not an end in itself.

At the same time that the existence of a military option strengthened America's diplomatic hand, the vigorous pursuit of a diplomatic solution was a critical prerequisite to resorting to arms. Indeed, perhaps the only way the military option could have been executed without serious damage to American relations with its regional allies and the international community would have been by first making a good faith effort to resolve the crisis through negotiation. Similarly, if negotiations failed, containment would still have been an available option. Since containment seemed tantamount to surrender to North Korean possession of nuclear weapons, and military attack risked general war as well as the destruction of the U.S.-ROK alliance, negotiation seemed the least bad *first* option.

One option that holds some attraction today but was *not* seriously contemplated in 1993 and 1994 was regime change *by military force*. A decade ago military enhancements were carried out, and major deployments considered, in order *to deter* North Korea from the use of force. But the only direct use of force considered by the United States at that time was confined to a possible attack against the Yongbyon nuclear facilities. Regime change through less ambitious means—ranging from simple containment and isolation of the

North Korean regime to the application of economic pressure through imposition of UN Security Council sanctions—also received no serious consideration in 1994.

At that time, some U.S. officials did speculate that the Kim Jong Il regime
would never last long enough to see the light-water reactors through to completion. But embracing a policy of "collapse"—essentially waiting for political
and economic rot to remove Kim Jong Il and his nuclear ambitions from the
scene—suffered from several significant flaws. First, no one could guarantee
that the regime would collapse soon enough to prevent acquisition, use, or
sale of nuclear weapons (a prudent view, in light of its continued survival
despite harrowing devastation in the intervening decade). Second, if there
were anything more dangerous than a nuclear-armed North Korea, it would
have been one on the brink of collapse, when its leaders might take desperate
measures with their plutonium in order to avert imminent demise. Third, had
Washington sought the removal of the North Korean regime, it would have
lost the support of key Security Council members, particularly China, which
in all likelihood would have stepped in to provide enough food and oil to keep
Pyongyang afloat. The arguments against regime change as a U.S. policy to
respond to the North Korean nuclear threat remain equally valid today.

Could the United States have *facilitated* a negotiated solution, perhaps letting others deal directly with Pyongyang while it planned and coordinated the
diplomatic efforts behind the scenes? After all, the North Korean nuclear
problem seriously affected the interests of its neighbors and the world. Why
could other key players not take center stage diplomatically? For such a strategy to succeed, two conditions need to be met. First, Washington's proxy
would need to have interests so closely aligned to its own that the U.S. government could entrust that party with a diplomatic mission on which the
safety and security of all Americans depended. It is hard to imagine any
administration assigning the protection of millions of American lives to *any*
third party, however closely aligned diplomatically. The protection of core
U.S. national security interests must be considered a non-delegable responsibility of the president. Specifically, the high priority the United States assigns
to nonproliferation appears to many South Koreans as a merely theoretical
concern, compared to what they view as the far greater risk that an aggressive
policy to thwart Pyongyang's nuclear ambitions could destabilize South Korea.

The second condition for what might be considered "diplomacy by proxy"
is that the proxy must have persuasive power over Pyongyang in order to succeed. Given North Korea's peculiar isolation, the countries with the interests
most closely aligned to the United States—for example, South Korea or even
Japan might be considered—are unlikely to meet this test. Part of the reason
is that much of Washington's ability to persuade Pyongyang flows from

uniquely American assets, such as the stature uniquely conferred by negotiating an agreement or some form of security assurance with the world's only remaining superpower.

No country other than the United States has been able to meet both conditions. Among the major diplomatic players, Japan is the one whose interests have been most closely aligned with those of the United States, though they are not identical. Nor could Japan reliably satisfy the second condition, as Pyongyang would clearly not accept Tokyo's representations as sufficiently binding upon Washington and Seoul. Among the interested governments, outside of the United States only China has seemed likely to persuade Pyongyang to reverse course. But clearly the United States could not rely on China to carry a purely American agenda undiluted by its own philosophy and preferences.

There is also a risk of allowing specific diplomatic forms—and forums—to dominate substance. In other words, while it is essential to have all relevant players—North and South Korea, Japan, China, Russia, and the United States—invested in any diplomatic solution to the North Korean nuclear issues, they do not all have to meet in the same place and the same time on every occasion in the effort to negotiate such a solution. First, as any veteran of multilateral diplomacy knows, the tough issues at the core of any major disagreement never get resolved in a plenary session of governments with widely divergent interests and complex relations among one another. Rather, as the preceding chapters suggest, diplomatic solutions are a product of complex, overlapping actions and negotiations carried out unilaterally, bilaterally, trilaterally, and multilaterally. The *real* deal gets cut in the back rooms and corridors, not in the chandeliered salons of diplomacy.

Second, ignoring that diplomatic reality and rigidly insisting on a specific format as a precondition to talks with North Korea gives Pyongyang the upper hand in controlling the pacing and escalation of the crisis it has created. If North Korea is threatening or taking actions inimical to U.S. national security, why should Washington allow Pyongyang to keep at it as long as the North eschews multilateral talks? It is not a gift or reward to North Korea, but rather an exercise of sovereignty in the service of U.S. national security, to ensure that senior American officials have a forum in which to convey their positions firmly and clearly to the North Korean leadership.

The Agreed Framework: A Balance Sheet

The discovery of the North Korean uranium-enrichment program and subsequent unraveling of the Agreed Framework inevitably leads one to ask whether it was a mistake from the beginning. Although some have taken that view, even President George W. Bush—despite his skepticism about the accord and the Kim Jong Il regime—has (however grudgingly) supported the Agreed Framework. Early in his administration, the president "reaffirmed" the U.S. commitment to the Agreed Framework in the joint statement issued with South Korean President Kim Dae Jung on March 7, 2001.[21] Three months later he approved a policy review that concluded that the United States should not abandon the Agreed Framework.[22] Subsequent statements by Secretary of State Colin Powell and Deputy Secretary of State Richard Armitage have been more forceful in their support, while others like Secretary of Defense Donald Rumsfeld predictably have been more skeptical.[23] In the summer of 2003, National Security Adviser Condoleezza Rice remarked that the Agreed Framework "in 1994 was probably exactly the right thing to do," though she properly concluded that the accord had been "badly frayed" to the point where it was unclear whether it could survive.[24]

In order to judge the Agreed Framework, two questions must be answered. First, did the Geneva accord advance U.S. national security interests at an acceptable price? Second, did North Korean cheating on the Agreed Framework defeat the security benefits expected by the United States?

To answer the first question—whether the Agreed Framework advanced American security interests at an acceptable price—one must analyze its costs and benefits fairly, without "double-counting." Obligations North Korea had already incurred—such as its agreement to safeguard its nuclear facilities pursuant to its NPT obligations and its agreement with the International Atomic Energy Agency—cannot "count" when tallying security benefits to the United States that are *attributable to the Agreed Framework*. If the accord provided *new* benefits to North Korea simply for complying with *old* (broken) promises, that would *not* be an acceptable price.

From that baseline, the Agreed Framework *did* impose fresh obligations upon North Korea, well beyond those entailed in the NPT and its IAEA safeguards agreement. Specifically, under its preexisting obligations, North Korea could argue that its existing nuclear production facilities—well suited to churning out bomb-worthy plutonium as well as reprocessing—were legal under the terms of the NPT provided they were safeguarded by the IAEA. The Agreed Framework, by contrast, required North Korea to shut down and dismantle its entire gas-graphite program: which meant the 5-, 50- and 200-megawatt nuclear reactors along with both reprocessing lines. It also allowed the United States to recan 8,000 spent fuel rods so that they could be stored indefinitely without risking radioactive leakage or requiring separation of the plutonium they contained. Eventually those facilities would have been dismantled and that spent fuel would be shipped out of North Korea. All of these measures would have been monitored by the IAEA.

The security benefits of the freeze were substantial and grew with each passing year that Pyongyang refrained from producing and separating more plutonium. (From Pyongyang's perspective, the opportunity cost of its continued adherence to the Agreed Framework kept rising each year.) U.S. projections of an unfettered North Korean plutonium production program showed that by the beginning of the twenty-first century, North Korea could have had hundreds of kilograms of plutonium and dozens or more nuclear weapons. Estimates also showed that if Pyongyang's ballistic missile program continued, it might be able to deliver those weapons to targets at increasingly greater ranges, including eventually the United States. The combined threat posed by North Korean nuclear and missile programs to the security of the United States, its close allies—South Korea and Japan—as well as its forces in Northeast Asia was clear.

Kim Jong Il may have viewed the North Korean nuclear program as the ultimate guarantee of his regime's survival, by providing access to a weapon that could deter any hostile force from attacking his regime. That is why stopping the North's plutonium production program was significant, requiring a major concession by North Korea.

Another way to assess the security benefits of the Agreed Framework is to consider how events might have unfolded in its absence. The odds favor a far more dangerous future, as an untrammeled North Korean nuclear program could provoke profoundly destabilizing events. Pressures to pursue nuclear weapons programs could emerge in Japan and South Korea, threaten their alliance with the United States, and jeopardize stability and prosperity throughout the region. Broad sectors of the Japanese and South Korean publics and ruling elites would likely oppose indigenous nuclear weapons programs. Yet when Japan's cabinet secretary Yasuo Fukuda remarked in 2002 that Tokyo might revisit its nonnuclear principles, despite uncorking a brief burst of criticism, Prime Minister Junichiro Koizumi easily brushed off calls for his adviser's resignation.[25]

If Seoul and Tokyo retained confidence in the reliability of the U.S. security guarantee against any possible North Korean nuclear aggression, nuclear ambitions among our Asian allies would likely be contained. But the risk of a regional arms race would be real and, even if contained, the internal debates over nuclear weapons could produce significant disruptions within Japan and South Korea as well as between those nations and other regional powers. If such a nuclear arms race were to begin, it might have a cascading effect. Taiwan, which had a rudimentary nuclear weapons program in the 1970s, could not be relied upon to stand idly by, and if it did not, China would certainly respond.

The danger of North Korea exporting nuclear weapons, material, or related technology to other countries or terrorists like Osama Bin Laden could compound the threat exponentially. A North Korea awash in bomb-making material would certainly be more tempted to earn hard currency from external sources. That temptation could grow if Pyongyang became desperate because of international isolation. The consequences could be devastating and virtually impossible to block, given the small size of a critical mass of plutonium and the porousness of international borders. This scenario is as stealthy as it is worrisome, as no one could have any confidence that the shipment of a critical mass of fissile material would even be detected by the intelligence community, either before or after it occurred. A detonation somewhere might well be the first evidence of such a transfer. The United States could not expect to prevent, deter, or defend against such an act.

Finally, the Geneva accord created an opportunity for North Korea to break out of its growing isolation. The political, economic, and security environment in Northeast Asia evolved rapidly during the early 1990s, as relationships frozen in place by fifty years of cold war confrontation began to thaw. The normalization of relations between South Korea and Russia, then China, promised greater contact and commerce among those nations. At the same time, the political changes as China evolved from a revolutionary to a status quo power, and as the Soviet Union disintegrated, deprived an increasingly desperate Pyongyang of a significant measure of outside support. As a lonely outpost of communist totalitarianism, North Korea continued to pose a nagging threat of confrontation and subversion. If the Agreed Framework could help smooth North Korea's transition from confrontation to cooperation with the international community, the world would have become safer and the North Koreans could regain some of the ground they had lost in their relations with their traditional patrons.

While this book has concentrated on the nuclear issues addressed by the Agreed Framework, the accord contained other provisions aimed at promoting just that transition—indicating, for example, the path toward normalization of relations with the United States and improvement in North-South relations. In theory, movement toward normal relations between North Korea and KEDO's charter members—the United States, South Korea, and Japan—could spawn increasing bonds of communication and commerce. Those bonds could sway North Korea away from its dangerous old ways, including its weapons of mass destruction programs. They could also help open the door for efforts to build peace and stability.

The 1994 Agreed Framework provided the political basis and context in

subsequent years for North Korea's initial, halting steps toward rapprochement with Seoul and the wider international community. While subsequent
events threw that rapprochement off course, its premise—that North Korea
would pose less of a threat to its neighbors and the world if integrated into the
international community than if left a persistent pariah—remains as valid
today as when it was attempted a decade ago.

Did the United States pay an acceptable price to obtain the benefits it
derived from the Agreed Framework? Over eight years, KEDO shipped North
Korea roughly 4 million metric tons of heavy fuel oil, worth $500 million.
That may have contributed up to 2 percent of North Korea's total energy supply and 8 percent of its electricity demand.[26] As for the light-water reactor
project itself, an aerial tour of the site would reveal substantial preparations
for construction, representing a significant financial commitment by South
Korea and Japan. But aside from that infrastructure and support provided to
some number of North Korean workers, the actual benefits remain unrealized.

Under the Agreed Framework, in 1999 the United States relaxed certain
economic sanctions against North Korea, allowing modest trade expansion.
Over the past five years, total U.S.–North Korean trade has amounted to $14
million, including $175,000 worth of imports from the North.[27] Compared
with the defense expenditures required even to deter a North Korean plutonium threat, much less remove it, the U.S.-origin benefits to North Korea were
quite modest. While the United States has provided large amounts of food
assistance as a humanitarian response to North Korea's deadly famine, that is
unrelated the Agreed Framework. As President Reagan said, "A hungry child
knows no politics."

The bottom line is that North Korea is no better off today than it was in
1994, before the accord was completed. Indeed, a strong case can be made
that—a decade later—North Korea is in worse shape. Its economy is in tatters.
In spite of KEDO heavy fuel oil shipments, energy shortages continue to stifle
economic growth. The food situation is still precarious, with Pyongyang
teetering on the brink of more significant shortages. North Korea's conventional military forces continue to pose a formidable threat by dint of sheer
numbers of men and artillery pieces, but looking past the crude number
discloses aging weapons and equipment, inadequate training, and under-
supplied troops.

While the benefits to North Korea from the Agreed Framework may not
have appreciably improved its situation, some might argue that they prevented the collapse of an undesirable regime. This seems unlikely, given the
role of China. North Korea may exasperate China's leaders, but the evidence

suggests that Beijing simply would not tolerate the collapse of the Pyongyang regime. The reason is simple: an imploding North Korea could promote political, economic, and social chaos on China's borders. It is no surprise, then, that substantial Chinese assistance mitigated the impact of North Korea's severe food shortages and economic decline over the past decade. For example, food shipments may have totaled twice as much as those sent by the World Food Program and three times the amount of American assistance. Other sources estimate Chinese assistance may have reached 1 million tons annually during the late 1990s.[28] Chinese energy assistance accounts for some 80 percent of North Korea's needs.[29] In short, the benefits under the Agreed Framework have been dwarfed by the food and oil assistance provided to North Korea by China.

But They Cheated . . .

The next question to consider is whether North Korean cheating alters an otherwise positive assessment of the Framework. American negotiators considered the prospect of North Korean cheating from the outset, harboring no more illusions about North Korean veracity than their predecessors did about the Soviet Union. That American assumption informed the U.S. design for the Agreed Framework, which linked every step by the United States and KEDO to a step by North Korea. Throughout the interagency discussions on the sequencing of the actions contemplated under the Geneva accord, U.S. officials explicitly sought to ensure that if, at any time, North Korea violated its commitments, then KEDO could terminate its performance and still leave its member states better off for having implemented the accord until that point. Most important, under the Agreed Framework North Korea would not be entitled to significant nuclear components needed to build the light-water reactors until it had returned to full compliance with its IAEA obligations including, if necessary, through special inspections.

So Washington knew it had to watch for cheating. From the time of signing the Agreed Framework, the United States kept close tabs on North Korean implementation of its obligations under the accord, while scouring for evidence on Pyongyang's nuclear activities. The initial news was positive, as North Korea proceeded to freeze, seal, and accept IAEA inspectors at its known nuclear facilities. Soon, however, the United States obtained evidence that North Korea may have diverted heavy fuel oil from allowed facilities. It quickly challenged the North Koreans on this point, and Pyongyang accepted monitoring of its power plants to deal with the problem. Later, when the United States obtained evidence that the North Koreans may have built a clandestine underground nuclear facility at Kumchang-ri, it pressed Pyong-yang and secured inspections of the site.

By the late 1990s, the U.S. government observed the North Korean pursuit of a significant uranium-enrichment program and, as noted earlier, was moving to deal with this and other issues (such as ballistic missiles) when time ran out on the Clinton administration. The Bush administration seems to have challenged the North on its uranium-enrichment efforts well before that program had matured to the point of producing weapon-usable mater-ial. As North Korea had yet to comply fully with its IAEA obligations at that time, KEDO had not yet provided the North with any significant nuclear components for the light-water reactors.

The existence of the clandestine uranium-enrichment program, while unacceptable and appropriate grounds for the U.S. suspension of benefits under the Agreed Framework, cannot erase the security benefits from the eight-year freeze on plutonium separation that the 1994 negotiations pro-duced. But it is fair to ask whether the existence of the Agreed Framework lulled the United States and others into an ill-advised complacency, which would facilitate Pyongyang's breakout into a highly enriched, uranium-based nuclear weapons program. The historical record suggests that this did not occur. Both the executive and legislative branches of the U.S. government con-tinued their close scrutiny of North Korean actions, in part through an annual appropriations process that required presidential certifications and reports to Congress as a condition of continued U.S. funding for KEDO.[30]

Concluding that the Agreed Framework was not a mistake, and that it suc-ceeded in advancing U.S. national interests, does not imply either that it was a perfect instrument or that it "solved" the North Korean nuclear threat. For example, the Agreed Framework would have better served American interests if some of the North Korean commitments could have been accelerated. It would have been better if Pyongyang had agreed to accept special inspections right away, or to ship the 8,000 spent fuel rods out of North Korea immedi-ately, or both. It would have been cheaper to secure the freeze in exchange for one light reactor rather than two, or in exchange for coal-fired plants rather than nuclear plants. Coal-fired plants would also have avoided the additional proliferation risks endemic to any light-water reactor project, especially the production of additional plutonium.

In fact, American negotiators pressed all of these points with the North Koreans and encountered fierce resistance. It was hard to imagine prevailing on all points outside of *The Land of Counterpane*, a poetic invention of Robert Louis Stevenson. The poem tells the story of a boy in his sickbed who marched his tin soldiers about and sent "ships in fleets/All up and down among the sheets" and over his counterpane, or bedspread. It is much easier to prevail if you get to move the soldiers on both sides of a conflict:

I was the giant great and still,
That sits upon the pillow hill,
And sees before him, dale and plane,
The pleasant land of counterpane.

But Geneva was not the Land of Counterpane. The North Koreans were not passive tin soldiers in a children's game, but rather shrewd adversaries playing, as one participant observed, as well as possible with a deuce-high hand. Moreover, in the land of counterpane the giant need not worry about the constraints that the American negotiators faced in maintaining congressional support, a common negotiating front with close allies and the IAEA, and the acceptance of the rest of the five permanent members of the UN Security Council. All of this had to be done against an adversary that sought every opportunity to drive wedges between the United States and the other key players.

By September 1994, staunch North Korean resistance on a number of issues put American negotiators on the horns of a dilemma. They could have ignored North Korean threats to restart the 5-megawatt reactor and to separate plutonium from the Yongbyon spent-fuel rods, dug in their heels, and waited until the North Koreans capitulated on all points. If they had done so, they would have risked a North Korean breakout from the fragile nuclear freeze on the operation of the 5-megawatt reactor and on separating the five bombs' worth of plutonium from the spent fuel rods at Yongbyon. Alternatively, the Americans could have concluded a deal promptly with North Korea in order to lock in the plutonium freeze, at the expense of deferring realization of some U.S. negotiating objectives until later in the implementation of the Agreed Framework.

In this instance, when the president, vice president, and principals considered the matter, they decided that they would attach the highest priority to *stopping North Korea from obtaining any additional plutonium.* All agreed, in essence, that it was more *urgent* to protect the present and the future than to unravel the past, by pinning down how much plutonium North Korea had indeed separated in its earlier reprocessing campaign. They were led to choosing the horn of the dilemma locking in the plutonium freeze, and deferring (but *not* abandoning) other objectives. In this, they were swayed by the concern that, despite its citizens' grinding poverty, the Pyongyang regime seemed more likely to unshackle its nuclear program long before—even if subjected to UN sanctions—it capitulated to every U.S. preference.

Once the president decided that the time had come to strike a deal, despite continued North Korean resistance to certain U.S. objectives, the question became one of choosing those objectives that were critical to stopping *future* North Korean access to separated plutonium. By definition, full satisfaction of IAEA safeguards concerns regarding resolution of questions surrounding *past* North Korean nuclear activities did not meet that test. The suspect waste sites were not going anywhere, and the agreement to wait some years to analyze those sites, provided that no significant nuclear equipment was shipped to North Korea in the meantime, seemed a worthwhile trade to secure the freeze. It would have been strange, indeed, to praise an agreement that solved the mystery of whether North Korea had produced a few kilograms of plutonium at the expense of missing the opportunity to stop the eventual production of hundreds of kilograms.

The harder issue related to the plutonium contained in North Korea's spent fuel. That *was* a plutonium issue, but no amount of negotiation proved capable of persuading the North Koreans to give up the rods for the precise reason the Americans wanted to take them away: the rods constituted North Korea's ultimate leverage. Once those rods left North Korea, that leverage would evaporate. In a relationship lacking mutual trust, such self-abnegation would have appeared to Pyongyang to be tantamount to unconditional surrender, well beyond the pale of negotiation. Ultimately, the Americans did gain a North Korean commitment to ship all the spent fuel out of country—but the shipments would start only when key components were delivered to the first new reactor, and finish by the time of completion of the second. In the subsequent contract for the supply of the light-water reactors, KEDO officials also succeeded in securing North Korea's commitment to ship the spent fuel produced by the new facilities out of North Korea.

When faced by a long-established, operational, and expanding plutonium production program, the Agreed Framework halted that program under international monitoring and secured agreement of its ultimate dismantlement. It could not "cure" the patient of its nuclear weapons ambitions or even its capabilities, as the U.S. government could not sway the hearts and minds of the North Korean regime and did not know (beyond Yongbyon) what additional nuclear capabilities and facilities existed, much less how to quash them. It did not preclude North Korean activities *outside* of the view of the inspectors and cameras at Yongbyon. It did not reduce the ballistic missile or the conventional military threats posed by Pyongyang. And it did not address North Korea's other aberrant activities, from its own human rights abuses and support for terrorism to its misguided political and economic system.

The decision to give the nuclear issue top priority was rooted in grim reality. Serious concerns about missiles, conventional arms, human rights, or even North Korea's past nuclear cheating (with the possible production of enough plutonium for one or two nuclear bombs) paled in comparison with the dangers the United States would face if North Korea's continuing plutonium program ran unchecked. And if the nuclear question were *tied* to the other issues, so that the nuclear question could not be settled absent progress on other issues, the likely effect would have been to overload the negotiations so that *none* would have been resolved. Once the Agreed Framework was signed, the United States did turn to other North Korean problems, beginning (once again) with the most urgent threat to U.S. and allied interests: North Korea's ballistic missile program.

Lessons Learned: The Road Ahead

What lessons do the crises of 1993 and 1994 hold for the impasse of today? Now, as then, the critical issue is North Korean access to bomb material, this time highly enriched uranium as well as plutonium. Now, as then, the consequences of failure would be grave: an untethered North Korea would be able to churn out bomb-making material each year for use in threatening its neighbors—or for export to terrorists or others. (The fastest route to al Qaeda would seem to run through Pakistan, North Korea's active trading partner in illicit arms and the likely source of the technology North Korea used to enrich uranium.) Now, as then, a difficult relationship with a newly elected South Korean president further complicates an already daunting diplomatic mission. Now, as then, the other regional powers—South Korea, Japan, China, and Russia—have important roles to play in resolving the crisis.

Mark Twain once observed that by sitting on a hot stove, his cat learned not to sit on a hot stove again. But the cat also learned not to sit on a cold stove. Even if one considered the Agreed Framework a hot stove, the question is whether the government could design a cold stove that could support a lasting and effective diplomatic solution to the North Korean nuclear challenge. To do so, it would have to consider *what kind* of agreement would advance U.S. interests and *how* the United States should go about negotiating such an arrangement. The 1994 crisis has relevance for today on both counts.

Lesson 1. Set strategic priorities; then stick to them. It may seem too obvious to dwell on this lesson, but setting and maintaining priorities is easier said than done. During the first North Korean crisis, the Clinton administration placed the highest strategic priority on blocking North Korean access to additional stocks of separated plutonium. Clarity on that point enabled decisionmakers to resist pressures inside the administration to press other (admittedly important) objectives—curbing Pyongyang's ballistic missile program and its threatening conventional force posture—to the point where they would jeopardize the resolution of the nuclear crisis.

Setting priorities and sticking to them has a number of advantages. First, it provides for discipline within one's own government and signals clarity of purpose to friendly and hostile nations alike. Second, a government that remains focused on its strategic priorities is less likely to waste precious time and bargaining leverage on objectives of little if any intrinsic importance (such as the timing of the exchange of North-South envoys). Third, setting priorities allows a modular approach to resolving a series of outstanding issues, picking them off in order of urgency. By contrast, the comprehensive approach in which all issues are linked to one another is prone to bog down and leave all issues, including the most important ones, unresolved.

Failure to set priorities quickly leads to stalemate. For example, the George W. Bush administration proposed a comprehensive approach in dealing with North Korea, a "bold initiative" that would offer energy and other carrots if North Korea verifiably dismantled its nuclear program and satisfied other U.S. security concerns.[31] Such an approach runs the risk of failure because it seeks full North Korean performance on all U.S. demands before offering significant U.S. performance on any North Korean demands. There was never any chance North Korea would accede to such a position, especially since time played in Pyongyang's favor as each passing day it enhanced its own nuclear capabilities. Since the president has made clear that the United States seeks a diplomatic resolution to the current crisis, some parallelism in performance will need to be negotiated if the parties are to achieve agreement on the core issues.

Failure to choose the right priorities can be equally damaging. For example, in 2003 the administration emphasized rejection of bilateral talks more than containment of North Korean plutonium, appearing to betray at least an initial preoccupation with form over substance. True, multilateral engagement will be indispensable in resolving the current North Korean nuclear crisis, as it was the last time, particularly in adding pressure on the North to abide by a settlement enforced by several governments. In particular, American success in promoting an active Chinese diplomatic role should be commended. But inflexibility on a matter of pure form may easily derail the broader strategy and lose sight of the strategic priority: stopping North Korea from having access to nuclear weapon material. The *strategic* point here is that any successful settlement must command multilateral support (see Lesson 3), but that is far different from insisting on who sits at which table in a specific negotiating session.

Lesson 2. Integrate carrots and sticks into a strategy of coercive diplomacy. If offered only carrots, the North Koreans will conclude that the other side is more desperate for a deal than they are and will likely continue on a path of defiance and increasing negotiating demands. Offering only sticks will tell the North Koreans that there is no benefit from complying with international demands, except avoidance of pain. They might as well continue down a dangerous path of defiance until their acts become so threatening that the international community will *have* to respond, by which time Pyongyang may have substantially strengthened its bargaining leverage. That is essentially what occurred after Assistant Secretary of State James Kelly challenged the North Koreans in October 2002 regarding their secret enrichment program.

The Clinton administration relied on both carrots *and* sticks to try to resolve the 1994 crisis, integrating them into a negotiating position that presented a clear choice.[32] If Pyongyang returned to full compliance with nonproliferation norms, then the international community would respond favorably, reassuring North Korea that compliance would enhance its national security, and even prosperity. It was easier to define the acceptable end state than to define a viable diplomatic path to reach it. Once the North Koreans were prepared to back down and comply with their nonproliferation obligations, they still sought a face-saving way to do so. This was the "escape valve" that President Clinton kept prodding his advisers to embed into the U.S. negotiating position and, deus ex machina, finally appeared in the form of Jimmy Carter.

At the same time, Pyongyang had to know that if it passed up the face-saving exit and continued to defy the international community, it would experience increasing isolation and hardship. In 1994 this coercive side of diplomacy came to the fore through a gradual military buildup on the peninsula and efforts to seek global support for economic sanctions. Ominous signals from Beijing at the time must have undermined the North Koreans' confidence that China would intervene to insulate Pyongyang from the effect of UN Security Council sanctions. These efforts put pressure on North Korea to back down when the crisis crested in June 1994. Arriving in Pyongyang at the critical moment, former President Jimmy Carter gave the North Koreans a face-saving way out. They took it.

Some have criticized Washington for taking too long to unfurl its diplomatic strategy during the first North Korean nuclear crisis. In particular, the United States has been blamed for not demonstrating more quickly to North Korea the benefits of a negotiated solution by meeting Pyongyang's demand in the summer of 1993 for light-water reactors. Looking back, one can indeed find evidence to support the view that the elements of the Agreed Framework could be discerned long before the October 1994 signing.

Practically speaking, however, it is unlikely that the United States could have short-circuited the tortuous road to the Geneva signing ceremony of the Agreed Framework.[33] First, given the half-century enmity between the United States and North Korea, it was understandable—indeed, inevitable—that U.S. officials responded skeptically to such an unprecedented request from Pyongyang. Indeed, U.S. officials remained unconvinced well after the July 1993 round of bilateral talks that Pyongyang was serious about its proposal to give up its gas-graphite nuclear program in exchange for light-water reactors. Second, the project presented enormous challenges—political, legal, and financial—that took time to resolve. Third, regardless of whether Washington wanted to move forward on the new reactor project or not, it needed multilateral support—particularly from South Korea and Japan—that needed to be painstakingly secured.

In the *Wizard of Oz*, Dorothy turned out to have had the power all along to return to Kansas just by clicking the heels of her ruby slippers; *but first* she needed to go through the Emerald Forest to appreciate why she even wanted to return to Kansas. Similarly, the Agreed Framework could not have been achieved on day one of the crisis; the parties first had to traverse the Emerald Forest of exhaustive negotiations, threats of UN Security Council sanctions, military buildups, and mounting global pressure in order to lay the groundwork for closing the deal.

Lesson 3. Use multilateral institutions and forums to reinforce U.S. diplomacy. Each of North Korea's neighbors has unique equities and assets that must be brought into the settlement. South Korea is the most directly affected, sharing the peninsula and innumerable ties of blood, culture, and history. The United States—a neighbor by virtue of the 37,000 American troops deployed across the Demilitarized Zone—has an unshakable security commitment to South Korea and broader political and economic interests in the region. Japan shares a complex history with Korea—-including its occupation of the peninsula ending with Tokyo's defeat in World War II, the painful issues of Japanese abducted by the North Korean regime, and ties between ethnic Koreans living in Japan and their relatives in the North. It also has the economic resources likely to be an essential part of any settlement with North Korea.

China—traditionally as close to North Korea as "lips and teeth"—has loosened its ties but remains more closely involved with Pyongyang than any other regional player. It also retains the most leverage of any outsider, as the provider of the majority of North Korea's fuel and food, without which

Pyongyang's economy could not survive. While Russia does not approximate that degree of influence, it is bound to the North by treaty and historical ties dating back to Josef Stalin. It can still contribute significantly to a diplomatic settlement of North Korea's differences with the world.

The Clinton administration worked closely with all of the other regional players in the quest for a solution to the nuclear crisis. It also made full use of all available multilateral institutions to bring pressure to bear upon North Korea in the effort to persuade it to comply with international nonproliferation norms. Toward that end, at the United Nations, Washington secured passage of UN Security Council Resolution 825, several presidential statements, and even a resolution from the unwieldy General Assembly. The IAEA Board of Governors was almost continuously engaged throughout 1993 and 1994, both in discussing the North Korean nuclear problem and in issuing multilateral pronouncements.

When the Clinton administration engaged in bilateral discussions with North Korea, it did so with multilateral backing—encouraged initially by South Korea and China, authorized by the UN Security Council. These bilateral talks in no way detracted from the administration effort to secure broad multilateral support for a negotiated solution if possible, and for the use of coercive measures if necessary. To the contrary, the showing of its good-faith bilateral efforts helped the United States make its case in multilateral forums.

Indeed, Washington sometimes might have put *too* much emphasis on multilateralism, by being too deferential to Seoul and Vienna. A case in point was the collapse of Super Tuesday over Seoul's insistence that the proposed North-South exchange of special envoys had to precede U.S.–North Korean negotiations. Washington's concerns over allied solidarity led it to accept that particular sequencing as a negotiating objective, even though it did not relate to the ticking clock on possible plutonium separation, or to U.S. security, or indeed to anything else beyond a matter of political pride. Little surprise, then, that Super Tuesday unraveled; it was held together by political expedience, not national security imperatives.

As for the International Atomic Energy Agency, at times "safeguards theology" created practical problems in blocking plutonium separation. In late 1993, during the implementation of the "tugboat strategy" of pulling Seoul and the IAEA toward Pyongyang, the agency kept shifting the goalposts by adding new conditions for "continuity of safeguards" inspections, making it difficult for the United States and North Korea to return to the negotiating table. Some U.S. officials felt the IAEA was piling on, that ensuring no diversion of North Korean nuclear material required fewer activities than it was demanding. But Washington had to be careful not to appear to muscle the nonproliferation watchdog, lest it inadvertently undermine the agency's inter-national credibility and reputation for impartiality. Fortunately, IAEA excesses were often kept in check through the skillful leadership of Director General Hans Blix who, in spite of North Korean intransigence, successfully walked the fine line between upholding IAEA standards and applying them flexibly enough to address real-world safeguards problems. His support would prove pivotal after the 1994 agreement was signed.

Lesson 4. Use bilateral talks to probe diplomatic alternatives. While multilat-eral diplomacy is indispensable, involving more governments—with varying motives, interests, and objectives—at best complicates and at worst dilutes or even undermines U.S. efforts. The United States should therefore use multi-lateral diplomacy but not be locked into it exclusively. As a sovereign nation, the United States must be free to use any mechanism—including bilateral talks—to advance its unique interests and objectives. In that sense, bilateral talks are not merely a "gift" to be conferred on other governments, but a vec-tor to convey U.S. perspectives unalloyed and undiluted by multilateral involvement.

Thus, after Super Tuesday collapsed, the administration to some degree eased its lockstep approach with other governments and allowed itself greater latitude to explore diplomatic solutions through bilateral discussions with North Korea. Nor did the United States allow the continuing friction between the IAEA, North Korea, and South Korea in the summer of 1994 to derail the Gallucci-Kang talks.

The use of the bilateral channel did not alter U.S. objectives; it just pro-vided another policy instrument in a pretty empty toolbox. Use of the bilat-eral channel allowed the Americans more leeway in exploring possible solu-tions informally with the North. It also provided an opportunity for the United States to focus especially on unique American concerns in a venue uncluttered by other considerations. At the end of the day, the bilateral chan-nel provided a mechanism to promote solutions that the U.S. government considered to be in its own interests as well as those of its multilateral partners and the rest of the international community. American negotiators sometimes envisaged outcomes that would satisfy its multilateral partners' needs, even if the partners were unwilling or unable (because of their negotiating con-straints or domestic political factors) to approve certain negotiating positions in advance. Of course, the trade-off is that although reducing the number of parties in direct negotiations can facilitate reaching a deal, it can complicate implementation to the degree that the arrangement does not adequately address the concerns of the governments whose cooperation is essential to success.

Today the Bush administration faces the same dilemma. It has relied almost entirely on multilateral talks, rejecting any but fleeting bilateral contacts with Pyongyang. This approach may give the key governments a greater stake in ensuring that an agreement is fully implemented, create greater pressure on Pyongyang by presenting a unified front, and provide an avenue for others to bring carrots or sticks to bear in the service of the collective diplomatic effort. The disadvantages include an inevitable muffling of U.S. positions in relation to Pyongyang, while also subjecting Washington to greater pressure to modify its own approach.

Most important, placing so much weight on the multilateral format of the discussions with North Korea allows Pyongyang to dictate the pace of the crisis. Pyongyang already makes the decisions on its own nuclear activities. Letting it off the hook of "confronting its accusers" also gives it the upper hand in deciding the tempo of the diplomatic effort. Rigid insistence on specific formats or conditions (as opposed to an "anytime, anywhere" offer for talks) permits the North Koreans—now liberated from the cameras, seals, and inspectors of the IAEA that they ejected in 2002—to continue their pursuit of nuclear weapons while sidestepping international pressure. (Of course, the United States could force the issue through such measures as IAEA Board of Governors' statements and UN Security Council actions, but the absence of actual negotiations with the North Koreans weakens U.S. efforts to show that diplomacy has been exhausted and that stronger measures are therefore required.) Since time is on North Korea's side, the United States and its allies should seek to force the issue by reasserting control over the pacing of the crisis.

In the Civil War, it was not enough for Abraham Lincoln to refuse to recognize the Confederate States of America. He had to take affirmative action to *interfere with* the Confederacy, which would have realized its strategic aims simply by carrying on its activities independently from—and unmolested by—the Union. Similarly, North Korea can realize its strategic objectives simply by continuing its current path until someone stops it. The longer real negotiations are delayed, the greater the nuclear capability—and bargaining leverage—the North will have accumulated. So whether a particular round of talks with North Korea is bilateral or multilateral is less important than that they occur sooner rather than later. (This is where setting priorities correctly comes into play.)

Lesson 5. South Korean support is crucial to any lasting solution of the North Korean nuclear problem. The role of South Korea is as complex as it is central to resolving the North Korean nuclear crisis. Seoul's support is critical, since any action or solution, whatever form it takes, will be on its peninsula. To that end, in 1993 and 1994 the United States and South Korea spent enormous amounts of time and energy working together to forge a common strategy. Contrary to popular belief in South Korea, time after time Washington deferred to Seoul or explicitly took its views into account. The record shows that South Korea had a remarkable degree of influence, even though its positions frequently changed.

Two notable exceptions to the rule merit separate mention. The first occurred when Seoul resisted the October 1994 decision to delay implementation of special inspections, in order to get a deal that would address the real and continuing threat of plutonium production by the North. The other exception occurred in 1995 when the United States cut a deal that finessed the name of the reactors to be built in North Korea. The theory was that this issue was far too trivial to justify destroying the Agreed Framework and far to obscure to ensure support for sanctions in the UN Security Council. In both cases, the United States parted company with the South Koreans only because its supreme national interest in blocking North Korean access to plutonium was on the line.

Some South Koreans have complained about being harnessed to an ally ready to sacrifice their interests on the altar of nuclear nonproliferation. The most notable example is President Kim's recent claim that he stopped President Clinton from starting a second Korean War.[34] In fact, the record discloses no eleventh-hour phone calls to the White House. President Kim was solidly behind the American drive for sanctions, and his government was well informed about the gradual military buildup on the peninsula as well as the more extensive deployments that were about to be considered. Seoul did not know about American consideration of a preemptive strike against Yongbyon, but it is clear from the record of the Principals Committee meetings that Washington would never have authorized an attack without prior consultation with Seoul. That consultation never became necessary after the June breakthrough that returned the nuclear issue to the negotiating table.

In important respects, the challenge of maintaining U.S.-South Korean solidarity is more difficult today than it was a decade ago. Then the majority of South Koreans, and their government leaders, had personal memories of the Korean War and its aftermath as well as serious doubts about Pyongyang's intentions. Now a younger generation has taken the reins of power, after years of a Sunshine Policy that has left many South Koreans feeling greater sympathy toward their brethren in the North and greater concern that their peace is more likely to be disturbed by Americans than North Koreans. For Americans, the deference once accorded to Seoul as facing the more imminent threat from the North has since September 11 been displaced by its own sense of vulnerability to the export of nuclear technology to adversaries and, to some, the prospect of North Korean ballistic missiles ranging the continental United States.

Unfortunately, the myth that the United States was willing to sacrifice the interests of its close ally in 1994 is widely accepted in South Korea and has colored Seoul's dealings with the current Bush administration. It reflects a long-standing Korean fear of abandonment dating back to the Taft-Katsura treaty of 1905, which essentially handed Korea over to Japan. When combined with the demographic changes just discussed, it is easy to see why the North Korean nuclear crisis can stress the U.S.-South Korean alliance. It will be important for U.S. and South Korean decisionmakers to recognize this reality as they chart a course for the alliance through the shoals of the current crisis.

Lesson 6. Take full advantage of China's continuing sway over North Korea. As the driving force behind the six-party talks in 2003, China assumed a much higher profile as a diplomatic player on the world stage. Its importance in addressing the North Korean nuclear crisis was already apparent in 1994. The first crisis broke during China's transition from unalloyed dedication to its alliance with Pyongyang to a more even-handed relationship between the two Koreas. That timing left China open to work cooperatively with Seoul, while giving Pyongyang greater reason to fear abandonment by its prime benefactor. Beijing understood both its own leverage as well as the grave consequences of a North Korean nuclear program and repeatedly, but quietly, nudged Pyongyang toward compliance with its nonproliferation commitments. Beijing's most important effort unfolded in the spring of 1994, when it tried its hand at mediation after North Korea's unloading of the fuel rods from the 5-megawatt reactor at Yongbyon and appeared to signal that Pyongyang could not count on China blocking the imposition of UN sanctions against North Korea.

Although Chinese officials have traditionally sought to downplay their influence in Pyongyang, they clearly retain greater leverage over the Kim Jong Il regime than any other player. Fortunately, China and the United States agree on two key objectives: (1) the Korean Peninsula should remain stable and secure, and (2) it should be free of nuclear weapons.

But this convergence of views between Washington and Beijing has limits. Specifically, China has a strong interest in avoiding political disruption in North Korea, which argues in favor of seeking a negotiated solution to the nuclear challenge and against taking steps that could induce regime change in North Korea. By 2003, however, some U.S. officials had apparently concluded that the North Koreans were inveterate cheaters with whom no agreement could be reached that would protect American interests. Under this view, agreements should therefore be eschewed in favor of the only practical way to head off North Korean possession of a growing nuclear weapon stockpile: regime change. Whether this would occur by force or by inducing a social collapse through encouraging massive refugee flows out of the North, the bottom line is that pursuit of this objective would drive a wedge between China and the United States.

China would not only object to steps intended to induce regime change in North Korea, it would actively oppose such efforts and likely step in to prevent the collapse of the Kim Jong Il regime. Thus sharing the same broad strategic aims regarding nuclear proliferation on the Korean peninsula does not necessarily translate into shared approaches. When those approaches differ, the U.S. efforts to encourage China to take the diplomatic lead in dealing with North Korea becomes a double-edged sword, increasing U.S. exposure to Chinese pressure at the same time that it increases Beijing's influence over the broader direction of the multilateral approach to North Korea. Since, as this book has concluded (for different reasons), forcing regime change is a losing nonproliferation strategy, the United States should continue to work with China in curbing North Korea's nuclear activities on the basis of the two objectives Washington and Beijing do share.

Lesson 7. Negotiated arrangements can advance U.S. interests even if the other party engages in cheating. Of course, it is possible to construct a deal that would leave the United States in a worse position if the other side cheated. An example would be an agreement that left the other side well positioned to break out of a treaty in a manner that would put the United States at an instant military disadvantage. Nazi Germany's rearmament in violation of the Versailles Treaty, combined with Europe's failure to respond, comes to mind. But it is also possible to construct a treaty that leaves the United States better off every day that the other party is compliant, and not significantly disadvantaged if the other party cheats.

Certainly, it would be a mistake to base a deal on trust. But as every American president concluded throughout the cold war, it is possible to construct a deal whose provisions, including those creating transparency, benefit the United States no matter what an aggressive and untrustworthy adversary does in the course of implementation. It is also possible to do so without submitting to "blackmail," if that term is meant to refer to a government's insistence on (1) being "paid" not to do harm, and (2) being "paid" more than once in order to keep commitments made through earlier agreements. That lesson is no less true today with respect to North Korea.

U.S. negotiators will always need to make hard choices. It would be desirable if any new deal includes comprehensive limits on North Korea's nuclear program, extending beyond known plutonium production facilities to encompass not only uranium-enrichment activities but also any nuclear weapons Pyongyang may have already built or obtained, as well as its research and development efforts. Such a commitment would be difficult to verify with confidence, even with "anytime, anywhere" inspections in North Korea. It is just too easy to cheat.

Should U.S. negotiators pass up stronger commitments if they cannot be confidently verified? What if a new deal imposes greater restrictions on Pyongyang with more extensive inspections than the 1994 accord but still leaves uncertainties? Would such a deal serve U.S. interests? Similar questions confronted the United States in 1994, when the president had to decide whether to seek more immediate limits on North Korea's threatening plutonium production program in lieu of immediate special inspections.

Reaching a deal is not always the best option. As noted earlier, the alternatives to engagement—military action or containment—were unattractive for most of the previous crises and may be unattractive today. But in June 1994 U.S. decisionmakers were on the verge of seriously considering a preemptive strike against the Yongbyon nuclear facilities, even in view of potentially dire consequences, out of concern that the North might be about to begin producing bomb-making material. Today, what would happen if North Korea ceremoniously unveiled a nuclear-tipped missile that was clearly threatening to its neighbors, the United States, and the world? Under certain circumstances, *no* deal may be the best option, leaving only acquiescence (masquerading as deterrence and containment) at one extreme and confrontation (possibly including military action) at the other. Extreme circumstances may leave only extreme options.

Lesson 8. Consider setting red lines. One way to try to avoid falling into a situation in which the president faces only extreme options is to set "red lines" for North Korea. Initially, the Bush administration seemed leery to do that on the assumption that "if you draw it, they will cross it." There is always a danger that Pyongyang will do just that, either deliberately or through miscalculation. In the spring of 1994, North Korea did cross a red line by unloading the 5-megawatt reactor and destroying important historical information contained in the spent fuel rods, triggering the march toward confrontation. The United States responded as it had warned that it would, by breaking off negotiations and returning to the UN Security Council to seek sanctions. But one month later, Pyongyang did not expel the IAEA inspectors monitoring the Yongbyon facility—nor did it reprocess the spent fuel—perhaps in part because of Jimmy Carter's trip but also because it knew that could trigger an American preemptive attack. In short, picking a clear boundary for acceptable

2thTHE LAND OF COUNTERPANE   407

behavior can prove a successful deterrent, but only if it is backed by the credible threat to escalate, including to the use of force. The United States should not be bluffing, and it must be clear that it is not.

For four decades, the greatest threat of nuclear conflict emerged from the superpower rivalry between the United States and the Soviet Union. The fall of the Berlin Wall set events in train that ended with the disintegration of the Soviet Union. The first major nuclear proliferation threat—of seeing four nuclear weapon states emerge full-blown at the end of the cold war—was averted when U.S. negotiators persuaded the newly formed nations of Ukraine, Kazakhstan, and Belarus to relinquish all of their nuclear weapons to Russia. The second threat—that Russia would become a source of nuclear weapons proliferation from the diversion of weapon scientists and fissile materials to hostile forces—spawned a series of U.S. initiatives under the seminal Nunn-Lugar legislation aimed at promoting the safe and secure dismantlement of the former Soviet nuclear arsenal.

North Korea posed the third great nuclear threat. Addressing that threat as a matter of national urgency led to the concerted effort described in these pages. The urgency was dictated not only by the dire consequences that unbounded North Korean plutonium production could have produced but also by the impending review and extension conference for the Nuclear Non-Proliferation Treaty, the cornerstone of global efforts to combat the spread of nuclear weapons. Had the United States failed to contain the North Korean threat in time, it would have torn a hole in the regime just at the moment when the nations of the world were gathering in New York to decide whether to extend the treaty indefinitely, or to let it lapse.

The Agreed Framework permitted the NPT conference to proceed with a North Korea that had reaffirmed its commitment to the treaty, accepted IAEA monitoring to ensure the continuation of the nuclear freeze, and promised ultimate North Korean acceptance of inspections to clarify remaining questions about its past nuclear activities and dismantlement of its existing program. The accord earned the support of the IAEA, and the NPT was successfully extended indefinitely and without condition, by consensus, in May 1995.[35]

The response of the United States to the North Korean nuclear challenge was pragmatic, guided by the overarching objective to stop Pyongyang's access to more separated plutonium. It was principled, gaining support of the world community through the UN Security Council, the IAEA, and other forums to support U.S. efforts to persuade Pyongyang to curtail and accept international limits on its nuclear activities. It was complex, involving constant scrutiny of U.S. interests and the effects of shifting events, continual consultations with friends and allies, and a difficult and protracted negotiation with the North Koreans.

Above all, the U.S. response was guided by a determination to prevent the nightmare of nuclear destruction threatened by the North Korean program. The U.S. officials involved in negotiating the Agreed Framework shared a fundamental commitment to advancing the nation's security. None would have advocated support for any accord that did not meet a simple test: would Americans be safer with the Agreed Framework than without it? As public servants, a decade ago we answered that question in favor of the Agreed Framework. As authors today, we reach the same conclusion.

That same question—will Americans be safer or not?—should guide the evaluation of any proposed U.S. response to the renewed nuclear threat in Korea. If grounded in a policy that forces North Korea to choose between a path of compliance with—or defiance of—the global norm against nuclear weapons proliferation, that question can bring the world to a safer future. North Korea will only be forced to make that choice if the path of defiance inexorably brings pressure that threatens the continued viability of the Kim Jong Il regime, while the path of compliance offers the regime the security assurances and improved relations with the international community that it seeks. We wish those entrusted with our national security well as they make the fateful choices that will shape the outcome of the current crisis. The stakes could not be higher.

Chronology

Early 1980s. North Korea begins construction of 5-megawatt reactor in Yongbyon

December 1985. North Korea signs the Nuclear Non-Proliferation Treaty (NPT)

January 5, 1986. 5-megawatt reactor begins to operate

December 1988. First official U.S.–North Korean contacts in Beijing

Spring 1989. Extended outage of 5-megawatt reactor

May 1991. North Korea joins the United Nations (UN)

September 1991. United States announces intention to redeploy tactical nuclear weapons worldwide

December 1991. North Korea and South Korea finalize nonaggression agreement and North-South Denuclearization Declaration

January 1992. South Korea announces suspension of Team Spirit 1992
North Korea signs IAEA fullscope safeguards agreement
U.S.–North Korean high-level talks (with Under Secretary Arnold Kanter in New York)

March 1992. North Korea and South Korea set up Joint Nuclear Control Committee for implementing the Denuclearization Declaration

April 10, 1992. North Korea Supreme People's Assembly ratifies International Atomic Energy Agency (IAEA) safeguards agreement

May 4, 1992. North Korea submits initial inventory of nuclear material
First IAEA ad hoc inspection

July 1992. Second IAEA ad hoc inspection; first evidence of "inconsistencies"

September 1992. Third IAEA ad hoc inspection

October 1992. United States and South Korea announce 1993 Team Spirit
exercise

November 1992. Fourth IAEA ad hoc inspection

High-level IAEA–North Korean consultations on discrepancies, in
Vienna; IAEA requests "visits to two suspect waste sites"

December 1992. Fifth IAEA ad hoc inspection

January 1993. IAEA team travels to Pyongyang to discuss discrepancies in
North Korean declaration

Sixth IAEA ad hoc inspection

February 9, 1993. IAEA requests special inspection of the two suspect sites

February 20, 1993. Further North Korean–IAEA consultations; Pyongyang
rejects special inspections

February 25, 1993. IAEA Board of Governors passes resolution calling for
North Korea to accept special inspections within one month

March 12, 1993. North Korea announces its intention to withdraw from the
NPT

March 18, 1993. Special Board meeting passes a second resolution calling on
North Korea to accept special inspections by March 31

April 1, 1993. Board of Governors adopts resolution finding North Korea in
noncompliance with its safeguards obligations; reports to the UN
Security Council

May 11, 1993. UN Security Council passes Resolution 825, which calls upon
North Korea to comply with its safeguards agreement as specified in
the February 25 IAEA resolution, requests the director general to continue to consult with Pyongyang, and urges member states to encourage a resolution

May 1993. IAEA inspectors allowed into Yongbyon to perform the necessary
work relating to safeguards monitoring equipment

June 11, 1993. High-level U.S.–North Korean talks in New York; in a joint
statement, North Korea agrees to suspend its withdrawal from the NPT
and agrees to the principle of "impartial application" of IAEA safeguards. The United States tells North Korea that for dialogue to continue it must accept IAEA inspections to ensure the continuity of safeguards, forgo reprocessing, and allow the IAEA to be present when
refueling the 5-megawatt reactor

July 1993. High-level U.S.–North Korean talks in Geneva; North Korea
agrees to resume discussion with South Korea and the IAEA on the
nuclear issue, United States agrees, in principle, to support North
Korea's conversion to light-water reactors

August 1993. IAEA inspectors allowed into Yongbyon to service safeguards monitoring equipment but given incomplete access to reprocessing plant U.S.–North Korean working-level talks begin in New York

September 1–3, 1993. IAEA consultations with government in North Korea on impartial application of safeguards

October 1, 1993. IAEA General Conference adopts resolution urging North Korea to fully implement safeguards

November 1, 1993. UN General Assembly adopts a resolution expressing grave concern that North Korea has failed to discharge its safeguards obligations and has widened the area of noncompliance. It also urges Pyongyang to cooperate immediately with the IAEA in the full implementation of its safeguards agreement

November 14, 1993. North Korea's withdrawal suspends North-South talks

December, 1993. U.S. commander in chief, U.S. Forces Korea, General Gary Luck, requests Patriot Missile Battalion to counter North Korean SCUD threat

December 5, 1993. IAEA Board of Governors meeting; Hans Blix, director general of the IAEA, states that he cannot give meaningful assurances about continuity of safeguards and that he cannot exclude the possibility that nuclear material has been diverted

December 29, 1993. United States and North Korea, in talks in New York, agree on an arrangement for a third round. North Korea agrees to accept the IAEA inspections needed to maintain continuity of safeguards at seven declared sites, and to resume North-South working-level talks in Panmunjom. In exchange, the United States agrees to concur in a South Korean announcement to suspend Team Spirit 1994 and set a date for a third round of U.S.–North Korean talks, which would be held only after the North's steps are completed

January 1994. North Korea begins talks with the IAEA in Vienna to discuss the scope of inspections necessary to provide continuity of safeguards

January 26, 1994. White House announces plans to send Patriot Missile Battalion to South Korea

January 31, 1994. North Korea's Foreign Ministry issues a statement accusing the United States of overturning the December 29 understanding; threatens to "unfreeze" its nuclear program

February 15, 1994. IAEA and North Korea reach an understanding on a comprehensive list of safeguards measures to verify that no diversion of nuclear material has occurred since earlier inspections in the seven declared nuclear installations

February 21, 1994. IAEA Board of Governors meeting

February 25, 1994. U.S.–North Korean joint statement outlines terms of December agreement

February 26, 1994. North Korean authorities issue two-week visas to IAEA inspection team

March 1, 1994. IAEA inspectors arrive in North Korea

March 3, 1994. Official "Super Tuesday" announcement: IAEA inspections begin, North-South talks begin, Team Spirit 1994 is suspended, and date is set for a third round of U.S.–North Korean talks

March 9, 1994. Second North-South meeting

March 12, 1994. Third North-South meeting; the parties reach an agreement, in principle, on an exchange of envoys

March 15, 1994. IAEA inspection team leaves Pyongyang, having conducted inspections without difficulty at all facilities except the reprocessing facility

March 16, 1994. Director General Blix calls a special session of the IAEA Board of Governors to informally report on the March 3–14 safeguards inspections in North Korea

Blix announces that the IAEA inspection team was unable to implement the February 15 North Korean–IAEA agreement, and thus the agency is unable to draw conclusions as to whether there has been diversion of nuclear material or reprocessing since earlier inspections

Fourth North-South meeting

March 19, 1994. Fifth North-South meeting; North Korea walks out, threatening to turn Seoul into a sea of fire; Team Spirit 1994 revived

March 21, 1994. IAEA Board of Governors passes a resolution finding North Korea in further noncompliance and referring the issue to the UN Security Council, with 25 approvals, 1 rejection, and 5 abstentions (including China)

Clinton administration announces Patriot Missile Battalion will be sent to South Korea

March 31, 1994. UN Security Council issues unanimous presidential statement calling on Pyongyang to allow the IAEA to complete inspection activities in accordance with the February 15 agreement and inviting Director General Blix to report back to the council within six weeks

April 4, 1994. President Clinton directs the establishment of a Senior Policy Steering Group on Korea (SSK) with responsibility for coordinating all aspects of U.S. policy on the current nuclear issue on the Korean Peninsula; Assistant Secretary Gallucci is asked to chair the group

South Korea announces Team Spirit 1994 will be held during the November time frame

South Korea drops North-South special envoys as a precondition to the third round

April 18, 1994. Patriot Missile Battalion arrives in South Korea

April 28, 1994. North Korea claims the 1953 Armistice Agreement is invalid and announces its intent to withdraw from the Military Armistice Committee

May 4, 1994. North Korea begins reactor discharge campaign.

May 18–23, 1994. IAEA inspectors complete March inspections and maintenance activities for the continuity of safeguards knowledge

May 20, 1994. IAEA reports to the UN Security Council that North Korea's decision to discharge fuel from the 5-megawatt reactor without prior IAEA agreement for future measurement "constitutes a serious safeguards violation"

May 25–27, 1994. IAEA–North Korean consultations on fuel monitoring, in Pyongyang

May 27, 1994. Director General Blix sends a letter to UN Secretary General Boutros Boutros-Ghali stating the IAEA–North Korean talks have failed, North Korea's fuel discharge is proceeding at a faster rate than before, and the IAEA's opportunity to measure spent fuel in the future will be lost within days if discharge continues at this rate

May 30, 1994. UN Security Council issues a presidential statement "strongly urging the DPRK only to proceed with the discharge operations at the 5-megawatt reactor in a manner which preserves the technical possibility of fuel measurements, in accordance with the IAEA's requirements in this regard"

June 3, 1994. Director General Blix reports to the UN Security Council on failed IAEA efforts to preserve the technical possibility of measuring discharged fuel from North Korea's 5-megawatt reactor

June 9, 1994. IAEA Board of Governors passes a resolution calling for immediate North Korean cooperation by providing access to all safeguards-related information and locations, and suspends nonmedical assistance to North Korea. The resolution receives 28 approvals, 1 rejection (Libya), and 4 abstentions (China, India, Lebanon, Syria); 2 members were absent (Saudi Arabia, Cuba)

June 13, 1994. North Korea officially withdraws from the IAEA

June 15–18, 1994. Former president Carter visits North Korea and receives commitment to permit IAEA inspectors and equipment to remain at Yongbyong, to establish U.S.–North Korean teams to recover remains of Americans killed in the Korean War, and to agree to an inter-Korean summit between Kim Il Sung and Kim Young Sam

June 20–22, 1994. North Korea's intention to reestablish the basis for dialogue is confirmed in an exchange of letters between Foreign Minister Kang and Assistant Secretary Gallucci

June 27, 1994. Agreement reached to hold the third round, starting July 8

June 28, 1994 North-South Korean summit between President Kim Il Sung and President Kim Young Sam announced for July 25–27

July 8, 1994. Third round of U.S.–North Korean talks begins in Geneva in a businesslike atmosphere and confirms Pyongyang's desire to convert to light-water reactor technology

July 9, 1994. Announcement of President Kim Il Sung's death postpones the third round until after the mourning period, and the planned July 25–27 North-South summit indefinitely

July 21, 1994. United States and North Korea agree to resume the third round on August 5

July 19–28, 1994. Delegation led by Assistant Secretary Gallucci visits Seoul, Tokyo, Beijing, and Moscow to discuss the provision of and solicit support for the conversion of North Korea's graphite-moderated reactors to light-water reactors, which are more proliferation resistant

August 5–12, 1994. Third round is resumed in Geneva; the United States and North Korea sign an agreement showing substantial progress toward an overall settlement. As part of the final resolution of the nuclear issue,

—the United States will provide light-water reactors to the DPRK, make arrangements for interim energy alternatives, and provide an assurance against the threat or use of nuclear weapons;

—North Korea will remain a party to the NPT, allow implementation of its safeguards agreement, and implement the Joint North-South Declaration on the Denuclearization of the Korean Peninsula; and

—the United States and North Korea will begin to establish diplomatic representation, hold expert-level meetings on the technical issues, and recess the talks, with resumption scheduled for September to resolve the remaining differences

September 23, 1994. Session two of the third round begins in Geneva

October 21, 1994. United States and North Korea sign the Agreed Framework United States hands over a presidential letter of assurance, and the United States and North Korea sign a confidential minute to the Agreed Framework

November 14–18, 1994. U.S. team of experts visits North Korea to discuss safe storage and disposition of spent fuel

November 23–28, 1994. IAEA team of experts visits North Korea to discuss details related to the monitoring and verification of North Korea's freeze on nuclear facilities

November 30, 1994. Experts from the United States and North Korea meet in Beijing for preliminary discussions on the light-water reactor project

December 6–10, 1994. North Korean team of experts visits Washington, D.C., to discuss technical and consular issues related to the planned exchange of liaison offices

January 9, 1995. North Korea announces lifting of restrictions on U.S. imports and on calls by U.S. vessels at DPRK ports

January 17–24, 1995. Second session of U.S.–North Korean talks on spent fuel in Pyongyang

January 19, 1995. First shipment of 50,000 metric tons of heavy fuel oil ($4.7 million) is delivered to Sonbong, North Korea

January 20, 1995. United States announces measures easing sanctions against North Korea in four areas: telecommunications and information, financial transactions, imports of North Korean magnesite, and transactions related to the future opening of liaison offices and other energy-related projects

January 23–28, 1995. IAEA–North Korean discussions continue in Pyongyang on implementation and verification of the freeze on nuclear facilities

January 28, 1995. Second session of talks on the U.S.–North Korean light-water reactor supply agreement, in Beijing

January 29, 1995. U.S. experts arrive in Pyongyang to survey sites for a future U.S. liaison office

February 15, 1995. Australia publicly announces its contribution of U.S. $5 million to KEDO (the Korean Energy Development Organization, later the Korean Peninsula Energy Development Organization)

Mid-February 1995. United States and South Korea agree that Team Spirit 1995 is not necessary

February 28, 1995. New Zealand publicly announces its contribution of U.S.$300,000 to KEDO

March 7–9, 1995. KEDO Preparatory Conference in New York

March 8, 1995. Treasury Department licenses a U.S. company to buy a one-year supply of magnesite ($5–10 million) from North Korea

March 9, 1995. KEDO is formally established as an international organization under international law; Canada, New Zealand, and Australia join

March 16, 1995. Federal Communications Commission publishes revised policy on common-carrier telecommunications services with North Korea

March 25–29, 1995. Third session of talks on the U.S.–North Korean light-water reactor supply agreement, in Berlin

April 4–8, 1995. North Korean experts arrive in Washington, D.C., to survey sites for a future North Korean liaison office

April 12–21, 1995. Fourth session of talks on the U.S.–North Korean light-water reactor supply agreement, in Berlin; talks break April 14–18

May 2, 1995. U.S. House of Representatives' National Security Committee approves Energy Department's reprogramming of $10 million in fiscal 1995 for the safe storage of spent fuel

May 27, 1995. North Korea tells IAEA inspectors that the spent fuel has to be delivered to the next stage of the nuclear fuel cycle for reprocessing, due to deterioriation

May 20–June 16, 1995. Fifth session of talks on the U.S.–North Korean light-water reactor supply agreement, in Kuala Lumpur; Thomas Hubbard and Kim Gye Gwan focus on reactor type and South Korea's central role

June 4–9, 1995. North Korea and the U.S. firm Minerals Technology reach agreement on a supply contract for 85,000 metric tonnes of North Korean magnesite, worth $5–10 million.

June 13, 1995. United States and North Korea reach agreement in Kuala Lumpur on South Korean reactors and the South's central role; KEDO will now enter into discussions with the North to conclude the supply contract

  KEDO Executive Board passes resolution 1995-12 reconfirming the Kuala Lumpur agreement by selecting Ulchin 3/4 as the reference plant and Korea Electric Power Corporation (KEPCO) as the prime contractor

June 16, 1995. North Korea sends letter refusing the visit of a U.S. liaison office technical team to inspect and survey the German compound in Pyongyang

June 17–18, 1995. North-South talks in Beijing at the vice minister level on the South Korean government's provision of rice to the North; an agreement is reached for 150,000 tons of ROK rice

June 17–24, 1995. U.S.–North Korean discussions on heavy fuel oil in Pyongyang reach ad ref agreement on verification measures for the heavy fuel oil and a delivery schedule for 100,000 metric tonnes of heavy fuel oil by October 21

June 21–27, 1995. U.S.–North Korean discussions on the safe storage and disposition of the spent fuel, in Pyongyang; North Korea approves the water treatment system and cannister design; the United States installs a chiller to slow fuel corrosion and cool the pond

June 22, 1995. North Korea informally notifies IAEA inspectors that it is willing to receive an IAEA team to discuss "technical issues" relating to the Agreed Framework

July 19, 1995. Stephen W. Bosworth is selected by KEDO's Executive Board to be an executive director

July 20, 1995. Yong Jin Choi (South Korea) and Itaru Umezu (Japan) are selected by KEDO's Executive Board as executive directors

July 23, 1995. A small U.S. technical team travels to North Korea to check on the operation of the chiller. North Korea makes progress on construction of a separate building to house the water treatment system

July 31–August 1, 1995. KEDO General Conference in New York

August 10, 1995. A three-person team travels to North Korea to install fuel-flow monitoring equipment at the Sonbong thermal power plant in advance of the next delivery of heavy fuel oil

Third round of North-South "rice talks"

August 15–22, 1995. KEDO's first light-water reactor site survey in the Sinpo Region

40,000 metric tonnes of heavy fuel oil delivered to North Korea

September 2, 1995. Spent fuel team begins installing water clarification system in the spent fuel basin

September 8–15, 1995. First KEDO–North Korean talks on the light-water reactor supply agreement, with South Korea and Japan participating

September 11–19, 1995. IAEA and North Korea resume discussions on outstanding safeguards issues; North Korea agrees to limited measurements of spent fuel prior to canning

September 16–22, 1995. KEDO team travels to Songbon, North Korea, to recalibrate the fuel-flow meters monitoring the heavy fuel oil

30,000 metric tonnes of heavy fuel oil delivered to North Korea

September 23–30, 1995. U.S. delegation travels to Pyongyang to survey the German U.S. liaison office facility and resume discussions on outstanding issues related to opening liaison offices

Gallucci travels to Europe to solicit a contribution from the European Union and its membership in KEDO

October 18–28, 1995. 30,000 metric tonnes of heavy fuel oil are delivered to North Korea—the last shipment for the year

October 24, 1995. KEDO's second light-water reactor site survey in the Sinpo Region

October 30, 1995. Tetsuya Endo travels to members of the Association of Southeast Asian Nations (ASEAN) to solicit contributions

November 4, 1995. Endo solicits ASEAN membership in KEDO

November 1995. Reprogrammed U.S. contribution of $4 million for fiscal 1995 is deposited in KEDO account

December 14, 1995. Principal Deputy Assistant Secretary for East Asia and the Pacific Thomas Hubbard meets with North Korean ambassador-at-large Ho Jong in New York for bilateral talks

December 15, 1995. KEDO and North Korea sign the light-water reactor supply agreement in New York

December 16, 1995. KEDO's third light-water reactor site survey in the Sinpo Region

Joint Statements
and Agreements

U.S.–North Korean Joint Statement
June 11, 1993
Geneva

The Democratic People's Republic of Korea and the United States of America held government-level talks in New York from the 2nd through the 11th of June, 1993. Present at the talks were the delegation of the Democratic People's Republic of Korea headed by First Vice Minster of Foreign Affairs Kang Sok Ju and the delegation of the United States of America led by Assistant Secretary of State Robert L. Gallucci, both representing their respective Governments. At the talks, both sides discussed policy matters with a view to a fundamental solution of the nuclear issue on the Korean Peninsula. Both sides expressed support for the North-South Joint Declaration on the Denuclearization of the Korean Peninsula in the interest of nuclear non-proliferation goals. The Democratic People's Republic of Korea and the United States have agreed to principles of:

 —assurances against the threat and use of force, including nuclear weapons;

 —peace and security in a nuclear-free Korean Peninsula, including impartial application of fullscope safe-guards, mutual respect for each other's sovereignty, and non-interference in each other's internal affairs; and

 —support for the peaceful reunification of Korea.

In this context, the two Governments have agreed to continue dialogue on an equal and unprejudiced basis. In this respect, the Government of the Democratic People's Republic of Korea has decided unilaterally to suspend as long as it considers necessary the effectuation of its withdrawal from the Treaty on the Non-Proliferation of Nuclear Weapons.

Agreed Statement between the United States of America and the Democratic People's Republic of Korea
August 12, 1994
Geneva

The delegations of the United States of America (U.S.) and the Democratic People's Republic of Korea (DPRK) met in Geneva from August 5–12, 1994, to resume the third round of talks.

Both sides reaffirmed the principles of the June 11, 1993, U.S.-DPRK joint statement and reached agreement that the following elements should be part of a final resolution of the nuclear issue:

(1) The DPRK is prepared to replace its graphite-moderated reactors and related facilities with light-water reactor (LWR) power plants, and the U.S. is prepared to make arrangements for the provision of LWRs of approximately 2,000 MW(e) to the DPRK as early as possible and to make arrangements for interim energy alternatives to the DPRK's graphite-moderated reactors. Upon receipt of U.S. assurances for the provision of LWRs and for arrangements for interim energy alternatives, the DPRK will freeze construction of the 50 MW(e) and 200 MW(e) reactors, forego reprocessing, and seal the Radiochemical Laboratory, to be monitored by the IAEA.

(2) The U.S. and the DPRK are prepared to establish diplomatic representation in each other's capitals and to reduce barriers to trade and investment, as a move toward full normalization of political and economic relations.

(3) To help achieve peace and security on a nuclear-free Korean Peninsula, the U.S. is prepared to provide the DPRK with assurances against the threat or use of nuclear weapons by the U.S., and the DPRK remains prepared to implement the North-South Joint Declaration on the Denuclearization of the Korean Peninsula.

(4) The DPRK is prepared to remain a party to the Treaty on the Non-Proliferation of Nuclear Weapons and to allow implementation of its safeguards agreement under the Treaty.

Important issues raised during the talks remain to be resolved. Both sides agree that expert-level discussions are necessary to advance the replacement of the DPRK's graphite-moderated program with LWR technology, the safe storage and disposition of the spent fuel, provision of alternative energy, and the establishment of the liaison offices. Accordingly, expert-level talks will be held in the U.S. and DPRK or elsewhere as agreed. The DPRK and U.S. agreed to recess their talks and resume in Geneva on September 23, 1994.

In the meantime, the U.S. will pursue arrangements necessary to provide assurances for the LWR project to the DPRK as part of a final resolution of the nuclear issue, and the DPRK will observe the freeze on nuclear activities and maintain the continuity of safeguards as agreed in the June 20–22, 1994, exchange of messages between Assistant Secretary of State Robert L. Gallucci and First Vice Minister of Foreign Affairs Kang Sok Ju.

Agreed Framework between the United States of America and the Democratic People's Republic of Korea
October 21, 1994
Geneva

Delegations of the governments of the United States of America (U.S.) and the Democratic People's Republic of Korea (DPRK) held talks in Geneva from September 23 to October 21, 1994, to negotiate an overall resolution of the nuclear issue on the Korean Peninsula.

Both sides reaffirmed the importance of attaining the objectives contained in the August 12, 1994, Agreed Statement between the U.S. and the DPRK and upholding the principles of the June 11, 1993, Joint Statement of the U.S. and the DPRK to achieve peace and security on a nuclear-free Korean peninsula. The U.S. and the DPRK decided to take the following actions for the resolution of the nuclear issue:

I. Both sides will cooperate to replace the DPRK's graphite-moderated reactors and related facilities with light-water reactor (LWR) power plants.

(1) In accordance with the October 20, 1994, letter of assurance from the U.S. President, the U.S. will undertake to make arrangements for the provision to the DPRK of a LWR project with a total generating capacity of approximately 2,000 MW(e) by a target date of 2003.

—The U.S. will organize under its leadership an international consortium to finance and supply the LWR project to be provided to the DPRK. The U.S., representing the international consortium, will serve as the principal point of contact with the DPRK for the LWR project.

—The U.S., representing the consortium, will make best efforts to secure the conclusion of a supply contract with the DPRK within six months of the date of this Document for the provision of the LWR project. Contract talks will begin as soon as possible after the date of this Document.

—As necessary, the U.S. and the DPRK will conclude a bilateral agreement for cooperation in the field of peaceful uses of nuclear energy.

(2) In accordance with the October 20, 1994, letter of assurance from the U.S. President, the U.S., representing the consortium, will make arrangements to offset the energy foregone due to the freeze of the DPRK's graphite-moderated reactors and related facilities, pending completion of the first LWR unit.

—Alternative energy will be provided in the form of heavy oil for heating and electricity production.

—Deliveries of heavy oil will begin within three months of the date of this Document and will reach a rate of 500,000 tons annually, in accordance with an agreed schedule of deliveries.

(3) Upon receipt of U.S. assurances for the provision of LWRs and for arrangements for interim energy alternatives, the DPRK will freeze its graphite-moderated reactors and related facilities and will eventually dismantle these reactors and related facilities.

—The freeze on the DPRK's graphite-moderated reactors and related facilities will be fully implemented within one month of the date of this Document. During this one-month period, and throughout the freeze, the International Atomic Energy Agency (IAEA) will be allowed to monitor this freeze, and the DPRK will provide full cooperation to the IAEA for this purpose.

—Dismantlement of the DPRK's graphite-moderated reactors and related facilities will be completed when the LWR project is completed.

—The U.S. and the DPRK will cooperate in finding a method to store safely the spent fuel from the 5 MW(e) experimental reactor during the construction of the LWR project, and to dispose of the fuel in a safe manner that does not involve reprocessing in the DPRK.

(4) As soon as possible after the date of this document U.S. and DPRK experts will hold two sets of experts talks.

—At one set of talks, experts will discuss issues related to alternative energy and the replacement of the graphite-moderated reactor program with the LWR project.

—At the other set of talks, experts will discuss specific arrangements for spent fuel storage and ultimate disposition.

II. The two sides will move toward full normalization of political and economic relations.

(1) Within three months of the date of this Document, both sides will reduce barriers to trade and investment, including restrictions on telecommunications services and financial transactions.

(2) Each side will open a liaison office in the other's capital following resolution of consular and other technical issues through expert-level discussions.

(3) As progress is made on issues of concern to each side, the U.S. and the DPRK will upgrade bilateral relations to the Ambassadorial level.

III. Both sides will work together for peace and security on a nuclear-free Korean peninsula.

(1) The U.S. will provide formal assurances to the DPRK, against the threat or use of nuclear weapons by the U.S.

(2) The DPRK will consistently take steps to implement the North-South Joint Declaration on the Denuclearization of the Korean Peninsula.

(3) The DPRK will engage in North-South dialogue, as this Agreed Framework will help create an atmosphere that promotes such dialogue.

IV. Both sides will work together to strengthen the international nuclear non-proliferation regime.

(1) The DPRK will remain a party to the Treaty on the Non-Proliferation of Nuclear Weapons (NPT) and will allow implementation of its safeguards agreement under the Treaty.

(2) Upon conclusion of the supply contract for the provision of the LWR project, ad hoc and routine inspections will resume under the DPRK's safeguards agreement with the IAEA with respect to the facilities not subject to the freeze. Pending conclusion of the supply contract, inspections required by the IAEA for the continuity of safeguards will continue at the facilities not subject to the freeze.

(3) When a significant portion of the LWR project is completed, but before delivery of key nuclear components, the DPRK will come into full compliance with its safeguards agreement with the IAEA (INFCIRC/403), including taking all steps that may be deemed necessary by the IAEA, following consultations with the Agency with regard to verifying the accuracy and completeness of the DPRK's initial report on all nuclear material in the DPRK.

Robert L. Gallucci
Head of Delegation of the
United States of America,
Ambassador at Large of the
United States of America

Kang Sok Ju
Head of the Delegation of the
Democratic People's Republic of Korea,
First Vice-Minister of Foreign Affairs of
the Democratic People's Republic of Korea

JOINT U.S.-DPRK PRESS STATEMENT
June 13, 1995
Kuala Lumpur

The delegations of the United States of America (U.S.) and the Democratic People's Republic of Korea (DPRK) held talks in Kuala Lumpur from May 19 to June 12, 1995, with respect to implementation of the DPRK-U.S. Agreed Framework of October 21, 1994.

Both sides reaffirmed their political commitments to implement the U.S.-DPRK Agreed Framework, and with particular regard to facilitating the light-water reactor (LWR) project as called for in the Agreed Framework, decided as follows:

I. The U.S. reaffirms that the letter of assurance from the U.S. President dated October 20, 1994, concerning the provision of the LWR project and interim energy alternatives continues in effect.

The Korean Peninsula Energy Development Organization (KEDO), under U.S. leadership, will finance and supply the LWR project in the DPRK as called for in the Agreed Framework. As specified in the Agreed Framework, the U.S. will serve as the principal point of contact with the DPRK for the LWR project. In this regard, U.S. citizens will lead delegations and teams of KEDO as required to fulfill this role.

II. The LWR project will consist of two pressurized light-water reactors with two coolant loops and a generating capacity of approximately 1,000 MW(e) each. The reactor model, selected by KEDO, will be the advanced version of the U.S.-origin design and technology currently under production.

III. The Commission for External Economic Relations, representing the DPRK Government, and KEDO will conclude a supply agreement at the earliest possible date for the provision of the LWR project on a turnkey basis. On the basis of this statement, the DPRK will meet with KEDO as soon as possible to negotiate the outstanding issues of the LWR supply agreement.

KEDO will conduct a site survey to identify the requirements for construction and operation of the LWR project. The costs of this site survey and site preparation will be included in the scope of supply for the project.

KEDO will select a prime contractor to carry out the project. A U.S. firm will serve as program coordinator to assist KEDO in supervising overall implementation of the LWR project; KEDO will select the program coordinator. A DPRK firm will enter into implementing arrangements as necessary to facilitate the LWR project.

IV. In addition to the LWR project, the two sides decided to take the following steps towards implementation of the Agreed Framework.

Experts from the two sides will meet in the DPRK as soon as possible in June to agree on a schedule and cooperative measures for phased delivery of heavy fuel oil in accordance with the Agreed Framework. KEDO will begin immediately to make arrangements for an initial delivery of heavy fuel oil, subject to conclusion of the above agreement.

The DPRK-U.S. Record of Meeting of January 20, 1995, on safe storage of spent fuel will be expeditiously implemented. In this regard, a U.S. team of experts will visit the DPRK as soon as possible in June to begin implementation.

U.S.-DPRK JOINT COMMUNIQUÉ (CALLS FOR PERMANENT PEACE ARRANGEMENTS)
October 12, 2000
Washington, D.C.

The United States and North Korea called for reducing tension on the Korean Peninsula, and for replacing the 1953 Armistice Agreement with "permanent peace arrangements" in a joint communiqué October 12.

The communiqué, which also hinted at a possible visit by the U.S. President to North Korea, came at the end of a four-day visit to Washington, D.C., by North Korean Vice Marshal Jo Myong Rok.

Jo came as a special envoy of Chairman Kim Jong Il, the ruler of the Democratic People's Republic of Korea (DPRK). He is the highest level official from Pyongyang to visit the United States, where he met with President Clinton, Secretary of State Madeleine Albright, Secretary of Defense William Cohen, and other U.S. officials and lawmakers.

"Recognizing the changed circumstances on the Korean Peninsula created by the historic inter-Korean summit, the United States and the Democratic People's Republic of Korea have decided to take steps to fundamentally improve their bilateral relations in the interests of enhancing peace and security in the Asia-Pacific region," the joint communiqué said.

Pyongyang and Washington, it added, agreed there are "a variety of available means, including Four Party talks, to reduce tension on the Korean Peninsula and formally end the Korean War by replacing the 1953 Armistice Agreement with permanent peace arrangements."

The two sides further agreed that Albright will visit the DPRK "in the near future to convey the views of U.S. President William Clinton directly to Chairman Kim Jong Il of the DPRK National Defense Commission and to prepare for a possible visit by the President of the United States."

Following is the text of the Joint Communiqué:

As the special envoy of Chairman Kim Jong Il of the DPRK National Defense Commission, the First Vice Chairman, Vice Marshal Jo Myong Rok, visited the United States of America from October 9–12, 2000.

During his visit, Special Envoy Jo Myong Rok delivered a letter from National Defense Commission Chairman Kim Jong Il, as well as his views on U.S.-DPRK relations, directly to U.S. President William Clinton. Special Envoy Jo Myong Rok and his party also met with senior officials of the U.S. Administration, including his host, Secretary of State Madeleine Albright, and Secretary of Defense William Cohen, for an extensive exchange of views on issues of common concern. They reviewed in depth the new opportunities that have opened up for improving the full range of relations between the United States of America and the Democratic People's Republic of Korea. The meetings proceeded in a serious, constructive, and businesslike atmosphere, allowing each side to gain a better understanding of the other's concerns.

Recognizing the changed circumstances on the Korean Peninsula created by the historic inter-Korean summit, the United States and the Democratic People's Republic of Korea have decided to take steps to fundamentally improve their bilateral relations in the interests of enhancing peace and security in the Asia-Pacific region. In this regard, the two sides agreed there are a variety of available means, including Four Party talks, to reduce tension on the Korean Peninsula and formally end the Korean War by replacing the 1953 Armistice Agreement with permanent peace arrangements.

Recognizing that improving ties is a natural goal in relations among states and that better relations would benefit both nations in the 21st century while helping ensure peace and security on the Korean Peninsula and in the Asia-Pacific region, the U.S. and the DPRK sides stated that they are prepared to undertake a new direction in their relations. As a crucial first step, the two sides stated that neither government would have hostile intent toward the other and confirmed the commitment of both governments to make every effort in the future to build a new relationship free from past enmity.

Building on the principles laid out in the June 11, 1993, U.S.-DPRK Joint Statement and reaffirmed in the October 21, 1994, Agreed Framework, the two sides agreed to work to remove mistrust, build mutual confidence, and maintain an atmosphere in which they can deal constructively with issues of central concern. In this regard, the two sides reaffirmed that their relations should be based on the principles of respect for each other's sovereignty and non-interference in each other's internal affairs, and noted the value of regular diplomatic contacts, bilaterally and in broader fora.

The two sides agreed to work together to develop mutually beneficial economic cooperation and exchanges. To explore the possibilities for trade and commerce that will benefit the peoples of both countries and contribute to an environment conducive to greater economic cooperation throughout Northeast Asia, the two sides discussed an exchange of visits by economic and trade experts at an early date.

The two sides agreed that resolution of the missile issue would make an essential contribution to a fundamentally improved relationship between them and to peace and security in the Asia-Pacific region. To further the efforts to build new relations, the DPRK informed the U.S. that it will not launch long-range missiles of any kind while talks on the missile issue continue.

Pledging to redouble their commitment and their efforts to fulfill their respective obligations in their entirety under the Agreed Framework, the U.S. and the DPRK strongly affirmed its importance to achieving peace and security on a nuclear weapons free Korean Peninsula. To this end, the two sides agreed on the desirability of greater transparency in carrying out their respective obligations under the Agreed Framework. In this regard, they noted the value of the access which removed U.S. concerns about the underground site at Kumchang-ri.

The two sides noted that in recent years they have begun to work cooperatively in areas of common humanitarian concern. The DPRK side expressed appreciation for significant U.S. contributions to its humanitarian needs in areas of food and medical assistance. The U.S. side expressed appreciation for DPRK cooperation in recovering the remains of U.S. servicemen still missing from the Korean War, and both sides agreed to work for rapid progress for the fullest possible accounting. The two sides will continue to meet to discuss these and other humanitarian issues.

As set forth in their Joint Statement of October 6, 2000, the two sides agreed to support and encourage international efforts against terrorism.

Special Envoy Jo Myong Rok explained to the U.S. side developments in the inter-Korean dialogue in recent months, including the results of the historic North-South summit. The U.S. side expressed its firm commitment to assist in all appropriate ways the continued progress and success of ongoing North-South dialogue and initiatives for reconciliation and greater cooperation, including increased security dialogue.

Special Envoy Jo Myong Rok expressed his appreciation to President Clinton and the American people for their warm hospitality during the visit.

It was agreed that Secretary of State Madeleine Albright will visit the DPRK in the near future to convey the views of U.S. President William Clinton directly to Chairman Kim Jong Il of the DPRK National Defense Commission and to prepare for a possible visit by the President of the United States.

Notes

Chapter One

1. Interview with U.S. official, 2001.
2. Interview with U.S. official, 2001.
3. Bruce Cumings, "Spring Thaw for Korea's Cold War," *Bulletin of the Atomic Scientists* (April 1992).
4. Michael J. Mazarr, *North Korea and the Bomb* (St. Martin's Press, 1995), p. 15.
5. Peter Hayes, *Pacific Powderkeg: American Nuclear Dilemmas in Korea* (Lexington, Mass.: Lexington Books, 1991), pp. 60–61.
6. Ibid.
7. Don Oberdorfer, *The Two Koreas: A Contemporary History* (Reading, Mass.: Addison-Wesley, 1997), p. 89.
8. Mazarr, *North Korea and the Bomb*, p. 16.
9. Alexandre Y. Mansourov, "The Origins, Evolution and Current Politics of the North Korean Nuclear Program," *Nonproliferation Review*, vol. 2, no. 3 (1995), pp. 25–26.
10. Oberdorfer, *Two Koreas*, pp. 252–53
11. Ibid., pp. 68, 72, 73.
12. The capacity of a nuclear reactor can be described either by its electrical power output, measured as kilowatts or megawatts (electrical), or by its total energy production rate, measured as kilowatts or megawatts (thermal). Since the efficiency of conversion of heat to electricity is typically about 33 percent, a 15-megawatt (thermal) (MWt) reactor would translate roughly into a 5-megawatt (electrical) (MWe) reactor. Research reactors are generally not used to generate electricity and so tend to be described in MWt, while nuclear power reactors used to generate electricity tend, naturally, to be described in MWe. The 5-MWe reactor that will feature prominently in this book is described politically; that is, its "electrical" nomenclature is part of the cover story that the reactor had principally electricity generation as its mission, whereas in fact the North Koreans never sought to link it to an electrical grid but *did* use it to produce plutonium. While it would be more accurate,

then, to describe the reactor by its thermal output (20–25 MWt), the reactor has become so widely known by its electrical output that this book will follow that convention and call it the "5-megawatt reactor."

13. Paul Leventhal and Steven Dolley, "The North Korean Nuclear Crisis," June 16, 1994, Nuclear Control Institute (www.nci.org/n/nkib1.htm).

14. *1993 CIA World Factbook* (http://es.rice.edu/projects/Poli378/CIA_Factbook/mkorea.html).

15. Association of Foreign Trading Agents of Korea (www.aftak.or.kr/aftak2001/about/econo_1.html); World Bank (www.worldbank.org/data/wdi2002/tables/table 4-1.pdf).

16. *1993 CIA World Factbook* (www.umsl.edu/services/govdocs/wofact93/wf940131/txt).

17. Oberdorfer, *Two Koreas*, p. 197.

18. Trip Report of William Taylor to North Korea, 1991.

19. Don Oberdorfer and Hajime Izumi, "The United States, Japan and the Korean Peninsula: Coordinating Policies and Objectives," Working Paper 11, prepared for the conference "Power and Prosperity" organized by the National Security Archive and the Institute for Global Conflict and Cooperation, University of California at San Diego, March 14–16, 1997, p. 5 (www.gwu.edu/~nsarchiv/japan/donizumitp.htm); Joel S. Wit, "North Korea: Leader of the Pack," *Washington Quarterly*, vol. 24, no. 1 (2001), p. 1.

20. Joel S. Wit, "Clinton and North Korea: Past, Present and Future," in David Albright and Kevin O'Neill, eds., *Solving the North Korean Nuclear Puzzle* (Washington: Institute for Science and International Security Press, 2000), p. 203.

21. Don Oberdorfer, "U.S. Steps Up Pressure on North Korea," *Washington Post*, March 18, 1993, p. A33.

22. Hayes, *Pacific Powderkeg*, p. 74.

23. George Bush and Brent Scowcroft, *A World Transformed* (Alfred A. Knopf, 1996), p. 542.

24. Ibid., pp. 544–45; President George Bush, "Address to the Nation on Reducing United States and Soviet Nuclear Weapons," September 27, 1991, Bush Presidential Library (http://bushlibrary.tamu.edu/papers/1991/91092704.html); "Bush to Cut U.S. Nuclear Arsenal," *Associated Press*, September 28, 1991, p. A1.

25. Oberdorfer, *Two Koreas*, pp. 259–60.

26. James Sterngold, "Seoul Says It Now Has No Nuclear Arms," *New York Times*, December 19, 1991, p. A3.

27. "News Conference of President George Bush," White House Briefing, *Federal News Service*, December 19, 1991.

28. "North and South Step Closer to Enforcing Denuclearization Declaration," *BBC Summary of World Broadcasts*, January 21, 1992.

29. *Soldiers Magazine*, August 1985.

30. "South Korea to Cancel 1992 'Team Spirit' Joint Military Exercise," *Yonhap News Agency* (hereafter, *Yonhap*), January 7, 1992.

31. "Briefing by National Security Advisor Brent Scowcroft," *Federal News Service*, January 8, 1992.

32. Interview with former U.S. official, 2001.

33. Interview with U.S. official, 2003.

34. Testimony by Hans Blix, Hearing before the House Committee on Foreign Affairs, 102 Cong. 2 sess. (Government Printing Office, July 22, 1992).

35. Oberdorfer, *Two Koreas*, pp. 269–70.

36. David Albright and Mark Hibbs, "Iraq's Quest for the Nuclear Grail: What Can We

Learn," *Arms Control Today*, vol. 22 (July/August 1992), pp. 3–11; Lawrence Scheinman, "Assuring the Nuclear Non-Proliferation Safeguards System," Occasional Paper (Atlantic Council, October 1992); Lawrence Scheinman, "Lessons from Post-War Iraq for the International Full-Scope Safeguards Regime," *Arms Control Today*, vol. 22 (April 1993).

37. "Joint Communiqué of the 24th U.S.-ROK Security Consultative Meeting," Washington, October 7–8, 1992; Oberdorfer, *Two Koreas*, p. 272; U.S.-Republic of South Korea 24th Annual Security Consultative Meeting, Defense Department Briefing, *Federal News Service*, October 8, 1992; Jane A. Morse, "DPRK Nuclear Weapons Capability Remains Top U.S., ROK Concern," United States Information Agency, October 10, 1992.

38. Donald Gregg, "Threats and Opportunities on the Korean Peninsula," Korean Information Center, *Federal News Service*, July 20, 1994; Oberdorfer, *Two Koreas*, pp. 272–73.

39. "South Korean Security Service Gives More Details of Alleged DPRK Spy Ring," *Yonhap*, October 8, 1992.

40. Oberdorfer, *Two Koreas*, p. 274.

41. Leon V. Sigal, *Disarming Strangers: Nuclear Diplomacy with North Korea* (Princeton University Press, 1998), pp. 46–47.

42. Gillen IAEA Chronology, 1986, p. 3 (hereafter, Gillen Chronology).

43. Interview with former U.S. official, 2002.

44. *North Korea News*, no. 669, February 8, 1993, pp. 5–6.

45. Interview with former U.S. official, 2002.

46. Gillen Chronology, p. 8.

47. David Albright and Kevin O'Neill, eds., *Solving the North Korean Nuclear Puzzle* (Washington: Institute for Science and International Security Press, 2000), p. 268; interview with former IAEA official, 2001.

48. "Pyongyang Sends Mixed Signal on Team Spirit Exercise," *FBIS Trends*, January 27, 1994.

49. Ibid.

50. Interview with former IAEA official, 2000.

51. Albright and O'Neill, *Solving the North Korean Nuclear Puzzle*, pp. 269–70.

52. Oberdorfer, *Two Koreas*, p. 175.

53. "New Ministers View Unification Policies," *Wolgan Chosun*, April 1993, pp. 158–65.

54. *Wall Street Journal*, August 19, 1993; "Major Officials Profiled," *Yonhap*, February 26, 1993.

55. Interview with Han Wan Sang, 2000.

56. "Kim Young Sam Calls for Building a New Korea," *BBC Summary of World Broadcasts*, February 26, 1993, from KBS Television Seoul in Korean, 0112 gmt, February 25, 1993.

57. Interview with former ROK official, 2000.

58. "DPRK Red Cross Demands ROK Release Yi In Mo," *Pyongyang Korean Central News Agency*, February 17, 1993.

59. Interview with former ROK (South Korean) official, 2000.

60. "Overall Review of DPRK Policy Planned," *Joongang Ilbo*, March 1, 1993; "ROK to Clarify Policy on DPRK Nuclear Program," *Yonhap*, March 8, 1993; "ROK to Unconditionally Return Yi In Mo to DPRK," *Yonhap*, March 10, 1993; "ROK Seeks Contact Meeting on Yi," *Yonhap*, March 11, 1993.

61. "Unification Minister Discusses DPRK Policy Review," Seoul KBS Television Network, February 28, 1994.

62. Interview with Gong Ro Myung, 2000.

63. "Kim Chong Il Orders Army Mobilization," Korean Central Broadcast Network, March 8, 1993; "North Korea Proclaims Semi-War State as Countermeasure Against Team Spirit," *North Korea News*, no. 674, March 15, 1993, p. 2; "Yonhap Notes Previous DPRK

Mobilizations," *Yonhap*, March 8, 1993; "Kim Chong Il Declares 'Semi-State of War,'" *BBC Summary of World Broadcasts*, March 9, 1993.

64. "North Korea Escalates Warlike Mood among Populace," *North Korea News*, no. 675, March 22, 1993, pp. 1–2.

65. Presentation by Gong Ro Myung, "Crisis on the Peninsula," public forum sponsored by Asahi Shimbun, March 2003.

Chapter Two

1. "Statement Notes Withdrawal," Korean Central Broadcast System, March 12, 1993.

2. Douglas Jehl, "U.S. Seeking UN Pressure to Compel North Korea to Honor Treaty," *New York Times*, March 13, 1993, p. 3; T. R. Reid, "Overtures Made to North Korea," *Washington Post*, March 17, 1993, p. A25.

3. "Government Meets in Emergency Session," *Joongang Ilbo*, March 12, 1993, p. 1; "Armed Forces Go on Nationwide Alert," March 13, 1993.

4. "Watanabe Criticizes DPRK NPT Withdrawal," *Kyodo News*, March 12, 1993.

5. "Spokesman on DPRK Withdrawal from Nuclear Pact," *Xinhua*, March 12, 1993.

6. Interview with former Chinese official, 2000.

7. "IAEA Reacts to DPRK Withdrawal from NPT," *Agence France-Presse*, March 12, 1993; "IAEA Holds Emergency Session," *Yonhap*, March 12, 1993; "IAEA to Discuss DPRK's Withdrawal from NPT," *Agence France-Presse*, March 15, 1993.

8. "North Korea Trifles with Doomsday," *New York Times*, March 16, 1993, p. 20.

9. David E. Sanger, "The Nonproliferation Treaty Bares Its Toothlessness," *New York Times*, March 14, 1993, sec. 4, p. 18.

10. "President on DPRK's NPT Withdrawal, Ties with Japan," *Nihon Keizai Shimbun*, April 30, 1993; "Further Comment on NPT Withdrawal," *Seoul Sinmun*, March 14, 1993, p. 4.

11. Interview with former ROK official, 2001

12. Interview with former ROK official, 2001; *Program and Markup of H. Con. Res. 189 and H. Con Res. 240,* Hearings before the Subcommittee on Asian and Pacific Affairs of the House Committee on International Relations, 102 Cong. 1 sess. (Government Printing Office, November 21, 1991).

13. Leslie H. Gelb, "The Next Crisis," *New York Times*, March 21, 1993, p. 17.

14. "ROK May Ask U.S. Troops to Remain," *Yonhap*, March 16, 1993.

15. "Pyongyang Seeks Talks with U.S. to Deflect UNSC Scrutiny," *FBIS Trends*, March 31, 1993.

16. "U.S. Requests Meeting with DPRK Counselor," *Joongang Ilbo*, March 17, 1993, p. 1; "U.S., DPRK Said to Hold Beijing Talks," Seoul KBS-1 Television Network, March 17, 1993; Don Oberdorfer, "U.S. Steps Up Pressure on North Korea," *Washington Post*, March 18, 1993, p. A33; Don Oberdorfer and R. Jeffrey Smith, "U.S., Asian Allies Discuss N. Korea Arms Inspections," *Washington Post*, March 24, 1993, p. A30.

17. "Yonhap Details Return," *Yonhap*, March 19, 1993; "Former North Korean Agent Yi In Mo Returns to Pyongyang," *North Korea News*, no. 676, March 29, 1993, p. 5.

18. Interview with former ROK official, 2001.

19. "Secretary Christopher and Spanish Foreign Minister Solana Remarks Prior to their Meeting," *News Transcripts Inc.*, March 15, 1993.

20. "ROK Seeks PRC Influence," Seoul KBS-1 Television Network, March 15, 1993.

21. "IAEA Resolution on Withdrawal," *Yonhap*, March 19, 1993.

22. Oberdorfer and Smith, "U.S., Asian Allies Discuss N. Korea Arms Inspections."

23. "Record of the Eight Hundred and Ninth Meeting," IAEA Headquarters, Vienna, GOV/OR 809, April 14, 1993.

24. R. Jeffrey Smith, "N. Korea Censure Seen as Turning Point in Arms Control," *Washington Post*, April 7, 1993, p. A23.

25. Interview with former U.S. official, 2001.

26. "Japan to Support UN Intervention," *Seoul Sinmun*, March 17, 1993.

27. Interview with former ROK official, 2001.

28. *Yonhap*, March 27, 1993.

29. "Pyongyang Takes Tough NPT Line, Sees U.S. Settlement Role," *FBIS Trends*, March 24, 1993.

30. "SDF Head Opposes Foreign Pressure on DPRK," *Kyodo News*, March 18, 1993.

31. Interview with Han Sung Chu by KBS, March 13, 1993.

32. Interview with former ROK official, 2001.

33. Interview with Chosen Soren official, 2001.

34. Interviews with former ROK officials, 2001.

35. "North Korea: Kim Chong Il's New Military Post," *FBIS Trends*, April 14, 1993.

36. "North Korea: Kim Birthday Events Signal Upcoming Succession," *FBIS Trends*, April 21, 1993.

37. Interview with former U.S. official, 2001.

38. Ibid.

39. "Pyongyang Seeks to Drive a Wedge between IAEA, Washington," *FBIS Trends*, February 10, 1993.

40. "Preparations for War in North Korea," Testimonies of North Korean Defectors, National Intelligence Service website (www.nis.go.kr/eng/north/defector_index.html [October 16, 2000]).

41. "Statement Notes Withdrawal."

42. Testimony of James Woolsey, Hearing before the Senate Committee on Governmental Affairs, 103 Cong. 1 sess. (GPO, February 24, 1993).

43. "NSP Head Opposes Military Sanctions," *Yonhap*, March 17, 1993.

44. Interview with former Japanese official, 2000.

45. Interview with former U.S. official, 2001.

46. "Pyongyang Berates IAEA, UN over Possible Scrutiny," *FBIS Trends*, April 7, 1993.

47. Interview with former U.S. official, 2001.

48. Ibid.

49. Interview with former ROK official, 2001.

50. "Russian Media Label North Korea's NPT Withdrawal an Unacceptably Adventurous Act," *North Korea News*, no. 680, April 26, 1993, p. 4.

51. Interview with former ROK official, 2000.

52. "North Korea: Sustained Interest in Talks with U.S.," *FBIS Trends*, April 21, 1993.

53. Interviews with American attending meeting and former U.S. official, 2001.

54. "Pyongyang Berates IAEA, UN over Possible Scrutiny."

55. Ibid.

56. Gillen Chronology.

57. Hans Blix, Statement to IAEA Board of Governors, June 11, 1993.

58. Gillen Chronology.

59. Gillen Chronology, pp. 16–17.

60. Gillen Chronology.

61. Gillen Chronology, pp. 17–20.

62. Gillen Chronology, p. 19–20.

63. "Blix BOG Statement," June 11, 1993; Gillen Chronology.

64. "U.S.-DPRK Talks to Follow UN Act," *Yonhap*, April 29, 1993; "Sources: UNSC Action on DPRK Said Delayed," *Yonhap*, May 7, 1993; R. Jeffrey Smith, "UN Members Agree to Urge N. Korean Adherence to Treaty," *Washington Post*, May 9, 1993, p. A28; Frank J. Prial, "UN Weighs Plea to North Korea," *New York Times*, May 9, 1993, p. 12.

65. Interview with former ROK official, 2001.

66. "NSP Head Opposes Military Sanctions," *Yonhap*, March 17, 1993.

67. "Pyongyang Affirms Continued Interest in Dialogue with Seoul," *FBIS Trends*, April 14, 1993.

68. Peter Hayes Report on trip to Pyongyang, May 8–11, 1993.

69. Interviews with former ROK officials, 2000.

70. "South Koreans Would Support Sanctions against North," Opinion Research Memorandum, United States Information Agency, June 7, 1993.

71. Interview with former ROK official, 2001.

72. "DPRK Business Said Ready for Reversal," *Chosun Ilbo*, May 25, 1993; "Inter-Korean Trade Continues, *Yonhap*, March 20, 1993; "Company Plans to Build Slate Plant in DPRK," *Chosun Ilbo*, April 21, 1993.

73. "President Holds Security Meeting on Issue," *Yonhap*, May 3, 1993.

74. Interview with former U.S. official, 2002.

75. Douglas Jehl, "U.S.-Korean Talks Sought on A-Pact," *New York Times*, May 18, 1993, p. A8.

76. "DPRK To Raise Six Items with U.S.," *Yonhap*, May 28, 1993.

77. "Zimbabwean President Visits Pyongyang," *North Korea News*, May 24, 1993, p. 6.

78. Interview with former U.S. official, 2001.

79. Peter Hayes Trip Report, May 8–11, 1993.

80. Testimony by Robert L. Gallucci, Hearing before the Subcommittee on East Asian and Pacific Affairs of the Senate Committee on Foreign Relations, 103 Cong. 1 sess. (GPO, May 26, 1993).

81. Interviews with former U.S. officials, 2001.

82. Nayan Chanda, "Great Leader's Gambit: Pyongyang Set for Nuclear Talks with the United States," *Far Eastern Economic Review*, June 3, 1993, p. 12–13.

Chapter Three

1. Interview with member of U.S. delegation, 2002.

2. Conversation with North Korean official, 1999.

3. C. Turner Joy, *How Communists Negotiate* (Macmillan, 1955).

4. Interview with member of U.S. delegation in New York, 2002.

5. Interviews with members of U.S. delegation, 2001.

6. Interview with member of U.S. delegation, 2001.

7. Interview with former U.S. official, 2001.

8. Interview with member of U.S. delegation, 2001.

9. Ibid.

10. Interview with former ROK official, 2001

11. "NK Energy Tech Tied to N-Issue: U.S.," *Korea Herald*, June 10, 1993.

12. "U.S., North Korea Hold Nuclear Talks," *Washington Post*, June 3, 1993, p. A26.

13. Interviews with U.S. delegation members, 2001.

14. Ibid.

15. "Sources: Foreigners Ordered to Leave," *Kyodo News*, June 3, 1993.

16. "DPRK Envoy: Sanctions 'Declaration of War,'" Seoul KBS-1 Radio Network, June 9, 1993; *North Korea News*, no. 687, June 14, 1993, p. 4.

17. Interviews with U.S. delegation members, 2001.

18. "DPRK Chief: Further Talks with U.S. Planned," Seoul KBS-1 Radio Network, June 4, 1993; "Discuss Further Things," *Yonhap*, June 5, 1993.

19. Interviews with U.S. delegation members, 2001.

20. "Successful Talks U.S. Responsibility," *Yonhap*, June 8, 1993.

21. "Joint Statement of the Democratic People's Republic of Korea and the United States of America," June 11, 1993, Arms Control Associate Fact Sheet.

22. Interview with U.S. delegation member.

23. Interviews with U.S. delegation members, 2001.

24. Ibid.

25. Interview with U.S. delegation member, 2002.

26. Interview with former U.S. official, 2001.

27. R. Jeffrey Smith, "N. Korea Won't Quit Nuclear Ban Treaty," *Washington Post*, June 12, 1993, p. A1.

28. "To Assure a Nuclear-Free Korea," *New York Times*, June 12, 1993, p. 20; Lally Weymouth, "Bearing Down on North Korea," *Washington Post*, June 18, 1993, p. A25.

29. John J. Fialka, "North Korea, after Reversing Stand on Treaty, to Hold Talks with U.S.," *Wall Street Journal*, June 14, 1993, p. A9.

30. "China Welcomes Progress in DPRK-U.S. Talks," *Xinhua*, June 12, 1993.

31. "Statement by Hans Blix to IAEA Board of Governors," June 11, 1993, p. 5; Gillen Chronology, p. 22.

32. "Interview on Positive DPRK Move," *Le Monde*, June 13–14, 1993.

33. "Seoul Proposes Resumption of Dialogue with DPRK," *Yonhap*, May 20, 1993.

34. "North Hints at Possibility of Holding Inter-Korean Summit," *FBIS Trends*, May 26, 1993.

35. Interview with former ROK official, 2001.

36. "North Hints at Possibility of Holding Inter-Korean Summit."

37. "Opposition Gives Guarded Welcome," *Korea Times*, May 27, 1993; "Glimmer of Hope in Proposal," Editorial, *Korea Times*, May 27, 1993, p. 6; "Daily Views Hidden Purpose of Proposal," *Chosun Ilbo*, May 27, 1993.

38. Interview with former ROK official, 2001.

39. Ibid.

40. "Prime Minister Proposes North Contact, June 5," *Yonhap*, May 29, 1993; "Premier Proposes 8 June Panmunjom Meeting," Pyongyang Korean Central Broadcasting System, June 4, 1993; "Hwang In Song Sends Message," Seoul KBS-1 Radio Network, June 7, 1993; "DPRK against Proposal," Seoul KBS-1 Radio Network, June 8, 1993.

41. Interview with former ROK official, 2002.

42. "News Conference in Civilian Style," *Yonhap*, June 3, 1993; "President Kim Marks First 100 Days in Office," Seoul KBS-1 Television Network, June 3, 1993.

43. "Commentary Criticizes ROK President," Pyongyang Korean Central Broadcasting System, June 5, 1993.

44. "Kang Song San Proposes 15 June Contact with South," Pyongyang Central Broadcasting System, June 11, 1993; "Premier Assesses DPRK Response," *Yonhap*, June 14, 1993; "North Suspends June 15 Contact with South," Seoul KBS-1 Radio Network, June 14, 1993.

45. "Seoul Accepts North Proposal for 24 June Contact," *Joongang Ilbo*, June 22, 1993, p. 2.

46. "North Postpones Response to South proposal," Seoul KBS-1 Radio, June 23, 1993; "Premier Issues Statement on North-South Talks," Pyongyang Korean Central Broadcasting System, June 25, 1993.

47. "Editorials Assess U.S.-DPRK Talks," SK1306232893, FBIS-EAS-93-112, June 14, 1993.

48. Interview with former ROK official, 2001.

49. Interview with member of U.S. delegation, 2001.

50. Interview with former ROK official, 2001.

51. Interview with former U.S. official, 2001.

52. Interview with former ROK official, 2001.

53. BBC Broadcast, June 24, 1993.

54. "Daily Sees Change in Kim's Stance toward North," *Korea Times*, June 29, 1993, p. 3.

55. "Kim Yong Sam: DPRK Manipulating Talks," *Yonhap*, July 2, 1993; David E. Sanger, "Seoul's Leader Says North Is Manipulating U.S. on Nuclear Issue," *New York Times*, July 2, 1993, p. 3.

56. Teresa Watanabe, "S. Korea, U.S. to Fete Good Bilateral Relations," *Washington Post*, July 10, 1993, p. A15.

57. Frank J. Murray, "Clinton Warns North Korea Not to Test Him," *Washington Times*, July 10, 1993, p. A1, and "Clinton Warns 'Renegade' N. Korea," *Washington Times*, July 11, 1993, p. 1; David E. Sanger, "Clinton in Seoul Tells North Korea to Drop Arms Plan," *New York Times*, July 11, 1993, sec. 1, p. 1.

58. Gwen Ifil, "In Korea, Chilling Reminder of Cold War," *New York Times*, July 18, 1993, p. 1.

59. Interview with former U.S. official, 2002.

60. Interview with former ROK official, 2001.

61. Interview with former U.S. official, 2001.

62. Warren Strobel, "North Korea Aims to Please U.S., Cancels Rallies," *Washington Times*, June 23, 1993; "DPRK-U.S.: Pyongyang Lowers Rhetoric on War Day Observance," *FBIS Trends*, June 30, 1993.

63. "DPRK Returning U.S. Remains Positive," *Yonhap*, July 9, 1993; "Clinton's Warning Irks North Korea," *New York Times*, July 13, 1993, p. A6.

64. "DPRK-U.S.: Pyongyang Lowers Rhetoric on War Day Observance."

65. "DPRK-U.S.: Pyongyang Mutes Criticism of President's Remarks," *FBIS Trends*, July 14, 1993.

66. Interviews with U.S. delegation members, 2001.

67. Interview with U.S. delegation member, 2001.

68. Interviews with U.S. delegation members, 2001.

69. Interview with U.S. delegation member 2001.

70. "Statement by Robert L. Gallucci, Assistant Secretary of State for Political-Military Affairs," U.S. Department of State, Office of Public Affairs, U.S. Mission, Geneva, July 19, 1993; Richard W. Stevenson, "U.S.–North Korea Meeting Yields Some Gains on Arms," *New York Times*, July 20, 1993, p. A2.

71. "Press Conference by Secretary of State Warren Christopher," July 21, 1993.

72. Interview with Danny Russel, 2002.

73. O Yong Hwan, "DPRK Not to Meet Goals of 3rd 7-Year Plan," *Joongang Ilbo*, August 2, 1993, p. 11; Yi Tae Hui, "North Korea's Request for Technology of Light-Water Reactors Reflects Its Power Shortage Situation," *Hanguk Ilbo*, August 9, 1993, p. 8.

74. Interview with James Laney, 2001; Mark E. Manyin, "North Korea-Japan Relations: The Normalization Talks and the Compensation/Reparations Issue," *CRS Report for Congress*, Congressional Research Service, pp. 1, 5.

75. Interview with U.S. government official, 2001.

Chapter Four

1. "Pyongyang Uses Armistice Anniversary to Boost Kim Chong Il," *FBIS Trends*, August 11, 1993.
2. Ibid.
3. Interview with former IAEA official, 2001.
4. Gillen Chronology, p. 23.
5. Gillen Chronology, p. 24.
6. David E. Sanger, "U.S. Warns North Koreans of UN Action on Nuclear Inspections," *New York Times*, October 15, 1993, p. A9.
7. "U.S. Awaits North Korean Actions after Progress in Nuclear Talks," *Arms Control Today*, September 1993, p. 21.
8. Gillen Chronology.
9. Ibid.
10. Ibid.
11. Ibid.
12. Ibid.
13. "Pyongyang Moves to Meet U.S. Conditions for Bilateral Talks," *FBIS Trends*, October 6, 1993; "Statement of the Minister of Atomic Energy of the Democratic People's Republic of Korea," October 11, 1993; James Sterngold, "North Korea Assails Atomic Unit, Asks U.S. Talks," *New York Times*, October 13, 1993, p. A14.
14. "Considers N.-S., U.S. Talks," *Yonhap*, July 9, 1993.
15. "Hints at Accepting Exchange of Special Envoys," Seoul KBS-1 Radio Network, August 15, 1993.
16. "Government Plans to Propose 8 September N.-S. Talks," Seoul KBS-1 Radio Network, September 2, 1993; "Picks 7 September Vice Minister Talks," *Yonhap*, September 2, 1993.
17. Interview with former ROK official, 2000.
18. "North-South Working Contact Held October 5," Seoul KBS-1 Radio Network, October 5, 1993; "Agree to Meet Again October 15," Seoul KBS-1 Radio Network, October 5, 1993; "Seoul Proposes North Send First Envoy," *Yonhap*, October 5, 1993; "Meeting Described as Tense," *Yonhap*, October 5, 1993; "Fail to Reach Concrete Agreement," *Yonhap*, October 5, 1993; "Inter-Korean Meeting on Special Envoys Makes Little Progress," *North Korea News*, no. 704, October 11, 1993, pp. 1–2.
19. "North-South Delegates Hold Contact October 5," Korean Central Broadcasting Network, October 5, 1993.
20. "North Korea Backs Out of Inter-Korean Talks for Envoy Exchange," *North Korea News*, no. 709, November 15, 1993.
21. "North-South Contact Cancelled after Interview," Korean Central Broadcasting Network, November 3, 1993.
22. Lally Weymouth, "Peninsula of Fear: Will North Korea Start an Asian Arms Race?" *Washington Post*, October 24, 1993, p. C1.
23. "Talks Conditional on S.-N. Talks," Seoul KBS-1 Radio Network, August 30, 1993; "Further on Conditions," *Yonhap*, August 30, 1993; "U.S. Conditions for North Talks Not Fulfilled," September 9, 1993; "Robert Gallucci Visits to Discuss Conditions," *Yonhap*, September 9, 1993.
24. "DPRK-U.S.: Pyongyang Mutes Impact of U.S. Official's Remarks," *FBIS Trends*, August 31, 1993.

25. "Newspapers Report on U.S. Letter to Pyongyang," FBIS-EAS-93-180, September 20, 1993.

26. Gillen Chronology; "Foreign Ministry Spokesman On DPRK-U.S. Talks," *Pyongyang KCNA*, September 22, 1994.

27. *North Korea News*, no. 673, March 8, 1993, p. 3.

28. Interview with member of Ackerman delegation, 2001.

29. Interview with former congressional staff member, 2001.

30. Interview with member of Ackerman delegation, 2001.

31. Michael Breen, "N. Korea Visit Is Useful, Ackerman Talks with Kim Il Sung," *Washington Times*, October 13, 1993, p. A11.

32. Interview with member of Ackerman delegation, 2001.

33. Ibid.

34. "North Korea: Kim Il Sung's Health," *FBIS Trends*, May 12, 1993.

35. "Rumors of Kim Il Sung Illness Spark Speculation," *Kyodo News*, February 10, 1993.

36. "Kim Il Sung's Health Care Methods Studied," *Chosun Ilbo*, January 1993.

37. Interview with member of Ackerman delegation, 2001.

38. Ibid.

39. Ibid.

40. Breen, "N. Korea Visit Is Useful."

41. James Sterngold, "North Korea Assails Atomic Unit, Asks U.S. Talks," *New York Times*, October 13, 1993, p. A14.

42. Interview with member of Ackerman delegation, 2001.

43. "Seoul Reconsiders Policy on Nuclear Issue," *Yonhap*, October 16, 1993; "N.-S. Contacts Positively Appraised," Seoul KBS-1 Radio Network, October 16, 1993.

44. Sanger, "U.S. Warns North Koreans."

45. Interview with former U.S. official, 2001.

46. "Mounting Concern that the United States was Led by North Korea's Pace," *Chosun Ilbo*, October 22, 1993, p. 6.

47. Sanger, "U.S. Warns North Koreans"; Daily Press Briefing, U.S. Department of State, October 15, 1993.

48. David E. Sanger, "U.S. Delay Urged on Korea Sanctions," *New York Times*, November 4, 1993, p. 9.

49. "Japanese Daily Cites Les Aspin," *Yonhap*, October 30, 1993, p. A1.

50. Television interview with Timothy Russert and Tom Brokaw, *Meet the Press*, November 7, 1993.

51. *North Korea News*, December 13, 1993, p. 7.

52. Interview with former U.S. official, 2001.

53. "Japanese Fear North Korea Developing Nuclear Weapons: Would Support Sanctions," United States Information Agency Opinion Research Memo, November 4, 1993.

54. Weymouth, "Peninsula of Fear."

55. "Joint News Conference Held 7 November," Seoul KBS-1 Television Network, November 6, 1993.

56. "Foreign Minister Han to Visit PRC 28 October," *Korea Times*, October 26, 1993, p. 2.

57. Barton Gellman, "Trepidation at Root of U.S. Korea Policy: Conventional War Seen as Catastrophic for South," *Washington Post*, December 12, 1993, p. 1.

58. Ibid.

59. Interview with General Gary Luck, 2001.

60. Michael Gordon, "Pentagon Begins Effort to Combat More Lethal Arms in Third World," *New York Times*, December 7, 1993, p. 15.

61. Interview with former U.S. official, 2001.

62. Jack Anderson and Michael Binstein, "North Korea: Loose Nuclear Cannon," *Washington Post*, March 29, 1992, p. C7; *North Korea News*, no. 702, September 27, 1993, p. 5.

63. Testimony of Secretary of Defense William Perry, Joint Hearing before the Senate Committee on Foreign Relations, 104 Cong. 1 sess. (Government Printing Office, January 1995), p. 15.

64. Tony Capaccio, "New Report: Air Strikes against Iraq's Key Nuke Site Were Wanting," *Defense Week*, January 10, 1994, pp. 1–3.

65. Ibid.

66. Ibid; Gordon, "Pentagon Begins Effort."

67. Interviews with former U.S. and ROK officials, 2001.

68. Michael Gordon and David Sanger, "North Korea's Huge Military Spurs New Strategy in South," *New York Times*, February 6, 1994, sec. 1, p. 1.

69. Interview with General Gary Luck, 2001; USFK Unclassified Briefing Papers.

70. "Legislator Sees Attack from North as Unlikely," *Seoul Sisa Journal*, December 30, 1993, pp. 30–32.

71. Anthony Lake, *Six Nightmares: Real Threats in a Dangerous World and How America Can Meet Them* (Little, Brown, 2000), p. 129.

72. Ibid.

73. "Blending Force with Diplomacy," *Time*, October 31, 1993, pp. 35–36.

74. Lake, *Six Nightmares*, pp. 128–51; Thomas Friedman, "U.S. Vision of Foreign Policy Reversed," *New York Times*, September 22, 1993, p. A13.

75. Warren Strobel, "Foreign Policy Mars Clinton's First Year: Clinton Fails to Define Foreign Policy in First Year," *Washington Times*, November 9, 1993, p. A1.

76. R. W. Apple, "Lights! Camera! Clinton at Work: Is Motion the Same Thing as Action?" *New York Times*, October 31, 1993, sec. 4, p. 1.

77. Dave McCurdy, "North Korea and the Bomb," *New York Times*, November 8, 1993, p. A19.

78. Interview with former U.S. official, 2001.

79. Arnold Kanter and Stephen Hadley, "North Korea: The Clock Is Ticking," Forum for International Policy.

80. Interview with former U.S. navy officer, 2001.

81. Interview with former ROK official, 2001.

82. Weymouth, "Peninsula of Fear."

83. Interview with former ROK official, 2001.

84. Kim Dae Jung, "Avenues to Korean Stability," *Washington Times*, October 13, 1993, p. A17.

85. Interview with former U.S. official, 2001.

86. "NSP Director Urges Package Deal on DPRK Issue," *Yonhap*, November 12, 1993.

87. "Too Early for Package Deal," *Yonhap*, November 13, 1993; "NSP Director Said Misquoted," *Yonhap*, November 13, 1993; "Commentaries on U.S. Reaction," *Foreign Broadcast Information Service*, November 1993, p. 15; "Nuclear Ambassador Appointed," *Yonhap*, November 16, 1993.

88. R. Jeffrey Smith, "U.S. Weighs North Korean Incentives," *Washington Post*, November 16, 1993, p. A31.

89. Interview with former ROK official, 2001.

90. "Ministry Denies U.S. Policy Change on DPRK," *Yonhap*, November 18, 1993; "Senior Official on Study of Team Spirit Issue," *Yonhap*, November 18, 1993; "Nuclear Ambassador Denies U.S. Package Deal," Seoul KBS-1 Radio Network, November 19, 1993.

91. Interview with former ROK official, 2000.

92. Ibid.

93. Interview with former U.S. officials, 2001.

94. Interview with former U.S. official, 2001.

95. Douglas Jehl, "U.S. May Dilute Earlier Threats to North Korea," *New York Times*, November 23, 1993, p. 6.

96. Interview with former U.S. official, 2001.

97. Ibid.

98. Jehl, "U.S. May Dilute Earlier Threats."

99. Interview with U.S. official, 2001.

100. Interview with former ROK official, 2001.

101. Ibid.

102. Ibid.; "Blue House General Secretary Profiled," *Hanguk Ilbo*, January 15, 1994, p. 2.

103. Interview with former ROK official, 2001.

104. Ibid.

105. Ibid.

106. Interview with former U.S. official, 2001.

107. Interview with U.S. official, 2001.

108. Alexander Sullivan, "Clinton Urges North Korea Not to Block Nuclear Inspections," United States Information Agency, November 23, 1993; "23 November Joint News Conference," Seoul KBS-1 Television Network, November 23, 1993.

109. Sullivan, "Clinton Urges North Korea Not to Block."

110. "ROK-U.S. Relations Change without Summit," *Kyonghyang Sinmun*, November 27, 1993, p. 4.

111. "80% Term Trip Productive," *Yonhap*, November 26, 1993.

112. "Probe Yi Tong Pok's Role in N.-S. Talks Ordered," *Yonhap,* November 22, 1993; "Yi Tong Pok Resigns from NSP," *Yonhap*, November 23, 1993.

113. "Han Wan Sang's Firing Analyzed," *Korea Herald*, December 24, 1993, pp. 2–4.

114. "Daily Assesses Changes with New Unification Minister," *Korea Herald*, January 14, 1994, p. 2.

115. Interview with former ROK official, 2001.

116. R. Jeffrey Smith, "S. Korean Holds Line on North: President Opposes Concessions until Direct Talks Are Reopened," *Washington Post*, November 23, 1993, p. A32.

117. Charles Krauthammer, "Talk Loudly, Carry a Big Stick," *Washington Post*, November 26, 1993, p. A31.

118. Interview with former U.S. official, 2001.

119. Ibid.

120. Ibid.

121. "DPRK Seeks Face-Saving Way to Meet U.S. Conditions for Talks," *FBIS Trends*, November 17, 1993.

122. "DPRK Return of UN Soldier Remains Reported," *Yonhap*, December 21, 1994; "DPRK Renews Call for Package Solution on Nuclear Issue," *FBIS Trends*, December 1, 1993.

123. "North Korea: Pyongyang Mutes Criticism of CIA Director," *FBIS Trends*, December 8, 1993.

124. Interview with former U.S. officials, 2001.

125. "Kim Young Sam, Clinton to Hold Summit 7 December 1993," Seoul KBS-1 Television Network, December 7, 1993.

126. "Consultations with ROK on North Korean Nuclear Issue," Draft Cable, December 7, 1993; Talking Points, December 7, 1993; "Meeting with Ambassador Han," December 7,

1993; "Kim Young Sam, Clinton Talk on Phone," Seoul KBS-1 Radio Network, December 7, 1993.

127. "Pyongyang Resists U.S. Pressure for Full IAEA Nuclear Inspections," *North Korea News*, no. 715, 1993, p. 5; Thomas W. Lippman, "North Korea Could Prove Sanction-Proof," *Washington Post*, December 25, 1993, p. A30.

Chapter Five

1. Lynn Davis, Undersecretary of State for International Affairs, "U.S.-North Korea Discussions on Nuclear Issues," State Department News Conference, Washington, January 5, 1994; "Clinton's Address before a Joint Session of Congress on the State of the Union," C-SPAN, January 25, 1994, p. 7.

2. "Kim Il Sung Stresses Talks with U.S. on Nuclear Issue," *FBIS Trends*, January 5, 1994.

3. Ibid.; "Radio Denounces Anti-Democratic South Regime," Pyongyang Korean Central Broadcasting Network, February 4, 1994.

4. "Pyongyang Concedes Economic Failure, Adjusts Priorities," *FBIS Trends*, December 9, 1993.

5. "Kim Young Sam Issues New Year's Day Message," *Yonhap*, December 31, 1993.

6. "Question, Answer Session," Seoul KBS-1 Television Network, January 6, 1993.

7. "South Korean Views on the Nuclear Issue," Briefing Paper, United States Information Agency, February 10, 1994.

8. Interview with ROK official, 2001.

9. Ibid.

10. Interview with former U.S. official, 2001.

11. Gillen Chronology.

12. Ibid.

13. Ibid.

14. Ibid.

15. "North Korea Continues to Reject Nuke Inspections," *Washington Times*, January 22, 1994, p. A1.

16. Alexander Simon, "The Patriot Missile: Performance in the Gulf War Reviewed," Center for Defense Information, Washington, July 15, 1996.

17. "Meeting with Laney, Luck, and Gallucci," Georgetown University School of Foreign Service, Washington, Spring 2000.

18. Interview with former U.S. official, 2001.

19. Michael Gordon, "U.S. Said to Plan Patriot Missiles for South Korea," *New York Times*, January 26, 1994, p. A1.

20. For example, "Government Reacts to Patriot Deployment Plan," *Yonhap*, January 27, 1994.

21. Interview with former ROK official, 2001.

22. "U.S. Reportedly to Sell Defective F-16 System," *Dong-A Ilbo*, January 20, 1994, p. 1; "Editorial Notes, Misgivings over Perry Document," *Korea Times*, February 5, 1994, p. 6.

23. "Rumors of Aircraft Carriers Deployment Denied," Seoul KBS-1 Radio Network, January 29, 1994; "Daily Reports ROK, U.S. Prepare for Team Spirit," *Joongang Ilbo*, February 7, 1994, p. 1; Michael Gordon and David Sanger, "North Korea's Huge Military," *New York Times*, February 6, 1994, sec. 1, p. 1; R. Jeffrey Smith, "North Korea Faces Inspection Deadline," *Washington Post*, February 7, 1994, p. A1; "South Korea Warns North of Plan to Hold War Game," *Washington Post*, February 1, 1994, p. A7.

24. "Senate Calls for Isolation of North Korea," *Reuters*, February 2, 1994; Carroll Doherty, "State Department: Clinton Lifts Vietnam Trade Ban After Senate Provides Cover," *Congressional Quarterly Weekly Report*, February 5, 1994, p. 256.

25. "Senate Calls for Isolation."

26. Interview with General Gary Luck, 2001.

27. "Government Reacts," *Hankyoreh Sinmun*, January 27, 1994.

28. "Han Holds Pre-Departure Briefing," *Yonhap*, February 8, 1994.

29. Interview with former ROK official, 2001.

30. Ibid.

31. "Han Holds News Conference 12 February," *Yonhap*, February 12, 1994.

32. "DPRK Accuses U.S. of Bad Faith, Threatens NPT Withdrawal," *FBIS Trends*, February 2, 1994.

33. Ibid.

34. Ibid.

35. "Pyongyang Mixes Harsh Rhetoric with Signs of Moderation," *FBIS Trends*, February 9, 1994.

36."Status of DPRK Missile Development Examined," *Chosun Ilbo*, March 20, 1994, p. 4; Barbara Starr, "N. Korea Casts a Longer Shadow with TD-2," *Jane's Defence Weekly*, March 12, 1994, p. 1.

37. "Current Operations on Bosnia, North Korea, Haiti and the Carribean," Hearing before the Senate Committee on Armed Services, 104 Cong. 1 sess. (Government Printing Office, May 10, 1995), p. 26.

38. "NUB Delivers Report on Trends in North Korea," *Dong-A Ilbo*, January 11, 1994, p. 5; "Defense Ministry Plans Future Oriented Policy," *Yonhap*, January 20, 1994.

39. Interview with former U.S. official, 2001.

40. Ibid.

41. Ibid.

42. "DPRK Envoy: No Immediate Accord on Inspectors," Seoul KBS-1 Television Network, February 4, 1994.

43. Jim Adams, "U.S. Defense Nominee Hopes No Force Needed in North Korea," *Reuters*, February 2, 1994.

44. Paul Lewis, "U.S. Urges China to Pressure North Koreans to Open Nuclear Sites," *New York Times*, February 5, 1994, p. 5.

45. Melanie Kirkpatrick, "North Korea's Unlikely Messenger," *Washington Post*, February 7, 1994, p. sec. 1, p. 5.

46. Ibid.

47. Ibid.

48. "President Kim Receives Visiting U.S. Pastor," *North Korea News*, no. 683, May 17, 1993, pp. 4–5.

49. Ibid.

50. "Graham to Deliver Kim Il Sung Message to Clinton," *Yonhap*, February 3, 1994.

51. Interview with former U.S. government officials, 2001.

52. Ibid.

53. "Foreign Ministry Spokesman Urges End to Pressure Campaign," Korean Central Broadcasting Network, February 12, 1994.

54. "DPRK: Yonhap Cites IAEA Spokesman on DPRK Inspection Agreement," *Yonhap*, February 16, 1994.

55. David Sanger, "North Koreans Agree to Survey of Atomic Sites," *New York Times*, February 16, 1994, p. A1.

56. Interview with former U.S. officials, 2001.

57. Martin Seiff, "Reports of Injury to Kim Disputed; N. Korean Expert Calls Him Healthy," *Washington Times*, February 18, 1994, p. A1.

58. "Chochongnyon Official on DPRK Succession," *Yonhap*, April 6, 1994.

59. Gillen Chronology.

60. "Pyongyang Ties Inspections to U.S. Action on Exercise Talks," *FBIS Trends*, February 23, 1994.

61. Interview with former ROK officials, 2001.

62. "Interview with DPRK Delegate Cited," Seoul KBS-1 Radio Network, February 25, 1994.

63. "IAEA Board of Governors Considers Safeguards Inspections in the Democratic People's Republic of Korea (DPRK)," Press Release, February 23, 1994.

64. "Agreed Conclusions of the United States-DPRK Talks," February 25, 1994.

65. "Agreed Conclusions."

66. "Recent Development in Nuclear Issue Assessed," *FBIS*, SK2802095794, March 1, 1994, p. 29.

67. "Pyongyang Signals Preference for Talks with U.S. over ROK," *FBIS Trends*, March 2, 1994.

68. "U.S. Department of State Dispatch," Bureau of Public Affairs, vol. 5 (March 14, 1994); "Ministry Announces Suspension of Team Spirit, *Yonhap*, March 3, 1994.

69. "DPRK Reiterates Stance against Preconditions for U.S. Talks," *FBIS Trends*, March 9, 1994.

70. "Foreign Ministry Comments on Envoy Exchange," *Yonhap*, March 5, 1994.

71. "Foreign Minister Interviewed on DPRK Issue," *Munhwa Ilbo*, December 31, 1993, p. 3.

72. Interview with former ROK officials, 2001.

73. Interview with General Gary Luck, 2001.

74. Interview with former U.S. official, 2001.

75. Thomas W. Lippman and T. R. Reid, "N. Korea Nuclear Inspection Begins," *Washington Post*, March 4, 1994, p. A1; Lynn Davis, Testimony Submitted for the Record, Senate Committee on Foreign Relations, 103 Cong. 2 sess. (GPO, March 3, 1994).

76. Institute for Defense and Disarmament Studies Chronology for 1994, March 28, 1994.

77. Interview with former U.S. official, 2001.

78. Interview with former U.S. official, 2002.

79. "Report by the Director General of the IAEA to the Security Council," March 23, 1994, addendum; "DPRK: Delay Possible in IAEA Nuclear Inspection," *Kyodo News*, March 10, 1994; R. Jeffrey Smith, "N. Korean Conduct of Inspection Draws Criticism of U.S. Officials," *Washington Post*, March 10, 1994, p. A34.

80. Smith, "N. Korean Conduct."

81. "Report by the Director General of the IAEA to the Security Council."

82. R. Jeffrey Smith, "N. Korea Adds Arms Capacity," *Washington Post*, April 2, 1994, p. A1; "Second Hidden Reprocessing Line Feared Open at Yongbyon," *Nucleonics Week*, March 24, 1994.

83. "DPRK Reiterates Stance against Preconditions for U.S. Talks," *FBIS Trends*, March 9, 1994; "Outcome of Contact Noted," *Yonhap*, March 3, 1994; "Spiked Words Reportedly Exchanged," *Yonhap*, March 3, 1994.

84. "March 9 N.-S. Contact Fails to Make Any Progress," *Yonhap*, March 9, 1994; "Representatives Conversation Cited," *Yonhap*, March 9, 1994; "South Senior Delegate Cited," Seoul KBS-1 Radio Network, March 9, 1994.

85. Smith, "N. Korean Conduct of Inspection"; "DPRK-ROK: North Depicts Moves to Avoid Deadlock in Talks," *FBIS Trends*, March 9, 1994.

86. "DPRK Appears Ready to Lift Barriers to Envoy Exchange," *FBIS Trends*, March 16, 1994.

87. Interview with former U.S. official, 2002.

88. Carol Giacomo, "U.S. Says N. Korea Did Not Cooperate on Inspections," *Reuters*, March 15, 1994.

89. "Talks Face Initial Difficulties," Seoul KBS-1 Radio, March 16, 1994.

90. Martin Sieff, "Sanctions in Cards for North Korea, Officials Tell Hill," *Washington Times*, March 18, 1994, p. A14; "Kim Sees DPRK Sanctions as Nearly Inevitable," *Yonhap*, March 18, 1994.

91. Robert Burns, "Hamilton: Resume Korean Exercises," *Philadelphia Inquirer*, March 19, 1994, p. 14.

92. "TV Airs Delegates' Remarks," Seoul KBS-1 Television Network, March 19, 1994.

93. Interview with former ROK official, 2001.

94. "Release of Closed Session N.-S. Talks Questioned," *Hankyoreh Sinmun*, March 23, 1994, p. 4.

95. "Pyongyang Breaks Off Talks with Seoul, Threatens War," *FBIS Trends*, March 23, 1994.

96. "First Shipment of Patriot Missiles Arrive," *Yonhap*, April 18,1994.

97. *Nightline*, American Broadcasting Corporation, March 23, 1994.

98. Stephan Barr and Lena H. Sun, "China's Cooperation on N. Korea Seen," *Washington Post*, March 21, 1994, p. A12.

99. "Kim Young Sam Chairs Ministers Meeting," *Yonhap*, March 21, 1994.

100. "ROK War Plan to Invade North Denounced," *Pyongyang KCNA*, March 30, 1994.

101. "Deputy Prime Minister Comments," Seoul KBS-1 Radio Network, March 19, 1993; "Reports Units Defensive Posture," *Dong-A Ilbo*, March 22, 1994.

102. Shim Jae Hoon, "Driven into a Corner," *Far Eastern Economic Review*, March 22, 1994.

103. Interview with former U.S. official, 2000.

104. "DPRK Sea of Fire Remarks Distorted by the South," Seoul KBS-1 Radio Network, April 13, 1994.

105. "Memorandum for the Record by the World Summit for Peace Delegation," May 1994.

106. Josette Shiner and Michael Breen, "Another Sharp 'No' from Kim Il Sung," *Washington Times*, April 19, 1994, pp. A1, A16.

107. Interview with former U.S. official, 2001.

108. Message from Nelson Sievering, U.S. Representative, to the IAEA Board of Governors, March 18, 1994.

109. French Foreign Ministry Statement, February 3, 1993; *Pyongyang KCNA*, February 11, 1994.

110. Message from Sievering to the IAEA Board.

111. Hans Blix, Statement to the IAEA Board of Governors, March 21, 1994.

112. "Results of the BOG Meeting on DPRK."

113. Talk given by former Chinese official at the American Enterprise Institute, Washington, December 2, 1993.

114. "ROK: Foreign Minister on PRC Role in Sanctions against DPRK," *Yonhap*, March 22, 1994.

115. Karen Eliot House, "Korea, Clinton's Cuban Missile Crisis," *Wall Street Journal*, January 5, 1994, p. A14.

116. "Pyongyang Threatens NPT Withdrawal," *FBIS Trends*, March 21, 1994.

117. Doyle McManus and Paul Richter, "Clinton and Yeltsin End Summit with New Unity," *Los Angeles Times*, January 15, 1994, p. 1.

118. Ibid.

119. Fred Hiatt, "Moscow Proposes Conference to Deal with North Korea," *Washington Post*, March 25, 1994, p. A25.

120. "Radio Reports Panov Remarks on Russian Aid," Korean Central Broadcasting System, March 31, 1994.

121. "Russia: DPRK Rejects Russia's Multilateral Approach Proposal," *Pravda*, April 2, 1994, p. 3.

122. "UN Disturbed over Korea Nuke Controversy," *Reuters*, March 24, 1994.

123. Interview with former U.S. official, 2000.

124. "Results of Han-Christopher Meeting Reported," *Yonhap*, March 31, 1994; R. Jeffrey Smith, "Perry Sharply Warns North Korea," *Washington Post*, March 31, 1994, p. A1.

125. UN Security Council Presidential Statement on North Korea, March 31, 1994.

126. Julia Preston, "UN Bows to China, Issues Mild Call to N. Korea to Permit Nuclear Check," *Washington Post*, April 1, 1994, p. A27.

127. "DPRK Calibrates War Rhetoric, Leaves Door Ajar for Talks," *FBIS Trends*, March 30, 1994; interview.

128. Interview with former U.S. official, 2000.

129. "DPRK-ROK-U.S.: North Sharpens Rhetoric on Patriot Missiles," *FBIS Trends*, March 30, 1994.

130. "WPK Secretary Delivers Report," *Pyongyang KCNA*, March 31, 1994.

131. "Significance Examined," *Pyongyang KCNA*, April 3, 1994; "Yi In Mo Meets with Secretaries," *Pyongyang KCNA*, April 4, 1994.

132. "DPRK Calibrates War Rhetoric."

133. "DPRK-ROK-U.S.: North Sharpens War Rhetoric."

134. "DPRK Hints at Willingness to Talk with IAEA on Inspections," *FBIS Trends*, April 6, 1993.

Chapter Six

1. "Another Chance for North Korea," *New York Times*, April 2, 1994, p. A18.

2. Don Phillips, "Sanctions a First Step, U.S. Warns North Korea," *Washington Post*, April 4, 1994, p. A1.

3. "Transcript of President Clinton Remarks in April 5 Event in Charlotte, NC," U.S. Newswire, April 6, 1994.

4. Interview with former U.S. government official, 2001.

5. Ibid.

6. R. Jeffrey Smith, "Perry Sharply Warns North Korea," *Washington Post*, March 31, 1994, p. A1.

7. "Patriot Deployment, Team Spirit Issue Viewed," FBIS-EAS-94-077, April 21, 1994; "Premeditated Military Buildup Maneuver," Pyongyang Korean Central Broadcasting Network, April 21, 1994; *Lessons from the Gulf War,* Hearing before the Military Readiness and Defense Infrastructure Subcommittee and the Coalition Defense and Reinforcing Subcommittee of the Senate Committee on Armed Services, 103 Cong. 2 sess. (Government Printing Office, April 18, 1994), pp. 22–23.

8. Dean Robert L. Gallucci, Ambassador James Laney, and General Gary Luck, Seminar at Georgetown University, Washington, Spring 2000.

9. Ibid.

10. Interview with former U.S. official, 2001.

11. Interview with James Laney, 2001.

12. "Background Information on U.S.–North Korea Relations, Nuclear Policy on the Korean Peninsula, International Atomic Energy Agency Inspections, and North Korea–South Korea Relations" (www.fas.org/news/dprk/1994/940412-dprk-usia.htm).

13. Interview with former U.S. military official, 2001.

14. "First Shipment of Patriot Missiles Arrive," *Yonhap*, April 18, 1994; Josette Shiner and Michael Breen, "Another Sharp 'No' from Kim Il Sung," *Washington Times*, April 19, 1994, p. A1.

15. "Ways Not to Link Exchange Examined," *Hanguk Ilbo*, April 3, 1994, p. 1; "Official on Talks Precondition," *Chosun Ilbo*, April 4, 1994, p. 1.

16. "Decision to Drop Demand on Envoy Swap Analyzed," *Yonhap*, April 15, 1994.

17. "Perilous Development," *Pyongyang KCNA*, April 19, 1994.

18. Shiner and Breen, "Another Sharp 'No' from Kim Il Sung," p. A16.

19. Mike Chinoy, *China Live: People Power and the Television Revolt* (New York: Rowman and Littlefield, 1999), pp. 342–45.

20. Ibid.

21. "Perry Calls Kim's Disavowal of Nuclear Arms Encouraging," *Associated Press*, April 19, 1994.

22. "U.S., N. Korea Readying for Talks, Report Says," *Japan Economic Newswire*, April 24, 1994; "Pyongyang to Allow IAEA to Monitor Fuel Rod Exchange," *Asian Political News*, April 25, 1994.

23. Interview with U.S. technical expert, 2001.

24. C. Turner Joy, *How Communists Negotiate* (Macmillan, 1955).

25. "North Korea Invites IAEA for Refueling, Sues for U.S. Talks," *FBIS Trends*, May 4, 1994.

26. *BBC Summary of World Broadcasts*, April 28, 1994.

27. JPRS-TND-94-011, May 16, 1994, p. 44; R. Jeffrey Smith, *Washington Post*, June 1, 1994, p. A22; *Guardian*, June 1, 1994.

28. David B. Ottaway, *Washington Post*, June 8, 1994, p. A25; "Pyongyang Replies Positively to IAEA Inspection Request," *Kyodo News*, April 21, 1994; Douglas Hamilton, *Reuters*, April 21, 1994.

29. Andrew Pollack, "U.N. Says North Korea Refuses to Allow Nuclear Inspections," *New York Times*, May 1, 1994, sec. 1, p. 6; Joan Biskupic and R. Jeffrey Smith, "N. Korea Keeps Nuclear Inspectors at Bay," *Washington Post*, May 1, 1994, p. A36.

30. Ibid.

31. "Pyongyang Threatens to Refuel Reactor without IAEA Presence," *FBIS Trends*, May 4, 1994.

32. Interview with U.S. official.

33. "North Korean Fuel Rods Are Being Removed," *New York Times*, May 15, 1994, p. A1.

34. David E. Sanger, "Nuclear Agency to Send a New Inspection Team to North Korea," *New York Times*, May 13, 1994, p. A7.

35. "Remarks by Secretary of Defense William Perry to the Asia Society," *Federal News Service*, May 3, 1994.

36. Interview with former U.S. official, 2001.

37. Speech by Prime Minister Eisaku Sato, National Press Club, Washington, November 21, 1969.

38. Interview with former U.S. official, 2001; "The Defense Agency Studied Its Offer of Airports and Seaports," *Asahi Shimbun*, March 23, 1994.

39. Sheila A. Smith, "The Evolution of Military Cooperation in the U.S.-Japan Alliance," in Michael J. Green and Patrick M. Cronin, eds., *The U.S.-Japan Alliance: Past, Present and Future* (New York: Council on Foreign Relations Press, 1999), p. 77.

40. Ibid., pp. 80–81.

41. NHK Television Special Series on Japan's Choice, "The Far East Emergency No. 2: What Will Japan Do?" July 1996.

42. Interview with former U.S. official, 2001; "The Plan of Support for the U.S. and Korea," *Asahi Shimbun*, April 15, 1994.

43. Interview with former Japanese official, 2001; "The Plan of Support."

44. "The Far East Emergency."

45. Interview with former Japanese official, 2001.

46. *Japan Times*, April 21, 1994, p. 4; *Asahi Shimbun*, March 23, 1994, p. 1.

47. United States Information Agency Poll, January 1994.

48. Interview with former Japanese official, 2001; "The U.S. Military's Request toward Japan Was Revealed," *Asahi Shimbun*, March 3, 1999.

49. Interview with former U.S. official, 2001.

50. Don Oberdorfer, *The Two Koreas: A Contemporary History* (Reading, Mass.: Addison-Wesley, 1997), pp. 314–15.

51. Interview with General Gary Luck, 2001.

52. Interview with former U.S. official, 2001.

53. Oberdorfer, *Two Koreas*, p. 315.

54. Interview with former U.S. military officer, 2001.

55. "IAEA Safeguards in the DPRK," IAEA, PR94/21, May 19, 1994.

56. Patrick Blum and Michael Littlejohns, "North Korea Violating Nuclear Pact," *Financial Times*, May 20, 1994, p. 5.

57. *Nightline*, Transcript 3388, May 18, 1994.

58. Jim Abrams, "U.S. Should Move toward Sanctions, Senators Say," *Associated Press*, May 16, 1994.

59. Jim Hoagland, "Thinking about Korean War II," *Washington Post*, May 12, 1994, p. A27.

60. Richard Perle, "The Best Defense against North Korea," *Wall Street Journal*, May 3, 1994, p. A14.

61. Donald Gregg, "Offer Korea a Carrot," *New York Times*, May 19, 1994, p. A24.

62. "U.S. Accepts North Korean Demand for New High-Level Talks," *Washington Post*, May 21, 1994, p. A20; Michael R. Gordon, "Citing Progress, U.S. Plans New Talks with North Korea," *New York Times*, May 21, 1994, sec. 1 p. 1.

63. Interview with former U.S. official, 2001.

64. Letter from Yang Hyong Sop, Chairman of Supreme People's Assembly, to Albert Gore, President of the Senate, April 26, 1994.

65. Warren Strobel, "Senator's Trip to Pyongyang Was Aborted," *Washington Times*, May 26, 1994, p. A1.

66. "North Korea Foils Efforts to Halt Its Nuclear Plans," *New York Times*, May 29, 1994, p. A1.

67. "Statement by the President of the Security Council," United Nations Security Council, S/PRST/1994/28.

68. CNN *Late Edition*, Transcript 35, May 29, 1994.

69. R. Jeffrey Smith, "U.S. Plans to Seek North Korean Sanctions," *Washington Post*, June 1, 1994, p. A22.

70. Ann Devroy, "War Talk by N. Korea Rejected," *Washington Post*, June 5, 1994, p. A1.

71. Ann Devroy, "U.S. to Seek Sanctions on N. Korea; Nuclear Inspectors Cite Lost Chance to Monitor Reactor," *Washington Post*, June 3, 1994, p. A1; "Report by DG on the Implementation," June 2, 1994, gov/2687/add.7.

72. R. Jeffrey Smith and Julia Preston, "Nuclear Watchdog Says N. Korea Steps Up Fuel Rod Withdrawal," *Washington Post*, May 28, 1994, p. A25; Michael R. Gordon, "Korea Speeds Nuclear Fuel Removal, Impeding Inspection," *New York Times*, May 28, 1994, p. A3.

73. Devroy, "U.S. to Seek Sanctions."

Chapter Seven

1. William Safire, "Reactor Roulette," *New York Times*, June 2, 1994, p. A23.

2. Charles Krauthammer, "Get Ready for War," *Washington Post*, June 3, 1994, p. A23.

3. Interview with former U.S. official, 2001.

4. Interview with former Japanese official, 2000.

5. Ibid.

6. Ibid.

7. Ibid.

8. Interview with Chosen Soren official, 2000.

9. "Tokyo to Prepare Fully for DPRK Sanctions," *Nihon Keizai Shimbun*, March 31, 1994, p. 2.

10. "Japanese Public's North Korean Worries," United States Information Agency (USIA) Briefing Paper, February 8, 1994.

11. Interview with former Japanese official, 2000.

12. "South Koreans Have Mixed Views on Nuclear Issue; But Many Would Still Support Sanctions," USIA Opinion Research Memorandum, May 19, 1994.

13. "Phased, Gradual Steps Supported," Seoul KBS-1 Radio Network, June 3, 1994; "President Phones Advisers about Nuclear Issue," *Yonhap*, June 3, 1994.

14. Interview with former ROK official, 2000.

15. Ann Devroy, "War Talk by N. Korea Rejected," *Washington Post*, June 5, 1994, p. A1; T. R. Reid, "Accord Near on N. Korea Sanctions," *Washington Post*, June 12, 1994, p. A1; "Sanctions Discussed with U.S.," Seoul KBS-1 Radio Network, June 3, 1994; "Japan Finalizes Concrete Steps," Seoul KBS-1 Radio Network, June 3, 1994.

16. Interview with former Japanese official, 2000.

17. "Kim Yong Sam Briefs Journalists on Russian Visit," *Hanguk Ilbo*, June 5, 1994.

18. Ibid.

19. Interview with former U.S. official, 2001.

20. "Han Optimistic on PRC Taking Part in Sanctions," *Yonhap*, June 7, 1994.

21. "PRC Virtually Refused Request on Sanctions," *Yonhap*, June 9, 1994.

22. "DPRK Seeks Third World Aid on Nuclear Issue, *Yonhap*, March 30, 1994.

23. David Ottaway, "North Korea Forbids Inspections," *Washington Post*, June 8, 1994, p. A25; "U.S. Presses for Sanctions against North Korea," *Reuters*, June 7, 1994.

24. ABC *Nightline*, Transcript 3403, June 8, 1994.

25. Don Oberdorfer, *The Two Koreas: A Contemporary History* (Reading, Mass.: Addison-Wesley, 1997), pp. 104–05, 317.

26. Interview with James Laney, 2001.

27. Jimmy Carter, "Report of Our Trip to Korea," June 1994.

28. Interviews with former U.S. officials, 2001.

29. "Jimmy Carter to Visit South Korea and North Korea," statement announcing former president Jimmy Carter's acceptance, June 9, 1994.

30. "Meets with President Kim," *Yonhap*, June 11, 1994.

31. Oberdorfer, *Two Koreas*, pp. 324–26.

32. Leon V. Sigal, *Disarming Strangers: Nuclear Diplomacy with North Korea* (Princeton University Press, 1998), p. 122.

33. Ibid., pp. 148–49.

34. Ibid.

35. Interviews with former U.S. officials, 2001.

36. George Bush and Brent Scowcroft, *A World Transformed* (Alfred A. Knopf, 1996), pp. 413–14.

37. Interview with former ROK officials, 2001.

38. "Significance of Choe Kwang Visit to PRC Viewed," *Joongang Ilbo*, June 7, 1994; "Strengthening of Ties Viewed," *Pyongyang KCNA*, June 8, 1994; "Envoy Denies PRC Warned DPRK on Negotiations," *Kyonghyang Sinmun*, June 9, 1994; "Political Observers Speculate on DPRK Delegation's Visit," *Kyodo News*, June 6, 1994; "Liu Huaqing Receives DPRK's Choe Kwang, Urges Dialogue," *Xinhua*, June 13, 1994.

39. "Phone Conversation Held," *Kyodo News*, June 14, 1994; "Japan's Support Reassured," *Kyodo News*, June 14, 1994; David E. Sanger, "Tokyo Reluctant to Levy Sanctions on North Korea," *New York Times*, June 9, 1994, p. A1.

40. "DG's Statement to the BOG on the DPRK," IAEA, Vienna, June 7, 1994; "IAEA, BOG to Discuss DPRK Nuclear Issue," *Yonhap*, June 9, 1994.

41. R. Jeffrey Smith and T. R. Reid, "North Korea Quits UN Nuclear Body, *Washington Post*, June 14, 1994, sec. 1, p. 1; David E. Sanger, "North Korea Quits Atom Agency in Wider Rift with U.S. and UN," *New York Times*, June 14, 1994, p. A1; Michael R. Gordon, "U.S. Is Considering Milder Sanctions for North Korea," *New York Times*, June 12, 1994; "DPRK-IAEA: Pyongyang Declares Withdrawal from IAEA," *FBIS Trends*, June 15, 1994.

42. Brent Scowcroft and Arnold Kanter, "Korea: A Time for Action," *Washington Post*, June 15, 1994, p. A25.

43. President Clinton, Address to Nixon Center, Washington, March 1, 1995.

44. Ibid; Oberdorfer, *Two Koreas*, p. 323; Ashton Carter and William J. Perry, "Back to the Brink," *Washington Post*, October 20, 1994, p. B1 (and a variety of press reports since then).

45. "Albright Says Draft on N. Korea May Be Ready Tuesday," *Reuters*, June 13, 1994.

46. Oberdorfer, *Two Koreas*, pp. 321–22.

47. "Pyongyang Makes Last-Ditch Effort to Save Talks," *FBIS Trends*, June 8, 1994.

48. "Pyongyang Claims U.S. Bad Faith, Hardens Nuclear Stance," *FBIS Trends*, June 8, 1994.

49. R. Jeffrey Smith and Ann Devroy, "Carter's Call from N. Korea Offered Option: Administration Seized on New Chance at Diplomacy," *Washington Post*, June 26, 1994, p. A1.

50. "Kim Young Sam Briefs Journalists on Russia Visit," *Hanguk Ilbo*, June 5, 1994.

51. "Kim Tok: DPRK Aims to Develop Nuclear Arms," *Yonhap*, June 13, 1994.

52. "Daily Reports Hoarding by Residents," *Korea Times*, June 16, 1994.

53. "Civil Defense Exercise Conducted Nationwide," *Yonhap*, June 15, 1994.

54. Interview with former ROK official.

55. "Government Decides to Strengthen Civil Defense," *Yonhap*, June 13, 1994.

56. "Defense Minister Assess Military Posture," Seoul KBS-1 Radio Network, June 9,1994; "Prepared to Cope with Any Event," *Yonhap*, June 9, 1994; "Defense Minister on Preparing for Provocation," *Yonhap*, June 15, 1994; "Defense Ministry Plans to Give Daily Briefing," *Yonhap*, June 16, 1994; "Kim Tok: DPRK Aims to Develop Nuclear Arms," *Yonhap*, June 13, 1994.

57. "Ruling Party Discusses DPRK with Ministers," Seoul KBS-1 Radio Network, June 15, 1994; "DLP Demand on Denuclearization Analyzed," *Chosun Ilbo*, June 16, 1994, p. 4.

58. "Opposition Party Urges Caution on Nuke Issue," *Yonhap*, June 3, 1994.

59. Interview with former U.S. official, 2001.

60. Testimony of General Gary E. Luck, U.S. Army Commander, United States Forces Korea, *Department of Defense Appropriations for Fiscal Year 1995,* Hearing before the House Committee on Appropriations, 103 Cong. 2 sess. (Government Printing Office, March 1, 1994), p. 611; interview with former U.S. official, 2002.

61. Interview with former U.S. official, 2001.

62. Ibid.

63. Ibid.

64. Ibid.

65. Ibid.

66. Interview with General Luck, 2001.

67. Oberdorfer, *Two Koreas,* p. 326.

68. Interview with former U.S. official, 2001.

69. Ibid.

70. Ibid.

71. Luck, *Department of Defense Appropriations;* "U.S. Non-Combatant Evacuation Exercise Denounced," Pyongyang Korean Central Broadcasting Network, June 7, 1994.

72. Carter, "Report of Our Trip."

73. Interviews with former ROK officials, 2001.

74. Interview with former U.S. official, 2001.

75. Interview with former U.S. official, 2003.

Chapter Eight

1. Jimmy Carter, "Report of Our Trip to Korea," June 1994.

2. Mike Chinoy, *China Live: People Power and the Television Revolt* (New York: Rowman and Littlefield, 1999), p. 350.

3. Interview with former U.S. official, 2002.

4. Interview with former U.S. officials and others, 2003.

5. Carter, "Report of Our Trip."

6. Interview with former U.S. official, 2000.

7. Carter, "Report of Our Trip."

8. Ibid.

9. Don Oberdorfer, *The Two Koreas: A Contemporary History* (Reading, Mass.: Addison-Wesley, 1997), p. 329.

10. Transcript of interview with Jimmy Carter, CNN, June 15, 1994; Oberdorfer, *Two Koreas,* p. 331.

11. Oberdorfer, *Two Koreas,* p. 331.

12. Press Conference by President Clinton, *Federal News Service,* June 16, 1994.

13. Ibid.

14. Special White House Briefing by Robert Gallucci, Assistant Secretary for Political-Military Affairs, *Federal News Service,* June 16, 1994.

15. Interview with former U.S. official, 2001.

16. Special White House Briefing by Robert Gallucci, Assistant Secretary for Political-Military Affairs, *Federal News Service,* June 16, 1994.

17. Ibid.

18. Ibid.

19. Interview with former ROK official, 2001.

20. Interview with former U.S. official, 2002.

21. Interview with U.S. official, 2001.

22. Oberdorfer, *Two Koreas*, p. 332.

23. Interview with Jimmy Carter, CNN, June 19, 1994; Leon V. Sigal, *Disarming Strangers: Nuclear Diplomacy with North Korea* (Princeton University Press, 1998), pp. 161–62; Oberdorfer, *Two Koreas*, p. 333.

24. Statement by the White House Press Secretary, June 18, 1994.

25. Michael R. Gordon, "U.S. Shift on Korea: Clinton Retreating from a Showdown," *New York Times*, June 18, 1994, p. A1.

26. Interviews with former U.S. officials, 2001.

27. Interview with former U.S. official, 2001.

28. Interview with former ROK official, 2001; Oberdorfer, *Two Koreas*, p. 334; "Kim Young Sam Accepts Proposal," *Yonhap*, June 18, 1994; Carter, "Report of Our Trip."

29. Kate Webb, "Carter Flays Sanctions, Arranges Inter-Korean Summit," *Agence France-Presse*, June 18, 1994.

30. Interviews with participants in June 19 meeting, 2001–02.

31. "Press Briefing by Assistant Secretary of State Robert L. Gallucci," *Federal News Service*, White House Briefing Room, June 19, 1994.

32. R. Jeffrey Smith and Ruth Marcus, "Carter Trip May Offer Opening; White House Wary of Ex-President's View N. Korea Crisis Is Over," *Washington Post*, June 20, 1994, p. A1.

33. Donald P. Gregg, "Korea: Toughness and Talk," *Washington Post*, June 17, 1994, p. A25.

34. Frank Sesno, "Jimmy Carter, Korean Peacemaker, Did His Trip to Korea Reduce the Threat of War?" CNN *Late Edition*, Transcript 38, June 19, 1994.

35. "The Carter Opening," *New York Times*, June 21, 1994, p. 16.

36. Smith and Marcus, "Carter Trip May Offer Opening."

37. Charles Krauthammer, "Peace in Our Time," *Washington Post*, June 24, 1994, p. A27.

38. Interviews with participants in June 20 meeting, 2001; R. Jeffery Smith and Ann Devroy, "U.S. Debates Shift on North Korea," *Washington Post*, June 21, 1994, p. A1.

39. "Americans Favor Resuming North Korea Talks—Poll," *Reuters*, June 18, 1994.

40. Press Conference with President Clinton, *Federal News Service*, June 22, 1994.

41. "Opening Statements from a News Conference," Brussels, Belgium, June 22, 1994.

42. Press Conference with President Clinton.

43. "Christopher Remarks on U.S.-DPRK Summit," *Seoul Sinmun*, June 26, 1994.

44. "North Accepts South's Call for Talks on Inter-Korean Summit," *FBIS Trends*, June 22, 1994.

45. "Statement by Press Secretary," White House, June 22, 1994; "Clinton Calls Kim on Resumption of DPRK Talks," *Yonhap*, June 22, 1994.

46. U.S. Department of State Daily Press Briefing, June 22, 1994, p. 2.

47. *Washington Post*/ABC News Poll, June 26, 1994.

Chapter Nine

1. Rich Jaroslovsky, "Washington Wire," *Wall Street Journal*, June 17, 1994, sec. A, p. 1.

2. Interview with Japanese official, 2001.

3. Peter Grier, "Stowing Its Threats, U.S. Will Hear Out N. Korea in Talks," *Christian Science Monitor*, July 7, 1994, p. 1.

4. Interview with former U.S. official, 2001.

5. R. James Woolsey and General James Clapper, Testimony in Hearings before the Senate Select Committee on Intelligence, 103 Cong. 2 sess. (Government Printing Office, January 25, 1994).

6. "North, South Agree on Summit, DPRK Upbeat on U.S. Talks," *FBIS Trends*, June 29, 1994.

7. Ibid.

8. "Arrival Statement by DPRK Delegation," U.S. Mission, Geneva, July 6, 1994; "Background Briefing by Senior U.S. Official," U.S. Mission, Geneva, July 1994.

9. "Kim Il Sung Dies of Heart Attack at 82," Special Report, *North Korea News*, July 1994.

10. Michael Breen, "North Korea Mourning Begins," *Washington Times*, July 11, 1994, p. A1; Kim Ju Yeon, "South Koreans Greet News of Kim's Death with Shock," Associated Press, July 9, 1994.

11. Breen, "North Korea Mourning Begins"; Kim Ju Yeon, "South Koreans Greet News of Kim's Death with Shock."

12. Breen, "North Korea Mourning Begins"; Kim Ju Yeon, "South Koreans Greet News of Kim's Death with Shock."

13. Breen, "North Korea Mourning Begins"; Kim Ju Yeon, "South Koreans Greet News of Kim's Death with Shock."

14. "Data on DPRK Missile Test Kept Secret," *Mainichi Shimbun*, August 14, 1994, p. 1.

15. Interview with former ROK official, 2001.

16. Ibid.

17. Ibid.

18. Patrick Worsnip, "Kim's Death Will Not Change North Korea's Policy," *Reuters*, July 11, 1994.

19. Ibid.

20. Interview with former ROK official, 2001.

21. Interview with former U.S. official, 2001.

22. Interview with former ROK official, 2001.

23. "30 North Korean Experts Assess Kim Chong Il," *Wolgan Joongang*, September 1994, pp. 192–205.

24. General James Clapper, Testimony in Hearing before Senate Select Committee on Intelligence, 104 Cong. 1sess. (GPO, July 25, 1994).

25. Interview with former ROK official, 2001.

26. Breen, "North Korean Mourning Begins."

27. Interview with former ROK official, 2001.

28. Ibid.

29. Interview with former U.S. officials, 2001.

30. "Clinton Statement on Death of North Korean President," *Associated Press*, July 9, 1994.

31. Interview with former U.S. official, 2001.

32. "Press Conference by Assistant Secretary Robert Gallucci," July 10, 1994, Geneva, Switzerland.

33. Bill Gertz, "Kim Jong Il Appears Assured of Succeeding Father," *Washington Times*, July 11, 1994, p. A9.

34. Interview with former U.S. official, 2001.

35. Interview with former ROK official, 2001.

36. Ibid.

37. "Foreign Minister: Seoul Ready for the Inter-Korean Summit," *Yonhap*, July 11, 1994.

38. Interview with former ROK officials, 2000.

39. "Sympathy in South Korea for Kim Angers Critics," *Reuters*, July 12, 1994.

40. "DP Lawmakers Retract Remarks about Kim Il Sung," *Yonhap*, July 13, 1994.

41. "Police Forces Arrest Condolence Delegation," Seoul KBS-1 Radio Network, July 16, 1994.

42. "Police Discover Secret Kim Il Sung Shrine," *Korea Herald*, July 16, 1994, p. 3.

43. "Seoul to Deal Sternly with Pro-North Students," *Yonhap*, July 18, 1994.

44. Interview with former ROK official, 2001; "Korean War Documents from Russia Disclosed," *Yonhap*, July 20, 1994.

45. "Government Position on Condolences Revealed," Seoul KBS-1 Radio Network, July 18, 1994.

46. Interview with former ROK official, 2001.

47. Ibid.

48. "Pyongyang Signals Orderly Succession, U.S. Policy Continuity," *FBIS Trends*, July 14, 1994; "DPRK Funeral Reflects Leadership, U.S. Policy Continuity," *FBIS Trends*, July 20, 1994; "Media Anomalies Reflect Slow Pace of Succession," *FBIS Trends*, July 27, 1994; interview.

49. "Media Anomalies."

50. Interview with former ROK official, 2000; T. R. Reid, "N. Korean Silent at Rite for Father," *Washington Post*, July 21, 1994, p. A21.

51. "DPRK Demands Delinking of North-South Ties from U.S. Talks," *FBIS Trends*, July 27, 1994.

52. Ibid.

53. Michael Breen, "Quiet Kim Shows Off Controls," *Washington Times*, July 21, 1994, p. 1.

54. "DPRK Demands Delinking."

55. James Sterngold, "The Key Issue on North Korea," *New York Times*, July 24, 1994, p. A14.

56. Interview with former ROK official, 2001.

57. "Kim Yong Sam, Clinton Discuss DPRK by Phone," *Yonhap*, July 15, 1994.

58. Interview with former ROK official, 2001.

59. "Senate Votes to Ban Aid to North Korea," *Associated Press*, July 15, 1994.

60. Interview with former U.S. official, 2001.

61. "Kozyrev: Russia to Help North Korea Change to Light-Water Reactors," *Ekho Moskvy* radio, Moscow (in Russian), 1800 gmt, July 15, 1994, reported in *BBC Summary of World Broadcasts*, July 18, 1994.

62. "Briefing by Ambassador Robert Gallucci," U.S. State Department, *Federal News Service*, August 2, 1994.

63. Interview with member of U.S. delegation, 2001.

64. "Gallucci Telephone Interview with BBC," August 9, 1994.

65. "Press Conference by Robert L. Gallucci and Kang Sok Ju at the DPRK Mission," August 12, 1994.

66. Alan Riding, "U.S. and N. Korea Say They'll Seek Diplomatic Links," *New York Times*, August 13, 1994, p. 1.

67. Steven Greenhouse, "U.S. Officials Urge Caution on Arms Pact," *New York Times*, August 14, 1994, p. 19.

68. Ibid.

69. "Press Conference by Gallucci and Kang," August 12, 1994.

70. "DPRK Minister on Special Inspections," *Yonhap*, August 14, 1994.

71. "DPRK-U.S.: Pyongyang Upbeat on Talks with Washington," *FBIS Trends*, August 17, 1994.

72. Greenhouse, "U.S. Officials Urge Caution on Arms Pact."

73. "Conflicting Policy on DPRK-US Ties Alleged," *Joongang Ilbo*, August 21, 1994, p. 2.

74. "Kim Dae Jung Proposes N.-S. Summit in Washington," *Korea Herald*, August 19, 1994.

75. "Poll: Majority Agree to Finance DPRK Reactor," *Joongang Ilbo*, August 19, 1994, p. 3.

76. "Agreement Reported," Seoul KBS-1 Radio Network, August 12, 1994; "Agreement May Hasten U.S. Expansion," Seoul KBS-1 Radio Network, August 13, 1994; "Papers Review U.S.-DPRK Talks, Agreement," SK 1308124994, FBIS, August 16, 1994, p. 48.

77. "Signs of Debate Emerge over Succession Issue," *FBIS Trends*, August 31, 1994.

78. Interviews with former ROK official, 2002.

79. "Contingency Plans for Abrupt Unification Noted," *Yonhap*, August 19, 1994.

80. Interview with former U.S. official, 2000.

81. Interview with former U.S. official, 2001.

82. Interview with U.S. intelligence official, 2001.

83. "President: Leaflets Significant," *Yonhap*, August 24, 1994.

84. "NSP Predicts Kim Chong Il to Succeed to Power," *Yonhap*, August 26, 1994.

85. Andrew Pollack, "Seoul Offers Help on Nuclear Power to North Korea," *New York Times*, August 16, 1994, p. A6.

86. "Seoul: North Must Accept ROK Model Reactor," *Yonhap*, August 29, 1994; "Pace of U.S.-North Rapproachement Questioned," *Yonhap*, August 31, 1994.

87. "Foreign Minister on North Nuclear Transparency," *Yonhap*, August 22, 1994.

88. "Reaction to Special Inspection Issue Reported," *Yonhap*, August 23, 1994; "President Stresses Importance," *Yonhap*, August 23, 1994.

89. "North Korea Reaffirms It Will Never Allow Special Nuclear Inspections," *North Korea News*, no. 750, August 29, 1994.

90. Interview with former U.S. official, 2001.

91. "Russian Official on Light-Water Reactor for North," Seoul KBS-1 Radio Network, August 26, 1994.

92. "Light-Water Reactor Issue Analyzed," *Seoul Mael Yongje Sinmun*, September 4, 1994, p. 2; "Conditions on Reactor for DPRK," *Hanguk Ilbo*, September 5, 1994, p. 1.

93. "Pyongyang Seeking to Buy German Nuclear Reactors," *Frankfurter Allgemeine*, September 8, 1994.

94. Interviews with members of U.S. delegation, 2001.

95. Interview with member of U.S. delegation, 2001.

96. Ibid.

97. Ibid.

98. "Memorandum from USIS Berlin to Gary Samore on Today's Press Conference," September 15, 1994.

99. Interview with former U.S. officials, 2001.

100. Paul Bedard and Gus Constantine, "Clinton Shows Support for Links to South Korea," *Washington Times*, September 9, 1994, p. A4.

101. "Tokyo May Change Stance on Light-Water Reactor," *Yomuiri Shimbun*, August 26, 1994, p. 2; "Japan Likely to Participate in DPRK Reactors," *Yonhap*, August 29, 1994.

102. "Resumption of DPRK Talks Reportedly Planned," *Nikon Keizai Shimbun*, August 7, 1994, p. 2.

103. Kim Cha Su and Pak Che Kyun, "Talking Security for Financial Cost on Light-Water Reactors," *Dong-A Ilbo*, September 12, 1994.

104. Interview with former ROK official, 2001.

105. Ibid.

106. "President Views Central Role in Reactor Issue," *Yonhap*, September 22, 1994.

107. "Lawmakers Collide over Light-Water Reactors," *Korea Times*, September 24, 1994, p. 2.

108. Interview with former ROK officials, 2001.

Chapter Ten

1. Robert Gallucci, Testimony in Hearings before the Subcommittee on Asia and the Pacific, House Committee on International Relations, 104 Cong. 1 sess. (Government Printing Office, February 23, 1995), p. 11.

2. Ibid., p. 9.

3. Bill Gertz, "U.S. Carrier Sails from Korea," *Washington Times*, October 6, 1994, p. A14.

4. Interview with former U.S. officer, 2001.

5. Interview with U.S. delegation member, 2002.

6. Interviews with member of U.S. delegation and former U.S. naval officer, 2001.

7. Interview with member of U.S. delegation, 2001.

8. Interview with Robert Carlin, 2001.

9. Sid Balman Jr., "U.S. Says Little Progress with North Korea," *United Press International*, September 28, 1994; Alexander G. Higgins, "Negotiators Look for Room to Bargain," *Associated Press*, September 28, 1994.

10. "Statement of the Spokesman of the Korean People's Army," Korean Central Broadcasting Network, September 27, 1994.

11. "DPRK, U.S. Diplomatic War Nerves Viewed," *Joongang Ilbo*, September 26, 1994, p. 6.

12. Interview with former U.S. official, 2001.

13. Interview with former U.S. official, 2002.

14. "U.S., North Korea Set to Resume Nuclear Talks," *Reuters*, October 5, 1994.

15. Michael R. Gordon, "North Korea and U.S. at an Impasse," *New York Times*, October 6, 1994, p. A7.

16. R. Jeffrey Smith, "Stalemate in North Korea Talks May Strain Relations, Officials Say," *Washington Post*, October 2, 1994, p. A30.

17. J. F. O. McAllister, "Back to Square One," *Time*, October 10, 1994, p. 51.

18. Interview with Robert Carlin and Danny Russel, 2001.

19. Interview with Robert Carlin, 2001.

20. Interview with member of U.S. delegation, 2001.

21. Interview with member of ROK delegation, 2001.

22. Ibid.

23. Ibid.

24. "All Party Members and Workers Should Exert All Efforts to Guarantee Dear Leader's Good Health and Longevity," *North Korea News*, no. 755, October 3, 1994, pp. 3–4.

25. "Kim Tae Chung to Meet with Carter," *Yonhap*, September 16, 1994; Interview with former ROK official, 2001.

26. James Sterngold, "South Korean President Lashes Out at U.S.," *New York Times*, October 8, 1994, p. A3.

27. Interview with former ROK official, 2001.

28. Interviews with members of U.S. delegation, 2001.

29. Interview with former U.S. official, 2001.

30. Interview with members of U.S. delegation, 2001.

31. Robert Evans, "U.S. Said Making New Offer in N. Korea Nuclear Talks," *Reuters*, October 12, 1994.

32. Interview with James Laney, 2002.

33. "U.S. Said to Offer N. Korea Five-Year Grace Period," *Reuters*, October 13, 1994.

34. Interview with former ROK official, 2001.

35. David E. Sanger, "Clinton Administration Reports Breakthrough in North Korea Nuclear Arms Talks," *New York Times*, October 15, 1994, sec. 1, p. 8.

36. Interview with former U.S. official, 2001.

37. T. R. Reid, "Seoul Hopes Carter Will Arrange First Summit of Korean Leaders," *Washington Post*, September 23, 1994; "Carter's Possible Visit to North Examined," *Yonhap*, September 18, 1994; "Dailies View Acceptance of Carter's DPRK Visit," SK 190904394, *FBIS*, September 19, 1994; James Sterngold, "North Korea Invites Carter to Mediate," *New York Times*, September 2, 1994, p. A7.

38. Interviews with members of U.S. delegation, 2001.

39. Interview with member of U.S. delegation, 2002.

40. Phillippe Naughton, "Geneva Talks Stalled, U.S. Says," *Washington Times*, October 16, 1994, p. A6.

41. Interview with member of U.S. delegation, 2001.

42. Interview with Thomas Hubbard, 2001.

43. Interview with member of South Korean delegation, 2001.

44. "Press Conference of Ambassador-at-Large Robert Gallucci," U.S. Mission, Geneva, Switzerland, October 17, 1994.

45. Interviews with members of U.S. delegation, 2001.

46. Interview with member of U.S. delegation, 2000.

47. Interview with Thomas Hubbard, 2001.

48. "Signing of Agreement Sketched," *Yonhap*, October 22, 1994.

49. Ibid.

50. "Press Conference Given by Ambassador-at-Large Robert L. Gallucci Following the Signing of the U.S.-DPRK Accord," Office of Public Affairs, U.S. Mission, Geneva, 7:00 PM, October 21, 1994.

Chapter Eleven

1. "United States-North Korea Accord," Transcript of Washington Briefings by President Clinton and Ambassador-at-Large Robert L. Gallucci, Office of Public Affairs, U.S. Mission, Geneva, October 18, 1994.

2. Ibid.

3. Ibid.

4. Ibid.

5. "Nuclear Breakthrough in Korea," *New York Times*, October 19, 1994, p. A22.

6. "Accord with North Korea," *Washington Post*, October 19, 1994, p. A22; "The Content of the Korea Accord," *Washington Post*, October 21, 1994, p. A24.

7. David E. Sanger, "Clinton Approves Plan to Give Aid to North Koreans," *New York Times*, October 19, 1994, p. A1.

8. R. Jeffrey Smith, "North Korea Pact Contains U.S. Concessions," *Washington Post*, October 19, 1994, p. A1.

9. William Safire, "Clinton's Concessions," *New York Times*, October 24, 1994, p. A17.

10. Caspar Weinberger, "The Appeasement of North Korea," *Forbes*, November 21, 1994, p. 35.

11. Jessica Matthews, "A Sound Beginning with North Korea," *Washington Post*, October 21, 1994, p. A25.

12. "U.S. Department of State Press Briefing," October 21, 1994, pp. 2, 6.

13. "U.S. White Paper on U.S.-North Korea Agreed Framework," October 1994.

14. Douglas Hamilton, "IAEA Concerned about Terms of U.S.-N. Korea Pact," *Reuters*, October 20, 1994.

15. *McNeil-Lehrer News Hour*, Transcript, October 21, 1994.

16. Gerald F. Seib, "In North Korea, Trouble Starts in Credibility Gap," *Wall Street Journal*, October 21, 1994, p. A20.

17. "U.S. Department of State Press Briefing," October 25, 1994, p. 6.

18. Warren Christopher, *In the Stream of History: Shaping Foreign Policy for a New Era* (Stanford University Press, 1998), p. 217.

19. Robert S. Greenberger, "To Senate Centrists Nunn and Lugar Falls Task of Steering Foreign Policy While Veering Right," *Wall Street Journal*, November 29, 1994, p. A24.

20. Interview with former U.S. official, 2001.

21. Christopher Burns, "UN Agency Praises U.S.-Korean Nuclear Deal; Dole Critical," *Associated Press*, October 20, 1994.

22. Interviews with former U.S. officials, 2001.

23. *Evaluating U.S. Foreign Policy*, Hearings before the House Committee on International Relations, 104 Cong. 1 sess. (Government Printing Office, January 12, 19, 26, 1995), p. 18.

24. *Implications of the U.S.-North Korea Nuclear Agreement*, Hearing before Subcommittee on East Asian and Pacific Affairs, Senate Committee on Foreign Relations, 103 Cong. 2 sess. (GPO, December 1, 1994), p. 6.

25. Ibid.

26. *North Korea News*, September 26, 1994, no. 754, p. 8.

27. "Presidential Statement on U.S.-North Korea Agreed Framework," United Nations Security Council, November 4, 1994.

28. "IAEA BOG Gives Green Light to Secretariat," IAEA Document PR 94/7, Vienna, November 11, 1994; "Statement by the DG to the BOG," IAEA document, Vienna, November 11, 1994.

29. "IAEA Negotiation Delegation Arrives November 22," Korean Central Broadcasting Network, November 22, 1994.

30. *Chosun Ilbo*, October 20, 1994; *Joongang Ilbo*, October 21, 1994; "South Koreans Have Mixed Reaction to the Nuclear Pact," United States Information Agency Briefing Paper, November 14, 1994.

31. R. Jeffrey Smith, "N. Korea, U.S. Reach Nuclear Pact," *Washington Post*, October 18, 1994, pp. A1, A28; "Government Puts a Positive Construction on the U.S.-North Korea Nuclear Accord," Korean Information Service, *FBIS*, October 18, 1994.

32. Han Sung Chu, "Larger View on the Expansion of the Diplomatic Horizon: U.S.–North Korean Agreement and the Direction of ROK Diplomacy," *Kukchong Sinmun Weekly*, October 31, 1994, p. 3.

33. "South Koreans Have a Mixed Reaction to the Nuclear Pact"; "Six out of Ten Willing to Pay for Reactors," *Joongang Ilbo*, October 21, 1994, p. 3.

34. Interview with former ROK official, 2002; "Task Force to Study Reactor's Financing Planned," *Korea Herald*, October 22, 1994, p. 2.

35. "South Korea Urges Inter-Korean Dialogue," *United Press International*, October 18, 1994.

36. Christopher, *In The Stream of History*, pp. 215–16.

37. Charles Aldinger, "U.S. Troops to Stay in S. Korea," *Washington Times*, October 21, 1994, p. 3.

38. *Kyonghyang Sinmun*, October 26, 1994, p. 3.

39. *Seoul Sinmun*, November 9, 1994.

40. Christopher, *In the Stream of History*.

41. "Takemura Seeks Burden Sharing on DPRK Issue," *Kyodo News*, October 25, 1994; "Tokyo Hedging on Financial Support for DPRK Reactor," *FBIS Trends*, October 26, 1994.

42. Interview with former U.S. official, 2001.

43. CNN, *Evans and Novak,* December 17, 1994.

44. Interview with former U.S. official, 2001.

45. *U.S.–North Korea Nuclear Issues,* Hearing before the Senate Committee on Energy and Natural Resources, 104 Cong. 1 sess. (GPO, January 19, 1995), p. 11.

46. Interview with former U.S. official, 2001.

47. Paul Blustein, "North Korea Hands Over Pilot's Body," *Washington Post*, December 22, 1994, p. A1; James Gerstenzang, "Copter Pilot Still in North Korean Hands, U.S. Seeks High-Level Talks," *Los Angeles Times*, December 26, 1994, p. 11.

48. Interview with Thomas Hubbard, 2001.

49. Ibid.

50. Jim Mann, "Episode Points to Limitations of Nuclear Deal," *Los Angeles Times*, December 30, 1994, p. 1.

51. *U.S.–North Korea Nuclear Issues,* Hearing, p. 11.

52. Interview with Thomas Hubbard, 2001.

53. Coauthor Joel Wit visited Pyongyang and made this observation.

54. *North Korea Nuclear Agreement,* Hearing before the Senate Committee on Foreign Relations, 104 Cong. 1 sess. (GPO, January 24, 25, 1995), p. 5.

55. Ibid., p. 16.

56. Ibid., p. 9.

57. *Security Implications of the Nuclear Non-Proliferation Agreement with North Korea,* Senate Committee on Armed Services, 104 Cong. 1 sess. (January 26, 1995), p. 5.

58. "Senators Paul Simon and Frank Murkowski Press Conference in Seoul," December 12, 1994, *Yonhap*, Seoul.

59. *North Korea Nuclear Agreement,* Hearing.

60. Ibid.

61. Ibid.

62. Leon V. Sigal, *Disarming Strangers: Nuclear Diplomacy with North Korea* (Princeton University Press, 1998), p. 200.

63. Interview with former U.S. official, 2001.

64. This account is based on recollections of James Pierce as well as relevant documents.

65. Interview with James Pierce, 2002.

66. Ibid.

67. Ibid.

68. Sigal, *Disarming Strangers*, p. 200.

69. Interview with former ROK official, 2002.

70. Sigal, *Disarming Strangers*, p. 200.

71. Interview with U.S. official, 2002.

72. Interviews with former U.S. officials, 2001.

73. Interview with former U.S. official, 2001.

74. Don Oberdorfer, *The Two Koreas: A Contemporary History* (Reading, Mass.: Addison-Wesley, 1997), p. 367; Sigal, *Disarming Strangers*, p. 202.

75. T. R. Reid and Lee Keumhyun, "S. Korea Accepts Deal with North on A-Power, Clinton Letter Eases Seoul's Concerns," *Washington Post*, June 14, 1995, p. A32.

76. Tom Mintier, "Text of Opening Remarks from U.S.–North Korea Briefing," CNN Transcript 715-1, June 13, 1995.

77. "South Korea to Build Light-Water Reactors in North: Gallucci," *Agence France-Presse*, June 13, 1995.

Chapter Twelve

1. James Brooke, "Indicted Hyundai Executive Plunges to Death in Seoul," *New York Times*, August 4, 2003, p. A6.

2. Plutonium bombs are implosion devices, requiring highly coordinated detonation of a number of charges around a plutonium sphere to drive the device instantaneously toward supercritical mass. Because of its atomic characteristics, however, highly enriched uranium can be fashioned into a far simpler "gun"-type assembly, where one slug of enriched uranium is "shot" into a larger quantity of the same material to create a super-critical mass. Indeed, the gun assembly is so simple and reliable a design that it would not require testing for the North Koreans—or their customers—to be confident that their bombs would produce a nuclear yield. (A workable plutonium implosion device might be achieved without testing, but it is a far greater engineering challenge than the uranium gun assembly.)

3. Takuji Kawata, "Korean Relations Run Aground by Sub Incident," *Daily Yomiuri*, October 23, 1996, p. 7.

4. Larry A. Niksch, "Korea: U.S.-Korean Relations—Issues for Congress," *Issue Brief for Congress*, Congressional Research Service, December 6, 2002, p. 4; Leon V. Sigal, "Did the United States Break the Agreed Framework?" History News Network, March 31, 2003 (http://hnn.us/articles/1353.html).

5. David E. Sanger, "North Korea Site an A-Bomb Plant, U.S. Agencies Say," *New York Times*, August 17, 1998, p. A1.

6. Susanne M. Schafer, "U.S. Views North Korean Missile Launch with Concern," *Associated Press*, August 31, 1998; "N. Korea Stirs Region's Worst Nightmares," *Financial Times*, September 2, 1998, p. 4.

7. Larry A. Niksch, "North Korea's Nuclear Weapons Program," *Issue Brief for Congress*, Congressional Research Service, August 27, 2003, p. 14.

8. Shigemi Sato, "U.S. Envoy Perry off to North Korea with Carrot-and-Stick Initiative," *Agence France-Presse*, May 25, 1999.

9. Howard W. French, "North Korea Says It Will Halt Missile Tests during U.S. Talks," *New York Times*, September 25, 1999, p. A1.

10. William J. Perry, "Review of United States Policy toward North Korea: Findings and Recommendations," Unclassified Report, October 12, 1999 (www.state.gov/www/regions/eap/991012_northkorea_rpt.html).

11. "U.S., N. Korea Issue Joint Communiqué in Washington," *Japan Economic Newswire*, October 12, 2000.

12. Steven Mufson, "Albright, N. Korea's Kim Meet for Historic Talks, *Washington Post*, October 24, 2000, p. A1.

13. Nicholas Kralev, "Bush 'Passed Up Chance to Reduce N. Korean Threat'; U.S. President Should Have Continued Clinton's Policy of Engagement, Madeleine Albright Says in Her Memoirs," *Straits Times*, August 9, 2003.

14. Mary McGrory, "Shadow on 'Sunshine Policy,'" *Washington Post*, March 15, 2001, p. A3.

15. George W. Bush, Statement by the President, Office of the Press Secretary, White House, June 13, 2001 (www.whitehouse.gov/news/releases/2001/06/20010611-4.html).

16. Interview with former U.S. official, 2003.

17. "North Korea Signs Two International Anti-Terrorism Treaties," *Associated Press*, November 29, 2001.

18. George W. Bush, State of the Union Address, Washington, January 29, 2002 (www.state.gov/g/wi/rls/14573.htm); "Remarks by the President at the 2002 Graduation Exercise at West Point," June 1, 2002.

19. Philipp C. Bleek, "Nuclear Posture Review Leaks; Outlines Targets, Contingencies," *Arms Control Today*, vol. 32 (April 2002).

20. "Unclassified Report to Congress on the Acquisition of Technology Relating to Weapons of Mass Destruction and Advanced Conventional Munitions," Central Intelligence Agency, January 1–June 30, 2002 (www.cia.gov/cia/reports/721_reports/jan_jun2002.html).

21. "Joint Statement between the United States of America and the Republic of Korea," March 7, 2001, Office of the Press Secretary, White House (www.whitehouse.gov/news/releases/2001/03/20010307-2.html).

22. George W. Bush, Statement by the President, Office of the Press Secretary, White House, June 13, 2001 (www.whitehouse.gov/news/releases/2001/06/20010611-4.html).

23. "U.S. to Start Contacts with NK in New York: Powell," *Korea Times*, June 9, 2001; "Joint Media Availability with Secretary of Defense Donald Rumsfeld and South Korean Defense Minister Kim Dong Shin following Their Meetings," Defense Department Briefing, Arlington, Virginia, *Federal News Service*, June 21, 2001; "U.S. Deputy State Secretary Urges North Korea to Resume Talks," *Yonhap*, July 7, 2001; "Joint Press Availability with Secretary of State Colin Powell and Korean Minister of Foreign Affairs and Trade Han Seung Soo," State Department Briefing, Seoul, South Korea, *Federal News Service*, July 27, 2001; "Rush of S.-N. Contacts May Help Doves in Bush Administration," *Korea Times*, August 15, 2002.

24. Condoleezza Rice, "Address to the International Institute for Strategic Studies," June 26, 2003.

25. Howard W. French, "Koizumi Aide Hints at Change to No-Nuclear Policy," *New York Times*, June 4, 2002, p. A10.

26. Mark E. Manyin and Ryun Jin, "U.S. Assistance to North Korea," *Report for Congress*, Congressional Research Service, March 17, 2003, pp. 19–22.

27. Ibid., pp. 22–24.

28. Ibid., pp. 10–11.

29. Ibid., p. 22.

30. Henry Sokolski, "Implementing the DPRK Nuclear Deal: What U.S. Law Requires," *Nonproliferation Review*, vol. 7 (Fall/Winter 2000), pp. 146–51; Niksch, "North Korea's Nuclear Weapons Program," p. 14.

31. Stephen Collinson, "Bush Says He Might Consider Reviving 'Bold' North Korea Initiative," *Agence France-Presse*, January 14, 2003; Glenn Kessler, "Bush Says He'd Consider Aid to N. Korea for Disarmament," *Washington Post*, January 15, 2003, p. A1.

32. Some say the Clinton administration used only carrots; see opening statement by Senator John McCain, *Security Implications of the Nuclear Agreement with North Korea*, Hearing before the Senate Committee on Armed Services, 104 Cong. 1 sess. (Government Printing Office, January 26, 1995). Others say they used all sticks; see Leon V. Sigal, *Disarming Strangers: Nuclear Diplomacy with North Korea* (Princeton University Press, 1998).

33. Sigal, *Disarming Strangers*.

34. Kim Young Sam, *Minjujueuireul Wheehan Naheh Tujeng* (My struggle for democracy) (Baeksan Seodang, 2000).

35. Tariq Rauf and Rebecca Johnson, "After the NPT's Indefinite Extension: The Future of the Global Nonproliferation Regime," *Nonproliferation Review*, vol. 3 (Fall 1995), pp. 28–41.

Index